Y0-CBU-290

AMERICAN IMPERIALISM
Viewpoints of United States
Foreign Policy, 1898-1941

THE WAR IN CUBA

Gonzalo de Quesada
and
Henry Davenport Northrop

ARNO PRESS & THE NEW YORK TIMES
New York ★ 1970

Collection Created and Selected
by
CHARLES GREGG OF GREGG PRESS

Reprinted from a copy in The Hoover Institution Library

Library of Congress Catalog Card Number: 79-111731
ISBN 0-405-02047-3

ISBN for complete set: 0-405-02000-7

Reprint Edition 1970 by Arno Press Inc.
Manufactured in the United States of America

THE WAR IN CUBA

BEING A FULL ACCOUNT OF HER

GREAT STRUGGLE FOR FREEDOM

CONTAINING

A COMPLETE RECORD OF SPANISH TYRANNY AND OPPRESSION;
SCENES OF VIOLENCE AND BLOODSHED;

Daring Deeds of Cuban Heroes and Patriots

THRILLING INCIDENTS OF THE CONFLICT; AMERICAN AID FOR
THE CAUSE OF CUBA; SECRET EXPEDITIONS; INSIDE
FACTS OF THE WAR, ETC., ETC.

TO WHICH IS ADDED A

FULL ACCOUNT OF OUR WAR WITH SPAIN, INCLUDING ADMIRAL
DEWEY'S GREAT NAVAL VICTORY AT MANILA DESTRUCTION
OF CERVERA'S FLEET; DOWNFALL OF SANTIAGO; IN-
VASION AND CAPTURE OF PORTO RICO; EVENTS
TO THE END OF THE WAR, ETC., ETC.

BY

Senor GONZALO de QUESADA

Chargé d'Affaires of the Republic of Cuba, at Washington, D. C.

AND

HENRY DAVENPORT NORTHROP

The well-known author

Embellished with many Beautiful Phototype Engravings

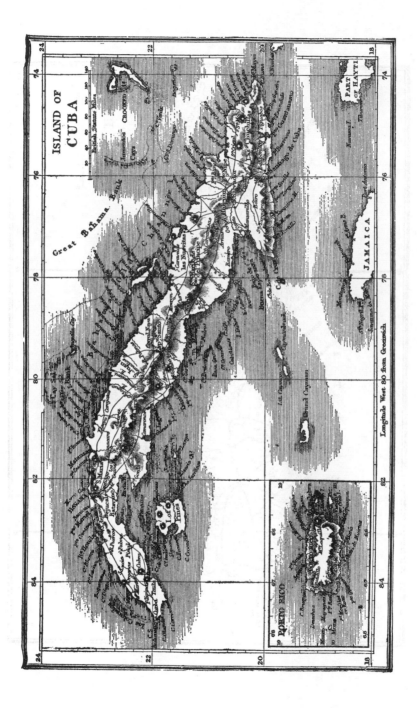

ISLAND OF
CUBA

PORTO RICO

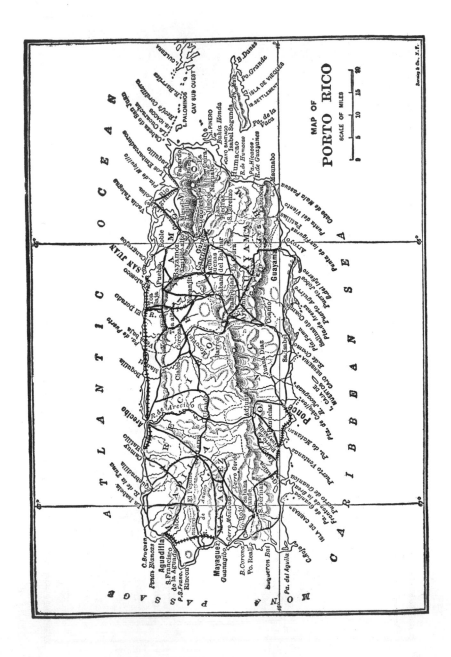

MAP OF
PORTO RICO

SCALE OF MILES

0   5   10   15   20

Berwig & Co., N.Y.

TO THE

ARMY OF CUBAN PATRIOTS,

WHO ARE

SACRIFICING THEIR LIVES IN THE CAUSE OF FREEDOM,

THIS VOLUME IS

DEDICATED

WITH THE HOPE AND BELIEF THAT

THEIR

GREAT STRUGGLE FOR INDEPENDENCE

WILL BE CROWNED WITH SUCCESS.

APPEAL TO AMERICANS.

By a Lieutenant from the Cuban Army.

To the American People!

As your forefathers fought for independence, so the brave army of my compatriots is struggling to make Cuba free. Read in these pages the causes, Progress and certain Triumph of the great Revolution. I have examined the proofs of this work and I find that the account here given is accurate and complete.

The terrible struggle of long-suffering Cuba, the true and heart-thrilling story of which is contained in this comprehensive volume, appeals to all freedom-loving people. Every person in America should know how just and holy is the cause for which so many Cubans are shedding their blood and giving their lives.

Francisco Bassols.

(Late Lieutenant of the "Regiment Prado n° 2" 1st Corps, 1st Division of the Cuban Army]

PREFACE.

THE eyes of the whole world are turned toward Cuba, eagerly watching her Great Struggle for Freedom. The American people recall the long and gory conflict that made this a free and independent nation. Their hearts beat high and their blood grows warm as they read of Cuba's gallant fight for Independence.

The Cuban people have the same reason for their Great Revolution that America had when she threw off the yoke of oppression. For long ages the beautiful " Queen of the Antilles " has suffered under the curse of Spanish tyranny and injustice. She has been robbed and impoverished. Just rights have been denied to her people. Repeatedly and gallantly she has fought to be free and has poured out her blood.

The whole tragic story is contained in this very comprehensive volume. The reader follows the silver-starred flag of the Cuban Patriots which waves from one end of the Island to the other. He sees an army of heroes fighting as Spartans fought at Thermopylæ, as sturdy Scots fought at Bannockburn, as the brave souls in our own Revolution fought at Bunker Hill and Yorktown.

PART I. treats of the Great Insurrection. Spanish brutality and injustice are pictured as they really are, and the reader fully understands why Cuba demands Independence from the atrocious rule of the haughty Castilian.

In a speech on the Cuban question, Congressman Robert R. Hitt, Chairman of the Committee on Foreign Affairs, used the following stirring words : " Americans, who are descendants of those who

iii

struggled through a contest against tyranny like that now being waged in Cuba, cannot be false to the memory of their fathers nor to the traditions and spirit of their history."

In this volume the opening scenes in the beginning of the war are vividly depicted. Then comes General Campos from Spain, with his Army of 75,000 troops. All the stirring incidents of the conflict are pictured in glowing colors—the successes of the Patriot Army, the downfall of General Campos, the arrival of General Weyler, secret expeditions, and pathetic stories of the war.

PART II. contains the complete History of Cuba from its discovery by Columbus to the present time. Striking portraits are given of the early Spanish rulers, and all the great events are vividly depicted. The story of Marti, the conspiracy of Lopez, the slaughter of the crew of the " Virginius," are told in all their thrilling details.

PART III. gives a picturesque description of Cuba, one of the loveliest gardens of the Tropics. This, like every other part of the work, has a peculiar charm to all readers. They behold the natural scenery of the far-famed Island; they see the people in their native homes; they learn all the manners, customs, peculiarities and characteristics of the Cubans, and find at the close of this most instructive volume that they have made a journey through every part of the " Queen of the Antilles."

This work stirs anew the sympathy of the American people for the brave Cuban Patriots who have resolved to free their beautiful Island from the oppression under which it has long suffered and bled. The conflict has been waged before, but never with such grim resolution and heroic bravery. The day of victory is not far distant.

> " Freedom's battle once begun,
> Bequeathed from bleeding sire to son,
> Though baffled oft, is always won."

CONTENTS.

PART I.

The Great Insurrection in Cuba.

CONTENTS.

PART II.

History of Cuba and Spanish Misrule.

PART III.

Picturesque Cuba: Manners and Customs of the People.

WAR-SONG OF THE CUBAN PATRIOTS.

HIMNO BAYAMÉS.

HIMNO BAYAMÉS. Concluded.

rir por la pa - tria es vivir. *En ca - de - nas vi - vir es - mo -*
die for one's country's to live; Life in chains is naught else but

ri *En o - pro bio y a - fren - ta su -*
dea h; In what shame and in - sult are we not

mi - - do, Del cla - rin es - cu - chad el so -
hum - - bled, Now the bu - gle, Hear you not the

ni - do, A las ar - mas va - lien - tes co - rred.
call,......... Then to arms val - iently and to field

PART I.

The Great Insurrection in Cuba

CHAPTER I.

The Long Struggle for Independence.

THE most glowing pages of history are those that record the proud achievements of patriots and heroes to gain national liberty and independence. Sparta had her Thermopylæ. Scotland had her Bannockburn and immortal Bruce. America had her Revolution, her Bunker Hill and Yorktown. Cuba has her patriot army, resolved that her fertile plains shall no longer be trampled under the heel of Spanish tyranny, and the warm sea that laves her rocky shores shall sing the anthem of the free.

"Queen of the Antilles!" Beautiful Cuba! For ages she has writhed under the oppression of the haughty Castilian. Spain, now in hopeless decline, once the mightiest nation of the globe, has had many of the richest of her colonial possessions, one after another, wrenched from her cruel grasp, and with desperate resolve sends the flower of her army to beat back the insurgent hosts and strengthen her hold upon this fairest gem of the West Indies.

The American people are alive to the situation. They recall the gory conflict that made themselves a free and independent nation. Their hearts beat high and their blood grows warm as they read the thrilling story of struggling Cuba and the brave deeds of her patriotic souls. To give here a complete history and description of Cuba's grand uprising, is all the advocacy that her sacred cause requires. It will be of interest to the reader to have, in the first place, a com-

2

prehensive sketch of the Spanish oppressions under which the people of Cuba have struggled for ages, together with their heroic efforts to obtain their freedom and independence. The history will be given later in detail, but from this general outline, a correct idea can be obtained of the causes which have led to the latest and greatest revolution. Since the beginning of the present century Cuba has been the scene of revolutions or uprisings of one kind or another. The direct aim of most, if not all, of these has been to free the island from Spanish control. The armed natives of the cities, joined by bands of stragglers and aided by filibusters, have struggled without organization against drilled, uniformed and comparatively well-equipped regular troops representing Spain.

Glowing Record of Brave Deeds.

For a long time insurrection was the term applied to these uprisings. At first, and indeed, until recently, it may be doubted if these uprisings had the genuine sympathy of the Cubans as a body, and consequently, they were foredoomed to be failures.

But the history of these struggles is replete with brave deeds and exhibitions of personal courage and strategy that would do credit to a body of men familiar with the science of warfare and accustomed to facing danger on the battlefield.

The Spanish colonies, Cuba excepted, gained their independence in 1820–21. Bolivar was their successful leader, and when he had fired the other provinces of Spain he turned his attention particularly to Cuba. But for a time his project failed; some Cuban revolutionists allege that it was the refusal of the United States to countenance such efforts which prevented their success. Be that as it may, the efforts of the islanders to throw off the Spanish yoke came to nothing material

But Bolivar and his fellow-conspirators were determined, and sought by every means in their power to stir up rebellion in the Island. Commissioners were sent to Cuba to create sentiment favorable to revolution. They were soon seized by the Spanish authorities and executed. Bolivar's plan came to a dismal end.

Revolution was in the blood of many of the Cubans, however, and not many years later it had manifestation. From 1848 to 1854 small and ill-planned uprisings took place. Certain elements in the South ern States assisted in encouraging these insurrections.

There was for some time in Southern circles a project looking to the annexation of Cuba to the United States, and its division into four States, each of which, of course, would have been entitled to representation in Congress, giving the South, perhaps, eight Senators and sixteen Representatives, and so throwing the balance of power here into the hands of the slavery advocates.

Captured and Put to Death.

The most important of these movements was that headed by Narciso Lopez, who had served in the Spanish army as a general of division, but who, on going to Cuba, espoused the cause of the revolutionists. He, with Crittenden, the Kentuckian, with a force of 400 Americans and 200 Cubans, set out from New Orleans, landed at Cardenas, on the north coast of Cuba, and captured it by assault.

The victory was a hollow one, for the time had been ill-advised and the country did not rise. Finding themselves without support, and seeing that without aid from the Cubans, they must be captured or driven into the sea, the invaders returned to Key West. The Cubans on that occasion regarded the movement as one solely in the interests of slavery, and believed its projectors to be inspired by mercenary motives.

But Lopez was not to be cast down by one failure. He made a second attempt, and landed at Bahia Honda. There he encountered a force of Spanish troops, under General Henna, and put them to rout. The Spanish commander was killed, and for the time the star of Lopez was in the ascendant. Still the country did not rise. Lopez, in the western end of the Island, where Spanish troops were strongest and the revolutionary spirit weakest, soon found himself surrounded and overpowered. Crittenden, who was to have joined him, remained on the coast, and finally attempted to escape by taking to the open sea in boats. He was captured, with fifty of his men, and all were put to death in Havana.   The execution was marked by atrocities, the news of which rang through the civilized world.

The forces of Lopez, overpowered by Spanish troops, were dispersed with ease.   The commander himself was garroted.   The Island was quiet for a time then, but not for long.   Other attempts to arouse the country up to 1854 were those of Pinto, a Spaniard of revolutionist tendencies ; Estrampes and Aguero, the last-named of whom freed all his slaves before he raised the rebel standard.   He was the first outspoken abolitionist in Cuba.   He and the other leaders were captured after a brief struggle and executed.

There were some unimportant risings after that, but none of note until after the American civil war.   This

GENERAL MAXIMO GOMEZ,
Commander-in-Chief, Cuban Army.

conflict abolished slavery.   Then the Southern States had no further object in meddling with Cuba.   The filibustering movements died out.   It remained for Cuba to attempt to work its own salvation.

In 1868 came the hour which thousands of patriots hailed as the dawn of deliverance, for on October 10 of that year Cespedes raised the five-barred flag at Yara.   He was a lawyer and logical above all things, so to begin with he freed his two hundred slaves, and they followed him to battle to a man.   The entire eastern end of the Island rose against the Spaniards at the call of Cespedes, but the men were without arms or discipline.   Their spirit was unquestioned, but they were of little utility against well-armed and disciplined forces.

Their leaders were Maximo Gomez, who is now commander-in-chief of the revolutionary forces ; Marmol and Figueredo.

The centre of the Island, called **Camaguey**, flocked to the standard of the Marques de Sta Lucia and the Agramontes in November, and as enthusiasm and confidence came with numbers the beginning of 1868 saw Las Villas in rebellion with 14,000 men, among whom there were not more than 100 armed with effective firearms. To oppose these unarmed and undisciplined enthusiasts there were 15,000 regulars.

The western end of the Island proved cold, but even there small uprisings were fomented. They were put down without difficulty. Aid from without was not wanting. In December, 1868, General Quesada landed with the first expedition from Nassau, bringing the first consignment of arms and munitions of war. The revolutionist cause prospered, and on April 10, 1869, a new government was constituted and a House of Assembly established. Cespedes was President of the provisional government, and Quesada commander-in-chief of the forces.

CUBAN COAT OF ARMS.

The government, which had little beyond its name, issued a proclamation giving freedom to all the negroes in the island—a matter which gave great offence to the Spaniards, even those of liberal tendencies.

Ten years of desultory warfare followed. The revolutionists held the centre of the Island and the mountains, but were unable to obtain any standing in the seaports, as their flag was not recognized there by the great powers, although it was duly saluted from time to time by the South American Republics. The United States did not recognize the revolutionists, despite the efforts of General Rawlings and Senator Sherman to that end.

Every effort was made to send arms to the insurgents. There were continual attempts at blockade-running. Some of these expeditions evaded capture, but others were taken by Spanish troops and the leaders were promptly executed. The most notable was that of the "Virginius," under Captain Fry. The "Virginius" put out from Kingston, Jamaica. The capture of the "Virginius" and the summary execution of American citizens by the Spanish authorities so excited this nation at the time that war with Spain seemed certain. This was one of the most notable incidents in Cuban history, at least in point of American interest.

Had the popular voice been heeded at that time ı peaceful solution of the difficulty would have been impossible. Feeling ran so high throughout the country that public meetings were held all over the country denouncing the execution as a butchery, and warlike preparations were begun in many cities. In some cases ships were prepared to go to sea in anticipation of an immediate declaration of war.

Tragic End of the Expedition.

The voyage of the "Virginius" was begun in November of 1873. The steamer was pursued by the Spanish warship "Tornado," and captured within sight of the Morant Point Lighthouse, at the east end of Jamaica. She was towed at once into Santiago de Cuba, despite the fact that she was flying the Stars and Stripes and was in British waters. Fifty-three of her men were shot in a public square in Santiago, in some instances after they had been given a trial lasting only ten minutes.

Among them was Captain Joseph Fry, who commanded the ship; Bernade Varona, W. A. C. Ryan, Jesus del Sol and Pedro Cespedes. There was no United States cruiser within reach of Santiago, but the British man-of-war "Niobe" arrived in time to prevent further slaughter of American and English subjects. Her commander, Sir Lambon Lorraine, acted with quickness and determination.

"Shoot another Englishman or American," he said, "and the Niobe will bombard the city."

Then the slaughter ceased. Both the United States and England protested through their representatives, and sent men-of-war to protect the other prisoners. The survivors were delivered up to the rescuing ships and brought to New York, and the "Virginius," with a hole in her bottom, sank off Frying Pan Shoals.

The return of the survivors and an accurate knowledge of the details of the shooting only served to fan into fierce blaze the fire of popular indignation.   The general voice was for war with Spain, and General Sickles, then American Minister in Madrid, had already asked to be recalled, and was preparing to leave the capital. Finally, however, the matter was adjusted diplomatically.   The Spanish Government paid an indemnity for the American subjects shot with General Ryan and Thomas Ryan, and the war cloud blew over.

But in Cuba the revolutionsts continued their fight for supremacy. For five years—until 1878—they strove against terrible odds in the centre of the Island and in the mountains.   At last they saw that the lack of arms and supplies and of money to purchase either had made the struggle a hopeless one, and they decided to make peace.

Promises of Reform by Spain.

A treaty was signed, by which Spain granted the native Cubans certain liberties, promised to reform their administration in some measure, and recognized the freedom of all the slaves who had fought in the Cuban army.   It had been a long and desperate fight.   Quesada had been succeeded as General-in-chief by General Thomas Jordan, formerly General Beauregard's chief of staff and a West Pointer. He lent much strength to the cause, but abandoned it as hopeless after a year's campaigning in the face of overwhelming odds, and with a few arms and scant supplies.   After him came Agramonte, but he died in a year, and then, when the rebel cause seemed to be prospering, General Gomez took command.   He invaded the western part of the Island and almost reached Matanzas, but he, too, saw that he could not gain ground with unarmed men and withdrew his forces.   That was in 1876, and from that time the revolution waned until the treaty of El Zanjon in February, 1878.

Still there was not entire quiet.   In the east end of Cuba General Maceo refused to recognize the treaty, and continued to fight for eleven months, only to fail in the end and be driven from Cuban soil. The treaty concessions were by no means liberal enough to maintain order for any length of time.   In 1880 General Garcia tried again.

for any length of time. In 1865, General Garcia

CITY AND HARBOR OF MATANZAS.

He was captured in 1875, but before surrendering shot himself under the chin, the bullet passing out at the forehead. He was sent to a fortress in Spain, and when he recovered made his escape to the United States.

Here he and Jose Marti. planned another expedition to Cuba. They landed and held their ground for six months, only to find that the country was not ripe for revolt. The Cubans, weary of continual turmoil and bloodshed, longed for quiet. At last Garcia was captured and sent once more to Spain. From this time dates the autonomist party, started by a group of men who maintained that experience would not justify further attempts to gain freedom for Cuba by force of arms, and that the Island's hope lay in peaceful measures alone. The party gained a footing very rapidly; in-

JOSE MARTI,
Late President of the Revolutionary Party.

deed, its existence and doctrine had much to do with the failure of General Garcia and the Cuban party of freedom.

Despite the efforts of the peace party, however, there were revolutionist leaders who were ready to try again. In 1884 Generals Gomez and Maceo visited the United States and Central America with a view of preparing for another invasion. The movement was opposed bitterly by the home-rule party in Cuba, and was abandoned. Small and ill-advised attempts at revolution followed from time to time after that, notably those headed by Limbano Sanchez, Benitez and Aguero.

The home-rulers, in the meantime, were attempting to get what concessions they could from Spain by peaceful means. In 1890 they became restless again. The peace policy did not prosper. Cuba was growing uneasy again. The concessions, small and unsatisfactory at all

times, began to be regarded as sops which Spain distributed to main
rain peace. They gave no promise of more liberal treatment in future
Men began to say that the native Cubans were cheated at the polls,
and in time their representatives went to the Cortes no more.

For fourteen years the home-rulers, led by such men as Govin
Montoro, Figueroa, Fernandez de Castro and Giberga, had made
most vigorous fights at the polls, and, notwithstanding conservative
frauds, had sent their best orators to the Spanish Parliament. It was
to no purpose. The home-rulers spoke to empty benches in Spain,
and no party there recognized them. They succeeded, nevertheless,
in forcing the conservatives in Cuba to modify their policy and aided
manfully to complete the emancipation of the negro, following the
Cuban Constitution, which declared that " all men are free." With
the economic party they forced the government to celebrate the
Spanish-American treaty, without which the fate of the Island was
sealed.

Divided on Important Questions.

The conservatives divided into two groups, one leaning toward
union with the Cubans on economic questions and hoping secretly for
the annexation of Cuba by the United States. They were demoral-
ized by the refusal of the liberals to go to the polls, the autonomists
having declared that unless the obnoxious suffrage laws which gave
the Spaniards a sure majority at the polls and disfranchised the Cuban
rural population were abolished, they would never go to the legislative assembly again.

The Spanish liberals really formed the economist party, to obtain
commercial concessions and secure a treaty with the United States,
and by joining hands with the Cubans they forced Spain's hand in the
matter. But this, like the other efforts to restore quiet and content,
proved a failure. The Cubans complained that in return for the treaty
and its benefits to the Island Spain imposed new taxes, which more
than counterbalanced all the good that had been done. Representatives were sent to the Spanish Parliament again, the home-rule con-
tingent demanding, as of old, electoral reform sufficient to guarantee
just representation.

It was then that the Cuban revolutionary party began to gain prominence—the party which has drawn the sword in the latest revolution—and asserted boldly that peaceful measures, looking to freedom and equality, had failed, and that Cuba must take up arms again and drive the Spanish soldiers into the sea. Such talk was dangerous on Cuban soil. Leaders of the party who were not already in exile left Cuba and began to plan from the outside, to raise money, to stir up the native population by secret agents—in a word to prepare the Island for one grand united effort to be free.

While this sentiment was being nursed at home and outside of Cuba the peace party was still at work on its own lines. In 1894 the reform wing of the Spaniards joined the Cubans in their fight against the Spanish conservatives. They secured some reforms, but these, the Cubans say, are a mere farce, as the proposition is the establishment of a council in Cuba in which the Spanish element will predominate. This council was to consist of thirty members, of which fifteen were to be appointed by the crown, and the remainder elected. The method of electing, the Cubans contend, would insure a majority for the Spaniards, and in any event the council might be dissolved at pleasure by the Captain-General, whoever he might be.

The Cubans want universal suffrage, and have been unable to secure it. as the Spaniards have insisted upon certain property qualifications.

CHAPTER II.

Spanish Tyranny and Injustice.

BY agreement that is practically unanimous outside of Spain, the people of Cuba have just cause for complaint. They have been the victims of extortion. They have been systematically robbed and hence impoverished. Time after time they have sought redress, and the answer has been a Spanish army, landed on their shores. They have asked for representation in the Spanish Cortes, and this has been granted so grudgingly that it has amounted to very little. They have plead long and earnestly for the correctior of abuses, only to find that the chains which bound them were riveted tighter.

Under such outrages it is no wonder that the people of Cuba have risen repeatedly to throw off the yoke of the tyrant, and in their gallant struggles have had the sympathy of nearly the whole civilized world.

War is a dire necessity. But when a people has exhausted all human means of persuasion to obtain from an unjust oppressor a remedy for its ills, if it appeals as a last resource to force in order to repel the persistent aggression which constitutes tyranny, this people is justified before its own conscience and before the tribunal of nations.

Such is the case of Cuba in its wars against Spain. No nation has ever been harsher or more obstinately harassing; none has ever despoiled a colony with more greediness and less foresight than Spain. No colony has ever been more prudent, more long-suffering, more cautious, more persevering than Cuba in its purpose of asking for its rights by appealing to the lessons of experience and political wisdom. Only driven by desperation have the people of Cuba taken up arms, and having done so, they display as much heroism in the hour of danger as they had shown good judgment in the hour of deliberation.

28

The history of Cuba during the present century is a long series of rebellions; but every one of these was preceded by a peaceful struggle for its rights—a fruitless struggle because of the obstinate blindness of Spain.

Cubans were deprived of the little show of political intervention they had in public affairs. By a simple Royal Decree in 1837 the small representation of Cuba in the Spanish Cortes was suppressed, and all the powers of the government were concentrated in the hands of the Captain General, on whom authority was conferred to act as the governor of a city in a state of siege. This implied that the Captain General, residing in Havana, was master of the life and property of every inhabitant of the Island of Cuba. This meant that Spain declared a permanent state of war against a peaceful and defenceless people.

Wandering Exiles.

Cuba saw its most illustrious sons, such as Heredia and Saco, wander in exile throughout the free American Continent. Cuba saw as many of the Cubans as dared to love liberty and declare it by act or word, die on the scaffold, such as Joaquin de Aguero and Placido. Cuba saw the product of its people's labor confiscated by iniquitous laws imposed by its masters from afar. Cuba saw the administration of justice in the hands of foreign magistrates, who acted at the will or the whim of its rulers.

Cuba suffered all the outrages that can humiliate a conquered people, in the name and by the work of a government that sarcastically calls itself paternal. Is it to be wondered then that an uninterrupted era of conspiracies and uprisings should have been inaugurated? Cuba in its despair took up arms in 1850 and 1851, conspired again in 1855, waged war in 1868, in 1879, in 1885, and has been fighting since the 24th of February, 1895.

But at the same time Cuba has never ceased to ask for justice and redress. Its people, before shouldering the rifle, pleaded for their rights. Before the pronunciamento of Aguero and the invasions of Lopez, Saco, in exile, exposed the dangers of Cuba to the Spanish statesmen, and pointed to the remedy. Other far-sighted men

CITY AND HARBOR OF HAVANA.

30

seconded him in the Colony. They denounced the cancer of slavery, the horrors of the traffic in slaves, the corruption of the office-holders, the abuses of the government, the discontent of the people with their forced state of political tutelage. No attention was given to them, and this brought on the first armed conflicts.

Before the formidable insurrection of 1868, which lasted ten years, the reform party, which included the most enlightened, wealthy and influential Cubans, exhausted all the resources within their reach to induce Spain to initiate a healthy change in the Cuban policy. The party started the publication of periodicals in Madrid and in the Island, addressed petitions, maintained a great agitation throughout the country, and having succeeded in leading the Spanish Govern· ment to make an inquiry into the economical, political and social condition of Cuba, they presented a complete plan of government which satisfied public requirements as well as the aspirations of the people. The Spanish Government disdainfully cast aside the proposition as useless, increased taxation, and proceeded to its exaction with extreme severity.

Outbreak of the Long War.

It was then that the ten-year war broke out. Cuba, almost a pigmy compared with Spain, fought like a giant. Blood ran in torrents. Public wealth disappeared in a bottomless abyss. Spain lost 200,000 men. Whole districts of Cuba were left almost entirely without their male population. Seven hundred millions were spent to feed that conflagration—a conflagration that tested Cuban heroism, but which could not touch the hardened heart of Spain. The latter could not subdue the bleeding Colony, which had no longer strength to prolong the struggle with any prospect of success. Spain proposed a compact, which was a snare and a deceit. She granted to Cuba the liberties of Puerto Rico, which enjoyed none.

On this deceitful ground was laid the new situation, throughout which has run a current of falsehood and hypocrisy. Spain, whose mind had not changed, hastened to change the name of things. The Captain General was called Governor General. The royal decrees took the name of authorizations. The commercial monopoly of Spain was named coasting trade. The right of banishment was transformed into the law of vagrancy. The abolition of constitutional guarantees became the law of public order. Taxation without the consent or knowledge of the Cuban people was changed into the law of estimates (budget) voted by the representatives of Spain, that is, of European Spain.

The painful lesson of the ten-year war had been entirely lost on Spain. Instead of inaugurating a redeeming policy that would heal the recent wounds, allay public anxiety, and quench the thirst for justice felt by the people, who were desirous to enjoy their natural rights, the Spanish Government, while lavish in promises of reform, persisted in carrying on unchanged its old and crafty system, the groundwork of which continues to be the same, namely : To exclude every native Cuban from every office that could give him any effective influence and intervention in public affairs ; the ungovernable exploitation of the colonists' labor for the benefit of Spanish commerce and Spanish bureaucracy, both civil and military. To carry out the latter purpose it was necessary to maintain the former at any cost.

Systematic Robbery of Cuba.

What use the Spanish Government has made of its power is apparent in the threefold spoliation to which it has submitted the Island of Cuba. Spain has not, in fact, a colonial policy. In the distant lands she has subdued by force, Spain has sought nothing but immediate riches, and these it has wrung by might from the compulsory labor of the natives. For this reason Spain to-day in Cuba is only a parasite. Spain robs the Island of Cuba through its fiscal regime, through its commercial regime and through its bureaucratic regime. These are the three forms of official spoliation ; but they are not the only forms of spoliation.

When the war of 1878 came to an end, two-thirds of the Island were completely ruined. The other third, the population of which had remained peaceful, was abundantly productive ; but it had to face the great economical change involved in the impending abolition

**DEADLY ENCOUNTER WITH THE SWORD AND THE
MACHETE**

The Machete, to which constant references are made, is the implement
used in cutting sugar cane. The weapon, however, is long and narrower
than the ordinary machete, and is very deadly in the hands of the insurgents.

CUBAN PATRIOTS FIGHTING FROM THE TREE TOPS

Concealing themselves in the tops of palm trees, the insurgents make attacks as represented in the engraving. This mode of warfare is adopted for the purpose of concealment from the enemy, and with practiced riflemen is most destructive.

UNITED STATES BATTLESHIP "MAINE."

The "Maine" was one of the Largest of the United States Warships. By its Destruction in the Harbor of Havana over 240 lives were lost.

ADMIRAL W. S. SCHLEY

DESTRUCTION OF THE BATTLESHIP MAINE IN THE HARBOR OF HAVANA

SANTIAGO DE CUBA

Formerly the Capital of Cuba, and now the chief town of the eastern department of the Island. Stands on a bay on the south coast, and has a harbor, deep, well protected and fortified. Population, 74,300

GENERAL MAXIMO GOMEZ

This is the portrait of the renowned Commander-in-Chief of the
Cuban Army. He comes from a distinguished family, to which
frequent reference is made in Spanish history. His great ability
as a general is equalled only by his ardent devotion to the cause of
Cuban freedom. General Gomez is over seventy years of age, and
is proud to devote his last days to the cause he has served so long.

GENERAL ANTONIO MACEO.

This late General was the second in command of the Cuban Army. He had long experience in the ranks of Cuban Patriots, was well educated, and was considered a very able commander. His achievements gave renown to the cause of the insurgents.

GENERAL CALIXTO GARCIA

This renowned Commander has long been a conspicuous figure
in Cuban insurrections. In the latter part of 1895 he was imprisoned
at Madrid; being liberated, he returned at once to the United States,
and was instrumental in organizing a formidable expedition to aid
the Cuban Patriots. He is considered one of the ablest and most
courageous Commanders among the Insurgents.

GENERAL MARTINEZ CAMPOS

CUBAN SUGAR TRADE—STREET SCENE IN MATANZAS

GENERAL WESLEY MERRITT

SCENE ON THE BATTLESHIP "MAINE"—DIVERS EXAMINING THE WRECK

GONZALO de QUESADA
Charge d'Affaires of the Republic of Cuba, at Washington, D. C.

SPIRITED CHARGE OF CUBAN CAVALRY

A large number of the Insurgents are cavalrymen. They are bold riders, accustomed to the peculiar characteristics of the country, and make their attacks with great dash and courage.

EXECUTION OF CUBAN SPIES

Many spies captured by the Spanish troops have been executed without the formality of a trial. The usual mode of execution is to bind them to trees, as seen in the engraving, while a detail of soldiers stands at a short distance from them and fires at the word of command.

of slavery. Slavery had received its death-blow at the hands of the insurrection, and Cuban insurrectionists succeeded at the close of the war in securing its eventual abolition.

Evidently it would have been a wholesome and provident policy to lighten the fiscal burdens of a country in such a condition. Spain was only bent on making Cuba pay the cost of the war. The Government overwhelmed the Colony with enormous budgets, reaching as high a figure as forty-six million dollars, and this only to cover the obligations of the State; or, rather, to fill up the unfathomable gulf left by the wastefulness and plunder of the civil and military administration during the years of war, and to meet the expenses of the military occupation of the country.

Oppressive Taxation.

The economical organization of Cuba is of the simplest kind. It produces to export, and imports almost everything it consumes. In view of this, it is evident that all Cuba required from the State was that it should not hamper its work with excessive burdens, nor hinder its commercial relations ; so that it could buy cheap where it suited her, and sell her products with profit.

Spain has done all the contrary. She has treated the tobacco as an enemy ; she has loaded the sugar with excessive imposts ; she has shackled with excessive and abusive excise duties the cattle-raising industry ; and with her legislative doings and undoings she has thrown obstacles in the way of the mining industry. And, to cap the climax, she has tightly bound Cuba in the network of a monstrous tariff and a commercial legislation which subjects the Colony, at the end of the nineteenth century, to the ruinous monopoly of the producers and merchants of certain regions of Spain, as in the halcyon days of the colonial compact.

If Spain were a flourishing industrial country, and produced the principal articles required by Cuba for the consumption of its people, or for developing and fostering its industries, the evil, although always great, would be a lesser one. But everybody knows the backwardness of the Spanish industries, and the inability of Spain to

3

THE GOVERNOR-GENERAL'S PALACE AND THE PLAZA DE ARMAS—HAVANA.

supply Cuba with the products she requires for her consumption and industries. The Cubans have to consume or use Spanish articles of inferior quality, or pay exorbitant prices for foreign goods. The Spanish merchants have found, moreover, a new source of fraud in the application of these antiquated and iniquitous laws; it consists in nationalizing foreign products for importation into Cuba.

As the mainspring of this senseless commercial policy is to support the monopoly of Spanish commerce, when Spain has been compelled to deviate from it, to a certain extent, by an international treaty, it has done so reluctantly, and in the anxious expectation of an opportunity to nullify its own promises. This explains the accidental history of the Reciprocity Treaty with the United States, which was received with joy by Cuba, obstructed by the Spanish administration, and prematurely abolished by the Spanish Government as soon as it saw an opportunity.

Seeds of Discontent and Dissension.

The injury done to Cuba, and the evil effects produced by this commercial legislation, are beyond calculation; its effects have been material losses which have engendered profound discontent. The " Circulo de Hacendados y Agricultores," the wealthiest corporation of the Island, in 1894, passed judgment on these commercial laws in the following severe terms:

" It would be impossible to explain, should the attempt be made, what is the signification of the present commercial laws, as regards any economical or political plan or system; because, economically, they aim at the destruction of public wealth, and, politically, they are the cause of *inextinguishable discontent*, and contain *the germs of grave dissensions*."

But Spain has not taken heed of this; her only care has been to keep the producers and merchants of such rebellious provinces as Catalonia contented, and to satisfy its military men and bureaucrats.

For the latter is reserved the best part of the booty taken from Cuba. High salaries and the power of extortion for the office-holders sent to the Colony; regular tributes for the politicians who uphold them in the Metropolis. The Governor General is paid a salary of $50,000, in addition to a palace, a country house as a summer resort, servants, coaches and a fund for secret expenses at his disposal. The Director General of the Treasury receives a salary of $18,500. The Archbishop of Santiago and the Bishop of Havana, $18,000 each. The Commander General of the "Apostadero" (naval station), $16,392.

Fat Salaries of Spanish Officials.

The General Segundo Cabo (second in command of the Island), and the President of the "Audiencia," $15,000 each; the Governor of Havana and the Secretary of the General Government, $8,000 each; the Postmaster General, $5,000; the Collector of the Havana Custom House, $4,000; the Manager of Lotteries, the same salary. The Chief Clerks of Administration of the first class receive $5,000 each, those of the second class $4,000, and those of the third class $3,000 each The major generals are paid $7,500, the brigadier generals $4,500, and, when in command, $5,000; the colonels $3,450, and this salary is increased when they are in command of a regiment. The captains of "navío" (the largest men-of-war) receive $6,300; the captains of frigates, $4,560; the lieutenants of "navío" of the first class, $3,370. All these functionaries are entitled to free lodgings and domestic servants. Then follows the numberless crowd of minor officials, all well provided for, and with great facilities better to provide for themselves.

In August of 1887, General Marin entered the custom-house of Havana at the head of a military force, besieged and occupied it, investigated the operations carried on there, and discharged every employee. The act caused a great stir, but not a single one of the officials was indicted, or suffered a further punishment. There were, in 1891, three hundred and fifty officials indicted in Cuba for committing fraud; not one of them was punished.

But how could they be punished? Every official who comes to Cuba has an influential patron in the Court of Madrid, for whose protection he pays with regularity. This is a public secret. General

Salamanca gave it out in plain words, and before and after General Salamanca all Spain knew and knows it. The political leaders are well known who draw the highest income from the office-holders of Cuba, who are, as a matter of course, the most fervent advocates of the necessity of Spanish rule in Cuba.

But Spanish bureaucracy is, moreover, so deep-rooted in Spain that it has succeeded in shielding itself even against the action of the courts of justice. There is a royal decree (that of 1882) in force in Cuba, which provides that the ordinary courts cannot take cognizance of such offences as defalcation, abstraction or malversation of public funds, forgery, etc., committed by officials of the administration, if their guilt is not first established by an administrative investigation. The administration is, therefore, its own judge. What further security does the corrupt office-holder need?

Why Cuba is Ruined.

The cause of the ruin of Cuba, despite her sugar output of one million tons and her vast tobacco fields, can be easily explained. Cuba does not capitalize, and it does not capitalize because the fiscal regime imposed upon the country does not permit it. The money derived from its large exportations does not return either in the form of importations of goods or of cash. It remains abroad to pay the interest of its huge debt, to cover the incessant remittances of funds by the Spaniards who hasten to send their earnings out of the country, to pay from Cuban money the pensioners who live in Spain, and to meet the drafts forwarded by every mail from Cuba by the Spaniards as a tribute to their political patrons in the Metropolis, and to help their families.

In exchange for all that Spaniards withhold from Cuba, they say that they have given her her liberties. This is a mockery. The liberties are written in the Constitution, but obliterated in its practical application. Before and after its promulgation the public press has been rigorously persecuted in Cuba. Many journalists, such as Señores Cepeda and Lópes Briñas, have been banished from the country without the formality of a trial. In November of 1891

Don Manuel A. Balmaceda was tried by *court martial* for having published an editorial paragraph relative to the shooting of medical students.

The newspapers have been allowed to discuss public affairs theoretically; but the moment they denounce any abuse or the conduct of any official they feel the hand of their rulers laid upon them. The official organ of the home-rule party, " El País," has undergone more than one trial for having pointed in measured terms to some infractions of the law on the part of officials, naming the transgressors. In 1887 that periodical was subjected to criminal proceedings simply because it had stated that a son of the president of the Havana " Audiencia " was holding a certain office contrary to law.

Right of Public Meeting Denied.

They say that in Cuba the people are at liberty to hold public meetings, but every time the inhabitants assemble, previous notification must be given to the authorities, and a functionary is appointed to be present, with power to suspend the meeting whenever he deems such a measure advisable. The meetings of the " Circulo de Trabajadores " (an association of workingmen) were forbidden by the authorities under the pretext that the building where they were to be held was not sufficiently safe. In 1895 the members of the " Circulo de Hacendados " (association of planters) invited their fellow-members throughout the country to get up a great demonstration to demand a remedy which the critical state of their affairs required. The government found means to prevent their meeting.

One of the most significant events that have occurred in Cuba, and one which throws a flood of light upon its political regime, was the failure of the " Junta Magna " (an extraordinary meeting) projected by the " Circulo de Hacendados." This corporation solicited the co-operation of the " Sociedad Económica " and of the " Junta General de Comercio " to hold a meeting for the purpose of sending to Madrid the complaints which the precarious situation of the country inspired. The work of preparation was already far advanced, when a friend of the government, Señor Rodriguez Correa, stated that the

Governor-General looked *with displeasure* upon and *forbade* the holding of the great meeting.   This was sufficient to frighten the " Circulo " and to secure the failure of the project.   It is then evident that the inhabitants of Cuba can have meetings only when the government thinks it advisable to permit them.

Against this political regime, which is a sarcasm, and in which deception is added to the most absolute contempt for right, the Cubans have unceasingly protested since it was implanted in 1878. It would be difficult to enumerate the representations made in Spain, the protests voiced by the representatives of Cuba, the commissions that have crossed the ocean to try to impress upon the exploiters of Cuba what the fatal consequences of their obstinacy would be.

A Bold Manifesto.

The exasperation prevailing in the country was such that the " Junta Central " of the home-rule party issued in 1892 a manifesto in which it foreshadowed that the moment might shortly arrive when the country would resort to " extreme measures, the responsibility of which would fall on those who, led by arrogance and priding themselves on their power, hold prudence in contempt, worship force and shield themselves with their impunity."

This manifesto, which foreboded the mournful hours of the present war, was unheeded by Spain, and not until a division took place in the Spanish party, which threatened to turn into an armed struggle, did the statesmen of Spain think that the moment had arrived to try a new farce, and to make a false show of reform in the administrative regime of Cuba.   Then was Minister Maura's plan broached, to be modified before its birth by Minister Abarzusa.

This project, to which the Spaniards have endeavored to give capital importance in order to condemn the revolution as the work of impatience and anarchism, leaves intact the political regime of Cuba. It does not alter the electoral law.   It does not curtail the power of the bureaucracy.   It increases the power of the general government. It leaves the same burdens upon the Cuban tax-payer, and does not give him the right to participate in the formation of the budgets.

The reform is confined to the changing of the Council of Adminis tration (now in existence in the Island, and the members of which are appointed by the government) into a partially elective body. One-half of its members are to be appointed by the government, and the other half to be elected by the qualified electors, that is, who are assessed and pay a certain amount of taxes.   The Governor General has the right to veto all its resolutions, and to suspend at will the elective members.   This Council is to make up a kind of special budget embracing the items included now in the general budget of Cuba under the head of "Fomento."   The State reserves for itself all the rest.

Treated as a Subjugated People.

Thus the Council can dispose of 2.75 per cent. of the revenues of Cuba, while the government distributes, as at present, 97.25 per cent. for its expenses, in the form we have explained.   The general budget will as heretofore be made up in Spain; the tariff laws will be enacted by Spain.   The debt, militarism and bureaucracy will continue to devour Cuba, and the Cubans will continue to be treated as a subjugated people.   All power is to continue in the hands of the Spanish government and its delegates in Cuba, and all the influence with the Spanish residents.   This is the *self-government* which Spain has promised to Cuba, and which it is announcing to the world, in exchange for its colonial system.   A far better form of government is enjoyed by the Bahama or the Turks Islands.

The Cubans would have been wanting not only in self-respect, but even in the instincts of self-preservation, if they could have endured such a degrading and destructive regime.   Their grievances are of such a nature that no people, no human community capable of valuing its honor and of aspiring to better its condition, could bear them without degrading and condemning itself to utter nullity and annihilation.

Spain denies to the Cubans all effective powers in their own country.

Spain condemns the Cubans to a political inferiority in the land where they are born.

Spain confiscates the product of the Cubans' labor, without giving them in return either safety, prosperity or education.

Spain has shown itself utterly incapable of governing Cuba.

Spain impoverishes and demoralizes Cuba.

To maintain by force of arms this monstrous regime, which brings ruin on a country rich by nature and degrades a vigorous and intelligent population, a population filled with noble aspirations, is what Spain calls to defend its honor and to preserve the prestige of its social functions as a civilizing power of America.

Rebellion against Oppression.

The Cubans, not in anger, but in despair, have appealed to arms in order to defend their rights and to vindicate an eternal principle, a principle without which every community, however robust in appearance, is in danger—the principle of justice. Nobody has the right of oppression. Spain oppresses Cuba. In rebelling against oppression, Cuba defends a right. In serving her own cause she serves the cause of mankind.

She has not counted the number of her enemies; she has not measured their strength. She has cast up the account of her grievances. She has weighed the mass of injustice that crushes her, and with uplifted heart she has risen to seek redress and to uphold her rights. She may find ruin and death a few steps ahead. So be it If the world is so indifferent to her cause, so much the worse for all. A new iniquity shall have been consummated. The principle of human solidarity shall have suffered a defeat. The sum of good existing in the world, and which the world needs to purify its moral atmosphere, shall have been lessened.

The people of Cuba require only liberty and independence to become a factor of prosperity and progress in the community of civilized nations. At present Cuba is a factor of intranquillity, disturbance and ruin. The fault lies entirely with Spain. Cuba is not the offender; it is the defender of its rights. Let America, let the world decide where rest justice and right.

CHAPTER III.

Why Cuba Demands Self-Government.

WE have already seen that there have been in Cuba repeated uprisings and the most heroic and self-sacrificing efforts to obtain independence. Every intelligent reader will conclude that there must have been grave and serious causes for this chronic state of discontent and revolution.

We will here allow a prominent, distinguished Cuban, whose intelligence and discernment are not to be questioned, state the case in his own clear and convincing manner. This gentleman is Tomas Estrada Palma, Delegate and Minister Plenipotentiary " Republica de Cuba." This gentleman says :

The cause of the present revolution in Cuba, briefly stated, may be said to be taxation without representation, a phrase certainly familiar to American ears and emphasized by the most important event in the history of the nation, the War for Independence. Is it not quite natural, especially in this progressive age, that an intelligent and spirited people like the Cubans should demand the right to govern themselves, especially in view of the fact that they have always suffered from misgovernment at the hands of their rulers?

For three hundred years, in the early history of Cuba, Spain almost forgot the existence of the Pearl of the Antilles, her attention being turned to Peru and Mexico, the countries of gold and silver. It is said that some of the Spanish officials even forgot the name of the Island, directing their dispatches to the Isla de la Habana.

All the laws for Cuba are made in Spain. The annual budget of the Island, that is, the annual estimate of revenue and expenditure, is made in Spain; all the employés in the governmental service on the Island come from Spain. The Spaniards decide just how much money shall be raised by taxes and all the Cubans have to do is, to

42

use an Americanism, " step up to the captain's office and settle." The annual taxation amounts to between $24,000,000 and $26,000,-000. Among the items of expenditure are $10,500,000 for interest on the national debt of Spain, nearly $7,000,000 for the army and navy, about $4,000,000 salaries for civil employés, $2,000,000 for pensions to retired military, civil and judicial officials or their widows, nearly $1,000,000 for the Judicial and $700,000 for the Treasury Department.

No money is appropriated to primary public education, and only an insignificant sum to works of public utility and higher education. The municipalities provide for primary education as best they can, though their means are very limited, all the available methods of raising revenue having been exhausted by the General Government. This taxation, for a country of 1,600,000 inhabitants, is an enormous burden, but does not represent the real amount of money taken from the people. For every dollar raised by taxation another dollar is stolen by the Spanish officials sent to the Island by the paternal Government.

Driven to take up Arms.

Under these circumstances it is not surprising that the Cubans should demand the right to self-government. It must be remembered that they have not resorted to physical force until peaceable methods to secure redress of their wrongs have failed. The people have vainly applied to the Spanish Cortes for the right of self-government, not only at a comparatively recent date, but for the past seventy years they have vainly endeavored to secure their rights by legislative means and have hoped to avoid a war.

The Spanish law-makers have invariably refused to grant them any real redress. I say real redress because the Cortes, about a year before the present revolution, offered a scheme of reform which would not have remedied any of the evils complained of, and was only intended as a sop to blind the eyes of the Cubans and keep them patient under the yoke of their masters. It did not, in any sense, provide for the self-government of Cuba. The Cubans would still be compelled to pay their enormous taxes, all the officials on the Island would still come from Spain as they have been coming from time immemorial.   The budget would still be made in Spain to suit the ideas of the rulers there, and the Cubans would have just as little as ever to say about the management of affairs on their beautiful Island.

Criminals Protected.

The Spanish Government always protects its officials in Cuba when they have been discovered in any crime.   It is very rarely that they are ever convicted of a crime, because the court officials are Spaniards and protect them in every possible way.   Once in a great while, however, a Spanish official may be found guilty ; but, when he is sent to Spain where he is to receive his punishment, he is invariably pardoned.   He uses the money which he has stolen from the Cubans to secure his release trom serving any sentence.

Mr. Edward A. Gilmore, an American, who was employed on a sugar plantation in Cuba for several years, gave the following illustration of Spanish justice in Cuba in one of the New York dailies. Mr. Gilmore says that there was an estate for sale in a town not far from Havana.   One of the Superior Judges wanted the estate and began negotiating for it.   At the same time a young Cuban lawyer decided that the estate was a property that would suit him.   He went to the owner, closed a contract with him, and the deed was made out.   When the Spanish judge heard that he had lost the estate he determined to secure it, notwithstanding it had been sold to another party.

He made a charge of fraud or some kind oi illegality against the young lawyer, had the case tried before himself, promptly decided against the young lawyer, throwing him into prison for an alleged violation of the law, and confiscated the estate.   Mr. Gilmore closes his recital of this incident by saying that this case is only one of a score of other cases of which he has personal knowledge.   "The arrogance and injustice of the Spanish rulers," he says, "and the long-suffering spirit, the humility of the Cubans under the outrageous oppression from which they suffer, are simply incredible to one who does not know the facts."

The attempt on the part of the Spanish Cortes to deceive, to humbug the Cubans into the idea that they were going to give them home rule, when they had no intention of so doing, certainly hastened the present uprising.   After suffering so many years from the injustice of their rulers, showing their discontent by several uprisings, notably the war of 1868 which lasted for ten years, the Cubans thought that Spain might finally reform the terrible abuses under which they had suffered so long.   But Spain gave them nothing. Now, Cuba is fighting for the reforms which she vainly tried to secure by peaceable means.

Hypocritical Promises.

Spain talked about giving Cuba home rule, but there was not the slightest intention of giving to Cuba even the kind of home rule that Canada enjoys.   Canada has her own Legislature, makes her own laws, and has her own government employés appointed from among her own people; and England, the mother country, only sends there a Governor-General.   But that is not the case with Cuba, and Spain would never give that kind of government to the Cubans, if they wanted it, which they do not.

There is really occasion for but very little commercial intercourse between Spain and Cuba, because the United States sends to the Island about everything that its inhabitants need, while, on the other hand, the United States is Cuba's great market for sugar.   Spain cannot buy her sugar.   Spain cannot supply her with flour.   The flour that reaches Cuba is first sent to Spain, and from there to Cuba, so that the Spaniards may collect a duty from the Islanders.   In that way the Cuban pays very dear for his flour, whereas he could obtain it very cheap if complete commercial intercourse existed between the two countries.

The great advantage which Spain has in Cuba, and will hold on to until it is forcibly wrested from her, is that she has her own officer on the Island to make up the budget, so that it will be to the profit of Spain without regard to the benefit of the Cubans.   She wants the Island to pay for her army and navy, consular expenses, and the salaries of the Spanish officials sent to Cuba, who steal from the people as much again as they are paid for their services. Oh no; Spain will never grant home rule in any sense of the word to Cuba, from which she derives such a large revenue for her lazy and venal officials.

The present uprising is, in every sense of the word, a real revolution, because it comes from the whole people.   The previous struggles for Cuban independence have generally been inspired by a few men occupying high positions.   At such times the mass of the people were not conscious of their rights, but, in the present great struggle, which we firmly believe will result in giving self government to Cuba, the whole people, the lower as well as the higher classes, have engaged their sympathies in the movement, and, as far as they are able to do so, they give their aid.   They have had their eyes opened to the legislative policy of Spain and her false promises of righting the

SALVADOR CISNEROS,
President of the Cuban Republic.

wrongs of Cuba.   They are indignant at the treatment they have received at her hands, both at home and in the Cortes, and they are thoroughly aroused to fight for the rights that they have been vainly demanding for the past seventy years.

It is not the fault of the Cubans that they have appealed to arms They would be only too glad to secure their liberty without the aid of war; but it has been plainly and repeatedly demonstrated to them that they cannot obtain their rights without a physical struggle. "Who would be free, themselves must strike the blow."   And so it is that in all orders of Cuban society, from the ignorant Negro to the intelligent merchant and the educated man of letters, all are inspired with one thought, all are animated with one resolve—the independence of Cuba.

The revolutionists in Cuba fight according to two methods, one is the guerrilla method, and the other is by massing their troops and fighting the Spanish forces in the open field. Whenever they can secure an advantageous position to meet the enemy in the open field they mass two or three thousand or more men, and battle with the Spaniards; then they divide their forces into bands of two or three hundred each and engage in guerrilla warfare. They are glad to meet the enemy face to face, and do so when they can secure an opportunity. The revolution has extended from the eastern part very far into the western end of the land. I should say that the revolution extends over four-fifths of the Island.

Arms and Ammunition.

It is not possible for the insurgents to fight in the towns along the coast, because they are guarded by Spanish war ships, still we have troops on the coast, and we are able to protect the landing of new-comers who are going to join our army, and also to land the arms and ammunition, which are continually being sent to the troops. Many of the firearms used by the insurgents have been captured by them from their enemies. Fourteen thousand rounds of ammunition were captured in one engagement alone.

I think there are some Cubans who are anxious that their Island shall be annexed to the United States as soon as possible; but there are many more, in fact a vast majority, who believe that the question of annexation is a long way off, and is not to be considered until the Cubans themselves have tried an independent government. This last-named class see no necessity for annexing Cuba politically to the United States, because she is already annexed to this country commercially. They see no reason why Cuba should form a part of the United States. When Cuba once secures her independence the Cuban people will then, through the exercise of the suffrage, decide the kind of government they will have.

It may possibly be that a majority of the people will decide that they want the Island annexed to the United States, or the vote may show a desire on the part of the Cubans to be an independent nation. That question is only to be decided after independence has been secured. The first and foremost thing before us now is to get rid of

BARTOLOME MASSO,
Vice-President of the Cuban Republic.

the Spanish Government. When once that has been done and Cuban independence has been secured the question of annexation can be decided.

We are now printing a pamphlet which will recite the causes of the war, the many grievances from which Cuba has suffered so long at the hands of Spain, and her determination to rid herself of the Spanish yoke. This history of Spanish rule in Cuba will be laid before our members of Congress. This will help them in their consideration of the Cuban question, and prove conclusively that our cause is as just as was the cause of the Americans in the Revolution.

There will be no argument about annexation. What we demand, what we must have first of all is independence. It is too late now to consider any scheme of home-rule, however feasible such a suggestion may have been in the past. " Independence " is the watchword of the Cuban, first, last and all the time.

On the twenty-fourth of February, 1895, the delegates of the revolution adopted their Constitution, solemnly declaring the separation of Cuba from the Spanish monarchy and the constitution of Cuba, as a free and independent State, under the name of the Republica de Cuba.

The officials of the New Republic were chosen as follows : President, Salvador Cisneros Betancourt, Marquis of Santa Lucia ; Vice-

President, Bartolome Masso ; Secretary of War, Carlos Roloff; Dele
gate and Minister Plenipotentiary, Tomas Estrada Palma ; General
in-Chief of the Army, Maximo Gomez ; Lieutenant-General, Antonio
Maceo ; Major-Generals, Serafin Sanchez, Francisco M. Carrillo.

From the united voice of the American press, from resolutions
offered in Congress, and every other possible source, there were
expressions of sympathy for the " Queen of the Antilles " in her
gallant struggle for liberty. The following poem aptly voices the
feeling of the American people :

For Cuba.

BY MAURICE THOMPSON.

Have you heard the call from Cuba
   Coming northward on the breeze ?
Have you seen the dark cloud hanging
   To the southward o'er the seas ?

It is a gasp for liberty,
   That shudders on the air ;
Spain has relit her torture-fires,
   And men are writhing there.

Oppression's tempest gathers force,
   Its tidal wave rolls high ;
Old Europe's shadow dims the stars
   We kindled in the sky.

The time is come for action,
   Now let the right prevail ;
Shall all our boasted sympathy
   With slaves downtrodden fail ?

Shall we be mockers of the faith
   By which our course was set ?
Shall we deny what we received
   From men like Lafayette ?

Help! help ! the swarthy patriots cry,
   While Spaniards beat them down,
Because they will not bend the knee
   To one who wears a crown.

4

The hoary, mediæval lie,
  That robes the power of kings,
And rivets chains on bleeding hands,
  Once more its logic brings.

At subtle diplomatic pleas
  Let free-born statesmen scoff;
Poor, drowning Cuba grips our skirt,—
  Shall Freedom shake her off?

Oh no! fling out the fleet and flag,
  To shield her from the storm,
And let that splendid Island feel
  The clasp of Freedom's arm.

Early it became evident that there was a strong feeling throughout America, extending to our lawmakers at Washington, in favor of the Cuban cause.   Senator Frye of Maine said:

"If Spain, by her actions at any time, justified us in so doing, I would seize and hold Cuba against the world.   This Island has been nothing but a sponge to be squeezed by Spain, utterly regardless of the interests of the people living there.   Annexed to our country it would soon become a paradise.   As the residents are entirely fit for American citizenship, I regard the acquisition of Cuba, as imperatively demanded, commercially and politically."

The revolution in Cuba was the subject of a good deal of anxious conversation among public men in Washington.   The fact that the previous rebellion lasted for ten years, and cost such a large sum of money to Spain, which, however, she has since shouldered on Cuba, led many of the public men to believe that the present outbreak would be much more serious.   It started out under much better conditions than the last rebellion, and the fact that Spain was sending such a large body of troops to Cuba conclusively demonstrated to the mind of the public that the revolution was a very serious affair.

While there was no disposition to act unfriendly to Spain, the sympathies of the public men in Washington were all with the Cubans. It was recognized that the Island had been outrageously treated by Spain and that the financial burdens imposed on it were more than the people could bear. Every fresh trouble would add to the burdens of Cuba because Spain makes Cuba pay the cost of putting down the revolution, and bear every item of expense incurred by Spain in behalf of Cuba.

A prominent Senator remarked that sooner or later Cuba would be a part of the United States, and that while people might smile over the outspoken words of Senator Frye and Senator Call on the subject, yet nine out of every ten members agreed with Mr. Frye and Mr. Call on this subject.

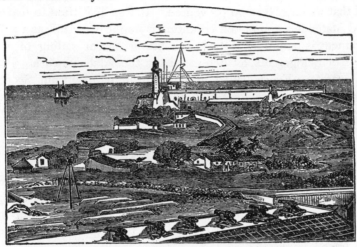

LAND VIEW OF MORRO CASTLE.

Owned by the United States, Cuba would be tremendously prosperous and would save this country from importing from any other nation sugar, tobacco, oranges and other things now largely imported. This feeling would lead to a good deal of aid being given indirectly to the revolutionists.

It was agreed that the Government would enforce the neutrality laws in every manner possible, but it would be absolutely impossible to prevent small expeditions from reaching Cuba from the coast of Florida. The Spanish Minister complained because munitions of war were allowed to be shipped from the United States to Central Ameri-

can States, when the Minister maintained that they were intended for
Cuban revolutionists.   But there is no law whatever to stop the sale
of munitions of war during a time of peace, even to Cubans, and
according to Spain, Cuba was now in a state of peace.   Even custom-
house officers were under a false impression in regard to this matter.
If Spain should declare a state of war in Cuba then the circumstances
would be different.

Minister Murauga notified this Government that a torpedo boat
was being fitted out in the United States for West Indian waters, and
asked that its departure be prevented.   If this boat tried to leave the
United States in a completed condition it might be seized, as a neutral
government is bound to restrain the fitting out or sailing of armed
cruisers of belligerents, as determined in the Alabama case.   But in
1879 Secretary Evarts ruled in reply to an inquiry from Secretary
Sherman, that " a torpedo launch, in five sections, ready to be set up,
though contraband of war, may be exported from the United States
without breach of neutrality."

From an Eminent American.

Our Consul General, Ramon Williams, of Havana, sent to the State
Department a remarkable argument against the continuance of Spanish rule in Cuba and in favor of tariff independence.   Reporting
under date of February 5, 1895, regarding the American flour market
in the Island, he wrote :

" Spain is the only country beside the United States that now sends
flour to the islands of Cuba and Puerto Rico.   But its importation
from Spain is done in violation of the natural economic law and at
the expense of Cuba by lessening the purchasing power of her
exports in their exchange for her imports; for there is scarcely a
vestige of natural economic tie remaining between these colonies and
their mother country, statistics proving, particularly in the case of
Cuba, that they have to send nearly all their exports for outlet to the
United States, the beet sugar of Austria, Belgium, France, Germany,
Holland, Russia and other countries having excluded the cane sugars
of all the West India Islands as well as those of Brazil and the

Hawaiian Islands from the markets of Europe, leaving them dependent on that of the United States. For the effects are tantamount to a second bounty wrought by Spanish legislation in favor of all other sugar-producing countries against Cuba and Puerto Rico."

Consul General Williams closed his report by instituting a comparison between the present economic policy of Great Britain toward her sugar-producing West Indian possessions and that of Spain toward Cuba, greatly to the disparagement of Spain.

Mr. Williams enclosed translations of articles published in leading newspapers of Cuba, and said:

" These publications will likewise convey to the department samples of the public discontent prevailing here against the commercial subjection in which the island is still held by the mother country."

Thousands of Troops.

Patriotic Cuban circles were much excited over the coming of General Martinez Campos with a couple of million dollars in cash, a lot of troops and a large personal prestige. It was the same old story of thousands of troops sent by the mother country to suppress Cuban insurrection. Without inquiring for the causes of the rebellious feeling, and seeking a lasting remedy, one in keeping with justice and humanity, the answer to Cuba's revolution was guns and General Campos. When he arrived he issued from Santiago de Cuba a proclamation offering pardon to all insurgents, with the exception of the leaders, who would lay down their arms and surrender. He made preparations to immediately pursue the members of the bands who refused to come in under the proclamation, and the warfare against them was to be waged vigorously.

Governor-General Campos pledged himself to carry out all the promised political and economical reforms for the Island if he was supported. He thought the rebellion would soon be crushed, but that the entire pacification of the Island would require a long time Campos warned the planters in the interior against aiding the insurgents.

A newspaper correspondent had an interview with the new Captain-

General of Cuba before he embarked for Manzanillo. He remained
in Santiago de Cuba only two days, and nearly every moment of
the time was occupied in making changes of military commanders,
receiving deputations and holding consultations with subordinates.
General Campos said he understood that the press of the United
States had sent several representatives to Cuba to study the situation.
He felt gratified that there was a desire to obtain facts, and he welcomed such investigation.   Asked if he proposed to take the field

A REVOLUTIONARY OUTPOST.

he replied: "I expect to go everywhere. I intend to direct the
movements of the army, and to conduct operations that will tend to
secure law and order throughout the island."

"Shall you remain here or go to Havana ?"

The Marshal replied indirectly; said he expected to leave Santiago
that evening, but would return.

"Are you taking any step in the "Allianca" affair ? "

The Captain-General shook his head slightly in a deprecating
manner, and said the subject was being considered by Señor Dupuy
de Lome, Spain's new Minister to Washington. "Señor Lome is a

diplomat," the General remarked, "and the question is for the diplo-
mats of Spain and the United States to consider. Spain desires to
be at peace with the United States and with all other nations."

He was asked how many revolutionists are in the field. "There
is no army," was the reply. "Small guerrilla bands are scattered
about the interior at the eastern end of the Island. The country is
thinly settled, and very difficult for an army to operate in. A few
men who know the paths can roam about in the chapparal, and their
capture is difficult. The United States had much trouble with
guerrilla bands during the Civil War."

He was asked what disposition would be made of the members of
Maceo's party, imprisoned at Guantanamo. The Marshal shook his
head emphatically, and said rather quickly: "They are in the hands
of the law." Then he added: "I do not propose to be severe without reason. When those in arms put them aside and submit, they
will be well received."

"How about the leaders?" The Marshal answered by referring
to his proclamation, in which amnesty was made the reward for surrender, but the leaders were not included. The Captain-General, at
the close of the interview, declined to issue to the correspondent a
special permit to travel in the interior, but said: "The country is
before you; go and see for yourself. Your passport as a citizen o
the United States will protect you in legitimate travel."

CHAPTER IV.

Beginning of the War.

BETWEEN April 1st and 12th, 1895, Marti and Gomez, the Cuban exiles, with a handful of companions, landed at Baracoa, on the eastern coast of Cuba, and proclaimed the republic. The effect of this bold move was instantaneous. The news spread from end to end of the Island, and although the friends of Cuba thought the movement ill-timed, hundreds of sympathizers flocked to the patriot standard. Like a prairie fire before a brisk breeze, the single spark of insurrection fired the dry tinder of the oppressed Cubans, and the rebellion grew in volume as it flew westward.

This is not Spain's first experience of the temper of her colony. For the past seventy years conspiracy, insurrection, rebellion and red war have followed one another in endless progression. A few words will suffice to explain the causes leading up to the latest revolution.

Cuba became a possession of Spain by the right of discovery on Columbus' second voyage. He named it Juana, after the son of Ferdinand and Isabella, and it has successively been known as Juana, Fernandina, Santiago, Ave Maria and Cuba, the latter being the native name of the " Queen of the Antilles." It was colonized by Spain, and its early history is a series of sacks and ravages by European foes. Not until the rule of Captain-General Las Casas, beginning 1790, did prosperity begin.

Under his guidance agriculture and commerce flourished, and the condition of the native population was ameliorated. The effect of his sagacious rule was felt for over thirty years, and when Napoleon deposed the royal family of Spain every member of the local government took oath to preserve the Island for their monarchy, and, going even further, they declared war against the French conqueror. This much to show the instinctive feeling of the colony toward the mother country.

56

Spanish coffers were empty with the restoration of the Bourbons in the person of Ferdinand VII., and Spain's mistress looked with hungry eyes upon the rich Island with her 1800 miles of sea coast, gemmed with prosperous ports, and her plantations of indigo, sugar, tobacco and fruit. It was Fortunata's purse wherein Spain might dip her fingers, and forever find it full to overflowing. With this discovery came oppressive taxation. With the gradual impoverishment of Spain came added demands. Then the deprivation of all civil, political and religious liberty, and the exclusion of Cubans from all public stations, and in order to enforce this the Cubans were taxed to support a standing army and navy—their jailors.

Conspiracy of the "Black Eagle."

With their oppression came their desire for liberty. In 1829 the Black Eagle conspiracy arose, the purpose of which was to throw off the Spanish yoke. It was suppressed, but was followed in 1840 by an insurrection of the colored population. After smouldering and blazing for a while the fires of insurrection were smothered only to break out eight years later in a genuine conspiracy of the Cubans under the leadership of Narcisso Lopez. This rebellion was quelled, and Lopez fled. In 1850 he landed in Cuba with 600 men from the United States. He made a third attempt in 1851, and together with most of his companions was captured and executed by the Spanish authorities.

The Reformist party, which sprang up at this time, succeeded in getting an inquiry of the abuses at Madrid, with the result, however of increased taxation. In 1868 the Advance party in Cuba rose in the district of Bayamo, and on October 10, 1868, signed a declaration of independence at Manzanillo. Their first successes were so great that almost all the Spanish-American republics recognized the insurgents as belligerents. After a war of ten years, that was confined to the mountainous regions east of the town of Puerto Principe, the rebellion was put down. To confine it to that locality the Spanish troops built a great fortified trench, known as La Trocha, across the entire width of the island, in the western portion of the State of

Puerto Principe. It was here that Captain-General Campos, the commander of the Spanish army, drew up his forces in the summer of 1895, to prevent the eastward march of the insurgents, who were now heavily reinforced.

All during the summer of 1895 the insurgents leaders were organizing their forces and receiving supplies of arms and ammunition. The people were flocking to the standard of revolt, and during October, 1895, Gomez and Maceo with ease penetrated the lines of the Spanish captain-general, crossing La Trocha, and causing the regular troops to fall back to a line just east of Remedios. The insurgents still pushing on, this was followed by a retreat of Campos to Santa Clara, in the province of Santa Clara, still further west.

Two Cuban Generals.

Gomez and Maceo were now in supreme authority, for Marti, the great leader of the revolutionary party, died just as the command started west. This blow to the insurgent cause was more than offset by the character of the people among which they found themselves. Of all the provinces of Cuba, Santa Clara is the most outspoken and loyal to the cause of liberty. The ranks of Gomez and Maceo were increased by thousands of volunteers of an intelligence and physical strength superior even to those of Santiago. Horses were procured in abundance, and the bulk of the insurgent army was formed into a speedy and well-equipped cavalry. They were armed with rifles, and carried with them an abundance of ammunition. Each man also carried a machete, which is a long, heavily-weighted iron knife, used by the sugar-planters to cut the cane, and by all travelers to open up paths through the heavy tropical underbrush. They are terrible weapons in the hands of the Cubans, and the Spanish troops fear them more than the rifles. The insurgents took no supply train with them. A stray pig or fowl supplied them with supper, while an ox meant dinner for a company. Thus prepared, they turned their faces toward the setting sun and Havana.

All this while Campos, the Spanish general, was "concentrating," according to the official dispatches. In other words, he was drawing dead lines across the Island at points where he announced that he would bring the insurgents to a pitched battle. Each successive dead line was further west than the one preceding it. And each time the insurgents slipped by the troops, leaving a harried country behind them. Railroads, bridges and roads destroyed, plantations burned and store-houses empty. The troops, under the spur of necessity, followed as rapidly as possible, leaving the insurgents in possession of the country to the east.

Landing of Expeditions.

In this way not only did the Cubans make this remarkable march westward, but they garrisoned it. In Santiago the insurgents kept the Spanish forces in the fortified cities, and in a short time two large expeditions successfully landed at that end of the island. One, armed with cannon, fired upon and crippled the " Nueva Espana," of the Spanish navy, while such leaders as Rabi, Martinez and Aguirre were fighting as valiantly there as were Gomez and Maceo in the province of Matanzas.

Similar reports came from Puerto Principe and Santa Clara, showing that the insurgents had complete control of the interior of these provinces. But Campos claimed that it was his plan to get the insurgents between his forces and Havana and crush them as a nut is crushed in a nut-cracker.

Then came decisive attacks by the insurgents. Campos was driven from pillar to post, changing his headquarters from Santa Clara to Cienfuegos, from Cienfuegos to Palmillas, from Palmillas to Colon, from Colon to Jovellanos, from Jovellanos to Limonare, from Limonare to Guanabana, and from Guanabana to Havana, where he was feted as a conqueror by the Spanish authorities, and where he received telegrams of congratulation from the Queen Regent of Spain and her Prime Minister.

Just prior to this noisy welcome, namely, on December 24, 1895, General Maximo Gomez, at the head of 12,000 men, by a feint turned the flank of the Spanish commander at Colon, and, passing the sleepy old seaport of Matanzas, marched straight on to a point only fifty miles from Havana, Campos, with all his 80,000 picked Spanish troops, to the contrary notwithstanding Christmas and New Year were passed, and the insurgents were still there, marching and coun termarching in three columns, holding Spain at bay, and waiting foi additional supplies of ammunition and arms before pushing on. The grave question now was what the insurgents would do ? Havana was in an agony of suspense and preparing for a siege. The loyalty of the citizens was unquestionable, as well as that of the Grande Civil or local militia. Campos and all his troops seemed unable to cope with the situation. It was believed that should the insurgents push on and take Havana, the defeat of Spain and the liberty of Cuba would arrive.

A Concise History of the Struggle.

These, in outline, are the main facts of Cuba's war during the firs³ year of its progress. The reader will be interested in another account from a war correspondent in Cuba, who had ample opportunity foi observation, and the accuracy of whose statements are unquestioned. Writing late in January, 1896, he says :

"The question of the United States recognizing the belligerent rights of the new Cuban republic is now receiving so much attention that a dispassionate and unbiased account of the state of affairs in Cuba may help some to a better understanding of the situation. In view of the misleading information and exaggeration of facts given out, on one hand, by Cubans in America, and, on the other, of the mis- representation and concealment of truth by the representatives of the Spanish side, facts gathered from the scenes of the war and the seat of its causes may throw light upon doubts which are entertained as to the wisdom of America's policy up to this time.

"The Cuban revolution is now within a few days of having turned its first year. It has passed all the bounds of previous insurrection. It has passed from the stage of organized rioting into actual war. It is no longer limited to a conflict between classes, or confined to any section of the Island. It has become a war between two peoples who are distinct in all the characteristics which mark the differences between nations. The recent successes have resulted in the best blood of Cuba's native-born population joining or aiding Gomez's armies, and have brought the issue to a point which means that the price of Spanish victory would be almost inevitably the extermination of some great families and the utter devastation of the Island.

" Such a victory would carry with it the accumulation of a war debt which would impoverish Cuba for two generations, and leave her a burden rather than a precious possession for the so-called mother country. Without the benefits which would come to the Cubans as the result of such recognition as they ask from the United States it is impossible for the revolutionists to hasten the issue of the war, and as Spain cannot drive them unwillingly into battles, only some event now entirely unforeseen can prevent the prolonging of the war for possibly a year or more.

The Two Armies.

" Both sides are weak, so weak that the question of which can hold out the longer is as important as the result of battles, perhaps more important than the result of the insignificant engagements which now monopolize all the reports from the field. On the side of Spain is an army drawn from a native population of 16,000,000. On the side of Cuba is an army drawn from a native population of 1,600,000. Dealing with the mere numbers one reason is apparent why Gomez avoids battles into which he might throw his forces with a certainty of victory. It is hard for him to replace his losses. Unless the killed were nearly sixteen to one the ease with which Spain could fill the gap in her ranks where they were nearer equal would be his weakness and practically turn his victories into disasters.

" Spain's army is made up of conscripts, unpaid, poverty-stricken, most of them too ignorant of military training to march in step at guard mount, and so youthful that regiment after regiment would not have an average age of above nineteen years; half-fed, with no commissary department or surgical service available after battles; so tender to the climate that ten die of disease to one in conflict, and so neglected in the hospitals that the wounded generally die of yellow fever contracted in the pest-houses to which they have been taken from the field, numbering with the Spanish Cuban volunteers recruited in the Island about 200,000 men ; 120,000 of these have come from Spain ; the other 80,000 are from the Island. Of them all, less than 500 are cavalry, and of this 500 at least one-half are only mounted infantry. They are all well armed. In commanders, Spaniards and Cubans, in proportion to the numbers, are equally supplied with veterans.

Fifty Thousand Native Cubans.

"The Cuban army numbers 50,000, half of whom are in small divisions, under captains or colonels, acting upon orders and in campaigns devised by Gomez and Maceo. At least 25,000 of them are mounted, but only 25,000 of them, according to the most trustworthy information, are supplied with modern arms. But the whole 50,000 are native Cubans, inured to the climate, safe in the fever season and unaffected by any hardship of march or exposure. Every farm estate and hut is their hospital. Every Cuban woman is a nurse for the wounded. Every farm and plantation is a source of food supply. Every Cuban is their guide and informant, prepared the next moment to lie like a Turk to a Spanish column. These 50,000 men are flushed with a year of almost uninterrupted successes, which have resulted in the downfall of one of Europe's greatest generals.

" Now, at the end of only one year, they have the whole Island at their command, except its city strongholds, with the Spanish armies cut off from communication with each other except by couriers on horses or protected steamers along the coast. Every railroad is paralyzed. The following year's revenues to Spain have been practically wiped out by the ruin of business and the destruction of the sugar cane. Havana itself has been declared by the captain-general to be in a state of siege. Gomez, with his army, has slept within sight of the city.

" The events which have led up to all this make a simple chapter of Spanish disaster and of Cuban successes, with occasional reverses, during which the more or less guerrilla warfare conducted in the early stages has developed into scientific campaigns, and also in the birth, on the 16th of September, 1895, of the Republic of Cuba. The war was started through the failure of Spain to put into force reforms in the government of Cuba which had been granted by the Spanish Cortes, after a tremendous effort on the part of the Island to procure relief from intolerable evils. It is generally believed that the Cortes did not act in good faith, but from a pressure to prevent a revolt from what was simple tyranny, and that there was never any intention to permit the reforms to go into operation.

" Calleja was then the Captain-General of the Island. He made a faint resistance when the first evidences of the preparation Cuba had been making for insurrection came to the surface in Santiago de Cuba, the extreme eastern province of the Island, and the stronghold of former revolutions. It is a rough country, where it was supposed the trouble would be confined. He declared the province and that of Puerto Principe, adjoining, to be under martial law.

Grand Uprising of Patriots.

" Between April 1 and April 12, Generals Gomez, Antonio Maceo, Jose Maceo, Cebreco, Crombet, Guerra, Marti and Borrero landed with men and arms, and they were joined by thousands of Cubans, who brought out from hiding-places arms and ammunition which they had been collecting and concealing for years. It was already apparent to Spain that the insurrection was to be serious, and by this time General Campos, then her greatest military chief, was already on his way to the Island with 10,000 men. He landed on April 16, 1895, at Santiago de Cuba, and made the mistake which has cost Spain the war and may in the end cost her all Cuba.

" He did not at once put the reforms in force, but announced that ' after peace was restored ' he would ' do all in his power to see that the reforms which had been granted by the Cortes were put in force.' It is true that already another and greater object was inspiring the Cubans—the liberty they now demand ; but, if Campos had then, instead of waiting three months, till the insurrection had gone beyond his control, granted the relief to Cuba which the Cortes had authorized, it would have almost inevitably resulted, notwithstanding what may be said outside of Cuba to-day to the contrary, in the restoration of peace, probably only temporary; but his course precipitated into the conflict all the elements which he might have used to prevent it.

"At the end of three months Gomez and Maceo had all Santiago and Puerto Principe in a state of insurrection. They started out with comparatively a handful of men. The most reliable sources agree that there were not more than 300. Thousands of Cubans joined them, furnishing their own horses and arms. Campos had declared that Puerto Principe would never rise against Spain, and he proposed at once a plan to make it doubly sure. He procured special concessions from Madrid for the foreign railroads, permitting them to import iron bridges to replace their wooden structures, and pledged them $20,000 a month until they had extended their lines and made connections to complete a continuous road through the country, using the money to employ the natives. This was to insure the peace of Puerto Principe and Santa Clara, both considered conservative, and to prevent the people joining the revolutionary party.

War's Dire Destruction.

"After the plan was announced the revolutionists burned out the wooden bridges, tore up the tracks in many places, and the roads have been, for all practical purposes, in their hands ever since. Campos, meantime, to prevent Gomez moving eastward, placed 10,000 troops on the border between the provinces of Santiago and Puerto Principe, but Gomez crossed the line on May 19, after a battle at Boca del Dos Rios, where a loss was suffered in the death of Gen. Marti, which was so great a blow to Cuba that Campos announced that the 'death blow to the bandits' had been struck.

"In Puerto Principe Gomez captured every town he attempted to take, among them Alta Gracia, San Jeronimo and Coscorro. He took Fort El Mulato, and in all the places secured large quantities of ammunition. So enthusiastic was his reception in the provinces of Puerto Principe and Santa Clara that in the latter 400 Spanish volunteers joined him with their arms. Places in this province that fell in rapid succession were Las Veras, Cantabria, Fort Taguaso, Guenia de Miranda and Cayo Espino.

SEN.
CUSHMAN K. DAVIS,
of
MINNESOTA

SEN.
GEORGE GRAY,
of
DELAWARE.

EX. SECT'Y.
of STATE,
WM. R. DAY.

SEN.
WM. P. FRYE,
of MAINE.

WHITELAW REID,
of NEW YORK.

AMERICAN PEACE COMMISSIONERS

GENERAL W. R. SHAFTER

1. BURNING A DESERTED VILLAGE. 2. ATTACKING A SPANISH
FORCE. 3. SPANISH PRISONERS BROUGHT INTO CAMP.

PALACE OF THE CAPTAIN-GENERAL—HAVANA

This palatial structure is on one side of the public square known as Plaza de Armas. It is ornamented with gardens of tropical plants, and the walls inside are decorated with paintings, illustrating events in Spanish history. Here the various Captain-Generals have had their residence. The Spanish flag may be seen constantly floating from the tower.

COUNTRY OX-CARTS.

Used for transporting sugar cane from the fields to the grinding mills

THE INDIAN STATUE ON THE PRADO—HAVANA

The Prado is a wide, capacious street, arranged as a boulevard, with rows of trees in the centre, a promenade for foot passengers, and on each side of this, the drives for carriages. The fine statue shown above is an object of interest and admiration to visitors.

SPANISH TROOPS FALLING INTO AN AMBUSCADE

The above represents the tragic affair at Manzanillo, when the Spanish troops experienced one of the most serious reverses of the protracted campaign. Lured into a cleverly planned ambuscade, the cavalry, smoking cigarettes and unconscious of danger, rode into a vertible death-trap.

AN INSURGENT ATTACK ON A FORT MANNED BY SPANISH TROOPS

Many Forts are scattered throughout the Island. The engraving represents a spirited attack on one of these by a detachment of the army of General Gomez.

INSURGENTS REPELLING AN ATTACK FROM BEHIND A BARRICADE OF
SUGAR HOGSHEADS

The engraving shows the Flag of the Republic of Cuba, which has a Silver Star on a Red Triangle, with wide
stripes of White and Blue.   Hogsheads form a convenient defense against attacks from the enemy.

A CAMP OF CUBAN INSURGENTS—COOKING A PIG

The Cuban army, being compelled to subsist on the products of the country, is not always able to obtain such a luxury as the one here represented. The view affords an excellent idea of the personal appearance of the patriot army and its uniform, if such it can be called.

MAJOR-GENERAL FITZHUGH LEE

SUGAR MILL DURING THE GRINDING SEASON

The cultivation of sugar cane is one of the principal industries of Cuba. The engraving represents a mill, with machinery for grinding the cane and preparing it for the process that follows

A CUBAN FARMHOUSE

This is a typical house among the agricultural classes. Most of the houses are one story, have thatched roofs, and have about them an air of negligence quite in contrast with the appearance of the fine mansions of many of the plantation owners.

ENGAGEMENT BETWEEN THE INSURGENTS AND SPANIARDS NEAR CAMAJUANI

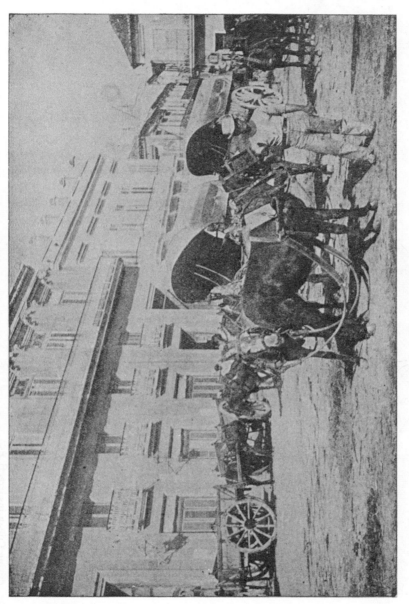

STREET SCENE IN HAVANA

The view shows the Plaza San Francisco, heavy vehicles covered and uncovered, and architecture of the buildings.

MORRO CASTLE—HAVANA

This strong fortress commands the entrance to the harbor, and is an object of great interest to the visitor, not merely on account of the history connected with it, but also by reason of the magnificent views of sea and land from its battlements. Here have been confined many prisoners of war captured by the Spanish during Cuban insurrections.

" The most important battle of the summer occurred at Bayamo in July, just as Gomez was near the Spanish line between Santa Clara and Puerto Principe. Campos decided to relieve the distress of the garrison at Bayamo and left Manzanillo, intending, after entering the town, to move quickly westward, driving Gomez into the Spanish line, while three other columns were to surround Maceo. Both bands were to be exterminated at once. On his way to Bayamo Campos was met by Maceo and Rabi at Peralajos, and in a twelve hours' battle, in which about 3,000 men were engaged on either side, Campos was completely routed.

" From that time on through the summer and far into the autumn, every day was marked by skirmishes, the taking of important places and the threatening of the larger towns. It kept the Spanish columns moving constantly, and the exposure in the rainy season killed thousands. It was, doubtless, Gomez's purpose to conduct his summer campaign to produce that effect, suffering nothing by it himself. He was then planning the great campaign of the winter, the execution of which resulted in the shutting up of Havana. He had accomplished the destruction of all methods of communication in the interior, to the east, and had issued his order against the grinding of sugar cane, for the purpose of cutting off Spain's revenues, and had announced that he would take his army clear through into the Matanzas province to insure obedience to his order.

" Amazing as this declaration was, it was fairly good evidence of Gomez's modesty. He had not only overrun Matanzas, but Havana province as well, burning plantations within sight of the city, where the owners disobeyed him, and finally subjugating the province of Pinar del Rio, in the extreme west."

5

CHAPTER V.

Insurgent Campaign in Western Cuba.

REFERENCE was made at the close of the preceding chapter to the spirited warlike operations of the insurgents in Western Cuba. Carrying the war into this section was simply threatening Havana, and this was one object of the insurgent leaders, Gomez and Maceo.

Enough of the history of the insurrection has been given to show the manner in which it was carried on during the first few months subsequent to the arrival of the Spanish General Campos and his army. All his boasts of conquest failed of fulfillment. He was slow to bring the insurgents to the point of battle, or if he did succeed in doing this, he failed utterly to accomplish his purpose of so vanquishing them as to stamp out what he was pleased to call the " Rebellion," and bring the country into a state of peace and quietude. It is more than probable that some of the skirmishes in which the Spanish troops claimed success were conducted by the insurgents more for the purpose of harassing Campos and his scattered forces than with the idea of obtaining any great substantial victory.

General Gomez and his commanding officers had a full knowledge of the country, knew all the strategic points, also knew that they were greatly outnumbered by the Spanish forces, and that they had only to hold their ground without being completely overthrown, and the proud army of Spain would be, partially at least, defeated by disease and the disastrous effects of the climate, to which they were not accustomed. Certain it is that after the operations of General Campos had been carried on for months, the insurgents were as strong and well-disciplined as ever, while in the provinces which they occupied they constantly received recruits from those dissatisfied spirits who were ready to join the patriot army in its daring and determined effort to throw off the Spanish yoke.

In order to understand the progress of events, it is necessary to describe the campaign of the insurgents in the province of Pinar del Rio.

When Gomez retired from this province he left Maceo there, and took up a position east of the Spanish line, where he remained near, but refused to give battle to the Spanish. He had been waiting for Maceo's work to be finished. All this time he has been within ten miles of Havana, and never more than twenty-five miles away. The highest officers in command of the field operations of the Spanish, commenting upon the strength of the new " wall of men," said that " if only Gomez were in so tight a place as Maceo, both would soon be wiped out, as they were hopelessly separated, Maceo burdened with wounded men, and Gomez between lines rapidly converging."

A March of Repeated Victories.

ı he truth is that they had not endeavored to meet, but Maceo had gone to the extreme end of Cuba, occupying its most western city, driving the garrison of that town down to the shore, where they fought on the sand-beach, under the fire of a Spanish cruiser out at sea. Maceo's march had been one of repeated victories. Towns surrendered without resistance; around others there were some slight encounters. Portions of several Spanish garrisons joined the revolutionists with their arms.

More than 2,000 recruits were made. The new government was established in the cities and towns of Mantua, San Cristobal, Remates, Palacios, Paso Real de San Diego, Guane, Consolacion del Sur, Pilotos, Alonso de Rojas, San Luis, San Juan y Martinez, and other less important places.

The capital of the province, Pinar del Rio City, was the one place of great importance that held out, but it was cut off from communication with its port, Colon, and was short of provisions. One supply sent by the Spanish for its relief, 100,000 rations, fell into Maceo's hands.

Maceo's march began as soon as he had left Gomez, near the lower border, between Havana and Pinar del Rio provinces. He had 2,000 mounted men, all armed, in divisions under Gens. Zayas, Varuna, Vivo and Gomez Rubio. Almost immediately the forces were divided, Maceo, with the main body, moving southwest, and a small division, under Varona, taking a western course through the northern country, to reunite with Maceo at the western extremity of the province. In this way it was designed to cover at once the sides of a great loop, embracing every important point in the province.

The Spanish Forces Scattered.

Gomez's retreat had been misunderstood by the Spanish, and when Maceo moved, the Spanish forces were scattered and unprepared to check him, being to the east, where they supposed the centre of operations was to remain, near Gomez. With trifling losses, and the wounding of but a handful of his men, Maceo entered Candelaria and San Cristobal on the same day, the third of his march.

In San Cristobal the Spanish flag on the government building was replaced by the emblem of the new republic, a mayor and city officials were appointed, resolutions were adopted by the new authorities, and, after all the arms in the town had been collected, and forty or fifty mounted recruits had been made, Maceo remained a day to rest his men and horses, and moved on the following morning at daybreak toward Palacios, just north of which lies Banos de San Diego. He took both these places, and the same scenes were repeated, the people decorating their houses and flying white flags from every roof as a token of their allegiance to the cause.

By this time the Spanish saw the trend of Maceo's plans, and Generals Nevarro and Luque were ordered to pursue the insurgent army, reinforcements at the same time being ordered to Pinar del Rio City. The garrison at Guanajay was strengthened, and an additional force was dispatched from Havana to proceed on a steamer along the south coast to Columa, to reach Pinar del Rio, if possible, before Maceo had arrived.

Nevarro made all haste, but was not out of sight of Guanajay, where he had left the terminus of the railroad, before he came upon burning cane fields, whose owners had disobeyed Gomez's prociamation against grinding. Navarro and Luque had together 5,000 infantry, 200 cavalry and 11 pieces of artillery. They found that the cattle had been gathered up by insurgents or hidden by their owners, but, learning that Maceo was at least two days' march ahead, they were able to move with freedom, and by forced marches came to the San Juan del Rio sugar estate, where the next day General Navarro met General Arizon's command, which had encountered Maceo's rear guard the previous day. Arizon had lost, as nearly as can be learned, five men, and had several wounded, and was waiting there to join Navarro's division.

General Navarro had sent a detachment after the smaller body of insurgents moving on the north, but further than a few encounters with some small bands, which may have been either skirmish lines or independent companies of insurgents, their pursuit was fruitless, and they arrived at Cabanas, on the north coast, the day after the insurgents had taken the place, disarmed the volunteer garrison, secured 11,000 rounds of ammunition, and retired with the loss of two men. This loss was confirmed by the Spanish official reports.

Fled in Disorder.

To come back to General Navarro, after being joined at the San Juan estate by Arizon's command, he moved on toward Quivera Hacha, and near there came up to Maceo, who had meantime established the insurgent government in Consolacion and Rio Hondo, and was preparing to move upon Pinar del Rio City. Near Quivera Hacha Navarro's skirmishers encountered a small band of mounted insurgents. There was rapid firing, and almost instantly 400 of the insurgents rode down upon Navarro's extreme vanguard, under Lieutenant La Torre, and came within fifty yards, shouting " Machete," firing but few shots and retiring without attacking.

The cry of " Machete," the name of the half-sword-like weapons which the Cubans use with such deadly effect in much of their fighting, terrified the Spanish, and considerable disorder followed. Fearing that all Maceo's army was at hand, lines of battle were quickly formed, the main body being well protected by a cactus fence. Two divisions were deployed right and left in cane fields, part of which had been burned. About 1,000 of Maceo's men were on higher ground, and although firing lasted twenty minutes, the losses on either side were not serious when the insurgents withdrew. None of Nevarro's cavalry or artillery took part in the action.

The Spanish followed them, prepared for an ambush at any moment, as the cane and underbrush were dense, but reached the Begona sugar estate safely, where, coming out into the open, they were within sight of 1000 of Maceo's men, two miles southwest, moving away. The Spanish during the day lost, according to the best information from both sides, about twenty-five men killed and wounded. Regarding Maceo's losses the Spanish report said: "The rebels must have lost several men."

Gen. Maceo at the Front.

The Cubans say they did not lose a man, and no dead were found on the field. At the Begona estate Gen. Navarro learned that he had been engaged with only a small part of Maceo's forces, and that the main command was at the Armendares estate.

The seat of operations at once changed to the vicinity of Pinar del Rio, Gen. Luque succeeding Gen. Navarro in command of the aggressive movements against Maceo, who, learning of the relief being sent to the city, tried to intercept it, probably in expectation of the valu· able capture which he subsequently made. His rapid progress with his cavalry, the Spanish following on foot, of course resulted in several days passing without an engagement. The first encounter took place on January 17, 1896, about five miles south of the city. It was nothing more than a skirmish, neither side suffering, and that night Gen. Luque left part of his forces at the village of St. Luis, through which Maceo had passed two hours ahead of him. He took his main body to Pinar del Rio.

During the night he learned that Maceo had taken a position at Tirado, commanding the road to Coloma, between Pinar del Rio and the coast. It was over this road that the wagon train from the coast was to bring up the supplies to Pinar del Rio. General Luque hastened at daylight to drive the insurgents back, but found Maceo strongly entrenched within three miles of the city. This was the morning of the 18th.

Luque came upon Maceo's vanguard under Colonel Velasco, but the moment the attack was made he found himself under fire from the tops of two low hills on both sides of the road, where the insurgents were well protected. They were in such an advantageous position that Luque sustained severe losses without inflicting much injury upon the enemy. So hot was the encounter that Luque withdrew and prepared to charge upon two points where the enemy were making a stand. With the San Quintin battalion he held the road, sending Colonel Hernandez to the right, while another division advanced on the left. The attack was successful. The Spanish made a magnificent effort under the withering fire, but both divisions swept Maceo's forces before them, not, however, until they had left the field scattered with their own dead and wounded.

The Spanish General Surprised.

For some reason the cavalry had not been used. The artillery was just coming up when the action had reached this point. The Spanish found that the enemy had, instead of being routed, simply fallen back and taken a position on another hill, and scattered firing went on for a considerable time, while Luque prepared to attack again. Then, against two thousand of Maceo's men, was directed all of Luque's command, over four thousand infantry, two hundred cavalry and eleven pieces of artillery.

At least half of Maceo's army, certainly not less than two thousand cavalry, had been moving to Luque's rear and came upon him, surprising him just as this second attack was being made.

For a time it was a question whether Luque's command would not be wiped out. They were practically surrounded by Maceo's men, and for fully an hour and a half the fighting was desperate. It is impossible to unravel the stories of both sides so as to arrive at a clear idea of the encounter. Hernandez's right wing had been weakened by the withdrawal of part of the San Quintin battalion, and when five companies of the insurgents fell upon him he suffered so quickly that Luque sent two battalions to his assistance. Hernandez then succeeded in gaining the hill, where one division of the insurgents was stationed, but not until a cavalry charge had been repelled and seven pieces of the artillery had been turned upon it.

When the cannonading ceased four companies of infantry charged up the hill and occupied it before the insurgents, who had been driven out by the artillery, could regain it. Shortly the hill on the left of the road was taken in the same way, and Luque, although at a great loss, had repelled Maceo's attack from the rear.

The insurgent forces then withdrew to a piece of woods and made another stand about a quarter of a mile from the field where the fight had taken place. General Luque, however, withdrew his shattered forces to Pinar del Rio.

The battle had lasted from 9.15 to 11.30. Maceo had about forty of his men wounded and left four dead on the field, taking away ten others. Twenty or more of his horses were killed. The Spanish reported that he had 1,000 killed; the next day reduced the number to 300, and finally to the statement that "the enemy's losses must have been enormous"—the usual phrase when the true number is humiliating. Luque's loss has never been officially reported. It is variously estimated between fifty and one hundred men, but his defeat was severest in the failure to save the supply train. Seventeen loaded wagons and twenty pack mules carrying 100,000 rations and perhaps 10,000 rounds of ammunition were in Maceo's hands at the end of the fight.

CHAPTER VI.

Downfall of General Campos.

WHEN the Spanish government sent tens of thousands of troops to Cuba, it evidently imagined the revolution would soon be smothered. General Campos had shown his prowess and military skill on many occasions and was considered the ablest commander in the Spanish army. It was thought that he would soon be able to overtake the insurrection and quench its fires. We have arrived now at a point where his complete failure must be recorded.

It was made plain that he had a larger contract on hand than he was able with all his hosts to carry out. Repeated dispatches had been sent abroad telling of his military movements and successes, but after he had been nine months in Cuba, the stubborn fact still remained that he did not hold the Island, and the fires of the revolution were burning higher and brighter than ever. The insurgents roamed over many parts of the Island at their own sweet will. Their leaders had not been captured and the promised era of peace had not come.

Secret expeditions from the United States had landed on the Cuban shores in spite of all the vigilance of Spanish ships on the sea and armed bodies of troops on land. Such aid was likely to be furnished to an unlimited extent. The sympathy of high officials in our government with the cause of Cuba was pronounced and emphatic. Arms and ammunition in some mysterious way were constantly shipped, and the spirit of revolution was fanned by the national sentiment of the United States. General Campos could not do impossibilities. The stars in their courses were fighting against him. The government at Madrid became dissatisfied, censorious, and was ready to recall its favorite general as unequal to the situation. The old

73

Spanish element in Cuba, sympathizing with the mother country, became restless and turbulent. The war was costing immense sums of money and nothing apparently was being gained. Heavier taxes would have to be imposed upon the people of Cuba, and this, together with the destruction caused by the movements of both the Spanish and the Cuban armies, frightened the people in the large towns and caused them almost to rise in rebellion, not merely against the insurgents, but against the home government.

About the middle of January, 1896, there was, at Havana, a strong feeling of distrust. On the Exchange the anti-Spanish sentiment was shown in something like seditious utterances. Several colonels and officers of volunteers who were present made speeches against Captain-General Campos, and a general protest was expressed against his military inactivity and over-humane policy

Proposition to Lynch the Captain-General.

One major of volunteers proposed that Campos be either forced to resign or be lynched, and the speech was met by cheers from various Spanish merchants. The majority of the representatives of Spanish business houses present signed a petition to close the Exchange, and many favored closing the stores as a protest against Campos' permanence in the Island.

A delegation from the volunteer corps' officers was named to wait on Campos and insist that Pando be called and given full military command and that Campos either radically change his political policy or else resign the governorship. The Spanish sentiment against him was increasing hourly, and trouble was feared. Several foreign vessels in the port, by the direction of their consignees, suspended the discharge of their cargoes, awaiting the outcome of the affair.

Lieutenant-General Marin was hurriedly called from Matanzas, and had a consultation with the Captain-General. Campos depended upon the regular forces and upon the fleet to support him in the event of trouble, but there were few troops in Havana, most of the columns being out after Gomez and Maceo, and, unfortunately, all the warships were away cruising up and down the coast.

A significant editorial appeared in the "Diario de Marino," the organ of the Reformist party, saying that the country and business circles could not longer stand the crisis, and openly intimating that if Campos could neither crush the revolution nor effect immediate peace the time had come for a new trial, as no time must be lost in the face of the growing strength of the rebel movement.

The next news was that Director-General Martinez Campos had decided to retire from the command of the Spanish forces in Cuba and from the direction of the campaign against the insurgents. This decision was arrived at after his conference with representatives of the three political parties in Cuba, when he found that two out of the three were unalterably opposed to him and his methods. General Martinez Campos did not tell the committee immediately of his decision, but it was understood that he was positive about it, and that his successor would probably assume command of the Spanish army as military governor of Cuba in a short time.

The General's Decision.

It was understood that at the conference General Campos asked each of the leaders his opinion. The leader representing the Autonomist party expressed complete satisfaction with the conduct of the campaign, but the leaders of the Reformists and Conservatives expressed contrary opinions. General Campos at the conclusion of the conference, informed the committee of his decision to consult the government at Madrid.

A more detailed account of the Spanish General's failure was given under date of Jan. 16th, as follows:

"More grave, every hour, is the state of affairs here, if the feeling of the people is a true barometer. Events now occurring are causing a loud protest against Campos' method in carrying on the war, and since Gomez has escaped from what Spain believed was a trap in which his downfall was inevitable he is spreading uninterrupted ruin wherever he goes. Spaniards are both angry and discouraged. And the Cubans in Havana are more cautious in their conversation not to say too much to reveal their interest in the insurgent victories.

"A demonstration was made in Havana yesterday, which the censorship has not yet permitted to be published in the local papers or sent out on the cable. A newspaper, the 'Diario de la Marina,' the most conservative organ, notwithstanding the Spanish control of all publications, published a strong editorial criticising as bitterly as the most diplomatic phrases could express, the fruitless results of the methods being used to 'suppress the rebels,' and, pointing to the gravity of the situation, declared, reservedly, that public opinion had reached such a stage that it could no longer refrain from giving expression to the general conviction that heroic measures should be adopted at once.

Bold Move by Spanish Merchants.

" This was followed later in the day by a meeting of the Produce Exchanges, in which, though its session was supposed to be executive, it is said a number of the merchants of the city participated. Some lively scenes occurred, and the body reached the point of passing resolutions condemning the methods of Campos, when they were side-tracked by a proposition that the merchants, in a body, should surrender their houses to the government and close their places of business as a more effective expression of their dissatisfaction. Business is being ruined. Prices are at war figures.

" Money is scarce, and to make clearer what may have forced others to join in the protests it may be mentioned that the bonds of the railroads are practically abandoned by the companies owning them, sold recently above par, and to-day, when offered by a man forced to sell, found no bidder at 50. The meeting of the merchants, however, adjourned without action after it was decided to make no further manifestation of displeasure for the moment than to compliment the newspaper mentioned for the stand it had taken.

" Only two weeks ago, when Campos returned from his unsuccessful pursuit of the rebels, the same merchants joined a great demonstration on the streets of the city, expressing the confidence of all parties in the wise methods of the Government and the ultimate successful crushing out of the revolution. That indicates the change of public sentiment and the increasing gravity of affairs. The majority, however bitter the criticism, seem to hesitate in demanding the retirement of Campos from the leadership, but express their desire that he shall change his methods and aggressively force an issue with the insurgents.

" A significant thing about it is that they do not offer one suggestion. If Campos, exercising the authority he possesses, commanding a besieged city, were to call these men before him and say, ' What shall I do?' they would retire as much at sea as they declare him to be. Chasing cavalry with poor infantry, when the troops are as well mounted as Gomez's forces, and as skillful in separating into several divisions, which flee in as many directions, to congregate later in a country they know so perfectly, is what Campos has been doing for a long time. And he has not met with marked success.

Indignant Protests.

" The protests are arising from the representative merchants of Havana. There are some of the richest and most prominent men of the Island in their number. All three parties, rigid as are their lines in other matters, are united on this point. They are old Conservatives who have long stood for almost anything, provided Spain was uppermost; the Reformists who demand more and want certain liberties for Cuba, and the Autonomists, who claim that they would retain Spanish sovereignty, but want Cuba to largely govern herself with an autonomy in reality, which Spain has in the past promised, but never fulfilled. These protests may move Campos to change his methods, even if he can devise any change that is promising, but it is probable that if any concerted effort is made to close the business places of Havana, he will deal summarily with the men who engage in it.

" He has manifested a disposition to do this already. When the railroad companies decided to suspend operations, he called the general manager before him. In a stormy interview which occurred, Campos, it is declared, said, ' If you attempt to do so, I'll seize all your property and use it for our own facilities.' The reply is said to have been: 'We wish you would if it will end the war. But the Government has not protected us; many of our engines are wrecked, our cars burned or destroyed in derailments, viaducts and tracks torn up, we can go no further alone without being ruined.'"

Thus it will be seen that there was widespread dissatisfaction with General Campos. To add to the general discontent, news came of another success gained by the insurgents. The details of the taking of the seaport Cabanas, on the north coast, west of Havana, were now coming in and being discussed in the city with more than usual interest. Of course it indicated that nearly all that was heard at first was more or less untrue. The burning of so many buildings in the large town of Bejucal, almost in sight of Havana, was given less importance now than the Cabanas incident, because Cabanas is a seaport, and the contention from the beginning was that the rebels had never taken a seaport, or at least one of any importance.

Wild Charge of Cavalry.

Gomez, it was now known, descended upon the town and demanded its surrender. The garrison refused. The gunboat "Alerta" was in the bay, and there were marines on shore for their assistance. Gomez's lieutenant, a dashing young fellow of about thirty, was fired on when he approached with the message, but he retired jeering at the soldiers who fired so wildly that not one shot took effect. Gomez's cavalry, it is said about 2,000 strong, descended with a rush on the city, and, invading the streets, drove the Spanish troops into the church.

The firing was resumed from the roof and tower of the church, but Gomez's men succeeded in setting fire to the structure, and the regulars were forced to surrender. Meanwhile the gunboat also retired. It stopped farther out in the bay, and, according to the Spanish reports, " placed several perfectly directed shells into the city, doing terrible execution." Gomez retired after he had sacked the town and burned a part of it, having taken 11,000 rounds of ammunition and a considerable quantity of arms. Despite the demonstration made over the marksmanship displayed by their gunboat, the government reported that only two rebels had been killed. No mention was made in the official reports about the loss on the Spanish side.

These details were not reassuring in Havana, because it was said by one of the leading Spanish residents of the city: "Gomez began by simply burning some cane fields in the far eastern end of the Island. Then he began to destroy great estates. Then he moved all over the Island. He began to burn little villages, and now he is not only taking such places as Bejucal, with 8,000 inhabitants, but has captured a seaport, occupied it as long as he wished and retired with rich booty. It is bad and growing worse. Great things must be done at once."

Another Important Capture.

In addition to this, word came into the city that another important town of 3,000 population had been taken and burned. Although Gomez was supposed to be still east of Havana, since his escape through "the wall" of men across the narrow part of the island, the town was San Jose de la Yeargas, west of Havana, in the province of Pinar del Rio, which Gomez invaded when his capture was planned. The report was even admitted as a "rumor" by some of the Spanish, whose admission that a rumor is circulating does not generally occur until after the exaggerated reports which the Cubans have been spreading have pretty generally been accepted as carrying more or less fact. It was said that the town was partially destroyed after the garrison had been driven out, and that the loss of life on both sides was small.

The truth about Gomez's successful operations within sight, almost, of Havana had not been permitted to go out by cable. He had been so successful that amazement hardly expressed the feeling of the Spanish. About ten days before this the statement reached the world that Campos had Gomez trapped; that the rebels had left the mountains at last and entered the open country in the narrow western province of Havana, on their way into the extreme western province of Pinar del Rio; that Campos had thrown "a wall of men" suddenly across the Island west of Havana from near Guanajay to the south coast and had hemmed in Gomez and his "band of raiders," cutting them off from their eastern strongholds, so that it was only a question of days before the whole outfit would be shot down or the residue marched into Havana with a bayonet at every man's back.

It was not made clear why Campos was in Havana when Gomez was crossing the open country back of the city. The Spanish said he stayed in the city because it was necessary to the laying of the trap. The Cubans pointed to the reason in the short campaign which Campos made some days before. His generals had been receiving his daily instructions to " go out and find the rebels; hunt them up and make them fight." They had been coming home empty-handed so long that he became dissatisfied and went out, saying: " I'll show you how."

He went eastward with a considerable column and met Gomez himself at Mal Tiempo. There was not a pitched battle, but some severe fighting occurred with the rear-guard, Gomez avoiding a decisive issue by his peculiar tactics in battle. At any rate Campos moved his headquarters next night toward Havana—" fell back," the Cubans called it. Campos called it an " advantageous change in the base of operations."

Fell Back to Havana.

The rebels continued their skirmishing and there were encounters where a couple of thousand men on each side were engaged, and the next night Campos fell back again. The next day came no change. It began to look as if Campos experienced less trouble than his generals in finding rebels, and for the third time Campos moved his quarters back nearer Havana. The next day he arrived in the city.

The Cubans said that Campos on his arrival was unstrung, that he declared the situation graver than he had before believed it to be. Some who were in the streets watching the return of the troops confirmed this, or refused to discuss it. And the Spanish said that Campos returned because he believed that Havana was to be attacked by the insurgents, and the defense of only 20,000 troops made it necessary for him to throw his column into the city at once. The Cubans called this a retreat.

It was when Campos was in the city, whatever the real cause may have been, that Gomez came within a dozen miles of Havana, burning villages and plantations right and left, cutting the railroad lines as he had been doing further out, and driving out after disarming the garrisons he found defending them. When Gomez got into the west he found the whole country ready to receive him. He was soon joined by more of his troops, and while all accounts vary it is fairly probable that he had 4,000 cavalry with him when Campos threw the "wall of men" across the island, and the censor permitted it to be announced to the world that the trap had been sprung.

The Garrison Surrenders.

The trap was still set, but Gomez passed "the wall" captured Bejucal, a town of 8,000 people only twelve miles south of the city, and was again east of Havana. Various reports were coming in about the taking of the city, most of them agreeing only that Campos left a strong garrison there, that it surrendered with slight resistance, and that the railroad station in the centre of the city, with thirty-five buildings, was burned. There was not the slightest doubt in Havana after the capture of Bejucal and the new move of Gomez occurred, that information of the movements of Gomez's generals indicated the gathering of ten or twelve thousand insurgent cavalry within the provinces of Matanzas and Havana.

The Spanish, in the information which they permitted Havana to receive, but cut off from the rest of the world, made no concealment of their alarm, although they would not of course permit any expression of just what they feared would occur. Yet they declared that they wished for nothing so much as a chance for a decisive battle.

Meanwhile, divisions of the Cuban army were apparently hurrying eastward to join Gomez. That they were doing so for some other purpose than to rescue Gomez was apparent from the nature of their progress. Gomez had no difficulty in carrying to a successful issue his western campaign and went back through "the wall" out of the trap without even one battle. Now, the troops he left behind had been ordered to join Maceo, and the first of them reached Matanzas under General Cespedes. They were less than one hundred and fifty miles

6

from Havana. Generals Jose Maceo and Rabi, with other divisions between Puerto Principe and Santa Clara, moved all in the same direction toward Gomez, but their progress was not made as if they had in mind at any time a fear for Gomez's safety while west of Havana. The Cubans said 25,000 mounted men were in these divisions. They may have had 10,000, but the insurgents were almost without exception finely mounted.

Furthermore, they controlled all the railroads in Cuba. They cut up the lines, burned bridges, destroyed rolling-stock, and ruined the business of the roads. Within a few hours they notified the engineers and conductors of the trains still moving on a few sections that they would be shot if they carried Spanish troops again.

No Protection from the Government.

The Spanish troops might man their own trains; but the first event to follow the new order was the announcement that the railroad companies would no longer attempt to repair their tracks or viaducts. They lost all their traffic and spent thousands upon thousands of dollars in repairing breaks, but the Spanish Government neither protected them nor gave them even a Spanish promise to pay the loss. Of course, considering the claim that the Cubans were rioters and raiders, and that actual war did not exist, the company expected the protection of the State from rioters.

From this time on the railroads were solely in the hands of the Spanish Government, theoretically; of the insurgents, practically. This action of the companies, which are largely owned by foreign investors, is received in Havana as significant of more than the mere deserting of a losing enterprise.

With affairs at this point the question at once arose whether the event for which all the world was waiting, the capture of Havana, was possible for Gomez, and whether Gomez would make the attempt

Gomez, in all probability, could have taken Havana. It is just as certain that Gomez knew the chances of his success in an attack. The question to be settled was whether he wished to do so.

He had done about everything he had said he would do since the first wave of the revolution gathered itself at the eastern end of the Island in February, 1895, for the sweep it had just finished in the western extremity. Yet he did not hold one large city. One hundred and thirteen thousand Spanish soldiers from abroad and 80,000 volunteers from the Island (according to the Spanish official figures) were holding the cities and towns of greater importance in every province. Gomez had not made serious efforts to capture any of the strongly garrisoned places. He filled the very streets and houses of the cities, however, with smoke from the blazing plantations outside, and passed and repassed with his troops in sight of the Spanish colors, but the Spanish defended the cities successfully, they said.

A Most Successful Advance.

Gomez has never attacked them. He may have exhibited great wisdom in not doing so. The Spanish say he did. Gomez always disappointed Campos. His progress from Cape Maysi to Cape San Antonio had been so successful, so skillful in tactics, so resourceful in avenues of retreat when they were temporarily necessary, and his objects were so uniformly attained, that it will be one of the greatest chapters in a new nation's history of its birth. The ease and apparent lack of seriousness with which he walked into Campos' trap and then walked out again is but one of a score of instances showing how his generalship proved to be more suitable to the exigencies of Cuban warfare than that of his enemies.

Therefore no reason exists for accepting the supposition of the Spanish that Havana was secure from attack so long as all the other cities on the Island were safe in Spanish possession. And a part of the alarm which was felt in Havana following the unexpected massing of Gomez's armies was due to the suspicion that he would possibly again execute exactly the opposite move from what the Spanish generals anticipated.

The foregoing facts and circumstances will give the reader a clear idea of the reasons which led to the recall of General Campos. He was unable to suppress the revolution, which had taken a firm hold on a large part of the Island. The more insurgents he condemned and executed, the more came forward to fill their places and risk everything in the cause of freedom. In many instances when he succeeded in getting into close quarters with his foes, they eluded him and slipped from his grasp.

The home government grew impatient and began openly to proclaim his incompetency. Realizing this and feeling that he was unequal to the task assigned him, General Campos signified his willingness to retire from the field. The government at Madrid believed that his measures were not sufficiently severe and thorough. It was much easier three thousand miles away to imagine how a war should be carried on than it was to win the battles on the ground. With a public demonstration and a show of regret General Campos left the Island.

CHAPTER VII.

General Weyler in Cuba.

THERE was a good deal of consternation in Cuban circles when it was announced that General Weyler was to be made Captain-General, and would soon appear to take charge of the Spanish army, and would suppress the revolution with a strong hand. He had been in Cuba before. He was there during the ten years' war, beginning in 1868. He gained the reputation of being an active, spirited commander. He also gained the reputation of being a butcher. His bloody acts followed him. It was believed that his reputation for wholesale butchery was the sole reason for his being sent to Cuba at this time.

But where were all the loud boasts of General Campos and Spanish officials that the fires of the revolution would soon be quenched and it would require but a few months to restore the Island to peace and tranquillity? It was plain that the insurrection was working mightily in the blood of the people. The sense of wrong, the memory of cruel deeds, a long and wearying oppression, the impoverished condition of the Island had stirred the spirit of Cuban patriots. So, at the end of a year's conflict, Cuba was still in arms, fighting for independence.

The steamer "Alfonso XIII." arrived at Havana, Feb. 10, 1896, having on board General Valeriano Weyler, the new Captain-General of Cuba; and Generals Enrique, Barges, Federico, Ochando, Miguel Melguiso, Marquis Ahumada, Luis Castellvi, Sanchez Bernal and Juan Arolas, the latter being the well-known hero of Jolo, Philippine Islands.

The entire city was brilliantly decorated in honor of the occasion, and the bay was a splendid sight, all the warships and merchant craft present being decorated with bunting. The wharfs were crowded

MILITARY PROMENADE—HAVANA.

with people at an early hour, and all the steamers and tugs were loaded with sight-seers. The Chamber of Commerce, the Bourse, all the big commercial houses and Government Departments, the Canarian Association, General Weyler's countrymen and others, crowded upon the chartered steamers or about the landing-place.

The troops and volunteers were turned out to a man, together with the fire department and police, and for a long time no such brilliant display had been witnessed in Havana. Among the high military officers present were Generals Suarez Valdez, Pando, Marin and Nevarro, Admiral Yanas and staff, Colonel Castanedo, Major Moriano and many others.

Enthusiastic Welcome.

General Weyler was welcomed by the City Council on board the "Alfonso XIII." He was presented with an address of welcome and assurance of loyalty. At 11 o'clock the Captain-General came ashore, and was received by General Marin and staff. The streets were packed with people, who displayed the greatest enthusiasm. In fact, rarely has a distinguished person been received so warmly as was General Weyler when he landed. There is no doubt that considerable real enthusiasm was manifested, in addition to the greetings which would naturally be bestowed upon the representative of Spain.

The balconies in all the streets about the water-front and in the vicinity of the Palace were full of ladies in holiday attire, and they showered flowers upon the new commander as he passed. Besides, numerous floral offerings of the most beautiful description, principally in the shape of crowns, were presented to the General, who expressed his thanks in each case in a few brief words. He seemed to be much pleased with his reception, and upon arriving at the Palace formally took over the duties of the captain-generalship, taking the oath of fealty over a crucifix and upon a Bible. General Marin administered the oath of office, and soon afterward he received the local military and civil authorities, the different corporations and the bishops and priests.

The German warships which were in the harbor saluted t/

arrival of General Weyler, as did all the Spanish warships in port and the forts ashore.   The Loyalists, of course, were out in the strongest force possible; but it may be said that the entire population of Havana turned out, and hardly a representative of the shipping or business interests of the city failed to make the day a holiday.   After the reception of the local military and civil authorities, corporations and clergy was completed, General Weyler appeared upon the balcony of the Palace and reviewed the troops.   His appearance before the public was the signal for a long outburst of the most enthusiastic cheering, the firing of cannon and the sound of martial music, all the bands in the city being stationed at different points.   In addition to the inhabitants of the city proper thousands of people flocked into the city from all directions before daybreak.

Restrictions upon the Press.

Accompanying General Weyler were Captains Gelaber and Linares, who are known as "military editors." They were to have charge of the press censorship, and it was rumored that there would be considerably more difficulty experienced in this connection by the correspondents in the future.   The press regulations had been considerably relaxed, and not much difficulty had been experienced in getting average matter upon the cable.   But, it was thought the new Captain-General would be very severe with correspondents who sent false accounts of Cuban successes or in any way brought about the publication of false news.   By this it was not meant that General Weyler intended to interfere with the proper liberty which the press can be allowed in war-time.   It really meant only that he would do everything possible to prevent the sending out of news undoubtedly false.

A disinterested observer of the situation wrote as follows under date of Feb. 10, 1896:

"So far as the general situation is concerned, there is not much change.   Indeed, no change of importance is expected for some days.   General Weyler will first devote himself to a complete review of the operations already undertaken, and he will then figure out the situation as it actually exists.   For this purpose, almost immediately after taking the oath of fealty, he caused orders to be sent to all the commanders in the field to draw up promptly and forward to head-quarters here complete returns of the condition of their commands, together with the state of railroads, telegraphs and public thorough-fares and the probable location and strength of the enemy in their neighborhoods.

Weyler Seeks to Learn the Situation.

" This action upon the part of General Weyler is supplementary to the regular report and returns which were handed over to him by General Marin after the new Captain-General had been sworn in. While it is no reflection upon General Marin or the other Spanish commanders here or in other parts of Cuba, the Captain-General took this step in order thoroughly to go over the ground himself, and possibly in view of the sensational reports which have been cir-culated by agents of the insurgents and others to the effect that large quantities of stores, arms and ammunition are missing from the dif-ferent depots and have found their way into the hands of the insur-gents.   Between this and the tales of wholesale dishonesty circulated here and elsewhere there is quite a difference, and nobody here believes that there has been any treachery of importance.

" General Marin, who has been appointed Captain-General of Porto Rico, is expected to leave for his new post to-morrow. The exact plan of campaign of General Weyler is not known, but it is believed that it will be a very different one from that of Campos. He is likely to call in all of the small detachments of troops, which have from the first had such a weakening effect upon the Spanish operations, and will try to drive the insurgents into a position from which they cannot escape without a pitched battle. General Weyler will also do everything possible to muster as strong a force of cavalry as he can. Considerable reinforcements of this branch of the service have already arrived here, and more are expected during the week.

" Some reports credit the insurgents with desiring to concentrate all their scattered detachments and columns into one body, and so bring the insurrection to a direct issue. But Spaniards here who are well posted on the situation say that there is no truth in the report that the insurgents will make any effort to risk a pitched battle."

Captain-General Weyler clearly defined the policy he intended to pursue in the conduct of the campaign for the suppression of the insurrection. Before he had been at Havana many hours he issued the following proclamation:

"To the People of Cuba: Honored by Her Majesty, the Queen, and her Government, with the command of this Island, under the difficult circumstances now prevailing, I take charge of it with the determination that it shall never be given up by me, and that I shall keep it in the possession of Spain, willing as she is to carry out whatever sacrifice shall be required to succeed, as she has been in the past.

"I rely upon the gallantry and discipline of the army and navy, upon the patriotism, never to be subdued, of the volunteer corps, and more especially upon the support that I should be given by the loyal inhabitants, born here or in Spain.

"It is not necessary to say that I shall be generous with the sub-dued and to all of those doing any service to the Spanish cause. But I will not lack in the decision and energy of my character to punish with all the rigor that the law enacts those who in any way shall help the enemy, or shall calumniate the prestige of our name.

"Putting aside at present any idea of politics, my mission is the honorable one of finishing the war, and I only see in you the loyal Spaniards who are to assist me to defeat the insurgents. But her Majesty's Government is aware of what you are and of what you are worthy, and the status of peace that these provinces may obtain. It will grant you, when it is deemed suitable to do so, the reforms the Government may think most proper, with the love of a mother to her children.

"Inhabitants of Cuba, lend me your co-operation and in that way you will defend your interests, which are those of the country.

"Long live Spanish Cuba!

"Your General and Governor,
　　　　　"VALERIANO WEYLER,
　　　　　　　"Marquis of Teneriffe."

To the Volunteers and Firemen.

General Weyler also offered the following address:

"Volunteers and Firemen: Being again at your head, I see in you the successors of the volunteers and firemen who fought with me in the previous war, and, with their bravery, energy and patriotism, brought about peace, defended the towns and cities and contributed most powerfully to save Cuba for Spain. Remember these virtues brighten your spirits, and, relying on my whole attention, my decisive support and my utmost confidence, lend me the same help and co-operation, and with the same ambition, save the prestige of your name and the honor of our flag, which, forever victorious, should fly over this Island.

"Soldiers of the army, I greet you in the name of Her Majesty, the Queen, and of the Government. Having the honor of being at your head, I trust that at my command you will continue to show the bravery in face of hardships proper for the Spanish soldier, and that you will confer new wreaths to add to those already attained under the command of my predecessors, Generals Martinez Campos and Sabas Marin.

"On my part, answering to the great sacrifice made by the nation and using the efforts of all arms and bodies in the work entrusted to each of the organic units, I will not omit anything to place you in the condition for obtaining the victory and the return of peace to this Island, which is what she longs for.

"Sailors, I have again the satisfaction to be at your side, and I again trust that, as in Mindanao recently, you will lend me your powerful co-operation to bring peace to this Island. Thus I expect surely that you will afford me a new chance to express my thanks and my enthusiasm to the Spanish navy."

To the Military Officers.

The following circular of General Weyler was addressed to the military officers :

" I have addressed my previous proclamations at the moment of my landing to the loyal inhabitants, to the volunteers and nremen, and to the army and navy.

" I may give you a slight idea of the intentions I have and the measures I shall follow as Governor-General-in-Chief, in accordance with the general desire of Spain and with the decided aim of Her Majesty's Government to furnish all the means required to control and crush this rebellion.

" Knowing this, and knowing my character, I may perhaps need to say no more to make you understand what is the conduct that I am to follow. But with the idea of avoiding all kinds of doubt, even keeping (as you are to keep) the circulars to be published, I deem it necessary to make some remarks.

Determined to Aid the Local Governments.

" It is not unknown by you that the state in which the rebellion has come and the raid made by the principal leaders recently, which could not be stopped even by the active pursuit of the columns, is due to the indifference, the fear or the disheartenment of the inhabitants. Since it cannot be doubted that some, seeing the burning of their property without opposition, and that others, who have been born in Spain, should sympathize with the insurgents, it is necessary at all hazards to better this state of things and to brighten the spirit of the inhabitants, making them aware that I am determined to lend all my assistance to the local inhabitants. So I am determined to have the law fall with all its weight upon all those in any way helping the enemy, or praising them, or in any way detracting from the prestige of Spain, of its army, or of its volunteers. It is necessary for those by our side to show their intentions with deeds, and their behavior should prove that they are Spanish.

" Since the defence of the country demands the sacrifice of her children, it is necessary that the towns should look to their defence, and that no precautions in the way of scouts should be lacking to give news concerning the enemy, and whether it is in their neighborhood, and so that it may not happen that the enemy should be better informed than we.

" The energy and vigor of the enemy will be strained to trace the course of our line, and in all cases you will arrest and place at my disposal to deliver to the courts those who in any way shall show their sympathy or support for the rebels.

" The public spirit being heatened, you must not forget to enlist the volunteers and guerrillas in your district, this not preventing at the same time the organization, as opportunity offers, of a guerrilla band of twenty-five citizens for each battalion of the army.

" I propose that you shall make the dispositions you think most proper for the carrying out of the plan I wish, but this shall not authorize you to determine anything not foreseen in the instructions, unless the urgency of some circumstances should demand it.

" I expect that, confining yourself to these instructions, you will lend me your worthy support towards the carrying out of my plan for the good of the Spanish cause.   WEYLER."

The People Alarmed.

It was considered that General Weyler's Proclamation was poorly adapted to quiet the storm of revolution.   When it was announced that he was coming, an alarm amounting almost to terror spread among the Cubans in the provinces, and every day that brought his landing nearer increased the panic.   In two days fifteen hundred people fled to Matanzas from the country south.   Others came into Havana from all directions.

In Sabanilla, after the Spanish garrison had killed the men to whom amnesty had been granted, in revenge for their losses and defeat by the insurgents, a reign of terror began in the city.   Women dared not leave their homes.   In many cases they were dragged out by the Spanish and by the drunken rabble of the town, who had license given to them at the same time that protection was withdrawn from the homes.   The whole matter was laid before the Captain-General, but he took no measure of relief.

A committee of citizens came to Havana from Jovellanos, another place where the same sort of murdering had been going on.   It was composed of both Spanish and Cubans.   They had no sooner returned unsuccessful in their mission to General Marin than the inhabitants began to leave, and more than half the population deserted the city.

The alarm spread to other places, and not without cause. Arrests of "suspects" were made in every town where there was a Spanish garrison. In Havana "suspects" were taken every day. Of a suspect's fate only one thing could be learned from the officials—"He was incommunicado." That meant that he was buried from the world. No one but the Spanish officers were then permitted to see him, and unless his arrest was observed by some one who knew him, not one word ever reached a friend or family to explain the cause of his disappearance.

The military executions are not public unless the victim is a "rebel chief" or a cause exists for a display. To be a "suspect" it is only necessary to be a "sympathizer," and "sympathy" is not defined. In a published statement made by Weyler just before he embarked for Cuba he is quoted as saying: "I will be inexorable toward spies and sympathizers," and he also omitted to draw the line. In Cuba it does not mean to extend aid or comfort.

Large Number of Arrests.

In five days there were forty-seven arrests in Pinar del Rio "on suspicion." From Jovellanos in Matanzas Province six hundred people fled because thirty-six "suspects" were arrested in two days. Some of these refugees reached Havana, and their story was that six of the prisoners were marched out of the city at night, that firing was heard, and that the guard returned without them. The friends of the victims were too much terrified to manifest their sympathy or attempt to recover the bodies, for fear of being themselves apprehended as suspects.

From Santiago people came to Havana with the same reports. At Hoyo Colorado, between Havana and Guanajay, the Spanish garrison took seventy-nine suspects within a few days. This town was peaceably held by the Cuban army for several days, and while the insurgents were there they hung some of the dissolute characters in the place, who had used their presence as an excuse for crime. After their retirement the Spanish moved in, and the wholesale arrests began.

Before General Weyler set out from Spain a cablegram from Madrid was published in the Havana newspapers quoting him as saying: " I desire the insurgents to remain in Havana and Pinar del Rio, because there the ground is suitable for wiping them out. I believe that suspects are quite right in fleeing from Havana, and when I arrive many more will go." It is significant that the newspapers of Havana in which the military censor caused this to be printed displayed the statement in black full-face type.

It is noteworthy that when Weyler was named as a possible successor to Captain-General Arias in 1894, Campos, who was not a candidate for the office—the choice lying between Weyler and Calleja—said: " If Weyler is nominated even the dead would rise from their graves to protest." Calleja was appointed because affairs in Cuba were already becoming unsettled, and the Spanish Ministry feared that Weyler's name alone would be dangerous to all interests. Whenever such methods were urged upon Campos, while he was in Cuba, he steadfastly resisted, and declared that humanity had a call upon any nation's acts in warfare.

CHAPTER VIII.

Horrible Story of Barbarity.

JUST previous to General Weyler's arrival some startling facts came out concerning the battle at Paso Real, between General Luque and General Maceo's division under Bermudez, Zayas and Chileno. From an official Spanish source and also from citizens of Paso Real, who were eye-witnesses of the battle, it was learned that the hospital was invaded, the wounded rebels killed, some of them in their beds, and that when the thirty-seven Spanish prisoners, taken in the battle outside the town, were about to be taken away, Bermudez, in retaliation for the butchery of his sick, ordered a line to be formed, and the thirty-seven were pinioned and shot.

The Cubans told a horrifying tale of the fight, and declared that the hospital was the real scene of which Luque wrote in his report : "I had the satisfaction of seeing at the end of the day sixty-two rebels dead."

Paso Real had been used for seventeen days as the insurgent hospital. Maceo had left all his wounded there when he moved into Havana province to operate with Gomez. The surrounding country was free, practically, from Spanish forces, except Luque's command in Pinar del Rio City. Maceo counted upon reaching the people with protection if they were threatened, and when word came to him that Luque had left for Paso Real, he sent Bermudez with 1,000 cavalry to hold the town. Luque, as he said in his report, marched twenty-seven hours, almost continuously, and when he reached Paso Real, he found only a small garrison there. His report says :

"The rebels made a strong defense, firing from the tops of houses and along the fences around the city. The Spanish vanguard, under Colonel Hernandez, attacked the vanguard, centre and rear-guard of the rebels in the central streets of the town, driving them with con-

96

ADMIRAL GEORGE DEWEY
THE HERO OF MANILA

UNITED STATES CRUISER OLYMPIA

Twin screw; length on water line, 340 feet; breadth, 53 feet; draft, 21 feet 6 inches; displacement, 5,870 tons; speed, 20 knots. Main battery, four 8-inch guns and ten 5-inch rapid-fire guns. Secondary battery, fourteen 6-pounder, and six 1-pounder rapid-fire guns, and four gatlings. Protected steel deck, from 2 to 4¾ 20 Officers, 290 Men. Cost, 1,769,000.

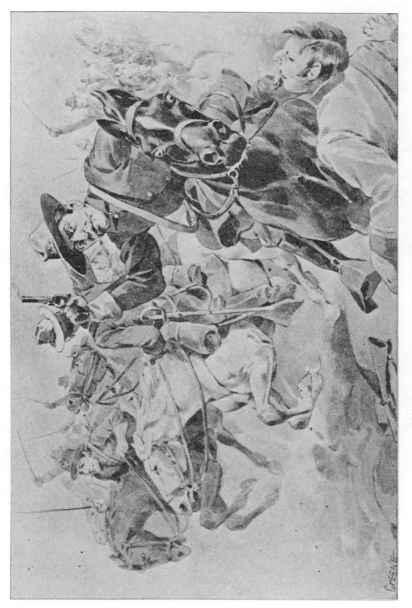

GALLANT CHARGE BY GENERAL WHEELER'S CAVALRY

UNITED STATES FORCES CAPTURING THE INTRENCHMENTS AT SANTIAGO

LANDING OF GENERAL SHAFTER'S ARMY NEAR SANTIAGO—CUBA

GENERAL TORAL SURRENDERING SANTIAGO TO GENERAL SHAFTER

ADMIRAL W. T. SAMPSON

BOMBARDMENT OF SAN JUAN BY ADMIRAL SAMPSON'S FLEET
THURSDAY, MAY 12, 1898

COMMANDER RICHARD WAINWRIGHT

CAMP OF UNITED STATES REGULARS IN CUBA

UNITED STATES BATTLESHIP OREGON

Twin screw; length, 348 feet; breadth, 69 feet 3 inches; draft, 24 feet; displacement, 10,288 tons; speed, 16.79 knots. Main battery four 13-inch, eight 8-inch and four 6-inch breech loading rifles. Secondary battery, twenty 6-pounder and six 1-pounder rapid-fire guns, and four gatlings. Armor on sides, 18 inches. 32 Officers, 441 Men. Cost $3,180,000.

UNITED STATES MONITOR MIANTONOMOH

Length, 259 feet 6 inches; breadth, 55 feet 10 inches; draft, 14 feet 6 inches; displacement, 3,990 tons; speed, 10 knots. Main battery, four 10-inch breech loading rifles. Secondary battery, two 6-pounder, two 3-pounder and two 1-pounder rapid-fire guns. Thickness of armor, 7 inches. 13 Officers, 136 Men.

LIEUT. R. P. HOBSON

TOTAL DESTRUCTION OF THE SPANISH FLEET NEAR SANTIAGO

GREAT AMERICAN VICTORY IN THE HARBOR OF MANILA

PREPARING A TORPEDO BOAT FOR ACTION

TOWN AND HARBOR OF CARDENAS.

tinuous volleys and fierce cavalry charges into the outskirts of the town." And all this is true.

Then General Luque says specifically that " up to this point we had killed ten insurgents." And there the citizens of Paso Real say that the report is also true, but that, having driven the insurgents out, the hospital was attacked, and twenty-eight men, or thirty-two (the accounts vary between these two figures), were killed. They declare that shots were fired through the windows upon men lying in cots, and that, when the doors were broken down, the rest were killed with the bayonet.

A Spirited Fight.

General Luque's report continues : " As Colonel Hernandez was pursuing them (the insurgents) out of the city, he encountered 1,000 cavalry drawn up in line of battle ready to attack him." This was Bermudez and his cavalry, who had come up at that moment. A Spanish officer who was in this fight said : " It was as hot as any fight we have ever had in this war. It seemed twice as if they were piling all over us. We just kept on firing, and I could see men going down on both sides. Sometimes we couldn't see anything for the smoke, but when it cleared the men only dropped so much faster that we wanted it back again. I came away at once when the fight was over, and I don't know what the losses were, but they must have been very large on both sides."

Of this the report says : " The Spanish forces advanced from one position to another, firing volleys. They were met by the enemy, whose cavalry charged, coming as far as the bayonet points of the Spanish soldiers. The first time we repelled them in straight lines, the second time in circular groups." From anything but a Spanish standpoint this peculiar progression of tactics would indicate that the Spanish straight lines were very seriously broken, and that the " circular groups " which followed were either accident or necessity, but General Luque says that it really meant that "the rebels were thus utterly dispersed and retreated in the direction of Palacios."

This part of the day's conflict was where the thirty-seven

Spanish were made prisoners. It was after the fight that Bermudez learned what had occurred in the town, and then he shot them and left their bodies on the ground, where they were buried that night by the Spanish, all in one grave. General Luque reported this fight as a great victory. There are Spanish school histories which say Nelson's fleet was defeated at Trafalgar. The Spanish newspapers at Havana were still referring to "the most glorious victory at Los Arrovos," where in the early fall one of their strong forces was utterly defeated, and the official Spanish report of Campos' defeat and retreat from Mal Tiempo still reads, "Our side had but seventeen killed."

A Disastrous Campaign.

Under date of February 8th, we have an account of the operations of the Spanish General Sabas Marin, who left Havana a short time before. His campaign in search of General Gomez was disastrous, and the official reports of Spanish victories were misleading. There were losses on both sides, but Marin accomplished absolutely nothing of what he intended to achieve.

The first misfortune which overtook the Spaniards was the rout of Carnella, on the very day on which Marin left Havana. Canellas left Guanajay in the morning with 1,500 infantry. His rout was known to Gomez, who sent Pedro Diaz with 400 infantry and 1,000 cavalry to engage him at the Saladrigas plantation, while the main army moved safely eastward, a few miles to the south. It was Gomez's intention to come up in the rear of Marin between the Captain-General's forces and the Spanish line.

Diaz reached Saladrigas early in the morning. Near the road the land is cut into small sections by stone fences, and a high fence fronted by a ditch faces the road. Just beyond this point is a sharp hill, around which the road turns. Behind the hill Diaz waited in concealment with the 1,000 cavalry for the sound of firing from the 400 infantry who were hidden behind the fence where Canellas was to pass. Nearly three hours they were lying there, when the head of the Spanish column appeared. The advance guard was allowed to pass, and the main body was completely in the trap when volleys were poured into them, fairly mowing them down. Canellas made a brave stand and attempted to dislodge the rebels, but his men were panic-stricken, and some of them had fled before he had his force under control.

As the first charge was being made Diaz came down upon his

THE OLD FORT HAVANA.

flank and rear with the thousand cavalry. The onslaught was irresistible. Half of Diaz's men never fired a shot, but howling "Machete!" they rode furiously upon the Spanish lines, cutting their way through with the ugly weapon of which they are such masters.

Diaz had not placed enough men behind the wall to hold it, and the Spanish succeeded in gaining it after a hot struggle. They were but little better off, however, as the insurgents took cover behind another fence on the opposite side of the field. Again they were dislodged and forced back, while from the first position about half of Canellas' force withstood the cavalry. Diaz, sheltered in underbrush and woods, kept up a scattered firing for over two hours, and then withdrew.

That night Canellas remained on the battle-ground. As soon as

Diaz was gone, picket lines were thrown out and the burying of the dead began. It was midnight when Canellas resumed his march toward San Antonio, and when he brought in what was left of his command Marin hastened back with all his force, to the main line and went down to Quivican.

No official report of this battle was issued by the Spanish. So far as the record shows it never occurred. A Spanish general admitted that Carnellas lost 200 men. An eye-witness of the fight, who reached Havana that night, said the loss was greater. Gomez's march was thus saved from interruption by Marin. The next day, while Marin was at Quivican, Gomez's forces were near Guira, in the Havana province. Gomez himself was that day at the Mirosa plantation, east of the Spanish line, with about 400 men. He had come down from the Bahia Honda district, through the same country Maceo was traversing.

Capture of a Railroad Train.

Next day, while Marin was moving trains loaded with men out over the branch road toward Guira for another move upon Gomez, occurred the second and by far the most serious of the Spanish disasters. It was nothing less. Diaz, until now unheard of as a rebel leader, came in behind Marin and captured a railroad train of twenty-nine cars directly on the trocha, two miles south of San Felipe. He took 1,000 Mauser rifles, 200,000 cartridges, two rapid-fire cannon and killed or captured the whole Spanish escort with the train. Then Marin returned again in all haste to Quivican.

This event has been embodied in an official report, but the report agrees neither with what the Spanish permitted to be printed in the Havana papers nor with the facts which were collected down the line. The rebels tore up the rails for a space of 300 yards. They were unmolested, as the Spanish had no idea that they would venture "into the face of death," as they say when referring to the trocha. Furthermore, Marin was out toward Guira, again engaged in surrounding Gomez.

Diaz, with 400 men, waited for the train in comparative security until 5 o'clock in the afternoon. It was guarded by only forty-two Spanish soldiers, and they were part in an armored car and part scattered along the top of the train. The engine ran on to the broken track and rolled over into the ditch. As soon as it struck, the rebels fired on the train, killing Major Lopez Tovezulla, who was in command, a lieutenant, a sergeant and fourteen of the soldiers. Then the rest surrendered their arms and the insurgents demanded the number of the car in which the rapid-fire cannon were stored. The soldiers declared they were left behind, and then the looting of the train began.

When all that the 400 men could carry had been loaded on their horses, and some mules taken from the train had been hitched to the cannon, Gen. Linares, who had heard the firing at San Felipe, came up with 2,000 infantry. The insurgents retired in the direction of Guira without waiting to engage with his force. Linares' men managed to save eight of the cars with part of their freight. The other twenty-two were burned, having been fired by the rebels. The train had one of the richest freights which had gone down the road in a long time. It was to be put on a steamer and sent to several ports on the south coast.

The insurgents not only knew the exact time of its passing, but of its contents, and the " Diario de la Marina," the Spanish newspaper in Havana, gravely requested in its leading editorial that Gen. Marin investigate to discover how the insurgents became informed and take precautions to prevent the repetition of such an unseemly occurrence.

The Spanish official report said that the Spanish guard did not surrender, and that they retained their arms. The only arms Gen. Linares brought back to San Felipe which he did not take out were some old shot-guns, muskets and muzzle-loading rifles. The Cubans declare that these were thrown away by the rebels when they secured the Mausers, and they are strong evidence that this Cuban version is the true one.

CHAPTER IX.

Men and Arms for Cuba.

FROM the beginning of the Cuban uprising constant attempts have been made to supply the insurgents with arms and ammunition from our own country. Secret agents were at work in many places, and Spanish spies were equally active. It was well understood that several expeditions had succeeded in effecting a landing in Cuba, and the supplies thus furnished had been of material help to General Gomez and his troops.

Our government officials, while sympathizing with the cause of Cuba, were nevertheless active in preventing the shipment of arms. But a sea-coast as long as ours, with a great number of ports, has afforded ample opportunity for expeditions to be fitted out secretly, and it seems impossible for Spanish gunboats to prevent entirely the Cuban army from obtaining supplies from outside sources.

The following account of the seizure of a vessel will be of interest to the reader: The iron steamer "Bermuda," flying the British flag, was boarded and seized by New York revenue officers off Liberty Island late on the night of Feb. 24. The "Bermuda" had been under the watch of Spanish spies for some time. They had reason to believe that she had been bought by Cuban revolutionists and was fitting out as a filibuster. She had been anchored off Liberty Island for several days, and there was evidence that she was preparing for sea.

At 11 P. M., just after a large party of Cubans had gone aboard, the revenue cutter "Hudson" steamed alongside, and a boarding party arrested all on the "Bermuda." At midnight the revenue cutter "Chandler" started down the bay to catch a lighter loaded with ammunition and look for another party of Cubans who had started to board the "Bermuda."

The "Bermuda" was an English-built steamer formerly running in the Outerbridge Line. She was purchased by a firm suspected of being in league with the revolutionary party. She was recently taken to the coal docks at Port Liberty, and there coaled up. Then she went to the Liberty Island anchorage. When the tug ran alongside the marshals and Pinkerton men swarmed aboard. No resistance was offered by the frightened crew and Cubans, who had just come aboard. Every man was seized. Among the captives were General Garcia and several other prominent Cubans. Several bags of gold were seized by the marshals and a quantity of ammunition.

Revolutionists Arrested.

General Calixto Garcia and about sixty other of the leading spirits in the Cuban revolutionary cause were brought to the Federal Building. The warrant upon which the 200 Cuban revolutionists were taken into custody was drawn in accordance with the section of the Federal Revised Statutes, which is a portion of what is known as the " Neutrality Act."

A great many of the prisoners found on the " Bermuda " and the two tug-boats were survivors of the expedition which left the New Haven river a month before on the " J. W. Hawkins," which sunk off the south shore of Long Island, a number of men going down with the wreck. Afterward the filibusters were watched by spies employed by the Spanish and United States governments. The surveillance led to the discovery that General Garcia and his followers had purchased the " Bermuda " to take a large company of insurgents to Cuba, with arms and ammunition. The " Bermuda," which had been granted clearance papers at the custom house to Santa Martha, United States of Colombia, was making ready to leave port when United States Marshals McCarthy and Kennedy made their raid. The steam lighter " Stranahan," which had left one of the Brooklyn piers, was seized, the ammunition in boxes, which was concealed beneath piles of cord-wood, and on the " Bermuda " were found several bags of gold coin.

The prisoners were released because their arrest was in violation of the instructions sent out from Washington by Attorney-General

Harmon, that suspicion merely was not sufficient ground for arrest, but that evidence of intention to violate the neutrality laws was required.

The trial of Captain Wiborg, First Mate Petersen and Second Mate Johansen, of the steamship "Horsa," on the charge of beginning a military expedition, to carry men and arms to Cuba, to aid in

MARINE WHARF—HAVANA.

the insurrection against Spain, was held in Philadelphia in the latter part of February, before Judge Butler in the United States District Court.

In the course of the proceedings, District Attorney Ingham called for the production by Captain Wiborg of the charter under which the "Horsa" made the trip from Philadelphia to Port Antonio, during which the alleged offence was said to have been committed. Mr. Ker, counsel for the defence, contended that if the "Horsa" was more than three miles out from the shore at Barnegat, when the men and ammunition were taken on board, the alleged offence did not come within the jurisdiction of the United States.

The Judge said that if it was proven that the defendants did not know where the men were going he would affirm the point. In reply District Attorney Ingham said that he did not rest the United States' case on that question. He relied on the testimony which was heard to show that there was an organization, and that it took place in the United States, and that under it men and arms were taken to Cuba.

Testimony of a Fireman.

The examination began with Oscar Svensen, one of the " Horsa's " firemen. The witness related that portions of the ship were repainted, and then, coming down to the time when the thirty or forty men were taken on board to be conveyed to Cuba, he said that he told the chief engineer that he did not wish to go along, and desired to go ashore. The witness said that the chief replied that his life was as dear to him as the lives of the witness and the men complaining with him were to them, and that the captain had said it was all right.

Svensen said he had taken five trips on the " Horsa;" that he knew Firemen Armstrong and Fredericksen of the vessel; also that nothing about money was said by the captain when the witness and the men with him had raised objections to going along.

Svensen said that some of the men taken on board on one occasion had an exercise. He had heard the cannon fired and saw the smoke. Regarding the boxes said to have contained ammunition, the witness said that a fellow from Jamaica had opened them. The pay of Svensen was $25 per month. To the question when he had first told his story and to whom, the witness answered by the statement that it was two weeks ago, and to a Pinkerton Agency man. The pay he received for giving information and his detention here was $2 per day and board.

After some further questioning by counsel, the witness, in answer to a question by the Judge, said that he shipped in Philadelphia, but that he did not know whether the other firemen were employed here or not. Svensen was shown a number of swords and machetes, some of which he designated as " banana snipes."

The next witness was Ludwig Gustav Jensen, who was also a fire-man on the " Horsa." Jensen said that he had wanted extra pay to go on the ship, after the thirty or forty men were taken aboard, and spoke to the chief engineer about it. The latter had said that if anybody was to get hung it would be him, the chief engineer, and not the crew. In reply to questions from the Judge, the witness described the cartridge boxes, said he saw six of the men taken on board drill, and described the rifles and guns.

The Captain on the Stand.

Edward N. Taxis and Herbert Ker testified that the machetes carried by the men were to be seen strapped to the waists or slung over the shoulders of nearly every inhabitant of the West Indies. Mr. Ker also testified that he had taken a trip to Africa on the " Horsa " last March, and was thoroughly familiar with the vessel. He said it was customary to paint the funnels and other portions of the vessel at sea, and he had often seen it done. During his trip to Africa he on one occasion happened to particularly notice the name on the stern of the vessel, and he testified that the name was in brass letters about six or eight inches high, and were raised about one inch.

Captain Wiborg was then called as a witness in his own behalf. Before beginning his examination Mr. Ker stated to the court that the mere making of an affidavit by any one in the court-room, who might hear this witness' testimony, would result in his life being forfeited should he ever set foot in Spanish dominion, and he thought it his duty, in order to protect his client as far as possible, to ask the court to forbid the publication of his testimony or to exclude every one from the court-room while he was being examined.

Judge Butler said the court was there to try the case according to the evidence, and had nothing to do with the risk the witness took in giving his testimony. He was not compelled to testify, and whatever evidence he gave would be voluntary, with the full knowledge on the part of the witness of the responsibility he was taking.

Captain Wiborg testified that he had been captain of the steamer " Horsa " two years. On the evening of November 9, 1895, he left Philadelphia for Jamaica between 7 and 8 o'clock. Before leaving port the name of the vessel was scraped off the side of the vessel on account of iron rust. He had regular clearance papers. The name of the vessel was also on the stern of the vessel in brass letters or composition. He had two boats and two horses, and a lot of empty boxes and barrels. He received a message to go opposite Barnegat and await orders, which he did.

He anchored four or five miles from shore. He anchored because the chief engineer told him part of the machinery was not working properly, and he should keep the ship in smooth water. While there anchored he received a message by tug telling him to take the men and boats on board and deliver the boats to the men when they called for them. The men walked through the port between decks when they boarded his vessel. He then proceeded southward and passed Waterland Island towards Jamaica. This route is called Crooked Island passage.

Off the Cuban Coast.

In taking this route to Jamaica, the captain said, it was necessary to sail along the coast of Cuba for about six hours. It was when his vessel was about six miles off the Cuban coast that a colored man, who was said to be a pilot, told him to stop the vessel and let the men off. He did so, and the men got into the boats, taking as many boxes as they could carry, and then asked him to tow them in towards shore a bit, which he did.

In answer to questions, the witness said that the men did not have the appearance of soldiers, and he had no knowledge that they were going to take part in the war in Cuba. In giving them passage he had obeyed orders, and had no right to refuse them. All told, he said, there were 39 men transferred to the "Horsa," and they brought a lot of boxes with them. They did not call upon him for meals, but brought their own food with them in the boxes, some of which contained canned goods and hardtack. He said the men had guns, but he did not think anything of that, as he had often seen passengers carry guns on his vessel. He saw the cannon which they brought, and at first he thought it was one of his own, as it was very much like them. The captain said that he had two cannons on the "Horsa."

one a small brass one, which was used in firing salutes, and the other of considerable size.

The following was Judge Butler's charge: " The defendants being, or rather having been at the time in question, officers of the ship, the first as captain, and the others as mates, are indicted jointly and also separately, in which indictments it is charged that ' they, within the territory and jurisdiction of the United States, did begin, set on foot, and provide and prepare the means for a certain military expedition and enterprise to be carried on from thence against the territory and dominions of a foreign prince, to wit: Against the Island of Cuba, the said Island being then and there the territory and dominions of the King of Spain, the said United States being at peace with the said king, contrary to the Act of Congress in such case made and provided.'

Was it a Military Expedition?

" The evidence heard would not justify a conviction of anything more than providing the means for or aiding such military expedition, as by furnishing transportation for the men, their arms, baggage, etc. To convict them you must be fully satisfied by the evidence that a military expedition was organized in this country to be carried out as, and with the object, charged in the bill; and that the defendants with knowledge of this provided means for its assistance and assisted it as before stated."

In commenting on the Judge's decisions, counsel for the defence said: " It has been decided that, 'it is no offence against the laws of the United States to transport arms, ammunition and munitions of war from this country to any foreign country, nor is it any offence to transport persons intending to enlist in foreign armies, and arms and munitions of war on the same ship. In such cases the persons transported and the shipper run the risk of seizure and capture by the foreign power, against whom the arms were to be used.'

" The Judge further charges that the putting out of lights and the taking on and transferring of passengers and boxes of arms on the high seas are acts which are perfectly lawful, in order to prevent capture by a Spanish man-of-war.

"If the Spaniards want to stop the landing of arms in Cuba, let them close the ports of the Island. This, of course, they won't do."

When the case was given to the jury, they deliberated twelve hours, then brought in a verdict of guilty against Captain Wiborg and his officers, who were sentenced to fines and imprisonment from one year to fifteen months. An appeal was taken, and the men were liberated on bail.

What Became of the "Bermuda?"

It is necessary at this point to anticipate a little the order of events and state what became of the steamer "Bermuda," referred to in the first part of this chapter. The quiet, easy-going people of Somers Point, N. J., Ocean City, Beesley's Point and Tuckahoe suddenly awakened, on March 17, to the fact that a big Cuban filibustering expedition has just cleared from their midst without one of them for a moment suspecting what the strange movements of the large body of swarthy-skinned visitors meant.

The steamer "Atlantic City" took the Cuban patriots, who reached Tuckahoe on the night of the 16th, out to the famous "Bermuda," which at 6 o'clock sharp gave five shrill signal whistles, announcing that she was awaiting them just off the Great Egg Harbor bar. Three hours afterwards the "Atlantic City" returned to her winter berth at Tuckahoe, having safely transferred her passengers to the "Bermuda," which promptly steamed away southward. The party consisted of General Garcia and his 32 compatriots, who left Philadelphia on the 15th, and about 30 other volunteers for Cuban freedom, who joined them in some mysterious way afterward.

In a clever manner the Cubans eluded the spies in the employ of Spain, who followed their tug down the Delaware on the night of the 15th. The tug started ostensibly for Cape Henlopen, where it was supposed the filibusters were to be put aboard the "Bermuda." The tug led the Spanish spies a merry chase about the Delaware Bay, and then, under cover of a heavy fog, slipped back up the Delaware, unsuspected and unnoticed, reaching Kaighn's Point, Camden, at an early hour on Monday evening, the 16th. Here a special train on the Reading Railroad awaited them, and the Cuban patriots were swiftly borne to Tuckahoe, which is only about eight miles from Great Egg Harbor Bay.

When the big party, which was said to have numbered fully 60, arrived at the little Jersey town, they began looking about for something to eat. There was no hotel of any consequence at the place, and, to make matters worse, no stimulants of any kind could be procured. Finally two handsome young Tuckahoe girls, who were on their way home from an evening sociable on the outskirts of the town, attracted the attention of the Cubans, and two of the best looking men of the party were delegated to interview them on the "grub" question.

Supper for Patriots.

The girls readily agreed to prepare supper for them, and were handed $50 each to stimulate them in their efforts to get a hurried meal for the hungry patriots. They were warned not to make any stir over the matter, and to say not a word to their neighbors until the party had left the place.

The Cubans ate their late supper in squads, and after liberally complimenting the accommodating girls left the house in the best of humor and quietly boarded the steamer "Atlantic City," which was lying at the wharf, above the drawbridge. The crew of the steamer were asleep at their homes in Tuckahoe, they having no knowledge whatever of the human freight which was taken aboard during their absence by Captain Reuben Young, of the "Atlantic City."

Meantime a man claiming to be Captain J. F. R. Gandy, of the steamer "Atlantic City," had journeyed from Tuckahoe to Somers Point, where he called on Deputy Customs Collector James Scull, and made application to have the certificate of inspection of the "Atlantic City" changed, so as to permit that boat to navigate anywhere along the coast within ten miles of the shore. The boat had been in service at the Inlet at Atlantic City in the summer of 1895, being one of the fleet of the Atlantic Coast Steamboat Company, an Atlantic City organization.

Captain Gandy informed Deputy Scull that he was in a big hurry to get the papers, and was willing to pay handsomely to have them hurried down to Tuckahoe. On being asked where he was going, he said he was engaged to take a party south, and would leave as soon as the weather would permit. It was still foggy when Captain Gandy reached Somers Point, on Monday morning, and he appeared to be very much irritated at the atmospheric outlook. He made a diligent search for the metropolitan morning papers, and paid any price asked for them. He started back to Tuckahoe by way of Beesley's Point. The inspection papers were mailed on Monday afternoon by Deputy Scull, and could not possibly have reached Tuckahoe before Tuesday morning.

General Garcia on Shore.

Captain Gandy had inquired if he could not sail without the papers, but was warned by Mr. Scull to wait until they reached him or he might get into trouble. The "Atlantic City" left Tuckahoe however, at 6 o'clock on Tuesday morning, long before the morning mail arrived there. She steamed to Ocean City, which is about five miles off, and anchored in the Ocean City channel.

Here the sloop-yacht "Black Ball," Captain Samuel B. Scull, put out to the "Atlantic City" and took a man, who has since been identified as General Garcia, ashore. The General remained on the little wharf, while the sloop carried out several loads of provisions for the consumption of the Cuban patriots aboard the steamer. The fact that Ocean City is a temperance town was a source of serious disappointment to the "Atlantic City's" passengers, almost all of whom were shivering with the cold after their cheerless night on the Tuckahoe River.

All Tuesday afternoon and night General Garcia and his men anxiously awaited a signal from the "Bermuda," which had left New York on Saturday morning. The cramped quarters aboard the "Atlantic City," and their desire to get away before suspicion was aroused as to the character and destination of the expedition, kept the Cubans in an uneasy state of mind. Not one of them, save

General Garcia, appeared above deck while the " Atlantic City " was anchored in the bay, and no one, not even Captain Scull, of the busy " Black Ball," was allowed aboard.

When at last the shrill screeches of the " Bermuda's " whistle resounded over the bay, a stifled cheer came from the impatient Cubans below deck, and all was activity aboard the little pleasure-steamer. The anchor was hastily weighed, and the " Atlantic City " swiftly headed for the open sea. As she cleared the Great Egg Harbor bar the men swarmed on deck, and cheer after cheer went up as they sighted the black hull of the " Bermuda " at a distance. Then, and not till then, did the people of shore towns suspect the true character of the mysterious party of Southern excursionists, as they had been frequently referred to.

Previous to that it had been industriously noised about that the " Atlantic City " had been chartered to take a party of laborers to Corson's Inlet, where, it was said, work was to be begun on the proposed new branch of the South Jersey Railroad to Ocean City. The whole details for the transfer of the Cubans from Tuckahoe had evidently been arranged on Saturday, about the time the " Bermuda " left New York.

The charter of the Philadelphia tug was a clever ruse to throw the Spanish spies off the track, and evidently worked perfectly in every detail.

8

CHAPTER X.

Imprisonments and Massacres.

EARLY in March the prisons of Cuba were groaning with the burden of thousands of innocents. "Suspect" was a terrifying word throughout the whole Island. Every town, village and city, from one end of the country to the other, was witnessing scenes that were heart-rending in their cruelty, but upon which it was impossible to look with anything except hopeless pity.

Men who had escaped were helpless to aid the victims, and to-morrow they might be in chains in the same cell. It required only an anonymous letter of denunciation addressed to the Spanish commander of the forces garrisoned in the town or at the nearest post. It might have been written by a debtor, an enemy, a spy whose services were valuable according to the number of his prey, or by some one whose designs might be furthered by removing the protection of women; but it needed only to be written, and a guard of soldiers were at hand, taking a man out of his bed at midnight, or from his table or his office, whence he was dragged to a military prison, chained into a gang of victims like himself, deprived of communication with any one, and, after a few days, a case having been manufactured against him, he was sent to Havana and thence to Africa, to spend in a living grave the brief period that he could survive the notorious horrors of the penal colony at Ceuta.

The extent to which this thing was being carried is almost incredible. There was no respect of persons, unless it was that the best men of the towns were a majority of the victims. To be simply a "suspect" meant, in nine cases out of ten, conviction and sentence to death or life servitude. In one instance twenty men were released just as they were about to be put aboard the steamer for deportation, because it had been discovered that the author of their "denuncia-

114

mento " was a sixteen-year-old boy, who had written an anonymous letter, probably inspired by the similarity between their names and those of some insurgent leaders.   And these men were all merchants and otherwise prominent citizens of Santiago.   Not a day passed without several companies of these prisoners reaching Havana.

Crowded Dungeons.

Morro Castle was overcrowded.   There, in the dungeons which have accumulated the poisons of three centuries, the poor wretches were crowded like sheep in slaughter-pens—ten, fifteen or twenty being crowded into a single cell, where the only light or air reaching them was through a grating which was not more than six inches high from the floor.   Unless some one could bribe a guard to give a blanket to a prisoner, the man was left to make the best that he could of bare stones.

An American correspondent who was in Morro but two days contracted a fever, although he was treated with exceptional consideration, as exceptions go in Morro.   But the herd, the natives who were being taken away in this manner in greater numbers than the armies lose in battles, the suspects to whom conviction had come without what Americans would recognize as a trial, these were mercilessly, inhumanly treated.   In Jaruco, Maceo, in raiding the town, forced the prison gates, and liberated thirty prisoners, who represented some of the best families of the surrounding country.   In Cienfuegos there were over fifty " suspects " held as political prisoners.

In Matanzas there were at one time eighty such men, and some of them were afterward brought to Havana.   From Pinar del Rio, Santa Clara, Santiago, Candelaria, Marianao and numerous other places, the same reports were coming.   There was hardly an hour of the day that women were not besieging the gates of the Palace with petitions. It was a wife pleading for husband, or mother for son, or children for father, but it was always the same plea, not for trial, nor to offer evidence of their innocence, but for mercy, always for mercy.

There seemed to be a blind conviction that there were no such things as trials or evidence, and no ground for hope in either of the shadowy forms that represent them. These wretched women reached the city, perhaps having walked for days, or may be they had horses or found some conveyance, but in any way they nearly all made a wearisome journey, having left all their worldly possessions or sold them to get means for reaching the city, since there were no railroad trains left to carry them.

Haggard and Frightened.

They were hollow-eyed, haggard and frightened, but in desperate earnest. They stood outside the gates or in the corridors of the Palace for hours. They made no scenes, as might be expected. They simply waited, waited, waited; put off on one pretext after another, hour after hour, till the day had passed. Another day and another, they were there, patient and waiting and pleading, but to no purpose. Some morning a familiar face in the crowd would be missing, and that day she might be seen with others down at the shore, watching the small boats loading with prisoners and going out to the great steamers about to leave with convicts for Africa. Possibly there was one last look, but no embrace or word of farewell. After that she was seen no more at the Palace.

It happened one day that one of these prisoners slipped off the steps while getting into the boat with the others and fell into the water. His arms were pinioned behind him and he was helpless, but he managed to struggle to the surface. As he raised his head none of the guard reached out to save him. The other prisoners were also pinioned and could not. He floated for a few seconds at the side of the boat, and then one of the soldiers pointed his rifle down into the man's face and shot him through the head. It was simply a murder. Nothing was done about it excepting to report that he was " shot while attempting to escape."

On Feb. 22nd there was a brutal massacre at Guatao, and the poor wretches made prisoners at the time were still confined in Morro Castle, while the government was investigating the slaughter of the eighteen citizens. There was no battle in or near Guatao at the time these prisoners were made, and that is the other side of the story of

Spain's prisoners of war. There were no prisoners made in battles. They were suspects, or, like the Guatao people, escaped from massacre. Official reports of engagements almost never made mention of a prisoner taken. Of twenty encounters reported not one return of a captive was recorded. It was always, " The enemy left five dead on the field," or some other number. It may be that the Cubans were skillful enough to avoid capture, but it was very common to have reports of captured Spanish soldiers.

No Spanish soldiers were ever " left dead on the field," but it was admitted by the Spanish generally, and it occasionally crept into a report, that Spanish prisoners had simply been stripped of arms and let go unmolested out of the rebel camp.

High-sounding Proclamation.

But General Weyler had seen the enormity of the abuses which brutal and ambitious officers had been guilty of, and went so far as to issue a proclamation against such wholesale arrests as followed his first decree. On March 6th he gave out the following notice :

" My attention has been called to the frequency with which civil and military authorities and commanders of forces in the country and towns are proceeding to detain civilians, who are afterward placed at my disposal to be deported from the Island, without the said commanders duly justifying the foundation which counseled such determination."

That was the Spanish way of saying that arrests had not been made upon official evidence. Then General Weyler urged that citizens who write anonymous letters should sign their names and testify freely, knowing that they would receive ample protection, and closed his decree with this warning :

" I will exact most strict responsibility from commanders who propose to me matters of this sort without accompanying them with the elements of justification already expressed."

General Weyler would not personally assume the responsibility of any man's execution or banishment without clear evidence of his guilt. It would not be possible to find a man who would more mercilessly execute the penalty of the law than Gen. Weyler, but he was honest. If he had had men in the field whose motives could have been trusted, innocent men's lives might have been safer than they were; but take such brutes as murdered sick men and beat women into insensibility at Guatao, who referred to their bloody work in a report saying: "Glory and infinite applause to our valiant men; worthy of all praise is the comportment of this column; all merit the consideration of your Excellency; their efforts made exceed all praise," and arm the leader of such a mob of assassins with a decree making men enemies who syn.pathize " in thought, word or action " with the insurgents, and it is doubtful if even the iron hand of General Weyler could hold them in check.

Shot for Raising a Flag.

A Frenchman was raising a French flag on his estate when a Spanish column came up, shot him dead, captured the flag and made off with it. This is another instance of Gen. Weyler's difficulty in controlling the irresponsibles, who made prisoners of " suspects," killed innocent people or committed other outrages, and left it to the government to square the matter. These were not isolated instances, but daily occurrences in all parts of the Island. The shooting of this French citizen occurred at the Olayita estate, near San Domingo. The Cuban commanders, Quintin Bandera, Guerra and Seraphim Sanchez were near the town, and passed so close that they were observed to have about 1,000 cavalry.

They were going in the direction of the Olayita plantation. Lieut.-Col. Arce and Major Rogelio Anino, with 450 men, followed them, leaving Guines. An encounter took place in a strip of woods on the edge of the estate, but it amounted to little. The insurgents had not enough ammunition to give battle, and the Spanish could do nething but worry them with so continuous a fire with Mausers from a distance. The insurgents replied with a few shots, and then broke into two detachments and left the woods, one force taking possession of the battery, and standing off the Spanish for two hours. There was a hot fight at this point.

The insurgents had a sheltered position in the buildings, and nursed their precious supply of cartridges until they were where their only alternatives were to retreat or to suffer a heavy loss of life if they remained till the Spanish could get in upon them. Then the order was given and they rode out, setting fire to the cane field over which they passed in order to make it impossible for the Spanish to follow them through the smoke and flames. When they left, the manager of the estate, Bernardo Duarte, ran out of the house with a French flag and was about to raise it, when he was shot dead.

Curious Spanish Reports.

A Spanish officer took the flag and carried it away. Duarte's body was left where he fell. He had taken no part in the fight. When the fight was going on Duarte was in the great stone house which was the owner's residence. The heavy walls were ample protection, and with all the inmates he was apparently safe, for he came out when the insurgents left to exhibit the sign of his neutrality. Here a curious thing was revealed by the Spanish report of the engagement, which said briefly, " We found also a woman and the seven farm hands dead."

There were really thirteen dead. The bodies were buried by workmen from an adjoining plantation. There was no one left to tell whether they were killed by the Spanish or the rebels. Even the Frenchman, Duarte, was shot with his flag in his hands, and the Spanish admitted killing him.

The hundreds of refugees coming into Havana declared that the Spanish were shooting the men who were on any estate where they could find that a rebel band was camped. Several owners of large estates within this province and Matanzas stated that this was undoubtedly true, and that some of their own men, who worked for them, had disappeared after a fight had been reported near their properties. Others deserted the places and came into the city, refusing to remain on account of the killing of people near them who were likewise caring for abandoned properties.

On March 5 Gen. Melquizo went out from Jaruco with two battalions of cavalry and infantry, and found some of Maceo's forces at the sugar estate Morales, near Casiguas, between Bainoa and Guines. The estate was occupied by a man named Jose Gregoria Delgado, said to be an American. His son, Jose Manuel Delgado, a doctor, was with him at the time the insurgents and Spanish came together. As usual, the insurgents made a stand in the buildings, because they afford excellent defense. Gen. Melquizo reported after the battle or skirmish, or whatever did actually occur, that "we found eighteen dead on the field."

It has developed since that fourteen of these dead men were the owner, Delgado, his son and their twelve workmen. Not a man was left alive on the estate. If this did not seem on its face to bear considerable evidence of a deliberate killing of these men, such an act would seem to be probable when the Spanish loss is mentioned. The Spanish official report said of this engagement that the Spanish had only two men wounded, none being killed.

No One Left Alive.

If the Spanish, entirely exposed, charged upon the insurgents, who were occupying protected positions in stone-walled buildings, and succeeded in dislodging them, and did so with no loss whatever there seems to be some reason for doubting that the fighting was severe enough to cause eighteen dead to the insurgents in actual combat. There was no one left on this estate alive, nor was there any one else from whom it would be possible to learn just what did occur, or why it was that not one man on the whole estate escaped death.

Not one of them was wounded. They were all lying there dead when people from the surrounding country went there and identified the bodies. It is a suspicious circumstance that they were not shot, but all were cut to pieces with swords.

It is easy to understand the alarm that spread over the whole Island as the consequence of such things as these. The stories of the refugees who were fleeing from every quarter into the cities, and chiefly into Havana, gave a dozen such instances. They were not tales of frightened negroes. Neither were they coffee-house fabrications of Cubans. A bookful of these tales could be collected. It was the men who had estates of their own, whose losses in one year alone amounted to anywhere from $50,000 to $200,000, who held on and exhausted every resource to save themselves and their properties, but who were compelled at last to give up and let everything go.

They were not men who pack up what few valuables they can carry away and then bring their families and servants long distances across the country to Havana, just for the pastime or amusement of lying about their reasons for coming. Where alarm had not driven out the poorer classes, destitution had done so. Forty-two cities and towns had already been burned and destroyed.

Great Scarcity of Provisions.

This does not indicate the homes of hundreds of others which have gone up in the flames of burning sugar estates. After the armies of both Spanish and insurgents consumed all the fruit and vegetables, and the railroads ceased carrying freight, food was almost beyond the reach of the poor. Great was the suffering in consequence of the scarcity of provisions, but a new system was put in operation which deprived even those who had a few dollars left from buying what they needed unless they stood in favor of the Spanish commanders of towns. This was a hard matter for people in a country where everybody was an insurgent, or of a family with representatives in the insurgent army.

If a man went to a store in any town outside of Havana he was compelled first to make out a statement of what he wished to purchase. He was limited to two cents' worth of salt, five cents' worth of flour, one pound of meat, one pound of rice and five cents' worth of coffee, and so on; but he was not permitted to buy oil, candles, medicines, or a multitude of other things. After the list was completed, the storekeeper and the customer had to appear before the Mayor of the town and swear that the articles were for the consumption of the purchaser, and not for the aid and comfort of any insurgent or sympathizer with the insurrection.

When this was done the whole formality cleared the way for the purchase of about one scanty meal for four persons. This, with the apprehension of suspects, was driving the country people out of their homes until whole districts were depopulated. Paso Real, Mantua, Baja, Guane, Tapaste, San Cristobal, and, in fact, nearly all the towns of Pinar del Rio Province, were admitted by the Spanish reports to be practically deserted.

In Havana and Matanzas provinces the same state of affairs existed. One man who passed through Guatao and Punta Brava said that where there had been 2,200 people all together a month before, less than 100 remained. Women came out and begged that he would give them food. They were crying, he said, and pleaded for relief to be sent out to them. There were a few children left in the places, and the desolation he described was something pitiful. The widows made by the massacre were chiefly those who remained. When asked why they did not get away, and so possibly find a place where they could get some relief, they replied that they could not make the journey.

Not a Rebel in the Place.

The government was investigating the massacre, and the method of the investigation indicated that a denial was in course of preparation. Here is a significant fact. The "Diario de la Marina," the government's most staunch supporter, published an item which said, "The Mayor of Guatao swears and forswears to Captain Calvo that at the time of the events in Guatao not a solitary rebel was in the place. Two days after the event this Mayor again met Calvo, who asked him if he had seen any insurgents there. He replied he had not. Notwithstanding, five minutes afterward Captain Calvo saw a group of eight men mounted, who ran away."

This was clearly to discredit the Mayor of Guatao. He confirmed the story of all the citizens, and swore that no insurgents were in the town when the massacre occurred. It also indicated that Captain Calvo, who was in command of the troops who committed the massacre, was conducting the investigation.

It would not be in keeping with the way all this was being done if the "Diario's" story were not declared by somebody to be untrue.

The gentleman above referred to was in Guatao at the time Captain Calvo was talking with the Mayor. He describes what occurred this way :

"I saw they were holding an excited debate about something, so I held up my driver till it was over. Then I talked to the Alcalde, and asked what occasioned all the fireworks between himself and the officer. He replied, 'I have just been asked about the rebels. I said I had seen four; he tells me, "You lie, you have seen a hundred." I have only seen four, and they are down that road now.'"

Charges Proved Untrue.

If the Mayor told the story just as it had occurred between himself and the officer a moment before, the account of it in the newspaper was an apparent attempt to clear the way for almost any sort of a report on the massacre. It would be easier after proving the chief witness unreliable to dispose of the stories of the women as attempts to shield their husbands. The government also took the ground that the insurgents were concealed in the church. This made it necessary to abandon the original charge that they were in the little thatched houses.

The authorities of Guatao opened the church and showed the officers, who went there to inspect it, that no horses or men could possibly have gotten into it. When this inspection was finished, the keeper of the church handed over the key, and the Mayor joined him in beseeching the Spanish officers to carry it away, so that what- ever might happen again they would be relieved of the responsibility for keeping the structure free from invasion.

Ten more prisoners were taken at the time this investigation, as it is called, was going on. A Spanish column came into Punta Brava from the east. At the same moment another came into the place from the west. The second one picked up ten men working in tobacco fields on the outskirts of the town. A storekeeper, recog- nizing them, went up to the lieutenant commanding, and said that the arrests were unjust, as the men were "pacificados," or peaceful citizens

CITY OF CIENFUGOS.

124

Then the lieutenant arrested the storekeeper. The two columns were at opposite ends of the main street, their officers disputing as to which was properly in possession of the place, as their orders were slightly conflicting, when a third column arrived with a captain in charge. He settled the difficulty by occupying the town himself, and after learning of the arrest of the ten tobacco-workers he liberated them all.

Heavy Guard of Soldiers.

The demonstrations against Americans in Havana were confined to individual encounters, where there were no serious results. A heavy guard of soldiers was quartered in a building near the Consul's office, and the patrolling of the streets was kept up with vigilance day and night. Where more than four men got together a soldier was at hand to scatter them. In the Plaza, when the military was playing, the crowds were constantly kept moving. An effort to get up a students' demonstration fell flat, because a majority of the students were in sympathy with the Americans.

There never was a time when the students were to be feared, on that account. The source of danger was the volunteers. A correspondent relates that he was talking with a hotel waiter after he had been away for a day. He said he was out doing duty as a volunteer. He was a little sawed-off ignoramus, and the correspondent was curious enough to ask him how his companions felt toward Uncle Sam.

" Muera Senor Sam," he hissed, bringing his fist down with a whack on the table.

" Death to Mr. Sam ?" I repeated. " Why so ?"

" He is going to help the insurrectors. We'll have to kill them all."

" But I'm an American ; would you kill me, too ?"

He seemed to be confronted by a situation for a moment only, when he said, sadly but earnestly :

" I am your friend, Senor, but I should have to kill you."

At that moment another Spaniard came up. " Senor, allow me to present my friend ——. As I was just telling this American gentleman, Spain will find every loyal son shoulder to shoulder, fighting till the last drop of blood is shed to avenge such an insult to our national honor as this uncalled-for interference of America."

This is not half-hearted hypocrisy. It is the way men talk who have been ruined by the collapse of every kind of business in the Island, and who want peace and prosperity restored at any cost. They are Spaniards, but they have been so long in commercial intercourse with the United States that their sentimental attachment to the theory of Spain's right to Cuba has been blunted by a period of successful business. All Cuba's enterprises are practically inseparable from the States, while Spain stands by as a third party, consuming half the profits that would naturally accrue to the other two. At such a price sentiment comes too high to maintain a secure position among hard-headed merchants.

The Cienfuegos houses resolved to boycott the United States, and proposed to do so by cancelling all their purchasing orders and refusing to sell to American buyers. This was considerable of a joke in its way. They would have to buy from Havana instead, and Havana would continue to buy direct from the States until war or something as serious should prevent. The merchants at Havana held a meeting to discuss retaliation of the same sort, but when it was pointed out to them that American houses would merely send out their own agents to sell their products they saw the danger ahead and contented themselves with resolutions praising the Cienfuegos merchants. They could afford to do that, as their commissions were being helped by the necessity of Cienfuegos buying here.

Two nephews of the Queen, the Princes of Caserta, were in an engagement in Sagua on March 3. The insurgents were led by Serafin Sanchez, Nunez and Alvarez. All that has ever been printed about the fight here was contained in a ten-line item, in which the insurgents lost thirty dead and forty wounded. The Queen cabled congratulations to General Weyler upon the glorious victory, and yesterday the insurgent loss was changed to read " 60 dead and 150 wounded." It is impossible to learn anything else here about the battle.

CHAPTER XI

Freedom for Cuba.

THE sympathy in Congress for the cause of Cuba received formal expression on February 28th. On that date the meeting of the Senate Committee on Foreign Relations resulted in action of a more vigorous character than the most ardent friend of the cause of Cuba was justified in expecting. The committee decided, after some debate, that it would not accept the wording of a resolution already adopted by the House Committee, but would cling to one of its own, which was looked upon as even stronger than any yet seriously considered—stronger because the committee capitulated to the sentiment represented in the resolution of Mr. Cameron declaring for the independence of the Cuban Republic.

It was agreed that when the question reached the voting stage Mr. Sherman, for the commiteee, was to recommend and urge the passage of the following, which was the language of the substitute reported by Mr. Morgan:

" *Resolved*, by the Senate (the House of Representatives concurring), That, in the opinion of Congress, a condition of public war exists between the government of Spain and the government proclaimed and for some time maintained by force of arms by the people of Cuba; and that the United States of America should maintain a strict neutrality between the contending powers, according to each all the rights of belligerents in the ports and territory of the United States."

As the day wore on in the Senate the crowds in the galleries and on the floor increased. The diplomatic gallery, for once, was well filled. Nearly every member of the House Foreign Affairs Committee was on the Senate floor, and they listened to the speeches with the greatest interest.

Mr. Lindsay, of Kentucky, addressed the Senate. He did not think that, in the present emergency, the subject ought to be controlled, in any way, by the past conduct of Spain to the United States. It was, in one sense, a question of humanity. War was being carried on at the very doors of the United States between the people of Cuba and the Spanish Government, and it would result either in the independence of Cuba or in the utter destruction of her people.

Sympathy for Cuban People.

Expressions of sympathy would avail nothing to the Cuban insurrectionists. If the United States intended to take any step to bring about a condition of affairs in Cuba different from that which had existed during the last seventy years, that step should be in the direction of the ultimate independence of Cuba.

It might be true—it was true—that affairs had not yet reached a point that would justify the United States in acknowledging the independence of Cuba. There was a state of things in Cuba that would justify the Government of the United States in considering a proposition for active interference in the struggle, for the reason that it seemed highly probable that, without such interference, either public order could never be restored in Cuba, or could only be restored after such suffering by humanity and such injuries to surrounding States, as would obviously overbalance the general evil of all interference from without. But the pending resolution proposed no such active interference. It proposed only that the good offices of the United States should be offered to Spain to bring about, not merely a cessation of hostilities, but an ultimate peace on the basis of Cuban independence—the only basis on which good government could ever be secured to the people of Cuba.

Spain owed to Cuba as much as Turkey owed to Armenia, as much as the United States owed to Venezuela. If Spain did not pay the obligations resting on her, and if her necessities prevented her doing so, then the time had come for steps to be initiated; and they could be properly initiated only by the government of the United States Overtures should be made to Spain for the sale of the

Island to the Cubans, the United States to guarantee the payment of the sum to be agreed upon.

Mr. Sherman, chairman of the Committee on Foreign Relations, addressed the Senate. He said that he did not disguise from himself the danger and possibility of hostile movements following the action of Congress. Spain was a sensitive, proud and gallant nation, and would not submit to what she considered an injustice. At the same time, his convictions were strong—made stronger every day—that the condition of affairs in Cuba was such that the intervention of the United States must be given, sooner or later, to put an end to crimes almost beyond description.

Called a Murderer and Criminal.

He quoted from a pamphlet written, he said, in a temperate style, to show what the Cubans had done in the way of establishing a government and carrying on the war, and containing an order of Gen. Maximo Gomez, as to the humane treatment of prisoners that might fall into the hands of the insurgents. And yet, he said, this man Gomez had been denounced as a murderer and barbarous criminal, like the one he would speak of after a while—Capt.-Gen. Weyler. Speaking of the insurgent Gen. Gomez, Mr. Sherman said that he was a man of standing and character—probably an idealist. But he ought to be, and would probably soon be, considered a patriot.

Mr. Sherman went on to say that he was not in favor of the annexation of Cuba to the United States. He did not desire to conquer Cuba, or to have any influence in her local autonomy. In his judgment Cuba should be attached to Mexico, because Cubans and Mexicans spoke the same language, had the same origin, the same antecedents, and many of the same circumstances.

Mr. Sherman sent to the clerk's desk, and had read extracts from a Spanish book, printed in a New York newspaper, reciting horrible cruelties charged against Weyler, some of the incidents being so bad that he directed the clerk to omit them. He spoke of these deeds as barbarous atrocities, and as inhuman cruelties, and said that Weyler was a demon rather than a general.

9

He denounced the idea of putting such a man in command of a hundred thousand troops, to ride rough-shod, kill and slaughter a feeble body of people ; and he declared that if this kind of policy is pursued by Spain in Cuba, and if the people of the United States be informed of it, there is no earthly power that will prevent the people of the United States from going over to that Island, running all over its length and breadth, and driving out from it those robbers and imitators of the worst men that ever lived in the world.

This statement was greeted by an outburst of applause from the crowded galleries, which showed the intense feeling awakened by the discussion of the subject of Cuban independence.

Belligerent Rights.

When the final vote on Mr. Sherman's resolution was taken in the Senate it was passed by a large majority, but there was an evident desire on the part of many in both Houses to grant belligerent rights to the Cubans, who had already maintained a state of war on the Island for over a year. Concerning this last proposition an eminent New York jurist expressed the following opinion :

" The mere recognition of belligerent rights on the part of the Cubans would not involve us in any complication with Spain. It is a different thing from recognizing the independence of the Cubans.

" The recognition of belligerent rights is merely the declaration of our opinion that the insurgents have established a stable government and are entitled to all the rights of war. This was what was done by Great Britain during our late war.

" Such a recognition, however, would not relieve the United States of its obligations toward Spain in the way of preventing the sending out of privateers or filibustering expeditions in aid of the insurgents from our ports. We established this proposition in the 'Alabama' arbitration against Great Britain.

" Furthermore, such recognition of a state of war between Spain and the insurgents in Cuba would give Spain the right to search our merchant vessels for goods contraband of war. This is the only respect in which our relations with Spain would be particularly altered by such recognition, as far as I can see."

"What would be our relations in case Congress should recognize the independence of Cuba?" was asked.

"That recognition might be treated by Spain as an unfriendly act, although I should hardly think that Spain would so regard it. It would not amount to a declaration on our part that we proposed to aid Cuba in the maintenance of its independence, and hence it would not necessarily be a *casus belli* (cause of war) as between us and Spain.

"Still it might involve us in serious complications, as we would be bound to regard the insurgent government as the only lawful government in the Island of Cuba, and to act accordingly and to disregard the rights of Spain. And such conduct on our part might lead to controversies with Spain which might furnish a *casus belli*. I do not personally believe, however, that such a result will follow in any event."

Probability of Bloodshed.

It was thought by many in Washington that if the Cuban insurgents were not quickly recognized as belligerents, and General Weyler maintained the reputation he had already acquired, it was not stretching speculation too far to assume that there was a probabilty of the bloody scenes of 1869 being re-enacted, when, under the orders of Gen. Burriel, American citizens were put to death in Santiago de Cuba.

The Captain-General of Cuba had issued a decree in which he said that all vessels which might be captured in Spanish waters, and which had on board men and munitions, and whose design was to give aid or comfort to the revolutionists, should be regarded as pirates, and that all on board, regardless of number, should be immediately executed.

Secretary Fish, then Secretary of State, made a protest against the butchery of the Americans, and maintained the right of the citizens of the United States to carry merchandise to the enemies of Spain, except such articles as were contraband of war, and which might be seized upon the high seas. Secretary Fish said the government could not assent to the punishment by Spain of any citizen of this country, except under the laws and treaties existing between Spain and the United States.

According to Halleck, one of the accepted authorities on laws between nations, "there is no law or regulation which forbids any person or government, whether the political designation be real or assumed, from purchasing arms from citizens of the United States and shipping them at the risk of the purchaser." The same authority says further: "Neutrals may establish themselves for the purposes of trade in ports convenient to either belligerent, and may sell or transport to either such articles as they may wish to buy, subject to risks of capture for violation of blockade or for the conveyance of contraband to belligerent ports."

Exceptions to the Rule.

"A belligerent cannot send out privateers from neutral ports. Neutrals in their own country may sell to belligerents whatever belligerents choose to buy. The principal exceptions to this rule are that neutrals must not sell to one belligerent what they refuse to sell to another, and must not furnish soldiers or sailors to either, nor prepare nor suffer to be prepared within their territory armed ships or military or naval expeditions against the other."

The position in which the United States would be placed by the recognition of the belligerency of the Cubans is clearly and tersely expressed by Justice Harlan, of the Supreme Court of the United States, in an opinion in the case of Ford vs. Surget. It is based on a careful and exhaustive study of the comity of nations, and the parts that appear applicable to the present situation are as follows:

"If the foreign State recognizes belligerency in the insurgents it releases the parent State for whatever may be done by the insurgents, or not done by the parent State, where the insurgent power extends.

"If it is a war, the commissioned cruisers of both sides may stop, search and capture the foreign merchant vessel, and that vessel must make no resistance and must submit to adjudication by a prize court: if it is not war, the cruisers of neither party can stop or search the foreign merchant vessel, and that vessel may resist all attempts in that direction, and the ships of war of the foreign State may attack and capture any cruiser persisting in the attempt; if it is war, the insurgent cruisers are to be treated by foreign citizens and officials, at sea and in port, as lawful belligerents; if it is a war, the rules and risks respecting carrying contraband or dispatches or military persons, come into play.

"The insurgents gain the great advantage of a recognized status (when belligerent rights are accorded), and the opportunity to employ commissioned cruisers at sea, and to exert all the powers known to maritime warfare, with the sanction of foreign nations. They can obtain abroad loans, military and naval materials, as against everything but neutrality laws.

What Rights are Acquired.

"Their flag and commissions are acknowledged, their revenue laws are respected, and they acquire a quasi-political recognition. On the other hand, the parent government is relieved from responsibility for acts done in the insurgent territory; its blockade of its own ports is respected, and it acquires a right to exert against neutral commerce all the powers of a party to a maritime war."

It was thought altogether probable that Spain would immediately enter a protest, if the belligerency of the insurgents was recognized, just as the United States did in the early days of the civil war, when France took that action. The then Secretary of State, William H. Seward, acknowledged the right of France to take such a step in these words:

"The President (Mr. Lincoln) does not deny—on the contrary, he maintains—that every sovereign power decides for itself, on its responsibility, the question whether or not it will at a given time accord the status of belligerency to the insurgent subjects of another power, as also the larger question of the independence of such subjects and their accession to the family of sovereign States."

As to the contention by Spain that war did not exist in Cuba; that there was a revolt against constituted authority, by a mob of rioters, this was pretty thoroughly disposed of by the opinion of the

Supreme Court of the United States about twenty years ago. It has never been changed or abridged.

"A civil war," said Judge Grier, giving the opinion in what is known as the Prize Cases, "is never solemnly declared; it becomes such by its accidents, the number, power and organization of the persons who originate and carry it on. When the party in rebellion occupy and hold in a hostile manner a certain portion of territory; have declared their independence; have cast off their allegiance; have organized armies; have commenced hostilities, the world acknowledges them as belligerents, and the contest a war."

The Resolutions Adopted.

After much discussion in Congress concerning the form that the resolutions should take, making the action of the two Houses concurrent, on April 6th, 1896, by the decisive and emphatic vote of 244 yeas to 27 nays the House of Representatives passed the Senate concurrent resolutions declaring that public war exists in Cuba, and granting belligerent rights to the insurgents.

Public interest in the Cuban question was manifested by the people of Washington, and long before the noon hour the Capitol corridors were thronged. When the House of Representatives was called to order there was standing-room only in the galleries, and long lines of waiting people filled the corridors before the entrance doors. There were no proceedings of unusual moment on the floor of the House. There was no debate and no opposition to the proceedings.

Congressman Hitt, of Illinois, Chairman of the Committee on Foreign Affairs, arose and demanded the regular order, and Speaker Reed put the question on the adoption of the conference report. The great, swelling chorus of ayes was followed by a feeble, scattering negative vote, and the Speaker was about to declare the motion carried when Mr. Hitt asked for the yeas and nays. Yielding to the appeals of many members, however, he withdrew it; but Mr. Tucker, of Virginia, demanded a record-making vote, and so the roll was called.

When Speaker Reed announced that " The yeas are 244 and the

nays 27, and the resolutions are adopted," the applause upon the floor of the House and in the galleries was roof-shaking in its intensity and continuity.

By its action the House agreed to the Senate resolutions, and disposed of the Cuban question. These resolutions are as follows :

Resolved, That, in the opinion of Congress, a condition of public war exists between the Government of Spain and the government proclaimed and for some time maintained by force of arms by the people of Cuba, and that the United States of America should maintain a strict neutrality between the contending powers, according to each all the rights of belligerents in the ports and territory of the United States.

Resolved, Further, that the friendly offices of the United States should be offered by the President to the Spanish Government for the recognition of the independence of Cuba.

CHAPTER XII.

Spanish Insults to the American Flag.

GREAT excitement was caused in Spain by the passage of the resolutions in the United States Senate relating to the independence of Cuba, and in a number of places the American flag was torn down and trampled upon by boisterous mobs. As showing the spirit by which the crowds were actuated, we give here a detailed account of the insults, which it is but just to the Spanish authorities to say they repudiated, calling out troops in some instances to protect our American officials and their residences.

At Madrid on March 2nd, 1896, there was a demonstration of students against the American legation, but before any overt acts had been committed the mob was dispersed by the authorities. The excitement over the Cuban question was intense. The prompt measures taken by the authorities to suppress disorder and prevent demonstrations, large forces of police being everywhere present, convinced the people that lawless acts would not be tolerated.

At Barcelona mounted gendarmes were kept busy patrolling the city and dispersing gatherings of persons plotting to vent their wrath upon the representatives of the United States Government there. Repeated attempts were made to attack the United States Consulate. The rioters were repeatedly charged by the police and scattered, only to form in some other place with a determination to mob the Consulate. Such tenacity of purpose indicated that mischief-makers were working upon the excited populace.

The greatest activity was displayed in the government dockyards, and every preparation possible was being made by the naval and military forces for an emergency.

The "Imparcial," a Madrid journal, declared that the utterances of the United States Senate constituted an "unqualified and unreasoning

THE MAGNIFICENT ESCURIAL—THE RESIDENCE OF THE KINGS OF SPAIN.

137

provocation," adding : " If the desire for war was on account of a fault in Spain, the Senators would be doing their duty.   But no provocation has been given to the United States, and the Americans judge rashly of the results of a Spanish-American war.   The obnoxious language of the Senate ought not to surprise any one. United States Senators are accustomed to exchange gross insults without crossing swords or exchanging bullets.   These are the cowards who are seeking war, and one awaits death with more coolness with a good conscience than with pockets filled with dollars."

The Spanish officials at Washington described the occurrences in Spain as merely the outbursts of a few excited Spanish youths, and claimed that the dispatches bore out this view, and there was no probability of any diplomatic trouble.   The prompt disavowal of the Minister of State to Minister Taylor was pointed to as evidence that the Spanish Government did not sympathize with the " mob."

"Down with the United States.'

An anti-American demonstration occurred at Cadiz, Spain, March 7.   A mob of about 500 students met in Genove's Park.   They carried two Spanish flags, and, after cheering some fiery utterances, paraded before the town hall with cries of " Long live Spain ! " " Down with the United States ! " etc.   Later, they proceeded to a tobacco factory and asked the manager to permit the workmen to join in the demonstration.   The manager, however, refused and called upon the police for protection.   The latter charged the mob with drawn swords, and several of the students were wounded before they were driven away from the vicinity of the factory.

After leaving that neighborhood the students made a demonstration in front of the military club.   There the police were again ordered to charge the mob.   This time the students showered stones upon the police and were dispersed with much more difficulty.   The authorities anticipated additional outbreaks.

The orchestra of the Grand Theatre at Barcelona played the national march, and the audience rose with enthusiastic shouts of Long live Spain ! " " Long live General Weyler ! " " Long live the army!" "Down with the United States!" etc. The audience, after leaving the theatre, was joined by very many other people, and paraded the streets, uttering similar shouts. The demonstrations took such proportions that the police were unable to disperse the crowds, and it became necessary to call out the gendarmes, who, with a considerable show of force, succeeded in quelling the disturbance,

There was an anti-American riot at Bilboa, Spain, March 9, and it was of greater importance than the previous so-called patriotic disturbances caused by the action of the Congress of the United States in regard to Cuba. About 12,000 people took part in the public demonstration. The excitement was started by a group of young

GENERAL WEYLER.

men at a street corner, who began cheering every soldier who passed by. Their conduct was soon imitated by other groups of people, until every soldier seen was cheered by the crowds, and some musicians who refused to repeat the national anthem were hustled, beaten and otherwise maltreated.

The excitement increased, and riotous groups formed in the main streets, cheering for Spain and denouncing the United States. The authorities did everything possible to maintain order. Almost the entire police force was turned out as soon as the populace assumed a threatening aspect, and the rioters were dispersed again and again. Eventually, however, the mob became so numerous and excited that the police were almost helpless.

After the first demonstrations of sympathy with the army the crowds had armed themselves with sticks and cudgels, and their numbers

were so great that the police were swept aside and an immense crowd
gathered on the leading thoroughfare, and marched towards the residence of the United States Consul, shouting, " Long live Spain!"
" Down with the Yankees! "

On their way to the Consul's residence they hurled stones through
the windows of stores and private residences, overturned a number of
vehicles, pulled several mounted policemen from their horses and
generally behaved in the most threatening manner. Stores dealing
in American goods received the most attention from the mob, and
the windows of the Consul's house were badly shattered, although
the police defended the building.

The mob then proceeded in the direction of the United States Consulate, evidently intending to stone the building as well. But the
authorities had taken the precaution to send a strong force of police
to guard that building and another detachment of police was stationed
across the streets leading to the Consulate. Therefore when the mob
neared the United States Consulate it was confronted by the police
with drawn swords. The mob halted, and then began pelting the
police most vigorously with stones and pieces of brick.

The policemen, however, held their ground, and a squad of the
officers charged the rioters. The latter began firing pistols at the
policemen, two of whom were wounded. This caused the police to
charge in a body, and, using their swords with good effect, the rioters
were dispersed, yelling and hooting at the authorities and shouting,
" Down with the Yankees! " and " Long live Spain! "

The police, who made a number of arrests, experienced considerable difficulty in escorting their prisoners to the depots. During the
whole afternoon there was more or less disorder. It was decided to
keep both the police proper and the gendarmes confined to barracks
until further orders, as there seemed to be danger of another outbreak.

The United States Consulate was guarded by a strong detachment
of gendarmes armed with carbines, revolvers and swords, and they
had instructions to protect the Consulate at any cost.

There was a serious anti-American riot at Salamanca March 9th.

The students, as usual, were the leaders of the disturbance. They carried Spanish and American flags and burned the latter amid the acclamations of the crowds which gathered to witness the "patriotic" demonstration.

Cheering for Spain.

Eventually the gendarmes charged the rioters and dispersed them temporarily. Later the students reassembled and gathered another mob about them. The prefect hurried to the scene and exhorted the students to disperse, but they hooted his utterances, cheering for Spain and denouncing the United States.

Finally the prefect was compelled to call upon the police for protection, and the gendarmes again charged the riotous students, who met the onslaught with showers of stones. Order, however, was finally restored, and the university was closed. The authorities feared there would be more outbreaks, and more elaborate precautions were taken to promptly suppress them.

A dispatch from Madrid, March 12th, was as follows: "Further demonstrations of students against the United States, as a result of the Cuban resolutions of Congress, have occurred. At Corunna two hundred students belonging to the University joined in a parade yesterday, cheered for Spain and burned an American flag. The police, however, succeeded in preventing the rioters from approaching the United States Consulate.

"At Alicante the Mayor and police, while dispersing a similar anti-American demonstration, were pelted with stones. A number of policemen sustained injuries.

"A dispatch from Barcelona says that on the arrival there last night of a train from Aragon two men were arrested upon a charge of carrying concealed weapons. When a search of their clothing was made, thirty dynamite cartridges and two daggers were discovered. The men asserted they had found the cartridges upon the road, and declared that they had come to Barcelona in search of work. The police discredit their story. The United States Consulate is being closely guarded."

CHAPTER XIII.

Horrors of Morro Castle.

HAVANA may, undoubtedly, be called a military city; for at every corner you meet a soldier, before nearly every public office there is a guard, and at various hours of the day and evening, and in various parts of the city, one's ear is greeted by the notes of the bugle, or the rattling of the drum; while many of the barracks and a fort or two are right in the midst of the city.

At night, sometimes, these sentries are troublesome with their challenging, in an open city; and if one approaches too near their posts, he hears the words, quickly rung out, "Who goes there?" (*Quien vive?*)   As a reply has to be made, the Habañeros say, "*España*," the regular pass-word.   An American finds no trouble in replying, "*Forastero*" (foreigner), or "*Americano.*"   But now-a-days, the latter might be dangerous, as the name does not seem to be popular.

A great deal of good sense has been displayed in uniforming the troops for this climate.   In lieu of the heavy cloth, the Cuban sol-diers are clad in simple linen, of various colors—white, blue and brown—than which nothing can look more soldierly.   Take, for instance, the infantry soldier, in full uniform.   He wears a sort of dark blue dungaree blouse, gathered at the waist to give it a natty shape, a pair of neat brown-drilling pantaloons, and a low-crowned cap of leather, with visor enough to be of some use.

In lieu of the stiff, uncomfortable coat collar, and the still more uncomfortable and unhealthy leather stock, he wears a neatly rolled collar, of red cloth, which, with his cuffs of the same, can be taken off when he sends his kit to the wash.

Others, again, are uniformed in pure white, with pretty "shoulder knockers," and collars and cuffs of red; while the cavalry and artil

142

lerymen wear loose short jackets, pants of blue linen, and broad palm-leaf hats. This uniform, far from being uncomfortable or unsoldierly, is just the opposite; and Spanish troops have the appearance of clean and well-instructed soldiers.

The Captain-General is the superior military chief of the Island, and commander-in-chief of its armies; while next to him in rank is the second chief, who has the rank of brigadier-general, and pay of ten thousand dollars per annum, and who is also the sub-inspector of infantry and cavalry. The corps of artillery and engineers have special sub-inspectors, with the title of *mariscales de campo*.

The fortresses of the Island, in which are nearly always the prisons and the barracks of the troops, have their own governors or commanders, with special staffs.

Large Standing Army.

The army consists generally of twenty-five or thirty thousand men, with its proportion of infantry, artillery, cavalry, engineers and marines. Each regiment has a colonel and lieutenant-colonel, a drum-major, and six contract musicians. The battalion has a first and second commander, an adjutant (lieutenant), an ensign, a chaplain, and a surgeon, a chief bugler, and a master armorer. These regiments are all known by names (not numbers), such as the King's, the Queen's, Isabel II. of Naples, of Spain, etc., which does much towards increasing the *esprit du corps* so necessary to make good soldiers.

There is also a battalion known as the "Guardia Civil," a fine body of men, who are scattered in small detachments throughout the Island, mostly as watchmen and police, or, perhaps, as spies. They are generally an intelligent set, handsomely uniformed in well-fitting, dark-blue coats, white pants, and broad-brimmed felt hats, neatly bound with white. One sees them on the wharves, in the opera-house, at the theatre, patrolling the paseo—in fact, everywhere in Havana.

A large percentage of the troops die every year when they first come from Spain, and therefore a large supply of recruits is necessary to keep the regiments up to their maximum. The pay of field, staff, and line is about the same as in our army, being double that which is received in Spain; though, as some of the officers declare, "half pay" is more at home (Spain) than double pay in Cuba, everything costs so much more on the Island.

Havana is said to be impregnable. If it is not, it ought to be, judging from the number of its stone walls, its frowning fortresses, and its ships of war; and yet it is not so strong as it looks. The day is past for the simple, old-fashioned ways of attack by buccaneers, and new modes of war make sad inroads upon the protection afforded by some of these old-time forts.

Warning to Filibusters.

The Morro and La Punta command the entrance. Across the bay is the Cabañas, with its guns pointing in every direction, and at the end of the bay the Fortress of Santo Domingo de Atares, which commands the bay and holds the city itself under surveillance. East and west, La Punta, El Morro, Cabañas, Number Four, Principe, San Lazaro, Pastora, and the Tower of Chorrera give notice to the adventurous filibuster to "keep off."

The Castillo de los tres Santos Reyes del Morro, and the Fortress of San Carlos de la Cabaña are the ones which every traveler desires to see, and which every one, if it is possible, should visit, as they are world-renowned, in addition to being well worth seeing, not only on account of their structure, but on account of the magnificent views of sea and land from their battlements.

In former years, it was a matter of some difficulty to gain entrance to these forts, and it is not now accomplished very easily. Of course, our consul is the person to secure passes to the forts; he always obliges such parties of Americans as desire to visit them, unless in war times. The authorities have a regular printed form of passes. Starting from the landing just outside the Puerta de la Punta, it is only a short pull directly across to the landing of El Morro.

Strolling up the slope from the landing, one begins to realize immediately the apparently great strength of the work. The slope itself which conducts up to the main gate of the castle is very strong with solid stone parapets on each side, and a road laid in mortar with small, regular-sized cobble-stones. To the left, almost on a line with the water, is the water battery known as the " Twelve Apostles,"—twelve iron guns, mounted on siege carriages, carrying twenty-four pound shot, and worked *en barbette*, which would give them great effect at short range on any vessel attempting to pass.

Although the soldiers of whom you ask questions in the fort either dare not or *will* not tell anything, yet they are useful guides. The walls here at the entrance are very thick, you notice, and form casemates, the one to the right being the guard-room, which is also occupied by the officer of the day, who sometimes strolls through the fort with foreigners.

A Dismal Old Fort.

In front of the entrance are the barracks and the storehouses, which seem to occupy the hollow square formed by the walls of this portion of the fort. They are of solid stone, with their rooms arched, ceiled, and paved in stone, the bunks of the men being simply cots. Looking towards the harbor is the casemate battery, mounting about eight guns. The whole of this first fort, which seems to be separated from the citadel by drawbridges, is very cramped and very dismal.

On the extreme corner of the fort, at the very mouth of the entrance to the bay, stands the O'Donnell light-house, a cylindrical tower of stone, seventy-eight feet in height from the wall of the castle, and fifteen feet in diameter, being altogether one hundred and fifty-eight feet above the level of the sea. The light is of the first order of Fresnel, fixed, but alternated with large reflectors that shine, every half minute, for about five or six seconds. It is ordinarily seen at a distance of eighteen miles, though in fine weather at a greater distance.

Near the light-house, but upon the terreplain of the portion above, is a small frame house, used as the signal-station, where are kept the signal-flags, which are displayed from the masts close by; there are so many flags and signals of all nations, that the interior of the house

10

looks quite like a dry-goods store. This portion of the fort is reached by a stone slope leading up between the quarters, or by a narrow spiral stone stairway inside the walls, coming out upon a concrete terreplain protected by stone parapets. pierced with embrasures for cannon.

From the parapet there is a fine view of the sea, the city, and the surrounding country. Here, also, can be seen the full lines of the land-face of the fort and the position of the others.

A Frowning Battery.

The moat is a dry and very deep one, the scarp walls of which are fully one hundred feet high, and the width full fifty feet. From the battlements one can see how much nature did for this fort in the beginning; for from the sea-side directly up to the counter-scarp, there is a natural *glacis*, commanded completely from every part by the guns *en barbette* in this part of the fort. The strongest battery, and the only one that really looks as though it were ready for work, is the one to the extreme right of the fort, entered by a covered way, and forming the sea-coast battery.

It mounts about twenty-four iron guns, of thirty-two pounds calibre, on siege carriages, and appears to be a very strong battery. Just after entering the fort, by the stone slope, inside the exterior wall, there is to the right hand a long stone-covered gallery, connecting the southern face of the fort with the covered way that leads to the sea-coast battery, as also to the road leading over to the Cabañas on the brow of the hill. This is a strong affair, arched, and lighted by long, narrow apertures. It is about one hundred yards long.

Morro Castle is not only celebrated for the beauty of its natural surroundings, but notorious because of the untold misery hidden within its walls. The historic structure, intended as a military stronghold, is admirably situated on a high elevation at the entrance to the harbor of Havana, and, as already stated, from that location an excellent view is obtainable of the land and water for many miles around. Viewed from a military point of observation, the castle, even with its natural advantages, is no longer a stronghold.

A bombardment by the elements controlled by the devastating hand of Father Time has created sad havoc with the architectural beauties of the old place, and what was at one time a really powerful fortification is nothing more than a crumbling mass of masonry. Cubans say that a sad tale of horror and misery can be told about the place for every one of the building stones used in the construction of the castle, and they now regard it as simply a shell where human suffering is carefully concealed from the light of civilization.

A House of Horrors.

While in Cuba an American correspondent viewed the castle from various points of observation. Fortunately for himself he did not view it from the inside, however, although several other American newspaper correspondents have been detained there under exasperating conditions.

" The castle is a grand old place from a distant point of view," writes the journalist. " In nearly every other consideration it is a House of Horrors. A mere mention of the name Morro Castle thrills the heart of the average Cuban with an ill-feeling, and they have a greater dread of confinement there than they have of the yellow fever.

" Political prisoners and suspects are taken there under a strong guard of armed men. They are taken there in boats about 6 o'clock in the morning, the soldiers having bayonets drawn ready for instant use. While on the way to the castle it would be almost certain death for a prisoner to show the least sign of insubordination, for the guards are authorized to deal summarily with their prisoners whenever occasion requires, and no hesitation occurs in taking full and instant advantage of that feature.

" Mr. Michaelson, the correspondent of a New York newspaper, and his interpreter were confined there as suspects. It required exertions of a most vigorous character for other Americans to discover the fact that Mr. Michaelson was really confined there. Murat Halstead and other Americans interviewed General Weyler, and finally gained from the Spanish commander a blunt admission that the New

York writer was in the castle. The treatment Mr. Michaelson received was almost brutal in its nature.

"He was compelled to sleep on the bare floor, and the interior of the whole castle is like a dungeon. Stimulants forwarded to the castle by his friends were never delivered to the prisoner. A hammock was not permitted to reach him until the day before he was liberated, and meals purchased at a hotel for his benefit were detained on the outside. His food was thrown to him as it might be given to a dog. Finally, a prison attendant who saw that he was a gentleman, gave him food on a tin plate, and then said in Spanish, 'I would like to have a little tip, if you don't mind, sir.'

Slow Death in Prison Vaults.

"While in the cell, the correspondent saw a rat of tremendous size. It was a black rat with a long gray beard, and approached Michaelson, he said, as if bent on opening hostilities. Michaelson took off his boot and hurled it at the animal, the missile striking the cell door with a loud noise. The rat was frightened away, and prison officials were attracted to the cell. They rebuked the prisoner for a breach of prison discipline, the noise not being permissible.

"The prison is a damp, unhealthy place, where no regard is paid to sanitary arrangements or conditions. A short confinement within its dreary walls is frequently attended with fatal consequences. The climate is such that dreaded fevers are disastrous in their results, the ravages of yellow fever being terrible in extent.

"The hospitals in and around Havana are so crowded with patients that frequently the military doctors send sufferers to hotels while the unfortunates are suffering from some dreaded disease. The announcement is made that the complaint is rheumatism or some other disease not of an infectious or contagious character, so that this method frequently results in many well persons being subjected needlessly to great dangers of contamination."

In April two hundred and twelve men were confined in two cells of Morro Castle. They were political prisoners, or "suspects," awaiting trial. Some had been there a week, some a month, some a year.

Two were American citizens; one a British subject. There was a boy of fourteen years, born in Spain, and not long enough in Cuba to dream of rebelling against the government.

There were men bowed in years, young men, merchants, professional men, clerks and farm laborers, all gathered in and thrown together, with little or no evidence of having aided or taken part in the insurrection. In the Cabanas fortress, close by, and in prisons all over the Island, were other unfortunates. Two thousand, three thousand, perhaps four thousand, altogether, for no man may know how many people Spain had behind the bars at this time in Cuba.

Like Subterranean Tunnels.

But of the 212 in the Morro. Each cell is about 20 feet wide and nearly 100 feet deep. They are of stone, arched above, and are more like subterranean tunnels than rooms for human beings. The only openings are at the ends. They are in the lower part of a building, within the outer walls, and having the appearance of being intended for storing supplies. They are damp and filthy, and are said to be infested with vermin. Nothing in the shape of chairs, benches or beds is provided. There are, however, hooks for fifty hammocks in each room. Friends of the prisoners supplied the hammocks; but, as there were 108 men in one room, and 104 in the other, more than half the number were compelled to sleep on the stone floor.

Water was furnished twice a day in separate cans, which once contained kerosene oil. Regular army rations were served. The sanitary arrangements were vile. Many men were taken from these cells to the hospitals before the slow-moving authorities saw fit to try their cases, or admit that they had no case.

One of the prisoners was Lopez Colona, who left Matanzas in the early days of the rebellion. Like Juan Gualberto Gomez, who died in Ceuta prison, Colona presented himself when Captain-General Calleja issued his proclamation granting amnesty to all insurgents who surrendered. He had been in prison more than a year, had neither been deported nor given a trial, and stood a good chance of dying in prison.

Another prisoner was Manuel Francisco Aguerro. He affirmed he was an American citizen, and though he was arrested in July, 1895, the American Consul said he had never before heard of the case. Aguerro was a general agent or manager of a traveling circus. He said he had visited the United States yearly to obtain features for his circus, and lived there at one time five years, when he took out citizenship papers. He had taken no part in the war, and was arrested in Guara, Havana province, July 7th, 1895.

All of the 212 in Morro Castle were white. One already mentioned was a smooth-cheeked Spanish lad of fourteen, who was clerk in a store in a small town in the interior of Havana province. He lost his position, and was walking along the highway to Havana when arrested, charged with being a rebel.

Aside from those named, the political prisoners are Cubans almost without exception. They are not in any sense prisoners of war. They are peaceable citizens dragged out of their homes, away from families dependent upon them for support, and sent to the Morro.

CHAPTER XIV.

Stirring Incidents of the Conflict.

IT is evident that there was no opportunity for General Weyler to fight a pitched battle with the entire insurgent army. The reason is plain. The insurgents were scattered and were not massed in large numbers. They were, indeed, separated into two divisions, the one under General Gomez and the other under General Antonio Maceo, but they were not to be found at any one point in very formidable numbers.

The insurgent generals exhibited great strategy in avoiding a pitched battle against overwhelming numbers. They knew every inch of Cuba. They could advance and retreat with the swiftness of the wind. They were well acquainted with all the natural strongholds, and could disappear whenever there was a certainty of being defeated or captured if they risked battle. Thus the war progressed and was not without incidents of the most stirring description.

On March 13th, Gomez and Maceo, who were in the province of Matanzas, separated, Gomez remaining in the vicinity of Jovellanos, while Maceo moved west. The Government troops directed attention to Maceo, who showed a tendency to retreat toward Havana. The columns commanded by Generals Bernal and Prats, Colonels Vicuna and Inclan, Tort and Molina and the Almanza battalion formed a combination to encircle Maceo and prevent his entrance to Havana province. The official announcement was made at the Palace of the combination of the seven columns. The result was anxiously awaited.

Later the Government announced that Maceo declined an engagement and entered Havana province. From other sources it was learned that Maceo discovered the combination, and with Lacret and Bandera's forces, numbering over ten thousand, fell upon the

151

Almanza battalion, which happened to be a raw one recently arrived from Spain, broke it to pieces near Los Palos, rode over the remains and crossed the Havana line, leaving the Government combination in the rear. Maceo passed south of Guines and struck the railroad north of Batanao, removed the track and telegraph wires from the trocha, and caused consternation in the block-houses along the strong line. In the vicinity of Pozo Redondo he burned two bridges, and was reported going in the direction of Pinar del Rio line.

General Weyler was very angry over the failure of the columns to prevent Maceo's return, especially since he had just proclaimed the province free of insurgents. The Government troops were rushed west in pursuit of Maceo, and the strong line was again strengthened. There was no improvement in the situation in the other provinces. The Spanish held only three towns in the Western province—Pinar del Rio, Candelaria and Artemisa.

In Matanzas many thousand acres of cane were burned, railroads destroyed and towns attacked. The rebels were more numerous than ever. The same was true of Santa Clara and Santiago provinces. General Weyler's recent decrees were being rigidly enforced, causing panic in many sections.

The Spaniards Killing One Another.

An untoward military accident occurred, growing out of a mis-understanding of the reply to a challenge, resulting in the killing of twelve soldiers and the wounding of a number of others. A small band of insurgents had set fire to the cane and buildings on a sugar estate near Marianao, Province of Havana. The smoke attracted the attention of two columns of Spanish troops who were advancing in search of the rebels. The column which first arrived on the estate entrenched themselves, as a precaution against any sudden attack from the insurgents, who were supposed to be near.

The second column, consisting of the San Quintin battalion, arrived on the scene after dark. As they approached the entrenchments of the first column they were hailed by the usual " Alerta " from a picket, and responded by calling out the name of their battal

ion—San Quintin.   The picket, confused by the sudden appearance
of the column, misunderstood the reply, taking it, from the similarity
of sound, to be Quintin Bandera, the name of one of the rebel
leaders.   He at once concluded that the insurgents were moving to
attack the column to which he belonged, and, without further parley,
discharged his piece and fell back to the entrenchments, where the
report of his rifle had caused all the troops to seize their arms and
prepare to repel an attack.

The second column had in the meantime continued to advance,
supposing that they had come upon the rebels for whom they were
looking.   They had not gone far before the first column poured a
volley into their ranks.   The second column returned the fire, and
then in response to an order fixed their bayonets and rushed forward
to take the entrenchments by storm.   As they went over the entrenchments the first column poured another volley into them, and
then when the troops came into close quarters it was discovered from
the uniforms and flags that a fatal blunder had been made.

It was reported that the losses on both sides in killed and wounded
were over thirty, but there was a strong suspicion that they were
much larger.

Defending Havana.

" Within three days," says a journalist, " I have made two journeys
out into the surrounding country, and have seen the hurried preparations for the defense of the city which are going on day and night.
I went clear across the Island to the south coast along the trocha,
and the work is astonishing.   Miles of trenches are being dug ; on
every high piece of ground commanding a quarter of mile radius has
been erected a stone fort with a boiler-iron roof and watch-tower,
and outside the limits of the city not a building commanding a street
or village, or a *hacienda* in the country remains which has not been
barricaded and garrisoned.   The numerous little forts are each capable of holding a hundred or a hundred and fifty men and a machine
gun has been sent out to half a dozen of them which are nearest the
city.

"It all looks very much like the hasty defense of a city about to be attacked, and the nature of the fortifications, outside the forts described, bears out this impression. The buildings utilized are topped along the four sides of the roof with a rampart of oil-barrels filled with sand, and when the supply of barrels has failed ordinary sugar sacks have been used in the same way. At Guanabacoa, east of the city in the direction of Matanzas, sardine boxes, flour barrels, empty cracker cases, old lumber and every sort of junk have been piled up in lines and filled with gravel.

The following letter, addressed to the American press, was received at Tampa, Fla., March 14th:

Outrages by a Despot.

"If the Government that unhappily rules the destinies of this unfortunate country should be true to the most rudimentary principles of justice and morality, Colonel Jull, who has been recently appointed Military Governor of Matanzas province, should be in the galleys among criminals. It is but a short time since he was relieved by General Martinez Campos of the military command at Cienfuegos, as he had not once engaged any of the insurgent forces, but vented all his ferocious instincts against innocent and inoffensive peasants.

"In Yaguaramas, a small town near Cienfuegos, he arrested as suspects and spies Mr. Antonio Morejon, an honest and hard-working man, and Mr. Ygnacio Chapi, who is well advanced in years and almost blind. Not being able to prove the charge against them, as they were innocent, he ordered Major Moreno, of the Barcelona battalion, doing garrison duty at Yaguaramas, to kill them with the machete and have them buried immediately. Major Moreno answered that he was a gentleman, who had come to fight for the integrity of his country, and not to commit murder. This displeased the colonel sorely, but, unfortunately, a volunteer sergeant, with six others, were willing to execute the order of the colonel, and Morejon and Chapi were murdered without pity.

"The order of Jull was executed in the most cruel manner. It horrifies to even think of it. Mr. Chapi, who knew the ways of

Colonel Jull, on being awakened at 3 o'clock in the morning, and notified by the volunteer of the guard that he and Morejon had to go out, suspected what was to come, and told his companion to cry out for help as soon as they would be taken out of the fort. They did so, but those who were to execute the order of Jull were neither moved nor weakened in their purpose.

A Ghastly Spectacle.

On the contrary, at the first screams of Chapi and Morejon they threw a lasso over their heads, and pulled at it by the ends. In a few moments they fell to the ground, choked to death. They were dragged on the earth without pity to the place where they were buried. All this bloody scene was witnessed by Jull from a short distance. Providence has not willed that so much iniquity should remain hidden forever. In the hurry the grave where these two innocent men were buried was not dug deep enough, and part of the rope with which they were choked remained outside. A neighbor looking for a lost cow saw the rope, took hold of it, and, on pulling, disinterred the head of one of the victims. He was terror-stricken, and immediately gave notice to the Guardia Civil and the Judge. These authorities soon found out that the men had been killed by order of Colonel Jull, and therefore proceedings were suspended.

"The neighbors and all civil and military authorities know everything that has been related here, but such is the state of affairs on this Island that General Weyler has had no objection to appointing this monster, Colonel Jull, Military Governor of Matanzas. Such deeds as enumerated are common.

"The people of the town of Matanzas, with Jull as Governor, and Arolas at the head of a column, will suffer the consequences of their pernicious and bloody instincts.

"That the readers may know in part who General Arolas is, I will relate what has happened in the Mercedes estate, near Colon. It having come to his knowledge that a small body of rebels was encamped on the sugar Estate Mercedes, of Mr. Carrillo, General Arolas went to engage them, but the rebels, who were few in num-

ber, retreated.   Much vexed at not being able to discharge one shot
at them, he made prisoners of three workmen who were out in the
field herding the animals of the estate, and without any formality of
trial shot them.   When the bodies were taken to the Central they
were recognized, and to cover his responsibility somewhat General
Arolas said that when he challenged them they ran off, and at the
first discharge of musketry they fell dead.

"It seems impossible that being so near the United States, so near
that country so free, cultured and generous, innocent peasants can be
butchered with impunity.   Not even in Armenia happens what is
being witnessed in Cuba.   The history of the Spanish dominion in
this unfortunate Island is a history of crimes."

Appalling Devastation.

Some idea of the devastation wrought by the war in Cuba may be
gathered from the fact that fifty-nine towns were destroyed in the four
western provinces.   Most of these towns were burned by the insurgents
for resisting attacks, or because they were being used as depots of
supplies for government troops.   In some cases, like that of Cabanas,
the Spanish troops demolished the town to prevent the insurgents
from occupying it.   Very little of the destruction was done wantonly
by either side.

When the insurgents, led by Maceo, entered Pinar del Rio every
town in the province except the capital city welcomed him with open
arms, and no property was injured.   Later the Government troops
entered the province, and, moving in strong columns, dislodged the
insurgents from town after town, establishing their own garrisons there.
Thereupon the inhabitants burned their own town, and nearly the
entire province was laid in ashes.   Spanish troops occupied the city
of Pinar del Rio, the towns of Candelaria, Artemisa and the port of
Colima.   All the rest of the province was in the hands of the enemy
A Spanish force was sent to establish a base of supplies at Guane.
Upon the approach of the column the residents burned their town.

In the general devastation of Pinar del Rio tobacco warehouses
were burned, and the indications were that this crop would not be

permitted to reach the coast. Banana and pineapple crops were also interfered with. Shipments from the interior to the sea-coast towns were so completely blocked that at Guines, in this province, cows were offered for sale at $4 each, pigs $1, turkeys 40 cents, and eggs and milk had no price. In Havana these things were worth four times the customary price, and codfish imported in large quantities for consumption in the interior was offered for one and one-half cents per pound, but a little more than the duty alone. Thousands of people were destitute, and had it not been for tropical fruits and the tropical climate starvation would have been theirs.

The following report from Defuniak Springs, Fla., under date of March 18th, shows that the friends of Cuba were active in supplying arms and ammunition:

Arrival of Munitions of War.

"The expedition of General Enrique Collazo, which sailed from Tampa about two weeks ago, was met at an appointed location in the Gulf by a steamer whose name is given as 'Jose Marti,' having aboard General Collazo, Major Charles Hernandez, and Miguel Duque de Estrada, a brother-in-law of Collazo. The main body consisted of ninety-eight able-bodied men, most of whom are prominent in society in Havana. The steamer will immediately sail for Cuba, intending to land on the northern coast, near Cardenas. The following is a list of the munitions of war taken:

"Five hundred Winchester rifles, 500 Remington rifles, 500 machetes, two rapid-firing field-pieces, and a large number of cartridges, caps and considerable dynamite. Sufficient accoutrements and equipments were taken for five hundred men.

"The Spanish Consul at Tampa was fully aware of the move, but on account of it being made on Sunday he could obtain no warrant to arrest the members of the expedition, the United States Marshal refusing to act without it."

The strength of the insurgent army at this time was close to 43,000 men. Cubans themselves estimated the number of men in the field as high as 60,000; but even if unarmed camp-followers, men in charge of provision trains, hospitals and camps were counted, it is doubtful if that number could have been found actually in service. There were thousands of Cubans who would willingly have cast their lot with the patriot army, but lack of arms and ammunition prevented.

The insurgent forces operated, as a rule, in zones or districts, and were organized on military lines. The columns of Gomez, Maceo, Lacret and Banderas were, however, limited to no one province, but passed from one to another, under direct orders of Gomez.

A Hand-to-Hand Encounter.

News was received at Havana of an important battle which was fought in the vicinity of Candelaria, in the Province of Pinar del Rio. The Government troops were unable to drive the insurgents back, and retired from their position with considerable loss. The Spanish forces were commanded by General Linares and Colonels Inclan and Hernandez, and the insurgents by Maceo and Banderas. The fighting was begun on a line parallel with the roadway. The Spanish forces deployed, the Tarifa battalion, a section of the Victoria cavalry and a detachment of artillery forming the vanguard and opening fire upon the enemy.

The insurgents returned this fire, and at the same time made an attack upon the rear-guard of the Spaniards, completely encircling their column. Having entirely surrounded the Government troops, the insurgents advanced upon the artillerymen with machetes. The latter made a vigorous resistance, using muskets and grenades with such effect as to check for a time the enemy's advance; but, with reinforcements, a second charge was made by the insurgents and a hand-to-hand engagement ensued. The battle terminated with a bayonet charge. After a hot fight, lasting two hours, the Spaniards were defeated, losing many killed and wounded. It was the intention of the enemy to prevent Colonel Inclan from proceeding to Candelaria.

The official report of the fight said the insurgents suffered a tremendous loss. The Spaniards lost two captains and five privates killed, and one lieutenant, four sergeants and fifty-four soldiers wounded.   General Linares arrived at Candelaria an hour after the conclusion of the engagement, when he reported his share in the battle.

A dispatch from Havana to the *Imparcial* at Madrid said: "Captain-General Weyler feels much hindered by the excessive degree of prudence he is compelled to observe during the discussion in the United States Congress of the question of the belligerency of the Cuban insurgents, which, moreover, prejudices the course of the war."

Mr. Armstrong, Secretary of the United States Legation at Madrid, said: "General Weyler is certainly in a very embarrassing position.   He is trying to quell an insurrection in a province in which 90 per cent. of the population are opposed to him, and as soon as he starts a friendly nation practically tells him that, while he may carry on the war, he must not shoot any one."

A detachment of Spanish troops near Cardenas, province of Matanzas, captured 151 cases of ammunition, nine cases of carbines, fourteen medical chests, twenty boxes of accoutrements and two boxes of cartridge caps.   These supplies, evidently intended for the insurgents, were found in three boats, which apparently belonged to some filibustering steamer off the coast.

Senor Dupuy de Lome, Spanish Minister at Washington, received the following cablegram on March 20:

"HAVANA, March 20.—The detachment of Veradero, near Cardenas, captured 150 boxes of ammunition for Remington and Winchester rifles, nine boxes of cavalry rifles, fourteen tin boxes of medicines, twenty knapsacks covered with oil-cloth, two boxes of explosives and three boats.   (Signed)   WEYLER."

The Spanish Minister was of the opinion that the war material mentioned was that of the Colazzo expedition, which was shipped from Cedar Key in the schooner "J. S. Mallory," captured by the United States revenue cutters, released by the authorities at Tampa, and afterwards transshipped somewhere near the southern coast of Florida to the steamer "Three Friends."

With the arrival at Philadelphia of the schooner "J. Manchester

Haynes" from Havana, came an interesting account of the state of affairs at the Cuban capital. For two months the schooner lay at Havana, and during all that time the insurgents tantalized the Spanish soldiers, who, notwithstanding the vigorous policy that was supposed to have been adopted, seemed to be unable to cope with the tactics employed by the patriots.

Flames from Burning Plantations.

Ninety thousand soldiers were quartered at Havana. During the time the "Haynes" was at that port the insurgent force, numbering about 6000, were at no time farther away from the capital than fifteen miles. The Spanish soldiers had possession of the city, but just outside havoc was being wrought by the insurgents. Flames from burning plantations could be seen at all times, and frequently a daring patriot would go almost into the capital and destroy property.

The Western Railroad, which runs from Havana, was a great sufferer. No sooner were the rails relaid than the insurgents tore them up again. An engineer, more daring than the rest, was warned by the insurgents not to venture out from the town, but, risking it, he was captured, and when the "Haynes" left Havana nothing further had been heard concerning him. The President of this railroad also lost cattle, which were in the western part of the city. The insurgents some weeks before raided that section and destroyed a large number of cows, and no milk could be had for several days.

Insurgent spies were said to enter Havana frequently to find out whatever news it was possible to learn, especially the plans of the Spanish. They then returned to the country, and the information thus obtained enabled the officers to direct their forces in a manner that baffled the Government troops.

The "Haynes" was at Havana when General Weyler arrived. War was to be pushed to a speedy end, it was declared, but there was no sign of an early termination of hostilities. When the United States Senate passed the resolutions favoring the recognition of the insurgents as belligerents, there was bitter feeling expressed by the Spaniards against this country. "Why," said one, "I could eat ten of those Americans myself!" Somebody remarked that it would be better for his country if he ate ten of the insurgents.

The insurgents seemed never to rest, but it appeared otherwise with the Spaniards. A small band of the insurgents would approach very close to the capital, but while the Government troops were pursuing them the time for eating would come. This settled it. The soldiers stopped to eat. After they had filled their stomachs with things good to eat and drink, they enjoyed their cigarettes. By this time the insurgents on their ponies were far away. This is quoted to illustrate the activity of one and the apathy of the other of the contending forces.

Capture of a Band of Insurgents.

Some days before the "Haynes" sailed for Philadelphia several bands of insurgents were captured. One band, numbering seventeen, headed by a negro chief, was marched through the town in the charge of a large regiment of soldiers. The soldiers with great glee kept swinging their swords near the chief's head. The entire band was taken to Morro Castle, where, it was believed, the chief would be shot. A Spanish commandant, who had been found giving provisions to insurgents, was executed in Morro Castle. An American sailor, who had been three years in Morro Castle, was released several weeks before. He had been put there for knocking down a policeman. The sailor was lounging around the docks when the "Haynes" departed.

A day or so before the schooner sailed from Havana an expedition was said to have been landed at Cabanas, a town to the westward of the capital. The gunboats did not seem to be able to prevent the landing of filibusters, who found it comparatively easy to get ashore on the coast from Santa Cruz to Havana. It was stated that property-owners and merchants were openly professing sympathy with the Spaniards, fearing that all that belonged to them would be confiscated if they appeared to favor the other side, but when the turning-point came, it was believed all would actively support the insurgents.

Owing to the destruction of the plantations very little new sugar

11

was coming into Havana from the country districts.   There was a lot of old sugar in the warehouses, but this the people did not care to send out because no new material was coming in.

Reference has been made to the expedition of the steamer " Three Friends," of Jacksonville, Florida.   We here give the complete story of the trip.   The steamer, in command of Captain Napoleon B. Broward, arrived at Jacksonville on March 18th, having succeeded in landing in Cuba General Enrique Collazo, Major Charles Hernandez, and Duke Estrada, besides fifty-four men taken off the schooner " Ardell," from Tampa, and the entire cargo of arms and ammunition of the schooner " Mallory," from Cedar Key.   It was by long odds the most important expedition that has set out from this country, and the Cubans at Jacksonville, when they learned that the " Three Friends " had safely fulfilled her mission, shouted   " Viva Cuba l " until they were hoarse.

Large Cargo of Arms.

They declared that it would change the character of the whole war, as the unarmed men would now be armed and those without ammunition would be supplied, and that Maceo, who had before been wary and cautious, would be more aggressive than he had ever been before.   The cargo of arms landed by the " Three Friends " and the "Mallory " was as follows : 750,000 rounds of cartridges ; 1,200 rifles ; 2,100 machetes ; 400 revolvers, besides stores, reloading tools, etc.

The " Three Friends " met the " Mallory " at Alligator Key.   The " Ardell " had just finished transferring the men to her.   While they were rendezvoused there behind the pines in a deep coral-walled creek three big Spanish men-of-war steamed slowly by, but they did not discover that there was anything suspicious-looking in shore, although with a glass men could be seen in their look-outs scanning the horizon, as well as searching the shore.   Sunday, about noon, no vessels being in sight, the " Three Friends " took in tow the " Mallory " and steamed southward under a good head of steam.

The " Three Friends " is a powerful tug, and by Monday night was close enough to the Cuban shore to hear the breakers. Several ship lights to the west were seen, one of which was evidently a Spanish man of-war, for she had a search light at her bow, and was sweeping the waves with it, but the "Three Friends" was a long way off and had no light, and so was out of the neighborhood of the Spaniard.

Shadowed by Detectives.

At ten o'clock that night, by the aid of a naphtha launch and two big surf-boats, which had been taken out of Jacksonville, the "Three Friends" landed the men and ammunition from her hold, and from that of the "Mallory." It took four and a half hours to complete the job. There were hundreds of men on shore to assist, and they did it silently, appreciating the peril of the undertaking.

The Cubans on shore recognized General Collazo immediately, and no words can describe their joy upon seeing him. He is a veteran of Cuban wars, and is one whom Spain fears. In fact, it is known that during his sojourn in Florida he was shadowed by detectives, who had been instructed to spare no expense to keep Collazo from reaching Cuba. When it was whispered that Collazo was really among them, they seemed not to believe their ears, but came forward and looked, and, seeing that there was really no mistake, threw up their arms and wept. Major Charles H. nandez and Duke Estrada were also enthusiastically welcomed.

It was reported that night that Maceo had received the arms of the first expedition that set forth three days before the "Three Friends" landed. They were not from the "Commodore," for they reported that they were now on the lookout for that vessel. They said, too, that at the end of the week four expeditions were afloat. Two, including the "Three Friends," had landed, and two more were on the way. Tuesday morning, as the "Three Friends" was returning, she sighted a steamer that answered to the description of the "Commodore." She was headed southward, and pushing along apparently at the rate of fifteen knots an hour. This vessel has an engine capable of driving a ship twice her size, and has a speed of seventeen knots an hour.

On Wednesday, March 3, General Collazo, Major Hernandez and Duke Estrada left Tampa, and reached Jacksonville the next day. They remained secreted at the house of a Cuban sympathizer until the 12th, General Collazo knowing that detectives had been on his trail for weeks. They intended to leave on the night of March 5th, but their departure was delayed, on account of the capture of the " Mallory," until the 12th. After release, the " Mallory " sailed with a part of the arms seized at Cedar Keys six months before, some on an island, some in a house, and some that had been jettisoned and had been released through the efforts of H. S. Rubens, general counsel of the Cubans. The schooner " Ardell " left Tampa the same night with fifty-four men and Brigadier-General Vasquez, a brother-in-law of General Collazo.

Escape of the Vessel.

Five tons of the " Mallory's " arms and ammunition were taken from her at Tampa and shipped to Jacksonville, in a sealed car, with instructions not to open until called for. When the car arrived in Jacksonville, one of the clerks of the railroad, not knowing of the orders, opened the car and unloaded it in the freight depot of the Florida Central & Peninsular Railroad, and this discovery led to all sorts of rumors. It was known that the boxes contained arms, as they were heavy, and they were labelled " Colt's Fire Arms Company." They were promptly removed to the warehouse of the President of the Friends of Cuba Club of Jacksonville.

The arms remained in this warehouse until the night of the 12th instant. Meanwhile the " Mallory " sailed from Tampa with the remainder of the cargo to Alligator Key, the appointed rendezvous. Alligator Key is about 100 miles south of Biscayne Bay. It is a part of the Florida reef, and, being well wooded, is an excellent place for the purpose. There the " Mallory " was joined by the " Ardell," where the two waited for the " Three Friends."

This vessel left the dock of the Alabama Coal Company in Jacksonville at 8 o'clock on the night of Thursday, the 12th inst., and proceeded to the dock, where she loaded with arms, ammunition and dynamite.   At 10 o'clock she sailed for the mouth of the river, but stopped at Bucki's on the way and took aboard General Collazo and his party, and A. W. Barra, who had driven out in carriages from the place where they were secreted.   At this point a large naphtha launch was taken on, as well as two large iron surf-boats, to be used in landing the arms, etc.

The steamer proceeded out to the bar that night, and at daylight of Friday, the 13th, she proceeded down the coast.   She arrived at Alligator Key Sunday morning, and then took in tow the " Mallory."

CHAPTER XV.

Pathetic Stories of the War.

ON the 4th of March, Dr. Delgado, an American citizen residing in Cuba, was wounded by brutal Spanish soldiers. There was a ghastly gash made by a machete across the side of his head, extending downward to the throat. It was sewed up by the doctors. The bullet-hole through his side was the most painful.

He had lived in New York, and had begun practicing medicine there as assistant to Dr. Alexander Mott. He came to Cuba in 1876 to claim property which belonged to him by inheritance. He grieved a great deal over the young men who were killed on the day of the massacre, when he escaped so miraculously to tell this story.

A newspaper correspondent heard the story of the butchery from Delgado's old father, who speaks good English. The old man was still suffering from the effects of the weeks which he spent in the damp cane fields with his wounded boy. Frequently, as he told the awful story, his face was convulsed with suffering, and tears flowed from his eyes. In his trembling hands he held the blood-stained bullet which fell from his side when they removed his garments. He said that he would bring it himself to Mr. Cleveland and would ask the President if there was no protection for Americans in Cuba.

"Our plantation," he said, "is called Dolores, the old name being Morales. It was about half-past one on the 4th day of March when a regiment of rebels, about 400 or 500 men, invaded the place. They told us that they were Maceo's men, and soon after them came Maceo, with twenty-four women, sixteen whites and eight mulattoes. I understood that these women were the wives of the officers.

"Maceo shook hands politely and asked if I would allow them to take breakfast with us. Of course there was nothing to do but to say yes, and the men spread themselves over about seventy acres of the plantation, the officers and the ladies coming into the house. They had provisions with them, but desired to cook and serve them, which they did. They sat down at the table, and were soon joking and laughing.

"Suddenly we heard rifle-shots. Hernandez yelled to his wife to hand him his machete. Then all went out and found that the firing had come from what seemed to be an advance guard of the Spanish troops. There was some skirmishing at a distance, and the insurgents rode away. They did not wish to fight on the plantation, as they were on another mission.

Bullets Cause Alarm.

"The Spaniards had fired the cane, thinking there were other insurgents hiding in it. Spanish bullets rattled on the tiled roof of the house, and farm-hands who were ploughing back of the house got frightened and wished to come in. So the doors and windows were unbarred, and six men and three women, wives of the farm-hands, came in.

"After a while I opened the window to see how matters stood and saw two cavalrymen and a captain, with two soldiers. My son and the farm-hands went out toward the burning cane in an attempt to save some oxen that were near the cane. When the captain saw them he shouted: 'Who are those people?'

"I told him they were our workmen, and he then gave orders to clear the house. They rushed their horses right through the house, the captain leading them. I took out my American papers and showed them to him to prove that I was a peaceful citizen.

"'They are the worst documents you can have,' said the captain. They answered my son in the same way, and the captain repeated the order to clear the house. Then they ordered us to march on as prisoners and told the women to stay back. My son asked them to let me stay back with the women, and they allowed me to do so. Of course, the women were panic-stricken and screaming when they saw their husbands taken away.

"We heard shots and then a second volley. One of the women

cried out: 'They have killed my husband!' Her words were true.
After about three hours I ventured out, and I saw coming toward the
house the old farm-hand, a man of about 70. He seemed to be holding a red handkerchief over his arm, but when I got nearer I saw
that it was covered with blood. He cried out when he saw me:—

"'They have killed them!'

"'My son! My son!' I cried.

"'He was the first one that they killed,' he said.

"I took the man in the house and tried to bind his arm, which had
been shattered by a bullet. I endeavored to pacify the women, and
told them that they should go to the nearest neighbors for help.
The two white farm-hands, who had been hiding in the cane, then
came over toward the house, while I was trying to quiet the women.
They were afraid to move, panic-stricken, and would not go for help.

"Suddenly a young man dashed up to the house at full gallop.
He drew his revolver and told the farm-hands to get cots and pillows and medicine to bring to the missing men in case any of them
should be still alive. He said he would shoot them if they disobeyed, and they did as he directed. They made up a litter, and we
walked on till we found the place where the men lay in a pool of
blood.

"I looked into my son's face and cried out: 'My son, my son.' He
opened his eyes and whispered, 'Father, they have killed us.'"

The old gentleman broke down in a passion of weeping at these
recollections of this awful scene. He led me in to the bedside of his
son, who then told me his story of the butchery.

"They marched us along," he said, "and I spoke to the General:
'General, I am an American citizen, and here are my papers from Mr.
Williams.'

"'They are the worst things you could have,' he said. 'I wish the
Consul were here himself, so that I could treat him thus,' and he
struck me three times in the face. Then he sounded the bugle calling
the volunteers, and ordered us taken to the rear-guard. Of course,
we knew that this meant death. They tied us in a line with our
hands pinioned. I knew the sergeant and said to him:—

" ' Is it possible that you are going to kill me ? '

" ' How can I help it ? ' he answered. Then the order was given and the soldiers rushed upon us with machetes. Their knives cut our ropes as we tried to dodge the blows, and the soldiers fired two volleys at us.

" The first shot grazed my head, and I dropped to the ground as though dead. The old farm-hand also threw himself to the earth. This act saved both our lives.

" The other four men who tried to fight were killed. At the second discharge a bullet pierced my side. When we all lay as though dead they came up and turned us over and searched our pockets—mine first, of course, as I was better dressed than the other men. One of the soldiers noticed that my breast moved and shouted out : ' This fellow is not dead yet. Give him another blow,' and he raised his machete and gave me a slash across the face and throat. Then I became unconscious."

Secreted in a Cane Field.

Delgado's father took up the story as his son left off : " The brave young man who brought us to the place where my son was, now jumped from his horse and gave orders to the men to lift my son on the litter, as we found he was the only man still living. We put a pillow under his head, and the two farm hands lifted the litter and carried it into the cane field.

" Meanwhile, the women relatives of the dead men came up and began to wail and cry. The young man, whom we afterward found was an insurgent leader, told them they should be quiet, as their lamentations would bring the Spanish troops upon the scene again.

" Then the litter was carried into the cane field. This young man said : ' You must immediately write to the American Consul. I will furnish you with a messenger, and you may rest safely in this cane field with your son. I will put a guard of 500 men around it so that they cannot burn it, as they do when they know people are hiding in the cane.'

" For five days I was in the cane field with my son. It rained upon us, and then I put the pilows over my son's chest, in order to protect him. I suffered greatly from rheumatism. Only the young man appeared and said that General Maceo had sent a guard to escort me back to my home.

"With my boy we were taken there and guard kept around our house. Then the messenger came back from the Consul, and I came on to Havana to see General Weyler, who had my son brought here to the city."

On the Sunday after Delgado was borne down the Prado on a covered litter, escorted by a gorgeous Red Cross detachment in Spanish uniform. There was so much theatrical display and pomp about the procession that it looked very much like a clever ruse to impress the newspaper correspondents, who, it was known, were in possession of all the details of the butchery.

No Protection for Americans.

Here is the story of the three brothers Farrar, all American citizens and joint owners of the coffee plantation Estrella, in Havana province, near Alquizar. It does not differ greatly from the experience of many other owners of estates in the interior, but as these men happened to be Americans and had made sworn statements protesting against the excesses committed by Spanish troops, and demanding damages, the affair became one of official record, and cannot be brushed away with a general denial. The papers were placed in the hands of Consul-General Williams, and Miguel Farrar, one of the brothers, furnished a copy of the statement. It is as follows:

"On Saturday, March 21st, the dwelling-house of the coffee plan-tation Estrella was the object of wanton attack by the column of General Bernat, operating in that region. The said building received cannon shots of grape and canister, breaking the door, one window, several piazza columns, and greatly endangering the lives of the families of my brothers, Don Tasio and Don Luis Farrar, both American citizens, the wife of the former being enceinte. There were two small children in the house. From my information it appears that the troops mentioned had sustained fire with a rebel band in Paz plantation, a quarter league from Estrella.

" The rebels having fled to Pedroso and Buena Esperanza plantations, the government troops advanced toward Estrella, in quite an opposite direction from that taken by the rebels. On arriving at the borders of Estrella plantation, the Spanish columns began firing cannon at the dwelling-house, and it was immediately invaded by soldiers, who ransacked it, carrying off from wardrobes all jewelry and men's clothing which they contained, as well as a sum of about $60 in money. They also took away everything found in workmen's dwellings, arresting at the same time twelve of the occupants, whom they conducted to Alquizar as insurgents. It should be observed that the cannon were fired solely at the dwelling-house of the owners, although there were twenty other buildings on the plantation, and the place was entirely clear of insurgents.

Immediate Indemnity Demanded.

" In consideration of all the above, and particularly on account of the danger to which his relatives were exposed, and also for the unjustifiable looting on the part of the regular troops in the service of a constituted government, the undersigned does most solemnly protest and asks an immediate indemnity for the damage suffered, which he values at $5,000, as all work has been stopped on the plantation and everything abandoned."

The Spanish official account of what happened on the Estrella plantation was as follows : " The column of General Bernat found several bands of rebels who fortified the houses of the coffee plantation Estrella, where they were beaten, and by artillery shots and cavalry charges the enemy was dislodged from his position. Twelve prisoners were captured, besides arms, ammunition and instruments to destroy railroad tracks. It is believed from the trails of blood seen in the place that the rebels had many dead and wounded. All the prisoners will be summarily court-martialed."

On March 25th twenty prisoners, taken in the operations around Artemisia and Alquizas, arrived in Havana. On being escorted through Obispo street to the palace they were followed by a constantly increasing mob, who shouted: " Viva Espana," and " Death to the rebels."

The men were kicked, beaten, and one had his head cut open by a flying missile. It was enough to make decent blood boil to see the poor wretches, with arms pinioned and a mob at their heels shouting for their blood. By the time the prisoners reached the Palace the mob numbered between 200 and 300. General Ahumada, the secundo cabo, or second chief of the government, came out and ordered the guards to disperse the mob.

A Heroine who Fought for Cuba.

An authentic account is given of a heroine who fell in defense of the Cuban cause. This woman was Senorita Matilde Agramonte, of Havana, who, after marching and fighting with Maceo's soldiers, fell dead at last, riddled with Spanish bullets.

Matilde was the last representative of one of the most widely known of old-stock Cuban families. Her ancestors were among the first Spanish settlers of the Island. In every insurrection that has occurred on the Island men of the Agramonte and Varona families have been found in the field. The wealth of the family has been counted by millions.

When uncles and brothers of Senorita Matilde followed General Maceo into battle they left Matilde on the ranch, in charge. The girl set out on a visit to Ciego de Avila. Upon her return she found nothing left but ashes and the bodies of the servants. She decided to join the army of General Maceo, and so the first female soldier to bear arms against Spain was enlisted.

The poor girl never saw but one battle. That was at the plantation of Olayita, in Quemado de Guines, province of Santa Clara. The patriots were overwhelmingly outnumbered To protect the main body in retreat, Maceo called for volunteers, who should remain behind and draw the fire of the Spanish.

Among those who stepped forward was Matilde. They carried out General Maceo's plan, but forfeited their own lives. Matilde stood shoulder to shoulder with the soldiers and fired her rifle. She was one of the last to fall.

The arrest of suspects continued during March at such a rate that the prisons were full, and epidemics among the prisoners were feared. The Remedios prison was in a terrible sanitary condition, with 200 prisoners in quarters which were very much overcrowded.

At Sagua there were 226 prisoners, and there was room for no more. The same state of affairs prevailed at many other points. The decrees of General Weyler were enforced with great harshness against the Cubans supposed to have Cuban sympathies. A state of panic, as a result of these decrees and the action of troops, prevailed in all portions of the Island occupied by the Spanish.

Where were the Prisoners?

The peaceable citizens had no fear of the insurgents, who followed more humane methods. It was absolutely impossible for correspondents to learn the whereabouts of the prisoners of war who were reported to be taken in the battles fought. The subordinate Spanish officers said that secret orders had been given to take no prisoners. The Cubans released all the Spanish soldiers captured. The Spanish gave no quarter. So many plantation employés and managers were butchered that the men dared not remain on the plantations, and the women were left in charge of them. The men hid in the woods at the approach of the Spanish column.

Here is the proclamation of General March, commanding the Third Division of the First Army Corps, issued from headquarters at Holguin, Santiago Province:

"Be it known that the forces operating in the territory of this division have orders to fire, without giving the signal to halt, on any person who travels at night on the roads outside the towns and hamlets, and for the purpose of preventing accidents this is hereby published for general knowledge." This illustrates the kind of war Spain was giving Cuba. Even the Spanish officers were disgusted at the methods used.

Under date of March 26th, it was reported that another blunder on the part of two Spanish commanders had once more led to fatal results.   The catastrophe which occurred at El Cano was to a great extent due to the darkness of the night, but now news came of columns mistaking each other for enemies in broad daylight, and continuing to fight until thirty men had been killed and over one hundred wounded.

With an absence of good taste, and even of common sense, this unfortunate affair was made a subject for self-glorification in the newspapers of Havana. They pointed exultingly to the proof afforded of the extreme valor and discipline of their army, which enabled them in so short a time to inflict such heavy damage.   Without desiring to detract from the acknowledged courage of the Spaniards, it may be stated that this made the fourth time within a few months that loyal battalions fired upon their own men. This argued, to say the least of it, an absence of coolness and judgment. the qualities most essential to a good commanding officer.

His Own Brother Among the Slain.

The manner of carrying on the campaign against the insurgents consisted in strong columns, which were supposed to be continually on the advance.   Three of these were kept within sound of shot of one another, while each leader had orders to attack the enemy anywhere, regardless of superiority of numbers or position, and to rely upon the support of the nearest troops.   Inexperienced generals and colonels were not capable of bringing this to a successful issue.

On the very first alarm they commenced an engagement either at long range or without proper investigation, to find subsequently to their dismay that they had actually been forwarding the cause of Cuban independence.   Some sad stories were told of the scenes that followed upon the battle at Santa Rosa.   One soldier, while engaged in succoring the wounded of the opposing column, discovered his own brother among the slain.

But in a fatal civil war such episodes are necessarily of frequent occurrence.   A colonel of the Guardia Civil, stationed at Cienfuegos, had two sons who, notwithstanding the fact of their being Spaniards, were strongly imbued with Cuban sympathy.   They joined the army of Gomez, and in the first action in which they took part one of them was killed by the regiment commanded by his father. One might hear over and over again of similar political differences in families throughout the Island.

A merchant of large fortune in Havana sent his eldest boys to the United States to keep them out of harm's way. Within three weeks they had returned with an expedition, and had been initiated among the insurgents. One still remained, Benjamin; but as he was only thirteen years of age, no apprehensions were entertained on his account. He was missing, however, one morning, and the anxious Spanish father hurried forthwith to General Weyler to report the circumstances and his fears that his son had taken to the woods. Messages were immediately dispatched in all directions, with the result that the juvenile warrior was captured asleep by the roadside, twenty miles from the capital, covered with dust and completely worn out by his long tramp.

A Singular Incident.

From these dreary records of battle and spoliation it is a relief to turn to an incident which took place at Bolondron, in Matanzas, though it can hardly be regarded as either admirable or edifying. It appears that sparrows in Cuba are looked upon as loyal subjects, and that good Spaniards have a respect for them which we are far from sharing in the United States. Now, there is a native bird called a pitirri, a very desperate character, who, from his absolute contempt for European prejudices, may almost be considered as an insurgent.

On the 19th of March, it is well to be accurate, an ill-conditioned pitirri got into an argument with a select flock of sparrows, and some very unparliamentary language was exchanged. In the investigation into the matter it has not been fully decided as to what was the origin of the discussion; but it is supposed to have had reference either to the elections or the question of belligerency. Whatever it was, however, the sparrows called upon the pitirri to retract or come on.

He selected the latter alternative, and for a few minutes there was little to be seen but a confused mass of plumage and dust. Though vastly outnumbered, the Cuban champion was game to the back-bone, and, though he carries a white feather or two in his general make-up, there was none in his disposition. The consequence was that courage and skill, as they deserve to do, triumphed. Six sparrows were stretched in the cold embrace of death upon the earth, while their companions withdrew to carry the melancholy tidings to the widows and orphans.

Some volunteers had witnessed the action from a distance, as is their custom, when they witness it at all, and their souls were wroth within them. Reinforcements were hastily summoned, and a guarded advance was made upon this prototype of Maceo. But the pitirri was satisfied with his exceedingly creditable performance, pocketed the stakes, and quietly flew away to his club among the palms. Slowly and sadly the poor, lifeless remains were lifted from the ground, and slowly and sadly they were borne by the volunteers to the barracks.

Here it was unanimously decided to honor the defunct birds with a public funeral. At first it was even proposed to bury them in the town cemetery; but it was finally arranged that the obsequies (or the " orgies," as Mark Twain's tramp would say) should take place in the plaza. The procession to the grave was worthy of the great occasion. Hundreds followed the bier, which was draped with the Spanish colors, and covered with wreaths and emblems.

The amazing part of this absolutely true story is that the cura, Father Gurna, actually headed the cortege. A volley of blank cartridges over the buried sparrows terminated the proceedings, and never, surely since Homer wrote of the frogs and mice, have the doughty deeds of such small deer been so magnificently recognized

CHAPTER XVI.

Successes of the Revolutionists.

A FTER Maceo's return to the Province of Havana his course may be described as one continued triumph. Every opposition which he met with was swept from his path. He defeated detachments, he destroyed military stations, he marched victoriously, until he was on the very borders of Pinar del Rio, when, according to the Captain-General, the rebellion had been crushed forever.

It was impossible to obtain perfectly accurate accounts of the engagement, which took place in the vicinity of Palos. The official reports stated that an encounter occurred without furnishing further details; but from what one could learn from other sources, two bands of the patriot army, commanded respectively by Maceo and Quintin Banderas, succeeded in partially surrounding the column of Colonel Tort, which they routed with heavy loss.

Directing their course to the southwest, the insurgents arrived on the evening of the 12th before the town of Batabano. Batabano is a small seaport, where vessels trading along the coast and passenger steamers from Havana are constantly putting in. The country in the vicinity is rich and fertile, while within a few miles the vast plantations of Melena yield annually the largest return of sugar in the Island.

The town was defended by a strong volunteer detachment, who were further supported by a Spanish gunboat at anchor in the harbor. As the Cubans advanced, the land and sea forces opened fire, and for a short time there was a brisk fusilade upon the insurgent ranks. These latter, who were, of necessity, sparing of their ammunition, returned the fire in moderation, but meanwhile pressed forward without an instant's pause.

As soon as Maceo had succeeded in effecting a lodgment in the outskirts of the town, the volunteer army fell back precipitately under shelter of the guns of the guard ship, and left Batabano in the hands of the invaders. The whole affair did not occupy quite an hour, and the losses on either side were only trifling.

The real disaster took place after the combat, for the insurgents then proceeded to set fire to the principal buildings, and as the flames spread with great rapidity, the entire town was quickly in a blaze. A few houses alone escaped, so that in place of the once prosperous seaport there remain nothing now but the blackened and crumbling ruins.

Destruction of a Beautiful Residence.

Later the hacienda of a Mr. Goicochea was also burned to the ground. This beautiful country residence was called Chico, and lay at a distance of only eight miles from the capital, near the small town of Arroyo Arenas. It was said to be one of the handsomest places in Cuba. The house was the very beau ideal of a planter's home, with its wide verandas, its spacious apartments and its enclosed court, filled with flowers and luxuriant palms.

The owner was a Cuban, but his sympathies were decidedly Spanish. Indeed, he had at his own expense raised and equipped a body of guerrillas, and in many other ways had shown his hostility to the cause of independence. The estate was partly devoted to the cultivation of coffee and tobacco, but, in addition to these, there were large pasturages, where about twelve hundred head of cattle and one hundred and fifty horses were at grass. A band of seven insurgents descended on the land early in the afternoon. They had chosen their hour with great judgment, as the guerrillas were absent and two men alone represented the garrison.

The dwelling-house and out-offices were set on fire, the carriages, of which there were many, and the farming implements were piled together and burned, and the ornamental grounds and gardens were laid waste. Not content with inflicting this wholesale destruction, the attacking party drove away all the stock, until the estimated loss is calculated to have amounted to over $200,000.

Now, these seven insurgents, though they were decidedly what the Highlanders call "men of their hands," were not for that reason deficient in reasoning capacity. They concocted a plot, which simply, as a ruse de guerre, may challenge competition. They terrified the two prisoners whom they had secured by announcing their determination to hang them both forthwith. Such a threat was naturally enough met by many prayers and entreaties, which were finally granted upon one condition.

This was that the released men should proceed to Marianao and there inform the officers in command that the Cubans intended to attack the village of El Cano that very night. Rejoicing at their escape, the two readily consented, with the result that six companies from the St. Quintin and Peninsula regiments were ordered to march at once to the threatened locality.

Spanish Troops Outwitted.

As El Cano had latterly been supposed to be in danger, it held a garrison of eighty men, under the command of a sub-lieutenant, who had taken the precaution to strengthen his position by a barricade erected midway down the single street. The wily insurgents knew all this well, and so they hovered around the outskirts to precipitate the mistake which they hopefully anticipated.

Shortly after nightfall the relieving column was heard approaching. "Quien vive," shouted the sentries, to which the reply, "Cuba libre!" came back instantly from the concealed patriots. The garrison, of course, concluded that they had to do with the enemy, and fired a volley upon their own men, who in their turn imagined that the town was in the hands of the insurgents. Under this delusion both sides continued to shoot, but as the defenders were behind walls, they suffered nothing, while the column speedily had many men *hors de combat.*

After this had gone on for some time the besieging column was ordered to charge into the town, and they managed to advance as far as the barricade. Here, however, they met with such a warm recep tion that the colonel decided to be satisfied with the half that he had gained, and to wait for daylight to resume the combat. With the morning came an explanation. The opposing forces beheld to their dismay that they had made a terrible mistake, and nothing remained but to count up the loss.

This was found to consist of thirteen killed and thirty-five wounded, including four officers and eight sergeants, all on the attacking side, for, so cleverly had the young sub-lieutenant disposed his men, that they had not suffered in the slightest degree.

One thing deserves mention, and that is that, though these Spanish soldiers were armed exclusively with Mauser and Remington rifles, many of the wounds were found to have been inflicted by other bullets, which leads one to conclude that the seven Cubans had not been altogether idle spectators of the affray which they had so successfully brought about.

A reliable newspaper correspondent in Cuba wrote, under date of March 21st, 1896, as follows:

Doubtful Victories.

"No unprejudiced person can any longer deny that hitherto the efforts of the Captain-General to cope with the rebellion have proved eminently unsuccessful. The army, with a few ultra-loyal Spaniards, rack their invention to smooth over the situation, while optimist newspapers improve upon the official reports of victories. When, however, we see such victories followed by the unchecked progress of the insurgents, it is not difficult to read between the lines.

" Nor is it even assuming too much to prophesy that the reign of Weyler will be brief. Martinez Campos, a soldier, and a brave one, to whose capacity as a commander is largely due the existence of the present reigning house of Spain, managed to weather the storm for ten months. He had not the honest support of his military colleagues, and was further impeded by secret and implacable intrigue.

" Under the circumstances, his failure was hardly to be wondered at. His successor, however, was the chosen of the most influential Spanish factions in Cuba, while the soldiers considered him as a man after their own heart. We were told of his surpassing energy, of his exceptional courage, and of his indomitable resolution. Of these we have seen nothing, unless it be an energy to frame oppressive proclamations, a courage to endure a guilty conscience, and a resolution to sustain the crimes of his subordinates.

"The last few days have shown more than ever the worthlessness of his plans. Gomez has returned to the province of Havana. Maceo, Quintin Banderas and Periquito Perez have triumphed in Pinar de Rio, and Nuñez and De Robau continue to harass Santa Clara.

A Young Hero.

"Among the many brave leaders of the insurgents there is perhaps none who has shown more heroism than young De Robau. After the breaking out of the revolution he was one of the first to join the standard of independence. At that time he was engaged to be married, yet with him the call of duty was paramount over every selfish consideration. After having served for some months with conspicuous credit, he was sent with his command into the neighborhood of his fiancé.

"The men hitherto, it may be imagined, had not paid much attention to their appearance, but now there was a regular conventional dress parade. A barber was requisitioned, accoutrements were furbished up, and weather-beaten sombreros were ornamented with brilliant ribands. When the metamorphosis was complete De Robau placed himself at the head of his dashing troop, and went in state to call upon the lady of his affections.

"His march was a triumph, as everywhere he was attended by crowds of enthusiastic people, who had long known him, and who now hailed him as a distinguished champion. How he sped in his wooing may be gathered from the fact that an orderly was soon dispatched for the village cura, and that there was a wedding which fairly rivalled that of Camacho, so often and so fondly recalled by the renowned Sancho. Since then the Senora de Robau has accompanied her husband throughout the campaign, sharing the hard fare and the dangers of the men, and adding another to the noble band of patriotic Cuban women, who vie with their husbands and brothers in fidelity to their native land.

Last Tuesday the insurgents gained an important victory. The columns of Colonel Inclan appear to have fallen into an ambuscade upon their march near Candelaria, when Maceo upon one flank and Banderas on the other poured in a heavy fire, inflicting serious loss. Nor was the misfortune confined to men alone, for it is now com-monly believed that the Cubans succeeded in capturing some pieces of artillery after a severe encounter with the gunners, who defended the cannon with great bravery.

" The same patriot forces routed Colonel Frances close to Guanajay and compelled him to fall back for support upon the brigade of General Linares at Artemisa.   That the wounded in both these en-gagements far exceed the official reports can be gathered from the large ambulance train which was sent out to the ground yesterday morning from Havana.   The increasing audacity of the insurgents, the comparative ease and impunity with which they roam from one end of the Island to the other, and the burning towns and villages which everywhere mark the line of their advance bear witness to the incapacity of the present administration.

" Nor do we hear anything further of that cane-crushing which was to have followed immediately after General Weyler's arrival. What has escaped the flames stands still uncut upon the fields, serv-ing as a refuge for homeless wanderers, or, as in the case of Dr. Delgado, as a hospital for unfortunate victims.   The elections, too, do not progress, and merely prove a bone of contention between the rival parties.

" Apropos, an amusing thing connected with these elections occurred here on Thursday evening.   It was reported that there was to be a conservative demonstration against the office of the ' Discu-sion,' a paper of decidedly liberal views.   Great preparations were made to repel the expected attack.   Editors held a council of war, reporters were mustered in force, and even the newsboys were pro-vided with defensive weapons.   One of these latter, about nine o'clock, when all were in breathless anticipation, very mischievously exploded a fire-cracker in the basement.

" In an instant there was a general stampede.   ' Sauve qui pent !'

was the word, and one of the most completely armed, a perfect walking arsenal, and who had previously boasted of his valorous intentions, got himself tightly wedged into a skylight, in a frantic effort to seek safety on the roof. Amid the universal alarm the newsboys alone were calm and undaunted, and would doubtless have been presented with a handsome testimonial had it not leaked out that they knew all the time that the whole affair was a practical joke. The announcement this morning that the 'Three Brothers' had successfully run the blockade and had landed her cargo of ammunition somewhere on the coast was received with much secret satisfaction by all the Cuban sympathizers in Havana.

The Insurgents Wage Destruction.

"Ammunition is one of the weaknesses of the insurgents; courage, ability and men they possess in abundance; but the lack of cartridges has interfered with many of their best-laid plans, and has often prevented them from availing themselves of favorable opportunities. Three or four rounds a man is nothing in an action, especially when the Spaniards are always so abundantly supplied.

"It is not possible, however, to imagine that anything could interfere with the prosecution of the war on Gomez's side. He seems determined this time to fight to the bitter end, and as Spanish incapacity becomes daily more apparent, the chances for final independence assume a brighter aspect. Should that cause eventually triumph, it is devoutly to be hoped that it may triumph soon. A long war in any country is a terrible evil, but in Cuba, in the way in which it is waged, it is exceptionally disastrous. Nearly sixty small towns have already been burned, in addition to railway stations and private houses, while the damage to the cornfields, the principal source of capital, is almost incalculable.

"Another year of such a conflict, and there will hardly be a dwelling left standing. Nothing but waste and ruins will mark the once smiling Island, and it must be long before industry and trade can revive. We have but a faint idea in Havana of the misery that exists in the interior. We can only gather a few facts, but they are still sufficient to show that in many places the people are reduced to the last extremity of destitution, and are face to face with famine. The commonest necessaries of life are almost unattainable, and milk and bread have become rare luxuries.

"The insurgents, among all this prevailing poverty, fare indifferently; but they are more inured to hardships and capable of enduring much without a murmur. It has often been asserted that they provide no comforts for their sick and wounded. So far is this from being the case that each one of the six provinces has now got its regular hospital, where Gomez's care has established a staff of medical attendants, and a strong garrison. The largest of all lies in that part of Santa Clara called the Isthmus of Zapata. It is a wild, swampy region, through which the natives alone can distinguish those precarious tracks, where the slightest deviation means being engulfed in the treacherous morass.

Hospitals for the Wounded.

"Puerto Principe has its hospital on the mountains of Cubita, and it stands in security on the lofty summit of the Gran Piedra. In Havana it is situated not far from Yagua, while in Santiago de Cuba and in Pinar del Rio there are asylums in the hills of Guaniguanico, and La Maestra. There are many smaller ones, as well, but not being so advantageously located, they are exposed to constant danger of capture, when the Spanish soldiers show little mercy to the suffering inmates.

"Perhaps no figure in this unhappy war is so familiar or holds quite so bad an eminence as does Morro Castle. Not even General Weyler, with all his imperfections on his head, can rival the grim old fortress. It is the first object which meets the eye on entering the harbor of Havana, and from its commanding position on a bold bluff over the sea, it seems to dominate the city. It was not until recently, however, that I had an opportunity of having more than an outside view of the prison.

"Commenced in 1589, in the reign of Philip II., of evil memory, it was not finally completed until the beginning of the seventeenth

century.   In 1642 it was captured by an English expedition under
the Duke of Albemarle, and remained the headquarters of the British
army during their occupation of Cuba.   It consists of a strong outer
fortification, where there are many cells devoted to those who are
called 'incommunicarods' or doomed to solitary confinement.
These are dreary rooms with floors and ceilings of stone, bare of
furniture and lighted by a single grated window.

Three Iron Doors.

" On the walls are the usual evidences of how the unhappy inmates
endeavored to while away the long, melancholy hours: Scraps of
poetry, interspersed with prose, all of a forlorn tendency and generally
signed with the name or initials of the captive.   The passage from
them into the interior leads through three iron doors, each one of
which is carefully locked and barred before the succeeding one is
opened.

" The quadrangle inside is nearly filled by a large building, which
constitutes the prison proper, and which is evidently of rather modern
construction.   Above, it is devoted to store-rooms and the kitchen
department, but underneath it is traversed from end to end by two
long passages, about twenty feet in width, closed at each extremity
by massive bars.   These passages contain the suspects awaiting trial,
and there, with nothing to protect them from the ocean breezes,
which blow fiercely owing to the northern exposure, and with no
beds or blankets, they remain for months and months.   They are
never permitted to go out, and can only take what exercise the limited
space admits of.

" Those who have relatives or friends may receive clothes, hammocks, and even food from them, but the less fortunate are condemned
to sleep upon the stones and to endure the cold and wet, which enter
freely through the open grating.   One of these rooms or passages
was occupied by 108 prisoners and the other by 104.   It must be
remembered that they are all still untried; in that stage, in fact,
where our law would consider them as innocent.   Here was a Spanish
boy of fourteen, with an honest, kindly face, who has only been a

few months in Cuba, and who, from his youth and country, can hardly be supposed to be an aggressive insurgent.

"Lopez Coloma is another inmate, a man who took part in the rising in Matanzas last February, but who surrendered in the following March under the amnesty proclamation of the Captain-General Calleja. For over a year Coloma has suffered for the faith which he placed in the word of a soldier and a Spanish Viceroy. In all probability he will share the fate of Jose Gomez, a history of whose sufferings and tortures his wife is said to possess recorded in his blood. Of the other prisoners I could hear of but little evidence against them; yet, be they ever so guilty, no man of ordinary feeling could witness without a pang the inhumanity to which they are subjected in Morro Castle."

CHAPTER XVII.

Pen-Pictures of the War.

ABOUT the middle of March it was announced at Havana that General Weyler would issue another proclamation, which, it was admitted in official circles, would threaten Cubans who had left the Island and were domiciled in the United States with the confiscation of their property, unless they returned at once to their homes. This measure, according to the official apology for it, was to punish "those conspirators against the cause of Spain, out of the country as well as within it."

While this looked like a wholesale campaign of robbery, there was unquestionably plenty of ground for Spanish anger at the work of the patriots who escaped from her clutches, and were acting so safely and so effectively for their cause in organizing expeditions, working up public sentiment and receiving assistance from the people of the United States to carry on the war.

They were called conspirators. If they remained where they were their worldly goods were to be taken. If they returned they would in all probability be arrested as traitors and shot or banished. In either case the application of the decree would bring their estates within the laws and they would lose them.

General Weyler's last preceding proclamations occasioned surprise by their mildness. The Cubans seemed to attach less importance to the provisions relating to the confiscation of their estates than to the articles providing for the disposition of the Civil Guard in the principal towns. The Civil Guard is a part of the regular army. It is, in fact, the better part, because the regiments of which it is composed are made up of picked men. At all times, in peace or in war, an army of these Civil Guards is maintained on the Island. They do police duty and preserve order in the country.

For over half a century Cuba has been under martial law, and these forces are continuously active. Peculiar powers have been vested in this institution, and with an extraordinary liberty in interpreting and enforcing laws, which has resulted in excesses against the property and even the lives of inhabitants, a protection has been thrown about them, so that for assault, extortion, libel, injury to property and a variety of other crimes a citizen has no redress.

The oppression and cruelties of which this department of the government has been guilty produced the bandits of Cuba. It was one of the multitude of evils which brought about the revolution, and besides its own criminality, it was the particular department of a corrupt administration with which the people were most often in contact. So many men have been assaulted and beaten to death by Civil Guards that a word has actually come into existence and taken its place in the Spanish language in Cuba to describe the action causing death in that manner—" compote."

Driven to Desperation.

Women have been subjected to indignity from these " protectors " of peace and good order, in the presence of male members of their families, who dared not resent it. These representatives of the " holy cause," as Spain terms her " mission " in Cuba, have been the agents of corrupt governors and mayors for assassinating men, under the old, old story of the prisoner attempting to escape, or in oppression and blackmail, until the ruin of the victims was accomplished.

In Camaguey the people were driven to a point which resulted in their seizing and hanging some of the Civil Guards, and for a time that put an end to their practices in that province. At elections, the whole Civil Guard is simply a political machine, so powerful and so perfectly handled that, except in a few districts, it controls the vote.

Manuel Garcia, one of the most dashing leaders in Gomez's army, who was killed by a Spanish spy sent into his company, was a bandit in Cuba before the war broke out. How he came to be an outlaw is a fair example of the fate of many citizens. He was a respectable storekeeper in Quivican, just a little way out of Havana, young

handsome and industrious, and was in love with a country woman.
They were about to be married when one of the Civil Guards
assaulted her. Garcia was immediately ordered to leave the country,
the authorities doubtless expecting that he would kill the man,
against whom it was impossible to bring any prosecution under the
law, because nearly all offences committed by members of the Civil
Guard are permitted to be tried by the Civil Guards themselves.

Beaten and Left for Dead.

He did not instantly shut up his store and abandon everything he
had in the world, and a few days later two of the Civil Guards
arrested him and took him to a place where he was stripped and
tied to a tree and beaten with a bamboo rod until he was left apparently dead. He was found shortly by some farmers who were hunting for lost cattle in the woods, and was carried to a house, where he
recovered. Garcia met two other guards on the road while making
his way back to Quivican. He said their salutation was: "If you
haven't had enough to cause you to obey the orders, we will see that
you get it now."

Whether this is true is of no importance ; but, whatever the
manner of their meeting may have been, it ended in Garcia killing
both with his machete and then fleeing for his life. A price of $5,000
was put upon his head, but he was never captured. In about a year
he appeared as the leader of a company of fifteen or twenty men,
and after 1892 he was a terror to the two provinces of Havana and
Matanzas.

The Spanish version of how Garcia became a bandit differs only in
the point that as a butcher he sold stolen meat; that he was a thief
and always a criminal, and that the respectable storekeeper of the
family was Vicente Garcia. It is interesting, however, to know that
after Manuel Garcia was a bandit " compote " was administered to
this respectable merchant for his brother's crimes, and the abuse
resulted in his also going to the woods and joining Manuel.

Strange as it may seem, Garcia carried on his depredations within
a radius seldom farther from Havana than twenty miles. At one

time he rode into his native city, Quivican, and turned the railroad station.   He held up a train, and in shooting killed the conductor, because a request for money which he had sent to the company had received no attention.   When the war broke out in 1895 he was one of the first to rise with a force in Matanzas.   He collected about 250 mounted and armed men within forty-eight hours, and Gomez per mitted him to attach himself and his followers to the invading army

A Heartless Assassination.

Garcia, however, did not live long enough to win any laurels as a fighter for the republic, although his bravery and spirit, and his perfect knowledge of the country, gained as a fugitive, made his services invaluable for a time.   It was possible to kill Garcia because of his new surroundings.   A brother of Fernandez de Castro, a sugar-estate owner, was kidnapped by Garcia, and a ransom of $14,000 had to be paid by Castro to secure his release. A friend of the Castros is said to have determined to avenge the act, and he enlisted in one of Garcia's companies.   He shot Garcia, and before he could escape was cut to pieces with the machetes of the chief's men.   It was said, and seems to be generally believed, that Garcia sent at least $25,000 to the States to be used in helping defray the expenses of an expedition.

Perico Delgado, the leader of the rebel forces in Pinar del Rio, and for a time Maceo's scout; Agüero, Matagas, Mirabal and Socorros, second in command under Delgado in Vuelta Abajo, were all bandits. Agüero and Matagas were killed.

We have referred to the history of Garcia to give an idea of the interest which attaches to General Weyler's plans for using this Civil Guard.   They were centered in all the principal towns, and as fast as surrounding villages were subdued detachments were sent into them. Moving and disseminating from central positions, the guard was eventually to acquire domination of the whole Island.   In every town the civil authorities were to be removed, and the commander of the Civil Guard was to exercise the function of mayor and general executive.   Into the hands of these leaders was given an arbitrary power which was fairly startling.

They govern by martial law, and are at liberty to exercise their own judgment in all emergencies. The first thing they do is to make up a list of loyal citizens in their towns and districts, and another list of rebels and rebel sympathizers, who have gone out to fight or who remain at home; and the amount of blackmailing done under threats of putting men's names in the wrong list is easily conceived. All public offices to which the people have elected men of their choice in recent years were vacated by this decree.

The conclusion of this plan, as outlined in the proclamation, contained an admission that the Spanish were operating largely on the defensive, since the rebel armies had invaded and taken possession of the whole country, province by province, except the few large cities. The language of this admission was that as rapidly as possible towns were to be fortified and placed " in a state of defense to prevent surprise." The other provisions of the proclamation, touching the confiscation of estates whose owners were insurgents, or who assisted them, were not particularly severe or improper.

The Cubans have their national anthem, some account of which will be of interest to the reader: " Wherever the armies of the revolution have gone they have carried it with them. The soldiers have sung it. Their bands have played it. In the festivities that celebrate their entrance into every town and village it has the most prominent place in the music. At the balls it is the last event for women, girls, men and boys to join in the chorus of ' Bayamesa's Hymn,' as it is called. The words and music are familiar all over Cuba, for the people are like the ruralists of Spain in one respect, their love for ballads.

"In times of peace the wandering minstrel with guitar or mandolin is as familiar a figure in the hill towns and villages of Cuba as in the romances of Spain. And everybody sings or can sing; except in those awful periods of butchery called ' wars with Spain ' and the subsequent recovery from devastation and poverty. Cuba is one of the happiest countries in the world. She is one of the richest. No man ever went to bed hungry in Cuba, except in war times. They seldom borrow their melodies. They make them.

"And, as if they were unconsciously sad, as if half a century of succeeding revolutions had burdened their very souls with lamentation, nearly all their songs have a plaintiveness that is striking to the ear of a stranger. Their nature has not been subdued, but their hearts have been broken. The 'Bayamesa's Hymn,' however, is in a robust F major, perhaps because it is so old, for one reason. It has been sung for many, many years as a Cuban ballad and has, in its entirety, some fifty verses, if all that have been sung to it were put together. But the theme never varies—'to arms, not for glory, but to break the chains of tyranny.' "

They Burned their City.

In the last war—the ten years' war—the city of Bayamo was to have been occupied by a Spanish army. The people were aware of the approach of the enemy, and, as the Russians did at Moscow, they burned their city, leaving nothing but its smoldering ruins to exhibit their hatred and horror of the invaders. To this day Bayamo of the seventies is simply a monument in crumbling walls to the patriotism of a people who had even before that inspired the Bayamesa's Hymn by their deeds.

It is impossible to give a translation which conveys all the intensity of the emotions aroused by the song, as it is one of those in which the melody seems to have sprung from the very syllables of the words, and neither can be separated from the other without injury. In turning the old ballad into a national hymn Cubanos has been substituted for Bayames.

Besides prohibiting this song or the playing of the music in Havana or other cities in Spanish possession, the authorities have had to suppress ballads which have been written by the Cubans caricaturing royalty and the " holy cause " of Spain. They have been prolific in turning them out, and one in particular, against which a special decree was issued from the Palace, was written with the music in waltz time, and the words beginning with and parodying that familiar sentence at the end of all Spanish reports of the battles with the Cubans, " Por nuestra parte no hay novedad "—on our part we had no loss.

The air was so catchy that it was soon being whistled and played all over Havana.   The Spanish authorities took it seriously, and they issued a decree making the death penalty for any one to utter the melody with words, and one can no longer sing of Spanish victories —at least to that tune.

Stirring Strains of Music.

All the revolutionary forces have bands and plenty of music. Always upon entering a town, if they are not taking it by fighting, they ride in with the band playing martial music.   The people turn out to welcome them—what people there are left—and the same young women who gave them all their smiles flee in terror when a Spanish column approaches their hamlet, for outrages or even murder are in store if they remain.   The Cuban soldiers are much given to personal adornment.

They wear the great five-pointed star on their hats, and the bands are braided with red, white and blue ribbons.   Their horses' bridles are gaudily tasseled, and the men are as expert horsemen as there are in the world.   They are welcomed, and their presence, the festivities, the dances, the stories of their battles, all go to make their coming a happy event.   When they leave the band plays the Bayames Hymn. This is in towns, of course, where the Spanish have no garrisons.   In the latter the coming of the insurgent army is an invasion with the firebrand and rifle, and the Bayamesa's Hymn gives way to a wild uproar of voices crying, " Viva Cuba Libre ! "

General Gomez introduced a new plan for the relief of owners of sugar estates, which was intended to result in saving several millions of dollars' worth of property that would otherwise go to ruin.   Permits were issued to planters who asked for them, which would let them plow and prepare land for planting cane, cut burned cane which was standing, and, in fact, perform almost any other work necessary to preserve their properties.   The grinding of cane was prohibited, as was the production of anything else which would benefit the revenues of Spain.   Gomez, however, became so confident that the war would be over within a year, that every possible measure to save

13

the sugar estates which obeyed the orders against grinding was to be taken.

If the burned cane was allowed to stand it would rot and fall, and leave the fields in a wretched condition, requiring an unusual amount of labor in weeding and cultivating and keeping the ground clean. The roots, however, would not be killed, but would sprout and grow after the rainy season. Cane which has not been cut will keep on growing, and if the war ended so that grinding could be resumed, the heavier and richer cane would produce so much sugar that a part of the losses would be offset. This gain would be material anyway, but it would practically amount to even more than the actual increase in the bearing of sugar, because the expenses of grinding for some time were not incurred.

Statistics Concerning Sugar.

We quote from a statement relating to the sugar industry:

"There are about 750,000 acres of cane under cultivation. Replanting, which covers the plowing of the ground and the care of the crop up to the time for cutting it, would cost about $25 an acre. Some of it would cost more. The introduction of American methods, substituting steam plows, cultivators and higher class of labor for the primitive means generally employed, has brought the cost down to $12 an acre in a few plantations recently replanted. Assuming the average to be $20 an acre, the loss facing the planter, in the event of a longer conflict, would approach $15,000,000. It would take Cuba years to recover, and many men would be hopelessly ruined.

"The importance of this new privilege is therefore apparent. No such condition existed in the ten years' war, because that revolution never extended over much more than half the Island. Many planters are already hastening to secure the advantages of the permission to work their land, but their great obstacle is the absence of labor. Three-quarters of the men working upon the estates last year are either in the rebel armies or have fled to the cities for refuge. Another embarrassment is the lack of money.

"The planters can secure no advances upon crops because there is to be no sugar produced. They cannot mortgage their holdings because lenders are putting out nothing in Cuba, and are striving instead to get every dollar away from the Island which they have there. Nevertheless, the new order of things is a benefit to the planters who can profit by it. Thousands of acres of cane will be saved, and plowing is already being done on several estates in Havana and Matanzas provinces.

"The orders are following so quickly the action of Congress that there is a general belief in a connection between the two events. There has never been a moment when the revolutionary leaders have not maintained that with belligerency rights from the United States the end of the war would be at hand within a few months. They are more confident of this now than ever before, since at the moment the granting of those rights seems to be at hand the bankrupt condition of Spain is also announced.

Is Spain Bankrupt?

"If Gomez foresaw the terrible blow to Spain which the cutting off her revenues from the sugar crop was to inflict, it was unquestionably a master stroke of policy, due to a degree of strategical foresight for which Spain had never given him credit. It is significant that even in Havana there was permitted to be published a cablegram from London, which read: ' The economical review, the " Statist," states that Spain is in bankruptcy, and that the war in Cuba may oblige her to confess this situation.'"

The paralysis of business which afflicted Cuba was manifesting itself in a new way. Spanish merchants who had been loyal to Spain all along were crying now for peace at any price. In conversation they admitted that they were holding off from day to day the inevitable crash, and that it was no longer a question of months, but of days, before the business houses of the Island would go down like a row of dominoes. If Cuba was to be lost, curiously enough they declared that they preferred annexation to the United States rather than attempting to live under the newly-constructed government.

There was a motive of selfishness or fear which accounts for this.

They believed that with the Cubans in power they would be shut out of everything and possibly subjected to such restrictions as the Cubans were now under, but they believed that under the government of the United States they would be allowed to hold their own within the limits of legitimate competition.

Facing Both Ways.

They talked about the "destiny of Cuba," they argued over "channels of commerce," and they discussed what they called "the inevitable tendencies of commercial control," and then the next moment raised their voices to proclaim their eternal loyalty to Spain and signed a memorial to General Weyler containing a pledge of "our unconditional adhesion to your Excellency and our willingness to sacrifice our fortunes and even our lives to retain Cuba under the bonds of Spain."

Some figures were prepared and printed, with the sanction of the Spanish, showing the sugar exports of the Island for two months, which, despite their source, indicated the affliction from which all business was suffering through General Gomez's orders cutting off the product. In 1895, on March 1, there had been received at the ports of the Island 319,326 tons of sugar. A year later the amount up to the same date was 53,298. This was notwithstanding the fact that the estates began grinding six weeks earlier than the year before, in fear of the rebels coming and in an effort to save all the cane possible before grinding would have to be suspended. Therefore the normal inflow of sugar stood as 319,000 tons, against 53,000 tons under pressure.

From Sagua, which, in 1895, at this date, had 204,000 sacks of sugar in hand, not one sack was marketed. The figures from Matanzas were, for the same date, 1895, 466,000 sacks; 1896, 59,000 sacks; from Cardenas, 1895, 323,300; in 1896, 1,294; from Cienfuegos, 1895, 266,200; in 1896, 28,000; from Caibarien, 1895, 150,-800; in 1896, 25,600; from Cuba, 1895, 81,000; in 1896, 10,700; from Zaza, 1895, 10,500; in 1896, none; from Trinidad, 1895, 14,496; in 1896, none. The entire export of sugar in 1895 was generally figured at 6,500,000 sacks, or between 975,000 and 1,000,000 tons. According to these official figures the exports of sugar for the same time in 1896 and the amount on hand were as follows:

	Tons.
Exports	76,076
Amount consumed	8,400
Amount on hand	55,489
Total	139,965
Amount of this which represents old stock left over	86,667
Remainder in sight	53,298

Under date of March 20th it was stated that the insurgent generals were still outwitting and outgeneraling the Spaniards with a completeness which would be ludicrous if the horrors of the Spanish attempt at brutal conquest were not always present in one's mind.

Maceo's invasion of Pinar del Rio had already attained such importance that it was designated "the second invasion." Although he had not started on his return, a brief summary of the events which had already occurred will show how important this invasion was to the issue of the war. The first event occurred two weeks before, when Maceo, who had been moving eastward through Matanzas, turned back toward the west. The seven Spanish columns, often referred to, were suddenly called upon to check him.

General Weyler's staff planned a manœuvre which would bring all tne forces into conjunction, surrounding Maceo's army at a point one mile from Coliseo. The orders were sent by telegraph to Generals Prat, Linares and Aldecoa and Colonel Hernandez requiring them to make that place at two o'clock in the afternoon. The telegraph operator let the message go correctly to General Prat, but changed the hour to six in the other messages; and when General Prat came upon Maceo he had about 3,500 men and the rebels over 8,000 cavalry. General Prat was forced to retreat with the column badly shattered.

A second combination was attempted two days later near Limonar.

where Maceo was apparently intending to cross the line into Havana province.   This also failed, for the reason that Colonel Tort with the Almancea battalion, a newly-arrived body of green recruits from Spain who had never seen fighting, attempted to hold the vital point on the lines.   Maceo's veterans swept down upon them and broke through the combination with a fierce fight which fairly wiped out the Almancea battalion.

Brave Telegraph Operator.

The Spanish retired in the direction of Limonar, carrying about 100 wounded; and, besides the nineteen dead they carried away, left seven on the field, which the rebels buried.   With these victories Maceo's road was clear, and after a few engagements of minor importance came the burning of the important town of Batabano. What the Spanish did to defend it is best told by their own report:

"When we saw the establishment, El Canon, belonging to Mr. Ricardo Ganidera, the first house burned, was in flames, the troops, in anticipation of what might occur, retired to the forts."

They were so whipped out that General Weyler, the day after the burning of the city, ordered the payment of $10 to each man in the garrison to enable him to buy clothing.   Here a gunboat lay out in the harbor and shelled the town while the insurgents were burning it, but Quintin Bandera happened to have four cannons, and when these unexpectedly opened upon the gunboat she put out to sea.

In this fight the cannon shots were passing over the roof of the little cable station where the line drops off shore, and the operator had to stand outside waving a lantern constantly to enable the gunners on the water to direct their shots over him or to one side.   He had to take his chances with the rebels when their cannons began to take part, and at one time he set down his lantern long enough to telephone to Havana: "Good-by, boys.   It's all up with us, and—" There the wire was cut.   He waved his light again till he saw the gun-boat leaving, and then lay flat down on the ground and waited. It was three days before the line was repaired and he was able to send word that he was still alive.

While this was going on the Spanish were setting a third line in a combination of troops to keep Maceo within Havana province and out of Pinar del Rio at any cost. Colonel Hernandez and Colonel Inclan, with nearly 3,000 men, were hurriedly sent in front of Maceo by trains down the western railway. General Ochando, the chief of General Weyler's staff, said that morning, the 13th: "They have entered this province again, but I have just given orders to bar their way into Pinar del Rio, and, although I don't know whether they will succeed in getting there or not, if they do they will never come out alive." Two days later Maceo's forces defeated Hernandez and Inclan at the Estate Neptuno, near Mangas, between Artemisa and Candelaria, and captured the mules with the ammunition and rations.

Sudden Attack from Ambush.

The next day occurred one of the hardest fights of the invasion. The troops of General Linares had begun to arrive to assist Hernandez and Inclan. They brought cavalry and artillery. The Spanish forces were moving along the road which lies between Candelaria and Guanajay. It was raining in torrents. Suddenly the whole division found itself in an ambush; 4,000 insurgents were behind stone fences on both sides of the road, and as soon as the fighting began they closed in front and rear. There was fighting for two hours. The insurgents used the ammunition they had captured the day before. They captured two cannons and more ammunition, and inflicted such losses upon the Spanish that a special train was sent out from Havana to bring in the dead and wounded. It was even given out at the Palace that the troops had suffered two captains killed, four lieutenants wounded and fifty-seven soldiers wounded. There were about fifty soldiers killed.

Of course, it was called a Spanish victory, and it was announced, "We dispersed the enemy with bayonet charges." The next day, the 18th, at Cayajabos, the insurgents took possession of the burned town for a camp. Gen. Linares, Col. Frances and Col. Inclan attacked them. Col. Francis arrived first. Gen. Linares and Col. Inclan heard the cannonading and rifle-fire and hurried on. The fight here lasted four hours, and the Spanish had four captains and seven lieutenants killed, the killed and wounded soldiers numbering nearly 300. The insurgents captured 1,000 rifles, and, on account of their strong position in the town, got through the day with about eighty losses, dead and wounded, as nearly as can be learned. Col. Francis was wounded and was brought back to Havana.

Maceo's Skillful Tactics.

This is an outline of the invasion. It is sufficient to show that Maceo's march was attended by every effort which the Spanish could exert to prevent his progress, that their resources were taxed to the uttermost, but that they failed at every point. He was still on his march. The Spanish were again behind him. Of his 12,000 men he suffered no appreciable loss; but captured some of the enemy's artillery, disabled one of their best leaders in Col. Frances, took 1,000 Mausers, and more than all these combined, he utterly destroyed the effect of Gen. Weyler's proclamation declaring that Havana and Pinar del Rio were cleared up and closed to the insurgent armies.

Gen. Gomez's movements were fully as significant as Maceo's invasion. Apparently satisfied that his lieutenant-general was perfectly safe in caring for himself, Gomez went back into Santa Clara, and crossed the Spanish military lines of that province, without firing a shot. Gomez had entirely disappeared from the official reports for three days, and then this was given out: " It is believed that Gomez is in Havana province." As if Gomez and 6,000 men could disappear and move around unobserved in a district hardly larger than Long Island. Gomez's move doubtless caused some embarrassment in the official reports, because they had him " driven " desperately into Santa Clara two weeks before, then he was being " harassed " back again and was " forced to make a union with Maceo," and later on they were " forced to separate." While Maceo was being fought and dispersed at every point on his invasion, Gomez was standing at a point near the centre of Matanzas watching the successful beginning of Maceo's march, and for some reason the reports dropped him there.   The reference to his being "believed to be" in this province may have been due to the disappointment of his having gone into Santa Clara while all attention was being directed toward Maceo.

The Spanish merchants of Havana raised a subscription in the shape of pledges, with the purpose of offering a reward of $50,000 for "the head of Gomez, dead or alive," and $30,000 for the head of Maceo, under the same conditions.   This was generally considered as one of the most practical suggestions which had been made for ending the war.

This horrible proclamation was issued at Holguin about the 20th of March: "Be it known, that all the forces who operate in the territory of this division have orders to fire without giving the halt to any person who travels at night on the roads outside of the cities and towns, and with the object of preventing any accidents this publication is made for general knowledge."

The butcheries of Balmaceda and every ghastly chapter of the ten years of blood were committed under a decree of which this was simply a reiteration.   Gen. March, who issued this decree, was a recent arrival in Cuba, and was in command of the Twenty-third Division of the First Army Corps.   He held the rank of brigadier-general.

Sanctioned by the Spanish General.

This bloody edict had the indirect sanction of Gen. Weyler, because he had not abrogated it, and because in his proclamations he conferred almost unlimited powers upon the commanders of army corps, and they in turn issued decrees and approved others published by the heads of their divisions.   As a consequence, scores of proclamations were coming out in all the provinces and zones of the Island, which carried the weight and authority of a proclamation from the captain-general, but which were thus given in a form that avoided the necessity of their coming to the eyes of the world with his signature.

There was no distinction of age or sex in Gen. March's decree. There was no responsibility placed upon the assassins who were thus given the lives of those whose homes were outside the cities, or who, for any cause whatsoever, passed out of the doors of their houses after sunset. There was no reason that the ruffians who were abusing thousands upon thousands of defenseless women and girls should leave any evidences of their crimes, or even await the absence of natural protectors. The robberies which so many Spaniards were protesting against in delegations which were visiting Gen. Weyler almost daily, were of course made safe by such a decree. Col. Molina's threatening to shoot down the owner of the Rosario estate, Ramon Pelayos, was something for which he did not have to answer, as he was safe under a similar decree covering the section of Matanzas province.

Thirsting for Blood.

There are Americans all through the Island, and naturalized Americans of Cuban birth (the distinction is simply in the degree of the hatred which the Spanish have for both), who might safely be put out of the way under a decree which said that every person should be killed without even a challenge. This was the state of affairs which the blood-thirsty "volunteers" had been crying for since the day that they welcomed Gen. Weyler's landing. Then they stood in front of the Palace bellowing, "Give us Cepero's head," and, "Blood to fertilize Cuba." Now they were following the prisoners who were brought into the towns, screaming: "Kill them! Kill the devilish insurgents! We want no more prisoners."

A batch of prisoners, pinioned and tied arm to arm, were attacked by a mob at the Machina as they were about to be taken from a steamer to the Cabanas and were beaten, kicked and bruised almost to death, while the guards stood by and looked on. If this was permitted in Havana, what could be expected beyond the city, where the whole Island was in darkness concerning the events that were taking place?

Every day made matters worse. The Guatao massacre resulted in the bestowal of honors upon the Marquis of Cevera by making him the military governor of Marianao, and Capt. Calvo, whom he sent to Guatao, and whose men committed the eighteen murders, was now in command of the troops, which were placed at the disposition of the

Marquis. The massacre on the Delgado estate, from which the American Dr. Delgado escaped miraculously, but not until four boys and two men had been shot and macheted to death, and an old man of 70 had been left for dead, was rapidly being forgotten, and Gen. Melguizo was still conducting the operations of his columns, and glorious victories were almost daily attributed to him in the Spanish official reports.

These reports describe the Delgado massacre, and the murder of 15-year-old Catarino Rubio, before her mother and sisters, while she was attempting to prevent the soldiers, who had shot her father, from stripping his body, as "victories" of General Melguizo's forces. Rape and death and destruction were sweeping over the western end of Cuba, annihilating the population or driving the people out of the country, and what property the insurgents were not destroying was being given to the firebrand by the Spanish.

Details of Another Massacre.

There were rumors of another massacre which was said to have occurred near the estate Esperanza, in the Sagua district. It was impossible to get any reliable details, but the following was published in the *Discussion*, a Havana newspaper:—" Major Goicochea, on the 16th, left the estate Esperanza with a detachment of guerrillas, and found a vanguard, which fired upon them. They rushed at them with machetes after the discharge, causing them a loss of six. Continuing the march, the column arrived at Bernigal, near to the Olayita estate, encountering the main body of the rebel force. Here an engagement took place, resulting in the dispersing of the enemy, and causing them nine more dead. I must remark," concludes the correspondent, "that the dead were all killed by machetes, and by the guerrilla Goicochea."

A force of Havana volunteers, under the command of Major Prudencia Noreiga, burned the buildings where the tenants lived on the San Jose estate in Manacas, Santa Clara, and then obliged the homeless people to go to the town of Placetas, where they might find shelter and food if they happened to have any friends. Before sending them off they made five of the men prisoners on the charge that they were insurgents, although one of them, Fermin Urrutia, was eighty years old.

The last that was ever seen of these prisoners alive was when some friends saw them digging a ditch around the fort at the Tahon Railway station, and the next morning five bodies were found dead on the San Pablo estate, so hacked with machete cuts that they were disfigured beyond recognition. In the pocket of one was a paper showing him to be Marcelino Herandez, one of the five prisoners. After this became known, the women who had gone on to Placetas sent Nicholas Valdivia to the commander, Noreiga, to ask what had become of their husbands. Valdivia was seen to enter the fort, but he was not heard of afterward.

Unprovoked Murder.

After General Prat was unsuccessful in capturing Maceo in the attempted combination near Coliseo, a detachment rode up to the Demante estate, owned by Laureano Angulo, and fired at four negroes who were standing near one of the buildings. They were all killed. One of them was holding a boy in his arms, who escaped. There was never any explanation of this, but it is supposed the Spanish troops believed they were spies. The people who had fled from the country into Matanzas, and some of them who came on to Havana, declared that the men were "pacificados," or farm hands, who were non-combatants.

The following graphic portraiture of General Weyler is from the pen of a journalist and gives an interesting account of the Spanish commander:

"Most men resemble their reputations, and if a life famously spent is in the mind of one who visits a character of world-wide repute, he quite naturally discovers peculiarities of facial expression and phy-sique which appear to account for the individuality of the man, fighter, philosopher, criminal, reformer or whatever he may be.

"All this is true of General Weyler. He is one of those men who create a first impression, the first sight of whom never can be effaced from the mind, by whose presence the most careless observer is impressed instantly, and yet, taken altogether, he is a man in whom the elements of greatness are concealed under a cloak of impenetrable obscurity. Inferior physically, unsoldierly in bearing, exhibiting no trace of refined sensibilities nor pleasure in the gentle associations that others live for or at least seek as diversions, he is nevertheless the embodiment of mental acuteness, crafty, unscrupulous, fearless and of indomitable perseverance.

"He is one of the most magnetic men in whose presence I have ever stood—yet not attractive. His overwhelming personality is irresistible—yet he is unpleasant of appearance. He turns the mind into a quick seeker for similarities, and one comes quickly. To me it was Marat. I have never seen a presentation of Marat that might not profitably be exchanged for a delineation of Weyler. It would account more satisfactorily for the power he attained—that domination of men with which it is so hard to candidly associate those pictures of the tyrant that are familiar to the stage.

No Appeal from Weyler's Decree.

"I am not saying that Weyler is a second Marat; but I recall Weyler's history, and that now his will is life or death to over a million and a half of people, that from his decree there is no appeal, that the making of the laws has been given to him by a decree so absolute that he may confer all his powers upon any subordinate.

"I have talked with Campos, Marin and Weyler, the three Captains-General to whom Spain has intrusted (thus far unsuccessfully) the reconquest of Cuba. Reconquest seems an ill-chosen word, but one of General Weyler's staff has so denominated this war, and Cuban revolutions can be settled only by conquests. Campos was an exceptional man. Marin was commonplace. Weyler is unique. Campos and Marin affected gold lace, dignity and self-conciousness. Weyler ignores them all as useless, unnecessary impediments, if anything, to the one object of his existence. Campos was fat, good-natured, wise, philosophical, slow in his mental processes, clear in his judgment, emphatic in his opinions, outspoken, and withal, lovable, humane, conservative, constructive, progressive, with but one project ever before him, the glorification of Spain as a mother-land and a figure among peaceful, enlightened nations.

"Weyler is lean, diminutive, shriveled, ambitious for immortality irrespective of its odor, a master of diplomacy, the slave of Spain for the glory of sitting at the right of her throne, unlovable, unloving, exalted—and doubtless justly—in self-esteem, because he is un-mistaken in his estimation of his value to his Queen. His passion is success, per se, foul or fair consequences or the conventional ideas of humanity notwithstanding.

His Mental Peculiarities.

"Imagine that man ever loving a woman! That is the first exclama-tion his presence suggests. They say that Weyler had a mother, and that he loved her. I know, for I have heard him say so, that he re-members something of his grandfather, who was a German, whence came his name. But there is not enough blood in his frail little body to warm into life those passions that revere the closer relations of womanhood, and mentally he is incapable of intellectual affections. What he lives for is completely epitomized in his person, and as others have been, I also was conscious of it the first time I saw him.

"That was in the Palace, of course. The gates were guarded by gaudy soldiers tinseled and polished. Every turn in the stairway and corridors was emblazoned with the arms and emblem of Spain. Officers of all ranks, groomed, barbered and powdered, were visible in scores. In the great Sala de Recibimiento were all military condi-tions from lieutenants to generals, whose hushed conversation and functional palaver were oppressive. On through this crowd and through more obstacles of formality to the presentation, the journey through the forest of gold lace terminated before the closed door of General Weyler's official abode. There an adjutant more bedizzened than the rest of the dazzling multitude trod softly to the portico, gently opened the way, retired again without a word, and we were alone in the presence of the man.

"And what a picture! A little man. An apparition of blacks-black eyes, black hair, black beard, dark—exceedingly dark—complexion; a plain black attire, black shoes, black tie, a very dirty shirt and soiled standing collar, with no jewelry and not a relief from the aspect of darkness anywhere on his person. He was alone, and was standing facing the door I entered. He had taken a position in the very centre of the room, and seemed lost in its immense depths. It is capable of holding four hundred people. Its vast marble floor is vacant of furniture, and its walls, of great height, are covered with portraits, larger than life, of the captains-general of Cuba during one hundred and twenty years. Voices echo in the cavernous chamber, and the ancient personages looked down upon an invasion of their quarter almost as if they, too, were receiving, with the living picture which will some day hang among them. It was like a stage-setting around this remarkable man.

Form and Features.

' It is not remarkable that I momentarily hesitated to make certain that this was actually Weyler. Doubt was dispelled with a look at his face. His eyes, far apart, bright, alert and striking, took me in at a glance. His face seemed to run to chin, his lower jaw protruding far beyond any ordinary indication of firmness, persistence or will-power. His forehead is neither high nor receding; neither is it that of a thoughtful or philosophic man. His ears are set far back; and what is called the region of intellect, in which are those mental attributes that might be defined as powers of observation, calculation, judgment and execution, is strongly developed. The conformation of his head, however, is not one that is generally accepted as an indication of any marked possession of philoprogenitiveness or its kindred emotions and inclinations. His nose is aquiline, bloodless and obtrusive. When he speaks it is with a high nasal enunciation that is not disagreeable, because it is not prolonged; and his sentences justify every impression that has already been formed of the man. They were short, crisp, emphatic and expressive.

" ' I have an aversion to speech,' he said. ' I am an enemy of publications. I prefer to act, not to talk. I am here to restore peace.

When peace is in the land I am going away. I am a soldier.
When I am gone politicians will reconstruct Cuba, and probably
they will upset things again until they are as bad as they are now.
I care not for America, England—any one—but only for the treaties
we have with them. They are the law. I observe the law and
every letter of the law. I have my ideas of Cuba's relation to Spain.
I have never expressed them. Some politicians would agree with
them; others would not. No one would agree with all of them. I
know I am merciless, but mercy has no place in war. I know the
reputation which has been built up for me. Things that are charged
to me were done by officers under me, and I was held responsible for
all things in the ten-years' war, including its victorious end. I do not
conceal the fact that I am here solely because it is believed I can
crush this insurrection. I care not what is said about me, unless it
is a lie so grave as to occasion alarm. I am not a politician. I am
Weyler.'

"Planted squarely on his tiny feet, which were set far apart, Gen.
Weyler talks with his hands in his trousers' pockets and a half smile
dimly playing over his features; but every word he utters is without
gesture or intonation which gives one thought the slightest emphasis
or importance over another. The great pictures of the captains-general of a hundred years seem to look down in admiration upon the
man in whose keeping Spain has intrusted all that their century of
labor has produced.

"For some reason there was no disposition on my part to reply in
those meaningless, commonplace but always necessary acknowledg-
ments of courtesy. Adroit phrases mean nothing to Weyler. I was
frozen by his atmosphere for the moment into a being remotely
resembling himself, and as dignifiedly, concisely, unconsciously perhaps as the tone of his conversation, I made the requests which had
led to my visit and retired. There again was the sea of gold lace,
the multitude of generals and lieutenants, the noisy clanking of swords
and spurs, the gaudy guards at the gate, all keeping up the appearances of military domination; but behind them in the recesses of the
Palace was the man, the memory, the Altogether of Spain in Cuba."

CHAPTER XVIII.

Side-Lights upon the Struggle.

THE intense sympathy for Cuba among the American people was voiced by the following editorial in one of our most widely-circulated journals, which was only one of many similar in sentiment that appeared in the newspaper press throughout the country: "Cuba bleeds at every pore, and Liberty goes weeping through a land desolated by cruel war and throttled by the iron hand of a foreign despotism. We hold that this government would be justified not only in recognizing Cuban belligerency, but also in recognizing Cuban independence on the sole ground of the rights and claims of outraged humanity. Take, for instance, the following proclamation of an almost general death sentence issued by Butcher Weyler:

"'Those who invent or circulate, by any means whatsoever, news or information which directly or indirectly favors the rebellion.

"'Those who destroy or damage railroads, telegraph or telephone lines, or interrupt communication by destroying bridges or wagon-roads.

"'Those who sell, carry or deliver arms or ammunition, or in any other way furnish or keep them in their possession. Persons knowing of the importing of such articles and not causing their seizure incur criminal responsibility.

"'Those who by word, or through print, or in any other manner belittle the prestige of Spain's army, volunteers, firemen or any other force operating in this army.

"'Those who by the same means endeavor to praise the enemy.

"'Those who furnish the enemy horses or other means of service in warfare.

"'Those who act as spies.

14   209

" ' Those who, having acted as rebel guides, fail to report imme-diately and prove that they were compelled to do so by force, fur-nishing on the spot proofs of their loyalty.

" ' Those who adulterate provisions for the army or combine to raise the price of the same.

" ' Those who use carrier pigeons, rockets or other signals to con-vey news to the enemy.'

" Then take Weyler's proclamation of February 16, in which he decreed that ' all the rural population must be driven within the Spanish lines, and that all the goods of country merchants should be conveyed to the Spanish garrisons.'   In consequence of Weyler's barbarous decrees the most harrowing scenes of savagery and bru-tality are of almost daily occurrence in this beautiful Island, which is situated a hundred miles from our Florida coast line.   In the midst of these horrifying and terrorizing spectacles Cuba extends her hands in supplication to this land of boasted freedom, asking for only a kindly glance of friendly recognition.

Americans cannot be Neutral.

" Shall we refuse them this small crumb of comfort from our boun-teous board?   Spain may have the right to expect American neutral-ity, but she has no right to demand indifference on our part to the fate of a brave people, whose territory almost touches our own, and is nearer to our National capital than are a number of the States of the Union, and whose heroic struggle for liberty was largely inspired by our glorious example of beneficent free institutions and successful self-government.

" Spanish rule in Cuba has been characterized by injustice, oppres-sion, extortion and demoralization.   She has fettered the energies of the people, while she has fattened upon their industry.   She smiled but to smite, and embraced but to crush.   She has disheartened exertion, disqualified merit and destroyed patience and forbearance, by supporting in riotous luxury a horde of foreign officials at the ex-pense of native industry and frugality.

" Then the climax of Cuba's wrongs and woes is reached in the advent of the bloody Weyler, who has turned the battle into a butchery, made war a double crime by justifying in its name wholesale rapine and murder, and transformed the honest soldier into a heartless brigand and a fiendish assassin.

" Spain has inverted social order, defiled domestic purity, outraged civic forms and laid waste the whole Island to satisfy an appetite for plunder and spoils that is as cruel as it is insatiable.   Irritated into resistance, the Cubans are now the intended victims of increased injustice.   But the inhuman design will fail of accomplishment. Cuban patriotism develops with the growth of oppression.   The aspiration for freedom increases in proportion to the weight of its multiplied chains. The dawn of Cuban liberty is rapidly approaching."

Spanish Soldiers Missing.

Some idea of the loose manner in which the war is carried on may be gained from the statement in official circles at Havana that there were 15,000 Spanish soldiers missing somewhere in Cuba.   The fact was communicated to the Madrid government, and the search for their whereabouts went on day and night.   They were, perhaps, lost only so far as the record was concerned, and might be accounted for in time, but such carelessness, or worse, upset official circles in Havana to something approaching a state of alarm, for 15,000 men, with 15,000 rifles and half a million cartridges, is an enormous item in the Spanish army.

The disappearance of the men would ultimately be traced, it was said, to one of three causes : Deaths in battle, the real number of which was concealed to hide Spanish losses ; details to positions in various parts of the Island, of which no record had been kept; or desertions to join the insurgents.   Very likely all three causes contributed to the discrepancy.   It is entirely improbable that the whole 15,000 took " to the woods," although the Spanish records showed that entire garrisons joined the insurgents with their arms in every province in the Island.

Possibly the extent of this loss was purposely kept out of the records, although there was no reason that, officially, it should not be known to the administration.   It was said that Campos stationed small bodies of fifty or a hundred men in numerous places, often doing so in circumstances which resulted in no official record of the division of a detachment being placed in the books at the Palace ; but careless-ness of that nature on such a grand scale not only seems out of the question, but the balance would have been shown as a result of the order issued by General Weyler for a report from every commander showing the number, position and condition of his force.

How to Account for It.

The responses to this increased the confusion, and there were re-ports from reliable sources that there were 20,000 men, instead of 15,000, to be accounted for.   The supposition that many losses in engagements were not sent in received support from the known falsity of those reports, which was repeatedly pointed out.   That 700 Spanish should attack 5,000 insurgents, that a battle lasting seven hours should ensue, and that only one Spanish soldier should be wounded (as was told in a report from Santa Clara) indicated that the Spanish soldiers had charmed lives, or that an enormous amount of lying was being done.   How far this was carried on in the past can be shown by a few figures, and they may account for the present difficulty.

During the ten years' war, a professor of languages in Havana, an American of Cuban birth, kept systematically a record of the Cuban losses reported in the authorized publications in Havana.   He made it all in detail, giving the date of each engagement, the locality, the number of men on each side, and the Cuban losses in killed, wounded, prisoners and horses.   At the end of the war his totals were as follows: Cuban losses—395,856 killed, 726,490 wounded, 451,000 prisoners, and a little over 800,000 horses killed or captured. The entire population of the Island was only a million and a quarter in the most liberal figures obtainable, or less than the number of killed, wounded and prisoners !

In curious contrast with this are the Spanish figures of their own losses, which follow.   To show their real significance we give also

the number of men the Spanish army had in the Island during each
of the years for which the losses are given:

	Losses.	Men.
1869	5,504	35,570
1870	9,395	47,242
1871	6,574	55,357
1872	7,780	58,708
1873	5,902	52,500
1874	5,923	62,578
1875	6,361	63,212
1876	8,482	78,099
1877	17,677	90,245
1878	7,500	81,700
Total	81,098	625,211

Of this number, the official record indicates that only 6,488 died in
battle or from wounds. In other words, 92 per cent. of the Spanish
losses were from fever. There never was a time when less than 14
per cent. of the army was in hospitals, and in 1874 18 per cent. of
the force was ineffective from sickness.

Comparing the Losses.

"A comparison of these losses," says a reliable authority, "with
the alleged Cuban loss is hardly more interesting than a comparison
with the Spanish losses in this present war. The conflict has lasted
just one year. The Spanish losses are now given for the twelve
months as 3,500, or at the extreme 4,000, killed or mortally wounded.
The exact figures cannot be available until the present cases in hospitals have completed their record. This is, at the higher figures,
only 4 per cent. and a fraction of losses from all causes, out of her
army of 113,000. The lowest percentage reported in the ten years'
war was 9⅝ in 1874, and the highest 19 and a fraction in 1876.
The curious differences here may be disposed of on the basis that
eighteen years have intervened between the two wars, that the improved methods of dealing death have been introduced, that hospitals
are better, and that the deficient arms of the insurgents are to be
taken into consideration.

" However, the relative conditions of the two armies more closely resemble each other than would at first be supposed, and where they do differ they indicate that the record of Spanish losses in this war should be greater than reported, and greater proportionately than it was in the ten years' war.   In both wars the insurgents have managed to keep themselves armed with practically the same weapons as their adversaries have had.   Their cry now is that they have not enough or they would have an army of 100,000 men in the field.

" In the ten years' war nothing like the present extent of the revolution was attained.   Gomez was only as far west as Matanzas, retreating instantly.   To-day the whole Island is in the hands of the Cubans, except a few cities.   Even Havana is in a state of siege, for the first time in 100 years."

Mainly Due to Volunteers.

The danger to American citizens, and the brutal outrages outside Havana, like the massacre at Guatao, were due chiefly to the volunteers recruited for the Spanish army right in Cuba.   The regular Spanish soldiers were either officers doing their best, according to their ideas, to save their country, or else were recruits who were utterly apathetic and were chiefly food for fever and the machete.   It was the brutish rabble of the dregs of Cuba that resorted to robbery and crime of every description—criminals whose only object in joining the army was the commission of crime on defenseless people—but the Spanish commanders were directly and personally to blame for their presence in the Spanish ranks, even Martinez Campos having recruited as many of these undesirable wretches as he could get hold of.   Campos kept them under control, in some measure, in connection with the regulars; but Weyler turned them loose in the rural districts.

General Campos admitted that the volunteers only were to be feared, and that Americans did not need to concern themselves.   At that time the danger was comparatively small.   General Marin, his successor, went so far when Consul-General Williams brought the subject to his official notice, after numerous appeals from American residents, as to say : " If it should become necessary I will use the regulars to shoot down any volunteers that attempt excesses."

General Weyler was sending the volunteers out of the city in great numbers, but several regiments remained at Havana. They were a hot-headed, ignorant, thoughtless mob, compared with the Spanish regulars, and were a continual source of trouble to the government. The volunteers prepared to send their colonels to Campos to demand that he adopt sanguinary methods of warfare, but Campos sent them word that any officer approaching him to criticise his generalship would be court-martialed. Then it was that the complications produced by these volunteers led to Campos' retirement. These volunteers made up the mob which lined the streets the day that Weyler arrived, yelling, "Blood to fertilize Cuba. Give us Cepero's head! Cepero's head! Cepero's head!" Cepero was the American citizen who was a prisoner of war in Morro Castle.

Discussing the Action of Congress.

Much was said at Havana by the Spaniards concerning the resolutions of Congress granting rights of belligerents to the Cubans. They cordially believed that the American people had a single selfish motive—the tearing of Cuba away from Spain. They admitted that there was no ground for the charges repeatedly published, that " recognition meant friendly assistance to organized bandits committing murder, arson and rape."

They declared that all America had in view was the ultimate annexation of Cuba. They acknowledged that the loss would be so severe to Spain that she would hazard all her resources of men and money until she could fight no longer to hold her possession. They felt that the unjust and obtrusive interference of the United States should be rebuked by other nations and that altercations would occur which might justify Spain in declaring war, although such an issue with the United States would not be resorted to until national honor was at stake.

An incident showed the treatment accorded to newspaper correspondents by General Weyler. Two of these were arrested, but were subsequently discharged.   Their names were Michaelson and Betancourt.

Their release was only provisional, pending the result of the investigation on the charge that they were at Guatao on the fatal day of the massacre and brought the news to Havana.   The only evidence against them was the report that two American correspondents had managed to get to the scene of the massacre.   Michaelson and Betancourt had been at Marianao, half way to Guatao, where the railroad ends.   Marques de Cervera received a call from them.   When he was requested that night, in a message from Havana, to furnish information as to who had been permitted to go to Guatao, he naturally suspected, having knowledge of no one else going that way, that Michaelson and Betancourt had eluded his vigilance and passed along that road.   There was no other evidence in the matter.

At 2 o'clock in the morning guards of soldiers invaded the room of each man—Michaelson's at the hotel and Betancourt's at his home. They made a thorough search in each case, looking through everything, examining every scrap of paper, peering into bureau drawers, clothes-closets and everything.   This process lasted two hours, so thorough and exhaustive was it, and they found absolutely nothing to sustain the position of the authorities.   Nevertheless, they removed both men to police headquarters, where they were kept until 6 A. M., when they were taken in row boats across the bay to Morro Castle.

There they were placed in solitary confinement in stone dungeons, with no cots, no chairs, no blankets, not a thing, indeed, to relieve their condition.   Mr. Murat Halstead and Consul-General Williams hastened to General Weyler to protest against this high-handed outrage ; but they were unable to see the autocrat until 5 P. M., because he was out calling and did not choose to have his social engagements interfered with by anything so trivial as duty or so absurd as humanity.

When these two gentlemen were finally successful in getting an audience with Weyler, he informed them that the offence charged to the prisoners—which was that of telling the truth—was very grave, indeed, and that it would take three days at least to investigate it.

At the end of two days they were released. They had received blankets and hammocks only just before their departure from Morro Castle, and too late to do them any good in their stone dungeons. No liquor or tobacco or anything else was sent to them during their incarceration, except some food, and that but little.

Gen. Weyler had been encouraged by the course of events after his arrival, and cabled to his home government to that effect. The progress of Gomez and Maceo back into Matanzas and toward Santa Clara was interpreted as a retreat from the neighborhood of Havana. That it was not a retreat, but rather an indication that they were conducting a new campaign, which the Spanish are unable to check, is shown by their movements.

The Two Generals Separate.

After the burning of Jaruco, the announcement was made that the Spanish columns, under Gens. Linares, Prat, Aldeco, Col. Hernandez and others, had the insurgents hemmed in; that they were in front of them to prevent their going back into Matanzas, and that behind them were all the forces at Havana and along the trocha. Maceo and Gomez separated at once, Maceo taking a northern course, and Gomez paralleling his march about twenty miles southward, and then they moved eastward simultaneously.

They burned and destroyed every obstruction to their progress, tearing up the railroads to prevent the transportation of the Spanish troops, and fighting at Catalina, Candela Hills, San Nicholas, Roque, Limonar, Tosca and the Guamacaro Hills, but nothing stopped the progress of either. Every battle was reported as a Spanish victory, in which the enemy were routed or dispersed or driven back; but the mere fact that the Spanish columns were still in front and re-porting encounters daily, and that Gomez and Maceo were moving irresistibly forward into the great sugar district, revealed the true state of affairs.

Their purpose in going there was disclosed by two things. Gen. Weyler, upon getting them surrounded in Havana province after Maceo crossed the trocha, issued orders to the planters of Matanzas and Santa Clara to begin grinding cane. Gomez's proclamation forbade their doing so, and they had stopped to save their estates from being burned. Gen. Weyler gave notice that by March 15 the Island would be so cleared up that they would be safe to proceed, but in order to profit by the thirty days which would intervene between his order and that date, he requested work to be begun at once, supposing he could hold Gomez and Maceo where they were and give the planters protection in the meantime.

Quintin Bandera started at once with 2,000 cavalry from Sancti Spiritus, and, hurrying by thirty miles a day marches, he swept into the sugar district to the assistance of the already large forces of insurgents there, and, encouraging them as well as reinforcing their numbers, he hurried on to facilitate the progress of Gomez and Maceo. On the 21st he met Gomez's forces near Najasa, for the latter had advanced more rapidly than even the insurgents anticipated, and was well into the centre of the province of Matanzas. Maceo had gotten even farther, and was northeast of Gomez's position, one of his detachments entering Cardenas, the seaport east of Matanzas, two days later.

Sugar Industry Prevented.

Bandera's command separated at once and came into Havana province. Four days later he camped, 2,000 strong, at the estate Benigno, Garcia Aguiar, in the district of Palma, near Sabanilla. He moved about in the same locality that Gomez occupied during Maceo's absence to conduct the campaign in Pinar del Rio, where he waited for Maceo, and from which place he went across the trocha to Maceo's assistance in clearing the way for the return of the latter's army.

The burning of cane was resumed. Wherever an effort was made to grind, the insurgents destroyed the estates. The planters were in a lamentable situation. If they attempted to grind, they were faced first by the absence of labor. It had gone to the woods, or fled to Havana. If they sent cutters into the fields or started fires under their boilers, the fire-brand was at hand. If they did not make any attempt, they would be " considered sympathizers with the insurgents and the enemies of Spain "—with all the penalties.   After everything else, if they did grind, by paying the Cuban republic for the privilege, the railroads were destroyed, and not a pound of their product could be transported out of the country.

Early in March Captain-General Weyler issued the following proclamation :

" I have promulgated an order that the teachers of divinity of the Provinces of Matanzas, Santa Clara, Puerto Principe and Santiago de Cuba, who, confessedly, have taken part in the movements of the insurgents, shall be pardoned on making their submission, surrendering their arms, and placing themselves under the surveillance of the lawful authority, provided they have not committed other crimes since the issuance of my last proclamation.   It will be a commendable circumstance that these submissions may be made by bodies of those affected.

Strict Regulations.

" The teachers of divinity who, without arms, shall come in under the same circumstances, will be immediately transferred to the encampments, forts, towns, and, in general, where they may be under the immediate vigilance of the troops, and all the teachers shall be under the control of the commandants in whatever jurisdiction they may be assigned.

" A record of those so attached to each column, encampment or fort will be kept, and their superiors will make a report every fifteen days concerning the conduct of the teachers, and will determine the time at which they will be permitted to reside in whatever place it may be deemed advisable to conduct them, placing them under the supervision of the local authorities or making any other disposition of them which may be considered proper.

" In the meantime they will become permanently attached to the military forces, and will give their attentions to the dying, and will be entitled to such rations as troops in the field or traveling.   These directions will not go into effect in the provinces of Pinar del Rio and Havana until these Provinces have extended to them the prevailing

law in the case of those who deliver themselves up to the authorities.   WEYLER."

"Havana, March 5, 1896."

Another proclamation was as follows:

" I make known to our harassed troops and to those who attempt
to demoralize them as they pursue eastward insurgent parties more
numerous than those whom they leave in the Provinces of Pinar del
Rio and Havana, that the time has arrived to pursue, with the greatest
activity and rigor, the little bands, more of outlaws than insurgents,
who have remained in the said provinces, and to adopt whatever
measures are necessary for the proper and immediate carrying out of
that intention. I hereby order:

Disposition of Troops.

" First—That the troops be divided into columns to operate in
both provinces, and that the ' Guardis Civil ' be re-established on the
lines of that now existing in Pinar del Rio and in a part of Puerto
Principe, and that in Havana and a part of the Province of Santiago
de Cuba, and that they occupy only the places remote from the present pacified or tranquillized districts until they are able to occupy the
positions which they held before (in the districts now in revolt).

"Second—The commander of each zone, or the corresponding
official who may be otherwise characterized in each place, shall be
the commander of the native army, and shall have municipal
powers, but in a less degree than those he exercises in the same
position with any garrison force of the army. In this case the
command of the native armies will devolve in accordance with
seniority of services.

" Three—Each community seeking to do so and applying to the
general staff of the army may arm a section of volunteers or guerrillas of thirty men, equipped as infantry soldiers, which force will defend the country and operate under orders of the military authorities
of the locality. Each section may be commanded by retired officers,
or deputed officials, or by persons of satisfactory qualifications

and antecedents, obtaining the pay of those holding second command of infantry, the appointment of the officials of these sections to be approved by the Captain-General.

" Fourth—Those who are in possession of arms must be placed in a state of complete defense and enabled to avoid a surprise.

" Fifth—The military governors of Havana and Pinar del Rio will present reports to the Captain-General for the guidance of the commander-in-chief of the Third Army Corps, and will send to the Governor-General proposals for the nominations of Mayors or Magistrates in the places where Guardis Civil exist, or, if they deem it expedient to expel those officials, retired persons or authorized persons who possess the necessary qualifications.

They Must Surrender.

" Sixth—The authorities of the villages who will show themselves friendly within a term of ten days, and those of the vicinity of the same, and all those within its limits that are engaged in the insurrection, are warned to surrender themselves within the space of fifteen days from the publication of this proclamation, otherwise they will be subject to arrest; and well-disposed persons will be set to their civil responsibilities, and, to effect this, it will be proposed to the Governor-General to nominate a body which will see to carrying this out.

" Seventh—If, in the case of insurgent parties who have robbed, sacked, burned, or committed other outrages during the rebellion, any one will give information as to the participation that such persons may have had in them, not only those who may have been in the rebel ranks, but also those who have succeeded them, or who have not remained in their homes, they will be fittingly punished; and, moreover, if any town or other places where robberies have been effected is known to them, they will be required to make identification that proper responsibility may be fixed.

" Eighth—Rebels who may not be responsible for any other crime, who within the term of fifteen days present themselves to the nearest military authority in both provinces, and who will assist in the apprehension of any one guilty of the foregoing offences, will not be molested,

but will be placed at my disposal. Those who have presented themselves at any earlier time will be pardoned ; those who may have
committed any other crimes or who obstructed any public cargo
proceeding to its destination, will be judged according to the antecedents, and their case will be withheld for final determination. He
who presents himself and surrenders arms, and, in a greater degree,
if there is a collective presentation, will have his case determined by
me. All who present themselves after the time mentioned in this
warning will be placed at my disposal.

"Ninth—All the authorities or civil functionaries of whatsoever
kind who do not hold a license for attendance upon the sick and who
are not found at their posts after the end of eight days in both provinces will be named to the Governor-General as ceasing to act for
the local authorities.

"Tenth—The planters, manufacturers and other persons who,
within the territory of the provinces warned shall periodically facilitate or even for a single time shall give money of any kind soever to
the insurgents, save and except in the case of their being obliged to
yield to superior force—a circumstance which will have to be examined in a most searching manner—will be regarded as disloyal
through helping the rebellion.

"Eleventh—For the repair of roads, railways, telegraphs, etc., the
personal co-operation of the inhabitants of the villages will be required, and in the case of the destruction of any kind of property,
the occupants of convenient habitations will be held responsible if
they do not immediately inform the nearest authority of such occurrences.   VALERIANO WEYLER."

One of the incidents of the struggle was General Antonio Maceo's
arraignment of General Weyler, soon after the latter arrived in Cuba.
General Maceo wrote as follows:

"Republic of Cuba, Invading Army,
            "Second Corps, Cayajabos, Feb. 27, 1896,
"General Valeriano Weyler, Havana:
"In spite of all that the press has published in regard to you I

have never been willing to give it belief and to base my judgment of
your conduct on its statements ; such an accumulation of atrocities,
so many crimes repugnant and dishonoring to any man of honor, I
thought it impossible for a soldier holding your high rank to commit.

" The accusations seemed to me rather to be made in bad faith, or to
be the utterances of personal enmity, and I expected that you would
take care to give the lie in due form to your detractors, rising to the
height required of gentlemen, and saving yourself from any imputa-
tion of that kind, by merely adopting in the treatment of the
wounded and of prisoners of war the generous course that has been
pursued from the beginning by the revolutionists toward the Spanish
wounded and prisoners.

Appeal Against Spanish Infamy.

" But, unfortunately, Spanish dominion must always be accompanied
by infamy, and although the errors and wrongful acts of the last war
seemed to be corrected at the beginning of this one, to-day it has
become manifest that it was only by closing our eyes to invariable
personal antecedents and incorrigible traditional arbitrariness that we
could have imagined Spain would forget forever her fatal characteristic of ferocity toward the defenseless and assassination in security.
For really it is difficult to believe everything we see in life, however
absurd it may seem.

" But we cannot help believing evidence. In my march during the
period of this campaign I see with alarm, with horror, how the
wretched reputation you enjoy is confirmed, and how the deeds that
disclose your barbarous irritation are repeated. What! must even
the peaceful inhabitants (I say nothing of the wounded and prisoners
of war), must they be sacrificed to the rage that gave the Duke of
Alva his name and fame ?

" Is it thus that Spain, through you, returns the clemency and
kindness with which we, the redeemers of this suffering people, have
acted in like circumstances ? What a reproach for yourself and for
Spain ! The license to burn the huts, assassinations like those at
Nueva Paz and the villa El Gato, committed by Spanish columns, in

particular those of Colonels Molina and Vicuna, proclaim you guilty before all humankind; your name will be forever infamous, here and far from here remembered with disgust and horror!

"Out of humanity, yielding to the honorable and generous impulses which are identified with both the spirit and the tendency of the revolution, I shall never use reprisals that would be unworthy of the reputation and the power of the liberating army of Cuba. But I nevertheless foresee that such abominable conduct on your part and on that of your men will arouse at no distant time private vengeances to which they will fall victims, without my being able to prevent it, even though I should punish hundreds of innocent persons.

"For this last reason, since war should only touch combatants and it is inhuman to make others suffer from its consequences, I invite you to retrace your steps, if you admit your guilt, or to repress these crimes with a heavy hand if they were committed without your consent. At all events, take care that no drop of blood be shed outside the battlefield; be merciful to the many unfortunate peaceful citizens. In so doing you will imitate in honorable emulation our conduct and our proceedings. Yours,

A. MACEO."

This appeal is valuable as showing the grievances of the insurgents, as well as their commander's bold and telling way of stating them.

An interview with General Weyler by a lady correspondent in Cuba will be of interest. She writes under date of March 13th:

His Excellency, Captain-General Weyler, graciously gave me an audience to-day. He received me with most charming courtesy; escorted me through his apartments and presented me with a bunch of roses from his own table. Before I left he had honored me with an invitation to dine with him at the Palace.

"Your Excellency," I said to him through my interpreter, "the American women have a very bad opinion of you. I am very much afraid of you myself, but I have come to ask the honor of an interview with you, in order that I may write something which will reassure the women of America that you are not treating women and children unmercifully."

"I do not give interviews," he said. "I am willing, however, to answer any question you wish to ask."

"In the United States," I said, "an impression prevails that your edict shutting out newspaper correspondents from the field is only to conceal cruelties perpetrated upon the insurgent prisoners. Will your Excellency tell me the real cause?"

"I have," replied the General, "shut out the Spanish and Cuban papers from the field, as well as the American. In the last war the correspondents created much jealousy by what they wrote. They praised one and rebuked the other. They wrote what their prisoners dictated instead of facts. They even created ill-feeling between the Spanish officers. They are a nuisance."

"Then I can deny the stories that have been published as to your being cruel?"

The General shrugged his heavy shoulders as he said carelessly: "I have no time to pay attention to stories. Some of them are true, and some are not. If you will particularize I will give direct answers, but these things are not important."

"Does not your Excellency think that prisoners of war should be treated with consideration and mercy?"

The General's eyes glinted dangerously. "The Spanish columns attend to their prisoners just as well as any other country in time of war," he replied. "War is war. You cannot make it otherwise, try as you will."

"Will not your Excellency allow me to go to the scene of battle under an escort of soldiers, if necessary, that I may write of the situation as it really is, and correct the impression that prevails in America that inhuman treatment is being accorded the insurgent prisoners?"

"Impossible," answered the General. "It would not be safe."

"I am willing to take all the danger, if your Excellency will allow me to go," I exclaimed.

General Weyler laughed. "There would be no danger from the rebels," he said, "but from the Spanish soldiers. They are of a very affectionate disposition and would all fall in love with you."

15

"I will keep a great distance from the fighting if you will allow me to go."

The General's lips closed tightly, and he said: "Impossible! Impossible!"

"What would happen," I asked, "if I should be discovered crossing the lines without permission?"

"You would be treated just the same as a man."

"Would I be sent to Castle Morro?"

"Yes," he replied, nodding his head vigorously. That settled it. I decided not to go.

"Why," I asked him, "is the rule 'incommunicado' placed upon prisoners? Is it not cruel to prevent a man from seeing his wife and children?"

"The rule 'incommunicado,'" said the General, "is a military law. Prisoners are allowed to see their relatives as a favor, but we exercise discretion in these cases."

"There are stories that prisoners are shot in Morro Castle at daybreak each morning, and that the shots can be plainly heard across the bay. Is this true?"

The General's eyes looked unpleasant again. "It is false!" he said, shortly. "The prisoners go through a regular court-martial, and no one could be shot at Morro without my orders, and I have not given orders to shoot any one since I have been here."

"Do you not think it very cruel that innocent women and children should be made to suffer in time of war?"

"No innocent women and children do suffer. It is only those who leave their homes and take part in battles who are injured. It is only the rebels who destroy peaceful homes."

"It is reported," I said, "that thirty women are fighting under Maceo. Is this true?"

"Yes," replied the General. "We took one woman yesterday She was dressed in man's clothes and was wielding a machete. She is now in Morro Castle. These women are fiercer than the men. Many of them are mulattoes. This particular woman was white."

"What will be her fate?"

" She will go through the regular form of trial."

" Will no mercy be shown her ? "

" Mercy is always shown to a woman. While the law is the same for both sexes there is a clause which admits of mercy to a woman."

" There are several Cuban women insurgents in Morro and the Cabañas. Would your Excellency," I asked, "allow me to visit them ? "

A Rigid Military Law.

" No," he said. " There is a law that no foreigner shall enter our fortresses. It is a military law. We can make no exceptions. You understand that I do not wish to be discourteous, senorita."

" Some of these women," I continued, " are said to be imprisoned for merely having Cuban flags in their homes. Is this possible ? "

" Treason," exclaimed the General, " is always a crime, punishable by imprisonment."

" There is a newspaper correspondent at present in Morro. What was his crime ? "

The General shrugged his shoulders again. " I know nothing about him," he said. " I think he has been freed."

" Do you not think that the life of a newspaper correspondent in Havana is at present a most unhappy one ? "

" I think it must be, for they make me unhappy. If they were all like you it would be a pleasure."

" Is it true that thumbscrews are used to extort confessions from prisoners ? "

" Not by the Spaniards. Rebels use all these things, similar to those that were used in the Inquisition tortures."

" What does your Excellency think of the Cubans as a race ? Do you not think them progressive and brave ? "

" With the progress of all nations the Cubans have progressed," he replied. " There are many Cubans in sympathy with Spain, but this insurrection is a blot upon the Cuban race which nothing can ever erase. It is a stain made with the blood of the slain and the tears of the women. It injures the Cubans themselves more than any other."

In the latter part of March Cuban circles in this country were elated over the successful landing in Cuba of the expedition sent out by the steamship "Bermuda." After her departure there was great anxiety among the Cuban sympathizers, and news of her safe landing afforded corresponding satisfaction.

Rafael Portuondo, Secretary of State of the insurgent Republic, said: "The successful landing of General Garcia and the ' Bermuda's' cargo of arms and ammunition is of greater moment to us than the outside world can imagine. We have hoped so long in vain for the administration of the United States to recognize our belligerency, that we have almost abandoned the idea of ever benefiting by the improved moral and international standing which such an act would give us in the eyes of other nations. We see now that we can expect but little aid from any one else; that we must carve our destiny with the Cuban sword—the machete.

"Diplomacy so far has availed us nothing. We have got to fight our way to freedom, and General Garcia is a fighter. He has faced death many times. He is feared by his enemies and loved by his friends. He will be a power in Cuba, and his safe arrival on the Island will be an important step toward securing her freedom. He will take immediate command of the department of the Oriente, which includes the provinces of Camaguey and Santiago de Cuba."

After Garcia's escape from Madrid in the fall of 1895, and his subsequent arrival in New York, every effort was made to enable him to reach Cuba with a respectable expedition. The failure of those efforts in the sinking of the "Hawkins" and the detention of the "Bermuda" are well known. Secretary Olney's order to release the "Bermuda" and arms seized on the "Stranahan" encouraged the Cuban officials in this country to make another attempt to leave the port, which was done in broad daylight.

On Sunday morning, March 15th, the "Bermuda" steamed out of New York harbor. She carried four rapid-fire Hotchkiss cannon, one twenty-pounder and one ten-pounder. These were by far the largest guns yet used by the insurgents.

Early in April was the time for holding elections in Cuba, and it

was claimed that Spain would receive a strong support.   Despite the
threats of the captain-general, the Autonomist party remained firm,
and refused to take any active share in the elections.   They intended,
indeed, to vote for two Senators, one for the University and the other
for Los Amigos del Pais, but here their efforts were to cease.

It was a serious predicament for General Weyler.   He pledged his
reputation on his ability to drive voters to the polls, hoping by that
act to prove to the government in Madrid that affairs were not in such
a really desperate condition.   Cuba had never been officially declared
to be in a state of war.   It was admitted that serious disturbances
existed; but, then, are not misfortunes liable to occur in the best
regulated households?   Have not the United States had riots in
Pittsburg and Chicago, and had not England to contend against the
Irish Land League?

And yet one is tempted to ask why people who arrived on board
the steamers were subjected to a rigorous inquisition.   Every Wednesday and Saturday, when the Tampa boat reached Havana, the
passengers were compelled to go to the Hotel Mascotte, near the
quay, and were there thoroughly searched.

Outside of the city, too, the country had not the appearance which
we are accustomed to see in times of ordinary tranquillity.   A trip
from Havana to Batabano, on the south coast, was exactly like jour-
neying through a desert.   At intervals of a couple of miles small
forts are constructed along the line, each with its garrison of twenty
or thirty soldiers, but, with these exceptions, no trace of human existence was to be seen.   A lonely and abandoned country stretched
away on each side.

Here and there a small green patch of sugar cane had escaped the
general conflagration, but for the most part the eye rested only upon
blackened stalks, over which the tall, slender palm trees waved like
sorrowing mourners.   Station buildings were heaps of crumbling
ruins, where, amid the general wreck, temporary fortifications of stone
and metal rails had been hastily put together, though for what purpose it was hard to imagine.

Every little village was occupied by troops, sentries were stationed upon every church, whose walls had been pierced for muskets, and round which deep trenches had been dug as an additional means of defence. These sacred edifices represented the citadel of the position, and, filled as they were with men who had signalized themselves by robbery and crime, one was forcibly reminded of the words which say: "You have made my house a den of thieves."

Batabano itself was half destroyed. In the recent attack the town hall and all the rest of the public buildings were burned, and yet there were ample accommodations for the few families who lingered on.

The port, called Surgidero, is about three miles distant. It is an important place, as it is the point of embarkation for Cienfuegos and Santiago de Cuba. So far it had escaped the insurgents, but there was a band lurking in the jungle close at hand who made constant demonstrations during the night, and kept the military authorities busy.

Embankments and Breastworks.

The precautions which were adopted for defence are interesting. A narrow, shallow trench was excavated for nearly a mile and a half outside the little seaport to protect it on the land side. Behind this trench the earth was thrown up into a low embankment, strengthened with a wattle breastwork, and guarded along the entire line by no fewer than twelve forts. A gunboat was close in shore, and as a guide to direct her fire, lanterns on high posts were set close together a few paces beyond the trench. She had a good deal of practice, for one of the inhabitants said that he counted thirty-seven shells which she discharged one night. Like Mr. Winkle's shot, however, they proved to be merely homeless wanderers, finding, contrary to the proverb, no billet anywhere.

At the railway station, the platform was crowded with people. They were emigrants, flying with their families and household goods from the terror which reigned throughout the land. But it was not a fear of the insurgents which compelled them to leave their homes. The Spanish army was the cause. The alcalde of Jovellanos, in Matanzas province, said that there was no safety for any one outside of the large cities.

This man was a Spaniard and a loyal subject. He officiated as Mayor of Jovellanos for two years, and was prosperous and respected. After soldiers were quartered in the town, he said, life had become unbearable. They plundered his store, notwithstanding his position as Chief Magistrate, and robbed the inhabitants at will. A Spanish guerrilla force, under the command of Lieutenant Salvador Paula, saw ten laborers working in a field in the outskirts of Jovellanos. When challenged these men replied: " Viva España ! " Yet they were immediately fired upon, though fortunately without any evil result to them. They were wise enough to fling themselves upon the ground, while an unfortunate Chinaman, who was feeding his horse close by, received a bullet in the leg. This poor creature limped up and showed the wound to Lieutenant Paula, who thereupon exclaimed : " O, you complain, do you? I will soon prevent your telling tales !" drew his machete and with one stroke cut off the Chinaman's head. This episode undoubtedly saved the workmen's lives.

Still Another Atrocity.

The guerrilleros, having gratified their taste for blood, departed, yet though the case, the Alcalde said, was reported to the commandant, General Prat, Paula and his gang were left unpunished.

Another atrocity was that of Colonel Vicuna, who, when marching with his column to the town, met three unarmed men upon the road. They were instantly arrested, and though there were no grounds for supposing them to be insurgents, Colonel Vicuna ordered them to be shot, a command which was carried out on the spot. Three days afterward the Alcalde read in the official reports in the newspapers that this very column had had an engagement with the insurgents near Jovellanos, and had killed three. The battle referred to was this cruel execution of inoffensive civilians.

Of a truth these official reports were merely useful as a record of what did not occur. No reliance can be placed in a single statement, unless it be the simple fact that something took place in a certain locality, while the circumstantial story and the result were complete fabrications. An account was given of an encounter near

Cardenas, where the Spaniards had one dead and four wounded. It was found subsequently that their losses amounted to sixty-two, of which no fewer than twenty-five had been killed.

In like manner the true account of the assault on Santa Clara is very different from that supplied from the Palace for publication. In a letter from an eye-witness of the whole affair, we find that the Cubans met with scarcely any opposition, and that General Bazan, so far from having ridden with his staff through the rain of bullets, sought refuge in the theatre until the enemy had retired. The insurgents patrolled the town all night long, and procured without difficulty the supplies which they required.

CHAPTER XIX.

The United States to the Rescue.

ON the 10th of April, 1896, our State Department at Washington sent to Madrid an important official despatch bearing on Cuban affairs. It was signed by Secretary Olney, and addressed to Minister Taylor. In it was laid down the attitude of the Administration on the Cuban question. The despatch was a lengthy one. Its four principal points were:

First. The President proposed that Spain accept mediation on the part of the United States, looking to a settlement of existing differences between the Spanish Government and the Cubans.

Second. It referred to the correspondence between the State Department and the Madrid authorities in 1870, in which Spain promised to inaugurate governmental reforms in Cuba, which promises, it was said, have not been fulfilled.

Third. That the present rebellion in Cuba is more serious and widespread than any which have arisen in recent years, and that the insurgents controlled practically all of Cuba except Havana and the near neighborhood.

Fourth. It assured Spain of the kindliest motives on the part of the United States in seeking to bring about a pacific condition of affairs in Cuba, and urged that the good offices of this country be accepted in the spirit proffered.

After the passage in the House of the Cuban resolutions the President and Secretary Olney were frequently in consultation in relation to the general affairs in Cuba and the wisest course for the United States to pursue in the matter. Few, if any, of the many friends of Cuba in Congress expected that the President would take steps in harmony with the provisions of the resolutions. The President decided that the question of recognizing a state of belligerency in the Island was not seriously to be considered. In reaching this decision he followed the advice of Secretary Olney, which was based on the precedent established by President Grant in his first administration, upon the earnest recommendations of Secretary Fish.

Our Government Offers to Mediate.

It having been determined not to recognize belligerency in the Island, the point to be decided was what, if any, steps should be taken in the matter. The President and the Secretary of State agreed that some measures were necessary. As a result of several important conferences, the President finally concluded that mediation on the part of the United States should be suggested to Spain.

As far as known the President did not discuss the proposed course with any other member of the Cabinet than Mr. Olney. In international affairs it was the exception when he asked for the views of any other Cabinet Minister. In the case of Cuba he did not depart from his rule, but drew up not only the outline of Mr. Olney's note to Minister Taylor, but suggested many of the paragraphs, and some of the sentences.

The President viewed the condition of affairs in Cuba as deserving of serious consideration. He recognized that conditions existed which were most unfortunate, and which were injurious not only to Spain, but to the vast commerce between the United States and Cuba. He realized, however, that Spain and this country are on terms of amity, and thought that vigorous proceedings on the part of the United States would result in the object aimed at being lost. This might mean a rupture of the friendly relations between Spain and the United States. The President was opposed to the adoption of any such course.

He looked upon the recognizing of a state of belligerency in Cuba as unwise and unjustifiable under the circumstances, and as certain to irritate the Spanish people. For the present, at least, he was of the opinion that the best course was to propose the good offices of this Government, looking to a settlement of the serious differences between Spain and the Cuban insurgents.

Secretary Olney's letter to Minister Taylor was written in the most careful, cautious manner. In referring to the proposition that Spain accept mediation on the part of the United States, he said that the attitude of this country in the matter is a friendly one, and that the United States could have no other object, as Spain must know, than to bring about a more satisfactory condition of affairs in Cuba. He complimented Spain to the extent of intimating that she is too great a Power to fear to do what is right, and that if the claims of the Cuban insurgents as to Spanish wrongs were based on fact, it was the duty of the Madrid Government to inaugurate a more just, lenient and humane policy toward Cuba.

Trying to Restore Order.

Such a course, it was pointed out, would tend to bring about quiet and restore order in the Island, and modify the growing impression throughout the world that many of the alleged evils in Cuba are the result of harsh treatment or the maladministration of the Colonial Government. As one reason for suggesting mediation in the case, Minister Taylor was informed that many of the citizens in this country interested in estates in Cuba, or in the commerce with the Island, were suffering on account of the rebellion. This fact and others, which the Secretary set forth, were, in his opinion, a sufficient justification for proposing to Spain that she accept the good offices of the United States looking to a settlement of differences between the mother country and her Island Colony.

The Secretary of State referred to the correspondence between the State Department and the Madrid Government in the first administration of President Grant, when Secretary Fish, by direction of the President, proposed that the United States should act as mediator between Spain and the insurgents. Spain then politely declined the good offices of this country, but intimated that the time might come when they would be acceptable to her. She promised, however, that a number of important governmental reforms should be instituted in Cuba, among others that the taxes in the Island should be equitably levied, that no unjust discrimination should be made against native

Cubans in the matter of holding offices, that the security of persons and property should be maintained, that the judiciary should be separated from the military authorities, and that greater freedom of speech, press and religion would be inaugurated. In those days slavery existed in Cuba, and partly at the instance of the United States, the Spanish Government passed a law of emancipation.

Spain's Promises Broken.

A number of other important reforms have not been brought about, however, and the Secretary pointed out that representatives of the insurgents in Washington contended that there was no probability of changes in law and custom being made. In a communication to the State Department, T. Estrada Palma, representing the insurgent party, stated that the causes of the revolution in the Island were substantially the same as those of the former revolution, lasting from 1868 to 1878, and terminating only on the representation of the Spanish Government that Cuba would be granted such reforms as would remove the ground of complaint on the part of the Cuban people.

Unfortunately, Mr. Palma said, the hopes thus held out have never been realized. The representation which was to be given Cubans proved to be absolutely without character. Taxes were levied anew on everything conceivable; the offices in the Island increased, but the officers were all Spaniards; the native Cubans had been left with no public duties whatsoever to perform except the payment of taxes to the Government, without privilege even to move from place to place in the Island, except on the permission of governmental authority.

Mr. Palma also complained that Spain had framed laws so that the natives had substantially been deprived of the right of suffrage. There was appropriated only $746,000 for internal improvements out of the $26,000,000 collected by taxes. Mr. Olney pointed out that if even part of the injustice and harshness alleged by the insurgents existed in Cuba, important reforms would appear to be demanded under the circumstances.

Secretary Olney informed Minister Taylor that from advices received from Cuba it was made clear that the revolution in the Island was more widespread than the ten years' revolution, and that the insurgents were reported to be masters of the situation, except in and near Havana. These conditions, in the opinion of the Secretary, went to show the extent of the insurrectionary movement, and the large number of persons engaged in it, and the effect was a serious blow to business throughout the Island, and operated necessarily greatly to the disadvantage of the commerce of the United States.

Much more was said in this connection in the despatch to Minister Taylor, but the drift of the statement was that the revolution had made greater headway than any preceding revolution in Cuba, and that the conditions were cause for grave concern on the part of the United States. Mr. Olney intimated that if the insurgents had not been successful in overcoming the Spanish forces and getting charge of the Island, it was equally true that Spain had not put down the rebellion.

A Friendly Proposition.

The Secretary concluded his lengthy despatch by directing Minister Taylor to assure Spain of the friendliness of this country in proposing mediation. His argument throughout was a strong one. Minister Taylor was instructed to lay the President's proposition before the Spanish Foreign Secretary at an early date, and to communicate the reply of the Madrid Government promptly upon receiving it.

What the feeling was at Madrid is clearly shown by the statement of a journalist, under date of April 16:

" As I am about to leave Spain a résumé of the present state of affairs here may be appropriate.

" Quiet reigns. It seems to me that the whole trouble will be amicably arranged. It is only necessary for Mr. Cleveland to make friendly overtures in order to get a friendly reply in regard to the reforms to be granted to Cuba. The present government has said as much. Laws have already been passed, and are only awaiting the cessation of hostilities to be enforced.

" Spain will strain every nerve to suppress the insurrection, although the government does not expect to succeed in this before the rainy season sets in.   On the contrary, preparations are now under way to send six thousand more soldiers to Cuba at the end of the summer. That will make a total of two hundred thousand men sent to the Island since the war began.

" The jingo threats of American interference have really strength-ened the present government.   Every Spaniard, whether conserva-tive, liberal or republican, would stand by the red and yellow flag, and afterward would fight it out among themselves.   The conserva-tives, who outnumber the liberals by three to one, are doing every-thing in their power, without compromising the honor of the nation, to avert war with the United States.

" The liberals are the jingoes of the Peninsula and they seem to think that Spain has been insulted quite enough already.   The republicans are very much in the minority just now and are confined almost entirely to the northern provinces.   They are against anything that is done by the government, and are consequently opposed to the pacific methods of Premier Canovas and his colleagues.   Even they would stand by the Crown in case of war.

Our Country Cordially Hated.

" While there is a deep-seated bitterness to the United States all over the country, there is very little open exhibition of it.   If the match were applied this feeling would explode with such violence that the lives of Americans would not be safe anywhere from Cadiz to San Sebastian.   The recognition of the Cuban insurgents as belli-gerents would be such a match.   The thousands of students in Madrid and Barcelona would start the trouble, and the infection would soon spread.   It should be remembered that there are 17,000 of these students in Madrid alone, and Madrid is only one of twelve university cities.

" If war came I doubt if Spain would attempt to hold Cuba for any length of time.   She would withdraw her troops and use them to defend the Peninsula from invasion.   Before that happened the effort would probably be made to attack Florida. Thirty merchant steamships, some of which are now being converted into cruisers, would be employed purely as privateers to harass American commerce. It is the boast of the Spaniards that they drove Napoleon back across the Pyrenees by guerrilla warfare, and they believe they could drive the Stars and Stripes from the seas by corsair methods.

"The regular Spanish navy would be kept near Cadiz and Barcelona, and it would not be an easy matter to capture Cadiz, which is quite as well fortified as New York. New and big guns have recently been mounted on the shore batteries. Torpedoes and torpedo boats are there without number. Barcelona also is well protected, and for that matter the defences of all the ports are being strengthened.

Scarcity of Food.

"Spain is so barren in food products that an invading army would have to depend entirely on its base for supplies. It could not live off the country. On the other hand, Spanish soldiers subsist on next to nothing. The private soldiers in the Spanish army honestly believe that in case of war Spain would win. They think this because the regular army of the United States numbers less than half the force now stationed in Madrid.

"Even though the Cuban rebellion is costing Spain one million pesetas daily, still Spanish money is but little more depreciated than it was three years ago, in time of peace."

The friendly efforts in the direction of mediation by the United States in Cuban affairs soon bore fruit. The State Department had information, it was reported, through Minister Taylor, at Madrid, that the Spanish authorities were making active preparations to put into effect the long-promised reforms in Cuba, which practically contemplated home rule for the Island.

The exact date when these reforms would be put into operation was not known. There was some criticism even in Spanish circles that these reforms were not inaugurated before the elections in Cuba. The war on the Island and the desire to crush it was the excuse offered for not sooner carrying out the laws enacted on March 15, 1895, by the Cortes.

Not only was it proposed to carry out the provisions of these laws, but the Spanish Ministry contemplated further reforms, which would be submitted to the Cortes for its approval. There were reasons for believing that the United States had taken an important part toward inducing Spain to adopt a more conciliatory course in regard to Cuba, and that in the role of meditator strong efforts were made by this country, especially after the arrival of the newly appointed consul, General Fitzhugh Lee, in Havana, to induce the Cuban insurgents to accept in a friendly spirit the contemplated changes in the administration of affairs in Cuba by the Spanish Government.

The Proposed Reforms.

The following is a copy of the laws enacted by the Cortes providing for the reforms. The internal affairs of the Island were to be under the control of a council of administration, to comprise thirty members, fifteen to be appointed by royal decree and fifteen to be elected according to the census under new methods of suffrage. The council, however, would be subordinate to the Governor-General. The conditions prescribed for appointment or election of councillors were these:

Besides a residence of at least four years on the Island, some one of the following qualifications were required:

To be or to have been president of the Chamber of Commerce or the Economic Society of Friends of the Country or of the Planters' Club; to be or to have been director of the university, or dean of the College of Lawyers of the capital of a province for a period of two years; to have been for a period of four years before the election one among the fifty largest taxpayers in the Island; to have exercised the functions of Senator of the kingdom or Deputy to the Cortes in one or more legislatures; to have been once or more than once president of the provincial Chambers of Deputies of the Island; to have been for two or more terms of two years each a member of the Provincial Commission, or for eight years a provincial Deputy; to have been for two or more terms Mayor in a capital of a province; to have been councillor of administration for two or more years previous to the promulgation of this law.

The councillors shall remain in office for a term of four years, the election taking place every two years alternately in the provinces of Havana, Pinar del Rio and Puerto Principe, and in those of Matanzas, Santa Clara and Santiago de Cuba. Havana shall elect four Councillors, Santiago de Cuba three and the other provinces two each. The whole number of Councillors shall be elected on the promulgation of this law. In ordinary cases the elections shall take place at the same time and by the same ballot as those of the provincial Deputies.

The Council shall examine the certificates of the members elected and decide as to the legal qualifications of the nominees of the people and of those of the Crown, and shall determine all questions relating to its Constitution in conformity to the law. In the first session of each year the Council shall appoint two vice-presidents and two secretaries, selected from the whole number of the Councillors. The Governor-General, whether permanent or provisional, shall be president of the Council.

The Council of Administration shall have charge of all questions relating to the constitution of municipalities and to the aggregation, segregation and demarcation of municipal districts. All questions relating to constitution of town councils, to matters pertaining to election, competency of nominees and the like shall be determined by the provincial Chamber of Deputies. Presidents of the municipalities will be those elected by the town councils among the town councillors, unless the Governor-General shall deem it expedient to replace them.

The Council of Administration shall decree whatsoever it may deem expedient for the conduct of the public works throughout the Island and of the telegraphic and postal communications, both by land and sea; of agriculture, industry and commerce and of immigration and colonization, of public instruction and of charities and health, without prejudice to the powers of supervision and other powers inherent in the sovereignty reserved by the laws to the national

16

government. It shall make up and approve the annual budget, making in it the necessary appropriations for the administrative department, the heads of which may be summoned for the council of the administration, but shall not have the right to vote. The council shall exercise such functions as the municipal and provincial laws may assign to it and such as are assigned by other special laws.

Everything Controlled by the Governor-General.

The Governor-General will continue to be the immediate representative of the national government in the Island of Cuba. He will have supreme command of all the forces on land and sea stationed on the Island. He will be the delegate of the Ministers of the Colony, State, war and navy, and all the other authorities of the Island will be subordinate to him. His appointment or removal will emanate from the President of the Cabinet, with the concurrence of the latter.

He will continue to have direct charge of all international questions, and will have an advisory council, composed of the Reverend Bishop of Havana, or the Reverend Archbishop of Santiago de Cuba; the Commander-General of the Navy, the Lieutenant-Governor, the President and the Attorney-General of the High Court of Havana, the head of the Department of Finance and the director of local administration.

In addition to the Island administrative reforms adopted by the Cortes of 1895, the Spanish Ministry considered a question of larger representation of native Cubans in public offices on the Island, and several important reforms in regard to customs and internal taxation.

Meanwhile the war went on in Cuba, and Captain-General Weyler, the man who was to accomplish so much, who was to crush the rebellion within a few months, and who was to repair the mistakes of Campos, only involved the loyal cause in fresh misfortunes. His columns were defeated, his heartless proclamations set at naught, and the very discretion which kept him in safety in his Palace, was a fruitful subject for all kinds of unflattering insinuations.

Says a correspondent: " Looking at him closely the other day I was struck more than ever with a curiosity to discover how it is that he has succeeded in inspiring people with any confidence in his character. He does not even possess the appearance of a great malefactor, such as one can fancy of a Danton or a Sulla, but, on the contrary, that of a very commonplace criminal, who would not look out of place in any police court in any city of the world.

"Perhaps it is due to the effect which he produces when, trussed up in uniform, with his ribband and stars, and the Cruz Laureada, the Spanish equivalent of the Victoria Cross, gained in San Domingo in all probability for some action like Melguizo's. He is then a butoned-up man like Mr. Tite Barnacle, who, we have it on the authority of Dickens, was consequently a weighty one. All buttoned-up men are weighty, all buttoned-up men are believed in.

Failure of General Weyler's Plans.

"Weyler has the bitter disappointment just at present of knowing that the latest of his carefully devised plans has failed in its effect. Maceo, with some six hundred of his followers, has crossed the formidable trocha near Cayujabos, though how he crossed it remains still a mystery. This military Figaro is accustomed to perform such feats and to appear in the most unexpected places without the slightest warning.

"The Spaniards, however, have a way of accounting for his last exploit which is more ingenious than probable. They say the insurgents disguise themselves as banana-sellers whenever they desire to pass through any fortified line. The soldiers imagine that they are innocent countrymen, and consequently never think of interfering with their passage. Of course not. Have not recent events shown the perfect impunity with which non-combatants are at liberty to wander everywhere in safety, and how considerate and gentle commanding officers have proved themselves of late?

"True to his policy of suppressing or distorting all news unfavorable to the Spanish cause, Captain-General Weyler has exerted himself to conceal the recognition of the belligerent rights of the insurgents by Congress. For many days the newspapers in Havana have been accustomed to announce that no telegrams had been received by them from the United States, but now they are forbidden to print even this notice, as doubtless too suggestive of coercive measures.

"And yet, of what avail is all this secrecy in such a case ? Does the government imagine that a fact unacknowledged, for that very reason ceases to exist, or do they cling to the hope of something in the chapter of accidents to avert its fulfillment ? The good tidings finally leaked out, despite all precautions, and brought joy and consolation to many a heart.

"It is still, however, too little circulated to permit of any effect being openly manifest. The streets are tranquil, people attend to their business as usual, and there is no appearance of any popular disturbance. There may, indeed, be none, or if there be it will surely follow upon some initiative proceeding in Barcelona or Madrid.

"The Spaniards in Havana are inveterate enough towards the United States, but then they live too near its shores not to recognize the power and importance which distant Spain has not yet learned to appreciate. They would like, had they a reasonable chance of success, to go to war, while in their hearts they must acknowledge how vain is the delusion of landing an invading army or of sweeping American commerce from the ocean. They have continually before their eyes, too, the desperate condition of affairs in this Island, and they can realize in a way which their fellow-countrymen cannot, the disastrous overthrow of the Captain-General's tactics.

"At this very time many of the people in the Province of Pinar del Rio have abandoned their dwellings, and are hiding in the sugar-cane to escape the brutalities of the columns, who are far more zealous in seeking such opponents than in following up the Cuban forces. One can imagine a conversation between a privileged stranger and a sentinel upon one of the innumerable forts along the tracks.

" 'What is that large body of men whom I see approaching from the hills ? '

" 'Oh, that,' replies the other carelessly; 'why, nothing but a crowd of fellows coming to sell fruit to the troops.'

" 'Your men are fond of fruit, then ? ' asks the stranger.

" 'Oh, passionately,' says the sentinel.

" ' But they have arms, I notice,' this a little anxiously, 'and they don't seem inclined to stop.'

" ' Why, you see how it is,' answers the soldier, ' the colonos all carry machetes, besides which, since that unfortunate affair at El Cano, we have to be cautious about firing upon stray parties.'

" ' But, I say, look there, they've surely got a Cuban flag.'

" ' Don't know, I'm sure. I'm color blind,' says the sentinel, resuming his rounds and dropping the conversation.

" It is, indeed, true that the Spaniards have been signalizing themselves of late by their lamentable mistakes. The last one did not certainly destroy any of their own men, but it resulted in the death of four women and two children. This was on the evening of the attack upon Hayo Colorado. About nightfall a body of insurgents crept through an open drain into the town, and had secured a safe position before their presence was recognized by the garrison or by the outposts stationed in the forts around.

Reckless Firing in the Streets.

" The invaders were left unmolested to procure such stores and supplies as they required, and it was only when their business was transacted and they had departed that the soldiers ventured to commence firing. The volleys which they then poured at random into the streets failed in their object, for the excellent reason that the enemy was not there, but they killed the women and children all the same.

" Strong measures are evidently to be taken with those planters who have failed to make at least some attempt at grinding. One of the offenders, Pedro Larrondo, of Sagua la Grande, in Santa Clara, has just been arrested for his obstinacy in this respect. In all probability he thought it wiser to suffer the loss of one year's produce than to incur the certainty of having his fields and buildings destroyed by fire; but it remains to be seen whether Weyler's anger may not prove more disastrous still than Cuban flames.

" Some men are now putting in large claims against the government for their many losses, alleging with reason that the order commanding all civilians to withdraw from the country into the towns, had left their plantations and farms completely at the mercy of the insurgents, and had also caused their cattle to die from want of water. But of what avail will it be even if these claims are admitted?

> " ' Honey from silk worms, who can gather,
> Or silk from the yellow bee ?" '

"And still more, who can expect to get compensation from a bankrupt nation, who do not pay their own army, and who have repudiated the many debts incurred in the last war in Cuba ?

"The spy system continues on the even tenor of its way in Havana, in a manner that is sometimes, though not often, exceedingly ridiculous. When we American correspondents assemble in a group we are generally aware of the same stunted individual, who hovers on the outskirts with an assumed air of innocence, which sits about as well on his Old-Bailey-looking countenance as a smile would on that of a rhinoceros. They are kittle-cattle, however, to deal with, these honored companions of the Spanish officers.

"They have methods of supplying evidence which have the merit, at least, of being unavoidable, and as they are never subjected to the cross-examination of their victims their carefully-prepared fabrications invariably triumph. It was, in all probability, to one of their well-devised schemes that Mariano Artiz, of Narcissa, near Saguajay, a Cuban of fortune and position, owes the fact that he is now a prisoner. An envelope directed to him was stopped at the post-office, in accordance with the system which holds no correspondence as sacred, and in it was found a letter to Maximo Gomez."

About the middle of April one of the staff officers of the Cuban army was in Philadelphia recovering from a wound received in a battle with the Spanish troops. He said that Gomez was again at the head of the insurgent forces and that Maceo would get away from the enemy, reported to have him hemmed in. Atrocities he declared continued. With the advent of the rainy season he said the patriots would inaugurate an offensive campaign.

The story he told of the progress of the war, of the atrocities perpetrated after General Weyler assumed command of the Spanish forces, and of the health of General Gomez, was one that will be read with interest, painful as it is in some respects.

Peraza (this officer's name) was a fine specimen of the patriotic volunteer. Fully six feet in height, but twenty-four years of age, and weighing 177 pounds, burned very dark by the tropical sun under which he lived, he looked to be a hard fighter. He was wounded in a charge by the cavalry of his division, a rifle ball entering his left shoulder. Failing to have it extracted in the camp hospital, he managed to get to New York by steamer, bringing with him some important military papers, and there the missile was located and taken out. He was awaiting a favorable opportunity to get back to the scene of strife.

Some Inside Facts.

In his statement he said: " I want at the outset to deny that General Gomez has been wounded or that he is dying of consumption, as has been reported through Spanish sources. He has been sick from liver troubles, but is in a fair way to complete recovery and is again at the head of his forces, as active as he ever was and as confident of ultimate success as at any time since he took the field. He has now directly under him an army of 12,000 men, most of whom are well armed.

" His total strength, counting the divisions of Maceo and other generals, is about 30,000. What is mostly lacking is ammunition. We meet the Spaniards and fight as long as our cartridges hold out and then divide into small groups, scattering in such a way that the government troops cannot reach us in force.

" As to the burning of the plantations, the Spanish reports are to a great extent false. When any of our generals attack a place containing Americans or other foreigners their property is respected and is not touched at all. Gomez has issued positive orders to protect the interests of such persons rather than to harm them. With regard to the reports of our losses in battle they are always exaggerated by the enemy.

" The latter never admit their own losses, but count those on our side as it may suit themselves. Our dead are always carried away and buried in the most convenient spots. None of our wounded are left on the field for fear the Spaniards would kill them outright. We send our wounded to the hospitals, located in the mountain fastnesses. Every division of our army has one of these places thus situated. There there are regular physicians, a few of them being from the United States. There are no Sisters of Charity, but there are Red Cross men and women, mostly Cubans.

"The recent successful expeditions have been a great help to us. We have got some more artillery, and it is being used under the direction of General Bandera in the province of Labillas. The rainy season begins about the 15th of this month. Then comes the yellow fever. It will decimate the ranks of the Spanish soldiers, because they are not acclimated. Our forces will, however, go on harassing the enemy and will be on the offensive all the time instead of on the defensive.

"General Weyler has not been any more successful against us than was Campos. In fact, less so. Our people think the former to be a coward at heart. Campos took the field, while Weyler has not shown himself at all. He remains in Havana and gives orders to his so-called volunteers—orders which lead to many atrocities.

"I have seen with my own eyes, on a farm in Lavinas, the bodies of men who had been shot down simply because they were known to sympathize with the cause of liberty. One of my own cousins who was captured by the Spaniards was hung to a tree and several shots fired into him. When we take wounded Spaniards we care for them, after taking away their rifles, until they are able to get back to their companions, when they are permitted to go. The killing of old men and old women by the Spanish volunteers goes on, no matter what the reports from government sources may say.

"Concerning the statement that General Maceo has been hemmed in, I can only say that once before he was in a far worse position than he now is. He is as cool and fearless as Gomez, and when he wants to get away I guess he will be able to do it."

The lieutenant was wounded in the left shoulder, "right nea the

Carolina State," he said.   General Lacret was endeavoring to join a portion of his column that had become separated from him, when he was attacked by the Spaniards numbering 3000.   Lacret had about 1000 men.   The fight lasted about two hours, when the insurgents retreated.   Peraza told of a little boy but thirteen years of age, who was in one of the fights.   A Spanish officer had had his arm broken by a rifle ball, but with his good hand he shot at the lad, hitting him in the left breast.   The lad fell with a cry of "three cheers for Free Cuba."   He was sent to the hospital and ultimately recovered.   These children, the lieutenant said, follow the insurgents from place to place and are permitted to remain because of the fear that they will be killed if sent away.

General Maceo Wins a Battle.

On April 15th news reached Havana that there had been heavy fighting in Pinar del Rio province.   Even official reports admitted that the Spanish columns were repulsed by General Antonio Maceo, with great loss of life.   The admission was very significant, in view of the circumstances and the character of official reports, which gave rise to a proverb that the Spaniards' loss was always one man whenever they were compelled to acknowledge defeat.

It was very difficult to obtain details of Maceo's victory.   The Spanish version alone was received.   All telegraph lines were cut, and news filtered to the city only by word of mouth.   The battle was west of the military strategic line, near Lechuza.   Government reports had previously located Maceo through an error at Lachuza, east of the line.

Further information received from private sources in Havana showed that this was the bloodiest engagement of the war.   The Spanish forces, under Colonel Linares, suffered overwhelming defeat at the hands of Antonio Maceo, who commanded a force of eight thousand men in a strong position.

Spanish reports placed Colonel Linares' force at fifteen hundred, of whom 450 were killed and 500 wounded.   The insurgents lost 200 killed and about 400 wounded.   The Spanish plan was for three battalions to attack Maceo simultaneously, but Colonel Echoverrea's battalion failed to arrive. It was stated that he was to be court-martialed.

Maceo led his troops into the thickest of the fight, and Colonel Linares' forces retreated in disorder. They finally made a stand on the wharf of the San Claudia plantation behind rude fortifications, until a warship came to their rescue. The Cuban forces on the shore made sad havoc with the troops as they embarked, shooting them down in their boats. In the battle the Amazons, a company of Cuban women, fought bravely.

In an effort to capture Colonel Linares, an insurgent, Alvarez, got separated. Seeing his danger, Mrs. Alvarez and several others followed him. Both husband and wife were caught in the Spanish lines and tried to fight their way back with machetes. Thinking that his wife was at his side still, Alvarez made his escape, but she was cut off at the last moment and was literally hacked to pieces by Spanish machetes. In his grief and chagrin Alvarez shot himself seriously.

"If You Live I Will Hang You."

General Maceo commanded him to appear before him. On demanding a reason for his crime, Alvarez said he could not endure life purchased by his wife's death. Maceo replied: " Pray God you may die, for if you live I will surely hang you. Cuba needs men too sorely to lose any except in the face of the enemy."

The news of the Spanish defeat produced a great sensation in Havana, and the censors were forced to admit many details.

Maceo's alleged heavy losses at La Palma, on the other hand, were corroborated by details received at Havana through non-official sources. The town was well fortified, and the rebel leader's attack was repelled. He directed his cannon on the town with his own hands. He was very anxious to capture it, as it contained large stores of ammunition and supplies. Two hundred volunteered and made the attempt. They crawled on their hands and knees through the fields, and about one hundred and fifty managed to enter the town. Ninety were shot from behind the walls before the others beat a retreat. Nearly all those killed were negroes.

An unusually large number of sugar plantations were burned. The losses from this source were said to aggregate $4,500,000 within a period of eight days. Property-owners ran equal risks from both sides. The Spanish troops passing estates shared by insurgents burned them, believing that the owners paid taxes to the insurgent government. The insurgents also continued their policy of destruction, and were determined to lay the country waste. The ruin was widespread, and the misery was growing greater.

The insurgents anxiously awaited a formal declaration of belligerency by the United States, and believed that every South and Central American government would immediately follow the example.

"A delay until August will mean the destruction of property worth $80,000,000 more," said one leader, grimly. "Weyler's regime has been marked by horrible cruelty, and minor officials feel or know that extreme measures will be approved."

Reports of massacres of innocent persons everywhere in the interior were, in fact, received daily in Havana. The Delgado incident was duplicated frequently, but the victims did not live to tell the tale.

Already there was a scarcity of horses in Cuba. General Weyler issued a decree that all owners of horses must have them examined by the government, so that all needed for the use of the troops might be bought. There was a promise of fair and prompt payment. Animals not fit for service were to be registered as worthless; others would either be taken or held subject to call, and branded to indicate their class. Owners failing to comply were to be deemed "unfaithful" to their country.

The threat had a terrible meaning in the existing condition of affairs, when executions of insurgents were too common to attract more than passing notice. Several persons living in Havana, on reading the orders, promptly decided to kill their riding horses to prevent them falling into the hands of the Spaniards.

"That is the only sensible plan," remarked a prominent man. "We don't want to help the enemy with animals. If the government took our horses we would have a small claim, and little chance of payment. We can't keep them safely, and the best way is to slaughter them."

Orders were given to the army to kill all horses and cattle in the country that could not be utilized, to prevent their possible use by the insurgents. Cavalrymen, whose mounts became too jaded to keep the line, must kill them. Passing troops were to use cattle for rifle practice, and whenever they saw horses they were to compare them with their own to see if an exchange was desirable.

Scarcity of food was reported everywhere in the interior of the Island. The price of meat rose in Havana. Game, which formerly abounded in the local market, could not be obtained, as there was no one to shoot birds in the hills except the troops. The fish supply continued good, although the fishermen were prohibited from going on the water except between sunrise and sunset, for fear of communicating with the insurgents.

Blood and Conflagration.

An interesting letter from General Gomez, the Cuban leader, concerning the war conditions on the Island, was received by President Palma, of the Cuban Junta. It reads as follows:

" SAGUA, CUBA, March 19.

" DEAR FRIEND:—The war continues more active and hard on account of the fierce character which General Weyler has given to it.

" Our wounded are followed and assassinated cruelly; he who has the misfortune to fall into the hands of the Spanish troops, perishes without fail. The peaceful country people only find death and dishonor.

" Cuba to-day, as in 1868, only presents pools of blood dried by conflagrations. Our enemies are burning the houses to deprive us, according to them, of our quarters for Spring. We will never use reprisals, for we understand that the revolution will never need to triumph by being cruel and sanguinary.

" We will go on with this war, the ultimate result of which you need not worry about—with success for the arms of the republic. We fight, when convenient to us, against an enemy tired out and without faith.

"My plans are well understood by my subordinates and each one knows what to do. Give us cartridges so that our soldiers can fight, and you can depend that in the Spring campaign the enemy's army will be greatly reduced, and it will be necessary for Spain to send another army, and I do not know whether it would be rash to say that perhaps Spain has not the money with which to do it.

"Everything that Spain orders and sends to this land, that she has drenched with the blood of her own children, only serves to ruin her power. And no man could be so well chosen as General Weyler, to represent in these times and in America the Spain of Philip II.

"Much is said and written about the recognition of belligerency by the American Government; this would be very advantageous to us, and is only doing justice, but as when we rose against tyranny, we only counted on the strength of our arms and the firm resolution of victory, we follow our march unconcerned, satisfied that what is to happen will happen.

"Your friend,
"MAXIMO GOMEZ."

Maceo Discusses his Western Campaign.

A letter from General Antonio Maceo, the insurgent Cuban leader, which showed his movements and the success met with, was received by Cuban leaders at Washington. It was dated at Cabanas, March 21, and read as follows:

"You know by my previous letters that the triumphant arms of the Republic were carried to the extreme western end of the Island. Everything that we desired has been obtained. The revolution is powerful in the provinces, which, as you know, were considered to be bulwarks of Spanish sentiment. Even the most remote places in the province of Pinar Del Rio responded admirably.

"ANTONIO MACEO."

Respecting the promises of Spain to institute reforms in Cuba, hoping thereby to end the insurrection, T. Estrada Palma, Cuban Delegate to the Government at Washington, said:

" The question of the supposed reforms is not a matter which at all concerns those who have already established an independent government in Cuba and have resolved to shrink from no sacrifice of property or life in order to emancipate the whole Island from the Spanish yoke. Spain must know by this time that while there is a single living Cuban with dignity there will not be peace in Cuba nor even the hope of it.

" If the right of thirteen British Colonies to rise in arms in order to acquire their independence has never been questioned, will there be a single citizen in this great republic who will doubt the justice, the necessity in which the Cuban people find themselves of fighting until they shall have overthrown Spanish oppression in their country and formed themselves into a free republic ?

Must be Fought to the Bitter End.

" Experience has taught us that as a people we have nothing to envy the Spaniards—in fact we feel ourselves superior to them, and from them we can expect no improvement, no better education.

" Let all know also that between the present revolution and the government of Spain there is no possible arrangement, if not based on the recognition of Cuban independence."

We cannot better close this tragic story of Cuba's gallant struggle for independence than by quoting the words of one of her distinguished sons :

" The population of the Island is, in round numbers, 1,600,000, of which less than 200,000 are Spaniards, some 500,000 are colored Cubans, and over 800,000 white Cubans. Of the Spaniards a small but not an inconsiderable fraction, although not taking an active part in the defense of our cause, sympathize with and are supporting it in various ways. Of the Cubans, whether colored or white, all are in sympathy with the revolution, with the exception of a few scattered individuals who hold positions under the Spanish Government or are engaged in enterprises which cannot thrive without it. All of the Cubans who have had the means and the opportunity to join the revolutionary army have done so, while those who have been com-

pelled for one reason or another to remain in the cities are co-
operating to the best of their abilities. If the people of the small
section of the western part of the Island, which yet remains quiet,
were supplied with arms and ammunition they would all rise to a
man within twenty-four hours.

Spanish Threats.

"This revolution of the whole Cuban people against the Government of Spain is what the Spanish officials are pleased to describe as
a disturbance caused by a few adventurers, robbers, bandits, and
assassins! But they have a purpose in so characterizing it, and it is
no other than to justify, in some way, the war of extermination which
the Prime Minister of Spain himself has declared will be waged by
his Government against the Cuban people! They are not yet satisfied with the rivers of human blood with which in times past they
inundated the fields of Italy, of the Low Countries, of our continent
of America, and only a few years ago, of Cuba itself! The Spanish
newspaper of Havana, *El Pueblo*, urges the Spanish soldiers to give
no quarter, to spare no one, to kill all, all without exception, until
they shall have torrents of Cuban blood in which to bathe themselves!

"It is well! The Cubans accept the challenge, but they will not
imitate their tyrants and cover themselves with infamy by waging a
savage war. The Cubans respect the lives of their Spanish prisoners,
they do not attack hospitals, and they cure and assist, with the same
care and solicitude with which they cure and assist their own, the
wounded Spaniards who may fall into their hands. They have done
so from the beginning of the war, and they will not change their
humane policy.

"The Spanish officials have also attempted to convince you that
the Cuban war is a war of races. Of what races? Of the black
against the white? It is not true, and the facts plainly show that
there is nothing of the kind. Nor is the war waged by Cubans
against the Spaniards as such. No. The war is waged against the
Government of Spain, and only against the Government of Spain and

the officials and a few monopolists who, under it, live and thrive upon the substance of the Cubans. We have no ill feeling against the thousands of Spaniards who industriously and honestly make their living in Cuba.

" But with the Spanish Government we will make no peace, and we will make no compromise. Under its rule there will be nothing for our people but oppression and misery. For years and years the Cuban people have patiently suffered, and in the interest of the colony, as well as in the interest of the metropolis, have earnestly prayed for reforms. Spain has not only turned a deaf ear to the prayers, but instead of reforming the most glaring abuses has allowed them to increase and flourish, until such a point has been reached that the continuation of the Spanish rule means for the Cuban people utter destruction."

PART II.

History of Cuba and Spanish Misrule.

CHAPTER XX.

Early Colonists and Rulers.

CUBA, the finest and largest of the West India Islands, was discovered by Columbus himself, on the 28th day of October, 1492, and was named by him Juana, in honor of Prince John, the son of Ferdinand and Isabella, the sovereigns of Aragon and Castile.

Upon the death of Ferdinand, the Island was called Fernandina. It afterward received the name of Santiago, as a mark of reverence for the patron saint of Spain, and still later, the inhabitants, to illustrate their piety, gave it that of Ave Maria, in honor of the Holy Virgin.

Notwithstanding these several titles, the island is still principally known by its original Indian name of Cuba; a name which it bore when the great navigator first landed on its shores, and which in all probability it is destined to retain.

With regard to the character of the aboriginal inhabitants of the Island, it is universally admitted by all the Spanish authors who have written on the subject, that they were disinterested and docile, gentle and generous, and that they received the first discoverer, as well as the conquerors, who followed in his track, with the most marked attention and courtesy. At the same time they are represented as being entirely given up to the enjoyment of those personal indulgences, and all the listlessness and love of ease, which the climate is supposed to provoke, and which is said to have amounted in the

eyes of their European conquerors to positive cowardice and pusilla-
nimity.

They seldom spoke until first addressed by the strangers, and then
with perfect modesty and respect.   Their hospitality was unbounded ,
but they were unwilling to expose themselves to any personal fatigue
beyond what was strictly necessary for their subsistence.   The cultivation of the soil was confined, as Columbus had observed, to the
raising of yams, garbanzos, and maize, or Indian corn, but as hunts-
men and fishermen they were exceedingly expert.

Their Costume and Customs.

Their habiliments were on the most limited scale, and their laws
and manners sanctioned the practice of polygamy.   The use of iron
was totally unknown to them, but they supplied the want of it with
pointed shells, in constructing their weapons, and in fashioning their
implements for fishing and the chase.   Their almost total want of
quadrupeds is worthy of notice.

Although the Island was divided into nine principalities, under nine
different caciques, all independent of each other, yet such was the
pacific disposition of the inhabitants that the most perfect tranquillity
prevailed throughout the Island at the time of the arrival of the invaders.   The several governments were administered in the simplest
form, the will of the cacique being received as law by his subjects,
and the age he had attained being in general the measure of his influence and authority, and of the reverence and respect with which
he was treated.   Their religion was limited to a belief in the immortality of the soul, and to the existence of a beneficent Deity—*un Dios
remunerador.*

But their priests were cunning, superstitious, or fanatic, pretending
to intelligence with malignant spirits, and maintaining their influence
over the people by working on their fears, and practicing the
grossest and most ridiculous extravagances.   No sanguinary sacrifices were resorted to, however ; still less could the gentle race be
chargeable with the horrid practices of the savage anthropophagi ;
and, according to the earliest Spanish authorities, they distinguished

themselves beyond any other Indian nation by the readiness and docility with which they received the doctrines of Christianity.

The town of Baracoa, which was called *de la Asumcion*, was the first that was founded, and was for some time considered the capital, until, in the year 1514, the whole of it had been overrun and examined. In that year, the towns of Santiago and Trinidad, on the southern side, were founded for the purpose of facilitating the communications of the new colonists with the Spanish inhabitants of Jamaica.

Founding a New Town.

Near the centre of the Island also were established, soon after this period, the towns of Bayamo, Puerto Principe, and Santi-Espiritus, and that of Baracoa was considerably enlarged. In the sequel, as there was no town toward the north, that of San Juan de los Remedios was founded; and on the 25th of July, 1515, at the place now called Batabano, on the south side of the Island, was planted a town with the name of San Cristobal de la Habana, in deference to the memory of the illustrious discoverer; but in the year 1519 this name was transferred to the place where the capital now stands.

The leaning of the Spaniards toward the southern side of the Island appears to have arisen from their previous possession of Jamaica and the Costa Firme; as till then they had no idea of the existence of the Floridas, or of New Spain; the expedition for the conquest of which, as well as the steps toward their first discovery, having been taken from the Island of Cuba.

The town of Baracoa, having first been raised to the dignity of a city and a bishopric, was declared the capital of the Island in 1518, and remained so till 1522, when both were transferred to Santiago de Cuba. In 1538 the Havana, second city of the name, was surprised by a French privateer, who reduced it to ashes. This misfortune brought the Governor of the Island, Hernando de Soto, to the spot, who lost no time in laying the foundation of the *Castillo de la Fuerza*, one of the numerous fortresses which still exist for the defence of the city. With this protection, combined with the advantageous geographical position of the harbor, the ships already pass-

ing, charged with the riches of New Spain, on their way to the
Peninsula, were induced to call there for supplies of water and
provisions.

In this way the Havana began to rise in importance by insensible
degrees, insomuch that in 1549, on the arrival of a new Governor,
Gonzalez Perez de Angulo, he resolved on making it his place of
residence. His example was followed by subsequent governors, and
in this way the city, although without any royal or legal sanction,
came to be silently regarded as the capital of the Island, until in
1589 it was formally declared so by the peninsular government, at
the time of the nomination of the first Captain-General, *El Maestre
de Campo*, Juan de Tejada, who was positively directed to take up his
residence at the Havana.

Residence of Early Chiefs.

In the annals of the Island the names of the first Governors and
of their lieutenants have not been recorded with a degree of accuracy
that can be altogether depended on. All that is known with certainty
is, that the early chiefs resided at Santiago de Cuba, from its being
the place where the largest population was collected, from its proximity to Jamaica and St. Domingo, and from its being the seat of the
ecclesiastical jurisdiction. For the Havana and other towns of in
ferior importance, lieutenants were appointed.

This system continued until the year 1538, when Hernando de
Soto, who, to the rank of *Adelantado* of the Floridas, added the office
of Governor of Cuba, having arrived at Santiago, passed a few days
there, and then proceeded to the continent. In his absence he left
the government of the Island in the hands of a lady, Dona Isabel de
Bobadilla, and gave her for a colleague, Don Juan de Rojas. This
Rojas had previously resided at the Havana, in quality of lieutenant-
governor; and it is from this date that the gradual transference of the
seat of power from Santiago to the Havana may be said to have
arisen. It was not till the year 1607 that the Island was divided into
two separate governments.

In 1545, Don Juan de Avila assumed the government, and to him

in 1547 succeeded Don Antonio de Chavez, to whom the Havana is
indebted for its first regular supply of water, bringing it from the
river called by the aborigines Casiguaguas, and by the Spaniards
Chorrera, a distance of two leagues from the city. At that period
the trade of the place was limited. The largest and wealthiest proprietors were mere breeders of cattle ; as yet agriculture was very little attended to, and any actua! labor performed consisted in exploring
the neighborhood in pursuit of the precious metals.

Obtaining Supplies at Havana.

To this governor succeeded Dr. Gonzalo Perez de Angulo, who,
according to the historian Urrutia, was the first who resided at the
Havana during the greater part of his administration. At this period the number of cattle and the practice of agriculture had so
much increased that the expeditions from the neighboring continent
obtained their supplies at the Havana, and from thence also large
quantities of provisions were sent to the *Terra Firma.* For some
time large profits were made by means of these exports, more especially ii the sale of horses for the troops ; but the continental settlements, having at length been able to provide for themselves, this
source of profit was dried up.

In the year 1554 the government was assumed by Don Diego de
Mazariegos, and, during his administration, the Havana was again
attacked and reduced to ashes by the French, notwithstanding the
protection supposed to be afforded by the Castillo de la Fuerza.
The other towns of the Island were also insulted, insomuch that the
bishop of the diocese was compelled to leave Santiago and take up
his residence at Bayamo, causing a serious misunderstanding between the ecclesiastical authorities and the civil governor.

To Mazariegos, in 1565, succeeded Garcia Osorio, and to Osorio,
two years afterward, Don Pedro Melendez de Avilez, who at the
same time held the office of *Adelantado* of the Floridas, administer-
ing the affairs of the Island for a number of years by means of a series
of lieutenant-governors. At this period, the hospital of San Juan
de Dios, and a church dedicated to San Cristobal, were erected at the

Havana. This church was built on the spot now occupied oy the residence of the captain-general.

Don Gabriel Montalvo was the successor of Melendez, and assumed the government in 1576. In his time the Franciscan con‑vent was erected, in spite of the opposition of the bishop; and prepa‑rations were made, by the building of suitable vessels, for the extirpation of the pirates by whom the coasts of the Island were infested. Don Francisco Carreno, the successor of Montalvo, assumed the command in 1578. In his time the weights and mea‑sures of the Island were regulated; and vast quantities of timbei were shipped to the mother-country, to contribute toward the con‑struction of the convent and palace of the Escurial.

Raids by Pirates.

During the administration of Don Gaspar de Torres, the successor of Carreno, who arrived in 1580, not only Cuba, but the neighboring islands of Jamaica and St. Domingo, were more than ever annoyed by piratical incursions. The expense occasioned by the attempts to suppress them was so great that it became necessary to impose a special tax, called *la sisa de piragua*, to cover it.

At this period was begun the cultivation of tobacco and the sugar-cane, the labor of which was found to be too great for the indolent aborigines, whose numbers had already been materially diminished by the state of slavery to which they had been reduced. It was to promote the production of these new luxuries that a royal license was first obtained for importing negroes from the coast of Africa.

The continued presence and increasing numbers of the pirates began to give a factitious importance to the castellanos of the fortress, which protected the harbor of the Havana, and sheltered the *lanchas* and *piraguas* and the *guardacostas* themselves. A military power thus insensibly arose, which, coming into collision with that of the civil governor, caused a great deal of disturbance and confusion.

The next governor, Don Gabriel de Lujan, who arrived in 1584, came to such a serious rupture with Don Diego Fernandez de Qui‑nones, the Castellano de la Fuerza, that the real audiencia of the district, at the instigation of Quinones, took it upon them to suspend Don Gabriel from his administration of the government, but some time afterward restored him.   On the application of the *Ayuntamiento*, the two offices were afterward combined and vested in the same individual.   During Lujan's administration, several hostile demonstrations were made against the Island; but none of them were seriously prosecuted.

The attacks of a diminutive enemy, the ant, became so alarming, however, that it was thought necessary by the Cabildo, or chapter of the diocese, to elect a new patron saint, and to confer that dignity on San Marcial, the bishop agreeing to celebrate his fiesta, and keep his day yearly, on the condition of his interceding for the extermination of the hormigas and vivijaguas.

Two Famous Fortresses.

The successor of Lujan, Don Juan de Tejada, was the first governor who arrived with the rank of captain-general, in which were included the same powers and jurisdiction enjoyed by the *vireyes* of the continental possessions of the crown.   Tejada was directed to commence the construction of the two fortresses now known as the Morro and the Punta, and for this purpose brought with him the Engineer Don Juan Bautista Antoneti; and he was authorized to negotiate with the provinces of New Spain for obtaining contributions by which to support the garrison, which at that time was limited for all the three fortresses to three hundred men.

After the building of the Morro was begun, it is said that Antoneti, having ascended the heights of the Cabana, remarked to those about him, that from that point the city and the Morro itself would be commanded. This opinion having been communicated to the government, the construction of the present fortress of the Cabanas was immediately determined on.   During Tejada's government the Havana received the title of *Ciudad;* the Ayuntamiento was increased to the number of twelve regidores; and a coat of arms was given to it by Philip the Second, bearing on a blue field three castles *argent*, in allusion to the Fuerza, the Morro, and the Punta, and a golden key to signify that it was the key of the Indies ; the whole surmounted by a crown.

Tejada was succeeded as captain-general in 1602 by Don Pedro Valdes, who made strong representations to the court on the subject of the excesses committed by the pirates, by whose incursions Santiago had been almost depopulated. The bishop, on returning there from Bayamo on a temporary visit, was seized, tied, stripped, and carried off by the pirate Giron, and detained for eighty days on board his vessel, until he was ransomed by the payment of two hundred ducats and five arrobas of beef by Don Gregorio Ramos who, after rescuing the bishop, succeeded in destroying the pirate.

A Subordinate Governor.

From the insecurity of Santiago, this bishop attempted, but without success, to establish his cathedral at the Havana. The supreme government, however, to stay the progress of depopulation at Santiago, resolved on establishing there a subordinate governor with the rank of *capitan de guerra*, and appointed to the office Don Juan de Villaverde, the Castillo of the Morro, who was charged with the defence of his new jurisdiction against the pirates.

The successor of Valdes was Don Gaspar Ruiz de Pereda in 1608; and that of Pereda in 1616 was Don Sancho de Alquiza. This last had been previously the Governor of Venezuela and Guiana, and he is recorded to have applied himself with energy to the working of the copper mines at Cobre in the neighborhood of Santiago; the superintendence of which was for some time annexed to the office of captain-general of the Havana, although it was afterward transferred to the lieutenant-governor at Santiago.

The annual produce of that period was about 2000 quintals, and the copper extracted is represented to have been of a quality superior to anything then known in the foundries of Europe. Alquiza died after having enjoyed his office only two years; and by a provision of the real audiencia, he was succeeded in the temporary command by Geronimo de Quero, the Castillo of the Morro, whose military rank was that of *sargento mayor.*

From this period till the year 1715, it appears that, in the nomination of captains-general, a declaration was constantly introduced to the effect that the castellanos of the Morro, on the death of the captain-general, should succeed to the military command of the Island; but since the year 1715 an officer has been specially named with the rank of *teniente rey* or *cabo-subalterno,* whose functions acquire an active character only on the death or incapacity of his chief.

Closing the Entrance to the Harbor.

Doctor Damian Velasquez de Contreras succeeded Alquiza in 1620, and Don Lorenzo de Cabrera, the next captain-general, was appointed to the command in 1626. A charge was brought against Cabrera, that he had sold a cargo of negroes in the Havana without a royal license; which being backed by other complaints, the licenciado Don Francisco de Prada was sent out to inquire into them, and by him the captain-general was sent home to the Peninsula, when de Prada assumed the civil and political jurisdiction, and assigned the military command to Don Cristobal de Aranda, the alcaide of the Morro. During the joint administration of de Prada and Aranda it was resolved to shut up the entrance of the harbor by means of a chain drawn across it, a resolution which is described by the historians of the period as having been exceedingly extravagant and absurd.

The next captain-general was Don Juan Bitrian de Viamonte, who began his administration in 1630, and projected the construction of two strong towers, the one in Chorrera, and the other in Cojimar, but the plan was not carried into effect until the year 1646. At this period a certain good woman, known by the name of Magdalena de Jesus, established a sort of female sanctuary, called a *beaterio,* which gave rise to the establishment of the first female monastery of Santa Clara.

Fears of an invasion of the Island by the Dutch now began to be entertained in the Peninsula; and as Viamonte's health was infirm, he was removed to the presidency of St. Domingo; and, in 1634. Don Francisco Riano y Gamboa was sent out to replace him. Gamboa introduced important reforms in the collection of the revenue. He established a court of accounts at the Havana, to which was afterward referred the examination of all public disbursements, not only for the Island of Cuba, but for Porto Rico, the Floridas, and that portion of the Spanish navy called the windward fleet, *la Armada de Barlovento.*

At first, a single accountant-general was named; but a second was afterward added, with instructions to visit alternately the various parts where the colonial revenue was collected or disbursed. During the government of Gamboa, also, a commissioner of the Inquisition came from Carthagena to reside in the Havana; to provide for whose support one of the canons of the cathedral of Santiago was suppressed. The bishops had for some time acquired a taste for residing in the capital, and other members of the ecclesiastical cabildo began to follow their example, soon degenerating into an abuse which loudly called for a remedy.

Spanish Possessions in America Threatened.

The successor of Gamboa was Don Alvaro de Luna y Sarmiento, who commenced his administration in 1639, and in the course of it completed the castle of Chorrera, two leagues to leeward of the Havana, and the Torreon de Cojimar, one league to windward.

In 1647, Sarmiento was succeeded by Don Diego de Villalva y Toledo, who, in 1650, was replaced by Don Francisco Gelder. During Gelder's administration, the establishment of the Commonwealth in England gave rise to serious apprehensions for the safety of the Spanish possessions in America; especially when it became known that, in 1655, a squadron had sailed by order of the Protector, the ostensible object of which was the reconciliation of the English colonies to the new form of government, but with the real design of capturing Jamaica.

It is scarcely necessary to add, that this design was successfully executed; that the Spanish defenders of Jamaica were dispersed, and the governor killed, and that many of the inhabitants removed in consequence to Cuba. An attempt on the Havana was also made by this expedition, but the assailants were successfully resisted. The failure is ascribed by the Spaniards to a sort of miracle performed in their favor. The invaders having landed on a very dark night, they became so terrified, according to the Spanish authorities, by the noise of the landcrabs and the flitting light of the fire-flies, which they took for an enemy in ambuscade, that they fled to their ships in the utmost disorder and confusion.

An Expedition that never Sailed.

The next captain-general was Don Juan Montano, who arrived in 1656. During his time the Spaniards of Jamaica continued to defend themselves under two distinguished hacendados, Don Francisco Proenza and Don Cristobal de Isasi; who, for their exertions in preserving the Island to the Spanish crown, received thanks and honors from the court. Orders were also sent out to the other Spanish settlements in America to lend their assistance to the Jamaica loyalists; and a strong expedition was prepared in the Peninsula, having the same object in view. In the end, however, in consequence of the sickness which prevailed on board the ships, the expedition never sailed, and the Spaniards were compelled to evacuate the Island.

Montano, having died within a year after his arrival, was succeeded in the command, in 1658, by Don Juan de Salamanca, in whose time the incursions of the pirates became more troublesome than ever, on all the coasts of Spanish America. As many of them had the audacity to sail under the flags of France and England, the court of Spain addressed itself to these governments on the subject, and received for answer that, having no countenance or authority from either, the Spaniards were at liberty to deal with them as they thought fit.

At this period the French, having established themselves in the island of Tortuga, began from thence by slow degrees, first on hunting parties, and afterward more permanently, to make encroachments on the neighboring coast of the Island of St. Domingo; until, in the end, they had completely taken possession of the western part of it, and created there a respectable colony. According to the Spanish authorities, the French colonists of St. Domingo formed an alliance

with the English in Jamaica, and, without the sanction of either of
their governments in Europe, made piratical incursions in the Spanish territories, and at length became so formidable that tne Spaniards
found it necessary to fortify their possessions, and to combine
together for their mutual protection.   The most remarkable of these
piratical leaders was the Frenchman Lolonois and the celebrated
Morgan.

The Walls of Havana are Built.

In 1663 arrived as captain-general Don Rodrigo de Flores y
Aldana, who in the following year was relieved by Don Francisco
Orejon y Gaston, previously Governor of Gibraltar and Venezuela.
Fearing the neighborhood of the English in Jamaica, Gaston applied
himself to the construction of the walls of the Havana; and to meet
the expense he was authorized to levy half a real on each quarter
of an arroba of wine, nearly equal to a gallon, which might be sold
in the city; but this having given rise to complaints, the Spanish
government, by a royal cedula, directed that $20,000 a year should
be raised for the purpose in Mexico; and that as much more should
be procured as the captain-general could extract by other means from
the inhabitants of the Havana.

The next Governor was Don Rodriguez de Ledesma, who assumed
his functions in 1670, and prosecuted the work of fortification with
the greatest ardor.   He also prepared a naval armament for the protection of the coast.   It was at this time that the working of the copper mines near Santiago was abandoned, and that the reconstruction
of the cathedral in that city was begun; but the greater part of the
slaves employed in the mines were sent to the Havana to work on
the fortifications.   During Ledesma's administration, a French party
landed in the eastern part of the Island, to the number of 800, under
the command of one Franquinay, with the intention of plundering the
city of Santiago, but they withdrew without doing any damage,
alarmed, according to the Spanish accounts, by hearing the mere cry
of "*al arma.*"

In 1675 the city of Santiago was destroyed by an earthquake, a
calamity from which the Havana and the western parts of the Island

appear to be exempt. Ledesma complained bitterly to his government that the English authorities in Jamaica countenanced and encouraged the attacks of the pirates, and applied for leave to make reprisals. He was succeeded by Don Jose Fernandez de Cordoba Ponce de Leon, who began his administration in 1680, and continued the work of fortification with energy.

In 1687 Ponce de Leon was replaced by Don Diego de Viana e Hinojosa, and to him, in 1689, succeeded Don Severino de Manzaneda y Salinas, during whose administration the city of Matanzas was founded, the first lines of it having been traced on the 10th of October, 1693, in presence of the captain-general, and many other persons of distinction. The etymology of the name Matanzas is much disputed by the antiquarians of Cuba, some ascribing it to the slaughter of Indians at the time of the conquest of the Island, contending that the supposed Indian name Yumuri, that of one of the two rivers between which the city stands, is in fact a synonym in bad Spanish for this general massacre.

Only One Left to Tell the Tale.

Others contend, with equal pertinacity, that it was the natives who killed the Spaniards, while passing from one side of the bay to the other, having mutinied against their masters and used their oars successfully as weapons of offence. Seven of the Spaniards are said to have attempted to escape, but were carried prisoners to a neighboring Indian town, where they were all put to death except one, who escaped to tell the tale of the *Matanza*.

The next captain-general was Don Diego de Cordoba Lazo de la Vega; to him in 1702 succeeded Don Pedro Nicolas Benitez de Lugo, who died soon after his arrival. The next captain-general was Don Pedro Alvarez de Villarin, who arrived in 1706, and died the same year. After him, in 1708, came the Marques de Casa Torres, ex-governor of the Floridas, who, having had some dispute with the auditor Don Jose Fernandez de Cordoba, was suspended from his office by the real audiencia.

The foundling hospital, or *Casa de Ninos Espositos,* vulgarly called

La Cuna, was founded in 1711 by Don Fray Jeronimo de Valdes, an institution which still exists, and, like that of St. Pierre in the Island of Martinique, is only resorted to by the white inhabitants, the presentation of a colored infant being a thing unknown. This fact, whether it arise from the sense of shame being stronger in the white mother, or from natural affection being stronger in the colored mother, is not unworthy of investigation.

Don Vicente Raja arrived as captain-general in the year 1716, bringing with him a royal *cedula,* declaring that in the event of his absence, illness, or death, the civil and military government should be transferred to the teniente rey; in case of his absence, illness or death, to the castellano del Morro; and failing the castellano, to the sergeant-major of the garrison; and failing him, to the senior captain of infantry, so as that in no case the civil and military jurisdictions should ever afterward be divided.

Sent to Madrid in Chains.

In the following year Raja returned to Spain, and in 1718 Don Gregorio Guazo arrived as his successor. Nothing material occurred during his administration, and he was replaced in 1724 by Don Dionisio Martinez de la Vega. In his time a serious difference arose on the occasion of an appointment to the office of lieutenant-governor of Santiago. On the 10th of May, 1728, Lieutenant-Colonel Don Juan del Hoyo took possession of the local government, and a few months afterward a royal *cedula* arrived prohibiting his admission. On this the captain-general required his removal; but the ayuntamiento opposed it, saying it was one thing to remove an officer, and another not to admit him. Lawyers were consulted on the point; and the Court of Chancery of the district was referred to, who decided that the ayuntamiento were in the right, and the captain-general in the wrong.

At this juncture the windward fleet, *la Armado de Barlovento,* arrived under the command of Don Antonio de Escudero, who, in his zeal for the royal service, and without any authority but that of force, laid hold of Del Hoyo, removed him from his employment, and carried him off to Vera Cruz. No sooner had he regained his liberty than he returned to the Island; and having visited the town of Puerto Principe, which at that time formed part of his jurisdiction, the peo ple rose against him, and having once more made him prisoner, sent him in irons to the Havana, from whence the captain-general had him carried to Madrid.

The next captain-general was Don Juan Francisco Guemes y Horcasitas, who arrived in the year 1734, and to him, in 1746, succeeded Don Juan Antonio Tineo y Fuertes, who died in the following year. He was the first captain-general who thought it necessary to establish a separate hospital for the reception of dissolute and incorrigible women; for which purpose the revenues of vacant ecclesiastical offices were to be applied.

Capture of the City by the English.

The date of the termination of the government of Martinez has not been very clearly defined; he was succeeded provisionally by Don Diego de Penalosa, as *teniente rey de la plaza*, and was replaced in 1747 by Don Francisco Cagigal de la Vega, who had previously been lieutenant-governor at Santiago. On leaving the command in 1760, the government was assumed provisionally by the Teniente Rey Don Pedro Alonzo; and he was relieved, in 1761, by Don Juan de Prado Porto Carrero, whose government was made so memorable by the capture of the city by the English.

The Habaneros themselves seemed desirous to commemorate the event by retaining English names for the points of the coast where the landing of the expedition was effected, and for the fortresses which were occupied preparatory to the descent on the Morro. In the Memorias de la Real Sociedad Patriotica there are also some interesting notices of the event.

The captain-general, according to some accounts, was apprised of the fact that the English were preparing an expedition for the invasion of the Island; but although he had made certain arrangements for the reception of the enemy, it is said that he never seriously believed that an invasion was about to take place. He made it his

business, however, to ascertain what number of men might be relied
on for the defence of the Island; and even the proportion of slaves to
whom arms might be safely intrusted. Juntas were frequently
assembled for the discussion of these matters during the three months
which intervened between the first rumor of the invasion and the
actual descent of the enemy.

At length, on the 6th of June, 1762, when a fleet of at least 250

OLD CATHEDRAL AT HAVANA.

sail had been reported as off the coast, the captain-general still refused
to believe that this was the hostile expedition; insisting that it must
be a homeward-bound convoy from Jamaica. On the morning of
that day he is said to have gone over to the Morro for the purpose
of observing in person the movements of the fleet; and when he found
that the garrison of the fortress had been called out under arms by
the *teniente rey*, Don Dionisio Soler, he expressed his disapprobation
of the proceeding—declaring it to be imprudent, and desiring that the
troops might be sent back to their quarters. After mid-day, however,
he received notice from the Morro that the ships of war were approaching the coast, and appeared from their manœuvres to be preparing to
effect a landing.

Confounded by his own previous incredulity, the governor at length gave orders to prepare for a vigorous defence. The consternation produced by the ringing of alarm bells and the moving of artillery was extreme. Such of the inhabitants as possessed arms made haste to put them in order, and those who were not so provided presented themselves at the *sala real* to ask for them; but there were only 3,500 muskets to be found, the greater part of them unfit for service, together with a few carbines, sabres, and bayonets. These were soon distributed; but in the end a great number of people remained unarmed for the want of needful supplies.

A Formidable Expedition.

The juntas were again assembled, consisting of the captain-general, the teniente rey, the marques del real transporte, general of marines, and the commissary-general, Don Lorenzo Montalvo, to whom were added the Conde de Superunda, as viceroy of Peru, and Major-General Don Diego Tabares, as Governor of Carthagena, who happened to be then at the Havana on their return to Europe. Orders were issued by this junta to Colonel Don Carlos Caro to resist the landing of the enemy on the beach of Cogimar and Bacuranao, which they seemed to threaten; adding to his own regiment, De Edimburgo, the rest of the cavalry then in the city, together with several companies of the infantry of the line, and a few lancers, amounting altogether to about 3,000 men.

The expedition sailed from Spithead on the 5th of March, 1762. Its chief object was, after seizing on the French possessions in the West Indies, to make a descent on the Havana, which was justly considered as the principal key to the vast possessions of the Spanish crown in the two great divisions of the American continent; the possession of which would effectually interrupt all communication between the Peninsula and the Gulf of Mexico, and thereby give the court of the Catholic king a distaste for the alliance with that of St. Cloud. The first rendezvous of the forces to be combined with the original expedition was at Martinique, and Sir James Douglas was ordered to unite his squadron, stationed at Port Royal, Jamaica, with

18

that of Sir George Pocock, at the Cape of St. Nicholas, in the Island of St. Domingo.

From this point of union the expedition had the choice of two courses in proceeding toward the Havana.   That which would have been the more easy of execution was to sail down the southern side of the Island, and doubling the western cape, present itself before the Havana.   But as this would have occupied more time, which the maintenance of secrecy rendered valuable, Sir George Pocock re-solved on following the shorter and more difficult as well as danger-ous course of the old Bahama channel, on the north side of the Island.   This resolution had the double effect of taking the enemy unprepared, and of obstructing the only course by which the French could send relief from St. Domingo.

On the 27th of May the admiral hoisted his flag, and the whole convoys, consisting of 200 vessels of all classes, were soon under sail for the old Bahama passage.   The "Alarm" and "Echo" frigates, sent in advance, discovered, on the 2d of June, five ships of the enemy, the frigate "Tetis," the sloop of war "Fenix," a brig, and two smaller vessels.   An engagement immediately took place, in the issue of which one of the light vessels escaped, the other four being captured.

On the evening of the 5th the "Pan" of Matanzas was visible ; and on the morning of the 6th, being then five leagues to the eastward of the Havana, the necessary orders were issued for the commanders of the boats of the squadron and the captains of the transports, with regard to the debarkation of the troops.   This duty was intrusted to the Honorable Commodore Keppel, at whose disposal were placed six ships of the line, several frigates, and the large boats of the squadron.   The admiral followed at two in the afternoon, with thir-teen ships of the line, two frigates, the bomb vessels of the expedi-tion, and thirty-six store-boats.   On presenting himself at the mouth of the harbor, for the double purpose of reconnoitering the enemy and making the feint of an attack to cover the operations of Commo-dore Keppel, he ascertained that twelve ships of the line and a num-ber of merchant vessels were lying at anchor within it.

On the following morning the admiral prepared his launches for landing a body of sailors and marines about four miles to the west-ward of the Havana. At the same time Lord Albemarle effected the landing of the whole of the troops, without opposition, between the rivers Bacuranao and Cogimar, about six miles from the Morro. A body of men having appeared on the beach, Commodore Keppel directed the " Mercury " and " Bonnetta " corvettes to disperse them; but a much greater number having soon afterward presented them-selves with the evident intention of disputing the passage of the Rio Cogimar with the main body of the expedition, Captain Hervey in the " Dragon " was sent to bombard the fort, which afforded the enemy protection, but which very soon surrendered, leaving a free passage for the advance of the invaders.

Resistance to the Invasion.

From the prisoners taken on the 2d of June in the " Tetis " and " Fenix," the presence of a naval force in the harbor became known to the English, together with the fact that most of the enemy's ships had completed their supplies of water, and were nearly ready for sea. Till then the governor, as has been stated, was almost wholly unpre-pared. The first notice he had of the actual approach of the expe-dition was obtained from the crew of the small schooner, which escaped from the pursuit of the " Alarm " and the " Echo."

As soon as he became convinced of the fact, the governor, as we have seen, assembled a council of war, composed of the chief officers under his command At this junta de guerra the plan of defence was arranged, and a firm resolution was taken to resist the invasion to the last extremity. The defence of the Morro, on the possession of which the fate of the Havana in a great measure depended, was intrusted to Don Luis de Valesco, commander of the " Reyna " ship of the line, to whose gallantry and perseverance Sir George Pocock, in his subsequent report to the admiralty, pays a just tribute of com-mendation. His second in command, the Marques de Gonzales, commander of the " Aquilon " ship of the line, followed in all respects the example of Valesco, dying sword in hand in defence of his flag.

The defence of the Punta Castle was in like manner assigned to a naval officer, Don Manuel Briseno, who had a friend in the same branch of the service for his second in command.   This arrangement gave deadly offence to the officers of the army, who thought themselves unjustly superseded in the post of honor and of danger; but it was urged in excuse, that naval officers were better acquainted than those of the infantry or the cavalry with the use of artillery ; and as the naval squadron had become useless by being locked up in the harbor, this was the only way in which they could be advantageously employed.

CHAPTER XXI.

War with Great Britain.

BEFORE the Governor could assemble the militia of the Island under arms, he thought it necessary to declare war by proclamation against Great Britain. When his whole force was at length assembled, it was found in gross numbers greatly to exceed that of the invaders. It consisted of nine squadrons of cavalry, including in all 810 men; the regiment of the Havana, 700; two battalions of the regiment de Espana, 1400; two battalions of the regiment de Aragon, 1400; three companies of artillery, 300; seamen and marines of the squadron, 9000; militia and people of color, 14,000—making a grand total of 27,610.

The greater part of the Spanish force was stationed in the town of Guanabacao, on the side of the bay opposite to the Havana, between the points where the invading forces had landed, in order to prevent them from turning the head of the harbor and attacking the city by land. The British force was divided into five brigades, amounting, with detachments from Jamaica and North America, to a total of 14,041 land forces. At daybreak, on the 7th, the troops were already on board the boats arranged in three divisions—the centre commanded by the Honorable Augustus Hervey; the right wing by Captains Barton and Drake; and the left, by Captains Arbuthnot and Jekyl.

The first brigade was also the first to land; and as soon as the troops had formed on the beach, Lord Albemarle took the command, and marched in the direction of the city, which he did without further molestation as soon as the Cogimar batteries had been silenced. His Excellency established his headquarters in Cogimar for the night; the troops were served with rations under arms, and several pickets were advanced to the eminences overlooking the

Havana. After a succession of attacks on the part of Lord Albemarle, and a continued bombardment of the castle, the Morro surrendered on the 30th of July, and the town itself on the 14th of
August, succeeding.

The spoils seized by the captors were of great value, and the distribution was a subject of much discontent; and it must be admitted
that the partition, which gave three or four pounds to a soldier or a
sailor, whose life was equally exposed with that of his superiors, and
100,000*l.* to an admiral or a commander-in-chief, was far from being
impartial.

Arrival of Troops.

The peace having been concluded in 1763, the Conde de Ricla
arrived at the Havana on the 30th of June, bringing the powers conferred by the treaty for the restoration of the British conquests in the
Island of Cuba, and accompanied by General O'Reilly, with four
ships of the line, a number of transports, and 2000 men for the
supply of the garrison. On their arrival they were received by the
English with every demonstration of respect. On the 7th of July
the keys of the city were formally delivered up to the Conde de
Ricla, on whom the government had been conferred, and the English
garrison was embarked on its return to Europe.

The restoration of the Island to the Spaniards is regarded by the
native writers as the true era from whence its aggrandizement and
prosperity are to be dated. It was during the administration of the
first governor that the new fortresses of San Carlos and Atares were
erected, and the enlargement and rebuilding of the Morro and the
Cabañas were begun. The old hospitals were placed on a better
footing, and new ones were built. The court of accounts, and the whole
department of finance, received a fresh impulse and a distinct form;
and an intendant was named, who, among other arrangements, for
the first time established the aduana, and created a custom-house
revenue, the duties having been first levied on the 15th of October,
1764.

The Conde de O'Reilly, as inspector-general of the army, succeeded
in organizing and placing on a respectable footing the regular troops.

as well as the militia of the Island. The city of the Havana having been divided into districts, the streets named, and the houses numbered, the truth came to be known, that the capital contained materials for the formation of a battalion of disciplined white militia. Beginning with the formation of a single company, the governor appointed lieutenants, sergeants, and corporals from the regular troops of the garrison, and, after a personal inspection, he followed the same course with the other companies.

New Battalions are Formed.

Adopting this principle in the other towns of the Island, he soon succeeded in realizing his ideas, and creating a considerable force on which the government had every reason to rely. When the two white battalions of the Havana and Guanabacoa were completed, it was still found that, with the addition of the stationary regiment of regulars and the other troops of the garrison, there would not be a sufficient force for the defence of the capital, so that the idea of forming two other battalions presented itself, the one of blacks, the other of people of color, and was immediately carried into effect.

Don Diego Manrique assumed the supreme command in 1765, but died within a few months after his arrival. He was succeeded in 1766 by Don Antonio Maria Bucarelli, who prosecuted with energy the construction of the fortifications begun by the Conde de Ricla. Bucarely paid great attention to the due administration of justice, and was distinguished by the affability of his manners, the facility he afforded of access to his person, and the readiness with which he heard and redressed the grievances of the people; making it a boast that he had succeeded in adjusting differences and compromising law suits which had been pending for forty years.

When afterward appointed viceroy of New Spain, the minister for the department of the Indies announced to him, by command of the king, as an unexampled occurrence, that during the whole period of his administration not a single complaint against him had reached the court of Madrid. Another of his merits with the people was the gentleness and address with which he effected the expulsion of the

Jesuits, who had come to the Island with Don Pedro Agustin Morel, and had acquired there large possessions. The church attached to their seminary is that which is now the cathedral of the Havana.

On the promotion of Bucarelli in 1771, the Marques de la Torre was named his successor, and became one of the most popular captains-general who have ever administered the government. He was replaced in 1777 by Don Diego Jose Navarro, who introduced great improvements in the administration of justice, and the police of the tribunals, and in regulating the duties and functions of the *abogados, escribanos, procuradores, tasadores*, and other officers and dependents of the courts of law, in which the greatest abuses had previously and have since prevailed.

Attempt to Recover the Floridas.

The base and deteriorated coin, which had been for some time in circulation, was also called in and abolished in the time of Navarro. In the course of the war which had again broken out between England and Spain, an expedition was prepared at the Havana for the recovery of the Floridas, which produced the surrender of Pensacola, and the submission of the garrison. This gave rise to a belief that the English would make reprisals on Cuba or Porto Rico, and led to the dispatch of reinforcements on a large scale to the garrison of the Havana.

The peace of 1783 soon followed, on which Lord Rodney prepared to return to England; and taking the Havana in his way, Prince William Henry, afterward William IV., having obtained leave from the admiral to go on shore, was so delighted with the city and the entertainments that were offered him, that he remained there three days, and did not return, if we may believe the Spanish writers, until Lord Rodney sent to his royal highness to say, that if he did not re-embark immediately, the squadron would set sail, and leave him behind. The Spanish general of marines, Solano, is said to have given the prince a breakfast which cost him $4000.

During the years which immediately succeeded the peace there appear to have been other changes in the colonial government besides those already noticed, beginning with Don Luis Gonzaga, followed by the Conde de Galves, Don Bernardo Troncoso, Don Jose Espeleta, and Don Domingo Ceballo. In the time of this first Espeleta there was again a great outcry as to the number of lawyers in the colony, and particularly at the Havana, where there were already no less than eighty-five abogados, with an equally liberal proportion of the inferior classes of the profession.

Steps were taken to prevent their increase, and a regulation was enforced on the 19th of November, 1784, prohibiting the admission of candidates and the immigration of professors of jurisprudence from the other colonies; and no lawyer who had studied his profession in Spain was to be allowed to practice it in the courts of the Island until six years at least after he had been called to the bar in the Peninsula.

Brilliant Epoch in Cuba's History.

Don Luis de las Casas arrived as captain-general in 1790, and the period of his administration is represented by all Spanish writers as a brilliant epoch in the history of the Island. To him it is indebted for the institution of the *Sociedad Patriotica*, which has ever since done so much to stimulate the activity and promote the improvement of education, agriculture, and trade, as well as literature, science, and the fine arts, combined with large and liberal views of public policy. To Las Casas, also, is the Island indebted for the establishment of the *Casa de Beneficencia*, having been begun by a voluntary subscription amounting to $36,000. The female department was at first a separate institution, situated in the extra-mural portion of the city, but was added to the other on the completion of the buildings in 1794.

In place of a monument to Las Casas, which he undoubtedly deserved as much as any of his predecessors, an inscription has been conspicuously engraved in the common hall of the school for boys, declaring that on its erection it had been expressly dedicated to the memory of the founder of the institution; reminding the young pupils that he had not only been the founder of the Casa de Beneficencia, but of the first public library, and the first newspaper which had existed in the Island, and of the patriotic and economical society. To increase the commercial prosperity of the Island he had the sagacity to perceive that his object could not be better accomplished than by removing, as far as his authority extended, all the trammels imposed upon it by the old system of privilege and restriction. During his administration, also, large sums were expended in the construction of roads, especially the great Calzada del Horcon and the Calzada de Guadalupe; but since then these highways have fallen so completely out of repair, as for the greater part of the year to have become next to impassable.

The Island Desolated by a Hurricane.

It was Las Casas, also, who introduced the culture of indigo; and during his time the long arrear of causes on the rolls of the courts of justice was greatly reduced. The hurricane, which desolated the Island on the 21st and 22d of June, 1791, afforded Las Casas a fresh opportunity for displaying the great resources of his mind in the promptitude with which he brought relief to the sufferers. In some districts the sudden rise of water in the rivers was most extraordinary, when the limited extent of land from sea to sea is considered.

On the bridge then just finished across the Rio del Calabazal the water rose to the height of thirty-six feet above the parapets; and in the town of San Antonio, where the wells are sunk into the bed of a subterraneous river, the water rushed up through the artificial openings, and inundated the whole country.

The French Revolution having communicated its irresistible impulse to the western parts of St. Domingo, the cabinet of Madrid took the alarm, and from the Havana and Santiago, Vera Cruz, the Caracas, Maracaybo, and Porto Rico, collected a force amounting altogether to 6000 men, the object of which was to suppress the insurrection. The sanguinary struggle which ensued, and the reverses which befell the Spanish troops, belong to another place. Suffice it here to say, by way of memorandum, that the interest of the Spanish Government in the Island of St. Domingo was definitely terminated by the treaty of Basilea soon afterward concluded with the French republic.

It was to the energetic measures of Las Casas, at the time of this revolution in St. Domingo, that the Island of Cuba was indebted for the uninterrupted maintenance of its tranquillity, in spite of the univer- sal persuasion that a conspiracy had been formed at the instigation of the French, among the free people of color, to provoke a similar revolution in Cuba.

Important Changes and Benefits.

On the occasion of his leaving the Island in December, 1796, a formal eulogium on his merits as Captain-General was recorded in the archives of the Ayuntamiento of the Havana, in which are enumerated the great benefits he had conferred on the community; among which the most prominent are the discouragement of gam- bling; the arrest of vagrants and vagabonds; the clearing of the jails of greater criminals, and the acceleration of the ends of justice in civil causes; the abandonment of a large portion of his own emolu- ments for the erection and support of the *Casa de Beneficencia* and other charitable institutions; the reduction and pacification of the maroons of Santiago; the suppression of the conspiracy among the people of color; the prohibition of the introduction of foreign negroes who had previously resided in other colonies, and the expulsion of those who had arrived from St. Domingo; the relief of the inhabi- tants from the clothing of the militia; the paving of the streets of the Havana; the making and mending of roads; the building of bridges, and the construction of public walks and alamedas; the erection of a convent, a coliseum, a primary school, a school of chemistry, natu- ral philosophy, mathematics and botany; the improvement of the Plaza de Toros, and the rejection of the profit which his predecessors had derived from the supply of provisions for the troops.

In this farewell eulogium he is also praised for the very question- able virtue of promoting the general prosperity by the copious intro- duction of Bozal negroes from the coast of Africa, which is stated to have greatly extended the cultivation of the sugar-cane, the bread- fruit tree, the cinnamon-tree, and other exotic plants of inestimable value. It is more easy to sympathize in the praises bestowed upon him for the great hospitality he showed to the unfortunate refugees from St. Domingo, and for the exertions he made and the liberality he evinced in the institution of the Patriotic Society, the formation of a public library, the publication of the Diario, and of the *Guia de Forasteros.*

Las Casas, in 1796, was succeeded in the government by the Conde de Santa Clara, whose noble and generous disposition, and the affability of his manners, made the loss of his predecessor less sensibly felt. It is admitted, however, that he gave no encouragement to education, that he had no taste for letters, and that in his time the social emulation which had previously prevailed sunk rapidly into apathy and indifference.

A People of Dilatory Habits.

It is a singular illustration of the dilatory habits of the people, and affords a sort of national characteristic, that for many years after the formal cession to the French of all interest in St. Domingo, the judges who exercised the supreme civil jurisdiction over the Island of Cuba and other Spanish settlements continued to reside in the ceded territory, so that, in consequence of the recommencement of hostilities with England, all communication by sea was so interrupted as to interpose an insurmountable barrier to the exercise of the right of appeal, and to the ordinary administration of justice. The royal cedula, for the removal of this tribunal to Puerto Principe, is dated on the 22d of May, 1797 ; but it does not appear at what precise date the actual translation took place.

Santa Clara was succeeded, in 1799, by the Marques de Someruelos, whose administration continued for a much longer period than the five years to which, by the practice, if not by a formal regulation of the Spanish government, the term of service of the captains-general of the colonies has been usually limited. The public works which serve to commemorate the administration of Someruelos are the old theatre and the public cemetery; the execution of which last was confided to the bishop, who pursued the object with zeal, and the work was completed on the 2d of February, 1806.

Its extent is not great, containing only 22,000 square yards; but the walls, the chapel, and the gateway, are on a scale which infers the outlay of a large sum of money. The chapel is ornamented with a painting in fresco representing the Resurrection, with the motto, " Ecce nunc in pulvere dormiam." Someruelos was thought by some to be stern and severe toward the poorer classes of society, and to reserve all his affability and condescension for the rich. On the occasion, however, of the great fire of 1802, which destroyed the populous suburb of Jesus Maria, leaving no less than 11,300 individuals without a roof to shelter them, the Marques, moved by their distress, circumambulated the town, going actually from door to door to petition for their relief.

Prospect of Another Invasion.

The belief again gained ground at the Havana, in 1807, that the English government contemplated a descent on the Island; and measures were taken in consequence to put it in a more respectable state of defence, although, from want of funds in the treasury, and the scarcity of indispensable supplies, the prospect of an invasion was sufficiently gloomy. The militia and the troops of the garrison were carefully drilled, and companies of volunteers were formed wherever materials for them could be found. The French, also, not content with mere preparations, made an actual descent on the Island, first threatening Santiago, and afterward landing at Batabano.

The invaders consisted chiefly of refugees from St. Domingo; and their intention seems to have been to have taken possession with a view to colonize and cultivate a portion of the unappropriated, or at least unoccupied, territory on the south side of the Island, as their countrymen had formerly done in St. Domingo. Without recurring to actual force, the captain-general prevailed on them to take their departure by a peaceful offer of the means of transit either to St. Domingo or to France.

The news of the abduction, by Napoleon, of the royal family of Spain reached the Havana by a private opportunity, at the moment when the cabildo was in session, when every member of it took a solemn oath to preserve the Island for its lawful sovereign. The official intelligence did not reach the city till the 17th of July, 1808; when it was brought from Cadiz by the Intendant Don Juan de Aguilar y Amat, who arrived in the American ship "Dispatch." The colonial government immediately declared war against Napoleon; and on the 20th, King Ferdinand VII. was proclaimed with general applause. The intelligence from Spain and the resolution of the captain-general were immediately communicated to all the colonial authorities in Spanish America.

Pretensions Firmly Resisted.

The events in the Peninsula soon began to be felt at the Havana; but the demands of the French intruders for the recognition of their authority were disregarded, and the public dispatches which came from them were destroyed. The Infanta Doña Carlota made similar pretensions, but these, like those of the French, were firmly resisted.

The foreign trade of the Island was reduced to such an extremity by the events of the war, that the local authorities of the Havana, the ayuntamiento, and the consulado, began seriously to deliberate on the expediency of throwing the trade open, and admitting foreign supplies on the same terms with those from the Peninsula. There was some division of opinion; but the majority were for a free competition on an equal footing between the Spaniard and the foreigner, on the ground that Spain alone was unable to purchase or consume the enormous mass of produce then exported from the Island; and so it was accordingly decided.

On the 21st and 22d of March, 1809, a serious disturbance arose, the object of which was to invite the return of the French to the Island; but this popular movement, although considered dangerous at the time, and viewed with alarm by the captain-general, was speedily put down by the display of firmness and resolution on the part of all who had anything to lose, and by the prompt offer of their personal services for its suppression. Proclamations were issued, a respectable force was collected, and the Marques de Someruelos presented himself in person to endeavor to pacify the discontented.

Tranquillity was restored at the end of the second day, with the loss of only two or three lives; but not without the destruction of a great deal of property. The French settlers in the rural districts were, in this respect, the greatest sufferers; and it had, in consequence, the effect of driving away several thousands of laborious and intelligent colonists, who were already deeply interested in the prosperity of the Island.

Soon after these events a young man arrived from the United States, of whose proceedings and character, as an emissary of King Joseph, the colonial government had been previously informed. This unfortunate person, Don Manuel Aleman, was not even suffered to land. The alguazils went on board; took possession of his papers and his person; a council of war was immediately assembled; but his fate was determined beforehand, and on the following morning, the 13th of July, 1810, he was brought out to the Campo de la Punta, and hanged for his temerity.

The revolutionary proceedings in the continental provinces of Spain were now in full career toward that independence of the mother-country which they have since achieved. In the meantime, the Island of Cuba enjoyed a degree of tranquillity quite remarkable under the circumstances of the sister colonies. This state of things was naturally, and not unjustly, ascribed to the political prudence and sagacity of the Marques de Someruelos. The colonial authorities petitioned the cabinet of Madrid for the farther prorogation of his government beyond the term to which it had been already extended.

But the very fact of his having given so much satisfaction to the colonists, if we may judge from experience elsewhere, was not likely to operate with the government of the mother-country in deciding on a farther extension of his stay. Instead of acceding to the prayer of the municipal functionaries of the Havana, the government of Madrid thought fit to mark its sense of the interference by instantly recalling the title of " Excellencia," which, on a former occasion, had been granted to the ayuntamiento as a special mark of the royal favor, and of which they were not a little proud.

The western districts of the Island were visited, in 1810, by another of those tremendous hurricanes, which sweep away so much life and property in these tropical regions. The city of the Havana was filled with consternation and dismay; the hopes of an abundant harvest were disappointed; in the harbor, so renowned for its security, the ships of war were driven from their anchors, and no less than sixty merchant vessels were destroyed.

In the time of Someruelos the Casa de Beneficencia was in danger of falling into decay; but in consequence of his earnest intervention, the Junta de Tabacos, which in Spain as in France is a royal mono- poly, consented to purchase 100 slaves, whose labor or whose wages were to furnish funds for the benefit of the institution; thus by an extraordinary perversion making the practice of cruelty and injustice toward one portion of the human family contribute to a work of charity in favor of another. The slaves were first employed in the manufacture of cigars, but have latterly been hired out for daily wages at whatever employment they could obtain.

Outbreak of a Negro Conspiracy.

A negro conspiracy broke out in 1812, which excited considerable alarm in the minds of the landed proprietors. That alarm was attended with its usual consequences: The negro leader, Aponte, and his associates were treated with unsparing severity, such as may be supposed to have been dictated much more by the fears of the *hacen- dados*, than by the strict justice of the case.

The successor of Someruelos was Don Juan Ruiz de Apodaca, afterward Conde de Benadito, who arrived on the 14th of April, 1812; and he, for the first time, combined the command of the naval force on the station with the office of captain-general of the Island. This un- precedented combination arose from the fear of the authors of the constitution of Cadiz, that their work and their representative would not be well received in this aristocratical colony His first duty on his arrival was to proclaim the constitution; and although it doubt- less excited an extraordinary sensation, it was not openly resisted.

The success of Apodaca in Cuba led to his promotion to the rank of viceroy of Mexico; and on the 1st of July, 1816, he was succeeded at the Havana by Lieutenant-General Don Jose Cienfuegos. In his time the third census of the Island was accomplished. This captain-general made himself exceedingly unpopular at the Havana by the severe measures of police he proclaimed and enforced for the suppression of projects of sedition, and for the preservation of the public tranquillity.

He resorted to an expedient which in other great cities would scarcely have become the subject of serious complaint—he caused the streets of the Havana to be lighted ; but this was only a part of the proceeding to which the citizens objected. He insisted, also, on closing up the public thoroughfares immediately after the conclusion of the evening service in the churches ; thus from that early hour confining the inhabitants to their own particular quarter of the city, and giving rise to clamorous representations and to the very disturbances which it was the object of the captain-general to prevent.

Arrival of a Convoy of Troops.

Señor Cienfuegos was for some time disabled by personal infirmity from the active administration of the government, and during that period his functions were performed by Don Juan Maria Hechavarria, as cabo subalterno ; but on the 29th of August, 1819, he was finally relieved by the arrival of his successor, Don Juan Manuel Cajigal, in the Spanish ship of war " Sabina " with a convoy of troops for the supply of the garrison.

The following year, 1820, from the events which took place in the Peninsula, was another period of trial and difficulty for a captain-general of the Havana ; but it is admitted by all parties that Cajigal succeeded, by the prudence and delicacy of his conduct, in avoiding the evils which might have been expected to arise from the difficult and extraordinary circumstances in which he found himself placed.

The extreme affability of his manners, and the perfect readiness with which he received and listened to all who desired to approach him, conciliated universal good will ; and it appears that the high estimation in which he was held by the inhabitants excited in his breast a corresponding feeling, as, on the termination of his com-

19

mand, he applied for and obtained the special grace from the king of being permitted to take up his permanent abode in the Island; and having retired to the town of Guanabacoa, he died there some time afterward, a simple but respected citizen.

The next captain-general was Don Nicolas Mahy, who arrived from Bordeaux in the French frigate "Therese," on the 3d of March, 1821; but such was the turbulence which prevailed in these troublesome times that he proved unequal to the task of controlling the storm, and at length sunk under the difficulties which surrounded him. He died on the 18th of July, 1822, but retained to the last moment of his life the direct administration of the affairs of the government.

Erection of a Famous Temple.

After his death the government was assumed provisionally by the *cabo subalterno*, Don Sebastian Kindelan; and on the 2d of May, 1823, the new captain-general arrived, Don Francisco Dionisio Vives, who was afterward raised to the dignity of Conde de Cuba. It was in his time that the fourth and last census of the Island was accomplished. It was under Vives, also, that the rural militia was organized, and that the construction of the fortresses of Bahia-honda, Mariel, Jaruco, and the Cabañas was begun or completed. It was he who divided the Island into three military departments; and it was under his auspices that the temple was erected on the Plaza de Armas of the Havana, on the very spot where, if tradition is to be believed, the first Christian rite was performed in the New World.

It is doubtless with the view of adding to the solemnity of the occasion that the temple is opened only once a year, on the anniversary of the day that Mass was first said there, in the presence of Columbus, to return thanks to Heaven for the success which had attended his enterprise. It was also in the time of Vives that the two lunatic asylums, *el Departamento de Dementes*, were added to the *Casa de Beneficencia;* and it is recorded of him that he never failed to preside at the meetings of the institution, and to animate by his presence the drooping zeal of his colleagues in the direction.

On the 15th of May, 1832, Don Mariano Roquefort took possession

of the government; and on the 1st of June, 1834, he was succeeded
by Don Miguel Tacon, whose administration terminated on the 16th
of April, 1838, when Don Joaquin de Espeleta, who had for some
time resided at the Havana with the rank of sub-inspector-general of
the troops, and second *cabo subalterno*, was promoted to the rank of
captain-general, not provisionally, as had been usual on former occasions, but *como proprietario*, to use a form of expression in constant
use, as applied to public offices in the language of Castile as well as
in that of France.

General Espeleta marked his career by a straightforward course,
strongly exemplified in his putting down all obnoxious and costly
practices to obtain licenses and passports, which were favored, both
by those preceding and succeeding him, from sordid and ignoble
motives. His uprightness could not, however, wash out the political
stain of his birth; for, by a mere chance, Espeleta was born at
Havana. He was consequently soon removed, and before the regular
term of five years, allotted to such offices in Spanish America.

Met by Opposition.

The Prince of Anglona, the next captain-general in order of time,
was a gentlemanly and courteous chief who, after one year's command in 1841, left the charge of the Island to the noble-minded Don
Geronimo Valdez, a man whose whole life had evinced a consistent
love of liberty, scarcely ever met with in a Spanish soldier, for such
he was. Being informed that there was a conspiracy on foot, and
that many young men talked in a revolutionary strain, he answered:
" I have a powerful army at my command; let the conspirators sally
forth, and I shall destroy them, but not before."

This liberality to the Cubans, and his conciliating course toward
the abolitionist Turnbull, who had landed at an unfortified part of the
Island, for some sinister purpose, among the blacks; and more than
all, his disinterested and faithful observance of the treaties condemning the African slave trade, brought on him the unrestrained attacks
of those engaged or concerned in it as capitalists or officials of government. He was consequently hurried from his station in the most

unceremonious manner, and the party who vainly endeavored to injure his name, charging him with motives treasonable to Spain, found in his successor a man better disposed to forward their selfish and sordid purposes, though for the same reason equally calculated to alienate the hearts of the inhabitants.

Valdez had the courage and honesty to issue, during his short command, upward of a thousand grants of freedom illegally withheld by his predecessors from so many Africans who, according to the treaty, had become free. He left the Palace of the captains-general of Cuba in the same high-minded poverty in which he had entered it.

In 1843, General Leopold O'Donnell took the command of the Island, and never was military despotism more successfully directed to destroy popular franchises, to establish individual oppression beyond the possibility of redress by altering existing institutions, and eminently to satisfy the avaricious thirst of the captain-general and his family and favorites. The bloody page of the negro insurrection, reported in another part of this work, was the most prominent feature of his governorship.

Strange Sources of Wealth.

At the close of one of General O'Donnell's balls, his wife sent for the baker who had supplied the entertainment, to come at 3 o'clock A. M., to take back the loaves not used! The baker refused, saying that he could not sell them except as stale bread, at a very reduced price. To this she replied that she had sent for him at so early an hour that he might have the chance of mixing it with the fresh bread he was to send around to his customers that morning. She was engaged in all kinds of profitable undertakings of the most obscure and common pursuits in life; monopolies of the most repugnant character were introduced for her advantage, based on the unbounded authority of a provincial tyrant. The cleansing of the sewers, and the locality fixed for the reception of the manure and dirt of the city were among the many sources of wealth which she did not scruple to turn to her advantage.

But nothing was so fruitful to this family of dealers, as the slave trade which, it was publicly asserted, furnished emoluments even to the daughter of the captain-general. O'Donnell was part owner of the marble quarries of the Isle of Pines, whither he, by his sole authority, sent to labor a great number of suspected or accused persons, without judgment or sentence passed on them. The agency for obtaining passports, and other services connected with government, as published in the Havana papers, exhibits a degree of immorality and defiance of public opinion hardly to be found in any civilized country.

General Frederico Roncali, graced by one of the numerous titles which Queen Christina has so profusedly and undeservedly bestowed within a very recent period, took the command of the Island in 1848. His ridiculous and perplexed action during the movement of the Round Island expedition, shows how weak the strength of bayonets is, where it is unsupported either by the confidence of the soldiery, or by the love of the people for their rulers.

Spanish Despotism Doomed.

The idea of marching out 4000 men, and stationing them in the central department of the Island, and announcing to the soldiers that they were to receive double pay as soon as the enemy landed, merely because 400 Americans had taken their abode in an island 700 miles off, is a tacit acknowledgment of the impending termination of Spanish rule in Cuba—that tottering column of European despotism in America. General Roncali's incapacity was never made more manifest, however, than in his management of the Rey affair. Don Cirilo Villaverde, author of a novel entitled " Cecilia Valdez," and other literary works, being accused of corresponding with the editor of the Cuban paper called La Verdad, was confined to the Havana prison during his trial, which he had no reason to expect should be fair or favorable in its results to him.

While there, a fraudulent bankrupt, by name Fernandez, being on the eve of escaping, through promises made to the jail-keeper Rey, of sharing with him the imaginary spoils of his bankruptcy, Mr. Villaverde succeeded in availing himself of the same opportunity to fly, and save himself, rather than trust to his innocence or the irregularity and corruption of Spanish military justice. The result, fully establishing the moral weakness of a government whose very agents turn against it, served to excite the anger and spiteful revenge of Roncali.

He therefore succeeded, through the consul at New Orleans, Don Carlos España, in abducting the jail-keeper, who was thereby destined to be severely punished, or generously rewarded should he act as witness against such influential creoles as were suspected of dissatisfaction to the Spanish government. It is not necessary to add anything further on this subject. The American public are sufficiently acquainted with the subsequent history of this ominous, sacrilegious and insulting act of the authorized menial of a European monarch on the heretofore respected soil of America.

Whatever moral qualities and honest wishes some of the captains-general may have possessed, they were compelled to follow out the restrictions and spoliations commenced by Tacon. The path of despotism, when justified by the national excuse of holding a distant colony, must always be one of inevitable and progressive oppression.

The historical sketch of Cuba is here concluded. The next chapters are designed to furnish an absrtact of its political history, including a notice of a formidable insurrection, with an account of the remarkable policy which has brought the Island to its present miserable condition.

CHAPTER XXII.

The Tyrannical Rule of Spain.

PREVIOUS to the eighteenth century, the history of the Island of Cuba is mostly occupied with accounts of the settlements commenced by the first Governor, Diego Velasquez; the noble defence of the Cazique Athuei, who was burned alive by order of the former; and the usual repartimientos or distribution of the territory and Indians among the Spanish settlers, which, through excess of labor, hastened the depopulation of the country. During that early period is also noticed the sailing of expeditions to more recently discovered and alluring regions; the beginning of the African slave trade, and the occasional descent and depredations of the buccaneers. The latter were so bold, from the scant population and absence of fortifications, that they carried off at one time the venerable Bishop Cabezas Altanurano, and at another, the very bells of the church and the cannons of the castle at Santiago.

Soon after the royal decree of 1530, liberating the native Indians, the remnants of this unfortunate race appeared to have congregated in towns such as Guanabac a, Guaisabana, Ovejas, and Caneyesarriba, and to have applied their efforts to simple husbandry and grazing.

But the advance of Cuba must have been extremely limited or doubtful, since the Bishop Almendares estimated the population of all the towns and cities in 1612 at 6,700 inhabitants.

The truth lies in the fact that, after having exhausted the Indian population, the Island was only held as a military post on the way to the mines of Mexico, with little else to occupy its reduced population than the raising of cattle on lands not appropriated. Till the latter years of the past century, commerce was not only confined to Spanish merchantmen, but to the periodical voyage of the fleet belonging to

295

the privileged India Company. Foreign trade has only been authorized in the present century, when the European wars, forcing the
Spanish flag from the seas, and the encroachment of contraband
trade, made it impossible to oppose it.

In the laws and municipal rights of Cuba, we notice the same independent and liberal spirit which prevailed in all the settlements of
Spain among the Moors, or elsewhere, as far as the Spanish settlers
and their descendants were concerned. Thus in the sixteenth and
seventeenth centuries, public assemblies of citizens were held to elect
the members of the corporations; free and bold charges were made
and sustained against governors; and no taxation was permitted
which was not sanctioned by these bodies, who exercised the same
prerogatives in the Spanish peninsula, during the long suspension of
representative government.

Peculiar Notions and Prejudices.

As to the commercial restrictions which prevented the growth of
this beautiful garden of America, they did not originate in any right,
expressed or implied, to control the fate of Cuba, on the part of the
European provinces, but in the peculiar notions of the age on
matters of political economy. Equally injudicious was the system
observed in the internal trade and relations between the several
Spanish provinces themselves, whose wealth and physical advance
are to this day obstructed by antiquated prejudices. Aside, therefore, from the measures adopted to nationalize the commerce and
trade of Cuba, or rather to direct their course by legislation, there
was not, until the last twenty years, any serious precedent or open
effort to justify a difference between the political rights of the Cubans
and the Spaniards on the soil of Cuba.

Were the conquest held as the foundation of such difference, the
privilege should certainly attach to the descendants of those who
shed their blood and used their means in the acquisition of the country—not to the emigration, much less to the salaried officers of the
government.

The recognition of the popular principle in the Sociedad Patriotica and Consulado, established near the close of the eighteenth century, and the vast influence derived therefrom, and which, in after times, gave a liberal tinge to the local administration, is especially worthy of notice.

Struggling for her own independence, and boldly confronting the ambitious and mighty chieftain of the age, Spain, at the opening of the nineteenth century, appeared in a noble attitude.   Actuated by the most sacred impulses of patriotism, and intensely engaged in the wars and policy of Europe, she could not and did not refuse whatever was requested by the Cuban assemblies.

Loyalty to the Mother Country.

Cuba, on her part, repaid the liberality of the mother-country by an unwavering loyalty.   Unseduced by the alluring prospect of independence, and undismayed by repeated invasions from foreign powers, she shut her eyes to the former, and boldly resisted the latter, at the liberal expense of the treasures of the Island, and the lives of the inhabitants.

This brings us to a period marked by fluctuations in the political history of Spain and her dependencies, and it is now to be seen what were their effect upon Cuba.

The political changes adopted in Spain in 1812 and 1820 were productive of similar changes in the Island; and when in both instances the constitution was proclaimed, the perpetual members of the municipalities were at once deprived of office, and their successors elected by the people.   The provincial assembly was called, and held its sessions.   The militia was organized; the press made entirely free, the verdict of a jury deciding actions for its abuses; and the same courts of justice were in no instance to decide a case a second time.

But if the institution of the consulado was very beneficent during Ferdinand's absolute sway, the ultra-popular grants of the constitutional system, which could hardly be exercised with quiet in Spain, were ill-adapted to Cuba, though more advanced in civilization, stained with all those vices that are the legitimate curse of a country

long under despotic sway.   That system was so democratic that the
king was deprived of all political authority.   No intermediate house
of nobility or senators tempered the enactments of a single elective
assembly.

This sudden change from an absolute government, with its usual
concomitant, a corrupt and debased public sentiment, to the full
enjoyment of republican privileges, served only to loosen all the ties
of decency and decorum throughout the Spanish community.   Infi-
delity resulted from it ; and that veil of respect for the religion of
their fathers, which had covered the deformity of such a state of
society, was imprudently thrown aside.   As the natural consequence
of placing the instruments of freedom in the hands of an ignorant
multitude, their minds were filled with visions of that chimerical
equality which the world has never yet realized.

The Rich Arrayed Against the Poor.

The rich found themselves deprived of their accustomed influence,
and felt that there was little chance of obtaining justice from the
common people (in no place so formidable as in Cuba, from the
heterogeneous nature of the population), and who were now, in a
manner, arrayed against them throughout the land.   They, of course,
eagerly wished the return of the old system of absolute rule.   But
the proprietors only asked for the liberal policy which they had
enjoyed at the hands of the Spanish monarch ; not, most surely, that
oppressive and nondescript government which, by separating the
interest of the country from that of her nearest rulers, and destroying
all means of redress or complaint, thrust the last offspring of Spain
into an abyss of bloodshed and ruin, during the disgusting exercise
of military rule, in punishing by the most arbitrary and cruel measures, persons suspected of engaging in an apprehended servile insurrection.

During the second period of democratic or what was called constitutional government, which commenced in 1820, the masonic societies came into vogue as they did in the mother-country.   They
adopted different plausible pretexts, though, to speak the truth, they

were little more than clubs for amusement and revelry. One of them, called the "*Soles de Bolivar*," went so far as to discuss whether, in case of a Colombian invasion, it would be more expedient to avoid a collision in the presence of the slaves, by giving way peaceably before the invading army.

Happily for Cuba, and certainly in consequence of the judicious interference of the United States, which foresaw in the preservation of its tranquillity the advantages of a fruitful commerce, the invasion did not take place. The difficulty of annexation, from the lesser influence the United States then possessed among nations and the controlling importance of the shipping interest in our country, made it unadvisable for Cuba to launch into a revolution unsustained, and in this way to experience a severe scourge, which, at that time, would have proved the principal if not the only fruits of independence to the first generation of its recipients. Under any circumstances the subsequent jealous policy of the Spanish government has been altogether unwarranted.

Schemes to Keep Cuba a Dependent Province.

A respectable portion of the old Spaniards residing in Cuba, were themselves desirous of upholding the constitutional system in the Island which they saw tottering in Spain. General Vives, who commanded at that time, regarded the circumstance with anxious solicitude, and very reasonably inferred that, if the constitution of 1812 was sustained in Cuba after the king's absolute power was acknowledged in Spain, the consequences would be fatal to its dependence, however rational and honest the views of the constitutionalists might be considered.

Hence his strenuous efforts in 1824, after the restoration of Ferdinand, to make the most of the wild and varying schemes which had been proposed in the " *Soles de Bolivar*," under the democratic institutions, and the relaxation of the reins of government. The greatly reduced Spanish military force at that time in the Island, and the fact that much of it consisted of regular regiments and native militia, are sufficient proof that to the solid good sense of the inhabitants, rather than any show of strength, should be attributed the immediate disappearance of those germs of disquietude. Not even the weakness of General Kindelan could induce the planters to lose sight of their chief interest.

Prosecutions and Imprisonments.

Though General Vives subsequently desired to impress the constitutional party with the idea that they might be carried farther than they meant to go, and with that view took especial care that a well-concerted scheme for throwing off the Spanish yoke should appear to have been devised, it must be acknowledged that notwithstanding he caused the prosecution and imprisonment of many individuals, and occasionally the ruin and misery of their families, he oftentimes also interfered to mitigate the appalling and unavoidable excesses of those menials of government who are every ready, under such circumstances, to exceed the wishes of the leading statesmen, and to make political difficulties subservient to the vilest purposes.   That which should have warned the Spanish ministry of the inexpediency of establishing such inappropriate institutions, brought upon the Island all its subsequent misfortunes; namely, the Royal Order of 1825.

By this order Cuba was placed under martial law; and the captain-general was invested "with the whole extent of power granted to governors of besieged towns."

The sad effects of this royal order, which the king only meant to be observed temporarily, and under a strict responsibility, "le mas estrecta responsibilidad," were not immediately felt. "Truth and justice compel me to assert," says one of the most enlightened Cubans, on being rejected from the Cortes, in common with all the deputies from the province, "that notwithstanding the terrible authority conferred on the captain-general by this royal order, Vives, who then held that office, far from putting it in execution during his long government, discovered that its application would be equally disadvantageous to Cuba and Spain.   Under a mild and conciliatory policy this Island became the refuge of many unhappy proscripts, who were expelled from the Peninsular territory by the arm of tyranny."

The judicious administration of the Count Villanueva, which had undoubtedly an influence materially advantageous to the country, was likewise calculated to make every one forget the depressed political condition to which the new law had reduced the inhabitants of Cuba. Under its fearful and comprehensive provisos, since become the scourge of the land, public bodies were respected. Some of them constantly consulted together on grave subjects, such as the rural and domestic police for the management of slaves, the imposition of taxes and judiciary reform, and enjoyed the privilege of printing their reports, without applying for the consent of the executive officers; and the press was moreover very far from being restricted as it now is.

The Problem of Slavery.

As a proof that the political servitude created by the royal order of 1825 was not intended to be permanent, an extract is made from an article on the dangers of the slave trade, published in a periodical of Havana, in 1832, under the despotic government of Ferdinand, and seven years after issuing the royal order above referred to. Immediately following a very precise detail of facts, of the numbers of imported slaves, and of the relative position of the races, we read:

"Thus far we have only considered the power which has its origin in the numbers of the colored population that surrounds us. What a picture we might draw, if we were to portray this immense body acting under the influence of political and moral causes, and presenting a spectacle unknown in history! We surely shall not do it. But we should be guilty of moral treason to our country, if we were to forget the efforts now making to effect a change in the condition of the African race.

"Philanthropic laws, enacted by some of the European nations, associations of distinguished Englishmen, periodicals solely devoted to this subject, eloquent parliamentary debates whose echoes are constantly repeated on this side the Atlantic, bold exhortations from the pulpits of religious sects, political principles which with lightning rapidity are spreading in both hemispheres, and very recent commotions in several parts of the West Indies, everything is calculated to awaken us from our profound slumber and remind us that we must save our country. And should this our beloved mother ask us what measures we have adopted to extricate her from her danger, what would those who boast themselves her dutiful sons, answer?

" The horrid traffic in human blood is carried on in defiance of the laws, and men who assume the name of patriots, being no other than parricides, cover the land with shackled victims. And as if this were not sufficiently fearful, with criminal apathy, Africans freed and brought to this country by English policy, are permitted to reside in our midst. How different the conduct of our neighbors the Americans!

Political Situation in the United States.

" Notwithstanding the rapid increase of their country; notwithstanding the white has constantly been four-fifths more numerous than the colored population, and have ten and a half millions to offset two millions; notwithstanding the importation of the latter is prohibited from one end of the republic to the other, while European immigration is immense; notwithstanding the countries lying upon their boundaries have no slaves to inspire dread, they organize associations, raise funds, purchase lands in Africa, establish colonies, favor the emigration of the colored population to them, increasing their exertions as the exigency may require, not faltering in their course, and leaving no expedient untried which shall prove them friends of humanity and their country. Not satisfied with these general measures, some states have adopted very thorough and efficient measures. In December, 1831, Louisiana passed a law prohibiting importation of slaves even from other states of the Union.

" Behold the movement of a great people, who would secure their safety! Behold the model you should imitate! But we are told, ' Your efforts are vain. You cannot justly reproach us. Our plantations need hands, and if we cannot obtain negroes, what shall we do?' We are far from wishing to offend a class equally deserving respect and esteem, including many we are happy to call friends. We are habitually indulgent, and in no instance more so than in that before us. The notions and examples to which they have been accustomed, justify in a great measure the part they act, and an immediate benefit and remote danger authorize in others a course of conduct which we wish may never be generally and permanently adopted. We would not rudely censure the motives of the planters.

"Our mission requires us only to remark, that it is necessary to adopt some other plan, since the change in politics is inconsistent with and hostile to the much longer continuance of the illicit traffic in slaves. We all know that England has, both with selfish and humane motives, made and is still making great efforts against it by means of treaties. She is no longer the only power thus engaged, since France is also taking her share in the enterprise.

"The United States will soon appear in the field to vindicate down-trodden humanity. They will adopt strong measures, and persever-ingly pursue the pirate negro-dealer. Will he then escape the vigi-lance of enemies so active and powerful? And even should some be able to do so, how enormously expensive must their piracy be! It is demonstrable that the number of imported negroes being then small, and their introduction subject to uncommon risks, their cost would be so enhanced as to destroy the motive for preferring slave labor.

"A proper regard to our true interests will lead us to consider henceforth other means of supplying our wants, since our present mode will ultimately paralyze our resources and be attended with baneful consequences. The equal distribution of the two sexes in the country, and an improved treatment of them, would alone be suf-ficient, not merely to prevent a diminution of their number, but greatly to increase it. But the existing disproportion of the sexes forbids our indulging in so pleasing a hope. We shall, however, do much to effect our purposes by discontinuing certain practices, and adopting a system more consonant to the good principles that should be our guide.

"Would it not be advisable to try some experiments that we may be able to compare the results of cultivating cane by slaves, with such other method as we may find it expedient to adopt?

"If the planters could realize the importance of these propositions to their welfare, we should see them striving to promote the introduction of white and the exclusion of colored hands. By forming associations, raising funds, and in various ways exerting themselves vigorously in a cause so eminently patriotic, they would at once overcome the obstacles to the introduction of white foreigners, and induce their immigration by the guarantees of good laws and the assured tranquillity of the country.

A Serious Emergency.

" We may be told that these are imaginary plans, and never to be realized. We answer that they are essays, not difficult or expensive, if undertaken, as we suggest, by a whole community. If we are not disposed to make the voluntary trial now, the day is at hand when we shall be *obliged* to attempt it, or abandon the cultivation of sugar. The prudent mariner on a boisterous ocean prepares betimes for the tempest and defies it. He who recklessly abandons himself to the fury of the elements is likely to perish in the rage of the storm.

"'How imprudent,' some may exclaim, 'how imprudent,' to propose a subject which should be forever buried in ' lasting oblivion ! ' Behold the general accusation raised against him who dares boldly avow new opinions respecting these matters Unfortunately there is among us an opinion which insists that ' silence ' is the true policy. All feel the evils which surround us, are acquainted with the dangers, and wish to avoid them. Let a remedy be suggested and a thousand confused voices are simultaneously raised ; and a significant and imploring ' Hush ! '—' hush ! ' is heard on every side.

" Such infatuation resembles his who conceals the disease which is hurrying him to speedy death, rather than hear its unpleasant history and mode of cure, from his only hope, the physician's saving science. Which betrays censurable apathy, he who obstinately rushes headlong to the brink of a mighty precipice, or he who gives the timely warning to beware ? Who would not thus save a whole community perhaps from frightful destruction ? If we knew most positively that the disease were beyond all hopes of cure, the knowledge of the fact would not stay the march of death, while it might serve but as a terrifying annunciation of his approach.

" If, however, the sick man is endowed with a strong constitution, that with timely prescription promises a probable return of health, it would be unpardonable to act the part of a passive spectator. We heed not that the selfish condemn, that the self-admiring wise censure, or the parricidal accuse us. Reflections of a higher nature guide us, and in the spirit of our responsible calling as a public writer, we will never cease to cry aloud, ' Let us save our country—let us save our country ! ' "

Nothing would more forcibly illustrate the rapid encroachment of despotism in the Island than the publication of a document like the above, or anything discreditable, or disparaging to the slave-dealers. Whoever should dare make the experiment, would most certainly do it at the risk of his life. Further comment on the progress of tyranny is unnecessary

20

CHAPTER XXIII.

A Wily Old General.

NOT to lose sight of the order of events, it must be borne in mind that immediately after the overthrow of the constitution, and precisely at the time the persecution for revolutionary opinions commenced under the order of 1825, the country was in its most flourishing and healthy period. The fruits of the several acts for promoting the country's welfare and the development of its resources, which owed their origin to corporations, before they had lost their vitality, had been gathered. Moreover, the judicious and liberal policy already described was continued by the intendant, who could then act with great independence. As chief of the financial department, the Count de Villanueva regulated the mode of keeping accounts, corrected abuses, introduced greater simplicity in the collection of taxes, and established several facilities beneficial to the merchants.

By means of his great influence at Madrid, he was enabled to supersede the captain-general in the presidency of the consulado, and directing the labors of that body, he made them subserve the development and improvement of the country. Availing himself of the general wealth, and of the increasing agriculture of the Island, he daringly taxed its products, and it is generally believed that it was during his administration, taxes of various kinds were imposed for the first time without the consent of those to be affected by them. He represented " de facto " the people of Cuba; was the chief fiscal agent; the friend and adviser of the captain-general; the favorite of Ferdinand's government.

A skillful and mighty authority like his could, at such a period, draw abundant resources from the country for the metropolis, and promote at the same time the interests of the former by reforming

306

abuses. To both these objects were his exertions successfully directed. To his discriminating judgment it was very evident that a vast territory, capable of great agricultural production, could not maintain its position, much less make progress, should its commerce be again limited to the mother-country. He was aware that the probable results of such limitation would be the total annihilation of the surplus revenue, of which they were so desirous at court; the immediate paralysis of agriculture, the fountain of the Island's wealth; and a very extensive contraband trade.

Public Improvements.

Villaneuva had the waters of the Husille brought into the city by a well-devised though costly plan; the roads near Havana macadamized, and a mud-machine erected to clear the anchorage and preserve the wharves. He established the more modern and rational system of selling at auction to the lowest bidder the performance of various services, particularly for the government or the public. He enlarged the Spanish navy from the navy-yard of Havana; the regular intercourse between the two countries by mail packets was his suggestion, and the Güines railroad is a crowning, ever-memorable and enduring monument of his enterprise and genius.

Amidst these improvements, beneficial to Spain and the Island, the count was enabled to make frequent and heavy remittances to the general treasury in Spain, which was so received by them that the demands were gradually augmented without any regard to the means of meeting them, and the inevitable consequence was the sacrifice of the necessities of the Island to the urgency of their payment. Thus it happened that the Bank of St. Ferdinand, the establishment of which was one of the acts which do honor to Villanueva, had no opportunity of doing any service to the public, as its capital was specially sent for from Madrid.

In brief, Count Villanueva's administration can in no way be better appreciated than by bearing in mind that whatever liberal and enlightened views he carried into practical effect, he had nothing similar to guide him or excite his emulation in all the Spanish territory.

His power in Cuba was great, his influence in Madrid had no equal, and his credit abroad was such that his promise and acceptance was a source of revenue at court. The authority of the Captain-General himself being eclipsed by his, it is certainly no matter of surprise that public bodies and individuals should have sunk into insignificance.

It was in such a state of political weakness and general prosperity that the enactment concerning the holding of property, which was the first liberal act of Christina's regency, found Cuba. Under it the inhabitants of the Island observed, as they always had done, the laws promulgated in the mother country. A number of members were added to the municipalities, equal to the number of hereditary members, and the former were by express proviso to be individuals who were highest on the tax list. Thus formed, these corporations elected the deputies who represented the interests of the Island at the Spanish Congress.

Deprived of Deputies to Madrid.

This slight political change, which enabled the corporations of Havana, Santiago de Cuba, and Puerto Principe to name three deputies in the "estamentos" without other free institutions, was certainly not calculated to alarm the royal authority, however jealous it might be supposed. Three votes, more or less, could not of course cause any uneasiness; but it is ever the consequence of free institutions, in just proportion to their worth, to diminish the importance of individuals. Here, then, was one of the causes of that strenuous opposition so successfully exerted to deprive the Island of deputies to Madrid.

Such a refusal, where there is an immense amount of productive capital to be benefited or injured, or destroyed by the enactments of government, and where the colony is not even allowed delegates to represent its interests at court, has no parallel in any civilized country professing to approve of liberal institutions.

The Island was at that time governed by General Tacon, whose short-sighted, narrow views, and jealous and weak mind, were joined to an uncommon stubbornness of character. Never satiated with power, it was through his influence that the wealthy portion of the community was divested of the privileges conferred on them by the estatuto. He even deprived the old municipalities of Havana of the faculty of naming the under-commissaries of police.

In his own immodest report of his reign, as it was justly termed, he enumerated the very extensive and costly buildings and public works he had constructed, and from the singular manner in which he accounts for procuring the ordinary means, we must suppose he had the power of working miracles. To sustain his absolute government by trampling on every institution, was the necessary consequence of his first violent and unjustifiable act. It was consequential upon his own and his followers' efforts.

Outrages on Personal Liberty.

For any power, any institution, not dependent on the palace of the captain-general, might be the means of denouncing abuses, of exposing the real deformity of his and their pretended patriotism ; and the numberless parasites whose interest ever was to blind the royal eyes, magnified the virtues of their hero, while they were rapidly accumulating fortunes at his side. In order to obtain credit in the management of the police, he displayed a despotic and even brutal activity in the mode of exacting from the under-officers, distributed in the several wards of the city, under personal responsibility, the apprehension and summary prosecution of criminals. They soon found that there would be no complaint, provided they acted vigorously and brought up prisoners. So far from presuming their innocence, or requiring proof of their crimes, those who were once arrested were put to the negative and difficult task of proving their innocence. The more unwarrantable the acts of his subalterns the more acceptable to him, since they, in his opinion, exhibited the energy of his authority. They trembled in his presence, and left it to persecute, to invent accusations, to imprison, and spread terror and desolation among the families of the land !.

It is but just to add, that the banditti and thieves and professed gamblers were terrified by his sweeping scythe, and became much more modest than they had been during the brief government of the weak and infirm General Roquefort, the predecessor of Tacon. The timid and short-sighted merchant who perceived this reform, did not comprehend or appreciate the illegality of the system, nor its pernicious effects on the future destinies of the country, and was the first to justify the man who dared interpose himself between the Spanish monarchs and their subjects, to silence every complaint of the latter, and to say to the former, " You shall never hear the petitions of your American vassals contrary to my pleasure."

The political servitude at that moment implanted in the country was new, and of course excited discontent, which was not unfrequently vented in the random conversation of young men.

Poor Carlist Prisoners.

The consequence of all this was, a regular system of espionage. The prisoners were distributed in the castles, because the jails were insufficient to contain them. In the dungeons were lodged nearly six hundred persons, the cause of whose detention nobody knew ; a fact authentically proved by a casual circumstance. In the streets, in the highways and fortresses, under a scorching sun, and during the unhealthy season, the poor Carlist prisoners, having surrendered themselves, trusting to the faith of liberals, were suffered to sicken and sink miserably into a premature grave.

Let it not be supposed, however, that his political persecution was confined to the enemies of the liberal institutions then existing in Madrid. The contrary may be adduced from the inconsiderate protection extended by him to the famous friar Cirilo Almeda, of whose machinations he appeared to approve, and from the fact that events favorable to the queen were at a certain period not permitted to appear in the distorted press of Havana.

His creed was soon ascertained. He considered those whom he thought likely to tear the veil from his tyranny, the veritable traitors, the enemies of the throne, and the advocates of independence in Cuba. He destroyed all freedom of discussion in the municipal body, usurped its powers, and frightened away such members as he thought would not bend sufficiently to his will. He constructed an enormously high, massive, level road through the widest avenue of the city, which has since been removed, at the expense of the same suffering community who had to pay for its erection, and to suffer its unhealthy effects while it remained.

General Tacon moreover established a privileged market for selling meat and fish, to the detriment of the public and the public revenue, and for the profit of himself and his nearest friends. Among other things it will there be seen how a man living at the table and board of Tacon, was subsequently found to be interested in the contract for the meat and fish market, without its being absolutely binding on him to perform the condition of paying in his amount of stock in order to be entitled to his share of the profits, which he did nevertheless receive.

A System of Robbery.

It will likewise be found that the party to that contract was illegally preferred to the more regular bidders. It may further be ascertained from that work that when the contractors obtained the grant and commenced exacting unauthorized fees, to the great injury of the public, a suit was instituted to investigate and reform the abuse at the tribunal of one of the alcaldes, and that the record was claimed and taken possession of by Tacon, who was charged with causing it to disappear, as it was stated in his successor General Espeleta's official answer, that it was not to be found in the archives of the captain-generalship.

Notwithstanding General Tacon's efforts at the first election under the estatuto, the voice of his Excellency Don Juan Montalvo y Castillo was raised in Madrid at the Cortes, and the misconduct of the former partially exposed. As it continued, Messrs. Armas and Saco were named for the second congress during his government, both very enlightened and able men, well acquainted with the circumstances, and friendly to the welfare of the Island, and as much opposed to the ultra-liberal or revolutionary ideas as desirous of removing from the Spanish peninsular government the shame and discredit of such lawless proceedings on the part of the chief metropolitan authority.

To discover imagined conspiracies, to commence suits blindly approved by his assessor, to expatriate, to vex, to imprison the citizens, these were Tacon's noble exploits. His artful reports found credit at court. He was therefore continued in his government, and the Spanish Cortes in 1836, by a majority exceeding thirteen votes, shut their doors, which had always been opened to American representatives, against the deputies of the Island, then elected and at Madrid. They were obliged to return without being allowed the privilege of uttering their grievances. This was the single but serious act of usurpation which robbed the descendants of the Island's conquerors of all interference in its administration and tributary system.

Some time after the oath to the constitution had been taken at Madrid in 1837, the Spanish General Lorenzo, commanding in St. Jago, encouraged by the encomiums and rewards conferred in former times and in similar instances, on such authorities as first followed the impulse given at the court of a political change, thought it his duty to conform to the plan most approved by all parties, royalist or liberal. viz.: to repeat the cry raised at the seat of government.

Brazen Display of Authority.

He therefore proclaimed the constitution. The wily old general who had so successfully deprived the country of all representative or delegate system, would not of course very quietly allow his fabric to be leveled to the ground. He made an ostentatious display of his authority, and though well satisfied of the pacific views of the eastern part of the Island, insisted upon fitting out an expensive expedition, which cost the inhabitants more than $500,000, and would have it proceed, notwithstanding that the commissioners sent by Lorenzo made a formal promise that the eastern part of the Island should preserve their system until the Queen decided, or would obey at once Tacon's order to annul the constitution, provided an amnesty were granted for the single act of proclaiming the same, their sole offence.

General Tacon again made use of his favorite weapon against the Islanders, applying it to General Lorenzo and the intendant of Havana, by perfidious suggestions calculated to impair their well-proven loyalty to their sovereign. Such improbable stories, the ill-disguised animosity of his passionate language, the cognizance by some impartial Peninsular tribunals of some of his grossly-imagined plans of conspiracy, all had an influence to force the Spanish court to acknowledge, without, for reasons of policy, publicly avowing it, the irregular and disorderly course of Tacon's administration, and he was removed from office.

The removal of General Tacon is said to have been effected by a compromise between the ministry and Olivar, acting as agent for Villaneuva, in which the rights of the Cubans were sacrificed to the latter's personal ambition. It was then agreed that no political assembly, or any rights whatever, should be allowed the Cubans, but that Tacon should be removed. This discreditable compromise was the undoubted origin of the immediate discontent and subsequent rapid adoption of the principle of annexation through the Island. Nothing was more efficient in drawing the mask from his face than the unskillfulness of Joaquin Valdez, his standing conspiracy-witness and confidential agent, who in framing one of his plans got into a strange dilemma by apprehending the intendant of Cadiz, and other respectable old Spaniards, supposed to be concerned in the plot.

It should be mentioned, to the honor of the Spanish name, that at the subsequent sittings of the Cortes, and before the removal of Tacon, as if the injuries which had been inflicted on Cuba called for immediate redress, it was generally admitted as a matter of course, what has since been artfully withdrawn from the sight of the congress, that the political condition of that distant colony should be attended to and ameliorated without delay.

A generous and high-minded Spaniard, Don Antonio Benavide, equally loyal to his country and desirous of the welfare of its inhabitants, clearly and ably insisted upon the adoption of any system in lieu of the omnipotence of the Captain-General. But the zeal and high sense of justice entertained by the congress could give no relief, where the agents of the local government were active, and the oppressed country had no delegates to maintain her rights.

The only result was a royal order authorizing Tacon to call a junta,

which he took care should be formed to his liking generally, composed of authorities named by government, in its pay, with three or
four private individuals among the general's pliant tools. This junta
was to propose special laws for the government of the Island. The
consequence was exactly what might have been expected. The chief
soon perceived that, however yielding the members might be, they
must draw up some rules ostensibly to restrain his untamed will, or
excite the ridicule of even the Spanish court.

After calling together and dispersing them instantly, under a show
of separating them into committees, he rendered the whole attempt
inefficient, and feigning fear of danger from the plots of the white
population, caused every feeling of justice to Cuba to be forgotten in
Spain. The only proposition which seems to have transpired from
the sitting of that strange, transitory, and expensive junta, was to
make the Island a vice-royalty and Tacon vice-king. Ludicrous as
as it may appear, it is no less true.

Black Men in British Uniform.

Notwithstanding it was under free institutions that Spain granted
the establishment of the mixed Anglo-Spanish tribunal at Havana,
for the cognizance of prizes taken from the African trade, it was
when the public bodies of the Island were without sufficient energy
to raise their spontaneous protest on political questions, that the Castilian name was humbled by the floating fortress which the English
anchored in the port of Havana, as a rallying signal for the blacks,
openly and malignantly avowed, and sufficiently evident from the
fact that it was manned by black men in British uniform.

These soldiers, distributed in the heart of the city, the greater
number liberated from slave-ships by the tribunal, who both during
and subsequently to their apprenticeship were left in the country in
direct communication with their bond-brethren, were the first instruments of spreading discontent among the slave population. Very
far from independent, and from representing the interest of the
wealthy planters, must have been the public bodies of the Island,
who thus patiently saw the germs of violent insurrection sown broad-

cast over the land, without most earnestly assailing the Spanish ministry with their complaints.

It was not, however, until about the year 1835 that the disproportion of the races became alarming. In 1837 General Tacon received an official communication from Madrid, enclosing a copy of a note from the Spanish minister at Washington, containing a vivid picture of the dangers to Cuba from the abolition efforts making in the United States and generally all over the world. He who had heedlessly given new life and development to the policy which Vives had only partially unfolded, and which consisted in separating the old Spaniards from the natives, was now made to feel that the co-operation of the country's *bourgeoisie*, in all their united effort, was requisite to oppose the encroachments of the abolitionists.

Immediate Danger.

The exposition of the minister at Washington, though abounding with contradictory opinions, was, in the main, exact. It predicted immediate danger. No public bodies existing which could be considered as emanating even indirectly from the people, rich or poor, he having discredited and crushed all such institutions, what could he do? He contrived to call a general meeting of the planters in the city of Matanzas, whose very judicious report provided for domestic and rural government, material defence, and funds to carry their plans into effect. The colonization of the Island by white inhabitants, which had been unlawfully terminated, was demanded by this meeting of planters, who also insisted upon the establishment of a rural militia.

In consequence of these requisitions, their resolutions on the first were not carried into execution. The immigration of whites has been materially obstructed by an influential party, who consider it hostile to the introduction of laborers more consonant to their taste and interest. General Valdez was latterly named captain-general, an honest and generous soldier, whose memory is still dear to the liberal party in Spain, wearing many honorable marks of worth, grey in the service of his country, but his capacity undoubtedly impaired by age, joined to a general ignorance of the colonies and of political affairs, common to all the military as a class.

A person observing the progress of English pretensions respecting Cuba, would certainly conclude that Lord Palmerston had himself chosen such a man, who, though beyond the reach of bribery, and incapable of willful wrong to his country, was, from his weakness, a suitable and manageable instrument. Let it, however, be said in his praise, that he had occasion to show that when the captain-general should choose to put an end to the slave trade, it would be in his power to do so.

Soon after his arrival, a series of by-laws made for the government of the slaves was published, wherein, instead of providing for the real circumstances of the occasion, the dominical rights of the master were suddenly attacked, yet not so much, perhaps, by their positive provisos, as by the appearance of interference at a period when the restlessness and uneasiness of the blacks required measures of an entirely contrary nature. The management of a slave country is always a difficult matter. To avoid the commission of great errors, in the condition of Cuba, would have been scarcely less than miraculous.

The actual feelings of the blacks could not, with certainty, be ascertained by individuals who had either recently arrived from Spain, or never attended on the estates but for a few moments, or during excursions of pleasure. Thus it happened, that many judicious planters, judging from the small and gradual changes in the domestic life of the blacks, foresaw the coming storm for years, while the government agent could not comprehend, and resolutely refuted, such opinions as they thought unnecessarily alarming, and decidedly against their interest in the African trade.

Mr. Turnbull, the English consul, who, from his European reputation, would never have been allowed to occupy the post of consul at Cuba, had the Cuban proprietors had an organ of complaint, other than the government agents, concerted incendiary plots, and boldly followed them, notwithstanding the timely interference of Garcia, one of the governors of the city of Matanzas.

CHAPTER XXIV.

Record of Atrocious Deeds.

SEVERAL incidents might be named, evident precursors of an insurrection, which, for many years before the repeated attempts, demanded a change in the system of the whole Island; a change which would have taken place under a government having the means and disposition to ascertain the true state of things.

For the better understanding of the subject, it must be remembered that the ancient balance of influence established by the Spanish law between the military class and the judicial or lettered part of the community, had been altogether lost; the former having been intrusted with every branch of the administration, even to the making of by-laws for the black slave population, which was submitted to the control of government agents, perhaps under the direction of their allies, the slave-dealers.

At the same time an ominous policy commenced; the colored inhabitants were particularly favored; had numerous meetings, called *cabildos*, and enjoyed even greater privileges than the whites—being formed into military bodies for public defence, whereas the whites could not form a militia for their own safety, even in moments of pressing danger, and in those places where the disproportion of the races was most frightful.

Laws were enacted purporting to alleviate the condition of the slaves; an apparent protection, calculated more to harass the owner than to realize the improvemeut of the former, without any attempt to instruct either. This was acompanied with the continuation of the slave trade, and the barbarous political oppression of the native creoles, whose every thought was looked upon with jealous suspicion. It seemed evident that the policy consisted in placing the lives and property of the inhabitants of Cuba in such imminent danger as to choke any feeling of resentment respecting the political changes which the Spanish government adopted for the exclusive advantage of the metropolitan part of the community.

Thus was the dissatisfaction of the blacks fostered. How else can be explained the cause of the progress made in the Island in that respect, and not in those slave-holding countries which surround it, and which, having a more frightful disproportion in numbers between the races, and greater freedom in the press and institutions, were withal enjoying comparative tranquillity ?

Threatened War of Races.

The bonds between master and slave were gradually severed; the affections destroyed; the mutual relations of the races, for which the Spaniards had been always distinguished, were broken; and while every one deprecated the perilous situation of the Cubans, the latter continued unarmed; the slave trade augmented the causes of fear; and no moral reform was adopted to soften the harsh features and discordant views of the subjected or of the dominant race. It seemed as if occasional ruptures, which should awaken the natives to a sense of danger, were the most acceptable offering to the administration.

Such did come to pass from time to time; what was the nature of these disturbances can, perhaps, be best understood by the following extract from the work of the Countess of Merlin, entitled " The Slaves in the Spanish Colonies;" who, though not a solid writer, has a style which savors of her sex, and is quite entertaining. She wrote somewhere about 1840:

" The suavity of manner of the Cuban toward his slave inspires the latter with a respectful feeling, which is akin to worship: there is no limit to this affection; he would murder his master's enemy publicly in the streets at mid-day, and would perish for his sake under torture, without giving a wink. To the slave, his master is his country and his family. The slave takes the family name of his lord; receives his children at their birth; shares with them the food which was prepared by nature in female breasts; serves them in humble adoration from earliest infancy.

" If the master is sick, the slave watches over him day and night; closes his eyes in death, and when this takes place, throws himself sorrowfully on the ground, cries wofully, and with his nails rends his own flesh in despair. But if a vindictive feeling is awakened in his bosom, he recovers his natural ferocity; he is equally ardent in his hatred and in his love; but very seldom does it happen that his master is the object of his revengeful fury.

" When an insurrection is not excited by foreigners (which, by the by, is not often the case), the cause of it may be traced to violent enmity toward the overseer. Here is a fact which proves the moral influence of the masters over the minds of these savages. A few months previous to my arrival, the blacks of the sugar estates of my cousin, Don Rafael, became insurrected. The slaves lately imported from Africa were mostly of the Luccoomee tribe, and therefore excellent workmen, but of a violent, unwieldly temper, and always ready to hang themselves at the slightest opposition in their way.

Protected by Slaves.

" It was just after the bell had struck five, and the dawn of the morning was scarcely visible. Don Rafael had gone over to another of his estates, within half an hour before, leaving behind him, and still in tranquil slumbers, his four children and his wife, who was in a state of pregnancy. Of a sudden the latter awakes, terrified by hideous cries, and the sound of hurried steps. She jumps affrighted from her bed, and observes that all the negroes of the estate are making their way to the house. She is instantly surrounded by her children, weeping and crying at her side.

" Being attended solely by slaves, she thought herself inevitably lost; but scarcely had she time to canvass these ideas in her distracted mind, when one of her negro girls came in, saying, ' Child, your bounty need have no fears; we have fastened all the doors, and Michael is gone for master.' Her companions placed themselves on all sides of their female owner, while the rebels advanced, tossing from hand to hand among themselves, a bloody corpse, with cries as awful as the hissing of the serpent in the desert.

"The negro girls exclaimed, 'That's the overseer's body!' The rebels were already at the door, when Pepilla (this is the name of the lady), saw the carriage of her husband coming at full speed. That sweet soul, who, until that moment, had valiantly awaited death, was now overpowered at the sight of her husband coming unarmed toward the infuriated mob, and she fainted.

"In the meantime, Rafael descends from the vehicle, places himself in front of them, and with only one severe look, and a single sign of the hand, designates the purging house for them to go to. The slaves suddenly become silent, abandon the dead body of their overseer, and, with downcast faces, still holding their field-swords in their hands, they turn round and enter where they had been ordered. Well might it be said, that they beheld in the man who stood before them the exterminating angel.

A Last Effort for Life.

"Although the movement," the countess continues, "had for a moment subsided, Rafael, who was not aware of its cause, and feared the results, selected the opportunity to hurry his family away from the danger. The *quitrin*, or vehicle of the country, could not hold more than two persons, and it would have been imprudent to wait till more conveyances were in readiness. Pepilla and the children were placed in it in the best possible manner; and they were on the point of starting, when a man, covered with wounds, with a haggard, death-like look, approached the wheels of the quitrin, as if he meant to climb by them.

"In his pale face the marks of despair and the symptoms of death could be traced, and fear and bitter anguish were the feelings which agitated his soul in the last moments of his life. He was the white accountant, who had been nearly murdered by the blacks, and having escaped from their ferocious hold, was making the last efforts to save a mere breath of life. His cries, his prayers, were calculated to make the heart faint. Rafael found himself in the cruel alternative of being deaf to the request of a dying man, or throwing his bloody and expiring corpse over his children; his pity conquered; the accountant was placed in the carriage as well as might be, and it moved away from the spot.

"While this was passing on the estate of Rafael, the Marquis of Cardenas, Pepilla's brother, whose plantations were two leagues off, who had been apprised through a slave of the danger with which his sister was threatened, hastened to her aid. On reaching the spot, he noticed a number of rebels, who, impelled by a remnant of rage, or the fear of punishment, were directing their course to the open plains, searching for safety among runaway slaves. The Marquis of Cardenas, whose sense of the danger of his sister had induced him to fly to her help, had brought with him, in the hurry of the moment, no one to guard his person except a single slave.

"Scarcely had the fugitive band perceived a white man, when they went toward him. The marquis stopped his course and prepared to meet them; it was a useless temerity in him against such odds. Turning his master's horse by the bridle, his own slave addressed him thus: 'My master, let your bounty get away from here; let me come to an understanding with them.' And he then whipped his master's horse, which went off at a gallop.

Fell a Victim to his Devotedness.

"The valiant 'JOSE,' for his name is as worthy of being remembered as that of a hero, went on toward the savage mob, so as to gain time for his master to fly, and fell a victim to his devotedness, after receiving thirty-six sword blows. This rising, which had not been premeditated, had no other consequences. It had originated in a severe chastisement, inflicted by the overseer, which had prompted the rebels to march toward the owner's dwelling, to expound their complaint. They begged Rafael's pardon, which was granted, with the exception of two or three, who were delivered over to the tribunals. A remarkable truth of the love of the slaves toward their lord, is the fact of their stopping, in the outset, the engine which was at the time grinding, and preventing the explosion which would otherwise have taken place.

"Not only do the inhabitants of Cuba forward the emancipation of

21

their slaves by procuring for them the means of gaining money, but
they often make the grant without any retribution.   A service of importance, a mark of attachment, the act of nursing the master's child,
assiduous care during the last illness, or the priority of services of
an old member of the family, are all acts rewarded by the gift of
liberty.   Sometimes the slave considers this benefit as a punishment,
and receives it weeping."

Anecdotes of Slaves.

These are very charming ideas.   It is a pity that the countess
should, by entering continually in the field of romance, get so far
from the regions of truth.   This remark, however, applies, in the
paragraphs quoted, only to the assertion that the slaves in any case
objected to being made free, or that such gifts were so common.
There are facts both pleasing to the philanthropist and worthy of
credit.   The following, from the touching pen of the lady of Merlin,
afford a happy illustration of them :

" Though the slave enjoys the right of holding property, at his
death it passes to the master ; but if he leaves children, the proprietor
never deprives them of the inheritance.   It sometimes happens that
the free negro makes his will in favor of his former master.   Here is
an example.   During the scourge of the cholera, an old woman was
attending the sick negroes of my brother.   She had continued in his
service, although she had freed herself many years before.

" Being taken with the disease, she called my brother and said to
him : ' My master, I am going to die.   These eighteen ounces of gold
are for your bounty ; this piece of money for my comrades ; and this
good old man, my husband, also, if your bounty will let him have an
ounce to help him on through life, it is well.'   The poor old woman
did not die, but had a most miraculous escape.

" I will refer to another anecdote, showing the lofty and delicate
feeling in the heart of a slave.   The Count of Gibacoa owned a
slave, who, being desirous of ransoming himself, asked his master
' how much he asked for him ?'   The answer was, ' Nothing ; thou art
free henceforth.'   The negro was silent, looked at his master, wept,

and went off. A few hours afterward he returned, bringing with him a fine *bozal*, or newly-imported African, whom he had purchased with the sum intended for his freedom ; and he said to the count : ' My master, your bounty had one slave before ; it has now two.'

" The blacks become identified with the affairs of their masters, and take part in their quarrels. The captain-general, Tacon, who, during the time of his government in Cuba, performed some few beneficent acts in this colony, but from his harsh and inflexible temper excited much ill-feeling, and took pleasure in humbling the nobility by his despotism, had persecuted the Marquis of Casa Calvo, who died while exiled. Some time afterward, and for the purpose of a magnificent banquet, which Tacon was to give the latter, he solicited the more renowned cooks of the city ; but the best of them was a slave to the Marchioness of Arcos, a daughter of the unfortunate Casa Calvo.

Would not Accept Liberty.

" Dazzled by the very height of his station, the general imagined that nothing would oppose his will ; and he asked the lady to allow him the services of the cook ; but she, as might be expected, refused. Mortified with the failure, the general offered the negro not only his freedom, but an additional and abundant gift, should he choose to enter his service ; but the negro answered : ' Tell the governor that I prefer slavery and poverty with my master to wealth and liberty without him.' "

These acts, however, of devoted fidelity on the part of the slaves are descriptive of a period in the history of the slavery of Cuba long since passed. Though the romantic and very youthful heart of the countess would have prolonged the dream, every one was soon awakened to the sad reality which covered the land.

Not very far apart, in time, from the insurrection of Montalvo, another took place somewhere near Aguacate. In 1842 there was one in Martiaro, for the second time. On the last occasion the slaves were made bold by the impunity which, through the deranged system of justice, and the influence of their owners, had been obtained for them previously. In the same year the captain of the district of

Lagunillas found an incendiary proclamation, which had fallen from the pocket of a foreign mulatto, who was employed as mason. A monk appeared on an estate near Limonar, under pretence of requesting alms for the Virgin, whose image he carried with him, and went on prophesying to the blacks that on St. John's day they would become free.

In July of the same year, the slaves of an estate near Bemba committed several acts of insubordination, and murdered a neighbor. An Italian hair-dresser was imprisoned in 1841 for receiving proclamations of an incendiary nature. The negroes of Aldama, under the very walls of Havana, refused to work, and claimed the right of freedom.

In January, 1843, a colored man, suspected by his companions of having revealed the particulars of the murder of an officer of government, by the name of Becerra, was assassinated by one of his own class, who, being afterward taken, committed suicide in jail. In March, 1843, there happened at Bemba an insurrection of five hundred negroes, belonging to the railroad company and others. Very soon after, there was another movement on a large estate; and before that year closed it occurred a second time. Soon after the insurgents made a formal rally, doing many bloody deeds, and murdering numbers of the whites of different ages and sexes.

The above brief retrospective view of a few only of the principal signs which were indicative of disquietude among the slave population is a very important part of Cuban history. The information received officially at Havana from the Spanish minister at Washington, and through the court of Madrid, as far back as 1834, in which the dangers which threatened the Island were fully shown, had been altogether slighted.

So also were these events, though marked with blood, and showing unequivocal symptoms of a coming storm. It gathered not in a single day, but came gradually on; and the humble landholder was doomed to see the clouds of destruction hanging over his property, amid the general apathy of the officers of government, who alone were intrusted with the care of that in which they felt no interest.

A rich planter having obtained, subsequently to the last bloody insurrection of November, 1843, by means of a negro woman, and by hiding himself during the night in the room where she slept with her husband, the particulars of a plan of devastation and bloodshed so extended as to make him shudder with horror, the local government seemed at length to awake from a sleep fraught with such imminent danger.

One of the immediate results was a meeting of the planters called in the city of Matanzas for the third of December. The meeting was held; a committee named to propose, on the seventeenth, a report, which report being unfavorable to the slave trade, the planters were not allowed to meet again, and the military administration went through those difficult circumstances, guided by its own incompetent intelligence, or by the suggestions of the ignorant.

How did they act? What system did they adopt to quell the general commotion among the colored population, which was so visible to every eye? The answer to these questions will be found in the ungrateful task which it is here necessary to perform.

All Considered Criminals.

Under the impression derived from some testimony obtained by the military tribunals, established for the occasion, and composed of officers of inferior grade, it was supposed that the conspiracy framed by the blacks comprehended every individual of that unfortunate class. No one was excepted: every one must be guilty; and those who would or could reveal nothing, were marked as the most criminal.

Acting upon this ground, a general investigation, or what was called "*expurgo*," was ordered throughout the whole land, and intrusted to the most ignorant officers, whose system of inquiry was reduced to questions implying the answers required, and accompanied by the most violent chastisement, often inflicted in such a manner as sooner or later to produce death. Suggestions were made of the utility of employing lawyers of eminent standing, whose ingenuity and capacity would have advanced the proceedings efficiently; but nothing of the kind met a hearing. The following are a few of the atrocious acts which resulted from conferring judicial powers upon military officers of an inferior class.

Under date of March 6th, 1844, the captain-general addressed a letter to General Salas, who presided over the military tribunal stationed in the interior, in answer to the dispatches of the latter, consulting him as to the necessity of using violent means in the prosecution of those *free* colored persons under indictment, who should refuse to discover their associates, and setting forth the good effects which those means had produced among the slaves. In this letter his excellency authorized these same means to be employed with the free colored population, and manifested his approbation of their chastisement in the country where they should be taken, and of the attendance of the officer, in order to certify the testimony!

Brutal Exercise of Authority.

These officers, thus raised by a power above the laws, and above the dominical rights of the owners of slaves, with very few exceptions, exercised their authority in a manner the most sordid, brutal, and sanguinary. Under the universal alarm raised, and extending to every hut, whoever was bold enough to insinuate a doubt respecting facts revealed under the most atrocious tortures, was deemed an abolitionist; although his interests and previous conduct presented a much safer guarantee of his opinions than the trust which should be placed in uneducated and hungry officers of the army. It was quite common for the latter to demand and obtain money from the accused, in order to save their lives, or their bodies from barbarous lashing.

One of these prosecuting attorneys, judges, and executioners, at one and the same time, namely, Don Ramon Gonzales, ordered his victims to be taken to a room which had been whitewashed, and the walls of which were besmeared with blood and small pieces of flesh from the wretches who had preceded them in this cruel treatment. There stood a bloody ladder, where the accused were tied, with their heads downward, and whether free or slave, if they would not avow what the fiscal officer insinuated, were whipped to death by two stout mulattoes selected for this purpose. They were scourged with leather straps, having at the end a small destructive button, made of fine wire.

At the spot called the farm of Soto, were butchered in this manner M. Ruiz, C. Tolon, George Blakely, and other freemen; and their deaths were made to appear, by certificates from physicians, as having been caused by diarrhœa. This new minister of the law had been formerly prosecuted for theft, extortion, and even deeper crimes, committed while he commanded the criminals' depot.

Inhuman Tortures.

Don Mariano F——— brought on himself the execration and odium of the whole city of Matanzas for his barbarous treatment of Andrew Dodge, a colored man, born free, who was generally beloved and esteemed, and was the owner of considerable property. He was tied to the ladder and flogged on three different occasions, but never avowed what he was accused of; and finally he was executed, in defiance even of those sanguinary laws of old, which instituted the ordeal of torture in ages called barbarous.

He also caused a free negro, Pedro Nuñez, to be tied hand-and-foot and hung to the ceiling of the house, keeping him in this painful position through the night, his body having been previously lacerated by the whip. Again, by threatening to inflict punishment, he obtained from the mulatto, Thomas Vargas, an affidavit against a man of the same class, called Fonten. He used to visit Vargas at his dungeon every day after sentence had been passed on him, to assure him sportingly that he would not fail to receive four bullets through his body. The prophecy was of course fulfilled.

Don Juan Costa, another of the acting officers, had likewise his share in this work of accusation ; and there were, in the process of his making, ninety-six certificates of an equal number of deaths of the indicted during the investigation. Of these, forty-two were freemen and fifty-four slaves. They all had died under the lash ; and that you may judge of the intensity of their sufferings, I will record what appears from the process, viz.: " Lorenzo Sanchez, imprisoned on the first of April, died on the fourth ; Joseph Cavallero, imprisoned

on the fourth, died on the sixth ; John Austin Molino, imprisoned on
the ninth, died on the twelfth ; and so on through an infinite number.

Don Jose del Pozo punished a negro one hundred and ten years
old, who died at the Matanzas jail.   Don Francisco Illas, the enlightened and humane fiscal officer, who appears among those of his
class as if to redeem the Spanish name from the dark stain brought
upon it by his associates, was called to certify to the death of this old
man ; but he drew back horror-struck from the spot when he beheld
a man so worn by age, having his body cut into pieces by the pitiless
lash.   The unfortunate victim had complained of the fiscal Pozo, accusing him of stealing from him forty-five dollars.   Del Pozo, after inflicting severe punishment, found sport in hanging the accused
victims on a tree, and then cutting the ropes to see them fall to the
ground in bunches.   He had been a journeyman tailor at Havana.

A Savage Boast.

Don Ferdinand Percher presented his process, having seventy-two
certificates of deaths of prisoners during the prosecution; twenty-
nine freemen and forty-three slaves.   " I have one hundred prisoners
in souse," said he once, before a number of respectable citizens, "and
if one escapes I am willing to have him nailed to my forehead."

Don Leon Dulzaides, in July, 1844, had a free negro placed in the
jail in what is called " campaign stocks," which is a most distressing
position of the body, the arms being arranged so as to hold the legs ;
and thus placed, ordered him to be whipped unmercifully, until he
should confess.   Another of the fiscals, who was acting in his official
character in the next room, was called by the cries of the victim, and
obtained for him a suspension of punishment.

Dulzaides demanded the punishment of death for twenty-seven
prisoners, but the council sentenced only two.   During the reading of
the sentence, he used to ask money of such as were saved from death.
Seventy prisoners of Don Jyacinth ——— died during the prosecution,
of whom thirty-five were freemen.   This fiscal was suspended from
office.

Don Miguel Ballo de la Torre, being on the estate of Oviedo, extorted from the negroes affidavits accusing their master, who, being absent, was apprised through his administrator or *econome*, that he was a lost man, but that the fiscal would save him, provided he paid two hundred ounces of gold. The administrator wrote several letters on the subject, which were handed to General Salas, president of the tribune, who wrote to the fiscal, ordering him not to continue the prosecution on that estate.

Don Manuel Siburu, fiscal of the prosecution against the English and American machinists, had demanded in his accusation the sentence of death upon an Englishman named Elkins. The members of the military tribunals, however, being intimidated by the consequences that might follow, and at the same time well aware that the testimony had been extorted by the lash, consulted respecting the case with General O'Donnell.

What the Treaty Guaranteed.

The latter answered, that they should proceed from what they found in the process, and look well to what they did; which, as there was no mention of the torture in the proceedings, meant that they should crown by their sentence the system of barbarous cruelty commenced by the fiscals. The consultation was repeated, and a similar answer obtained.

At the same time, Mr. Crawford, the English consul at Havana, officially informed the captain-general that he was aware that the British Majesty's subjects were being indicted and judged at Matanzas in a manner different from that adopted toward Spanish subjects; that as the testimony had been obtained by forcible means, whatever had been done was null; that there existed a treaty between the two nations, wherein it was stipulated that no Englishman should be judged in the Spanish dominions by special tribunals or committees, but by the regular order of the Spanish laws for Spaniards.

The consul was persevering in his demand, and the captain-general, embarrassed also by the consultations aforesaid, was obliged to give up; and he consequently ordered that the prosecution against foreigners should be placed in the hands of Don Francisco Illas, to be made anew. This able officer soon perceived that nothing was to be met with in what had been done but falsehood, infamy, and calumny, disconnectedly thrown together by the stupid Siburu.

Within two months afterward the prisoners were declared innocent, and liberated. It was in the presence of this same Siburu, that another of his prisoners, the aged and respectable mulatto, Ceballos, well known and esteemed by the merchants of Havana, suddenly expired on being shown the place of torture.

Shifting the Guilt on Another.

Don Pedro Linares had three old Indians whipped in Cardenas, two of whom died, who lived in that neighborhood, and had resided on the Island since the acquisition of Florida by the United States, whence they had come, from their attachment to the Spanish nation. Don Pedro Acevedo, fiscal of the proceedings against the negroes on the coffee estate of Domech, who had been accused of possessing poison (which, by the by, was never found) for the purpose of killing their master, so contrived it as to throw the guilt on a young white man, a native of the Canary Islands, aged between nineteen and twenty-one, who was executed, declaring his innocence to the last moment of his life. On being exhorted by the priest to pardon his enemies, he complied with the request, excepting the fiscal, Acevedo, whom he could not pardon.

Don Pedro Llanes, another of the fiscals, filled up the measure of his crimes, which cried so loudly for punishment, that he was at length accused of numberless robberies, extortions of money, and all kinds of wickedness, and at last was stopped in his dark career, and imprisoned in the Havana jail. There, under the stingings of conscience, he placed in the hands of General O'Donnell two hundred and fifty ounces of gold, which had been the fruits of his rapacity; and soon after committed suicide by cutting his throat. Don Manuel Mata, lieutenant-colonel of the Carlist ranks in 1834, another of the fiscals, was imprisoned at Havana for excesses and robberies committed in his official character during these disgraceful proceedings.

The remaining fiscals, Gala, Gherci, Flores Apodaca, Cruces,

Custardoz, Marcotegui, Maso, Llorens, Sanchez, Rosquin, Baltanas, Alvarez Murillo, and Domenech, traversed the country in every direction, and strictly obeyed the orders they had received; some whipping or torturing free colored or slave individuals, and extorting false testimony and accusations, and others seizing horses, cattle, furniture, and whatever was owned by the free colored persons, all which they sold and converted into cash. It is hardly necessary to say, that the fiscals took from their victims every cent which they possessed.

It is but justice to add, that the fiscals named Mendoza, Arango, and Illas are honorable exceptions to this host of miscreants. Signor Illas, above all, has called forth the approbation of all the feeling part of the community, and of the friends of justice and humanity, for his able, judicious, disinterested, and impartial conduct and deportment in the cases of the French coffee-planters and the English and American machinists, as well as of all who fell under his control.

Prisoners Sentenced to Death.

In the cases under the direction of the fiscal Ballo, this officer did not demand that sentence of death should be pronounced on any of his prisoners; the tribunal nevertheless sentenced two. The fiscal Lara demanded death for only one, and the tribunal sentenced four. The sergeant intrusted with the custody of the prisoners in the military jail at Matanzas is said to have collected twenty thousand dollars in cash for prison-fees and other arbitrary charges exacted from the prisoners.

In the city of Matanzas, the general persecution of the colored race was converted by the fiscals into means of gratifying their lewd passions upon the distracted daughters, wives, and sisters of their male victims. So far did they carry their barefaced impudence, that a ball was given by several of the fiscals, and attended by the consulting lawyer of the military tribunal, where none but women of color appeared. At a late hour of the night, the doors were closed; and all the inmates being in a state of disgraceful nudity, one can imagine what scenes of revelry and debauch followed.

Acts of such low and stupid infamy serve to show how the several channels of civilization are interwoven, and how easy it is for man, when once authorized to trample on any of the salutary restraints of society, to mock and despise whatever comes in the way of his most sensual appetites.

And now, in order justly to estimate the trust placed in the hands of these agents of military justice, the nature of their duties should be stated. They had separately the jurisdiction of a tribunal, with power to imprison and call before them whomsoever they would interrogate. The testimony which they obtained was received privately, no one being present except the fiscal and the witness. The fiscal would write down and sign the declaration, the blacks and the majority of witnesses knowing neither how to read nor write.

A Mockery of Justice.

Not even the notary, who is required to be present at the affidavits before the ordinary tribunals, appeared on these occasions to check the arbitrary, malicious, or blind impressions of the fiscal. Officers of the army were named to act as counsel for the individuals indicted, whether colored or white, free or bondsmen. These counselors, incapable through lack of talent or learning, were not allowed to read the proceedings regarding the persons whom they were to defend. All the instruction they had must be derived from a hasty and general abstract of facts made by the same fiscal, whose last duty was to demand the sentence which, in his opinion, should be imposed on the criminal.

Too much blame should not be attributed to the chief who, commanding the Island at this delicate period, could not be approached by the wisdom and intelligence of the land. The invariable and jealous policy which, for many years, has directed the administration of Cuba, drew away from the absolute military authority whatever was enlightened and spirited. Men of vulgar habits and little education were the natural upholders of a barbarous system; and it was not easy to find officers of superior worth to act under a cruel impulse, and to execute sanguinary orders; so that this strange course was unavoidably placed in the most incapable or polluted hands.

With regard to the truth of the conspiracy, and whatever ground it originally had, it has been so much embroiled and connected with incoherent, false, and improbable testimony, adduced by the fear of punishment, that a general opinion is fast gaining ground at the present day that it never existed, and that the few reports and conversations of a rebellious nature, mentioned with some plausibility in the course of the investigations, are the constant and latent workings of the slaves, which, in all ages, have accompanied the institution of slavery.   This would be a difficult matter to decide.

The events which preceded the general and scourging inquisition, together with the simultaneous and visible impudence of the free colored race, were certain indications of a disturbed state of mind in at least some sections of the country.   On the other hand, the indictments followed up by different fiscals, and the use of the torture without obtaining satisfactory evidence to dispel all manner of doubt as to the existence of a plot, speak against its credibility.   It can also be alleged that the very ignorance of the prosecutors, and the irregularity of their mode of procedure, were calculated to hinder the discovery of a plot, without deciding that it had positively no foundation.

It is more likely that the conspiracy was in its infancy; and that when the avenging storm which swept over the land was heard from afar, it increased the number of the discontented, who, through despair, prepared for some last acts of devastation and blood.   There i one painful reflection, which fixes itself upon the considerate observer of events.   While foreigners, after long delay, obtained a hearing of their cases, and after being paraded through the country, tied hand-and-foot on horseback, and kept in a filthy dungeon, were declared innocent, the white creoles, who had been imprisoned with equal injustice, remained still incarcerated, and their cases undecided, because they had no consul to claim for them the rights of civilized man !

CHAPTER XXV.

Story of Marti, the Smuggler.

ONE of the most successful villains whose story will be written in history, is a man named Marti, as well known in Cuba as the person of the Governor-General himself. Formerly he was notorious as a smuggler and half pirate on the coast of the Island, being a daring and accomplished leader of reckless men. At one time he bore the title of King of the Isle of Pines, where was his principal rendezvous, and from whence he dispatched his vessels, small, fleet crafts, to operate in the neighboring waters.

When Tacon landed on the Island, and became Governor-General, he found the revenue laws in a sad condition, as well as the internal regulations of the Island. As already stated, Tacon governed Cuba four years, from 1834 to 1838. The Spanish marine sent out to regulate the maritime matters of the Island, lay idly in port, the officers passing their time on shore, or in giving balls and dances on the decks of their vessels. Tacon saw that one of the first moves for him to make was to suppress the smuggling upon the coast, at all hazards; and to this end he set himself directly to work. The maritime force at his command was at once detailed upon this service, and they coasted night and day, but without the least success against the smugglers. In vain were all the vigilance and activity of Tacon and his agents—they accomplished nothing.

At last, finding that all his expeditions against them failed, partly from the adroitness and bravery of the smugglers, and partly from the want of pilots among the shoals and rocks they had frequented, a large and tempting reward was offered to any one of them who would desert from his comrades and act in this capacity in behalf of the Government.

At the same time, a double sum, most princely in amount, was

334

offered for the person of one Marti, dead or alive, who was known to be the leader of the lawless rovers who thus defied the Government. These rewards were freely promulgated, and posted so as to reach the ears and eyes of those whom they concerned; but even these seemed to produce no effect, and the Government officers were at a loss how to proceed in the matter.

A Mysterious Figure.

It was a dark, cloudy night in Havana, some three or four months subsequent to the issuing of these placards announcing the rewards referred to, when two sentinels were pacing backwards and forwards before the main entrance to the Governor's palace, just opposite the grand plaza. A little before midnight, a man, wrapped in a cloak, was watching them from behind the statue of Ferdinand, near the fountain, and, after observing that the two soldiers acting as sentinels paced their brief walk so as to meet each other, and then turn their backs as they separated, leaving a brief moment in the interval when the eyes of both were turned away from the entrance they were placed to guard, seemed to calculate upon passing them unobserved.

It was an exceedingly delicate manœuvre, and required great care and dexterity to effect it; but, at last, it was adroitly done, and the stranger sprang lightly through the entrance, secreting himself behind one of the pillars in the inner court of the palace. The sentinels paced on undisturbed.

The figure which had thus stealthily effected an entrance, now sought the broad stairs that led to the Governor's suite of apartments, with a confidence that evinced a perfect knowledge of the place. A second guard-post was to be passed at the head of the stairs; but, assuming an air of authority, the stranger offered a cold military salute and pressed forward, as though there was not the most distant question of his right so to do; and thus avoiding all suspicion in the guard's mind, he boldly entered the Governor's reception-room unchallenged, and closed the door behind him.

In a large easy-chair sat the commander-in-chief, busily engaged in writing, but alone. An expression of undisguised satisfaction

passed across the weather-beaten countenance of the new-comer at
this state of affairs, as he coolly cast off his cloak and tossed it over
his arm, and then proceeded to wipe the perspiration from his face.
The Governor, looking up with surprise, fixed his keen eyes upon
the intruder.

"Who enters here, unannounced, at this hour?" he asked, sternly
while he regarded the stranger earnestly.

"One who has information of value for the governor-general. You
are Tacon, I suppose?"

"I am. What would you with me? or, rather, how did you pass
my guard unchallenged?"

"Of that anon. Excellency, you have offered a handsome reward
for information concerning the rovers of the gulf?"

"Ha! yes. What of them?" said Tacon, with undisguised interest.

"Excellency, I must speak with caution," continued the new-
comer; "otherwise I may condemn and sacrifice myself."

"You have naught to fear on that head. The offer of reward for
evidence against the scapegraces also vouchsafes a pardon to the
informant. You may speak on, without fear for yourself, even
though you may be one of the very confederation itself."

"You offer a reward, also, in addition, for the discovery of Marti—
Captain Marti, of the smugglers—do you not?"

"We do, and will gladly make good the promise of reward for any
and all information upon the subject," replied Tacon.

"First, Excellency, do you give me your knightly word that you
will grant a free pardon to *me*, if I reveal all that you require to
know, even embracing the most secret hiding-places of the rovers?"

"I pledge you my word of honor," said the commander.

"No matter how heinous in the sight of the law my offences may
have been, still you will pardon me, under the king's seal?"

"I will, if you reveal truly and to any good purpose," answered
Tacon, weighing in his mind the purpose of all this precaution.

"Even if I were a leader among the rovers, myself?"

The governor hesitated for a moment, canvassing in a single
glance the subject before him, and then said:

"Even then, be you whom you may; if you are able and will hon-estly pilot our ships and reveal the secrets of Marti and his followers, you shall be rewarded as our proffer sets forth, and yourself receive a free pardon."

"Excellency, I think I know your character well enough to trust you, else I should not have ventured here."

"Speak, then; my time is precious," was the impatient reply of Tacon.

"Then, Excellency, the man for whom you have offered the largest reward, dead or alive, is now before you!"

"And you are—"

"Marti!"

The governor-general drew back in astonishment, and cast his eyes towards a brace of pistols that lay within reach of his right hand; but it was only for a single moment, when he again assumed entire self-control, and said:

"I shall keep my promise, sir, provided you are faithful, though the laws call loudly for your punishment, and even now you are in my power. To insure your faithfulness, you must remain at present under guard." Saying which, he rang a silver bell by his side, and issued a verbal order to the attendant who answered it. Immediately after, the officer of the watch entered, and Marti was placed in confinement, with orders to render him comfortable until he was sent for. His name remained a secret with the commander; and thus the night scene closed.

The Smuggler Kept his Word.

On the following day, one of the men-of-war that lay idly beneath the guns of Morro Castle suddenly became the scene of the utmost activity, and, before noon, had weighed her anchor, and was standing out into the gulf stream. Marti, the smuggler, was on board, as her pilot; and faithfully did he guide the ship, on the discharge of his treacherous business, among the shoals and bays of the coast for nearly a month, revealing every secret haunt of the rovers, exposing their most valuable depots and well-selected rendezvous; and many a smuggling craft was taken and destroyed.

22

The amount of money and property thus secured was very great; and Marti returned with the ship to claim his reward from the governor-general, who, well satisfied with the manner in which the rascal had fulfilled his agreement, and betrayed those comrades who were too faithful to be tempted to treachery themselves, summoned Marti before him.

"As you have faithfully performed your part of our agreement," said the governor-general, "I am now prepared to comply with the articles on my part. In this package you will find a free and unconditional pardon for all your past offences against the laws. And here is an order on the treasury for—"

He Controlled the Fish Market.

"Excellency, excuse me. The pardon I gladly receive. As to the sum of money you propose to give to me, let me make you a proposition. Retain the money; and, in place of it, guarantee to me the right to fish in the neighborhood of the city, and declare the trade in fish contraband to all except my agents. This will richly repay me, and I will erect a public market of stone at my own expense, which shall be an ornament to the city, and which at the expiration of a specified number of years shall revert to the government, with all right and title to the fishery."

Tacon was pleased at the idea of a superb fish-market, which should eventually revert to the government, and also at the idea of saving the large sum of money covered by the promised reward. The singular proposition of the smuggler was duly considered and acceded to, and Marti was declared in legal form to possess for the future sole right to fish in the neighborhood of the city, or to sell the article in any form, and he at once assumed the rights that the order guaranteed to him.

Having in his roving life learned all the best fishing-grounds, he furnished the city bountifully with the article, and reaped yearly an immense profit, until, at the close of the period for which the monopoly was granted, he was the richest man on the Island. According to the agreement, the fine market and its privilege reverted to the government at the time specified, and the monopoly has ever since been rigorously enforced.

Marti, now possessed of immense wealth, looked about him, to see in what way he could most profitably invest it to insure a handsome and sure return. The idea struck him if he could obtain the monopoly of theatricals in Havana on some such conditions as he had done that of the right to fish off its shores, he could still further increase his ill-gotten wealth. He obtained the monopoly, on condition that he should erect one of the largest and finest theatres in the world, which he did, locating the same just outside the city walls.

Many romantic stories are told of Marti; but the one we have here related is the only one that is authenticated.

CHAPTER XXVI.

The Conspiracy of Lopez.

THE result of the movement in the western department, under Tacon, showed the Cubans that they had nothing to hope from Spain, while the cruelties of General O'Donnell increased the great discontent and despair of the people. They now became satisfied that the hope of legal reform was but a chimera: and a portion of the liberal party, seeing no issue from their insufferable position but that of revolution, boldly advocated the intervention of arms. In 1848 a conspiracy was formed in Cienfuegos and Trinidad, with the purpose of throwing off the Spanish yoke; but it was soon discovered and crushed by the imprisonment of various individuals in the central department.

The principal leader in this movement was General Narciso Lopez, who succeeded in effecting his escape to the United States, where he immediately placed himself in communication with several influential and liberal creoles, voluntary and involuntary exiles, and established a correspondence with the remnant of the liberal party yet at liberty on the Island, at the same time being aided in his plans by American sympathy. The result of the deliberations of himself, his correspondents and associates, was to try by the chances of war for the liberation of Cuba.

Many of the leading patriots of the Island undoubtedly believed that the government of the United States would second their efforts if they should decide to unite themselves to our republic, and boldly raise the banner of annexation. A portion of the Cuban liberals adopted the motto, " Legal Reform or Independence ; " and these two factions of the patriots did not henceforth act in perfect concert with each other—a most fatal error to the interests of both. Time and circumstances favored the war and annexation party ; the people were more than ever discontented with a government which so oppressed them by a military despotism, and by the enormous weight of the unjust taxation levied upon them. We may here remark that the increase of the public revenue, in the midst of so many elements of destruction and ruin, can only be explained by the facility with which the captain-general and royal stewards of the Island invented and arranged taxes, at their pleasure, and without a shadow of propriety, or even precedent.

The colored population of the Island, both slaves and free, hated the Spaniards, for good reasons. The war party, moreover, reckoned on the genius of a leader (Lopez), " the first lance of Spain," trained to arms, equal in talents to any of the Spanish generals, and beloved by the Spanish troops, as well as by the Cuban population; and they relied, also, as we have said, on the sympathy and ultimate aid of the United States government.

Many False Reports.

It is undoubtedly true that interested parties in this country, prompted by mercenary motives, increased this latter delusion by false reports; while the Cuban conspirators, in turn, buoyed up the hopes of their friends in the United States, by glowing accounts of the patriotic spirit of the creoles, and the extent of the preparations they were making for a successful revolt.

General Lopez was actively arranging the means for an invasion, when, in 1849, the United States government threw terror into the ranks of the filibusters, by announcing its determination to enforce the sacredness of treaty stipulations. This, for a time, frustrated the intended invasion.

In 1850 Lopez succeeded in effecting his first descent upon the Island. Having succeeded in baffling the vigilance of the United States government, an expedition, consisting of six hundred and fifty-two men, was embarked on board two sailing-vessels and the steamer " Creole," which conveyed the general and his staff. In the beginning of July the sailing-vessels left New Orleans, with-orders to anchor at Contoy, one of the Mugeres Islands, on the coast of

Yucatan; the general followed, on the "Creole," on the 7th. At the time when the troops were embarked on the "Creole" at Contoy, fifty-two of the number, who had been deceived as to the nature of the expedition, refused to follow the general, and were left on the island, with the intention of returning to the United States in the two schooners.

General Lopez, after gaining some information from a fisherman he encountered, resolved to land at Cardenas, on the northern coast of the Island, a hundred and twenty miles east of Havana. He calculated that he could surprise and master the garrison before the Captain-General could possibly obtain intelligence of his departure from New Orleans. His plan was to master the town, secure the authorities, intimidate the Spaniards, and then, sustained by the moral influence of victory, proceed to Matanzas by railroad.

War-Ships Hastily Despatched.

Roncali, the Captain-General, having received intelligence of the landing at Contoy, dispatched several ships-of-war in that direction, to seize upon the general and his followers. The latter, however, escaped the snare, and effected his landing on the 19th. The garrison rushed to arms, and, while a portion of the troops, after immaterial loss, retired in good order to the suburbs, another, under the command of Governor Ceruti, intrenched themselves in the government house, and gave battle to the invaders.

After a sharp skirmish, the building being set on fire, they surrendered; the Governor and two or three officers were made prisoners, and the soldiers consented to join the revolutionary colors! Meanwhile a body of one hundred invaders seized upon the railroad station. The engines were fired up, and the trains made ready to transport the invading column to Matanzas.

But now came a pause. General Lopez, seeing that the native population did not respond to his appeal, knew that as soon as the news of the taking of Cardenas should be circulated he would be in a very critical situation. In fact, the Governor of Matanzas was soon on the march, at the head of five hundred men. General Armero sailed from Havana in the " Pizarro," with a thousand infantry, while two thousand five hundred picked troops, under the command of General Count de Mirasol, were sent from Havana by the railroad.

Lopez saw that it would be madness to await the attack of these formidable columns, unsupported save by his own immediate followers, and accordingly issued his orders for the reëmbarkation of his band, yet without relinquishing the idea of landing on some more favorable point of the Island.

That portion of the garrison which, in the beginning of the affair, had retreated to the suburbs, finding itself reinforced by a detachment of cavalry, attempted to cut off the retreat of the invading general; but the deadly fire of the latter's reserve decimated the horse, and the infantry, dismayed at their destruction, took to rapid flight. The " Creole " accordingly left the port without molestation, and before the arrival of the government steam-frigate " Pizarro."

The Spanish prisoners were landed at Cayo de Piedras, and then Lopez, discovering the " Pizarro " in the distance, made for the American continent, where the steamer was abandoned. General Lopez was arrested by the authorities of Savannah, but liberated again, in deference to the public clamor. The " Creole " was seized, confiscated and sold. The invaders disbanded; and thus this enterprise terminated.

A less enterprising and determined spirit than that of General Lopez would have been completely broken by the failure of his first attempts, the inactivity of the Cubans, the hostility of the American government, and the formidable forces and preparations of the Spanish officials.

He believed, however, that the Cubans were ripe for revolt; that public opinion in the United States would nullify the action of the Federal government; and that, if he could once gain a foothold in the Island, the Spanish troops would desert in such numbers to his banners that the preponderance of power would soon be upon his side; and, with these views, he once more busied himself, with unremitting industry, to form another expedition.

Meanwhile, the daring attack upon Cardenas, while it demonstrated the determination of the invading party, caused great anxiety in the mind of General Roncali. True, he had at his disposal an army of more than twenty thousand regular troops; but he was by no means sure of their loyalty, and he therefore determined to raise a local militia; but, as he suffered only Spaniards to enlist in it, he aroused the jealousy of the Cuban-born inhabitants, and thus swelled the force of opposition against the government. General Lopez was informed of this fact, and based new hopes upon the circumstance.

The Tyranny Continued.

The Spanish government, having recalled Roncali, appointed Don José de la Concha Captain-General of the Island, and the severity of his sway reminded the inhabitants of the iron rule of Tacon. It was during his administration that Lopez effected his second landing at Playitas, sixty miles west of Havana. Several partial insurrections, which had preceded this event, easily suppressed, as it appears, by the Spanish government, but exaggerated in the accounts dispatched to the friends of Cuba in the United States, inflamed the zeal of Lopez, and made him believe that the time for a successful invasion had at length arrived. The following is from a narrative of one of the invaders : " The general showed me much of his correspondence from the Island. It represented a pervading anxiety for his arrival, on the part of the creole population. His presence alone, to head the insurrection, which would then become general, was all they called for; his presence and a supply of arms, of which they were totally destitute. The risings already made were highly colored in some of the communications addressed to him from sources of unquestionable sincerity."

He was so confident, at one time, of the determination and ability of the Cubans alone to secure their independence, that he wished to embark without any force, and throw himself among them. It was this confidence that led him to embark with only four hundred ill-armed men on board the little steamer " Pampero," on the 2d of August, 1851. This force consisted mostly of Americans, but embraced forty-nine Cubans in its ranks, with several German and

Hungarian officers; among the latter, General Pragay, one of the heroes of the Hungarian revolution, who was second in command to General Lopez on this occasion.

Many of the foreign officers spoke little, if any, English, and mutual jealousies and insubordinations soon manifested themselves in the little band. They were composed of fierce spirits, and had come together without any previous drilling or knowledge of each other. It was not the intention of the commander-in-chief to sail direct for Cuba, but to go to the neighborhood of St. John's river, Florida, and get a supply of artillery, ammunition, extra arms, etc.

The Invaders Effect a Landing.

He then proposed to land somewhere in the central department, where he thought he could get a footing, and rally a formidable force, before the government troops could reach him. But, when five days out, Lopez discovered that the " Pampero " was short of coal; as no time could be spared to remedy this deficiency, he resolved to effect a landing at once, and send back the " Pampero " for reinforcements and supplies.

At Key West he obtained favorable intelligence from Cuba, which confirmed his previous plans. He learned that a large portion of the troops had been sent to the eastern department; and he accordingly steered for Bahia Honda (deep bay). The current of the gulf, acting while the machinery of the boat was temporarily stopped for repairs, and the variation of the compass in the neighborhood of so many arms, caused the steamer to run out of her course on the night of the 10th; and when the morning broke, the invaders found themselves heading for the narrow entrance of the harbor of Havana !

The course of the steamer was instantly altered; but all on board momentarily expected the apparition of a war steamer from the channel between the Morro and the Punta. It appeared, afterwards, that the " Pampero " was signalized as a strange steamer, but not reported as suspicious until evening. The " Pampero " then made for the bay of Cabañas; but, just as she was turning into the entrance, a Spanish frigate and sloop-of-war were seen at anchor, the first of which immediately gave chase; but, the wind falling, the frigate gave it up, and returned to the bay to send intelligence of the expedition to Havana.

The landing was finally effected at midnight, between the 11th and 12th of August, and the steamer was immediately sent off to the United States for further reinforcements. As it was necessary to obtain transportation for the baggage, General Lopez resolved to leave Colonel Crittenden with one hundred and twenty men to guard it and with the remainder of the expedition to push on to Las Pozas, a village about ten miles distant, whence he could send back carts and horses to receive it. Among the baggage were four barrels of powder, two of cartridges, the officers' effects, including the arms of the general, and the flag of the expedition. From the powder and arms they should not have separated, but have divided that, against contingency.

The Invasion a Failure.

In the meantime, seven picked companies of Spanish troops of the line had been landed at Bahia Honda, which force was strengthened by contingents drawn from the neighborhood. The march of the invading band to Las Pozas was straggling and irregular. On reaching the village, they found it deserted by the inhabitants. A few carts were procured and sent back to Crittenden, that he might advance with the baggage.

Lopez here learned from a countryman of the preparations making to attack him. It was no portion of his plan to bring the men into action with regular troops, in their present undisciplined state; he proposed rather to take a strong position in the mountains, and there plant his standard as a rallying-point, and await the rising of the Cubans, and the return of the "Pampero" with reinforcements for active operations.

As soon as Lopez learned the news from Bahia Honda, he dispatched a peremptory order to Crittenden to hasten up with the rear-guard, abandoning the heavy baggage, but bringing off the cartridges and papers of the expedition. But the fatal delay of Crittenden separated him forever from the main body, only a small detachment of his comrades (under Captain Kelly) ever reaching it. The next day, while breakfast was being prepared for them, the soldiers of the expedition were suddenly informed, by a volley from one of the houses of the village, that the Spanish troops were upon them.

A Spirited Battle.

They flew to arms at once, and the Cuban company dislodged the vanguard of the enemy, who had fired, at the point of the bayonet, their captain, Oberto, receiving his death-wound in the spirited affair. General Enna, a brave officer, in command of the Spanish troops, made two charges in column on the centre of the invaders' line, but was repulsed by that deadly fire which is the preëminent characteristic of American troops. Four men alone escaped from the company heading the first column, and seventeen from that forming the advance of the second column of attack. The Spaniards were seized with a panic, and fled.

Lopez's force in this action amounted to about two hundred and eighty men; the Spaniards had more than eight hundred. The total loss of the former, in killed and wounded, was thirty-five; that of the latter about two hundred men killed, and a large number wounded! The invaders landed with about eighty rounds of cartridges each; the Spanish dead supplied them with about twelve thousand more; and a further supply was subsequently obtained at Las Frias; the ammunition left with Crittenden was never recovered. In the battle of Las Pozas, General Enna's horse was shot under him, and his second in command killed. The invaders lost Colonel Downman, a brave American officer; while General Pragay was wounded, and afterwards died in consequence.

Though the invaders fired well and did terrible execution, they could not be prevailed upon to charge the enemy, and gave great trouble to the officers by their insubordination. The night after the battle, Captain Kelly came up with forty men, and announced that the Spanish troops had succeeded in dividing the rear-guard, and that the situation of Crittenden was unknown. It was not until some days afterwards that it was ascertained that Crittenden's party, attempting to leave the Island in launches, had been made prisoners by a Spanish man-of-war. They were taken to Havana, and brutally shot at the Castle of Atares.

About two o'clock on the 14th of August, the expedition resumed its march for the interior, leaving behind their wounded, who were afterwards killed and mutilated by the Spaniards. The second action with the Spanish troops occurred at the coffee-plantation of Las Frias, General Enna attacking with four howitzers, one hundred and twenty cavalry, and twelve hundred infantry.

Wandering in the Mountains.

The Spanish general attacked with his cavalry, but they were met by a deadly fire, thrown into utter confusion, and forced to retreat, carrying off the general mortally wounded. The panic of the cavalry communicated itself to the infantry, and the result was a complete rout. This was the work of about two hundred muskets, for many of Lopez's men had thrown away their arms on the long and toilsome march.

The expedition, however, was too weak to profit by their desperate successes, and had no means of following up these victories. Plunging into the mountains, they wandered about for days, drenched with rain, destitute of food or proper clothing, until despair at last seized them. They separated from each other, a few steadfast comrades remaining by their leader. In the neighborhood of San Cristobal, Lopez finally surrendered to a party of pursuers. He was treated with every indignity by his captors, though he submitted to everything with courage and serenity. He was taken in a steamer from Mariel to Havana.

Arrived here, he earnestly desired to obtain an interview with Concha, who had been an old companion-in-arms with him in Spain ; not that he expected pardon at his hands, but hoping to obtain a change in the manner of his death. His soul shrank from the infamous *garrote*, and he aspired to the indulgence of the *cuatro tiros* (four shots).

Both the interview and the indulgence were refused, and he was executed on the first day of September, at seven o'clock in the morning, in the Punta, by that mode of punishment which the Spaniards esteem the most infamous of all. When he landed at Bahia Honda, he stooped and kissed the earth, with the fond salutation, " *Querida Cuba*" (dear Cuba)! And his last words, pronounced in a tone of deep tenderness, were, " *Muero por mi amada Cuba*" (I die for my beloved Cuba.

General Lopez was born in Venezuela, South America, in 1798 ; and hence, at the time of his execution, must have been about fifty-two years of age. He early became an adopted citizen of Cuba, and espoused one of its daughters.

The remainder of the prisoners who fell into the hands of the authorities were sent to the Moorish fortress of Ceuta ; but Spain seems to have been ashamed of the massacre of Atares, and atoned for the ferocity of her colonial officials by leniency towards the misguided men of the expedition, granting them a pardon.

Cause of the Conspiracy.

This uprising, or rather attempt at revolution, was all due to the despotic policy pursued by Spain. It is impossible to conceive of any degree of loyalty that would be proof against the unparalleled burthens and atrocious system by which the mother country has ever loaded and weighed down her western colonists. They must be either more or less than men if they still cherish attachment to a foreign throne under such circumstances. But the fact simply is, the creoles of Cuba are neither angels nor brutes; they are, it is true, a long-suffering and somewhat indolent people, lacking in a great degree the stern qualities of the Anglo-Saxon and the Anglo-Norman races, but nevertheless intelligent, if wanting culture, and not without those noble aspirations for independence and freedom, destitute of which they would cease to be men, justly forfeiting all claim to our sympathy and consideration.

During the brief intervals in which a liberal spirit was manifested towards the colony by the home government, the Cubans gave proof of talent and energy, which, had they been permitted to attain their full development, would have given them a highly honorable name and distinguished character. When the field for genius was comparatively clear, Cuba produced more than one statesman and man of science, who would have done honor to a more favored land.

But these cheering rays of light were soon extinguished, and the fluctuating policy of Spain settled down into the rayless and brutal despotism which has become its normal condition, and a double darkness closed upon the political and intellectual prospects of Cuba. But the people are not, and have not been, the supine and idle victims of tyranny which Spain depicts them. The reader will remember the several times they have attempted, manacled as they are, to free their limbs from the chains that bind them. It is insulting and idle to say that they might have been free if they had earnestly desired and made the effort for freedom.

Parallel Cases in History.

Who can say what would have been the result of our own struggle for independence, if Great Britain, at the outset, had been as well prepared for resistance as Spain has always been in Cuba? Who can say how long and painful would have been the struggle, if one of the most powerful military nations of Europe had not listened to our despairing appeal, and thrown the weight of her gold and her arms into the scale against our great enemy?

When we see how—as we do clearly—in a single night the well-contrived schemes of an adroit and unprincipled knave enslaved a brilliant and war-like people, like the French, who had more than once tasted the fruits of republican glory and liberty, who had borne their free flag in triumph over more than half of Europe, we can understand why the Cubans, overawed from the very outset, by the presence of a force vastly greater in proportion than that which enslaved France, have been unable to achieve their deliverance.

Nay, more—when we consider the system pursued by the government of the Island, the impossibility of forming assemblages, and of concerting action, the presence of troops and spies everywhere, the compulsory silence of the press—the violation of the sanctity of correspondence—we can only wonder that any effort has been made, any step taken in that fatal pathway of revolution which leads infallibly to the *garrote*.

If Cuba lies at present under the armed heel of despotism, we may be sure that the anguish of her sons is keenly aggravated by their perfect understanding of our own liberal institutions, and an earnest, if fruitless, desire to participate in their enjoyment. It is beyond the power of the Spanish government to keep the people of the Island in a state of complete darkness, as it seems to desire to do. The young men of Cuba educated at our colleges and schools, the visitors from the United States, and American merchants established on the Island, are all so many apostles of republicanism, and propagandists of treason and rebellion.

They Only Await the Opportunity.

Nor can the captains-general with all their vigilance exclude what they are pleased to call incendiary newspapers and documents from pretty extensive circulation among the " ever faithful." That liberal ideas and hatred of Spanish despotism are widely entertained among the Cubans is a fact no one who has passed a brief period among them can truthfully deny. They await only the means and the opportunity to rise in rebellion against Spain. We are too far distant to see more than the light smoke, but those who have trodden the soil of Cuba have sounded the depths of the volcano.

The history of the unfortunate Lopez expedition proves nothing contrary to this. The force under Lopez afforded too weak a nucleus, was too hastily thrown upon the Island, too ill prepared, and too untimely attacked, to enable the native patriots to rally round its standard, and thus to second the efforts of the invaders. With no ammunition nor arms to spare, recruits would have only added to the embarrassment of the adventurers.

Yet had Lopez been joined by the brave but unfortunate Crittenden, with what arms and ammunition he possessed, had he gained some fastness where he could have been disciplining his command, until further aid arrived, the adventure might have had a very different termination from what we have recorded in an early chapter of this book.

Disastrous as was the result of the Lopez expedition, it nevertne-less proved two important facts : first, the bravery of the Cubans, a small company of whom drove the enemy at the point of the bayonet; and, secondly, the inefficiency of Spanish troops when opposed by resolute men. If a large force of picked Spanish troops were decimated and routed in two actions, by a handful of ill-armed and undisciplined men, taken by surprise, we are justified in believ-ing that if an effective force of ten thousand men, comprising the several arms of cavalry, artillery, and infantry, had been thrown into the Island, they would have carried all before them. With such a body of men to rally upon, the Cubans would have risen in the departments of the Island, and her best transatlantic jewel would have been torn from the diadem of Spain.

American Sympathy for Cuba.

That the Spanish government lived in constant dread of a renewal of the efforts on the part of Americans and exiled Cubans to aid the disaffected people of the Island in throwing off its odious yoke, is a notorious fact, and there were evidences in the conduct of its officials towards those of this government that it regarded the latter as secretly favoring such illegal action. Yet the steps taken by our government to crush any such attempts were decided enough to satisfy any but a jealous and unreasonable power.

President Fillmore, in his memorable proclamation, said, ' Such expeditions can only be regarded as adventures for plunder and robbery," and declaring Americans who engaged in them outlaws, informed them that " they would forfeit their claim to the protection of this government, or any interference in their behalf, no matter to what extremity they might be reduced in consequence of their illegal conduct." In accordance with this declaration, the brave Crittenden and his men were allowed to be shot at Atares, though they were not taken with arms in their hands, had abandoned the expedition, and were seeking to escape from the Island.

In a similar spirit President Pierce alluded to our relations with Spain in his inaugural address, in the following explicit terms: "Indeed it is not to be disguised that our attitude as a nation, and our position on the globe, render the acquisition of certain possessions, not within our jurisdiction, eminently important, if not, in the future, essential for the preservation of the rights of commerce and the peace of the world. Should they be obtained, it will be through no grasping spirit, but with a view to obvious national interest and security, and in a manner entirely consistent with the strictest observance of national faith."

Honorable Attitude of our Government.

A subsequent proclamation, emanating from the same source, and warning our citizens of the consequences of engaging in an invasion of the Island, also attested the determination to maintain the integrity of our relations with an allied power.

No candid student of the history of our relations with Spain can fail to be impressed by the frank and honorable attitude of our government, or to contrast its acts with those of the Spanish officials of Cuba. A history of the commercial intercourse of our citizens with the Island would be a history of petty and also serious annoyances and grievances to which they have been subjected for a series of years by the Spanish officials, increasing in magnitude as the latter have witnessed the forbearance and magnanimity of our government.

Not an American merchant or captain, who had dealings with Cuba, but could furnish his list of insults and outrages, some in the shape of illegal extortions and delays, others merely gratuitous ebullitions of spite and malice dictated by a hatred of our country and its citizens. Instances of outrage so flagrant occurred, that the executive felt bound to call the attention of Congress to them in a message, in which he pointed out the great evil which lay at the bottom, and also the remedy.

"The offending party," he said, "is at our doors with large power for aggression, but none, it is alleged, for reparation. The source of redress is in another hemisphere: and the answers to our just com-

23

plaints, made to the home government, are but the repetition of excuses rendered by inferior officials to the superiors, in reply to the representations of misconduct. In giving extraordinary power to them, she owes it to justice, and to her friendly relations to this government, to guard with great vigilance against the exorbitant exercise of these powers, and in case of injuries to provide for prompt redress."

It is very clear that if, in such cases as the seizure of a vessel and her cargo by the port officers at Havana, for an alleged violation of revenue laws, or even port usages, redress, in case of official misconduct, could only be had by reference to the home government in another part of the world, our trade with Cuba would be completely paralyzed. The delay and difficulty in obtaining such redress, in too many cases, prompted extortion on the one hand, and acquiescence to injustice on the other.

Seizure of American Vessels.

In 1851 two American vessels were seized off Yucatan by the Spanish authorities on suspicion of being engaged in the Lopez expedition; in the same year the steamship "Falcon" was wantonly fired upon by a Spanish government vessel; in 1852 the American mail bags were forcibly opened, and their contents examined by order of the Captain-General; the "Crescent City" was not allowed to land her passengers and mails, simply because the purser, Smith, was obnoxious to the government of the Island.

The "Black Warrior," fired into on one voyage, was seized for a violation of a custom-house form. More than once, on specious pretexts, were American sailors taken from American vessels and thrown into Spanish prisons. In short, the insults offered by Spanish officials to our flag so multiplied that the popular indignation in the country reached an alarming height.

It is difficult for a republic and a despotism, situated like the United States and Cuba, to live on neighborly terms; and to control the indignation of the citizens of the former, proud and high-spirited, conscious of giving no offence, and yet subjected to repeated insults, is a task almost too great for the most adroit and pacific administration. Had she possessed more foresight and less pride, Spain would have long since sold the Island to the United States, and thereby have relieved herself of a weighty care and a most dangerous property.

"So far from being really injured by the loss of the Island," said Hon. Edward Everett, in his able and well-known letter to the British minister rejecting the proposition for the tripartite convention, "there is no doubt that, were it peacefully transferred to the United States, a prosperous commerce between Cuba and Spain, resulting from ancient associations and common language and tastes, would be far more productive than the best-contrived system of colonial taxation. Such, notoriously, has been the result to Great Britain of the establishment of the independence of the United States."

Bold Utterances in Congress.

The following remarks are quoted from a conservative speech of Mr. Latham, then member of Congress from California. They present, with emphasis, some of the points we have lightly touched upon.

"I admit that our relations with Spain, growing out of that Island (Cuba), are of an extremely delicate nature; that the fate of that Island, its misgovernment, its proximity to our shores, and the particular institutions established upon it, are of vast importance to the peace and security of this country; and that the utmost vigilance in regard to it is not only demanded by prudence, but an act of imperative duty on the part of our government. The Island of Cuba commands, in a measure, the Gulf of Mexico.

"In case of a maritime war, in which the United States may be engaged, its possession by the enemy might become a source of infinite annoyance to us, crippling our shipping, threatening the great emporium of our southern commerce, and exposing our whole southern coast, from the capes of Florida to the mouth of the Rio Grande, to the enemy's cruisers. The geographical position of Cuba is such that we cannot, without a total disregard to our own safety, permit it to pass into the hands of any first-class power; nay, that it would be extremely imprudent to allow it to pass even into the hands of a power of the second rank, possessed of energy and capacity for expansion."

"Rich in soil, salubrious in climate, varied in productions, the home of commerce," said the Hon. O. R. Singleton, of Mississippi, "Cuba seems to have been formed to become 'the very button on Fortune's cap.' Washed by the Gulf-stream on half her borders, with the Mississippi pouring out its rich treasures on one side, and the Amazon, destined to become a 'cornucopia,' on the other,—with the ports of Havana and Matanzas on the north, and the Isle of Pines and St. Jago de Cuba on the south, Nature has written upon her, in legible characters, a destiny far above that of a subjugated province of a rotten European dynasty.

"Her home is in the bosom of the North American confederacy. Like a lost Pleiad, she may wander on for a few months or years in lawless, chaotic confusion; but, ultimately, the laws of nature and of nations will vindicate themselves, and she will assume her true social and political condition, despite the diplomacy of statesmen, the trickery of knaves, or the frowns of tyrants.

"Cuba will be free. The spirit is abroad among her people; and, although they dare not give utterance to their thoughts, lest some treacherous breeze should bear them to a tyrant's ears, still they think and feel, and will act when the proper time shall arrive. The few who have dared 'to do or die' have fallen, and their blood still marks the spot where they fell. Such has been the case in all great revolutionary struggles. Those who lead the van must expect a sharp encounter before they break through the serried hosts of tyranny, and many a good man falls upon the threshold of the temple.

> "'But freedom's battle once begun,
> Bequeathed from bleeding sire to son,
> Though baffled oft, is always won.'"

CHAPTER XXVII.

The Bitter Ten-Years' War.

SOON after the events narrated in the preceding chapter a Reformist party sprang up, desirous of coming to a settlement which should insure the rights of the colony without impairing the interests of Spain, and after protracted efforts this party succeeded in obtaining an inquiry at Madrid on the reforms needed by Cuba; but the only alteration decreed was that of a new system of taxation, more depressive than the former. Great sympathy had long been shown for the Cubans by the people of the United States, and in 1848 President Polk had gone the length of proposing through the American ambassador at Madrid a transference of the Island to the United States for a sum of $1,000,000.

A similar proposal was made ten years afterwards in the Senate—the sum suggested being $30,000,000—but after debate it was withdrawn. When the Spanish revolution of 1868 broke out the advanced party in Cuba at once matured their plans for the liberation of the Island from the military despotism of Spain, rose in arms at Yara in the district of Bayamo, and made a declaration of independence, dated at Manzanillo, on the 10th of October of that year. This insurrection soon assumed formidable dimensions in the eastern portion of the Island; on the 18th of October the town of Bayamo was taken, and on the 28th the jurisdiction of Holguin rose in arms.

Early in November the patriots defeated a force which had been sent against them from Santiago de Cuba, and the greater number of the Spanish-American republics hastened to recognize the Cubans as belligerents. During subsequent years, in spite of the large and continued increase of the number of troops sent from Spain and organized by the Spanish authorities in the Island, the yearly campaigns up to the present time have shown that in the eastern interior the Cuban patriots are practically invincible, and that by maintaining a guerrilla warfare they can attack and harass and even defeat their enemies who may be bold enough to act on the aggressive.

In the long war above referred to, the insurgents were never accorded belligerent rights by any power strong enough to take Spain by the throat and force her to conduct operations under the reasonable humanities of modern war. The peculiar form of Cuba renders the control of every port easy to the Spanish navy; and although battles were won and campaigns steadily conducted for ten years by the insurgents, the United States government chose to close its eyes to the truth. The real facts were, not that a state of war was not fully demonstrated, but the " Alabama " claims were in the air, and we were ready first to turn our backs on Cuba in order not to prejudice our money case against England, and after the payment of the award, the precedent was still too fresh.

Balmaceda's Proclamation.

The South American republics which recognized Cuban belligerency were powerless, and Europe remained indifferent. Thus Spain, left unrestrained by foreign powers, worked her will with a cynical frankness that laid bare her full savagery. The war having begun, General Count Balmaceda published the following proclamation :

" Inhabitants of the country! The reinforcements of troops that I have been waiting for have arrived ; with them I shall give protection to the good, and punish promptly those that still remain in rebellion against the government of the metropolis.

" You know that I have pardoned those who have fought us with arms ; that your wives, mothers, and sisters have found in me the unexpected protection that you have refused them. You know, also, that many of those we have pardoned have turned against us again.

" Before such ingratitude, such villainy, it is not possible for me to be the man that I have been ; there is no longer a place for a falsified neutrality ; *he that is not for me is against me ;* and that my soldiers may know how to distinguish, you hear the order they carry:

" 1st. Every man, from the age of fifteen years upward, found away from his habitation (finca), and who does not prove a justified motive therefor, will be shot.

" 2d. Every habitation unoccupied will be burned by the troops.

" 3d. Every habitation from which does not float a white flag, as a signal that its occupants desire peace, will be reduced to ashes.

" Women that are not living at their own homes, or at the houses of their relatives, will collect in the town of Jiguani, or Bayamo, where maintenance will be provided. Those who do not present themselves will be conducted forcibly.

" The foregoing determinations will commence to take effect on the 14th of the present month.

" EL CONDE DE BALMACEDA.

" Bayamo, April 4, 1869."

Tyrants Quoting the Bible.

Spanish tyrants are always deeply Christian, so that it can hardly be supposed that Balmaceda, in using solemn words of the Saviour, did so unconscious that the source of his phrase is the source of divine compassion to men.

A month later, Mr. Fish, then Secretary of State, correctly branded this proclamation as " infamous," and wrote in a letter to Señor Lopez Roberts (Spanish Minister to the United States):

" In the interest of Christian civilization and common humanity, I hope that this document is a forgery. If it indeed be genuine, the President instructs me in the most forcible manner to protest against such mode of warfare."

We have not forgotten the wanton butchery of Americans in the " Virginius " affair. It remains of value as a proved example without which we should be slow to believe that Spanish generals habitually shot insurgents captured in battle, as in fact they did. A published record of the Spanish barbarities of the war gives in detail a list of 2,927 " Martyrs to Liberty,"—political prisoners executed during the war,—and of 4,672 captured insurgents whose fate has never been made known. There were 13,000 confiscations of estates,

1,000 being those of ladies whose only crime was the love of Cuban liberty.

The experience of American newspaper correspondents, like O'Kelly, in rebel camps and Spanish prisons, confirms the revolting character of the Spanish conduct of the war; and there are extant letters of Spanish officers which throw gleams of light into the darkness of the period.   A specimen or two are enough.

Last Words for Cuba.

Jesus Rivocoba, under date of September 4, 1869, writes:

"We captured seventeen, thirteen of whom were shot outright ; on dying they shouted, 'Hurrah for Free Cuba, hurrah for Independence.'   A mulatto said, 'Hurrah for Cespedes.'   On the following day we killed a Cuban officer and another man.   Among the thirteen that we shot the first day were found three sons and their father ; the father witnessed the execution of his sons without even changing color, and when his turn came he said he died for the independence of his country.   On coming back we brought along with us three carts filled with women and children, the families of those we had shot ; and they asked us to shoot them, because they would rather die than live among Spaniards."

Pedro Fardon, another officer, who entered perfectly into the spirit of the service he honored, writes on September 22, 1869 :

"Not a single Cuban will remain in this Island, because we shoot all those we find in the fields, on the farms, and in every hovel."

And again, on the same day, the same officer sends the following good news to his old father :

"We do not leave a creature alive where we pass, be it man or animal.   If we find cows, we kill them ; if horses, ditto ; if hogs, ditto ; men, women, or children, ditto ; as to the houses, we burn them : so every one receives his due,—the men in balls, the animals in bayonet-thrusts.   The Island will remain a desert."

Balmaceda himself paid a visit to the plantation home of the Mora family, and, there being no male patriots on whom to wreak his lust for blood, butchered and burned the sisters Mora and left their home in ashes. A mere enumeration of authentic cases of Spanish inhumanity in the last insurrection would fill volumes and exhibit one of the blackest episodes of history.

The following paragraphs are from an able article by Mr. Clarence King, on the question, "Shall Cuba be Free?" and published in " The Forum ":

"In Spanish character survives a continuous trait of the Pagan cruelty of Rome, reinforced and raised to fiendish intensity by the teachings of the Inquisition. Had the United States, by one stroke of her pen, recognized Cuban belligerency, as was her moral duty, all the Caligula-Torquemada atrocities would have been stopped, and the war for freedom gone on to victory unstained by the blood of women and children. President Grant lost this noblest opportunity of his civil career by miserable anxiety about the ' Alabama ' claims.

Willing to Stake Everything.

" Cubans are under no delusion as to the fateful step they have taken; the men who survived the scourge of the ten-years' war, in rushing to arms again, act in full consciousness of what they are doing, and willingly face the cruel odds. If this were a first effort to acquire freedom it might be attributed to the over-confident enthusiasm of a brave people inexperienced in war and its train of suffering and grief, and ignorant of the combination of money, material, and men their enemy can hurl against her.

" But these are the very people who half a generation ago fought ten years, and felt the shock of 200,000 Spanish soldiers, and suffered as no modern combatants have done. They enter this war as bravely as before, but with eyes open and with memory loaded down with visions of agony and blood. Of that adoration of liberty which is the only sure foundation of modern representative government, this insurrection is as pure and lofty an example as the course of human history can show.

" That all the material advantages of war are against them can easily be seen. In the first place, Cuba is a long, narrow Island about seven hundred miles in east-and-west extent, by a north-and

south breadth of twenty-one to one hundred and twenty miles It
possesses a truly remarkable series of great and small harbors: the
more important ones roomy and landlocked, like those of Havana,
Cienfuegos, Santiago, and others of the type; and the small but often
admirable ones strung at short intervals along the whole 2,000 miles
of sea-coast.   The greater harbors are fortified.

" Spain has a respectable navy, and has, in fact, occupied all the
chief and several of the small harbors with fifteen vessels of war. She
has, besides, a fleet of light-draught gunboats, partly in use and partly
under contract on the Clyde, and soon to be available for cruising
perpetually along the short intervals of shore between the various
harbors which are occupied by larger war-vessels.   In her centuries
of neglect of useful public works in Cuba she has built practically no
wagon-roads, so that if the insurgents possessed artillery, which they
cannot obtain, they could not, save by an almost superhuman effort,
move it to concentration for the capture of one of the ports.

Harbors Blockaded.

" Spain, on the other hand, holds the few rudimentary roads within
the theatre of war, and whatever use of field guns is possible is therefore for Spain alone.   Not only is every important harbor under
effective blockade against insurgent people and freight, but it is
a secure base of supplies.   Practically seventy miles would be a
maximum distance for any considerable operation from a safely-
maintained—even an unthreatened—base, and the average cannot be
above fifty miles.

" Spain therefore begins her campaign to quell the Cubans with a
cordon of impregnable bases, to which at all times she has unre-
stricted access by a sea on which not a single Cuban flag floats,
except on some hovering, unarmed sea-tug or timid blockade-runner
which avoids the ports and creeps in under cover of darkness to bring
a handful of patriots or some boxes of arms.   By means of this complete chain of fortified and occupied harbors, Spain can pour in the
whole resources of the nation in men, supplies, and munitions, without
a moment's interruption or a shadow of danger.   These resources are

a peninsula population of 17,000,000 to draw from, and a standing army, which, on a peace basis, carries 115,735 men, and reaches in nominal war resource something more than 1,000,000.

"Financial advantage is also wholly with Spain. Although bent under a debt of over a thousand millions of dollars, and her fiscal affairs in such wretched condition that there has been no parliamentary endorsement of expenditures since 1865–67, and the Tribunal of Accounts has not dared to publish the national books since 1869,— nevertheless Spain is a nation still possessing the shattered remnants of a public credit.

"She can vote bonds, and there is even yet a price at which they can be sold. Her soldiery face death with courage, in spite of Napier's epigram that "Spaniards are brave behind walls, cowards in the field, and robbers always,"—their conduct in action in Cuba disproving the middle term of an otherwise correct characterization.

"The Spanish *Military Gazette* gives the figures of the national forces in Cuba as follows: 60,000 regulars, the chief part of which are infantry, but including cavalry, 2,596; artillery, 621; engineers, 415; public-order officers, 676; civil guards, 4,400; marines, 2,700; guerrillas, 1,152; the whole under one captain-general, seven division generals, one auditor, one military intendant, one sanitary inspector, and the usual complement of staff and line officers. Besides this there are about 40,000 Cuban militia recruited from the loyal classes and used chiefly for garrison purposes. There are fifteen warships and nineteen vessels in purchase.

"All Cuba has a population of about 1,600,000, of which more than half are in garrison cities and regions so overawed by the power of Spain that they cannot successfully rise until the national forces are shattered in the field. Of the portion in revolt (about two-thirds of the area and one-third of the population) it is probable that of the total number of a sex, age and physical condition to bear arms, the figure would not exceed the actual peace force of the Spanish army, to say nothing of the 17,000,000 which the enemy have to draw upon.

"Impoverished by centuries of financial oppression, the Cuban patriots are poor, their slender resources are the sum of innumerable small contributions. Few in number, empty of purse, they stand within this tight-drawn ring of Spanish fire. Cut off from any but dangerous and clandestine introduction of arms and medicines; lacking supplies to form a base; with not a cent to pay a single soldier or officer of their little army; with only a skeleton medical corps,—in short, almost nothing to make war with,—these brave souls are facing, not death only, but Spanish death.

One Great Graveyard.

"The region under revolution is one great graveyard of those fallen in the ten years' revolt, yet Cubans are undaunted by the numbers or resources of their foe. Beside this far-reaching patience of valor a single act of heroism like Thermopylæ is pastime; compared with the raggedness, hunger, and privation which Cubans bravely choose to accept, Valley Forge was a garden party. For ten years these same men with the same slender resources held the arms and pride of Spain at bay, and then capitulated to promises which were made only to be broken.

"Of Spain the insurgents have no fear but if the United States rigorously prevents the shipment of arms and munitions from our shore, we can discourage, we can delay the triumph of patriotism, but in the end we cannot prevent it. In this war, or the next, or the next, Cuba will be free. Although these men are our near neighbors, although we are to them the chosen people who have won independence and grown great in freedom, yet they have never made the slightest appeal to us for active aid in their struggle.

"They expect no good-Samaritan offices. They look for no gallant American Lafayette to draw sword for them and share the penury and hardships of their camps. They ask nothing. But I happen to know that they are at a loss to comprehend how a great people to whom Heaven has granted the victorious liberty for which they are fighting and dying, should let months pass in cold half-silence, without one ringing 'God-speed!' to cheer them on into battle.

"It is doubtless explicable enough that a people whose own business is so essentially materialistic as ours, and who mind it so absorbedly, should remain carelessly ignorant of the real Cuban question and the moral attitude of the Island people; but is it fair, is it generous, is it worthy of the real blood of freedom that still flows from the big American heart? Already a change is coming, and isolated expressions of genuine sympathy are becoming frequent. The time will come, and that not long hence, when the voice of America will ring out clear and true.

"The Cuban war hangs before us an issue which we cannot evade. Either we must stand as the friend of Spain, and, by our thorough prevention of the shipment of war supplies to the insurgents, aid and countenance the Spanish efforts to conquer Cuba into continued sorrow, or we must befriend Cuba in her heroic battle to throw off a mediæval yoke. Let us not deceive ourselves! Spain alone cannot conquer Cuba; she proved that in ten years of miserable failure. If we prevent the sending of munitions to Cuba, and continue to allow Spain to buy ships and arms and ammunition here it is we who will conquer Cuba, not Spain. It is we who will crush liberty!

"To secure victory for Cuba it is necessary for us, in my opinion, to take but a single step; that is, to recognize her belligerency; she will do all the rest. That step the government will doubtless hesitate to take at the present state of the struggle, because as yet the insurgents have neither instituted a government nor established a capital. In the last insurrection they did both, besides maintaining a state of war for ten years.

"That a state of war exists is virtually admitted by the proclamation of Governor-General Campos, who in addition to the army under his command, consisting of about 60,000 regulars and 40,000 militia, calls for heavy reinforcements, and the Spanish war office has been obliged to order out the first class of reserves. Moreover, a commander-in-chief routed in battle and fleeing, his 'rear-guard fighting bravely all the way into Bayamo,' to use his own words, connotes nothing less than war.

"When the Cuban government is set up, as it soon will be, we shall have equally as good international authority and precedent to recognize a state of war in the Island as Spain did for our own Confederate insurgents forty days after the shot on Fort Sumter. We can return to her, in the interests of liberty, the compliment she then paid us in behalf of slavery. The justice will be poetic. With all possible decorum, with a politeness above criticism, with a firmness wholly irresistible, we should assist Spain out of Cuba and out of the hemisphere as effectually as Lincoln and Seward did the French invaders of Mexico in the sixties.

"Moreover, according to American precedent, neither a state of hostilities nor the setting up of a civil or military organization is positively necessary to entitle a people to belligerent rights; for before either of these conditions was established in 1838, we went so far as to issue a proclamation for 'prevention of unlawful interference in the civil war in Canada.'

"Our record toward Spain is clear. We heartily approved when George Canning invoked the Holy Alliance to prevent her from recovering her American provinces, and in 1825 we refused to guarantee her perpetual possession of Cuba in exchange for commercial concessions to ourselves.

"Our obligations to her are measured by an easily terminable treaty, which, however, while in force, in no way prevents us from recognizing Cuba's belligerency. Is it difficult for us to decide between free Cuba and tyrant Spain? Why not fling overboard Spain and give Cuba the aid which she needs, and which our treaty with Spain cannot prevent? Which cause is morally right?—which is manly?—which is American?"

CHAPTER XXVIII.

Butchery of the Crew of the "Virginius."

ONE of the most cold-blooded massacres on record was that of the crew of the "Virginius," a ship that was rendering aid to the insurgents and was captured by the Spanish. Nothing in all the annals of crime, not even excepting the bloody and savage massacres of Armenia, was more brutal or inhuman than this wholesale slaughter of the gallant captain, officers and crew of that ill-fated vessel. Even though forfeiting their lives, the manner in which they were executed shocked the civilized world. After the first firing some were left still alive, yet writhing in the throes of death. These in some instances had the muzzles of guns rammed into their mouths and their heads were blown off.

With such an inhuman record, and many others to match it in the long ages of Spanish barbarities in Cuba, it is not strange that both the sympathy and the indignation of the American people have, from time to time, been aroused to the highest pitch, and it is only by national forbearance, unjustified as many believe, that Cuba has not been snatched from the grasp of her tormentor. The following is the full and tragic story of the butchery of the crew of the "Virginius."

In 1873 American sympathy for the Cuban struggle for freedom ran high, and we were apparently near war with Spain. To go further back, twenty years before there had been a proposition for the United States to buy Cuba, and it had been haughtily if not contemptuously rejected by Spain. That proposition was the outgrowth of the desire of the Southern political leaders to increase the slave territory and strengthen the pro-slavery representation in Congress by the manufacture of the new States carved out of the Island of Cuba.

In 1873 the situation had changed for the better in the United States as well as in Cuba. The United States had repudiated slavery.

America's sympathy with Cuba's aspirations for independence, and their desire for the acquisition of Cuba, so far as such desire existed, was sincere, and inspired by lofty if not wholly disinterested impulses. This sympathy animated the American people without regard to partisan affiliations and without accruing benefit to either of the great political parties at the expense of the other. Singularly enough—and the fact is now generally forgotten—Spain was at that time a republic under Emilio Castelar.

Unfounded Hopes.

Americans believed that the leopard was going to change its spots. They were urged to wait; that once peace was restored Cuba would share the enlightenment that had begun to shed its beams over Spain and her possessions. All Castelar's eloquence and sophistry were employed in the effort to impress this view upon those in authority in Washington, and not without effect.

But Cubans resident in this country, especially in New York and other coast cities, nearly all of them naturalized, and all of them rich, thought they knew Spain as well as Castelar, and took no stock in her conversion to republican principles, much less in her willingness either under a republican or monarchical form of government, to do anything for Cuba in the way of loosening the ties binding her like whip-cords, not like ties of affection, to the mother country.

They encouraged their brethren in chains to revolt. They sent money and men and arms for the reinforcement of the revolutionists. Filibustering expeditions were common. One of the best ships engaged in these expeditions was the "Virginius," flying the American flag, commanded by Captain Frey, of New Orleans, an American citizen and a veteran of our civil war, and manned in part by American and British sailors. The "Virginius" slipped in and out of Cuban harbors with wonderful success; but the pitcher went to the well once too often.

In October, 1873, the "Virginius" was captured in neutral waters, near the British Island of Jamaica, towed into Santiago de Cuba, declared a pirate and fifty-two of the officers and crew were executed against the protest of the United States Consul.   The whole thing was irregular.   A fraudulent use was made of the Stars and Stripes, and the flag could afford the ship no protection.   International law had been set at naught by capturing the ship in neutral waters, and in executing the captured, some of whom were naturalized citizens of the United States.

The incident served to inform the world of the wholesale, lawless butchery going on in Cuba, and distinguished by Spain as legitimate war.   The four principal officers, Gen. Washington Ryan, Varona, Jesus del Sol and Pedro Cespedes, were marched to the slaughter-house of Santiago de Cuba and murdered.   They were in irons when they were marched against the low, square structure of adobe. Fifteen feet above them the red tile roof projected.   At their feet there was a ditch to catch rain-drops.

Shocking Barbarities.

They were made to kneel, facing the wall.   The wall above them was pitted deep with the bullets that flew over their heads.   As they fell into the ditch the cavalry rode over their warm bodies, and military wagons crunched and slipped on the bodies.   Negroes cut off their heads and carried them on pikes through the city, and the mutilated bodies were dumped into a pit of quicklime.

The North American continent thrilled with indignation in view of this outrage.   The press voiced the demand of the people for apology, indemnity, revenge and the recognition of the Cubans, unorganized as they were, as belligerents.   The government seemed to share the popular feeling to a considerable degree.   War between Spain and the United States seemed to be imminent and unavoidable.

Our poor little navy, consisting of wooden vessels of antiquated models and of ironclads dusty from disuse, was patched up as quickly as possible and ordered to rendezvous at Key West, whence it might descend upon Cuba in a night.   Admiral Scott commanded the North Atlantic Squadron, such as it was.   The flagship was the old " Worcester," Capt. W. D. Whiting.   The " Wyoming " was there under Commander Cushing, and the " Juniata," under Lieut.-Com-

24

mander Merriman. Capt. Jouett commanded the side-wheeler " Powhatan," with the " Ossipee," the " Pawnee " and some others, eleven or twelve in all. The dispatch boats were the " Pinta," Capt. Gorringe (afterward of " Obelisk " celebrity); the " Dispatch," Capt. Frederick Rodgers, and the " Fortune," Lieut.-Commander F. M. Green. Then there were the ironclads which came very near swamping on their tedious cruise down the coast.

Only for a Bluff.

These war vessels, insignificant as they appear in retrospect and unformidable as they must have looked then in the eyes of naval experts, made a very pretty and warlike show as they lay at anchor in the harbor of Key West, and if they had put in an appearance promptly at Havana would have commanded some respect from the expected enemy. But a half bluff is worse than no bluff at all.

It was soon apparent that the government at Washington did not mean business any farther than requiring the surrender of the " Virginius," and of the surviving members of her crew, and an in· demnity, trivial in amount, for the blood of those American citizens whose nationality could be proved beyond peradventure. The State Department did not share the belligerent disposition of the Navy Department. Secretary Fish was able, patriotic and incorruptible, but somehow or other the legal representatives of the Spanish Government managed to block the way, and Spanish diplomacy, then as now, was plausible and resourceful.

Whatever the cause, the naval display at Key West was feeble and ineffective. Our flagship, at least, like the British flagship, should have gone to Havana. As a matter of fact, Admiral Scott had to make an excuse and get express authority to send over a dispatch boat, and was dependent upon the newspaper correspondents, or one of them, for news of what was going on in his immediate front.

From the versatile pen of Major Moses P. Handy we quote a graphic description of the bloody tragedy :

" There was as much newspaper enterprise then as now, although you may not think so. Every New York journal sent correspondents to the front. The New York 'Herald' was represented at first at Key West by W. B. Stephens and Karl Case, who were reinforced by James A. Cowardin and 'Modoc' Fox, and finally by J. A. McGahan, one of the most famous of war correspondents, who came from the European station on one of our men-of-war, and Julius Chambers. The 'Tribune' bureau was in my charge, and we also had Ralph Keeler at Santiago de Cuba and W. P. Sullivan, now a New York broker, at Havana. McGahan, Stephens, Cowardin, Case and Fox are now dead.

Rivalry to get the News.

"The race between the correspondents for news was very hot. Every man as the representative of his newspaper was on his mettle, and enterprise was at a premium. McGahan had the advantage of being ward-room guest on a man-of-war. Fox was paymaster's yeoman on the 'Pinta,' the fastest boat in the navy. When we learned that the 'Virginius' was to be surrendered we all realized that that event would end the campaign. The point then was to be in at the death, and to obtain the best if not the exclusive story of the ceremony and attendant circumstances. The lips of the government officials were sealed as to the time and place appointed.

" In fact the programme was arranged at Washington by the Secretary of State and the Spanish Minister and communicated confidentially to Admiral Scott. However, I managed to get at the secret, and, thus armed, 'stowed away' on the 'Dispatch,' which was the vessel appointed to receive the surrender. Captain Rodgers commanded the 'Dispatch,' but the receiving officer was Captain Whiting. The fleet captain and the other officers of the detail were Lieutenant Adolph Marix, Master George A. Calhoun and Assistant Engineer N. H. Lambdin. With them were thirty-nine sailor men from the 'Pawnee,' who were to man the surrendered vessel as a prize crew. All of these people except Captain Whiting were ignorant of their instructions, not even knowing their destination, and the pilot taken aboard before leaving Key West had sealed orders.

"We left Key West on a Sunday night at 10 o'clock. We were in the open sea before I ventured to make my appearance on deck, present myself to the officers, declare myself a stowaway, and verify my information as to their mission.   The next morning at 10 o'clock the blue hills of the Cuban coast rose above the horizon and the bow of the 'Dispatch' was directed toward Bahia Honda, the obscure little port selected for the function.

"It was about noon when we passed an old fort called Murillo, commanding the entrance to the harbor.   Speed was then slackened, and the vessel crept cautiously along the narrow, but clearly marked channel, which leads to the smooth water where the 'Virginius' was supposed to be lying.

Raising the Stars and Stripes.

"As soon as the 'Dispatch' was sighted from the shore, the Spanish flag, bearing the crown, notwithstanding the republic abolishing that monarchical emblem, was flung to the breeze.   We discovered a black side-wheel steamship lying about a mile beyond the fort.   It was the 'Virginius.'   No other craft, except two or three coasting steamers, or fishing smacks, was then visible, and it was not until we were about to come to anchor that we discerned a Spanish sloop-of-war lying close under the shore, about two and a half miles away.

"Very soon a boat from the Spanish man-of-war came alongside of the 'Virginius,' and immediately the Stars and Stripes were raised by Spanish hands, and again floated over the vessel which carried Ryan and his unfortunate comrades to their death.   At the same moment we saw, by the aid of field-glasses, another boat let down from the Spanish vessel.   It proved to be the captain's gig, and brought to the 'Dispatch' a naval officer in full uniform, who proved to be Senor de la Camera, of the Spanish sloop-of-war 'Favorita.' He stepped briskly forward, and was met at the gangway by Captain Rodgers and Captain Whiting.

"After an exchange of courteous salutations, Commander de la Camera remarked that he had received a copy of the protocol providing for the surrender of the 'Virginius,' and that the surrender might now be considered to have taken place.   Captain Whiting replied that under his instructions the following day was named for the surrender, and that he could not receive it until that time. Meanwhile he would thank the Spanish officer to continue in possession. Nine o'clock on Tuesday morning was then agreed upon as the hour, and after informing the American officer that there was coal enough on board of the 'Virginius' to last six days, salutes were exchanged and the Spanish officer retired.

"The next morning, half an hour ahead of time, the gig of the 'Favorita' came over to the 'Virginius.' It contained oarsmen and a single officer. As the latter stepped on deck a petty officer and half a dozen men, who had stood watch on the 'Virginius' during the night, went over the side and remained in a dingy awaiting orders. At 9 precisely by the bells the American flag again flew to the flag-staff of the 'Virginius,' and at the same moment a boat containing Capt. Whiting and Lieut. Marix put away from the 'Dispatch.' As they ascended the accommodation ladder of the 'Virginius' the single man on deck, who proved to be Señor de la Camera, advanced and made a courteous salute.

Account of the Surrender.

"The officers then read their respective instructions, and Capt. de la Camera remarked that in obedience to the requirements of the government and in execution of the provisions of the protocol, he had the honor to turn over the steamer 'Virginius' to the American authorities. Capt. Whiting accepted, and, learning that a receipt was required, gave one in due form. A word or two more was spoken, and the Spaniard stepped over the side, signalled to his oarsmen, and in ten minutes was again upon the deck of his own vessel. Beside the surrendering and receipting officers, I was the only witness of the ceremony.

"While the Spanish officer was courtesy itself, we were all impressed with the fact that the ceremony was lacking in dignity, and that the Spaniards had purposely made that lack as conspicuous as they dared. It appeared that the 'Virginius' was towed to Havana by the first-class man-of-war 'Isabel la Catolica,' the commander of which retired immediately and left the surrender to be made by the commander of the 'Favorita,' which had been in the vicinity of Bahia Honda for several months engaged in surveying duty. The surrender should have taken place either at Santiago de Cuba or at Havana, and a Spanish officer of like rank with Capt. Whiting should have discharged the duty.

Bad Condition of the Vessel.

"A quick survey by our officers showed the 'Virginius' to be in a most filthy condition. She was stripped of almost everything moveable save a few vermin, which haunted the mattresses and cushions in cabin and staterooms, and half a dozen casks of water. The decks were caked with dirt, and nuisances recently committed, combined with mold and decomposition, caused a foul stench in the forecastle and below the hatches. In the cabin, however, the odor of carbolic acid gave evidence that an attempt had been made to make that part of the vessel habitable for the temporary custodians of the ship.

"Our officers were reluctant to put the men into the dirty forecastle and stowed them away into hardly more agreeable quarters afforded by the staterooms of Ryan and his butchered companions. Some attempt seemed to have been made, as shown by the engineering survey, to repair the machinery, but a few hours' work put the engines in workable order. The ship was leaking considerably and the pumps had to be kept going constantly to keep the water down. After a few hours of hard work we got under way, but had only gone 200 yards when the engines suddenly refused to do duty, and it became necessary for the 'Dispatch' to take us in tow.

"As we passed the fort at the entrance to the harbor the Spanish flag was rather defiantly displayed by that antiquated apology for a fortification, and there was no salute for the American flag, either from the fort or the surrendering sloop-of-war.

"We had a hard time that night—those of us who were aboard the 'Virginius.' It seemed hardly possible that we could keep afloat until morning. During the night the navy tug 'Fortune,' from Key West, met us and remained with the convoy. At noon the next day, when we were about thirty miles south-southeast of Dry Tortugas, the vessels separated, the 'Virginius' and 'Dispatch' going to Tortugas and the 'Fortune' returning, with me as a solitary passenger, to Key West whence I had the honor of reporting the news to the Admiral.

Cheers from Excited Spaniards.

"It was the general opinion among the naval officers that the Sania had endeavored to belittle the whole proceeding by smuggling the 'Virginius' out of Havana, by selecting an obscure harbor not a port of entry as the place of surrender and by turning the duty of surrender over to a surveying sloop, while the 'Tornado,' which made the capture, lay in the harbor of Havana and the 'Isabel la Catolica,' which had been selected as convoy, steamed back to Havana under cover of the night. The American officers and American residents in Cuba and Key West agreed that our government ought to have required that the 'Virginius' should be surrendered with all the released prisoners on board either at Santiago de Cuba, where the 'Tornado' brought in her ill-gotten prey and where the inhuman butcheries were committed, or in Havana where she was afterward taken in triumph and greeted with the cheers of the excited Spaniards over the humiliation of the Americans.

"An attempt was made to take the 'Virginius' to some northern port, but the old hulk was not equal to the journey. On the way no pumping or caulking could stop her leaks, and she foundered in mid-ocean. The government had been puzzled to know what disposition to make of her, and there was great relief in official circles to know that she was out of the way.

"The surrender of the surviving prisoners of the massacre took place in the course of time at Santiago, owing more to British insistence than to our feeble representations. As to the fifty-three who were killed, Spain never gave us any real satisfaction. For a long time the Madrid government unblushingly denied that there had been any killing, and when forced to acknowledge the fact, they put us off with preposterous excuses. 'Butcher Borrel,' by whose orders the outrage was perpetrated, was considered at Madrid to have been justified by circumstances. It was pretended that orders to suspend the execution of Ryan and his associates were 'unfortunately' received too late, owing to interruption of telegraph lines by the insurgents to whose broad and bleeding shoulders an attempt was thus made to shift the responsibility.

'Butcher' Borrel Promoted.

"There was a nominal repudiation of Borrel's act and a promise was made to inflict punishment upon 'those who have offended;' but no punishment was inflicted upon anybody. The Spanish Government, with characteristic double dealing, resorted to procrastination, prevarication and trickery, and thus gained time until new issues effaced in the American mind the memory of old wrongs unavenged. Instead of being degraded Borrel was promoted. Never to this day has there been any adequate atonement by Spain, much less an apology or expression of regret for the 'Virginius' massacre.

"Newspaper correspondents having figured in this sketch, I cannot close it without referring to the fate of one of my colleagues whose death undoubtedly lies at the door of the Spaniards. Ralph Keeler was his name. He was more magazinist than newspaper man, and had achieved reputation by his stories of actual experiences in vagabondage, written, I think, for the 'Atlantic Monthly.' We all expected great things of him as a war correspondent.

"After the surrender of the 'Virginius,' he was expected to cover the surrender of the prisoners, but having some misgivings as to whether he would understand what was required to get ahead in the dispatch of the news to New York, I laid plans to cover any default by securing a report from another source. My misgivings had more substantial foundation than I knew, for poor Keeler was probably dead at the moment when his instructions were filed in the telegraph office.

"He disappeared as effectually as if the earth had opened and swallowed him. How, why or when he died his friends never knew.

It is believed, however, that he was another victim of the hatred which in those days inflamed the Spanish breast against every citizen of the United States. Circumstantial evidence indicated that he was assassinated by Spanish volunteers, and I have always thought of my genial and gifted colleague as one of the murdered Americans now vaguely remembered as the victims of the Spanish bloodthirstiness in the matter of the unavenged ' Virginius ' incident."

PART III.

Picturesque Cuba:
Manners and Customs of the People.

CHAPTER XXIX.

First Impressions of the Island.

CUBA! Beautiful "Queen of the Antilles," the land of the cocoa and the palm—of the golden banana and the luscious orange —well may the hearts of thy sons and the dark, lustrous eyes of thy maidens glow and glisten with pride at the praises of thy sunny Isle! How few Americans there are who have formed any correct conception of "Life in the Tropics!" To the generality of us, Cuba suggests the idea of heat and yellow fever, of venomous reptiles and insects, slaves and sugar, oranges and ever-blooming flowers—an idea in a great degree erroneous.

Few, indeed, can realize that, leaving the snow-clad hills of New York harbor in the depth of winter, in three and a half or four days they will be sailing over the placid waters of the bay of Havana, under a tropic sun, which even in mid-winter rivals that of our own land in its season of dog-day heat, and will see around them the verdure-clad hills, with the graceful palm and cocoa-tree clear against the pure blue sky of the beautiful Isle, so truly called "the most precious jewel of the Spanish crown."

Yet there are many Americans who, each year, either for purposes of health, business, or pleasure, flock to Havana, all glad to avoid the inclement weather of the icy north; and even with all their traveling it is difficult to get any reliable information as to what preparations

378

one needs to make before starting; unless, indeed, some of one's acquaintances have been there, and even then it is very limited.

To him, therefore, who has any intention of making a visit to the Island of Cuba with the purpose of staying there some time, of traveling over the Island, and of really enjoying its beautiful scenery, its oddities of manners and customs, or even of trying its numerous medicinal waters, we recommend to pick up a little Spanish, even if it be only enough to ask for something to eat, to give directions about luggage and such other every-day necessities as occur to the traveler in any land.

Not Great Travelers.

The Cubans themselves are not a traveling people, and, to use the words of one of their own authors, " have little fancy for traveling, be it on account of the bad roads, that now are disappearing with the advent of steamboats and railroads, or be it from the love with which the localities where we are born and pass the first years of our infancy inspire us,—where exist our interests, and where gather round our sweetest memories.

Few foreigners go much away from Havana or Matanzas, or perhaps Cardenas, and the people have not yet learned the necessities of those who travel for curiosity or health; and therefore to us, accustomed as we are to have our traveling made easy, many things will seem hard, uncomfortable, and strange, unless one is able by a few words of Spanish to smooth away the rough peculiarities of places and people not accustomed to a traveling public.

And yet, with all the inconveniences and peculiarities that the traveler experiences after leaving Havana, he is compensated for all of these by the perfect novelty of the sights and scenery he meets with, and by the extreme change in the manner of life, he is accustomed to, although he may leave behind him some greater conveniences in quitting the prominent places like Havana and Matanzas, where, after the novelty of the streets, the architecture of the houses, and the odd appearance of the stores, etc., are worn off, he is reminded of the city life of his own land constantly. The social life of the better classes is much the same, the world over ; they eat, and drink, and visit pretty much as they do in all the great capitals of the world.

But it is in such towns as Trinidad and Santiago de Cuba, and in such pretty villages as Güines, San Antonio, and Guanajay, or among the coffee-places of the Vuelta Abajo, and the sugar estates of the Vuelta Arriba, that the stranger sees the original habits aud customs of a people who are always loth to change; and it has been truly said that Cuba is more Spanish than Spain ; for here it is out of the world, in some degree, while there effort is made to keep up with the new ideas of the day.

Cuban Hospitality.

A more kind-hearted, hospitable people than the Cubans, particularly to " Los Americanos," it would be difficult to find ; no trouble is too great for them if you can make them comprehend the *purpose* of what you desire ; and the " oiling of the palm " is just as effectual amongst these primitive peope of the interior as in more civilized lands. Many of the people speak English, a great many French,—which, in fact, is the household language in some parts of the Island,—and many of the young men one finds have been regularly educated in the United States.

In arranging money matters, unless one is very extravagant indeed in his daily expenditures, five dollars gold per day is a very fair allowance for ordinary expenses while on the Island for simply living and traveling ; while, of course, if one desires to be extravagant or make purchases, there are just as many ways of getting rid of money as in other places.

The provision for these expenses can best be made by a letter of credit. As exchange on London is generally at a premium in Havana, a bill of exchange even up to ninety days on some well-known house can be disposed of to advantage ; as, however, there is not the same system of banking in Havana as there is with us, the best arrangement for the general traveler is to take a letter of credit on some well-known house in Havana. He will then only have to pay for money as he uses it, he has no trouble in carrying money with him, and such houses will furnish letters of credit to other parts of the Island, which is a great convenience.

An amount of silver in ten-cent pieces, which pass readily as the " real sencilla,"—say from twenty to fifty dollars' worth, will be found very convenient for the thousand and one daily expenses of the traveler, small change being scarce. Other silver coin it is not advisable to take, since our twenty-five cent pieces pass for only twenty cents (*peseta*), and the half dollars (*medio peso*) for only forty cents. American gold passes readily, being generally at a premium of seven or eight per cent.; and if you can supply yourself with the Spanish doubloons at their intrinsic value of sixteen dollars, they will pass for seventeen dollars in Cuba, as that is their value fixed by the government to keep the coin in the country.

Letters of Introduction.

Letters of introduction to business men in Havana are really not worth the paper they are written on, no matter by whom written, or in whose favor given; for the merchants receive such hosts of them that it would be impossible, even had they the inclination, to show attentions to the bearers. Many amusing incidents we could give of persons with really strong letters, presenting the same under the impression that at least some ordinary civility would be shown them, when on the contrary they were astonished by the very blunt question addressed to them, without preface, of—" Well, what do you want ? "

Letters to planters or citizens will be found very useful and are generally well and politely received, particularly those to the owners of sugar and coffee estates, than whom a more hospitable, kindly people it is hard to find. They are generally very glad indeed to entertain you at their places, if they themselves are living there; or if not, and you desire to visit a sugar estate, are kind enough to forward you, with a letter, to the administrator of the estate, who constantly lives upon it, and will take good care of you.

Clothing for a stay on the Island needs to be of the very lightest summer kind; and one can wear, almost without intermission, linen clothes, or a light suit of summer woolens.   The nights during the winter months are quite cool and agreeable for sleep, but the middle of the day is always warm, the average temperature in Havana being about eighty degrees.   Clothing, particularly linens, of all kinds can be purchased, of the best kinds and makes, in Havana, and at very reasonable prices; and there are certain styles of dresses that can be much better purchased there than at home, some of them being made specially for the Cuban market.

A suggestion, prompted by experience, we would here make to any one intending to leave the traveled routes (as in fact it applies as well to the towns, where they have no baggage carts), and that is to have one's baggage in the shape of good-sized valises (*maletas*), for these can be easily handled, can even be put in the car with the owner, and, in the country, strapped on the back of mules or horses, which is the common mode of transportation the people are familiar with.

Singular Beds and Mattresses.

If the traveler is an invalid, and proposes to go to other places than Havana and Matanzas, it will be well to provide himself with an air-pillow, and, if he cannot sleep on a somewhat hard bed, an air-mattress also.   Few of the hotels even in Havana are provided with mattresses to the beds, and the pillows are generally stuffed with hard cotton or hair, the beds being a simple sacking bottom, covered with a linen sheet.   This may seem, at first, a great hardship, accustomed as we are to our patent spring-mattresses; but they are much cooler and, after a little experience, as comfortable for that climate as are mattresses.

Half a dozen towels will not be found amiss, as at some of the smaller places the supply is somewhat short.   And in speaking of invalids who are very far gone with any organic disease, very few indeed are ever very much benefited by a stay on the Island, any more than that they avoid the inclemencies and changes of a northern winter; though there are cases in which some wonderful cures have been effected, particularly in the Island of Pines.

For the overworked man of business, however, the debilitated or weakly person, or one whose system has from some cause or other become reduced, the climate and scenes of Cuba will work wonders; and all such cases generally go back at the end of the winter completely restored. But the poor consumptive, who has left it till it is too late for anything in this world to do him good, only comes out here to have his high hopes entirely dispelled, particularly when he finds so many of the ordinary comforts to which he is accustomed, and which are so necessary to the invalid, entirely unheard of.

It is safe for the stranger to visit the Island any time after December, though January and February are the gay months, and he can remain until even the first of June, though in May they have it very hot indeed, and also some little fever amongst the shipping. If it is necessary for the invalid to leave home in October, before the winter of the north sets in, he can visit the Island with safety, but will find it pleasanter to go directly to some of the "places of *recreo*," as they are called, near the city,—which are simply pretty villages, such as Guines, Marianao, and Puentes Grandes, where good accommodations can always be had.

Merry Christmas.

There is, however, not much to be done or seen before January, if one wants to make simply a pleasure trip of it; for at Christmas almost all the families visit their estates and distribute presents to the hands, making a week's regular holiday of it; after which the grinding season begins on the sugar plantations, and the business of the town becomes quick and active. Carnival season, the week before Lent, is the jolly season of the year, when everybody gives up to the spirit of pure enjoyment and mischief; and it is then the Habañeros are seen unbending from their usually dignified manner, and giving loose rein to their tastes for balls, masks and spectacles.

Holy Week, the closing of the Lenten season, has also its attractions in a country so thoroughly Romanistic as Cuba; and the processions and ceremonies of the church, some of which are carried on with great solemnity and splendor, will interest the Protestant traveler.

Many persons make the trip to Havana and back solely for the sea voyage, from which they derive great benefit, simply staying over one steamer. We have known business men in New York, who would not tear themselves away until actually sent away by their doctors, take the voyage out, remain ten days in Havana, and return thoroughly recuperated men—so wonderful is the effect of the sea air in the Gulf Stream, and the immense let-up afforded by the entire change of customs, scenes and language at Havana.

As the steamers are large and well patronized, their accommodations are of the very best class, and one is always sure to find pleasant company on board with whom to while away agreeably the short passage of even four days.

> " We left behind the painted buoy
>   That tossed at the harbor-mouth :
> And madly danced our hearts with joy,
>   As fast we fleeted to the South.
> How fresh was every sight and sound
>   On open main or winding shore !
> We knew the merry world was round,
>   And we might sail forever more.
>
> Warm broke the breeze against the brow.
>   Dry sang the tackle, sang the sail ;
> The lady's head upon the prow
>   Caught the shrill salt, and sheered the gale.
> The broad seas swelled to meet the keel,
>   And swept behind ; so swift the run,
> We felt the good ship shake and reel,
>   We seemed to sail into the sun."

"Will make Cuba in the morning, sir," says the captain ; and so we stroll forward to watch the porpoises as they race along with the steamer through the blue water, or amuse ourselves watching the tiny mariner, the nautilus, as it floats lightly on the wave. With night comes the never-failing pleasure of leaning over the vessel's stern with some charming fair one, watching the ever-sparkling beauties of the phosphorescent light in the vessel's wake, and enjoying that indescribable pleasure of a tropical night at sea.

" Cuba is in sight, sir; can see it through your window," says the
steward, rousing you up on the morning of the fourth day out; and,
turning over in your berth, there, sure enough, are seen the hills of
Cuba, and the indistinct outlines of the Morro Castle—looking, as
you see them through your window, like some beautiful painting to
which the oval of the dead-eye forms a frame.

We are fortunate in arriving so opportunely, for, had we arrived
the previous evening after sundown, though it were still daylight, we
would have been compelled to lie outside all night, as no vessels are
allowed to enter after evening gun-fire, at sundown.   There are the
signals flying in the morning breeze from the watch-tower of the
grim Morro Castle; and as we approach more nearly, we distinguish
our dear old bunting, rivaling with its stars and stripes even the
bright sky and sparkling waves.

First View of Havana.

And now we have before us a full view of Havana and its surroundings—the Morro Castle to the left; to the right, the city, with
the fort of La Punta (historic, too) on its extreme point—the white,
blue, and yellow-colored houses, with their red-tiled roofs, looking
fresh and bright in this breezy January morning.

Still later, we are passing within easy stone-throw of the grim-
looking Morro, from whose frowning battlements the sentry hails as
we go swiftly by; there, to the left, the white walls on the abrupt hills
of the Cabañas fortifications; to the right, again, the bay side-walls of
the city, with the roofs of houses and towers of churches piled up in
close proximity; and there, fresh and green, like an oasis in the desert of stone houses, the small but pretty Cortina de Valdes, looking
so invitingly cool in the shade of its trees; some of the other Paseos
in the outer portion of the city being marked out by the long, regular rows of green trees that stretch away until they are lost in the
distant buildings.

How one's heart leaps at such a quaint, novel scene as this!
Havana, around whose walls cluster so many memories of the once
haughty Spanish Dons, whose foundation dates back nearly two cen-

25

turies before our own noble country was settled; what visions of
gold-laden ships, of wild, reckless, murderous freebooters, expeditions
of gallant early adventurers and discoverers, and more lately the
realization of numerous passages of Irving's and Prescott's glowing
descriptions, come flooding upon one as he sees for the first time this
apparently beautiful city!

Still swiftly gliding on up the bay, passing as we go the Spanish
men-of-war and vessels of all nations sailing in and out, we see to
great advantage this far-famed beautiful bay; a turn to the right, and
we see the long line of covered wharves, with the shipping of the
world lying side by side, waiting the completion of their cargoes; to
the left, the white walls of still another fort—the Casa Blanca—that
commands the city, and farther on in front of us we see the little
town of Regla, with its immense warehouses of solid stone and cor-
rugated iron for storing the sugar of the Island, as substantial and
handsome in their structure as any the world can show.   And now
we are at anchor.

The custom-house officers come on board, and the steamer is surrounded by a perfect fleet of small boats, that are a cross between a
market-wagon and a scow, from which rush a horde of hotel-run-
ners, all expatiating upon the merits of their particular hotels, some
of them in the most amusing broken English.

These boats, by-the-by, are afloat what the "volante" is ashore;
and the traveler must needs use many of them if he wishes to see
anything of the bay and surroundings of Havana.   Small boats are
not allowed to carry more than five passengers, or the large ones ten!
"From ten and a half o'clock at night until the firing of the signal
gun at daybreak in the morning, no boats will be allowed to pass in
the bay."   The traveler is, however, on all long trips, advised to
make a bargain with the boatman, using care that he is not over-
charged.

Having made up our mind before leaving the steamer as to which
hotel we propose to patronize, we point out our baggage to the
runner of that hotel, who will take charge of it, and we shall have no
further trouble about it, except to pass it at the custom-house on

landing. The runner has also a boat, into which we go, and have no trouble about fares, the which are settled for, and with the baggage charges will be found in his hotel bill " all right."

Now comes the fun. The passengers crowd into the little boats, a pile of baggage is stowed forward, the sail is set and away skims the little tub to the custom-house, each one trying to get there first. Arrived there, the voyager has his first experience of a *Cosas de Cuba* in the shape of a stalwart negro who takes a trunk, no matter how large, from the boat, places it on his head, and in the most nonchalant manner walks off with it to the examining office as though it were a trifle instead of a trunk on his brain, if he has any at all of that organ. The officers are very easy and polite in their examination of baggage, passing everything almost with a merely nominal examina- tion, particularly if the keys are politely and readily produced.

Hacks and Hotels.

And now we are in Havana, and free to go where we like, notwith- standing those two military statues at the door, who look at us so fiercely as we go by. Outside the custom-house will be found hacks, which for twenty cents will carry the traveler where he wants to go.

But here we are at our hotel, and plenty of hotels there are to satisfy every taste and purse, though somewhat different from our great caravansaries. The ease and comforts (or lack of such, as we know them) of one of the hotels are most acceptable with their *café con leche* or chocolate at early morning, their eleven o'clock breakfast of luscious fruits and cool salads, and their abundant and pleasant dinners at five or six o'clock.

After dinner comes the delicious drive on the " Paseo," where magnificent equipages, lovely women, and well-dressed men, added to the beautiful surroundings of stately, graceful palms, and avenues of tropical trees, make up a scene that will vie with anything the world can show, the day ending, maybe, by a charming stroll in the magnificent grounds of " El Jardin Botanico," at the Governor- General's, where, at no expense, and without let or hindrance, one can wander for hours at a time through a garden that in its luxuriant magnificence of trees, fruits and flowers rivals anything the eye has ever seen in America.

" *Café solo o con leche ?* " (coffee with or without milk) is about the first thing one hears of a morning in a Spanish hotel, as " Boots " puts his head in at the door to make the inquiry ; and as, to make use of a common expression, "you pay your money and you have your choice," you will very quickly decide, if you want to get into Cuban ways, to have it thus early in the morning *con leche.* Our reasons for this are that in Cuba the custom is, on first rising, to take only a cup of coffee or chocolate, with a bit of dry toast or roll, which satisfies the appetite until the regular breakfast-hour of nine, ten, or eleven o'clock ; and experience has taught that coffee *with* milk on an *empty* stomach is better than the coffee without (or *cafe noir*), which is best as a digestor *after* meals. Fruit, also, in the morning on rising is used, and is very palatable ; but a little experience will show that the Cuban fashion of *beginning* the breakfast with fruit is best.

Excellent Restaurants.

Havana, city as it is of quite two hundred and fifty thousand inhabitants, with abundance of travel at certain seasons of the year, does not boast of one first-class hotel, as we understand the word, though there are several where the traveler, if he is not too particular, can be tolerably comfortable. There is no giving the reason for this—the fact is so, and though there are numbers of excellent restaurants kept by Spaniards and French, yet there are but few hotels kept by those people that are more than passable.

The city is large, there are constant arrivals of people from other portions of the Island, and in the winter season there are crowds of travelers from abroad ; and yet, if you discuss the matter with a Cuban, he will only shrug his shoulders, and remark, " It won't pay."

But what more can be expected from a city that does not possess a chimney in its whole vast extent of private dwellings ? Who ever heard even of *a house without a chimney?* They don't need them here, you say ? Well, how do you account, then, for the absence of the other things ?—you can't say they don't need them.

CHAPTER XXX.

Curious Sights in Havana.

TO see the curiosities of Havana and its neighborhood properly there is necessarily involved, in addition to a large expenditure of shoe-leather, much expenditure of *reales* and *pesetas* in cab hire. Although there are few passenger railways in Havana, yet from the abundance of all kinds of public vehicles it can not be said that they are missed much, since, if it is desired to go to any particular spot, all that is necessary is to wait in front of your hotel or at the corner of the street, and inside of three minutes you will have your choice of perhaps a dozen vehicles, that are constantly passing in every direction, and which, for twenty cents, will carry you to any part of the city.

These comprise various kinds and styles; but the one most in use to-day, and the latest novelty, is the "Victoria," a very comfortable four-wheeled affair, with seats for two, and in front a seat upon the box for the driver of the one horse required to draw it. All of these vehicles are the property of a few owners.

Such is the constant busy travel, that there is always a great demand for them, even at what would seem a high price, in comparison with what the *caleseros* (drivers) are allowed to charge the passengers; and yet the owners could rent out a greater number still, each driver, at that rate, making from two to four dollars per day.

Wherever you go in the city, you see a constant stream of these carriages going in every direction, without and with occupants; those that are not occupied have a little tin sign hanging over the box, "*Se alquila*" (to hire). One of the owners of a line of these carriages had made over $100,000, and was desirous of selling out and going back to his *belle France*, whence he originally came.

Although the popular name of the "volante" has made it familiar even to the foreign mind, there is in fact a great mistake about that conveyance—since the volante proper was a different affair in times gone by, and is to-day, from what is now called volante, which in truth is really the "quitrin." The old volante is now almost extinct, or used simply by some business man to drive to and from his place

OLD VOLANTE.

of business, or is found in a very dilapidated state in some of the interior towns of the Island.

It, like the volante vulgar, is a two-wheeled affair, with long shafts, which rest upon the horse or mule, upon whose back sits the driver in a clumsily-made big saddle. The shafts have one end resting upon the axle, the other upon the horse, on the same principle as the poles of the old-fashioned litter; and the

volante body is also on the same principle, being with its huge leather springs, constantly in motion from side to side. The main difference between the two vehicles is, that the old volante does not lower its top, which is permanent, while the vo-lante or quitrin of to-day permits of the top being lowered or raised at

VOLANTE AS IT IS.

pleasure—a very great improvement and convenience.

As public vehicles in Havana, these are fast giving entire place to the carriage and the Victoria; but the private quitrin is, and always will be, one of the *cosas de Cuba*, for it is the only vehicle used on the bad roads by the families in going to and from their places, while in the city it is splendidly adorned and decorated with silver-platings and rich stuffs—the most elegant and handsome affair in which the Señoritas can take their airings, and show off their handsome persons.

It is amusing sometimes to see these long-poled conveyances attempt to turn one of the corners in the usually narrow streets of the old town. It is a matter of considerable difficulty, the horse and rider appearing as though they would have to enter some store-door to get out of the way of the volante behind it, and is the occasion of much hard swearing. A few years ago the volante was the only conveyance seen; and now, on the contrary, one sees carriages of all kinds and styles, of as fine and striking appearance as anything in Central Park.

But the volante or quitrin of the livery-stable is, *par excellence*, another affair, as any one will find out to his cost who orders one innocently from the stable without inquiring its expense. When, however, he sees it drive up with two fine horses, the *calesero* in a stunning red livery, covered with gold lace, high boots coming almost up to his waist, and the horses decked out in harness that reflects the sun from a hundred silver-plated buckles, rings, and knobs, he begins to have a glimmering that this is going to cost something, and must " be settled " for.

Different Kinds of Vehicles.

On the public stands can also be had two-horse carriages, usually **very** comfortable barouches, and used generally for a party of four or five for a drive on the Paseo. The livery-stables, also, furnish very handsome carriages of the same kind, which, with the two-horse volantes, can be had at all times by applying at the hotels, as they generally have some particular stable at which they get carriages. The prices are in all cases quite high enough.

An American traveler in Cuba relates the following incident: " Cabmen appear to be the same the world over; and I shall not soon forget an amusing episode that took place on our first departure from Havana. One of these fellows, of an early morning, had carried us to the depot, and upon settling with him I gave him double fare in consideration of his putting our trunks in his wagon. This was a proceeding so unusual, that he immediately thought I must be a novice indeed, and demanded double the fare already paid him. I politely declined to comply with his request, on the ground that I had already paid him double; whereupon he stormed and swore that he was being robbed, very much to our amusement and that of the bystanders. I could not resist laughing in the fellow's face at his cool impudence, which aggravated him so much that he thrust the fare back into my hand, vowing he would take nothing.

"I thanked him very kindly, and, with the utmost gravity, told him I would drink his health, and raising my hat to him, politely bade him good-by ; and, showing my ticket, was about entering the cars, when the fellow was so taken aback at this peculiar way of meeting him, that he rushed at me, holding out his hand, and remarked, 'Ah, you are an American ; give me what you please !' upon which I returned him his gift, and left him with a smile upon his countenance, and the remark, ' A pleasant journey to you, sir ; ' when, had you seen him five minutes previously, raving and lamenting, you would have truly thought he really meant what he said."

In the Public Markets.

It is always a matter of interest to the traveler in any land to know how and from where the supplies of food for the people generally come ; and this is best seen by a visit to the public market-place, where not only the material with which they are fed can be seen, but a great deal may be learned of the manners and habits of a certain class of the people themselves.   Therefore, as fruit is said to be best in these warm climates before breakfast, we will stroll down to the markets, and while doing a little inspection duty, make an investment in some of the fruits of the country.

The most convenient one inside the city is that of the "Mercado de Cristina," in the Plaza Vieja, situated at the corner of Teniente Rey street and San Ygnacio.   Here, in the centre of a hollow square, the sides of which are formed of ranges of stores of all classes, faced by an arcade, is one of the great marts for the sale of vegetables, fruits and meats for the supply of the city.   It is a large stone build-ing apparently, though really a simple quadrangle, open to the sky, occupying the whole of a square, and was erected in 1836, during Tacon's administration.

The arcade of stores is filled with shops of all kinds, but princi-pally occupied in the sale of such "notions" as will please the country people or the negroes, while the Plaza is filled with immense piles of onions, and cabbages, and sweet potatoes, which are the principal productions of the Island in the vegetable way; and there are smaller piles of oranges, green mangos, pine-apples, and other tropic fruits, new in name and appearance; clusters of the plantain, or banana, as we call it, of various colors, and pyramids of the green cocoa fruit meet the eye at every turn, all presided over by dusky negroes in all varieties of costume, or swarthy Cubans, the native country people. These come in from the surrounding country with their products, raised upon the small *estancia* in the neighborhood of the city. Here and there, too, may be seen the patient donkey, with his load of greer fodder, giving comic life to the scene.

Wholesome Vegetables.

The plantain, of which we see such large quantities exposed, is the vegetable upon which the lower classes depend for food, and which is cooked in various ways; and with the "*tasajo*" (jerked beef, or fish), constitutes the diet of the poor. Of the many delightful vegetables that grow in such abundance in our summer season, there is not a single one to be seen. Of berries of any kind there is not one raised upon the Island, owing to the great heat, which burns them up, it is said. The market presents a very different appearance from one of ours, with its profusion of everything arranged in the tidy-looking stalls, and presided over by clean-looking vendors.

Here it is very different; a great proportion of the market people are negroes, most of whom are free, and such a chattering as they keep up, particularly the women, who are scolding, laughing, or railing at each other in the most deafening way. It is very amusing to walk along in front of the little tables, or more usually the piles of fruit on the ground, and buy some of the queer-looking fruits you see, and which are totally unheard of by the names which the negroes give them, many of them, nevertheless, being quite palatable.

The little banana and the orange are, however, the most agreeable of all, tasting very pleasant and cool in the early morning before one's breakfast; but there are others that are very luscious when eaten perfectly ripe and in season, and which the market people will gladly tell you all about, as soon as they find you are a stranger,— particularly an " Americano."

The choicest of these, after the luscious pine-apple, orange, and banana, are the delicious " *anon*," the " *zapote*," and the " *mamey colorado*," the latter sometimes called " angels' sweetmeats ;" any of which, if they happen to be in season, will please the palate of the stranger, if he is fond of rich, luscious fruits ; many persons find them too rich and sweet.

Having heard so much of the milk of the cocoanut when drank fresh from the green fruit, you seize this opportunity to get a new experience of a *cosas de Cuba* ; and, negotiating for a good large one, for which you pay *un medio* (five cents), the negro takes a huge sharp knife, and slices off the top of the fruit, in which he punches a hole from which you are to drink. Seizing it with both hands, you raise it to your mouth like a water-jar, and empty the contents, as you think, down your throat ; and sweet, cool, and pleasant it certainly is to the palate, only this is rather an awkward and inconvenient way or drinking it, as you find on examining your shirt front, which has received a good share of the contents.

A much more convenient way is to carry the green cocoanut to one's hotel, and there, pouring out the milk into a big glass add plenty of ice and a little brandy, and it makes a delicious drink— sweet and wholesome—pronounced capital as a diuretic.

Strolling through the market, one sees every variety of Cuban peasant and negro—many of the latter coming into town only to bring a small quantity of the sugar-cane, which is bought and eaten by the people with great zest. Then, in going through the stores surrounding the market, one sees innumerable strange sights and articles, a busy throng of buyers and sellers of all kinds of merchandise, of oddities and antiquities of architecture ; and, perhaps, heard above all the din and bustle, are the loud nasal tones of the lottery-ticket vender, calling out in his protracted high key the number of the tickets he has for sale.

From here we will stroll over to the fish market, or " Pescaderia," as it is called, and see another *cosas de Cuba*. This is situated over on the other side of the town, on the bay side, and we reach it by going directly along the street Mercaderes, on the lower side of this market, which comes out directly opposite the fish-market, in Empedrado street.

It is a well-built stone building, with the lower portion open on the side facing the street, and supported by pillared arches, which give the place somewhat the appearance of an arcade. In the interior, as permanent structures, in lieu of tables, are square stone forms with tiled tops, upon which the fish, fresh from the sea, are exposed for sale, and which are of great variety, many of them resembling ours—such as the flounder, and bass, and one something like the blue-fish. All the fish on the coast are very fine, with some few exceptions,—as the *pez espada, gato, picua,* and some others that have the peculiarity of making persons sick, or poisoning those that eat of them.

The Lively Shark.

Of all the many species (and there are said to be one hundred species and more), the *pargo* and the *rabi-rubia* are the best, being somewhat scarce, except during the prevalence of north winds in the winter season, when they sell as low as twelve cents per pound. The shark, small and large, in pieces or whole, may also be seen here for sale, under its name of "*tiburon*," the which abounds in these waters, and from it is extracted the oil. It is very fierce, and many accidents happen each year from persons recklessly going in to bathe in some of the bays frequented by these creatures, who attack the swimmers without hesitation, and gobble a leg or arm, or maybe the whole person; the little ones, that are called "*cazones*," are eaten.

Their fish are not all brought from along the coast, but many of the larger fishermen have properties on the coast of Yucatan, and bring the fish from there, as also from Florida and the Tortugas. Generally, however, the first come from the coast in the neighborhood, many being caught just off the bay.

At the little village of Chorrera, directly on the coast and about two miles from Havana, is, however, the great fishing place for this district, and one can go out any time, taking the passenger (horse) cars at the station opposite the Tacon theatre, and going out there. The cars leave every hour, take about half an hour to go, and return the following hour ; fare twenty cents.   On the way out, the traveler passes through a portion of the city he is not otherwise likely to see, that is parallel with the coast, passing by, also, the large charitable institution, the Real Casa de Beneficencia, at the corner of the street Belascoin.

A Large Donation.

This is a flourishing institution, being an asylum for destitute orphans and the prevention of vagrancy, by putting all vagrants therein.   It was established during the time of Las Casas, in 1790–96, and in 1802 enjoyed the protection of the Marquis-Governor Someruelos, who at one donation bestowed twenty-five thousand dollars.   It is a fine, large building, and has beautiful grounds.

The village of Chorrera itself is a small place, celebrated as being the first site of Havana, and as being the place where the English attacked and landed, the commanding officer of the fort or castle blowing it up and retiring.   There is now a queer-looking tower, with portcullis, still there for protection, though the Fort Principe commands the place.

It is rare indeed that a meal in Cuba is served without fish, for even in the interior some of the streams are abundantly supplied.   It is stated by one of the old authors that that was the reason all the settlements were located on the coast of Cuba by the early inhabitants, in order to be convenient to the supplies of fish.

In connection with the inhabitants of the deep, there is one that they have in Cuba, known as the *manati*, a species of sea-hog, somewhat resembling those met with in Florida—different from the sea-calf or cow—that frequents the mouth of the rivers, and even mounts up on the earth.   From its flesh they make *tasajo*, its oil is useful and medicinal, and from its skin canes are made that are very beautiful, but very expensive.

Of the shell-fish there is a great variety,—amongst them the lobster, the craw-fish, and (best of all) the shrimp, both salt and fresh water, which is *par excellence* the most delicious thing they have on the Island, being as tender and resembling the white meat of the crab.   They are eaten simply boiled, and served cold with a little salt, or made into a delicious salad.   Some of them are quite large, and resemble a lobster-claw, are considered very wholesome, and used in great profusion all over the Island.   *Camarones*, bear in mind, is the name for them in Cuba, and they are identically the same as those we have south.

The Cuban oysters are quite small, and it would take a dozen of them to make one of our noble York river oysters or chincoteagues ; but they are nevertheless very good, being very appetizing, eaten at breakfast, as they have the briny and somewhat coppery taste of the French oyster.

Fish and Fishermen.

To finish up the morning's walk before breakfast, let us take a Victoria out to the other market of Tacon—unless, indeed, you want to turn the corner here, go up those old stone steps, and take a stroll along the Paseo de Valdes, which is cool and shady at this hour in the morning.   Then, too, perhaps, at this end near the steps, we may see some odd kind of fish we have not seen in the markets, for this is also frequented at times by fishermen, who do a small trade with the negroes, cutting up the small fish, even into quarters and halves, to sell to those villainous, filthy-looking negroes, who are probably too lazy to work to buy themselves better food.

On our way out, since it is a fine, breezy morning, and the sea is coming in heavily, we will pass by the Puerta de la Punta, and see the surf beating on the rocks in a most beautiful, violent way, dashing the spray high in air.   This is always the case after a norther; and it is a most attractive sight, either after or during one of these blows, to come out here on the point and see the ocean worked up into a state of fury, entirely different from its usually calm, placid appearance ; and here, just outside the gate, is always to be seen a lively party in that cove-like place with the gravelly shore—for here gather, of a morning, sometimes as many as a dozen or more negro drivers, with their two and three horses each, and entirely naked, except a short pair of pants.

They swim the animals into the salt water, which is most excellent for them. It is a jolly sight, when the sea is rough, to see these fellows, laughing, shouting and singing, enjoying their bath on horseback, the sea breaking clean over them at times, and the horses bracing themselves against the shock with their hind quarters to the waves.

The odd-looking building you see in the background is the old Bateria de la Punta, and the end of the new building is part of the government ordnance shed; the circular-looking iron affairs scattered along the shore being the old-fashioned sugar-pans.

Special Types of Cubans.

And now for the Plaza de Vapor, which is a market very similar to that of Cristina, known more generally as " Mercado de Tacon." It is situated at the corner of Galiano and Reina streets, or *calzadas*, the name generally given to fine, wide streets like avenues. This market is rather better in appearance than the others, being elevated some distance above the ground, and is two stories in height, with very good-sized stores around its four sides, with the portico facing on the street, the market itself being inside the square.

Here we have the opportunity of seeing to advantage special types of the lower class of Cubans,—countrymen as well as citizens. Here, for example, is the *malojero*, who comes from some distance in the country simply to bring that load of *maloja* that he has on the back of his horse, and which is the product of an inferior kind of corn that does not run to seed, and is raised with so little trouble that these lazy fellows prefer to let it grow on their places rather than trouble themselves to plant crops that require cultivation and attention.

The *guajiro*, or small property-owner from the country, is also seen here in his glory, with his varied stock of produce seeking a market. There is rather greater profusion of fruit here, but the meat carts with their uninviting loads are in appearance bad enough to take one's appetite away, as he sees these sides and quarters swinging to and fro, or piled up one upon the other in these small carts which bring the beef from the *mataderos* on the outskirts of town, no butchering being allowed within the city limits.

The shops, and in fact the whole market, present the same general appearance as the others; if you see one you see them all, with, perhaps, this difference—that there is always a great variety in the colored human nature, which at times presents itself very grotesquely to one's notice.

CHAPTER XXXI.

Famous Localities and Buildings.

ONE of the best and pleasantest ways of getting an idea of Havana within the walls, and particularly that portion of it lying on the water side, is to hire a carriage by the hour, and start early in the morning, or, if more convenient, after an early dinner in the afternoon, when the sun is sufficiently down to make it cool.

There is always this advantage in going anywhere within the old city in the afternoon—that almost the entire general buisness of the city is confined to this portion of it; and as most of the mercantile houses do no business after four or five o'clock, that portion of the city at the water side does not present as lively an appearance as in the early hours of the morning, when the business community, taking advantage of the freshness and coolness, attend to most of their business out doors and upon the quays, which thereby present a much more stirring and active picture to the stranger. On the contrary, outside the walls in the afternoon all is life, fashion, and pleasure.

We direct the driver to enter the city by the extreme north gate, known as La Puerta de la Punta, which is the entrance at the extreme end of the city on the bay, and where commenced the walls of the old city, which are here entered by an ordinary stone arch, some twenty-four feet long, the sides of which were casemates for storing artillery implements, etc., while the top of it formed a battery *en barbette*, with terreplain, stone rampart, and a slope leading up from the ground; while mounted for defence were some half-dozen rusty, old-fashioned carronades that would be no earthly use in case of need; across from it can be seen the Morro.

Inside the gate and extending along the street, parallel with the water, quite up to the Maestranza, is a stone covered way, with a

400

stone parapet to serve as breastworks in case of need. Outside the
gate and to the left is the landing quay, or the point used for landing
and embarking timber, horses, etc., and a good place whence to start
for the Morro Castle, there always being a boat or two there. Continuing down Cuba street, we come to a fine, large building on the
left hand, evidently a modern affair, built of brown stone, and several
stories in height.

Here are the offices and officers' quarters, and in fact the headquarters of the artillery, known as the " Maestranza," or Parque de
Artilleria.   Keeping on down past the building, we come to the street
Chacon, turning into which to the left we can go inside the arsenal
belonging to the Maestranza, where is a large supply of ordnance of
various kinds, and a number of old bronze cannon, bearing some very
antique inscriptions and strange names, such as the " Peacemaker,"
the " Thunderer," etc.

Stone Seats and Delightful Breezes.

Immediately opposite to this is the entrance to the Paseo de Valdez,
which extends along the bay side to Empedrado street. We direct
the carriage to meet us at the other end, and then find it pleasant to
stroll down the walk. Though the Paseo is not now in the best
order, it has still a pretty row of trees, stone seats, and always a
delightful breeze, and commands a fine view of the fortifications across
the bay.

At the entrance there is a sort of an arch and fountain erected,
which, though now in sad repair, has been in its day quite handsome,
and, as its tablet informs us, was erected by the corps of Royal Engineers, in 1843, the slab upon which is the inscription being marble
from the Isle of Pines, and on the top of which are grouped different
symbols of the military and particularly the engineer profession.
Here, of an early morning, it is pleasant to stroll, if you have nothing
better to do, and hear the music of the military bands performing
inside the walls of the Cabañas opposite, and which comes softly and
pleasantly mingling with the breeze of the ocean, which is only a short
distance off.

26

Entering the carriage, we drive through the street Tacon, passing the Pescaderia and the Intendencia, which is directly in front of La Fuerza, the oldest fort in the city, and around which cluster many traditions of antiquity, of assaults and defences, and attacks of pirates and enemies. Desiring to enter and see it, we pass around into the barrack yard on O'Reilly street, and are permitted to go through it. It is still a star-shaped bastioned fort, having a good line of fire upon the entrance and the bay, and having fine, large quarters near it for the troops.

An Ancient Fort.

This old fort dates back as far as the time of Fernando de Soto, the conqueror of Florida and discoverer of the Mississippi, who, being governor of the Island, gave orders to the engineer, Captain Aceituno, to build, in 1538, this fort, allowing for the purpose the sum of $4,000, —the which was paid by the inhabitants of Havana and Santiago de Cuba, for the purpose of having a fortified place on this side the Island. It was completed six or seven years after it was commenced. At the beginning, it was simply a quadrilateral of walls of double thickness, twenty-five yards high, with arched or casemated terreplains, and a bastion in each angle, the whole encompassed by a foss. In subsequent years, it has suffered various reforms, but still is of the general form as when first erected.

The portcullis and the barracks of the troops were erected in 1718 by Don Guazo, the then Governor-General. De Soto's wife, it is said, died here, after waiting many years for news of her gallant husband. The statue on the top of the castle is that of an Indian, who (so runs the legend) was the first to receive Columbus on landing. Opposite is the public square, known as the Plaza de Armas, and on the west side of that is the residence of the Captain-General of the Island. The large building adjoining the square of La Fuerza is the headquarters of the military governor of the city, the official who grants permission to visit the Morro Castle and Cabañas, at the written request of the consul.

The sentries and guards on duty are worthy of a little attention from those fond of military matters. They are generally picked men, whose "get up" is quite unimpeachable when on duty during the day, being clad in a uniform of pure white, with trappings, "neat and gay" of red cloth, and who, in their comfortable linens, look "natty" and soldierly.

Passing around the square to the lower or east side, we come to what is known as "El Templete" (little temple), at the corner of Ena Street. Tradition relates that in 1519, on the removal of the city to its present site, there was celebrated under an old ceiba tree the first mass in commemoration of this event; and upon this same spot was erected, in 1828, the present temple to perpetuate it. It is a substantial stone building, not very large, erected in imitation of a Grecian temple, with a portico and pillars, standing some distance back from the street, from which it is protected by iron railings connected with heavy stone columns, the whole resting upon a solid base of stone. Within this railing stands the stone column that marks the spot where the old tree grew.

A Celebrated Hostelry.

As we enter the square of San Francisco, the old yellow building at the left-hand corner is the former "Hotel Almy," probably one of the most celebrated in its day of any in the city. It was there that Dr. Kane, the arctic explorer, died, the hotel occupying the second story over the warehouse. On the opposite side of the Plaza, the antique, worn-looking building is the old church of San Francisco, which has had its formerly sacred halls turned into a custom-house store-room. This old church, it is said, was in its day the best church in the city. It was consecrated in 1737, and shut in 1843. Its tower to-day is the most elevated one in the city, the immense weight of which is supported upon the arches of the principal doorway.

It is a singular-looking old building, and has undergone some changes since its occupation for business purposes. The towers have been despoiled of their bells, and an additional door knocked in its side. The front of the church, in the narrow street Officios, cannot be seen to advantage ; but in the niches, of which there are two, one on each side of the front, there are queer old statues, in stone, of monks, one of whom, from his peculiarity of attire, is readily perceived to be a Franciscan.

As one looks at these *hard* old boys, that have stood here for so many ages, he is struck with the thought of what capital sentries they have made.   Posted, each one of them in his niche, like a sentinel in his sentry-box, they have stood here, doing that which they were placed here to do, without any relief ever passing around in so many years to make a change for them.

"These Stolid Old Fellows."

There they have stood, year after year—aye, scores upon scores of years, too—and seen these portals, that once swung back only for the entrance of the devout and prayerful, open for the entrance of the worldly, with their bales of goods ; there, calm and immovable, they have seen the busy throngs of ages past go by, and yet still they stand impassive and inanimate as in days of yore, as the busy throng of to-day still goes by, many of whom, throwing but a casual glance at these stolid old fellows, perhaps know not, and care less, that this was the first place where their mothers' mothers knelt and prayed.

Though the world has changed, though governor after governor has come and gone, though the small group of houses that once was the original town has grown into a vast assemblage of what is now a fine city, though other churches have been erected—aye, even amid the roar of the tempest and the lashing of the stormy waves which in the wild fury of a tropical storm have dashed almost to their very feet—there they stand still, not a muscle changed or a position altered since they were first posted in their stony guard-houses, on guard.

Passing through the handsome iron gateway which separates the square from the quay, you enter upon the landing, known as the " Caballeria," being a portion of the continuous wharves that extend from the Castillo La Fuerza to the marine barracks and quarters, and the whole of which is devoted to shipping purposes. Here, any morning, you will find a busy throng of merchants, clerks, etc., talking, and smoking, and driving their bargains—for this is, in fact, the Exchange—while the active portion of the business is done by sturdy negroes and swarthy laborers of many climes.

The whole series of quays is covered so completely with roofs that one may walk a considerable distance free from exposure to the sun, amusing oneself in examining the variety of vessels—of which there are crowds, side by side—from every nation in the world.

In this ocean-loving city of Havana, boatmen take the place of the persistent cabmen who assail one the moment of coming from a depot. Here, the moment you put your foot upon the quay, every boatman imagines you must want a boat, and a crowd gathers round you immediately, each vociferating the name of his boat, and you have considerable difficulty in getting away from the swarthy, piratical-looking fellows who cease not to accost you with—" *Quiere bote, Señor?*" all desirous of securing you for a *paseo* on the water.

A Gorgeous Boat.

And now we are catching the fresh breezes from the bay on the Quay de Machina, or machine wharf, which is the landing used for the men-of-war, and is, in fact, a naval storehouse on a small scale. The objects that will probably interest the stranger here are the state barge of the Captain-General, a very large and gorgeous affair of a boat, as also the very diminutive garden, about the dimensions of a good-sized parlor, seeming to be made simply to see how small a garden can be.

It is quite pretty, though, with miniature walks, shrubbery, and flowers, and also a fountain containing gold and silver fish, the whole affair being surrounded by an iron railing, and guarded by some nautical individual, who takes great delight in showing you through, particularly if one tips him a trifle.

Just beyond the quay of the Machina are the ferries for crossing over the bay to the little village of Regla, where are the wonderfully large storehouses for storing the sugar; also, the depot of the railroad for Matanzas and for Guanabacoa.

The boats run every five minutes to the other side, the fare upon which is ten cents each way. They are exceedingly well-built boats, having all been made in the United States (as in fact are nearly all the steamboats in Cuban waters), and are kept in very good order, more so than most of our ferry lines. If one has nothing better to do of a morning, it is quite a refreshing trip to go and return on one of these boats, since there is a fine view of the different portions of the bay, the shipping and the city; add to which there is always a fine breeze felt on them when in motion.

Stretching from these ferries, almost continuously, are what are known as *paseos*, or promenades. They are a species of boulevard, in fact, running parallel with the bay, laid out in trees and a well-made walk, with solid stone wall, erected at the water side, and fountains and stone benches scattered at intervals throughout their length, some of the former being very pretty and tasteful in their designs.

Stone Fountain with Military Trophies.

The first and most imposing of these paseos is that of the "Alameda de Paula," erected, in 1802, by the Marquis-Governor Someruelos. It is also called Salon O'Donnell (after the marshal of that name, who was inspector of the Island), and is situated between the quay De Luz and the bastion of "Paula," overlooking the bay. It has seats of stone, trees on the land side, and a breastwork on the water side formed of a balustrade composed of plaster concrete, with ornaments of the same, alternated by iron railings. In the middle there is a semi-circular *glorieta*, or stone look-out, furnished with seats, behind which is a handsome stone fountain, having in its centre a marble column with military trophies and national symbols in very good taste.

Next to this one is that of the "Paseo de Roncali," from which one has a fine view of the upper part of the bay, with the castle of Atares in the background, and fine views of the surrounding country. This is a beautiful place of a moonlight night to get a view of the bay, but is not much frequented. This castle of Atares that you see in the centre of the bay is said to be the one where young Crittenden and his fifty fellow-prisoners—all young men from the United States, who had come out in the Lopez expedition—had been captured, and were there shot, being brought out, twelve at a time, compelled to kneel down, six at a time, in front of the other six, and thus were all gradually murdered.

Protest by the English Consul.

A noble story is related of old Mr. Crawford, the then English consul, who, disgusted as every one else was by the inaction of our consul, Mr. Owens, when seeing these poor fellows shot down, went to the authorities, and told them that these massacres must cease; that, though these men were Americans and filibusters, they were yet human beings, belonging to the Anglo-Saxon race; and that, if the shooting did not cease, he would throw the English flag over them on the score of humanity. All honor to such a noble, brave spirit! And we are glad to say it was appreciated by the Americans living at the port at the time, for they presented him with a handsome set of silver.

As a matter of curiosity, to see what is understood by a navy-yard in Cuba, it is well to pay the "Arsenal" a visit, where is at once the naval dock, navy and store yard, situated at the extreme southwestern corner of the town, just outside the walls where they commence at the water side.   It is entered from the city by the Puerta del Arsenal, and, with its pretty officers' quarters and green trees, looks quite attractive from the outside.

At present it certainly does not amount to a great deal, though it has ship-houses, docks, machine-shops, and other things peculiar to naval construction.   In days past, however, the arsenal of Havana was very celebrated.   In 1722 they began building vessels of war, and quite a large number were built; and the vessels obtained such a good reputation from the excellent quality of wood used that an arsenal was, in 1728, regularly constructed, and finished in 1734.

Cannon were also cast, at one time, of bronze, the copper being furnished on the Island from the Cobre mines; but everything in this way seems to be at a stand-still, the yard deserted, and no work of any important nature being carried on. The dock is capable of dock-ing a vessel of one thousand tons, and their engine is of only twenty horse-power. Everything is very different from the bustle and life and extent of our navy-yards.

Guards Mounted at the Gates.

And now we will finish up our morning by returning by the way of " Los Ejidos," a street running inside and parallel to the old walls. Here were some of the most interesting features about Havana, giv-ing it that old air of walled antiquity, and offering some attractions to the student of history in the events so closely connected with their construction. Some are still standing, in tolerably good order, though they all have a somewhat dilapidated look, and are all to be torn down. A good smart cannonade would knock them to pieces very quickly.

They are of not much use now, for they may be said to be in the very heart of the city, and would be of no avail in a strong attack against the city, as a city, except as a *dernier resort* for a small body of men. Guards are, however, still mounted at some of the gates, and cannon yet frown from the grass-grown battlements ; and the moat, with time and indifference, has become filled with all manner of structures—even truck gardens being laid out in some of them.

These gates and walls used to be of great interest to most travelers, as they were for so many, many years, connected with the history of the old city of Havana ; and though as walls they no longer stand, yet the expression has become so familiarized that one still hears " in-side the walls " and " outside the walls " freely used.

As portions of these walls are still in existence, and the trenches also, with their nondescript appearance, it may not be amiss to give here some historical facts pertaining to them.

Some of the gates were constructed with an eye to architectural beauty originally, but are now among the memories of the past. The best of them was the Puerta de Tierra, near the Ursulinos con-vent, on Sol street, which still looks well, and had a somewhat imposing design. The gates of Monserrate were probably more used than any other of the gates, there being two of them—one of egress, and the other ingress, for the busiest streets of Obispo and O'Reilly.

As early as 1589, under the superintendence of the Governor and engineers Lejada and Antonelli, these walls were traced out, destined to take an important part in the defense of the town from the repeated attacks of the pirates, and have lasted nearly three centuries.

If the old adage be true, that "the nearer the church the farther from God," then we fear much the people of Havana have no hope of future salvation; for to almost every square in the old city, within the walls, there seems to be a church of some kind, to many of which are attached religious societies or organizations.

Priests with Three-cornered Hats.

The priesthood and the church have probably a greater share in the life of the Cubans, particularly with the female portion, than anything else that goes to make up the sum of their simple daily life; and as one strolls along the street, he is met at almost every turn by some priest of some particular order, either in shovel or three-cornered hats, or, perhaps, like a stout old Franciscan—whose vows prevent him from having anything *comfortable* in this world—forced by the heat of the sun to forget his resolution of baring his head to the elements, and sporting an enormous palm-leaf, that answers the purposes of both hat and umbrella.

The superior authority of the secular portion of the Cuban Church is the Captain-General, as Vice Royal Patron, and as his deputy in the Arch-bishopric of Cuba, the Commanding General of the Eastern Department. There are attached to the church a number of dignitaries of different grades, all drawing salaries in proportion to their rank; while the government of the church is divided into four vicarages and forty-one parishes, the grand Cathedral being situated in the town of Santiago de Cuba. Besides the churches actual, there are a number of convents, monasteries, etc., belonging to the different orders of St. Domingo, San Francisco, Jesuits, San Agustin, etc., etc.

The Cuban Church, in comparison with that of other countries, is said to be poor, especially in the Arch-bishopric, the temples needing the magnificence and those church ornaments that the traveler on the continent of Europe admires so much.   Notwithstanding, in some of the principal towns there are a few imposing structures, interesting from their great antiquity and ancient style of architecture, while upon special occasions the services carried on are tolerably rich and imposing.

The first church that the traveler from any land (and particularly we Americans) will desire to visit, is the Cathedral, not from any great beauty of itself—though it is perhaps the most interesting church edifice in the city of Havana—but since within its walls lies ensconced beneath a simple slab all that remains of him who gave to the world, from his combined wisdom and courage, not only a new continent, but also a new theory of a world—Columbus.

Magnificent Old Church.

This old church, now the most magnificent one in the city, is very odd indeed, seen from the outside.   Constructed of a peculiar colored brown stone, now blackened by age, it has no great beauty in its exterior architectural design; but yet, with its two queer old towers, its façade of pillars, niches, cornices, and mouldings, it is a striking looking edifice.   It was erected in 1724, for a college of Jesuits, who at the time occupied the site where now is the Palace of the Captain-General.   It is composed of the church edifice itself and the capacious buildings adjoining for the use of the priests of the order.

It was, in November, 1789, constituted into a cathedral; has one large doorway in the centre, and two smaller ones, one on each side of that, with a solid stone piazza, reached by short flights of stone steps, at its front.   There is also a side entrance by means of a stone court, on the other side of which are the dormitories of the priests.

The church is shown to strangers at any hour of the day, by inquiring of any of the priests you meet in the courtyard, and it is also open every morning and evening for Mass; though it is best seen in the morning, when the soft sunlight comes into the building, giving good effect to the shadows and shades of the massive pillars and arches; while the kneeling devotees serve to illustrate the great size of the structure by comparison.

The grand altar is very handsome, as is also the choir in the rear. The carving of the stalls is exceedingly fine, being done in polished mahogany, in very light and graceful designs.   At intervals around the church are several very beautiful altars, formed with solid pillars of mahoga-
ny and cornices and moulding of the same material, richly gilt upon the most promi-
nent parts.   Each one of these altars is devoted to some particular saint, and boasts of some very good altar-pieces, copies of Raphael, Murillo, etc.

The grand object of interest, however, is the "Tomb of Columbus;" and it is astonishing how many people there are who come to Havana that are ignorant of the remains of Columbus being in the precincts of Havana—having been transferred from the place of his death.

TOMB OF COLUMBUS.

History tells us that Columbus died in Valladolid, Spain, on Ascension-day, the 20th of May, 1506; that his body was deposited in the convent of San Francisco, and his obsequies celebrated with funeral pomp in that city.   His remains were afterwards transported, in 1513, to the Carthusian Monastery of Seville, known as "Las Cuevas," where they erected a handsome monument to him, by command of Ferdinand and Isabella, with the simple inscription, borne upon his shield, of—

À CASTILE Y LEON,

NUEVO MUNDO DIO COLON.

In the year 1536, his body and that of his son Diègo were re moved to the city of St. Domingo, in the Island of Hayti, and interred at the principal chapel.   But they were not permitted to rest

even there; for, on the 15th of January, 1796, they were brought to Havana, and interred in their present tomb, amidst grand and imposing ceremonies, participated in by the army, navy, and church officials, and an immense concourse of spectators. To use the words of a Spanish author: "Havana wept with joy, admiration, and gratitude at seeing enter within its precincts, in order to guard them forever, the ashes of Cristobal Colon."

The ashes, it is understood, were deposited in an urn, which was placed in a niche in the wall, at the entrance and to the left of the chancel of the cathedral.   Over this has been placed a slab of stone, elaborately carved, in a stone frame, and representing the bust of Columbus in the costume of the time, a wreath of laurel around his head, and symbolical emblems t the foot of the medallion, upon which is inscribed, in Castilian :

> "Oh, rest thou, image of the great Colon,
>   Thousand centuries remain, guarded in the urn,
>   And in the remembrance of our nation."

Well may the question be asked: Where, then, were all the muses when they inscribed such lines as these?

CHAPTER XXXII.

Celebrated Avenues and Gardens.

FOR a simple drive outside the walls, on the Paseo, in order to see and be seen, the afternoon hour of five or six o'clock is decidedly the best; but for combining pleasure with the business of sight-seeing, the cool, breezy hours of early morning are best, even though one does not then expect the pleasure of seeing the bright-eyed occupants of the elegant quitrin on his journey.

The driver is directed to start from the end of the Prado, which opens directly upon the sea, with the Morro Castle opposite, on the other side of the entrance, while close at hand is the queer old fort of La Punta, originally a bastioned, star-shaped fort, now somewhat rambling in its form. This is, also, one of the antiquities of Havana; for on the very spot where it now stands landed the pirate, Robert Baal, when he attacked and burned the city, in 1543. San Salvador de la Punta, which is its original name, was begun at the same time as the Morro, and by the same engineers, in 1589, and finished in 1597.

To the left of the Prado, directly on the sea, can be seen the various sea baths. Now facing toward the city, we begin our journey down the street Prado, or Paseo Isabel, a wide, capacious street, arranged as a boulevard, with rows of trees in the centre, beneath which are, at intervals, stone seats, and a promenade for foot-passengers, and on each side of this, again, the drives for carriages. The sides of the street are occupied by rows of fine buildings—private dwellings, many of them—with pillared porticoes, and tasty fronts of white or blue. This drive was first begun in 1771, and in 1772 was first opened. In 1797, under Santa Clara, it was extended, and several fountains erected upon it, and in Tacon's administration it received some improvements.

After leaving the Punta, the first building that we notice is the large yellow one to the left hand, occupying a whole square. It is the Royal Prison, and general headquarters of the council—singular combination—the front on the Paseo being used as quarters and offices, while the rear part, facing towards the walls, is the public prison for malefactors.

This was also erected in 1771, and is in the form of a hollow square, the courtyard of which is used by the prisoners for exercise; and they can be seen any day through the iron-grated gates or windows as well also as much of the prison as one wants to see. The student of physiognomy will find some interesting subjects at these windows any day, about twelve o'clock, when the prisoners are sometimes allowed to receive, through the gratings, packages from their friends, being first inspected by the sentries always on guard in the narrow, barred passages which separate the outer and inner world.

Where Lopez Met his Death.

The large open space beside the dungeon is used as a parade-ground; and it was here that the unfortunate Lopez met his death, dying like a brave man, after the unfortunate expedition, which induced by the promises of the Creoles, he had conducted to Cuba, and in which he was defeated. Here, as already stated, in the presence of a vast body of troops, on the 1st of September, 1851, he was garroted, his last words being: " I die for my beloved Cuba."

Scattered along the Paseo, at different intervals, are various fountains of stone and marble, many of them of very handsome design, and a few of them of some antiquity, though nearly all of them appear to be dry. On the right-hand side of the Prado is the Gymnasium and Fencing School, where is the best gymnasium in the city, with a very excellent instructor in calisthenics and dumb-bell exercise, as well also as a good French master-at-arms. The Cubans are, many of them, very fine gymnasts; and of a morning, from seven to nine, there is generally a very good class exercising under the supervision of the instructor.

To the left is the theatre of Villa Nueva, a rather poor affair, and used mostly as a French theatre, or for the smaller Spanish dramatic companies. It is built of wood, principally, and never seems to be well filled. It has now become a historical place, from the fact that it was here the troops fired on the audience while attending a representation, during the ten years' war.

On the Prado, opposite the gates of Monserrate, is what is known as the " Parque de Isabel," a portion of the street being laid out with grass-plots, gravel-walks, trees, and handsome iron settees, while in the centre is a marble statue of Isabel II.

The Field of Mars.

On the Paseo is the large square known as the " Campo de Marte," or field of Mars, where the troops are generally in the habit of exercising early in the morning, or during the winter about two o'clock in the day. It is a square somewhat in the form of a trapezium, with its longest side about two hundred and twenty-five yards in length, and surrounded by an iron railing upon a base of stone, combined with pillars of stone at regular intervals, and upon the top of each one of which is an iron bomb-shell, of large size, by way of ornaments.

It has four principal entrances, closed by iron gates, upon the top of the posts of which are placed bronze mortars; and as the columns are large and well built, the gates have a good effect. They are called after the distinguished men who bore the names of Colon, Cortes, Pizarro, and Tacon, the latter being the founder of the square, which at various times has suffered considerable damage from the tornadoes. It is now repaired and beautified.

Directly opposite the square, in the centre of the Paseo, is the beautiful Glorieta, and fountain of India, surrounded by noble *palmas reales*. The fountain is a work of considerable beauty, carved out of Carrara marble, and erected at the expense of the Count of Villa Nueva. It is one of the most beautiful of the public fountains, and does equal credit to the taste and heart of the patriotic citizen who erected it.

Nearly opposite the fountain, on a small paseo leading from the Prado, is the Circus, and on the other side of the Campo de Marte is the magnificent private residence, or in fact palace, of the Aldama family, which was one of the richest in Cuba, and owned a number of the finest sugar estates in the Island, but since confiscated, owing to the family having interested themselves in the rebellion of 1868.

The Queen's Street is a fine wide street, upon which there is generally seen more life of an afternoon than on any other, although on some portions of it the buildings are not so fine as in the other streets. At its junction with the Paseo Tacon, there commences one of the prettiest drives about the city, having double rows of trees, with a promenade for foot passengers, and a fine, wide carriage-drive, which is the fashionable one of an afternoon, and where splendid equipages may be seen to advantage. At different intervals along this Paseo there are fountains erected, statues, and *glorietas;* and of a fine day, with its beautiful women, elegant equipages, and long rows of shady trees, it presents a perspective and near view perfectly charming.

Beautiful Botanical Gardens.

Nearly at the end of the Paseo is a fine gateway, giving entrance to the beautiful gardens known as the Botanical Gardens (*Jardin Botanico*), and adjoining which are also the beautiful gardens belonging to the country place (*Quinta*) of the Captain-General, known as "Los Molinos." These are all so very beautiful and interesting that the stranger will, if he have time, want to pay them several visits, both morning and evening, as they offer more attractions than any public place pertaining to Havana. Even in the middle of the day, when it is too hot to go anywhere else, this is a cool, pleasant, shady place, in which to pass the midday hours. They are open day and night, and any one is allowed to enter and stroll through the beautiful walks, shaded and surrounded by most exquisite tropical flowers, shrubs, and trees.

Nothing can be more delightful, of a warm morning or evening, than a saunter through these magnificent grounds, rivaling in their beauty, luxuriance, and novelty any garden that we have in the United States. The best plan, on a casual visit, is to leave your carriage at the entrance of the Botanical Gardens, and direct the driver to meet you at the entrance to the Quinta, some distance above; and you can then, after strolling through the gardens, pass into those of the Captain-General, and, enjoying them, sally out by the magnificent Avenue of Palms that leads from the gateway to the house. In the Botanical Gardens there are specimens of almost every tropical plant, and directly in the centre is a large stone basin, filled with the finest water-lilies, and in the middle of that a rustic fountain, made of shells.

Lovers' Romantic Walk.

Passing from these gardens, you enter those belonging to the Quinta, which are somewhat larger, and contain some very beautiful walks,—one of which, nearly one hundred yards long, is as complete a lovers' walk as the most ardent pair could desire. It is formed of the rose of the Pacific Ocean, growing to a good height, and covered with flowers of a light pink color, the bushes forming a handsome green and fragrant arch over the head of the pedestrian.

There is an artificial fountain or cascade, formed, also, by permitting the waters of a small creek to pass over artificial rocks, which form underneath a damp and, it must be said, unattractive cavern; while the waters are carried off by a canal, upon the surface of which rest the pleasure-boats of his Excellency, the banks being shaded by the overhanging trees, and inhabited by some curious breeds of ducks. An aviary or two there are also, filled with some species of doves of different kinds, while in the centre of the gardens stands the comfortable house of the Captain-General and the buildings pertaining thereto.

The avenues of palms in these gardens will strike the visitor with astonishment, as something surpassingly graceful, beautiful, and majestic; while he can study to advantage the cocoa and plantain trees, with which the gardens are filled. The whole place would be perfect in itself, in the way of a garden, were it not that it has been necessary to run a railroad through the middle of it, the noise from the passing trains of which breaks at times inharmoniously upon the ear as one saunters enjoyingly through the fragrant and otherwise quiet paths.

27

The gardens seem to be divided off under different names, as may be seen by the sign-boards, at different places, designating the gardens of San Antonio, the Queen, the Wood of the Princess. A military guard is in and about the gardens all the time. It has been the custom for the Captains-General to spend their summers here; but it having got abroad that the place was unhealthy, it has not been so often occupied lately, the Governors going out to Marianao or Puentes Grandes. Be that as it may, it is a lovely spot for the stranger, on his winter visit, to stroll into and pass his time agreeably, whether sauntering through the shady walks with some lady friend, or smoking his fragrant Havana beneath the stately palms.

View of the Surrounding Country.

From these gardens, if the traveler is anxious for exercise, he can mount up to the fort upon the hill, known as the "Principe," whence there is a good view of the surrounding country, always provided the sentry will allow him to pass. The fort itself is small, though somewhat old, having been built, in 1763, for the protection of the village and bay of Chorrera.

Leaving now the Quinta, we have a very pretty view of the continuation of the Paseo, with its rows of trees that shade the road so nicely, and which have attained such a luxuriant growth that it makes this, with reason, one of the most charming portions of the afternoon drive of the Habaneros. Turning again into a fine, wide avenue, known as the "Calzada de la Infanta," we drive over to a long, handsome street, known as "El Cerro" (the hill), and leading out to a little village of that name. It is a very handsome street, about three miles long, lined on each side with the beautiful and comfortable residences of the fashionable and wealthy, for whom this with its surroundings is the principal place of residence, particularly in the summer.

Here is an ample field for the study of tropic architecture, hardly any two houses being alike, yet all with the same general plan, very different indeed from our ideas of comfort, and yet probably the best plan that can be adopted for this climate. Not only on the "Cerro," but everywhere in the cities, is the stranger struck by the peculiarities of this Cuban architecture, with its enormous windows, without a particle of glass, but grated with strong iron bars, the single story of height, the tremendous doorways, their massive doors studded, many of them, with numerous brass knobs and decorations, all bearing the appearance of having been built for defence from outside attack.

Houses of Singular Construction.

Upon the Cerro, the houses are modernized somewhat, having their stables and carriages in their rear, and in front stone piazzas, elevated some distance above the level of the street. Passages are not at all frequent in the houses, and the principal entrance opens directly into large and cool halls, which are in fact rooms and furnished as such, laid with marble-tiled floors, and connected with the rooms beyond by large archways.

These halls are usually the dining-rooms, where always there is a breeze from the open courtyard or through the wide *sala*, or parlor, at the entrance; the whole being devoid of curtains, and exposed to the eye or curiosity of every passerby. The ceilings are uncommonly high, and the houses are, without exception, open on the interior side to the *patio*, or courtyard, which affords, even of the warmest days, a chance for some air.

This *patio* takes with those in the cities the place of our gardens; all the rooms open to it, and where there is a second story, a gallery runs around the entire square, having either blinds or fancy-colored awnings for protection from the sun's rays, which have full scope in the open centre of the square.

This secures a free circulation of air, a shady place in which to sit or walk, and very often, when the *patio* is laid out with walks, flowers, fountains, and orange, pomegranate, or mignonette trees, a charming place in which to dream one's idle hours away.

Here are also to be seen some superb specimens of the cactus, which in Cuba grows to an immense size, and possesses great strength, for a plant of this kind, in its branches, some of which will bear a man seated on them. In the trenches around Havana are also other fine specimens, which have a very odd appearance at times from the large quantities of fine dust that settle on them. On our return, we pass through the "Calzada Galiano," one of the finest streets in the city, and always having new charms, with its width, pillared porticoes, and regular architecture, to say nothing of the constant life there visible.

The great charm of Cuba for the traveler from the United States is the entire change of appearance of matters and things from what he is accustomed to. From the time of landing at Havana, with one's mind filled with the Spanish life as described in Irving's "Alhambra" and "Granada," or as written in Prescott's works, there is an additional pleasure of seeing, verified with one's own eyes, those peculiarities of houses, climate, and people, described somewhat in those works.

Charm and Novelty Everywhere.

From the moment of entering the bay of Havana, where one sees the city before him, with all its oddities of colors, and shapes, and styles of its walls, with an occasional palm or cocoa tree to give a marked type to its appearance, to the time of turning his back upon the luxuriant Coffee Mountains of the east, or sugar-cane clad prairies of the valleys, there is one constant charm of novelty, and very often ridiculously so.

The first thing that strikes the novice, in wandering through the old town of Havana, is the solidity of the buildings and the narrowness of the streets, the smallness of the sidewalks of which will cause him at first some considerable annoyance in stepping off into, perhaps, the muddy street, for the purpose of giving the "right of way" to some pedestrian who is keeping to the right, "as the law directs;" or, when disgusted with the constant getting out of the way, he takes to the middle of the street, and is suddenly punched in the ribs by the shafts of some volante, whose driver has gauged his pulling up so nicely that he just avoids running over you.

Then the houses, hardly ever more than one story high—never more than two—with their tremendous doors and windows; when, if the door is open, you see a handsome flight of stone steps, perhaps, leading to the upper story, the walls all gaily painted in white and blue, or yellow; the entrance probably taken up with a gorgeous quitrin, or, perhaps, a handsome carriage, according as to whether the family are wealthy, and occupy the whole house, or only well-off, and keep the upper stories, renting out the lower ones, which are probably filled with merchandise. Notice, now, this great door to the large and showy mansion. It is shut; but see how resplendent it is with brass decorations, latches, hinges, door-plates, or studded with quaintly-shaped brass-headed bolts, with shining handles.

Is it wonderful that an American, with his national character for impudence, should follow in the steps of the courtly and stately Spaniard, when he sees a pair of lovely eyes peeping at him from behind the curtain of the barred window, and, doffing his hat, should exclaim, with antique gallantry, "Señorita, I put myself at your feet," or " the surprising beauty of your lovely eyes will not permit of my passing by, Señorita, without doing them homage?"—grateful if he is rewarded, as he always will be, by bright glances from the dark-haired damsel, who, with a stately smile, utters her " *Gracias Señor,*" in return for what she deems only due tribute.

Peculiar Types of Character.

Here's a contrast! Now mark that great negro, with his ridiculous-looking wheelbarrow, appearing as though it had come out of the ark, such is the simplicity of its construction; the negro himself, without head-covering, with as little clothing as the law allows (if there is any law in such matters), generally ragged pants, and a portion of a shirt only.

Here we are in the ever-busy street O'Reilly, which, like Obispo or Ricla, one never gets tired of wandering in. Do not imagine for a moment, if you want to find any particular store, that you must ask for Mr. Smith's or Mr. Jones's establishment; oh, no,—these people do not generally travel under their own names; but, like a hotel, stick up something that is unique, expressive, or easily remembered. As a consequence, you have "The Nymphs," "The Looking Glass," " The Little Isabel," the " Green Cross," which you see gets its name from the big Maltese cross, built into the wall of that corner store, and hundreds of other funny, curious, and expressive names.

Just look down that street, this hot February day.   See those fancy-colored awnings, stretching across all the way down, to keep the warm sun away from our heads ; those handsome shop windows, or the stores themselves, in fact, with their shelves almost upon the street,

PINE-APPLE PLANTATION.

all reminding one of the descriptions of Eastern bazaars, were it not that the well-dressed men that are scattered through the non-coated, cool-looking people, show the presence, in a civilized land, of capital tailor's work.

And now, while intent upon the sights, you hear a shout of " *Cuidado! cuidado!* " (take care), behind you, and jumping out of the way, in the expectation that your last hour is come, you are convulsed with laughter at the cause of your alarm, in a most ridiculously small donkey pulling a big cart, while upon the back of the donkey, perhaps, are piled a dozen folded blankets or cloths ; upon top of which, again, is a great cumbersome saddle, big enough and heavy enough for a French cuirassier.

Poor little donkey! He has just twice as much load as is necessary to carry, but the plucky little fellow goes sturdily along as if it
was all right.   Now, turning a corner, we are suddenly taken aback
by a negro girl, with a white child in her arms, out for an airing, we
suppose, from the nature of the apparel, which consists of just th*
amount of hair usually found on the heads of children, and which
probably the novice thinks is a little too airy for the public streets of
a city like Havana.

Only his Head to be Seen.

" Halloa! what's up now, in this narrow street we are going
through?" you will ask, as, looking ahead, you see it completely
stopped up with a mass of green vegetable matter that is coming
down on you with hardly any perceptible propelling aid; however,
now it is near, you descry the long-eared head of a small donkey,
or perhaps a Cuban horse, almost buried under a load of green fodder,
piled upon and beside him in such manner that nothing is to be seen
except the head and feet of the little fellow, who, while thus buried,
has not even the satisfaction of a quiet little chew of the material
that surrounds him, for his mouth is muzzled up in a curiously netted
muzzle of twine.

This fodder constitutes, with corn, the only food given to horses in
Havana, and is all brought in from the surrounding country on the
backs of mules, sometimes ten or twelve in number, strung together
like a lot of beads, head and tail.   No oats are raised, or grain of any
kind, in the Island, except the small sweet ears of Indian corn which
is grown everywhere, and the stalks of which, with the tender tops of
the sugar-cane, make up the only food to be had for horses.

There's another fellow bawling out at this early hour something
he calls " *leche, leche ;* " and which we find to be milk he is carrying
around in those immense tin cans, stuck away in the straw or palm
panniers hanging over his horse's back, and which, with the hot sun
and the motion, would soon get churned to butter, or rather oil, the
'atter being the way they use it on the Island.

Again is heard a peculiar clattering, as if crockery was being hardly dealt with, and which is found to proceed from the hands of a peripatetic " Chinois," who takes to the street for a market for his wares. Here he is, now, a regular thorough-going " John China-man," who, after having served out his time as a Coolie on perhaps some large sugar estate, has become imbued with the ambitious desire of being a merchant, and no longer remaining in his hard-working way of life as a " *trabajador* " in the hot sugar fields.

Having saved sufficient money from his hard earnings, or, what is more likely, made his capital by gambling with his more verdant and less fortunate fellows, he has started in trade, with a bamboo yoke carried over his shoulders, and pendant from the ends of which hang two large, round baskets, filled with crockery of all kinds.

Clad in thin, wide pantaloons, a blue dungaree shirt, with a broad palm-leaf hat on his head, and his feet thrust into loose, heelless slippers, he perambulates the streets, seeking to tempt the cautious housewife into purchasing something of him—not by the dulcet sounds of his voice (which sounds like a turkey-gobbler), but by the insinuating music of the wares themselves, emitted in a peculiar sound and way by the half-dozen saucers he carries in his hand, and which he is constantly throwing up gently, and letting them fall one upon the other with a sharp, continuous, rattling sound that will bring the indolent housewife quickly to the window, if she wants anything in that line. No danger of his breaking them in this way of making himself known, for the Chinese are celebrated for their sleight of hand, and this is evidence of it.

Now we hear the fruit-venders crying out their wares, as they walk beside their pannier-loaded horses. " *Naranjas, naranjas, dulces* " (oranges, sweet oranges), he cries ; which, in the season pro-per for them, you can buy of him, the largest and ripest kind, for a *peseta* (twenty cents) the dozen, or less,—as well as other fruits of the country. Although the oranges are ripe all the year round, there seems to be a profusion of them in the early Spring months, unless, as is the case some years, they are somewhat scarce from the torna-does having destroyed many of the trees.

Look at this ridiculous sight,—that fellow, a poultry-dealer, going up the street there ahead of us, mounted upon his donkey, his feet projecting out in front, while he is high up on the pack that holds his large, square panniers of chickens, which he has brought in from the country to dispose of, and which he carries safely in the baskets, corded over the tops with a net work, or more frequently a cloth, the *pollos* sticking forth their heads from time to time, and doubtless wondering, as they keep up their cachinating, why their master is thus treating them to this morning's *paseo*.

Now we meet a "*dulce*" seller. As a general thing they are neat-looking mulatto women, rather better attired than most of the colored women one meets in the street. They carry a basket on the arm, or perhaps upon the head, while in their hands they have a waiter, with all sorts of sweetmeats,—mostly, however, the preserved fruits of the country, and which are very delicious, indeed,—much affected by ladies.

We need not have any hesitation in buying from these women, as they usually are sent out by private families, the female members of which make these *dulces* for their living, the saleswoman often being the only property they own, and having no other way (or, perhaps, too proud, if they have) of gaining a livelihood.

Here is something that won't strike you quite so agreeably. Did you ever see anything more disgusting than that great negro wench, —a large clothes-basket on her head, a colossal cigar sticking out from between her thick lips, while she walks along, majestically trailing an ill-fitting, loose dress (probably the only article of apparel she has on) after her slip-shod strides? She puts on airs, occasionally, if you scold her for spoiling your clothes, that you have rashly trusted her to wash for you.

CHAPTER XXXIII.

Sugar-making in Cuba.

A BOOK on the Island of Cuba without a chapter on sugar-making would hardly be complete. If the cultivation of the cane is also added, on the same place where the cane is raised, and by the same proprietor, the manufacture of sugar, such places being called in the Cuban dialect *ingenios*, or sugar estates, the carrying on of which requires a large amount of capital, a great degree of intelligence, and much mechanical skill.

These *ingenios* vary in size from five hundred to ten thousand acres, though the results of their crops are not always in proportion to the number of their acres, that depending more particularly upon the nature of the soil of the particular locality in which they are situated, and the degree of intelligence and amount of labor with which they are worked. Each one of the *ingenios* is, in some degree, like a small village, or, as with the larger ones, quite a town, in which are substantial edifices, numerous dwellings, and expensive machinery, together with a large number of inhabitants, the different officials necessary for their government and management representing the civil officers, except with, perhaps, greater power.

The buildings upon a first-class sugar estate are generally a dwelling-house (*casa de vivienda*), which, from its size, style, and cost, might sometimes be called a palace, some of them having, in addition to numerous other conveniences, small chapels in which to celebrate the religious services of the estate, the dwelling being occupied by the owner and his family, if living on the estate ; if not, by the *administrador*, who is charged with the care and management of the estate in the absence of the owner, and who, in fact, may be said to be the man of the place.

There is also the house occupied by the *mayoral*, as he is called the chief of the negro laborers, whose business it is to follow the

478

laborers to the field to see that they do their work properly, and that sufficient amount of cane is cut to keep the mill constantly supplied with material to grind; in fact he has a general supervision of all the agricultural duties of the estate, receiving his orders only from the owner or *administrador*, as the case may be. The *mayorales* are generally very ordinary men, of no education, the intelligence they possess being simply that gained by long experience in this kind of business.

The *maquinista*, or engineer, is really the most important man upon the place, as upon him depend the grinding of the cane and the care of the mill and its machinery—that it is kept in good and running order, so that no delay may take place in the grinding season. His quarters are generally in some part of the mill, where he manages to be pretty comfortable.

American Engineers.

These engineers are mostly young Americans, with now and then an Englishman or a German; but the Americans are much preferred on account of their superior intelligence and assiduous attention to their business. Their pay is from one thousand two hundred to two thousand five hundred dollars for the grinding season, which begins about December and ends nearly always in or before June, most of the engineers going over to the States to pass the summer, or, as they express it, " to have a good time."

The Hospital is always an important building on these places, as it is the only place where the sick can be treated and properly taken care of. It is usually arranged with a great deal of care and neatness, the building being divided off into different wards for men and women, and also for contagious diseases; it is generally in charge of a hospital steward, who has quite an apothecary shop in his charge, and who receives his instructions from the attending physician, who also attends a number of the estates in the same locality, visiting each one generally every day, and receiving compensation at so much per year. As a matter of simple economy, to say nothing of charity, the invalids get the best of treatment, and are not sent back to work until they are completely restored, though while convalescing they are required to do light work, such as making baskets, hats, etc.

The Nursery is also quite an important place, and is highly amusing to visit, for here the future hopes of the plantation are cared for. These little black, naked sinners, running and tumbling over each other in great glee, are generally kept in a large room, with rows of cradles or cribs on each side, in which each little one is kept at

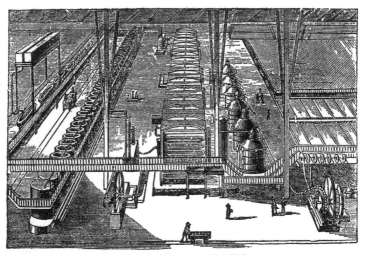

INTERIOR OF A SUGAR-MILL.

night, the old women who are too feeble to work any longer being retained as nurses in charge, while the mothers of the little ones are out at work in the fields, being allowed, two or three times a day, to return and suckle such infants as need the mother's milk.

It is very amusing to enter one of these nurseries when the children are being fed, and see their gambols and antics, and the expression of the little ones' eyes as they see the white master, as he is called, and with whom they keep on friendly terms, enter their quarters. They all appear to be happy and jolly, and make as much noise and have as much fun as would satisfy any "radical" in the States. Poor things, they happily know nothing of the hard lot in store for them.

But the most important of all the buildings is, of course, the Sugar-mill, which generally consists of the engine-house, where is all the machinery and power for grinding, boiling and working the cane and juice, and the purging and drying-houses. The engine-house is generally an extremely large roof, supported by pillars and posts, and entirely open on all sides—in fact, nothing more than a very well constructed shed to keep off the sun and rain, the floor being mostly paved with brick, and the stairways leading from one portion of the building to another being of solid stone. In fact, one of these mills of the first class is a very handsome affair—everything about it, the engines and the machinery being kept in the most scrupulously clean order, equal to a man-of-war.

How the Employees Live.

On the larger places there are generally what are called barracoons, or quarters for the workmen. They are large buildings, constructed of stone, in the form of a quadrangle, on the inner side of which are the rooms for the negroes, to which there is only one main entrance; this is shut at night when the hands are all in.

On the outside, and much better built, there are rooms occupied by the different white men connected with the place and not otherwise provided for; probably, also, a long row of stables for the many horses usually kept upon places of this kind, and of which there is no lack, either for work or play.

On other places, again, the negroes live in *bohios*, or huts—some few constructed of stone, but most of them simply log or cane huts, of the most ordinary description, thatched with palm-leaf or grass, and making no attempt at comfort, but simply serving as shelters from the rain. In the Southern States the miserable habitations called cabins are bad enough; but these are worse; though, to be sure, in a climate like this it does not matter much about shelter—all one wants is shade.

The Purging-house is generally of very great extent, being two stories high, and of great length. The floor of the upper story is simply a series of strong frames, with apertures for placing in them

the *hormas,* funnel-shaped cylinders of tin or sheet-iron, into which
is put the molasses to drain into troughs beneath.   One side of this
house is open, in order to permit the *gavetas,* or large boxes upon
wheels, into which are put the forms of sugar, to be run in and out
conveniently.   In these boxes, which are immensely large, the sugar

SECTION OF PURGING-HOUSE.

in forms is broken up and exposed to the air and sun, for the purpose
of thoroughly drying it.

The number of these *hormas* is something wonderful, there being in
some of the houses as many as twenty thousand.   Beneath the upper
floor are a number of troughs, each trough having a slant to a main
trough.   Over the minor troughs are the mouths of the aforesaid
funnels, which permit the molasses draining from the pans of sugar
above to run into the troughs, which again convey it to large vats or
hogsheads, called *bocoyes,* each of which holds from twelve to fifteen
hundred gallons.   It is in this process that they make the distinction
of the different sugars—*blanco,* or white; *quebrado,* or broken; and
the common, dark-colored sugar called *cucurucho.*

In making these three qualities of sugar, a layer of moist earth or clay is placed upon the top of the pans of crystallized syrup, from which the moisture, draining constantly through, carries off all the imperfections, leaving the pans full of dry sugar in the form of solid cases, and generally of three colors; that nearest the top, pure white; next below that, the discolored; and at the bottom of that, the moist or dark colored.

If, however, it is desired to make only a *moscabado* sugar, which is of a rich brown color, and does not require the same time or pains as the finer qualities, the syrup is simply put in the large hogsheads, before described, and allowed to drain off in the natural way without the process of "claying" it, as it is called. This, of course, makes more sugar of an average inferior grade, which weighs more, having the molasses in it; and this is the sugar generally preferred by sugar refiners.

Various Workshops.

Besides the above, other buildings there are, of different kinds, necessary to large establishments like these, such as cooper, carpenter, and blacksmith shops; while there are also, on the best estates, gas works, at which is manufactured the gas with which the mill and buildings are illuminated, it being found much cheaper and cleaner to manufacture and use gas than oil.

Of the persons directly in charge of making the sugar there are one or two upon each place whose business it is to see to the boiling and refining of the sugar, and who are known as sugar-makers, receiving for their services from eight hundred to one thousand dollars each per annum.

It is calculated that to every one thousand boxes of sugar, consisting of four hundred pounds each, it is necessary to have from fifty to seventy-five hands; for, of course, the greater supply of labor there is, the better are the chances of making the sugar of superior quality. Of these laborers the larger proportion are negroes, while upon nearly every place there are more or less Chinese or Coolies, all of whom are divided into classes and divisions, according to the labor for which they are desired.

Guardianes, or guardians, are stationed in small huts at the entrances to the estates, and act as porters, though their lodges are nothing more, usually, than a simple shelter hut, of grass or palm-leaf, the occupants being generally old men unfit for hard labor. Firemen attend to keeping up the furnace fires, which are generally placed in a cavity, or sort of cellar in the ground, upon one side of the mill there being left a large space in front of the furnaces into which the carts, upon backing up to its edge, empty their loads of mashed cane, the only fuel used to generate steam. These carts are rude, rough affairs, invariably drawn by either one or two yoke of oxen.

The Bill of Fare.

The bulk of the hands used in the general operations of the place, cutting cane, plowing, etc., are known as the *gente,* or "people." They are pretty well taken care of as regards food, at least in quantity if not in quality; they get *tasajo,* or dried beef, *boniatos,* or sweet potatoes, rice, and plantains which answer for bread, and of which they are very fond, eating them either roasted or fried.

The clothing they wear is limited, not only in quality, but quantity, the children usually going about stark naked—the women with only a calico dress on, and the men wearing only their pants. It is rather a novel sight, at the eleven o'clock halt from work, to see these people gathering for their rations.

Attached to every estate is the *potrero,* or corral, where are herded the cattle used in doing the hauling on the place, and also those intended for supplying the hands with meat.

Of the cane itself there are several species known in Cuba. The *criolla,* or native cane, is the oldest known, being that brought to Spain by Columbus, on his second voyage, from the Canaries, but is thin, poor, and not very juicy; that of Otaheite, which is large, thick, and preferred by the sugar-makers, being introduced into the Island in 1795; that of the Cristallina, last introduced, and cultivated by many as preferable to that of Otaheite, a cartful of which will give a pan and a half of dry sugar, amounting to about sixty pounds.

The height attained by the cane, averaging as it does six or eight feet, and sometimes reaching twenty, the length of joint, the color, and many other particulars, vary with different species, with the character of the soil, and with the mode of culture adopted. The stems are divided by prominent annular joints into short lengths, from each joint of which there sprout long, narrow leaves, which, as the canes approach maturity, drop off from the lower joints.

The outer part of the cane is hard and brittle, but the inner consists of a soft pith containing the sweet juice, which is elaborated separately in each joint. This is very nutritious, and is eaten in large quantities by the negroes, who in their leisure moments are generally supplied with a piece at which they constantly suck, having prepared it by stripping off the outer skin, which leaves in a good piece of cane almost a solid lump of sugar.

The cane is propagated by slips or cuttings, consisting of the top of the cane with two or three of the upper joints, the leaves being stripped off. These are planted, either in holes dug by hand or in trenches formed by a plough, about eight or twelve inches deep, the earth being banked up upon the margin, and well manured; two or more slips are laid longitudinally at the bottom of each hole, and covered with earth from the banks to the depth of one or two inches.

In about a fortnight the sprouts appear a little above the earth, and then a little more earth from the bank is put in the hole, and as the plants continue to grow, the earth is occasionally filled in a little at a time, until, after four or five months, the holes are entirely filled up.

The planting takes place in the intervals of the rainy season, which commences regularly in June, and lasts until October or November, the cutting taking place immediately after the Christmas holidays, and continuing on up to May, even, in some cases.

The maturity of the cane is indicated by the skin becoming dry, smooth, and brittle, by the cane becoming heavy, the pith gray, approaching to brown, and the juice sweet and glutinous. It is usual to raise several crops in successive years from the same roots, the plan, I believe, being to plant about one-third of the grounds every year.

When the cane is ripe for cutting, the mill is put in complete run-

28

ning order, and the hands, under the charge of the *mayoral*, proceed
to the field of now green cane, each negro—man, woman, or child—
armed with a *machete*, or knife of peculiar construction, something
like a butcher's cleaver, and very strong and sharp. Spreading themselves out over the field, they begin the cutting of the cane, first by
one cut at the top, which takes off the long leaves and that part of
the cane which is worthless, except as it is used for food for the
cattle; a second cut is then given as near the root as possible, the
cane falling carelessly to the ground, from which it is gathered as
wanted.

A Lively Scene.

A field in the cutting season presents a lively sight, with its three
or four hundred laborers superintended by the *mayoral* on horseback,
its carpet of cut cane, and its long lines of slowly-moving carts, with
their noisy drivers, while the sea of standing cane, sometimes extending for miles and miles, is stirred by the gentle breeze into waves of
undulating green.

The carts being now piled up with the cane, and the fodder left
upon the ground to be carried off another time, they drive back in a
long line to the mill, where they empty the cane under a large shed,
close to that portion of the mill wherein is the crusher.

This pile of cane generally becomes immense, as the carts keep
continually bringing it in faster than the mill can grind during the
day; and at night, work in the field, as a general thing, ceases—a
portion of the hands going in the early part of the evening to get
their rest, while the others keep feeding the cane to the mill.
Towards morning, when the stock on hand gets low, the negroes are
called up, and sent out to the field to keep up the supply of cut cane,
the engine never ceasing to run night or day, unless in case of accident, during the whole of the grinding season.

The cane being deposited under the shed at the mill in sufficient
quantities, the engine is started, and the machinery put in motion.
The cane is then thrown by the hands upon an endless inclined flexi-
ble conductor, formed of strips of wood and links of chain, which,
being constantly in motion, and passing round a cylinder near the

crushers, throws the cane into their jaws, by which the juice is completely pressed out of it, and passes in a continuous stream into the troughs beneath, while the refuse cane is carried out on the other side into a wooden trough, from which it is taken by hand, placed in carts, and carried off to the furnaces.

These crushers, or *maquinas de moler*, as they are called, consist of three immensely large, solid, iron rollers, placed horizontally, revolving, one above and two beneath, in a kind of pyramidal form, the opening between the upper and first lower one being larger than that between the upper and second lower one, in order to form more of a mouth with which to draw in the cane from the feeder.

The juice, as it now runs out in a liquid state, is an opaque fluid, of a dull gray or olive-green color, of a sweet, pleasant taste, and is known by the name of *guarapo*. It is quite thick, and holds in suspension particles of the cane and refuse, which are separated from it by filtration. This liquid is so exceedingly fermentable that it is necessary to clarify it immediately. It runs from the mill by means of troughs or conductors, passing in its course into pans of copper, pierced with holes like a cullender, through which the liquor runs, leaving its refuse matter on the surface to be disposed of by a man constantly in attendance for the purpose.

It is then forced, by means of pumps, into large tanks, from which it is conveyed by a trough to the clarifiers, which are large kettles heated by steam. In these, defecation takes place, the process being assisted by four or five ounces of lime to every four hundred and fifty gallons of boiling liquid contained in each kettle. Sometimes more lime is required, this depending entirely upon the density of the juice.

In connection with these vats, which are known as clarifiers, there is generally used a test paper, by which the juice is tested as it comes from the mill, to ascertain the amount of acidity in it. This is a simple chemically-prepared paper, of a blue color, which, on being put into the liquid, turns to a red color, more or less intense according to the degree of acidity in the juice.

From the clarifiers, the juice, after settling, is filtered through vats, filled nearly up to the top with bone-black, which is usually used two or three times, or until the juice changes color or does not run off well. The length of time which the bone-black is used is the real secret of the difference in some sugars ; and, as proof of this, on the estates where the finest sugars are made, the bone-black is changed every eight hours ; while on the estates where the poorest sugar is made, it is changed only once in two or three days.

From these clarifying vats there are three copper troughs,—one for molasses, one for cane-juice, and one for syrups. From these three troughs as many pipes lead to large tanks, which are simply receptacles for the material accumulating. From these tanks, again, the liquor is conveyed to the vacuum-pans, the principle of latent heat being made use of to evaporate the cane-juice.

These vacuum-pans are three in number, the first of which is for juice, the second for syrup, and the third a strike-pan, as it s called. The vacuum-pan consists of a close copper vessel, perfectly air tight, the middle portion cylindrical, and from six to seven feet in diameter, the upper portion convex or dome-shaped, and the bottom also convex, but less so than the top. The bottom of the pan is double, the cavity between the inner and outer bottom forming a receptacle for steam ; and there is also a coiled steam-pipe just over the upper bottom. There is one pipe of communication with the vessel of clarified syrup, one with the vessel which is to receive the crystallized sugar, and one with an air-pump, and there are numerous valves, gauges, etc.

In using the pan, a quantity of liquid sugar is admitted, and the air-pump is set to work to exhaust all the air from the pan in order that the contents may boil at a low temperature. To enable the person who superintends the process to ascertain when the syrup is sufficiently evaporated, the pan is supplied with a very ingenious appendage called the proof-stick, by which a little of the sugar can be taken out, and its state ascertained by the touch. Some of the pans have a small glass window, through which can be seen the liquid in a boiling state.

The clarified juice from the tank before mentioned is pumped into the first pan, from the first into the second, it having now become syrup of twenty-eight degrees density; thence it is pumped into syrup clarifiers, then skimmed, then run again through filters of bone-black; out of these filters it goes to the syrup-trough, and thence to the syrup-tank before mentioned.

It is now ready for the third or strike-pan, being drawn up by the vacuum at the option of the sugar-maker, and when the pan is full, it is discharged by a valve into the strike-heater, a double-bottomed kettle with a sufficient amount of steam to keep the sugar warm, and create a certain degree of crystallization; from this it goes into the moulds, or *hormas*, before described.

Common Grades of Sugar.

These moulds are then run on small railway trucks into the purging-house, and then through the different finishing processes before described. The molasses that drains off in the purging-house is afterwards re-boiled and made into a common grade of sugar, known as molasses-sugar. The best molasses comes from the *moscabado* sugar, since it has not passed through so many purifying operations, and, therefore, has more saccharine matter in it.

The sugar being thoroughly dried, sorted, and pulverized, is carried into the packing-room, where, ranged upon a slightly elevated frame, are the empty packing-boxes, capable of holding four hundred pounds each. These are filled with the loose sugar, a gang of negroes or coolies range themselves on each side of the rows, with broad, heavy packing-sticks in their hands, and thus all together they pound away, keeping time with their strokes, and making music with their voices. This seems to be a very primitive way of packing the sugar, taking as it does so much time; but no other plan has ever been successfully tried.

The sugar being now tightly packed in the boxes, the latter are closed up and strapped with narrow strips of raw hide. and are then shipped to market.

The foregoing process of sugar-making differs, of course, in some respects, on different estates; but the general method is the same, the differences being generally due to some variation in the kind of machinery,—some of the manufacturers, for instance, still clinging to the old-fashioned method of boiling the sugar in open pans, which of course allows a great deal of valuable matter to escape; others not going through so much of the refining process with the crop.

In concluding this chapter, it may interest the reader to know that sugar-making was first tried in Cuba as far back as 1535, when a grant of land was made for that purpose on what is now known as the Cerro, near Havana, though good authorities state that it was in Havana itself, and at Regla, on the other side of the bay, in 1598, that really paying sugar estates were established.

CHAPTER XXXIV.

Description of Far-Famed Matanzas.

OF all the towns in the Island of Cuba visited by travelers, Matanzas is the one that gives entire satisfaction to the generality of visitors. Built with regularity and in good style, it lies prettily at the foot of surrounding hills, on the shore of the beautiful bay of Matanzas, while through its limits run two small rivers, which empty into the bay and serve to give additional character and beauty to the place. Away from the grand rush of travel that fills up Havana in the winter, Matanzas gets a smaller share of attention which, from its many attractions, it more richly merits than almost any place upon the Island.

The inhabitants are polished and hospitable, and there is great wealth amongst them, while the women are remarkably pretty (naturally). These things, with the natural beauties of the city, make it the pleasantest place for an invalid, or any one desiring to pass several months on the Island without traveling.

Matanzas, now the second city of the Island in riches and commerce, is situated at the depth of the bay of the same name, formed by an arm of the sea, into which empty the waters of the rivers San Juan and Yumuri. The city proper is bounded on the north by the river Yumuri, and on the south by that of San Juan, while on the east side are the brilliant waters of the noble bay.

It is said that the town is built upon the sight of a former Indian village, known by the early discoverers by its original appellation of "Yucayo." Some thirty families, having emigrated from the Canary Isles, located themselves upon the spot, or in the neighborhood; for Manzaneda, to effect a settlement, had purchased from Charles II. about one hundred and fifty acres of land, with the adjoining *corral* (a cattle-field), known as Matanzas, which signifies "slaughter-pen."

The same name is retained to-day, with the addition of those of its patron saints, San Severino and San Carlos.

The above regular settlement took place on the 10th day of October, 1693, which was on a Saturday, and on Sunday, Bishop Compostello arrived. On Monday, the ground having been previously marked out, he laid the first stone for the future church or cathedral, with the celebration of a grand Mass; at the same time were traced the lines of the castle, known as San Carlos, still standing as a fort upon the Punta Gorda.

Like many of the towns of the Island, Matanzas was threatened at various times by attack from buccaneers and enemies, and has even had naval engagements off its harbor; but its most serious loss was in 1845, when there took place, in the month of June, a great conflagration, which destroyed over two million dollars' worth of property.

Handsome Houses and Stores.

It is now, however, a pretty, well-built city, with a really fine public square—the Plaza de Armas—which is prettily laid out with walks, shrubbery, and flowers, with a fine statue of Ferdinand VII. in the centre. On the east side are the residence and offices of the *commandante*, while on the other three sides are well-built, handsome houses and stores, with one or two cafés, the whole having a very fine appearance.

There is only one church, a large antique-looking old building, remarkable for nothing except the rough architectural beauties of its towers, particularly the taller one of the two, which has some considerable height. There is a fine new theatre, the handsomest on the Island; also a number of public buildings, none of which are remarkable in any way.

That portion of the town lying to the south of the river San Juan is known as "Pueblo Nuevo," in which is situated the railroad depot, and in its outskirts several beautiful country places, the river being crossed by well-built bridges of solid stone. On the other side of the river Yumuri, this portion of the town is known as Versailles, reaching to the very foot of the hill, known as the "Cumbre," from the summit of which is seen the beautiful valley of the Yumuri; while on the hills facing the bay stand the military hospital and the barracks of Santa Isabel, capable of containing over fifteen hundred men. Close to it, on the extreme edge of the bay, is the beautiful paseo of Versailles, the favorite drive of the inhabitants, of an evening. At the end of the paseo is the small castle and fort of San Severino.

The object of greatest attraction, however, to the passing traveler are the " Caves of Bellamar," situated to the south-east of the city, about two and a half miles, and reached by a very pleasant hour's drive, a portion of the way being by the sea-side. This trip is usually made in the early morning, though it is a pretty drive at any hour, and the caves are worth going to see several times.

Resembling Scenes in Venice.

Having ordered your volante (if only gentlemen are in the party, g' on horseback) the night previous, you will find, at six o'clock in the morning, waiting your coming, a two-horse volante and driver; for which you will be charged about six dollars and thirty-seven cents for the excursion. On the way out, you cross the stone bridge over the San Juan, known as the " Belen Bridge," and pass through the town beyond, known as " New Town." These rivers running through the city in this way give it a particularly Venetian appearance, and views taken from one or two blocks upon the river bank might be readily mistaken for scenes in Venice.

In the new town there is a handsome street that the traveler should direct his driver to go through *en route* to the cave; it is called the " Calzada de Esteban," and contains together, in one block, a collection of private dwelling-houses, the newest, most tasteful and beautiful seen in Cuba. The houses are large, beautifully built, with very imposing and handsome pillared fronts and porticoes, generally with large and luxuriantly-flowering gardens, while the combination of iron-railing of pretty designs, with stone pillars and bases, gives a most charming effect.

There will, also, be noticed here the happy use made of prettily-colored tiles in the formation of terraces (if we may so call them) to the fronts of the piazzas. There is a pleasing effect to this style of architecture in Cuba, when, if the same style were adopted with us, it would be pronounced too gaudy, or ginger-bread looking; while here, from the peculiar climate, where the sky is always so beautifully blue, and the sun brightly hot, the high colors used in architecture seem in harmony with those of nature.

Leaving now the town behind us, and passing by some straggling houses, we come out by the side of the bay, whose emerald-green waters wash gently the sandy shore, and from whose blue distance come the cooling ocean breezes of early morning; while across the bay are the verdure-clad hills that over-top the valley of lovely Yumuri; the picture being completed on our right hand by green banks and hills, overshadowed by the tall and graceful palm, or the fan-like branches of the cocoanut tree.

Entrance to the Cave.

Turning off from the sea-side, and winding up a rugged and stony road, some distance up the hills, upon the top of the plateau, we come to the "Cave House," a large frame building erected over the entrance to the cave, and containing the visitors' register, as also numerous specimens of the crystal formations of the cave. In the centre of the building is the stairway leading into the entrance of the cave.

We would advise all visitors to the cave to divest themselves of any superfluous clothing in the way of coats, shawls, vests, etc., which they can leave in charge of the attendant; for the atmosphere inside is quite warm, and, with the exercise, gets to be, before coming out, quite oppressive.

Well, we pay our dollar each; the *muchacho* takes his one candle, and, following him, we descend the stairs into the cave. After a few paces, we cross a small wooden bridge, and find ourselves in the "Gothic Temple." Even in the obscure light (though in this particular place one or two lanterns are hung up) one can see that it is very, very beautiful, with its millions of crystals, its thousand weird forms, and gloomy corners. When the candle is placed behind some of the columns or projecting crystals, their transparency produces a most lovely effect, their colors varying from the purest white to amber and the most tender of rose tints.

This temple is quite two hundred feet long, and about seventy wide, and is about one hundred and fifty feet from the entrance of the cave; and while it far surpasses in richness and splendor the temple of the same name in the Mammoth Cave, it does not equal it in size or solemn grandeur, though, as far as the ease and comfort with which the cave is seen, it is far ahead of the Kentucky cave, as the proprietor has had enterprise enough to make strong bridges, plank walks, and, when necessary, strong iron-railings for protection from slipping.

"A Dream of Fairyland."

The Mammoth Cave leaves upon the mind an impression of solemn, gloomy grandeur, and one peoples it with gnomes and demons. This cave is a dream of fairy-land, with its sprites and lovely fairies keeping gay revel to soft music; and one almost expects to see shooting from the crystal shadows some lovely Undine or beauteous naïad. One becomes thus dreamy under the influences of the names of some of the most striking places, many of which, the *muchacho* says, "some call one thing and some another;" for every pillar has its great name—as "Columbus' Mantle," and every mass is likened unto the "Guardian Spirit," or more sacred "Altar," while without the "Cloak of the Virgin" it would not be a Cuban cave.

This "*Fuente de Nieve*" (fountain of snow) is one of the loveliest portions and most striking objects in the cave; but it contains attractions enough to bring one here again and again, when he can get the chance. The cave is thus far opened about three miles in extent, and its greatest depth below the surface of the earth is five hundred feet. It has been opened about twenty years, having been first discovered in an accidental way, by one of the workmen of Senor Don Manuel Santos Parga, who, while working near by, saw his lever sink through the hole which proved to be the entrance to the cave. " Who has not seen the Caves of Bellamar has not seen Cuba." The views of the valley of the Yumuri should by all means be seen both at sunrise and sunset. This excursion should be made on horseback, by young people, as it is a beautiful road of an afternoon, winding up the hill, the town being left behind until it becomes only a confused mass of buildings in the distance; while to the right hand is the bay with its shipping and forts, and beyond, the hazy landscape; and after a short ride, a full and splendid view of the ocean breaks upon you. The ascent is a steep one, though over a very fair road, particularly for horses, and the change in the atmosphere can be noticed almost immediately after the first turn on the hill, while before the return at night it is quite cold, so that a shawl will not be amiss for lady travelers.

The Far-famed Yumuri.

After about an hour and a half continuous ascent, the road suddenly winds around the brink of a grassy precipice, and there, spread out at one's feet, lies the far famed, poetically described, beautiful valley of the Yumuri, with its patches of green and gold, and its groups in twos and threes of graceful waving palm-trees, while meandering through its grassy banks is the little stream of Yumuri, looking like a silver ribband, except where, here and there, its waters are golden-hued from the setting sun; and over all these hangs that air of perfect stillness—that grand, quiet solitude—which one often realizes amid such noble expanses of nature as this.

All travelers are in the habit of stopping to see a sugar-house in the vicinity, and get a view from the top of the dwelling. One can get a general idea of sugar-making, though on a very small scale; or he can taste the boiling *guarapo* (sugar-juice) from the trough, and, if he is consumptive, " sniff" the odors of the boiling sugar, said to be so beneficial to weak lungs.

Says a traveler: " Our interview with the little black *niños* was highly amusing. On entering the court-yard of the negro quarters, a dozen little black imps, of all ages and sexes and sizes, perfectly naked, rushed towards us, and crossing their arms upon their breasts, fell upon their knees before us, and jabbered and muttered, out of which could be distinguished, " Master, master, give us thy blessing," which we interpreted to mean "tin;" whereupon we scattered sundry *medios* amongst them. Hey! presto! what a change! The little black devils fell over one another, fought, tugged, and scrambled to secure a prize; while any one who had been lucky enough to obtain a coin, marched off in a state of dignified delight, his distended little stomach going before him like a small beer-barrel, while the owner of it kept shouting out, '*Medio, yo tengo medio*' (five cents, I have five cents)."

Sublime Scenery.

There is another view of this charming valley of the Yumuri to the west of the town, out over the hills, known as the "Abra de Yumuri," or "Boca," as it is sometimes called. The view is of the whole valley, from the left bank of the river, with the grand, majestic opening in the rocks, as though they had been sundered expressly to let the river through.

From the top of the hill can be seen the picturesque towers of the city, and the waters of the bay, with all its shipping displayed therein while in the background, towards the south, are seen the distant hills that extend from the hill of San Juan to those of Camarioca, looking like blue clouds against the roseate sky.

The livery stables of Matanzas furnish very fair teams, and the saddle-horses are also very good; they can be had by ordering them at your hotel. Ladies who are not accustomed to riding much will find riding the Cuban ponies a very easy affair indeed; for their gait is a species of amble—what we call racking—and our fair novices in equestrianism pronounce it "divine."

Securing a stylish turn-out, about six o'clock in the evening, we will drive down to El Paseo, which is on the extreme edge of that portion of the city known as Versailles, and immediately on the shore of the bay, whence come, morning and evening, the delightful sea-breezes which everybody comes down here to get.

This paseo is a pretty drive, about half a mile long, and beyond it a road of about the same length to the castle. It is laid out with gravel-walks, rows of trees, and a stone parapet, with iron-gates at each end of the drive; and if the stranger wants to see the beauty and fashion of Matanzas, it is here that he can do so, particularly on Sunday afternoon—that being the great day. Quite as many elegant equipages can here be seen, in proportion to the population and size of the place, as in Havana.

Starting from the front gate, they drive the whole length of the paseo, turning at the other end and retracing their course; and this they do for an hour or more at a time, until there is a perfect string of carriages following one another around and around. Towards eight o'clock, if it is the night of the *retreta* (always Sunday), when the band plays at the Plaza, most of the carriages file off to that square.

Grotesque Street Scenes.

One of the most delightful pleasures in Matanzas is that of the bath at the *Ojo de Agua* (eye of water), where, on the bank of the Yumuri River, some springs of pure, cool water burst forth, and many of the young men walk out in the fresh mornings, and get a dip.

The reader will be interested in the following description by a tourist in Cuba:

" It was our good fortune to be in Matanzas during the last three days of the Carnival; and while the whole time was occupied by noisy processions and grotesque street masqueraders, the crowning ceremonies were on the last Sunday night; then the whole town used every effort to wind up the season in a *feu de joie* of pleasure and amusement. In almost every town of any importance there is an association of the young men, generally known as 'El Liceo,' organized for artistic and literary purposes, and for social recreation.

" A fine large building is generally occupied by the association, with ample space for theatrical representations, balls, etc.; in addition to which there are billiard-rooms, and reading-rooms, adorned, probably, with fine paintings. In Matanzas, this association is known as 'El Liceo Artistico y Literario de Matanzas,' and is a particularly fine one, being composed of the *élite* of the city, with a fine large house, to which they made an addition by purchasing the 'Club,' beautifully situated upon the Plaza.

"Thanks to our letter of introduction, we were, through the kind offices of members, permitted to enjoy the pleasures of their grand ball, called the 'Piñata,' which was indeed a very fine affair, attended by the beauty and fashion of Matanzas. The ball commenced at the sensible hour of eight o'clock in the evening; and at entering, each one was required to give up his ticket to a committee of managers, who thus had a kind of general inspection of all those admitted.

"Passing through the main hall, which was ablaze with light reflected from the highly colored walls and polished marble floor, we entered a *Sala de reception*—which, even at this early hour, was quite full, and which opened into the ball-room. Dear me, what a sight it was! Such crowds of beautiful women, such pretty dresses, such elegant *coiffures*, in which, from the abundance of the raven tresses of the Señoras, no '*rats*' or '*mice*' were necessary—at least, I don't think there were; but then we men are *so innocent!* I do not think I ever saw so many beautiful women together.

Great Array of Female Beauties.

"The ball-room was a long, large hall, at the other end of which was a pretty stage, for theatrical representations; on each side of the room was an arched colonnade, over which were the galleries, where the bands were posted. Ranged in doubled rows of chairs the full length of the room, in front of the colonnade, sat hundreds of dark-eyed angels—calm, dignified, and appearing, most of them, to be mere lookers-on; not a black coat among them. All of these, with the exception of a few courageous ones that were facing all this beauty, were huddled together at the other end of the room, wanting the courage (it could not be the inclination) to pay their respects to *las Señoritas*.

"What is exactly the trouble in Cuba between the gentlemen and the ladies I have never been able quite to understand. The men are polished and gentlemanly, as a general thing—sufficiently intelligent, apparently; while the ladies are dignified and pretty. And yet I have never seen that appearance of easy and pleasant intercourse between the sexes which makes our society so charming.

"I am inclined to believe that it is the fault of custom, in a great degree, which surrounds women in Cuba with etiquette, iron bars, and formality. This would seem to apply to the natives only; for nothing can be kinder, more friendly, and courteous than the manners of the Cuban ladies to strangers, at least, judging from what is seen. It may be as a lady with whom I was arguing the point said: ' It is very different with strangers, Señor, and particularly with the Americans, who are celebrated for their chivalric gallantry to ladies.' Now, I call that a very pretty national compliment.

"Taking the arm of my friend, we walk up and down to see, as he expresses it, ' who there is to be presented to ;' and faith, if beauty is to be the test, it would seem to be a hard matter to make up one's mind, there is so much of it; but after a turn or two around the room, this form is gone through with, and one begins to feel at home and ready to enjoy one's self.

"When one finds ladies (and there are numbers) who have been educated abroad, either in the United States or Europe, he finds them highly accomplished and entertaining. Several that I had the pleasure of meeting on this and other occasions spoke French perfectly, some English, and one or two both of these in addition to their native tongue.

"But let us return to the ball, which is all this time going on with great *éclat*. It opens with the advent upon the stage of a dozen or more young men, under the direction of a leader, in some fancy costume very handsomely made, who, after making their bow to the audience, go through some novel kind of dance. The performers take this means of filling up the intervals of the general dance, and amusing the audience."

Galops, quadrilles, and waltzes are on the programme ; but the prevailing dance here, as everywhere on the Island, is, or used to be, the creole dance or waltz called " *La Lanza*"—a quiet, graceful dance, and the only one which, owing to the heat of the climate, can be enjoyed with any degree of comfort. The following description of the dance, written by a Cuban author, gives the best idea of it :

"Though there are known and executed in the Island all the

modern dances, yet preponderating over them and eclipsing them all is the irresistible *Danza Criolla*—true Cuban specialty. It is nothing else than the old-fashioned Spanish contra dance, modified by the warm and voluptuous character of the tropical climate. Its music is of a peculiar style—so much so, that any one who has not heard it played by one already initiated in its mysteries, will attempt in vain to play it, though he may have it perfectly written before him.

Pretty and Amusing Ceremony.

" It is now getting late, and the rooms are terribly warm; the fans of the long rows of lovely sitters, who have not moved out of their places the whole evening, keep up a constant flutter, and one begins to sigh for a breath of fresh air, and relief from the discomforts of a full-dress suit; but the grand affair of the evening is yet to come off, we are told, and so we linger on, and are finally rewarded by the grand ceremony of the *Piñata*, from which the ball takes its name.

"This word I can hardly give the meaning of as applied to this ceremony, which consists in having pendant from the ceiling a form of ribbands and flowers, the ribbands numbered and hanging from the flowers, the rights to pull which are drawn like prizes in a lottery. Of these ribbands, one is fastened to a beautiful crown of flowers, which, when the ribband to which it is attached is pulled, falls into the hands of the lucky person, who has then the privilege of crowning any lady he may deem worthy of the honor, ' Queen of the Ball,' to whom every one is obliged to yield obedience, homage, and admiration. There is, also, the same opportunity afforded to the ladies to crown a king. The whole ceremony is pretty, and creates much merriment and amusement.

" This ceremony over, at midnight we sally out into the open air. But what a sight greets us there! Lights blaze in such profusion that it seems more than day; music and dancing are everywhere; songs, deviltry, and mirth have taken complete possession of the place; while people of all ages, sexes, and colors are mixed together, in what seems inextricable confusion, intent upon having a good time in the open air, while their masters and betters are doing the same

29

thing under cover. This is a Carnival sight indeed, and only to be seen in a tropical climate.

"Some one suggests that we go down to the theatre, as the fun only commences there after midnight; and so we go there, passing a soldier or two on guard, to see a new phase of life in the form of a *mascara*, or ball of the lower class, known as the '*Cuña*,' where people of all colors and sexes go who are not required to show certificates of character (and could not do it if they were) other than a golden dollar, which is taken at the door.

A Hilarious Crowd.

"Truly it is a mob indeed—a dancing, noisy, masked mob, who, amidst shouts, the din of music, and the shuffling of feet, are going through *all* the figures of the *danza criolla*, most of which are entirely unknown to its more refined female admirers. Keep your hand on your pocket-book, my friend, and cover up your watch-chain with your coat, as you go through the crowd; and more than all, don't tread on any one's toes, unless you are prepared to 'hit out' quickly."

If, while at Matanzas, the traveler wishes to visit a Cuban watering-place—the Cuban Saratoga, in fact—it can be easily done, any day, by taking a ticket for Madruga. Now, unless indeed thou art an invalid, troubled with partial paralysis, stiffened with rheumatism, or suffering from some other unfortunate malady, think not of going there, even if thou feelest for a moment the growing influence of a Cuban's description of the waters and place.

Madruga is a small village, to the south-west of Matanzas, about two hours' ride by railroad, and can be easily reached twice a day, being on the direct road to Havana, by way of the long route. Madruga is simply a watering-place, and as such is celebrated for its mineral springs, which are certainly very beneficial—and wonderful, if all the accounts be true that are given of them. The season begins for the fashionable world about the middle of April, though the baths are taken all the year round by the villagers and strangers.

The hotels are not by any means first class, and are entirely different from anything we are accustomed to; but any one desiring particularly to try the waters, can make himself pretty comfortable. Though there are some inducements on the score of health that might tempt one to make a prolonged visit, yet we advise all those who have any thoughts of staying there to run down from Matanzas before moving their baggage, just to "look before they leap."

The village itself is an ordinary country village, the principal part of it being around the Plaza, and is situated on high ground, in a beautiful rolling country, celebrated for being remarkably healthy. Its public buildings are confined to one small, neat church, in addition to the baths, which are all public. These are the property of the town, having been presented to it by Don José O'Farrell, Governor-General in 1820, on condition that the town should keep them in order and have them in charge. They are in direct charge of the captain of the district, and are kept in repair by the contributions of the people of the village, who find it to their interest to attract strangers to their town.

The baths are all more or less impregnated with sulphur, some iron and magnesia, and some potassa, and are said to be sovereign cures for rheumatism, paralysis, weakness of the stomach, scrofula, and some other complaints.

The baths are very pleasant to take, the water being rather cold. They are taken early in the morning, and then, after the *siesta*, in the middle of the day, a glass or two of the water being drank after each bath. Invalids from all parts of the Island come here, and it is not a very pleasant sight to go into the bath-room, sometimes, and have the eye displeased and the mind shocked by the cases of paralysis, rheumatism, etc., that are there presented.

With a jolly party, one can have a pretty good time at Madruga —bathing, riding on horseback, and walking to the tops of the neighboring hills, from which fine views may be had. The view of the "Valley of Glory," from the top of the hill "Cupey," is very fine, as are also some of the other views, and the change of temperature from the country below is very agreeable.

Far as the eye can reach are seen the waving fields of sugar-cane, darkened here and there by patches of woods or clumps of palms; while in the foreground are the tall, white chimneys of the sugar-mills belching forth their black smoke. In the distance there is just the faintest glimpse of the hazy sea, the distant mountains and hills seeming to fade quite away into it.

Mode of Conducting Funerals.

One sees a good deal of primitive life in a village like this, off of the main route of travel, and away from the "grand world" influ-ences. Observe the method of conducting funerals. First come the small boys, with white linen gowns over their clothes, short enough to display their ragged pants and dirty boots, the boy in the centre bearing a tall pole, upon the top of which is a silver cross partially draped, while each of the other boys carries a tall candlestick.

Behind them comes the priest, in shabby attire, in one hand his prayer-book, from which he is chanting from time to time, while in the other hand, the sun being hot, he holds an open umbrella; behind him, again, comes tottering along a venerable old man, personating whilom the acolyth, the bell-ringer, the sacristan, or other church functionary, as may be necessary, and now croning out in his dreary voice, as he goes swinging the burning censer, the *second* to the chants of the priest. The coffin then makes its appearance, formed of rough boards, but covered with black paper-muslin, and borne upon the shoulders of four of the villagers, a crowd of whom, all uncovered, bring up the rear.

Here, as in all other Catholic countries, the spectators uncover their heads at the passing of the funeral cortége. At the church are further ceremonies of reading prayers, burning candles, and sprink-ling the coffin with holy water; after which the priest goes his way, and the procession take up the line of march for the new-made grave in the dilapidated and neglected cemetery, where the coffin is depos-ited without further ceremony. No females are present during the whole affair.

This humble funeral is a very different affair from what one could see in the larger cities, and particularly Havana, with its ostentatious display of the corpse upon a sumptuous catafalque or under a crystal urn, its crying and screaming women, its long line of carriages, and its various ceremonies, arranged and provided for by a "funeral agency."

A family in mourning in Cuba not only dress in dark clothes upon which there is no lustre, but they keep the windows of the house shut for six months; in fact, by an ordinance of the government, it is now prohibited to display the corpse to the public through the open windows, as was formerly done, both they and the doors being now required to be shut.

An Attractive Village.

The traveler can leave Madruga for Havana or Matanzas, passing on his way to Havana the beautiful little village of Güines, where many people stay during the hot season.   There is no particular attraction here, except that the village is pretty, and the country around attractive, there being some pretty rides and drives, and the horses being very good.   The road to Havana runs through a very beautiful country, amid lovely scenery, and is a very pleasant ride.

Near to Matanzas, on the road to Bemba, is a very pretty little town, known as Limonar, one of the pleasantest places on the Island, and most desirable for the invalid, as the air is fresh and very invigorating.   From there, one can drive over to the baths of sulphur, at San Miguel, which, in the early spring months, are well patronized by the people of the district.

From Matanzas, there are a great many pretty drives to neighboring places, where lovely views can always be had ; and it is as much owing to this fact as to the pleasant society of the town that Matanzas is so popular a place with the stranger.

After Yumuri, one of the most extended and pleasing views is that from the Hill of Paradise, looking down into the Valley of the Magdalen.   A picture, vast and interesting, is offered to the eye of the spectator by this magnificent panorama.

Imagine a space some fifteen miles long, surrounded by hazy mountains, in a country slightly rolling with verdure-clad hills, which serve as points for the eye to rest on; graceful groups of palms and other trees, and the picturesque edifices of an immense number of *ingenios;* the whole limited in the distance by the city of Matanzas— the bay with its shipping; beyond which is seen the almost atmospheric sea uniting with the azure sky.

If the traveler, being at Matanzas, desires to visit Cardenas or Sagua la Grande (and he will do neither, if he takes our advice, unless business compels him), he has the choice of two routes—by cars or by steamboats. This latter, however, we will not take into consideration—the boats being small and dirty, and irregular in their trips.

CHAPTER XXXV.

A Quaint Old Town.

WHAT a glorious morning it is, as we come in sight of the superb Bay of Nuevitas!—the very perfection of a May-day; but such a May-day as few northern eyes have ever seen, with the brightness of the verdure, and the purity of the wondrous atmosphere and sky. And then the water—it is so hard to resist the temptation of its sparkling clearness and depth, and of its seductively cool appearance, and not make a dash overboard.

Irving, in describing the feelings of Columbus on arriving off this very spot, says: "Columbus was struck with its magnitude and the grandeur of its features; its high and airy mountains, which reminded him of those of Sicily; its fertile valleys, and long, sweeping plains, watered by noble rivers; its stately forests, its bold promontories, and stretching headlands, which melted away into the remotest distances."

But we have entered the bay, which gradually opens out into an immense land-locked sheet of water. On its extreme southern side lies the small town of Nuevitas itself, with its few white-walled houses glaring in the morning sun. The bay is said to be the second one in size on the Island, containing within its area a space of fifty-seven square miles, though its depth is not very great.

On the 14th of November, 1492, Columbus anchored in this bay, to which he gave the name of Puerto Principe, erecting a cross upon a neighboring height in token of possession, and passing a number of days in exploring the collection of beautiful islands in the vicinity, since known as "El Jardin del Rey," or the King's Garden. This, it is said, was the foundation of the town of Nuevitas, which was originally known as Santa Maria; but it was not until 1513 that a permanent settlement was made under Diego Velasquez, when the

455

principal town was removed to the Indian village Caonao, and soon afterwards to the town of Camagüey, now known by its name of Puerto Principe. Nuevitas, a town of about six thousand inhabitants, gets its importance simply from the fact that it is the port of entry for the city of Puerto Principe, situated in the interior, at forty-five miles distance.

As a modern town, it made its commencement in 1819, under the name of San Fernando de Nuevitas. It is a growing little place, and is becoming the depot of shipment of a good deal of the sugar and molasses of the neighborhood, as well as of large quantities of hides.

Sponge and Turtle-fishing.

There is also an interesting branch of commerce pursued here, though not amounting to a very large trade. This is the sponge and turtle-fishing, carried on by almost an entirely distinct set of people from those ashore. The sponges are those mostly used on the Island, and a rough calculation estimates the annual production at one hundred thousand dozen, worth one dollar per dozen, which is quite a business for a people who carry it on as they do.

The turtle-shell is prepared usually for export, the meat being sent to the markets of the vicinity in which the turtles are caught. It is quite an amusing sight to see the habitations of these people, dotting some portions of the bay, and, as it is almost perpetual summer, their life is not a very unpleasant one.

Puerto Principe is connected with Nuevitas by a railroad forty-five miles long, and is, probably, the oldest, quaintest town on the Island —in fact, it may be said to be a finished town, as the world has gone on so fast that the place seems a million years old, and, from its style of dress, a visitor might think he was put back almost to the days of Colon.

The road to the town runs through a fine, rolling country, affording many beautiful views, and, from the hills around the place itself, not only the town, but the neighboring country, can be seen to advantage. But may heaven help you, O stranger! if you wander to Puerto Principe without having some friends to depend upon; for it is sadly deficient in hotels. It is, probably, for this reason that the Cubans, as a people, are so hospitable that they will not allow their friends to go to hotels, and even to strangers who have been presented to them they insist on showing this attention.

Lest we be misunderstood in relation to this matter, we wish to say that it is the custom in Cuba for one friend visiting the town of another friend to stay with him at his house, the kindness being returned as occasion demands; and no one having the slightest claim to a courtesy of this kind need hesitate to accept it, either on the plantations or in the interior towns. This can be done without fear of disturbing the hospitable household of the host, for he gives you what he has himself, and, as a general thing, every one in Cuba lives in a free, open-handed way, with abundance of rooms, servants, and an extremely profuse table.

Cuban Hospitality.

In many cases, too, it is as much a kindness to the giver of the invitation to accept it as for him to extend it, for the simple reason that there is not much travel or intercourse on the Island, and the stranger, whether from some other part of the Island or from abroad, has news to impart, a novelty to give, or business to transact with his host. The stranger may be sure the courtesy is sincere when extended with, "Frankly, Señor, I wish you to stay with me, and I shall order your baggage to my house."

Santa Maria del Puerto Principe is situated in the heart of the grazing country, from which business it derives its importance. Its streets are narrow and tortuous, many of them entirely unpaved and without sidewalks; its buildings comprise several queer old churches, various convents, large quarters for the troops, a tolerable theatre, and a fine lot of public buildings for government officers. The general style of architecture, though Cuban, offers many peculiarities to the artist or antiquarian.

This town has always been looked upon with suspicion by the authorities on account of the strong proclivities its people had for insurrection; and its sons have had a greater or smaller share in almost every revolution that has taken place in the Island. It has received its baptism of blood in the cause of liberty for "free Cuba," having sustained a siege, been attacked, and almost starved out.

Although there is not much in the actual town to occupy the traveler, the surrounding country affords fine opportunities for studying some peculiarities of the Island not so advantageously seen elsewhere as here. First among these are the *potreros*.

Potrero, in the Castilian, really means a horse-herd, a pasture-farm; but in the Cuban dialect, it has a somewhat different meaning. In the early days of Cuba when land was plenty and the government liberal in the disposition of it, they called all grounds or properties, whether belonging to the crown or to private persons, used for the purpose of sheep-folds or cattle herding, *haciendas or hatos*.

A Cuban Stock-farm.

These were large extents of ground, of circular form, with a radius of over nine thousand yards, the centre of which only was marked out, where the pens and buildings were usually erected. The *corral* was also a circular tract, one quarter the above size, that is to say, with a radius of four thousand five hundred yards, intended for the care of smaller cattle, sheep, pigs, etc. its centre being also marked by the hog-pen, or the fences of the sheep-folds.

Owing to the difficulty of always laying out the exact lines (caused by the location of woods), the surveyors adopted the method of describing polygons, with a large number of sides, each of which was equivalent to so many yards. The spaces left between these polygons, almost circular, were considered as the property of the crown, and were known as *realengos*.

But as time advanced, and the government kept on increasing these gifts, without any particular reference to the line of demarcation in the land, many centres of the new farms or folds were fixed in such a manner that, in drawing their boundary-lines according to their radii, they cut those already established, one new circle falling within an old one, creating thereby inextricable confusion, which ended in every man going to law with his neighbor about the boundary-lines;

and from this came the belief that every Cuban had a farm and a lawsuit.

Many of these tracts were then, by the decision of the court, divided, and afterwards, by the will of their owners, sub-divided into small lots, appropriated for the various uses of cultivating grain, raising cattle and fruits, while others were again cut up and laid out in town lots. Out of these divisions came all the different rural establishments known as cattle farms, farms proper, and small truck-gardens, and which, under various names, bother the stranger or the student of Cuban life.

The largest of all the above is the *potrero*, where cattle are raised, fed, and looked after with care; while in the *corrales* they are left to run wild in every direction, getting water from the running brooks, and only attended to, from time to time, by the keepers. But the *potreros* are large places, encircled by walls of stone piled up, or stone-fences. Not only the cattle of the place are taken care of, but those also belonging to neighboring *ingenios*, or farms, are fed and attended to.

The raising of cattle is a very profitable business indeed, particularly as no attention is paid to the fattening of beef, but the cattle are sold just as they are thought to be fit for market. The consequence is, that it is rare indeed that a piece of beef fit to roast is seen—at least as we know it.

It is a great sight to see these immense herds of cattle, scattered over extensive plains, with here and there large clumps of palm or cocoa trees affording shade, while, at regular intervals, long stone walls serve to separate the herds. Many of the fiercest bulls used in the bull-ring come from this district; and when so noted upon the play-bills, an audience is sure to be attracted by the superior " sport " they offer.

Valuing the cattle at the lowest prices, and calculating from various reports as to the number of such on the Island, it is estimated there is represented, by the stock of these cattle-places and at the sugar and coffee estates and smaller farms, a capital of twenty-one millions of dollars. This is exclusive of horses and mules, too, of which there are large numbers raised upon the Island, the value of which is estimated at two millions of dollars.

At one time, camels were introduced into the Island, in the hope that they would answer the purposes of transportation; but they did not do well, for, strange to say, the smallest insect, the *nigua*, that buries itself in the feet and there procreates, utterly ruined all of them.

At almost all of these places, the beef is cured by putting it, salted, in the sun, and it then is known as *tasajo* (jerked beef); and prepared in this way, it will keep for two or three weeks, being used principally for home consumption, that which is prepared for market requiring more curing. This is the great article of food amongst the masses of the population, and is found sometimes even upon the table of the better class, when no strangers are present. Large quantities of the hides of the cattle are exported, while the bones are made into "bone-black," of which immense quantities are required by the sugar manufacture of the Island.

Unique Breed of Horses.

From Puerto Principe come, also, some of the finest horses raised on the Island. The Cuban horse is not supposed to be a native either of the Island or of these climes—in fact, if we believe the accounts of the early discoverers, the animal was not known upon this continent; for, in every case when the natives first saw a horse, they were struck dumb with astonishment, showing that they had never seen one before.

It is, therefore, suspected that the Cuban horse of to-day, peculiar breed as it is, is simply the result of some of the Spanish stock transferred to the Island and affected by the peculiarities of the climate in its breeding. At all events, it is a fine animal now, with a short, stout, well-built body, neat, clear limbs, fine, intelligent eyes, with a gait for long journeys under the saddle not to be surpassed. These horses have sturdy necks, heavy manes, and thick tails, and, seen on the plains, where they are raised, and before being handled and dressed, they present a very rough and wild appearance. Their gait is something peculiar, it would seem, to themselves; and on a well-

broken horse the greatest novice in the art of riding need not hesitate
to mount.

The *marcha*, or fast walk, is simply the easiest gate in the way of
a walk; and *el paso*, or the rapid gait of the horse, is something like
the movement of our pacing horses, or, as they call it in the Southern
States, a single-footed rack, only it is a great deal more easy. Some
of the horses have a movement so gentle that a rider can carry a full
glass of water without spilling. It is for this reason that the Cuban
horses are so much admired by lady travelers fond of horseback
riding, for they can ride miles and miles without experiencing the
slightest fatigue.

If we were to tell all the wonderful stories about the performances
of these horses, the reader would be incredulous; but this we can
say, that, day after day, the Cuban horse will journey from forty-five
to sixty miles without showing the slightest sign of giving out, and
on forced rides, seventy to eighty miles is no unusual occurrence.

Plaited Tails and Fancy Ribbands.

The price varies, according to circumstances, and it is amusing to
see with what care those owned by wealthy people are created.
Owing to the sticky nature of the mud of the country roads, it has
been the custom to plait the tails of all the horses (the end being
fastened to a ring in the cantle of the saddle), and to crop the manes.
But in the cities, especially, is great display made in plaiting the tail
with fancy ribbands, and the mane is trimmed with mathematical precision.

Judging from experience, we should say that all Cuban horses were
good, even-tempered animals. The Cubans explain this by saying
that the horse is one of the family, as in town he is kept in some portion of the *patio*, usually near the kitchen, and in the country he is
treated with even more familiarity.

One of the first things in a Cuban house that strikes the stranger
with its novelty is the guava with cheese, which may mean either
guava jelly or marmalade; and from this universal custom, one wishes
to know what is this guava they make so much use of; and as Puerto

Principe is a place noted for its manufacture, we will give here a description of it.

In some of the towns of Cuba, such as Trinidad, Santiago de Cuba, and Puerto Principe there is a class of women remarkable for their beauty, whose race it would be hard for the stranger to tell, with any degree of certainty—some appearing even lighter in color than Cubans; others, again, like the far-famed octaroons of Louisiana; and still others, of the light mulatto order—all resembling each other, however, in the wonderful blackness and brilliancy of their eyes, the jet of their hair, and a certain indescribable grace of outline and movement of figure, having in it a dash of that voluptuous languor that we believe peculiar to the Orient.

Makers of Sweetmeats.

Who they are, and what their fathers and mothers have been, it would be hard to say. Some of them, however, claim to have " gentle blood " running in their veins, and, if appearances are worth anything, with good reason. Be that as it may, they are the seamstresses, very often the lady's maids, but more frequently the manufacturers of the delicious preserve known as " *Jalea* " and " *Pasta de Guayaba.*"

The *dulce* or sweetmeat of guava, then, is of two kinds,—the jelly, a pure, translucent, garnet-colored substance. similar to our currant-jelly ; and the marmalade, an opaque, soft substance, similar to good quince marmalade, and of about the same color, or darker.

Both of these are made from the same fruit, though prepared in a different way ; and there are also two kinds of the fruit,—one known as the *guayaba del Peru,* which is very scarce, and the other, *guayabas cotorreras*, the common red apple-bearing tree, which is the one most found in Cuba ; the fruit of the former being of a greenish color in the inside, while that of the latter is either red, yellow, or white.

The fruit is small and edible, having a fragrant but peculiar odor, and a sweetish taste ; and the making of the jelly is an extremely simple operation, as follows : The fruit is cut in halves, and separated from the seeds; then gently stewed; then the sugar, thoroughly boiled to a syrup, is cleared. The guava is now strained through a bag, and the juice only being united with the syrup, it is all boiled until it reaches a proper state of consistency, when it is taken out, put into moulds of the different-sized boxes required, and allowed to cool and get firm, when it is placed in long, shallow boxes of various sizes, lined with paper, then closed up, papered to keep out the air, and labeled for market.

A Rare Delicacy.

The paste is made in the same way, except that only the seeds are taken out, and the whole fruit incorporated with the syrup is used to make the marmalade, which by many is considered the richer for that reason. To any who have ever tasted the guava jelly it needs no recommendation; but to those who have not, and who wish a "new sensation," we advise them to try it, being careful, however, to buy the small, flat boxes, which are the best, the round boxes usually being filled with very poor stuff. Large quantities of this sweet-meat are exported each year, and there are many manufactories of it in Havana; the best, however, comes from Puerto Principe and Trinidad.

Hot as it may be in Cuba, there is some way of keeping cool. You can get up in the morning, when the breeze is always fresh and strong, transact your business, and return to your breakfast, where, in some sweet-smelling, flowered court-yard, you can, by keeping quiet, and, with the aid of refreshing drinks, keep cool. The afternoons bring the delicious sea-breeze, that carries with it new life for the *paseo*, or the music in the evening. But your landlady cautions you, as you sit in your room, looking out upon the blue sea, where lies, far away, your northern home, "Not to make any noise." You ask: "Why?"

"Because there is a poor, sick stranger in the next room."

"Is he very sick?"

"Yes, but he will go away in a day or two."

"What's the matter with him?"

"He has a very bad case of yellow fever."

Notwithstanding you are told that you are not a fit subject for the fever—that there is no danger, you think it just as well to anticipate your neighbor's departure, particularly as Havana is no longer the gay place it was early in the winter. The opera season is over, 'he circus is closed, and even the bull-fights offer no attraction. The hotels, where once during the past months it was a hard matter to get lodging-room, are now dull and deserted, and the long, gaunt faces and bearded chins of Americans are no longer seen in the cool precincts of the Louvre, sipping their cobblers or cold rum-punches.

CHAPTER XXXVI.

Here and There in Cuba.

IF the traveler in Cuba desires to see its most beautiful portions, and also some of its prettiest, quietest towns, he will do well to make a trip along the south coast, from Batabano to Santiago de Cuba, stopping at Trinidad, and, if he likes, taking the steamer at Santiago home to the States. Or if he desires to visit the British West Indies, he can do so by means of the French steamers running from that place.

The trip is a very enjoyable one, even for ladies, the boats are large and fine, and the accommodations on board them excellent; the voyage is as pleasant and beautiful as a summer trip on the Hudson, or as a sail on Lake George, the sea being generally as calm as a lake. With a good party and plenty of light reading it is as agreeable a trip as can be taken.

Leaving Havana at 5.45 in the morning, the traveler reaches Batabano at 8 o'clock, and goes immediately on board one of the steamers lying at the wharf; and he should immediately see the cabin-boy and make his choice of a stateroom, which should always be taken in the upper cabin, if one can get it there. An eye after one's baggage will not be amiss now, for they do sometimes make mistakes.

And now we are afloat and have time to look about us, and we already feel quite at home from finding the boat and machinery are "Yankee notions," being made either in New York or Philadelphia, while the cheerful looks and courteous manners of the passengers demonstrate that we are in good company. Acquaintance will be easy if the traveler is able to speak any Spanish ; if not, all he has to do is to look pleasant, like the rest of the people, and watch his chance of finding some one who speaks English, and who will be delighted to explain to the stranger, in his own tongue, the beauties of the Cuban shore.

Ten o'clock, and there goes the breakfast bell. No hurry, gentlemen, everybody is provided for, and there is none of that scrambling and struggling for a seat at the table, so disgraceful to us Americans on our boats; no, everything here is quiet and orderly, and ladies go leisurely to their table in the upper cabin, and the men to theirs arranged in a cool place on the main deck.

Now you will want your Spanish bill of fare, for the table is bountifully supplied with the best of food cooked in the best Spanish fashion, while there is an ample supply of ice and *vino catalan* to wash it down with; don't hurry, either, my friend, these people don't propose to make a labor of what should always be a pleasure.

Bold Coast and Rocky Islands.

The coast for some distance after leaving Batabano is quite low, and generally marshy; but, on nearing Cienfuegos, it gets higher and even mountainous. To the right, some distance from the coast, and inside of which the steamer always keeps on her passage, are low keys or rocky islets, known as *Los Jardines*, and likely to prove very dangerous to the navigator, if not acquainted with their locality.

Many of the passengers, after breakfast, seat themselves at a table with the game called "Loto," at which they all gamble more or less. Even the chambermaid is a party to the gambling speculation, for she goes about the boat offering you a ticket in a raffle for a gold watch, or something else, and finding as many purchasers among the ladies as among the men. And so the day slips round, and we have the beauties of a moonlight night in a tropic sea, which add vastly to our pleasure before turning in for the night into our cane-bottomed berth, over which is simply thrown a sheet—a capital idea for boats in warm weather, for such beds, being cool and quite elastic, are most comfortable.

We arrive off the harbor of Cienfuegos some time during the night, but as vessels are not allowed to enter any of the ports of the Island at night, particularly during war times, we have to wait until daybreak, when we get under weigh and enter that beautiful port by the light of the rising sun. The bay is a very extensive one, the entrance itself being quite narrow, with a lighthouse on the extreme point, and stone forts upon the adjacent hills at the mouth, none of which appear to be very strong.

Anchorage for Large Vessels.

The bay has anchorage for vessels of the largest class, while the high hills that surround it afford ample shelter from any stormy winds that may blow. It was this bay that Columbus visited on his first voyage, and Padre las Casas, in speaking of it, calls it the most magnificent port in the world, comprising within its shores six square leagues. Herrera, also, describing the port and bay of Cienfuegos, as seen by Ocampo in a voyage round the Island, says: "There was Ocampo very much at his ease, well served by the Indians with an infinite number of partridges, like those of Castile, except somewhat smaller. He had also abundance of fish (*lizas*, skate). They took them from this natural fish-pond, where there were millions of them just as safe as if they were in a tank attached to one's home."

The steamer reaches the wharf about six o'clock, and, as she remains until eleven, the traveler has ample time to go ashore and see the town or try the excellent oysters, of which they have large quantities. Probably no place on the Island offers greater advantages for seeing sugar-making in its most favorable aspects than Cienfuegos, as it is surrounded by an immense cane-growing district, with some of the best estates on the Island.

Still, keeping close to the coast, we begin to see some of its mountainous beauties; for, sailing within a mile or two of the shore, we have a constantly changing panorama of green hills, that come down to the very water's edge, while, in the distance, they stretch away until some of their tops appear to be holding up the heavens.

We know not if Tennyson was ever in the tropics in person, but he must have been there in mind when he wrote, as though filled with their ardor:

"Oh, hundred shores of happy climes,
How swiftly streamed ye by the bark!
At times the whole sea burned; at times,
With wakes of fire we tore the dark;
At times a craven craft would shoot
From heavens hid in fairy bowers,
With naked limbs and flowers and fruit,
But we nor paused for fruits nor flowers."

Breaking in upon our romantic musings comes the sound of the hand-bell, and we wonder what it can be for. Our late breakfast was over only an hour or so ago. It cannot be anything to eat; no, innocents, it is only something to drink, in the shape of *frescos*, which may be made either of lemons or oranges, placed nice and cold, in large pitchers, for you to help yourself to at discretion.

Small Hands and Ruby Lips.

It is an attractive sight to see these pretty Cuban women sipping their *frescos*, holding the glasses to their ruby lips with the smallest hands imaginable; while, perhaps, peeping out from beneath their dresses, are the tiny feet for which they are celebrated, evidently never intended by nature to walk on. "To be sure" (we think we hear some uncharitable lady reader say), "if I made as little use of my hands and feet as they do, I could have such trifling appendages." Nevertheless, they are very pretty, and we think most of the Señoritas are positively aware of the fact, from the way they display them.

About four o'clock in the afternoon, we arrive in sight of those high and beautiful mountains of Trinidad, a continuation and part of the range which we have been seeing all day, known as the "Guana-huya;" and, at last, we see Trinidad—beautiful Trinidad—on this balmy south coast, which, seen from some distance out at sea, looks, as it lies far up the mountain side, its white walls glistening in the golden light, like a babe nestling on its mother's breast. It takes some time to get up to its port, for in front of the bay there is a large narrow point of land, which, with the main land, forms the bay and port of Casilda.

Reaching this, we steam around the point, and then, retracing our course in the direction from which we have come, we see, upon the shore of this beautiful bay, the little village of Casilda, which is the port of entrance for Trinidad. There are two other ports of entrance, though not in use—that of "La Boca," to the south-west, where empties the river Táyabo, and that of the river Musé, to the south-east.

The anchorage in the bay is not a very good one, as the water is so shallow that it necessitates the loading of vessels by lighters, unless they happen to be quite small. The town has quite an extensive series of wharves and warehouses, the principal portion of the shipping business being done down here, though the town itself is a straggling village, with a few large warehouses and the depot of the railroad which connects it with Trinidad.

A Hotel in Trinidad.

If the traveler can find a volante, we would advise him to take that and ride up, unless the cars are ready to start, for sometimes there is a delay of several hours after the arrival of the boat, before the train gets off, and as the distance is only three miles, over a good road, with beautiful views, it is quite as pleasant to go in a volante as in the cars, though somewhat more expensive. It is an ascent all the way.

One is not very greatly struck with the appearance of the town of Trinidad upon getting out at the depot, for the streets lying immediately in its neighborhood are anything but attractive, though they are rather antique and rugged, looking as if you had come to some third-rate village.

One has to look out now for his own baggage, engaging a cart to carry it, and seeing himself that it is put upon the cart, which is then driven to the designated hotel. Generally there is not much choice of hotels in Trinidad, and the best way is to examine all of them that are tolerable enough to go to, before deciding.

Says a traveler, speaking of a large boarding-house: "Our first experience there was very amusing. After securing our room, we ordered the waiter to provide us a dinner, hot, good, and as quickly as possible, which instructions were received with a frequent ' *Si,* Se or, warm and quickly, Señor.' A few minutes finds us seated at table, and prepared to enjoy the said dinner.

" 'Serve the soup, waiter.'

" 'There is none, Señor; there is theatre to-night, sir.'

" We try the fish. ' Why, confound it, this fish is as cold as a stone.'

" 'Yes, Señor, do you go to the theatre to-night?'

" 'Hang the theatre, we want dinner! What else have you?'

" 'Salad and meat, Señor.'

" We try the oil; it is bad. The meat turns out to be pork. We are hungrily, furiously angry by this time, and, jumping up from the table, we ask if we can have a dinner or not.

" 'But, Señor, I am going to the theatre to-night; are you not going?'

" 'Hang the theatre!' we roared, thinking the man was crazy, ' bring out our baggage and (in a theatrical manner) we will go hence.'

" Waiter (humbly, but sullenly): 'If the gentlemen will wait I will warm the fish, and give them some good oil. I have some most splendid boiled ham, with some fine fruit; and if the gentlemen will have patience till to-morrow, they shall live like lords.'

" We relent, having no other place to go to, and make a tolerably fair meal, but the climax was reached next morning, when, having had an elegant breakfast, at which mine host was present, I remarked to him, ' We are glad to see that you do have good meals here some-times; our dinner of yesterday was a disgrace to your house, sir.'

" 'Yes,' he replied, very coolly, 'I know it was, it was that boy's fault (pointing to the waiter); he wanted to go to the theatre on a free ticket.'

" The waiter makes some deprecatory remark.

" 'You lie, scoundrel,' said the old man, with much vim, 'I heard you.'

" 'Why, where were you?' I asked, rather astonished that, as he had heard the row, he had not made his appearance.

"' In the room there, lying down.'

"' Well, why did you not come out and attend to your guests ?'

"' *No valia la pena*' (it wasn't worth while), in a perfectly innocent manner ; 'the boy wanted to go to the theatre.'"

Trinidad de Cuba is a pretty, rambling, hilly town, of about fifteen thousand inhabitants, situated on the side of the mountain of the *Vijia* (watch tower), and elevated about four hundred feet above the level of the sea, from which it is distant some six miles, and from Havana, by land, about two hundred and seventy miles.

A Fertile Country with Grand Scenery.

Exposed to the combined breezes of sea and mountain, with a most delicious climate, it is reputed to be the healthiest town upon the Island, while, from its beautiful situation in a rich and fertile country, its exquisitely grand and extended views, the beauty of its lovely maidens, and the general hospitality of its inhabitants, it would be, were there only a good hotel, the most attractive town upon the Island for the sojourn of the invalid traveler. Here one can find quiet, kindness, and every inducement for taking pleasant exercise in the way of walks, rides and drives.

Historically, we don't know that it has much to interest the general traveler, and yet it was here that that " gay Lothario," gallant adventurer, and sagacious but cruel conqueror, Hernan Cortéz, came after parting with his uncertain employer and governor, Velasquez, of whom he took " French leave," with all the vessels and men fitted out for the conquest of Mexico ; here it was, too, that he added means and men to that same expedition, the history of which seems, at the present reading, like some wondrous fairy tale.

Trinidad is also one of the oldest towns on the Island, having been settled by Diego Velasquez in 1513, and suffered in its earlier days, like many other Cuban towns, from various attacks of pirates and enemies, one of which was made, in 1702, by the English corsair Grant, who, with three hundred men, invaded the town, and made good his retreat, without suffering for his intrepidity. The bay of Casilda is also famous as being the battle-ground of three British men-of-war with the Spaniards, under Don Luis Bassecourt, whose command consisted of militia and a few veteran pickets; but the English were compelled, nothwithstanding, to withdraw after three days' fighting.

The streets of the city are, with some exceptions, narrow and tortuous, and many of those upon the edge of the town entirely unpaved, while the houses in the best streets are generally comfortable, well-built, stone houses, some of which are really magnificent private edifices.

Peculiarities of the Houses.

The houses of Trinidad differ from those in Havana in not having dividing walls to separate the dining room and the saloon, but in their place they have, generally, open stone arches, which, while separating the apartments in some degree, yet add to their beauty and comfort by permitting a free circulation of air and affording a charming prospective of marble floors, mirrored arches, and richly furnished rooms. Some of the streets are quite odd in their appearance, with their rough tiled houses, their narrow pavements, and the funny names which are seen, just as in Havana, stuck up over the store doors.

The " Campo de Marte " is a fine large place at the southeast end of the town, with barracks and drill-grounds for the troops. But the plaza, *par excellence*, of Trinidad, and in fact of all Cuba, for it is certainly a most gracefully beautiful square, is known as the " Plaza de Carillo," situated nearly in the centre of the town, and opposite which is the governor's house.

The square is most beautifully laid out, with vines and shrubbery shading the stone walks, on either side of which is a profusion of flowers, while in the centre of the square there is erected a graceful dome-like arbor, completely covered with flowering vines. Extending around the square is a broad stone paseo, which is separated from the main garden by a tasty iron railing, and from the street by a stone base. A profusion of gas-lights are ranged at intervals around the square, which at night, when illuminated, have a most beautiful effect.

The square is always open, but the *retreta* is only about three times a week, one of those times being Sunday. On such occasions the plaza is brilliantly lighted, and the music, the soft breezes, and the delicious fragrance of the flowers, are enjoyed by throngs of "fair women and brave men." The *Vijia* is probably the greatest attraction to the town proper, for no matter how often we go up, there is always some new beauty discovered, either in land, or sea, or sky. It is very easily reached on horseback, to its very top; is a pleasant walk before breakfast, or can be easily gained by elderly people in a volante, which can go nearly to the top. No one, however, can be said to have seen *La Vijia* who has not visited it both at sunrise and sunset; let us try it.

Scene of Wonderful Beauty.

It is a fine bracing morning, and, having had our bath and coffee, we sally out at the door of our hotel, and find in the dusky morning (it is not yet daybreak) our horses, ordered the previous evening, awaiting our coming; they are not " much," but they will do to carry us up the hill. So, mounting, we wind through various streets of the upper town, and come out at last by the rustic road leading past the military hospital, which is about half-way up the mountain.

Leaving these below us, we strike a rough, steep road, ascending which we get far above the town, and begin to take in something of the vast scene, which at this early hour of the morning is somewhat indistinct. Higher and higher we go at a slow pace, until at last we reach the top, where is a small house or hut in which lives the signal-man, and in front of which is the mast where signals are made to the town below, of any approaching vessels. Here we leave our horses, and on foot proceed by a path leading beyond the house, that takes us to the very summit.

What a scene bursts upon us here! We seem to be on a high point, around which are vast seas of mist and vapor, that, floating far below us, look like grand lakes, while some, not so distant, are yet more opaque, resembling solid fields of cotton; but now over the distant eastern hills, the first rays of the rising sun begin to shed their light, and, gradually getting higher and higher, the orb of day rises, in all its magnificence of blazing golden glory, over the top of the neighboring mountain.

The scene now rapidly changes, the vast bodies of vapor that hung like a pall over the whole face of the lower valley, are now rapidly dissolved by the warm rays of the risen sun, and then we have unfolded to our astonished vision, piece by piece, the loveliest bits of hill and dale, of fields of waving cane, as bright and green as the emerald water of the ocean itself. The neighboring hills, too, in their glittering and verdure-clad robes, deign to appear, one by one, gorgeously gilded by the morning sun.

Turning to the south we have the town and the country between it and the sea clearly defined, while beyond is the sea itself extending its blue waters until lost in the hazy clouds of the distant heavens ; and this scene is not the same with every morning, for there is always some difference of light and atmosphere that gives a changing beauty to the views.

Magnificent Sunset View.

The scene is changed; it is now the evening hour of sunset, and seated upon the rocks we gaze at the same scenes in a different light. Everything is quiet and peaceful—not a sound is heard from the great world below. We see the people moving like mere specks in the streets of the town—even the trains of cars, winding swiftly over the long black trail, look like small boxes endowed with some supernatural power of motion, for we hear no noise of engines.

We look up the valley, and from clumps of green foliage shoot up here and there the tall white chimneys of the sugar mills, puffing out their black smoke, which rises in clouds, higher and higher until it vanishes away into air; the little stream that wanders between its wooded banks looks, as we catch a glimpse of it here and there, like a silver ribband. And then the sea, too, as blue as blue can be, with not a perceptible ripple on its surface, but quiet as a lake, while a white sail here and there seems to make a boundary between sea and sky, which latter is assuming all those beautiful golden crimson tints peculiar to a tropical sunset, and yet so beautifully graduated one into the other that it is hard to say where the blue leaves off and the gold and grander tints begin.

But hark, even now there is a sound—a quiet soft musical sound—that comes stealing up the valley as the sun is slowly going down, and which truly harmonizes with the scene,—the vesper bell. How *apropos* the lines of Byron to such a scene, and such an hour as this:

> " Sweet hour of twilight !
> Soft hour which wakes the wish and melts the heart
> Of those who sail the seas, on the first day
> When they from their sweet friends are torn apart ;
> Or, fills with love the pilgrim on his way,
> As the far bell of vesper makes him start,
> Seeming to weep the dying day's decay.
> Is this a fancy which our reason scorns ?
> Ah ! surely nothing dies but something mourns."

There, far down in these peaceful valleys, that look so calm and still, and which even seem to fill one's breast with prophetic sadness, have taken place some sharp, fierce struggles—where a little band of patriots, badly armed and equipped, but with stout hearts, in a good cause, have essayed to plant firmly the flag of freedom. Now forward, now backward, sometimes in good success up to the very foot of the hill of Trinidad they have pressed, and yet again been forced back amidst the shades of these palmy groves, or the shelter of the waving cane. These grand old hills have witnessed horrid deeds of cruelty in the beautiful plains below, which rival in brutality and bloodthirstiness any that the page of history yet can show.

On the other side of the valley, the highest peak which the traveler is able to see, and one whose top is frequently hidden in fleecy clouds, is the " Pico de Potrerillo," one of the highest mountains in Cuba, being some three thousand odd feet above the level of the sea. It is said that the view from there is even more grand and extensive than that from the Vijia, but it is a long ride, and involves the necessity of staying in its neighborhood over night.

The drive to the " Loma del Puerto " is a very beautiful one that should be taken by every traveler at Trinidad, presenting, as it does, grand and beautiful views of the hill " Del Puerto" and a portion of the valley.

This valley is said to be the most beautiful of the Island seen from this side, as there one sees the beautiful perspective of mountains, that rise to good height at the depth of the valley, and towering above which is seen the "Pico de Potrerillo." Within the boundaries of the valley there are no less than fifty *ingenios*, some of them of the finest class. It is watered by a number of beautiful streams, two of which, the Ay and the Agabama, unite and form the river Manati, which empties into the sea to the east of Casilda, and which is navigable some seven miles, and by which the planters send their sugar and molasses to the shipping points.

Mineral Springs.

In this same river of Ay there are sulphurous mineral springs, the water being delicious to drink; and in the centre of the valley, and on its banks, is a village of the same name as the river, prettily situated in a grove of trees—in fact, the whole of the valley is one scene of beauty. The railroad from the Casilda runs through the valley some distance, and if the time-table is so arranged that the traveler can go from Trinidad in the morning and return in the evening, he will be delighted with his trip.

On the way back from the Loma del Puerto, the tourist can visit the magnificent place of Recreo, " Quinta," or country house of the Cantero family, which is situated a short distance from the town, at the head of the beautiful valley, and at the foot of the mountains, which rise up behind it forming a majestic background to the lovely beauties of the place. It is a lovely walk to this estate of an early morning from Trinidad, and one can go in and walk around these beautiful grounds with constant and renewed pleasure.

In the north of the town is the *barranca*, as it is called, a place of very rapid descent, leading from the town down into the valley, the road being dug out of the side of the hill and paved with stone as far down as the bank of the river Tayabo, which flows by the town at this point. Here the washerwomen have established their city laundry, as it may be called, and a ridiculous and not very decent sight it is of a wash-day to see men and women, many entirely naked. seated upon the rocks or half immersed in the water, washing, slashing and pounding the clothes with pieces of stone, and if the traveler has been unfortunate enough to trust any of them with his wardrobe, he will learn to his cost with what effect.

This *barranca* is also a lovely stroll of an evening, when the shadows of night are stealing over the quiet hills and valley below, giving them a peculiarly quiet and sombre hue.

The Public Buildings.

There are several public buildings and churches in the town of Trinidad, which offer nothing in particular to the traveler, except it may be the extreme filthiness of the hospital for women and children, and the dreary jail-like appearance of the *carcel* or dungeon; while of the churches, the only one of any size is that of San Francisco. The church of Santa Anna is small and old, and *Paula*, at the Plaza de Carillo, not much better.

On Palm Sunday, doors and windows are decorated with the graceful branches of the *real* palm, and it is a great day with church and state, the morning Mass being celebrated with great pomp at the church of San Francisco. The governor and staff, in full uniform, the town council in sombre full dress, the officers of the troops stationed in the town, " pipe-clayed and mustache waxed," are all there to assist.

Trinidad, in the winter or gay season, is a very hospitable, pleasant place for the stranger. Almost every night there is a ball or party, and in the daytime there are frequent excursions made up the before mentioned lovely valley. There is no pleasanter place to spend a winter in than Trinidad de Cuba, and any traveler not caring to travel over the Island, but who wants quiet, rest, and pleasant enjoyment, should winter there.

And now the boat is in, and will start in a few hours. We order our volante, make our preparations and bidding adieu to our kind friends after giving a knuckle-breaking shake of the hand to the jolly old landlord, we turn our backs upon the varied attractions of this city, carrying away with us a lively memory of its beautiful scenes, lovely women and hospitable people, the delightful ride down the mountain forming a fitting close to our exceedingly pleasant stay in Trinidad.

CHAPTER XXXVII.

Life in the Coffee Mountains.

A TRAVELER who is familiar with every part of Cuba, furnishes the following interesting account of the cultivation of the coffee plant, which furnishes one of the chief exports of the Island :

" Our horses are all saddled and bridled, and the party, consisting of five persons, is ready to mount. Our cigars are lighted, and, mounting the sturdy beasts that have some work in prospect, we ride off in the fine bracing air fresh from the mountains.

" My future host, like most of the inhabitants of this section of the country, was a descendant of the old original French settlers, refugees from the terrible massacres of St. Domingo, who, coming to the Island of Cuba, settled themselves, as much as possible, in their old occupations of sugar-making and coffee-growing. French, therefore, by birth, educated in the United States from a boy, and living constantly amongst Spaniards, he had the happy faculty of being able to speak either French, English, or Spanish, as a mother-tongue, in addition to which he spoke the Creole dialect—a compound of vile French and some little Spanish, which is the usual language of the negroes and the plantation.

" A young Englishman, amusing himself and at the same time making money by traveling all over the world as a photographer, was one of our number, while two Cuban planters, one of them a nephew of our host, made up the party.

" We rode through some lovely valleys, covered with sugar-cane, and then, striking the hills, began the ascent of those mountains known as the ' Yateras,' which appeared quite near to the village of Catalina when we started, but now seemed to recede almost as we advanced. Our journey was to be about eighteen miles in extent, continually ascending until we should reach the very summit of the mountains, where the finest coffee grows, and which is now known as the coffee district.

"Gradually getting to the foot of the hills, and then ascending them for some time, we begin to take in the beauties of our road and the advantages of our position. We have left now the flat country behind us, and are coming into clumps of forests, with occasionally a *hacienda*, or farm, and now and then a small coffee place, and at last we strike the steep mountain path.

Beauties of Mountain and Landscape.

"Now, turning in our saddles, we begin to see the magnificent beauties of the landscape. Far above us, the wild, high mountains are raising their forest-clothed crests, while around is a broken country of hills with small valleys in their midst, and far away, below us, we catch glimpses through the turnings of the road of the level green plain of the earth below. Mossy rocks, strange trees, beautiful ferns, and curious hanging vines, or graceful festoons of moss we see upon either side of the road, and here and there a wax-like looking tree pushes out to our view from the thick roadside foliage the golden but bitter fruit of the wild orange, which tempts us in vain.

"Occasionally we hear shouts from some of the invisible labyrinths of roads followed by the head of some coffee-laden mule emerging around the curve, and, perhaps, succeeded by twenty or thirty others, all with their loads of coffee following their leader, to whom they are attached head and tail, down to the village.

"The air is pure and dry, about the temperature of that of the White Mountains in summer, with that peculiar feeling of rarity and lightness so agreeable to breathe in. Our journey is enlivened by pleasant converse and these beautiful scenes, varied by occasionally meeting some very gentlemanly French planters on their way down; and at last we begin to near the summit, when Mr. L——, my host, tells me to prepare myself for the most beautiful view I have seen.

"A little incredulous, after seeing Trinidad, I prepare myself to enjoy, perhaps, some wild or extensive view; when, upon turning a high, rocky point in the road, we have presented to our view nearly such a scene as Church has endeavored to depict in his 'Heart of the Andes,' though here, of course, there are no mountains so high. Farther than eye can pierce extends the wonderful distance in this view of the 'Plain of Guantanamo,' where sea and sky appear to fade away into fairy mist before meeting each other. We see a vast plain of cane-fields, which at this distance appear as simple pastures, while farther away the strong light of early morning gives the appearance of lakes of silver. Near us and above us rise the majestic hills, covered with innumerable gigantic forest trees.

"Now we come in sight of our destination, which we see, as the road skirts around the mountain, to be a lovely place, nestling in the shadow of the great hills behind it, while in front is a lovely valley, teeming with the luxuriant vegetation of the tropics.

"At the cross-roads we bid good-by to our planter friends, promising to pay them a visit, and putting spurs to our horses, we gallop up between the walls of the *secaderos* (coffee dryers) to the door of mine host, where, dismounting, we are cordially and pleasantly received by Madame and her two beautiful children, of whom, with my usual penchant for handsome children, horses, and dogs, I became very fond.

A Danish Custom.

"There is a good old custom amongst the Danes, I believe, that when the first toast is drunk, it is to the 'roof' of the house which covers every one in it—meaning thereby that it is all one family strangers included. This same custom might appropriately be kept up amongst the French coffee-planters of the mountains; for when you take your seat at the table, you are immediately installed as one of the family circle.

"And how, O reader! can I adequately describe to you that most delicious life in those lofty mountains?—the pure air, the morning rides, the beautiful effects of nature, which were impressed indelibly on my memory by my ever unsatisfactory attempts to transfer their loveliness to my sketch-book. Let us try a day or two together, and see if we can form an idea of this life, so pure, so fresh, so natural.

31

" Rising at six o'clock, we all meet around the family board, where each one takes his simple cup of coffee, with, perhaps, a biscuit, the children being supplied with milk. The gentlemen then mount their horses, the little ones go off with their governess, and we leave Madame in charge of the establishment, while we gallop off to ride over the place and see the hands at work in the coffee groves, or, perhaps, making a new road, or clearing off the timber of the forests for a new coffee-field.

" Try to imagine any beautiful mountains that you have ever been on, covered with woods, two or three thousand feet above the sea, with a temperature always the same the year round, the road dug out of the very mountain side, the vegetation as luxuriant as it is possible to be, with vines, ferns, wild orange trees, and shrubs, from the branches of which moss hangs down in graceful festoons ; and more than all, the wonderful, curious parasites, which, graceful and beautiful as they are, carry certain death to any forest denizen they twine their arms around. Here is one called the ' *cupey*,' taken in one of the paths in the Calderones mountains.

Trees Squeezed to Death.

" It is a parasite which entwines itself around the ceiba, or other tree, and in course of time entirely kills it. It originates on the tree itself, and throws its roots downwards, which, in the course of their growth, entwine the tree in such a manner that eventually its trunk is compressed as if in a vice, and life very soon becomes extinct. The parasite, with its roots continually descending, takes strong hold in the ground. Sometimes, however, it shares the fate of the tree whose death it has caused, inasmuch as when the original tree dies, the strength of the parasite has not been sufficiently matured to support its own weight alone, and it therefore falls to the ground with its victim.

" There is a great number of curious smaller plants, some of which we know, others that we never heard of before—fit studies for the botanist. Here is the ' *ladies' collar*,' an herb with a large leaf, shaped like the old style of collars worn by ladies, from which it gets its aame. There is the old familiar plant of the castor oil, of which we as children have no pleasant recollections.

"This grows in great quantities all over these mountains, and is prepared by the superannuated negro women, who select the beans and clean them ready for extracting the oil. I was very much amused with an old woman, perfectly blind, who seemed to pick out the perfect and imperfect seeds with the greatest facility, while she sat croning over her task on the stone floor of the coffee-dryer.

"Still wandering along, we come out upon an opening in the woods, and, looking down, we see the new fields being prepared for coffee; which is simply done by cutting down the timber upon the side of a hill favorably situated, and burning off the brush. The seed is put in with those of the plantain, the cacao, or the palm, and left to grow. One of these fields looks exactly like one of our western clearings.

"Let us turn now into this grassy path that looks as if it would bury itself deep in the woods; a step or two more, and just look at that! what a curious combination of strange trees, warm sunlight, and graceful foliage!

"One tree quite common throughout the Island is a species of parasite, somewhat peculiar even for a tropical country, known as the *jaguey;* it has the same peculiarities as the *cupey*, but with the exception that after its roots take hold in the ground they unite and form one trunk of many pillars, becoming a sturdy tree, while the original tree dies out and decays; leaving a hollow space in the centre of the parasite. In this it only follows the usual fate of this variety of trees as observed elsewhere.

"It is supposed the origin of these parasites is from the ordure of the birds who carry the seed and deposit it in the tree, where it appears to take root in the branches as a simple vine, gradually assuming size and strength, until finally it causes the death of its host. Usually, every morning, I visited with my host some neighboring estates, where we were always cordially received and welcomed, and immediately the disposition of the house was put at my service by the courtly owners.

" At eleven o'clock, breakfast was served, which was the same substantial meal as in the low country, except there was a greater variety of fine vegetables—yams, potatoes of various kinds, delicious watercresses fresh from the cool brooks, and several that we are not acquainted with, such as the *apio* and the *yuca*, the latter one of the most useful plants on the Island, of which there are four classes known, but only two are indigenous to, and used on, the Island. From this they make the *cassava* bread, and it is generally used boiled as an esculent; starch is also made from it in large quantities.

" The *chayote*, which, cooked in a certain way, is as good an imitation of apple-sauce as can be made, is an odd-looking fruit, resembling a big, rugged pear, growing on a vine which is very tender and graceful, and when twining itself around some cacao or plantain tree, has a very pretty appearance.

A Curious Fruit.

" The *mamey* is also a curious fruit, of a peculiar shape, like a large sweet potato, with a rusty brown skin, which, when cut in two, displays one long, milky-white seed, and surrounding it the rich, reddish-brown color of the fruit, resembling a nutmeg-melon. To my taste it is too ' sickish,' having no juice, but being of a dead-ripe flavor.

" Here in the mountains I found that siesta-taking, after breakfast, prevailed, notwithstanding the fact that, even in the middle of the day, the sun is not too hot to go out in, except in the depth of summer. In lieu of my siesta, while the rest of the household were dozing, I would frequently stroll off on foot, somewhere in the vicinity of the house, to sketch, always being sure, when seated on some log or rock, of having the companionship of one of the many beautiful lizards that abounded, and that were so tame that they ran all about me, being perfectly harmless, too.

" One little fellow amused me very much. I had taken up a comfortable position, with my back against a cocoa-nut tree, when this little fellow came running down the tree and looked over my shoulders, apparently with the greatest eye to criticism. I turned my head to watch him better, but, as he did not seem to mind me, and kept perfectly quiet, I 'took' him, with his bright, knowing look. Some of these lizards are perfectly beautiful, with their exceeding brilliancy of color, those with stripes of green and black across their back, and with little jet eyes, being charmingly pretty.

"The *chameleon*, that we have heard so much about, it was not my good fortune to meet the whole time I was on the Island. I was struck with the entire absence, also, of venomous insects and reptiles. The worst thing they have is the scorpion, whose bite, though not considered dangerous, is very painful.

Troublesome Insect.

"The 'jigger,' as it is vulgarly called, is an insect that often occasions more trouble to strangers than anything else, being a small insect that gets under the toe-nails, and, if not taken out, makes its nest, inflames the foot, and causes much pain; it can then only be removed with the knife.

"'Monte de Verde' is, probably, the finest estate in this section of the country, being a very large and well-regulated property, situated in a lovely valley, amidst surrounding hills. The house is large and handsome, with a beautiful flower-garden in its rear. The fruit and vegetable-gardens are very large and very fine; and some attempts have been made to cultivate the strawberry, this being the only portion of the Island where that berry is found. Here among the mountains it grows wild, though never very large. In fact, there are no berries such as we have, upon the Island, as far as my experience goes.

"The loveliest place that I saw was the one known as the 'Orangeries,' which, high up among the mountains, was itself built upon a plateau, from whence an ascent to the top of the still higher hills was made. It was a fine stone house, built something in the style of some of the Swiss chalets, and finished in its interior with the beautiful polished wood of the country. It commands a splendid view of the adjacent mountains and the valley beneath.

"Some of the roads around these different estates were very lovely.

The light fell upon them, tempered by the thick, screening branches of the fragrant orange plants, the lovely jessamine, or the delicate heliotrope ; while hanging temptingly within one's reach was the large and brilliant-looking pomegranate, which here grows to a size as large as the orange

"To the naturalist, the botanist, or the artist, this section of country offers every inducement for a visit. Rare plants, curious insects, and superb and novel views meet one at every step. At the same house with me was stopping Mr. Cleinwerche, a Prussian artist of great talent, who had passed some time in various parts of the Island, painting its striking scenes, which he informed me surpassed any he had ever seen in the many lands in which he had traveled.

Delightful Excursions.

"Our afternoon rides were here always as agreeable as those of the morning ; in fact there was no time during the day that it was not cool enough to exercise, either on foot or on horseback ; and many were the rides we had to the house of some neighbor, where, stopping to dine, perhaps, we returned in the evening over mountain paths made bright for us by the rays of the moon, which added new beauties to the scene ; or, if the moon did not favor us, there was always the bright peripatetic candle-bearer, the 'cucullo,' by whose brilliant light one can not only walk, but even read.

"This insect is about the size of our roach, and has somewhat its appearance, being perfectly black, with two small, bright eyes in the back of its long head, on each side of which extend two small, sharp horns, or feelers. These two eyes, in connection with another in the point of its breast, are the live orbs that give out the bright light, the three together, when the insect has its wings spread, appearing in the dark nights as one brilliant, by the light of which one can see to read a letter.

"They are used, it is said, by anxious lovers, at their stolen nocturnal rendezvous ; and it may be for this reason they are such great favorites with the ladies, who wear them in their belts, their hair, and under their thin, gauzy dresses, which they wear of an evening ; the effect as may be imagined, is as novel as it is beautiful. In some parts of the Island they also make pets of them, by keeping them in little cages, feeding them on sugar-cane, and bathing them !

"A wonderful natural curiosity I saw here, also, in the form of vegetable lace, made from the bark of a tree called '*guana.*' A small piece of this, not larger than one's thumb, is taken, a thin slice cut from it and moistened in water ; after which the women pull it with their hands, first one way and then the other, until it opens out into, apparently, the finest threads, looking exactly like the best mull. The ladies take this, embroider it, put an edging of real lace on it, and wear it for neckerchiefs.

Flower of Holy Week.

"There is one flower I was particularly struck with, known as the ' Flor de Pascua,' as well from its profusion as its great beauty. This is the special flower of Holy Week, from which it receives its name, from the fact that about this season it comes out in all its brilliancy of color. It is a simple bush, with the leaves growing in graceful clusters, which then become of a bright vermilion color ; while the flower itself is of a most delicate cup or vase-like form (something in the shape of an Etruscan vase,) the colors upon which are a most delicate gradation from white to rich pink. It has also the most exquisitely formed stamens. I have seen it but once in our hot-houses.

"I must confess to being disappointed in the number of birds of Cuba, or else I was not very fortunate in seeing them during my stay. At all events, I remarked frequently, in the woods, the absence of those sweet-singing birds so numerous with us ; and as I have read so much and heard so much of the brilliant plumage of the birds of the tropics, I was disappointed in not seeing them. Chirping-birds abound, and the most brilliant bird I saw was the *tocorroro*, a bird belonging to the woodpecker tribe.

"In the country beyond these mountains of the Yateras, which is still a wilderness, there are, I am told, a great many attractions for the scientific man, in the large numbers of strange birds, insects, and reptiles.

" It was the last of April before I left the Coffee Mountains, and the rainy season, as they call it, had then set in.   This only added to my pleasure ; for the rain, as far as I saw it, consisted of a splendid shower either once or twice a day, which had the effect of making the air even more bracing than before.   Sometimes, in the middle of the day, it would rain for a couple of hours as though the very flood-gates of heaven had broken open, and then, having exhausted itself, it would clear up, the sun would come out in new glory, and we would have a most beautiful afternoon and evening.

" For the invalid traveler I can imagine no more perfect country or .ife than that of the Coffee Mountains of the Yateras.   Breathing :he purest of air, living luxuriously upon the astonishing profusion of natural supplies, enjoying a climate that from day to day and week to week does not vary a degree, and experiencing the exhilarating and invigorating effects of the constant exercise on fine horses that becomes a daily habit, the sick man needs to despair indeed if he is not recuperated by such a life as this.   Unfortunately, unless he is recommended to some of the hospitable people of that section, there is no means of living, unless, indeed, he has a taste for ' camping out,' which, amid such scenes and in a climate like this, would be no hardship.

" If, in some happy day for the Cubans, their Island shall be blessed with a more liberal government and a more tolerant religion, which will be followed by a strong tide of emigration, these hills, mountains and valleys of the Calderones and Yateras will be the chosen spots of the Island ; for here, with comparatively little expense and less trouble, can be made the most beautiful homes in the world for those fond of rural life and the beauties of nature.

" As for me, the benefit I derived in health and strength, and the great pleasure I experienced from a short sojourn amidst the scenes and the people of the Yateras, have given me memories never to be forgotten, and I shall ever treasure them up as we treasure the fairy visions of our youth."

How few of us, as we sit in our cozy dining-rooms after dinner, of a cold winter's day, sipping our coffee, think or know of the trouble, the time, and the labor that is taken, far off under the hot sun of the tropics, to give us that little cupful of mahogany-looking fluid; of the sweat and the toil of its cultivation; of the processes, machinery, and journeys necessary before it comes to us! Few of us know whether it grows like corn on a cob, or beans in a pod; and few there are who will not be astonished when told that it grows and looks on the tree very much like a cherry.

The Coffee District.

Although coffee is now grown, more or less, all over the Island of Cuba, and at one time was as largely cultivated in the valleys and plains as is at present the sugar-cane, yet now the portion of the Island where most of the coffee-raising is done is in the district and near the town of Cuba, and in the jurisdiction of Guantanamo. Land in this portion of the Island has been so cheap that planters have found it to their interest, as their old places became worn out, to sell them, and come with their means to these beautiful hills, where the climate was healthy, the crop of coffee better, and the land to be had for a song.

In addition to this, coffee culture, for various reasons, has in some degree declined, principally owing, it is said, to the United States placing an almost prohibitory tariff on Cuban coffee in favor of Brazil, which empire receives our flour and grain at a nominal tariff, while in Cuba there has been always a tax upon our exports of that kind. Be this as it may, it is certain that many of those who formerly planted coffee now make sugar, partly because they can use their large number of hands to greater advantage, and partly because, owing to the uncertainty of the coffee crop, the price has varied from three to thirty dollars per hundred pounds.

The *cafetales* most noted for their richness and for the excellency of the fruit, one finds in the range of mountains known as the Sierra Maestra, vicinity of Cuba, in the Vuelta Abajo, and in the districts of Alquizar and San Marcos. From the fact that these latter are old places, that have been established a long time, they are possessed of all that degree of elegance and magnificence for which they are originally celebrated; nevertheless, the mountains of Guantanamo are now considered the coffee regions of Cuba, and there the cultivation is on the increase, while in other places it has decreased rapidly.

After the *ingenios*, the *cafetales* are the most extensive agricultural establishments carried on in Cuba—the latter exceeding the former generally in their handsome appearance and care. Their size varies from one hundred to one thousand acres, or even more in the mountains. The number of hands employed in the low country is as high as one hundred, but generally averages to every one thousand acres about fifty or sixty negroes.

How Coffee was Introduced.

The first coffee plantation was established in 1748, the seeds being brought from Santo Domingo by one Don José Gelabert, of whom it is related that it was his intention when he came to make only a garden. He established himself at a short distance from Havana, but the cultivation of coffee did not really commence until the arrival of the French from Santo Domingo, about 1795.

In addition to the cultivation of coffee, large amounts of rice, plantains, potatoes, cacao or chocolate, and all kinds of fruit are raised; the seeds being planted in the same fields with the coffee, in order that the trees may eventually afford the shade which the coffee-plant requires. The *guarda rayos*, or roads that lead up to the dwellings, are generally shaded by these plants, or by long rows of palm or cocoa, and in some cases a beautiful, graceful species of poplar, all of which form very charming avenues or drives.

The *cafetal* has also its *batey*, or square, like the *ingenio*, formed by the different buildings, which latter are not generally so extensive as on the sugar-estates, consisting of the dwelling-house, the storehouses, the stone terraces for drying the coffee, the stables, the negro quarters, and the coffee-house where the fruit is prepared, this being generally the largest of the structures. The number of subordinates required is small from the small number of hands employed; and although there are sometimes administrators to the *cafetales*, in general they are managed by the proprietor with the assistance of the *mayoral*, who may be white, but who is generally the most intelligent negro on the place.

It is computed by some authorities that, in good seasons, a crop is produced in about the following proportions: To every two hundred and sixty-four acres, two hundred thousand trees can be planted, which will produce, on an average, sixty-two thousand five hundred pounds of coffee, which, at the rate of twenty-five dollars per bag of one hundred pounds, will give the nice little return of fifteen thousand dollars for the cultivation of over two hundred and sixty-four acres. From that, of course, have to be deducted the expenses, which vary according to locality and circumstances, or the number of hands employed.

Description of the Plant.

In the past few years, owing to the gradually increasing scarcity of negroes, many improvements have been made in the use of labor-saving machines, some of which are worked by steam-power in lieu of the old-fashioned way of working by water-power.

Coffee is an evergreen shrub, with oblong, pulpy berries, which are at first green, then bright red, and afterwards purple. That portion of it used as the coffee of commerce, and which, when ground and boiled, we drink, is a secretion formed in the interior of the seed, and enveloping the embryo plant, for whose support it is destined when it first begins to germinate. It is raised from the seed when green or dried in the air, and then planted in the ground, where it is left to grow for forty days, at which time the shoot appears, if the weather is favorable.

The number of seeds planted in one hole is ten or a dozen, the holes being made with a knife or pointed iron. These are made in regular rows, being carefully marked out, with a space of four inches between each plant, and four and a half inches between each row. The shoots having begun to appear and gain size, are carefully and regularly weeded, about once a month, for two years; at the end of which time those plants that have attained to the height of thirty inches are cropped. At the end of the third year, they begin bearing in small quantities; at the end of the fourth year, they are in full bearing, and continue giving good crops, if the land is good, for twenty-five or thirty years; at the end of the sixth or seventh year, they require pruning; and after ten years, they only bear good crops every alternate year.

At the end of February, the bearing plants begin to blossom, and in cold places, even as late as March and April, continuing even up to June. Now is the time to see a coffee place in its beauty. Far as the eye can reach, is one vast sea of green, wax-like looking leaves, upon bushes the branches of which are now in their luxuriant growth, mingling one with another; and scattered over this sea of green are the beautiful white blossoms, looking at a distance, like millions of snow-drops, or, on being closely examined, resembling a most delicate Maltese cross of milky wax. In bunches, as they cluster thick around the stem, they resemble the flower of the jessamine, possibly even more delicate.

Clusters of Red and Golden Fruit.

It is hard to conceive anything more beautiful, particularly if looking over head, you see the banana tree, with its clusters of green and red and golden fruit peeping out from their large, green leaves. At the end of each bunch there is a curiously formed, acorn-shaped, and regal purple-colored bud or blossom. Add to this sight the red, yellow, and purple fruit of the cacao, and the rosy-cheeked pomegranate, and you have an idea of this land, lowing with milk and honey—the milk, if you desire it, being found in the clusters of green cocoa-nuts that hang far above your head.

The coffee-blossom remains in flower about two days, and then are formed the berries, the size of gun-shot, until at maturity they attain the size and appearance of very small cherries, or, to be more exact, cranberries. This maturity is attained usually by the month of September, and the picking season then begins, although it is now the rainy season. As the berries are ripening all the time, the picking season lasts as late as November sometimes. If the months of July and August are dry months, with no rain, the berries become scorched with the hot sun. Coffee is a fruit which requires a genial but even temperature, there being hardly any possibility of its having too much rain.

The picking is done by the hands on the place—men, women and children all going through the rows, each one with two bags and a basket (according to the capability of the hand), which they are required to fill during the day with the round, rich, red berry. Each of these berries contains two seeds, side by side. The bags being filled are brought to the house on the backs of mules, and there received by the overseer, who measures the fruit for the purpose of seeing how much each negro has picked, and whether he has performed his proper amount of labor.

The best trees yield half a pound, but the average is a quarter of a pound per tree. The berries are now ready for the pulping-mill, which is a large wooden wheel, set vertically in a circular canal with ribbed or clinker-built wooden sides, in which are placed the berries for the purpose of having the rind taken off, the operation being performed by the wheel, which is worked either by steam or water-power, passing over them. This apparatus generally occupies the lower floor of the coffee-house, usually a large frame or stone building.

The Pulp in Ferment.

The pulp is now placed in a large, dry, stone basin, of about the form and size of a small swimming bath, and allowed to remain there and ferment for twelve hours, for the pupose of more completely separating the rind and the beans; water is then let into the basin, and all the gum, which is a sort of slimy, mucous matter that in the old process deteriorated the coffee, is washed off.

Then the coffee is taken out of the water and placed in the *secaderos*, where the berries are spread out to dry in the warm rays of the sun, which they do in from seven to nine days, if there is no rain. These *secaderos*, or drying-floors, are large stone basins, quadrangular in shape, about fifty or sixty feet long by twenty or thirty feet wide, arranged in a sort of terrace, side by side, and sometimes a dozen in number, the brow of the hill on which the dwellings stand being usually selected to build them upon. They are about three feet from the ground, built of stone, with plastered floors having an inclination from the centre to the sides, to drain off the water in case of rain, they being entirely uncovered, but having a stone wall around them about a foot high.

Should it come on to rain while the berries are thus exposed, they are hurriedly swept up into large heaps in the centre, and over them is placed a sort of covering similar to a small wigwam, made of thatch or palm leaves, and impervious to water, there being two handles to lift them by. The moment it ceases to rain, the berries are spread out again until thoroughly dry. They are covered in the same way at night to protect them from the dew.

Each berry now resembles a round bean, or the kernel of a small hazel nut, having its exterior pellicle quite dry and dark-colored, in which state it is placed away in the store-house until the whole crop is gathered, each batch of green fruit undergoing the same process as fast as it comes in.

Ready for the Market.

Now the preparing of the fruit for market takes place, the first operation of which is placing the dry berries again in the pulping-mill, the wheel of which, being put in motion, cracks off the dry skin, and the two grains of coffee fall out, just of the shape in which we see them for sale ; thence, it is put in the fanning-mill, identically the same as that used by our farmers to separate the grain from the chaff.

Being now free from all extraneous substances, the beans are placed again in the pulping-mill for the purpose of being polished, or colored ; for think not, O reader, that coffee comes to us of its natural color without a little " doctoring ; " as to every thousand pounds of grain there is added half an ounce of lampblack, and the wheel now travels over and over it, until it assumes the fine green color it has when we get it. This is called the polishing process, and some planters use for the operation charcoal made of cedar-wood ; others, again, use soapstone and powdered white lead, according to the shade they wish to give it. For the European market, the latter is used, which gives the coffee a dark-grey color.

Now it is ready for the sorting-room, in which there is a circular sieve with several compartments of different-sized wire, which, worked by machinery, revolves. From the room above, and directly over the sieve, there is a wooden box or pipe, leading down into a wooden funnel-shaped reservoir, for the purpose of conducting the grain from the room into the sieve, the quantity being governed by a wooden stopper in the side of the trough. The grain, being placed in this reservoir, runs slowly into the revolving cylinder through an opening in its first compartment, and from thence into the others, being assorted in its passage through the different-sized wires of the sieves into three kinds.

Different Qualities.

El caracolillo is the small round coffee, one grain of which only is found in each berry, and resembles the celebrated Arabian coffee, "Mocha," from which it also takes its name. This is the most prized, bringing usually a dollar or two extra per bag; its flavor is not really better than that of other coffee, except that the grain, being smaller and round, is more easily and thoroughly roasted; the bean also presents a much better appearance to the purchaser.

This small grain, strange to say, is supposed to be a disease in the coffee, as, generally from want of rain, or from some freak of nature, the grain appears in this stunted form. Great care is used in sorting so as to secure the best of coffee, free from dirt, pebbles, and decayed berries. This is done by the negro women picking over all the coffee. They are arranged on two sides of a long table, in a well-lighted room, used expressly for this purpose.

It is quite a novel sight to see twenty or thirty of these women in their oddities of dress, or even the scarcity of it, picking away from the great piles of beans before them, and filling huge baskets with the bright green grain, keeping up all the time a monotonous chanting, in which each one takes a part, interrupted now and then by a stranger, whose advent is an era in the lives of these out-of-the-world people, and who immediately address him with: " *Da me medio, mai tre* " (give me five cents, master).

The second quality of coffee, called *el primer*, or *lavado* (first or washed), is that of which the largest quantities are made, being the coffee in its usual size, of two grains to the berry, sound and large. The third quality is the poorer or refuse coffee, the most of which is retained upon the place and used or sold at a low price for domestic consumption. The fine Caracolillo coffee is very carefully re-sifted and picked over by some specially skillful hand.

The coffee, being now ready for market, is placed in strong canvas bags, in which we see it, and each one of which contains about one hundred and seven pounds. It is then forwarded to the commission merchant in the town, to be sold for account of the owner, or is sometimes bought outright by the merchants.

The transporting of the coffee to market is a business of itself, and is generally carried on by some native Indian, the owner of large numbers of mules, though on some of the estates where horses are plenty the proprietors send down their own trains. These consist of from a dozen to thirty or forty horses or mules, which have upon their backs the most old-fashioned, useless packs that can be made, being simply huge walls of straw, sometimes covered with canvas, rarely leather, roughly put together, and retained upon the horses by girths and ropes, or canvas breeching, which sometimes are fancifully decorated with fringe, as is also the head stall, particularly of the leader, who has also a string of bells upon his neck, in Spanish muleteer fashion. Upon there rude pack-saddles the coffee is strapped, a bag on each side, over which a cloth or matting of the palm is thrown, to keep it from the rain. Each train is now arranged with the head of one horse tied to the tail of the one in front of him, the guide and his assistant mount their horses, and the train is started down the mountain to the village.

It is quite a novel as well as pretty sight to see these trains taking their way down the hill-side; the long line of mules, with their curious burdens, winding in and out of the romantic road, the gay appearance of the leader, the musical sound of his bells, and the shouts of the *muleteros*, all serve to make up a picture strange and interesting.

CHAPTER XXXVIII.

Rural Life and Customs.

"NO traveler," says N. P. Willis, "except for some special or overruling reason, leaves willingly Havana;" but as we like contrast, and are fond of seeking the *Cosas de Cuba*, both of town and country, we seek the contrast, as Baron Humboldt writes it, that "one encounters in leaving the capital (Havana), for the country, and exchanging its civilization, partial and local, for the simplicity of manners and customs that reigns in the isolated farms and little villages of the Island."

Besides this, for an invalid traveler who has been passing all his winter in the tropics it is not wise, even if safe, to go north until the chill of winter days is there thoroughly thawed from the atmosphere by the genial rays of an early June sun; and as Havana has no longer attractions for us out of season, we turn to the country.

There is much pleasure, too, in wandering about among some of these little villages in the bright, hot days of the Cuban spring, when the early rains for an hour or two each day only serve to brighten up the landscape and freshen the air a little. Making, therefore, our headquarters in such places as Güines, where there are tolerable accommodations, and where such lovely views of the valley of Güines are afforded from the " Hill of Fire," we run out to San Antonio or Marianao, where we get a sea breath, with a whiff of ocean, fresh and strong, or even to Mariel or Cabañas, twenty-five miles along the coast.

There is the *pueblo* of San Cristobal, too, in the Vuelta Abajo, in a beautiful country, easily accessible by railroad, and at a short distance from which are the romantic Falls of the Rosario. This, too, is the district sanctified in the cause of freedom by the struggles and final capture of Lopez, in his unsuccessful attempt at revolution, his fate being sealed almost within sight of this beautiful cascade ; for, having had an engagement with the Spanish troops, he with seven companions fled, when they fell into the power of a party of sixteen of the peasants of that section, and being sent up to Havana, were there garroted.

In another chapter there has been given an account of the manner in which the subdivisions of land in Cuba obtained their names, and it only remains now to speak specially of one of these, first of which is the " Estancia," the most humble of the rural properties, but nevertheless the one that produces or can produce the best returns to its cultivator.   Situated in the vicinity of the cities or of the large villages, its purpose is to raise for their markets garden stuff, small meats, fruits, chickens, eggs, milk, cheese, and other articles of general and necessary consumption ; also forage, or fodder rather, for the horses maintained in the towns.

Antiquated Farming.

The size of these places varies from a dozen acres to one hundred and twenty-five, many of them being cultivated by tenants only, who pay a rent of about two hundred dollars per year for thirty or forty acres.   This system of farming, so opposed to the real advancement of agriculture, and the indolence natural to the laborers accustomed to expect from the fertility of the soil what their labor ought at least to assist in bringing forth, keep these places in a state of backward ness.   Only a small part is devoted to garden stuff, which requires care, while not much more is put in melons, plantains, and potatoes, more than one-half usually being sown with *maloja*, a kind of corn, which grows without giving good grain, and is cut green for the fodder of animals which prefer it to any other kind of grass food.

The fruit-trees are not renewed, and the principal care of the *estanciero*, or farmer, is the raising of chickens and cows; and it is from this reason, in part, that there is a scarcity of garden stuff and fruits in the local markets—a scarcity that is augmented when they cheapen the other products, and when the crop of beans, onions, potatoes, peas, etc., does not amount to the smallest part of the quantity consumed, although the towns are surrounded by innumerable acres of uselessly fertile land.

In many of these *estancias* the cultivation of the soil is abandoned for the business of lime-burning and the raising of sufficient fodder for the oxen that draw the lime to market. The dwelling-houses on these places are small and of moderate expense in construction, and the number of negroes does not exceed, on the best of these places, five negroes to every forty or fifty acres, the land being worth about sixty dollars per acre.

A Succulent Vegetable.

The sweet-potato is the principal vegetable raised on these *estancias*, and is mostly of two kinds—the white and yellow. It is similar to ours, and is eaten in the same way, and is produced all the year round. The white (or Irish) potato is not raised on the Island in any quantity, being poor and small; large quantities are, therefore, imported.

" *El ñame* " is *the* tuber, solid and heavy, juicy, white or yellow, and very nutritious, being stewed with meat. This name is given it by the negroes, though its Indian name is " *aje.*" It weighs five or six pounds, and has even been known to weigh as much as twenty-five pounds. The negroes prefer it to any other vegetable, making several dishes from it by compounding it with other things. It is of somewhat the same nature as the yam.

Platanos are raised also in large quantities. On all these places are raised lettuce, cabbage, and many nutritious seeds, most of which flourish the year round. Where the *estancia* is large, and managed with judgment, there are a great many fruits of various kinds raised; but it would be hard to find in the whole Island an orchard, such as we understand one to be. Our system of intelligent gardening, farming, and fruit-raising would prove very profitable; for the whole Island is a perfect garden naturally, and with very little attention, almost everything grows in abundance.

Gardening as a business does not seem as yet to be followed by the Cubans, and the only flower-gardens that one sees are those attached to private houses, or, occasionally, small ones near the towns. Some of these private gardens are remarkably beautiful, laid out with great taste, and presenting, when they are confined simply to flowers, a most brilliant appearance with their very highly colored plants. At Marianao, Matanzas, and around Havana, one sees these in perfection; but the most lovely gardens, combined with fruits, are those attached to fine sugar-estates, if we except such as the Cantero gardens, at Trinidad, and the public gardens on the paseo Tacon.

The Bee Industry.

Upon the *fincas*, or small country places, attention is paid more particularly to raising and keeping bees, from which large quantities of wax and honey are produced, the former being quite an important article of export. There are two kinds of bees used on the Island, the *comun*, or exotic, brought from Florida, and the *criolla*, or native bee. The little honey produced by the latter is used by the Cubans for medicinal purposes, the dark-colored wax, under the name of "virgin wax," serving as lights for the poor of the country.

The imported bee creates one of the principal sources of rural riches, as its products are exported in considerable quantities, its honey even being sent abroad, while the white and yellow wax produced are well-known articles of commerce; in addition to which, large quantities are retained for domestic use in the churches, at funerals, etc.

In a district where these rural places are of a good class, and *potreros* are found, it is pleasant to mount one's horse, and ride round amongst them, as the owners, particularly of the better class, are quite intelligent about their own business, and always kind to the stranger; having, notwithstanding their rustic life, a certain air of easy politeness, peculiar to the people of the Latin race. And almost the first thing you are asked, even in the humblest of these *finca* residences, is, " *Quiere cafê, Senor ?* " (Will you have coffee, sir), of which beverage these people are very fond. The houses are often very humble affairs indeed, as regards material, though they may be ample in number of rooms, with numerous outbuildings.

They are usually composed of one story, roughly constructed of poles, palm-leaves, and thatch, put together in such a way as to be impervious to rain, yet light enough to admit plenty of air, especially as the doors, if there are any, always stand open. A living-room, with a sleeping-room or two, all on the same floor, which is often of earth, make up the main building, while a simple roof connects it with an outbuilding, where is the kitchen, in which are performed the household and other duties of the women.

Many of these women, be it said to their credit, are more industrious than the men, as they attend to their domestic duties, often weave cotton cloth for home consumption from the small amount of cotton raised, and have a general superintendence over the place. Cotton, by-the-by, though it cannot be said to be one of the products of the Island, does grow in sufficient quantity to manufacture out of it a rough kind of cloth, used by the country people. Every attempt to cultivate it systematically has been a failure ; and yet in the Coffee Mountains one may see beautiful cotton growing wild, in small lots, but the moment it is attended to and looked after, strange to say, it ceases to flourish.

It is upon these rural places also that the Cascarilla cosmetic powder, so great a favorite with Cuban ladies, is prepared from the egg-shells ; and the extent to which this is used may be imagined, when it is estimated that there are over one hundred thousand pounds consumed every year.

The last of the rural places we are called upon to notice is the " Hacienda de Crianza," or *sitio*, as it is called—an uncultivated, unenclosed place, where the cattle are allowed to run wild, unattended except by the *montero*, who goes about on foot, or the half-savage *sabanero*, who, being mounted, rides in amongst the herd. Their united business is to scour the fields every day, and pick out the newborn calves, with their mothers, and take care of them for fifteen or twenty days at the houses or sheds; to see if there are any dead animals, or to pick out those ready to send to market or kill for consumption.

" The rural population of the Island," says a Cuban author, " has rusticity, but not that boasted simplicity of the European laborer. Our *guajiro* (countryman) is astute though frank, boastful though brave, and superstitious if not religious. His ruling passions are gambling (particularly at cock-fights, of which he is very fond), and coffee, which he drinks at all hours; his favorite food, pork and the platano, usually roasted."

His costume consists of a pair of loose pantaloons, girdled at the waist with a bit of leather, a shirt of fancy-colored linen, a handkerchief of silk or cotton tied around his neck, or, more frequently, about his head, upon which is a broad-brimmed hat of *yarey*—a species of common palm-leaf—while his usually bare feet are thrust into common leather pumps or slippers. Rarely does he wear a coat, even if he owns one, and his shirt is worn more generally outside than inside his pants.

Takes Life Easy.

He never works regularly, nor does much else than direct the cultivation of his property, look after the cattle, or, perhaps, act as carter or teamster. Sometimes he may plow, or sow a little grain, or even pick fruit; but if he employs negroes he makes them do the work. Sometimes he does a little trading on his own account, and may, perhaps, keep a sort of country-store and tavern, if his place is on a public road. He travels on horseback, armed invariably with the *machete*, and often carrying a sun-umbrella, taking care to stop at every tavern on the road, where he is ready to talk with any one he meets, or accept an invitation to drink.

La guajira (country woman) is not so talkative as the husband, particularly with strangers, to whom her partially Castilian blood makes her, at first, ceremonious and dignified, even rising to receive them. She can mount a horse, though she usually rides with her husband, sitting in front of him, upon the neck of the horse almost, while his right arm encircles her. She dresses in the most simple manner (often a little too much so) in a *camison*, or frock, with a kerchief around her neck; seldom wearing stockings, except on state occasions—of a ball, visit, etc., her head often being covered with a huge straw hat when she moves about, but otherwise dressed with the utmost care to display to advantage her superb hair.

These country people all have manners and customs peculiar to themselves, even their food being different from that of the cities; and it is amongst them one can study the Cuban cuisine. They have but two meals a day, always accompanied by coffee, which they also take on rising in the morning, at night-time, and at any hour of the day they fancy, or may have a guest. Civilization has found its way even to the homes of these simple people; and, on the richer and larger places, English beer is now generally used, and ') strangers even champagne is presented.

Entertaining Guests.

So natural a custom is it with these hospitable country people to entertain the guest, that, does he happen to be present when a meal is announced, he is not even honored with an invitation, but he is expected, as the most natural thing in the world, to seat himself at the table and partake of their food, whatever it may be. To refuse to do so, unless he has the excuse to make that he has lately eaten, would be considered an offense. As the service of the table, in most of the cities, at all the hotels, and many of the best private houses partakes of the nature of French cooking, it is only in the rural parts one can see the *bona fide* Cuban dishes.

The daily meals of the more humble farmers consist of fried pork and boiled rice in the morning, and, in lieu of bread, the roasted plantain. At dinner, they make use of cow-beef, jerked beef, birds, and roasted pig; but usually this meal consists of roasted plantains, and the national dish of *ajïaco*, or what we should call an Irish stew. This dish is to the Island what *olla podrida* is to Spain. It is composed of fresh meat, either beef or pork—dried meat of either—all sorts of vegetables, young corn, and green plantains. It is made with plenty of broth, thickened with a farinaceous root known as *malanga*, and has also some lemon-juice squeezed into it. It is toothsome, cheap, and nutritious—quite equal to the French *pot au feu.*

Boiled rice is never dispensed with at any meal, and the cooking of it is understood to perfection. It is used mixed in all their stews, or with a simple sauce of tomatoes. *El aporreado* is made of half raw meat, dressed with water, vinegar, salt, etc., which operation is known as *perdigar* (or stewing in an earthen pan); then mashed and stirred together, it is fried slightly in a sauce of lard, tomatoes, garlic, onions, and peppers. Hashes are always good upon the Island—town or country—even if one does not know who made them. The *tasajo brujo*, or jerked beef bewitched, so called from the fact that it grows so much larger in cooking, is the dish found almost everywhere, and cooked in many ways.

Amusements of Country People.

It is almost always a savory dish the traveler need not be afraid of, particularly if he has had army experience. There are some other dishes, but with the knowledge of the above the stranger will be safe to accept an invitation to dine with any of the *hacendados*, and it will also be seen that Cuban cookery is not such a fearful thing as we have been led to believe; for little or no oil is used, and the small quantity of garlic used is so disguised in other things that few people could tell it. These country folks also have their special amusements as well as cookery. First upon the list stand the cock-fights.

Every village, or *pueblo*, has a patron saint, for whom there is a special *dia de fiesta*, which all the villagers and people in the vicinity celebrate with masses, etc, at the village church, and afterwards by games, dancing, and sports, the women taking part also as spectators if in no other way. But usually they are divided into two parties, each party being distinguished by the color of the ribbon it wears, and which gives its name to the band.

Each party elects a queen, chosen for her grace, beauty, or good style, and the admirers of each are known as vassals, and they give their presence to the amusement going on. When the performers belonging to one party or the other are successful, the vanquished party with its queen and vassals has to render homage to the rival queen. The goose-fight is another one of their sports, and a very cruel one it is ; for in a plaza or smooth field two forked poles are set up, and from one to the other a rope is stretched; in the middle of this a live goose is hung, firmly tied by the feet.

The place is now filled with spectators, while five, ten, or fifteen mounted *guajiros* pass at full gallop in front of the goose, and attempt to seize the head, which has been well greased, and separate it from the body in their full career. Of course many unsuccessful attempts are made, and the bird usually dies before the efforts are successful, but he who succeeds in this *glorious* attempt is declared *victor*.

Feasts and Celebrations.

Las loas (or prologues) are practiced in the country villages in their religious feasts and civil celebrations,—as processions of the Holy Virgin or the Patron Saint, etc. A little girl, dressed (or undressed) as an image, is conducted, publicly, in a small cart profusely decorated with banners, flowers, and branches; before her, march on horseback four or six men, in costumes of Indians, and behind, others clad as Moors. A band plays, and the procession, which is composed of almost all the people of the village, when arrived at the appointed place stops, and the child stands up and recites or declaims her *loa*, a composition appropriate to the subject of the celebration.

Altares de Cruz—the custom of forming altars in the houses in the first days of May, in order to celebrate the invention of the Holy Cross, is preserved very generally in the interior of the Island, but with a character almost entirely profane. The altar is erected modestly in a sleeping-room of the house, on the 3d of May, or day of Santa Cruz, and on every day of the first nine, the guests gather before it, to dance, sing, play, and eat and drink at times. On the first night, the master of the house delivers a branch of flowers to the guest that he chooses, and the latter contracts, in receiving it, the obligation to re-form the altar, and pay the expenses of the next night's entertainment, he himself taking the name of the godfather.

The second night arrived, the godfather or godmother renews this performance of the branch upon another victim, and it thus happens that each altar has a new godfather for each night, and as every one endeavors to do better than his predecessor, it happens that the last night winds up the festival with a superb supper and a full orchestra.

Mamarrachos is the name given to the individuals on horseback, who, in a great part of the Vuelta Arriba, ride, masked and grotesquely costumed, through the streets, during the Carnival or other seasons of merry-making. Surprise parties are very numerous, not only amongst the country people, but at the watering-places during the season.

The country dances, however, are something especially peculiar, many old-fashioned customs and figures being retained, although the usual waltzes and contra-dances are danced, too, while the former are less formal, being the social meetings of intimate friends or neighbors.

The especial dance is the one known as the *zapateo*, and is peculiar to this Island. It is danced to the music of the harp, the guitar, or the songs of the *guajiros*, by both women and men, and has a good many peculiar figures, the principal object appearing to be for the women to see how many men they can tire out, as they give every now and then a signal to their *vis à vis* "to leave," when he is replaced by another. A low humming or singing is kept up by those present, broken every now and then by the loud plaudits of the spectators at the success of some dancer.

In many sections of the country one still finds sugar estates, almost as they were originally, in the possession of owners of moderate means and little intelligence, who have not availed themselves of the advantages afforded by improved machinery and scientific modes of making sugar.

Some of the places, again, are so poor in soil and product, having been worked for so many years without intermission, that the owners do not deem it worth while, even if they can afford the outlay, to put up new mills and machinery,—much preferring to try new land. Still, the country is improving in its agricultural pursuits of all kinds, though in none has it made such rapid strides as in sugar-making.

Cuba is divided, rather indefinitely, into two unequal portions—the "Vuelta Arriba," or higher valley, and the "Vuelta Abajo," or lower valley. General usage seems to settle the point, that the "Vuelta Abajo" is all that fertile low country lying to the west of Havana; at all events, it is only from that section that the true "Vuelta Abajo" tobacco comes, and it is also there that one finds not only sugar but coffee-growing estates.

Beautiful Section of Country.

Guanajay is a small and prettily-situated village on the grand mail route, that runs through the "Vuelta Abajo." The town lies in the heart of a beautiful section of country, some twelve miles from the sea. To the north of it, between it and the sea, are any number of fine, large sugar estates, beautifully situated in a rolling country, which extends to the very borders of the ocean, upon which, and within a short drive, are the towns of Mariel and Cabañas, upon bays of the same names.

The best properties known as *vegas*, or tobacco farms, are comprised in a narrow area in the south-west part of the Island, about twenty-seven leagues long by about seven broad, shut in on the north by mountains, and on the south-west by the ocean, Pinar del Rio being the principal point in the district.

These vegas are found generally on the margins of rivers, or in low, moist localities, their ordinary size amounting to about thirty-three acres of our measurement. The half of this is also most frequently devoted to the raising of the banana, which may be said to be the bread of the lower classes. A few other small vegetables are raised.

The usual buildings upon such places are a dwelling-house, a drying-house, a few sheds for cattle, and, perhaps, a small hut or two, made in the rudest manner, for the shelter of the hands, who, upon some of the very largest places, number twenty or thirty, though not always negroes—for this portion of the labor of the Island seems to be performed by the lower classes of whites. Some of the places that are large have a *mayoral*, as he is called, a man whose business it is to look after the negroes, and direct the agricultural labors; but, as a general thing, the planter, who is not always the owner of the property, but simply the lessee, lives upon, directs, and governs the place.

Guided by the results of a long experience, transmitted from his ancestors (says a Spanish author), the farmer knows, without being able to explain himself, the means of augmenting or diminishing the strength or mildness of the tobacco. His right hand, as if guided by an instinct, foresees what buds it is necessary to take off in order to put a limit to the increase or height, and what amount of trimming is necessary to give a chance to the proper quantity of leaves. But the principal care, and that which occupies him in his waking hours, is the extermination of the voracious insects that persecute the plant. One called *cachaga* domesticates itself at the foot of the leaves; the *verde*, on the under side of the leaves; the *rosquilla*, in the heart of the plant; all ot them doing more or less damage.

Fighting a Plague.

The planter passes entire nights, provided with lights, cleaning the buds just opening, of these destructive insects. He has even to carry on a war with still worse enemies—a species of large, native ants, that are to the tobacco what the locust is to the wheat. This plague is so great at times, that prayers and special adoration are offered up to San Marcial to intercede against the plague of ants.

Tobacco of the best quality, such as is produced in the choice vegas of the "Vuelta Abajo," is known by its even tint of rich dark brown and freedom from stains, burning freely, when made into cigars, with a brown or white ash, which will remain as such on the cigar, some-times, till it is half smoked, without falling off.

The city of Havana has the honor of being the first place in which tobacco was grown. Its culture commenced in 1580, there being nothing heard of the now-famed "Vuelta Abajo" until 1790. This culture is one that has increased very rapidly in the Island; it being stated upon good authority that, in 1827, there were only five thousand five hundred and thirty-four tobacco farms, while in 1846 there were more than nine thousand, and in 1859 some ten thousand, which shows a very rapid increase indeed; and it is now estimated that the tobacco crop alone of the small portion of the Island under cultivation is worth from eighteen to twenty millions of dollars annually.

Thirty-three acres of ground produce about nine thousand pounds of tobacco. From these figures, taking the bale at one hundred pounds, and the average price of the tobacco at twenty dollars per bale (though this is a low estimate, for the crops of some of the vegas are sold as high, sometimes, as four hundred dollars per bale), an approximate idea may be formed of the profit of a large plantation, in a good year, when the crops are satisfactory.

Thrifty Palm-trees.

The volante with three horses shows a peculiarity of fashionable volante-riding in the country; the *calesero* riding one horse and guiding the other two, the three being harnessed abreast; the Señoras, meanwhile, reclining at their ease, escorted by their mounted attendant.

The palm-tree is probably the most useful if not the most beautiful tree in the Island of Cuba, and is found in every portion of it, giving at once character and beauty to the scenery; and that known as the *palma real* (royal) is only one of the twenty-two varieties which are enumerated in this majestic family of the tropics. Its feathers or branches fall airily and gracefully from the top of a cylindrical trunk of fifteen or twenty yards in height; in the centre of the branches is the heart or bud of the plant, elevating itself perpendicularly, with its needle-point like a lightning-rod.

This heart, enveloped in wrappers of tender white leaves, makes a most nourishing and delicious salad; it is also boiled like cauliflower, and served with a delicate white sauce. In either way it is a very agreeable esculent for the table. The branches, numbering from twenty to twenty-two, are secured to the trunk by a large exfoliated capping, and between each scale there starts out one of the feathers or branches. At the foot of these burst little buds, which open into delicate bunches of small flowers, followed by the fruit or seed, which is used as nourishment for the herds of hogs on the breeding-farms; it is also used as a substitute for coffee amongst the poor people of some portions of the Island.

The trunk of the palm is a cylinder or tube, filled with milky fibres, which, torn off in long strips from top to bottom, are dried, and make a narrow, thin kind of board, with which the peasants form the walls of their rustic habitations; while the branches serve as roofs or covering to their lightly constructed houses; though for this latter purpose are also used the leaves of nearly all the palms.

The leaves serve for roofs and for lining the walls of the huts, and for general purposes of shelter for the country people of Cuba; while they are used also as wrappers for bales of tobacco and other materials. Torn into narrow shreds, they answer for tying packages in lieu of twine.

El yarey is another of the palms that merits especial mention; for from it they make the excellent palm-leaf hats that are commonly worn on the Island amongst the country people and the villagers, the manufacture of which constitutes one branch of industry amongst the women, and for which they get from one to two dollars per hat.

Famous Watering-Place.

If there happens to be a party of friends together they can make the trip to San Diego, and pass some weeks there agreeably enough, taking care, however, to carry with them some light reading, of which none can be had either in Spanish or English, in the town. The country around is quite picturesque, and, like almost all parts of Cuba, beautiful in the novel character of its scenery and vegetation, while there are numerous objects of interest to visit in the neighborhood. Of course, in a place like this, if the traveler can speak no Spanish, he is thrown entirely upon his own resources, unless, indeed, he makes, as he is likely to do, the acquaintance of persons who can speak English.

One of the excursions which can be made in the neighborhood, is that to the "Arcos de Caiguanabo," which is the official name given to the "doors" or caves formed by the river San Diego, passing through a peculiar natural formation of rocks, a magnificent and imposing arch divided by a grand pillar, the arch being about one hundred feet wide, one hundred feet long, and sixty feet high, the river running quietly beneath it.

Beneath this portal, and on a level with the river, upon its right bank is the first cave, the entrance to which is straight and stony, and suddenly opens into a large chamber filled with quantities of stalactites, or specimens of concrete petrifactions; columns large and small, and, in fact, a thousand figures of fantastic and capricious shapes, which a fertile imagination can liken to a number of things. This saloon receives the light by two apertures that permit also of exit on both sides of the hill.

A Journey to the Caves.

Beyond the arch, and reached by a narrow path made at the foot of the range of hills, for a short distance, is the second cave, which presents the same characteristics as the first. From this cave there is a descent, when, following the base of the hills for the distance of about one hundred and eighty feet, another ascent is made by a path to the third cave, called the "Cathedral," to enter which it is necessary to have torches, as the light penetrates no farther than the entrance. The dimensions of this chamber are larger than those of the others. The world-wide custom of inscribing names is here noticed.

The journey to these caves is made mostly on horseback, and it is quite the fashion to come out on breakfast picnics here amid these wild and picturesque scenes. Those who have been fortunate enough to visit the caves of Bellamar, near Matanzas, will not appreciate these so much.

The cave of "Taita Domingo," said to be the identical cave inhabited by that hardly-treated but diseased negro who discovered the baths, is to the northeast of the town, and is a large gloomy cavern not yet explored. With a good guide and much labor the traveler can also make the ascent to the top of the "Loma de la Guira," from which can be had a fine view of the surrounding country, and the north and south seas ; the former about eighteen miles distant, and the latter about twenty-five.

A walk or ride up to the "Casita de la Loma," or as it is more properly called, "Hermosa Vista" (beautiful view), which is the hill seen to the north from the Plaza of Isabel II., is good exercise and pleasant occupation.

In addition to the shooting, which can be had in the mountains, there are the usual diversions in the way of balls and dancing, at which there are frequently present very pretty girls, whilst for those whose taste runs that way there are occasional "cock-fights."

In returning from San Diego, it is more convenient to return by the western railroad. This can be very pleasantly and quickly accomplished by taking a horse or volante to San Cristobal and the cars from that place.

Distinguished Cuban Patriots:

The Founders of Liberty.

BY GONZALO DE QUESADA,

CHARGE D'AFFAIRES OF THE REPUBLIC OF CUBA.

N O one man can be said to be the author of a revolution, which is a complex result of many heterogeneous elements.

The Cuban revolution, more than the work of any one man or of any group of patriots, is the natural consequence of the secular and unique policy of spoliation of the mother country. Like a torrent—and this popular and unanimous uprising is an irresistible one—this revolution has been growing in magnitude and power as years of constant oppression, deluded hopes, and repeated mockery have passed; its turbulent waters, at times in apparent serenity, now sweep to the sea, from the gray peaks, crowned with blue, of Santiago and Pinar del Rio, over the eternal green meadows and poetic palm-groves of the Central Provinces –to-day in imposing desolation—overwhelming the tottering ruins of mediæval despotisms, the institutions of slavery and immorality.

And when the inexhaustible Cuban fields, purer and more fertile by this necessary commotion, shall teem again with the undulating foliage of the canes, when our vegas and cafetals shall blossom as they never did before, with their snowy flowers, and our gorgeous birds shall in delightful harmony intone the hymn of love and remembrance for the heroes who have fallen; when the black clouds of the blessed hurricane shall have disappeared, there shall rise on his gigantic pedestal of copper and iron mountains, illumined by the sun of liberty, in proud contemplation of his people, happy and redeemed, the sublime figure of the truest and bravest of patriots— of the Cuban genius—José Marti.

If ever there was a directing hand in a revolution it was that of

José Marti in the Cuban. He had calculated the time when the tempest would break forth, and had prepared the conditions so that the torrent would not find any obstacles in its way; he had prophesied its march and triumph. The originality of this extraordinary man consisted in this intuition, in this ability to forecast the events which were to follow with such mathematical exactness.

His life is like the symbol of his country's history; in his diverse and versatile accomplishments, in the salient virtues of his character, he embodied those of his native land; even in his glorious death and his immortality we see the future of Cuba which must give even her blood to conquer her deserved place among the great.

A Noble Patriot.

Marti was born when Cuba was still under the painful impression of the execution of Lopez and Aguero, two years before the liberal Catalan Pinto was garroted for aspiring to Cuba's independence. Of Spanish parents, Marti was animated, always, as are all the Spaniards and Cubans who fight to-day for the tri-color flag, by the highest aims; he did not and could not hate the Spaniards as individuals; he wanted Cuba for all the honest inhabitants of the Island; he would sever the connections between an old country, incapable by its constitution and traditions to understand modern life and to keep pace with civilization, and a new country situated in the very heart of a continent devoted to progress and freedom.

He would drive from the victim the vampire which has for five centuries sucked her best blood; he would make Cuba independent of Spain; he would not exterminate his ancestors, as the ancestors would exterminate his children; he would constitute a nation of cordiality, of enterprise; father and child reconciled under a generous regime; the laboring peasant of Spain, employing his energies in a better work than butchering his cousins, and his cousins dignified and raised to freemen; where all, whatever be their race, creed or nationality, could live in peace and prosperity.

From his Valencian father, an officer in the Spanish army, there came to Marti that decision and bravery which stood by him in many a dark hour of his existence; from his mother he inherited that tenacity and virtue which overcame all the difficulties of his life, filled with agony and almost a constant struggle from his childhood to his early grave.

Born in the Capital, where vice finds an easier hold, Marti saw with his own eyes the subtle plans of Spain to enervate the Cuban youth by offering all the facilities of prostitution, and at the same time undermining his manhood by gambling in all its forms: the Royal lottery which Spain authorizes because she derives from it a large income, the Monte, the Chinese dens, the cock-pits; by tempting him with voluptuous music and dance; by discouraging every legitimate pastime, anything that could strengthen or elevate him; and Marti's life was the immaculate example, in his school and college days and in his subsequent career, of virility and virtue.

Story of His Early Life.

His early years were passed in the country, where he acquired that love of nature which afterwards was revealed in his poetry; he was a precocious child whom it was impossible to keep away from books; many a time he was surprised in the stillness of the night by his parents, who looked with disfavor on his literary proclivities, reading by the light of the moon or by the phosphorescence of the Cocuyos, fire beetles, a stray volume of Dumas "The Three Musketeers," or an old edition of the Quixote or some sonnets of Fray Luis de Leon.

Thus his inclinations for the romantic, as well as for the highest models, commenced when he could hardly spell; his first verses were his first punishments; he was to be a clerk and not a poet, and he was chastised; but his imagination, his love of the beautiful, his exquisite taste afterwards gave remarkable fruits.

The family, which was well-to-do, was forced to come to Havana. Marti, from his open-air surroundings, was now to become, not yet thirteen years of age, an office boy, thrown into the company of an arrogant and stupid Spanish shop-keeper and of vulgar emigrants, who looked on the little Creole with disdain and jealousy. The boy mastered arithmetic wonderfully, and in a few weeks he was keeping the books of the firm; he was doing all the work, while the relatives and friends of the foreign proprietor were getting all the benefits of his industry.

But the lad was of steel; he was helping his family, the father was yielding slowly; he had consented to his going, after business hours, to the school of Mendive, the famous Cuban poet. Marti did not complain; the old booksellers had become his friends; they would allow him to handle the old tomes and the new volumes, which it was his custom to care for as if they were human beings, and would wonder at the brawny youngster, who would devour a work standing in front of those cases which were his only temptations. Marti was happy because an old wig-maker, seeing his fondness for the drama, would send him with the blonde tresses for the leading lady, or the fierce mustachios for the villain, and there behind the scenes he could follow the plays and comedies, which years afterwards he could repeat from memory.

Thrown into Prison.

There sprung up between Marti and his master, Mendive, a most loyal friendship; Marti afterwards became his favorite pupil, the manager of the school, and in 1869, when the delicate poet was confined to prison for his political opinions, it was the tender regard for his necessities, the devotion with which Marti attended to his family and the gentleness and constant affection of the grateful boy, which consoled the venerable educator in his hours of trial.

It was shortly afterwards that the martyrdom of José Marti commenced. He was sixteen, when he published his first clandestine newspaper, in Havana, in favor of the revolution; for this, for his essay of a tragedy in which he symbolized the Cuban struggle, and for his disinterested action of claiming, in order to save a friend, the authorship of an article against the Government, he was thrown into prison, the first reward of the Cuban for his love of Country!

So proud was he that he refused from his parents, Spanish, who did not sympathize with his ideas, any aid; so rebel was he that he would not let his mother ask for pardon in his name! On being exiled to Spain, he fearlessly exposed before the metropolis, without complaining of his own experiences, the horrors that he had seen committed: the old men bastinadoed to death, the innocent children wounded by the swords, the contemptible vices fomented by their keepers, the men who died for want of food, the sick agonizing, in the midst of the laughter of their tormentors.

All this he put into pages which are to-day just as true as they were a quarter of a century ago, and which would constitute by them- selves a catalogue of crime sufficient to call forth the indignation of civilized people. The remedy which he then asked for these abuses, moved not by the love for his compatriots, but by his pity for human beings, is still forthcoming; the same atrocities depicted, the same terrible deeds are of daily occurrence in the same blood-stained Morro, in the unhealthy Cabañas, in the overcrowded and filthy jails.

A Brilliant Scholar.

By dint of perseverance, with his once robust health shattered by the twelve months spent in physical and moral torture, supporting himself by the few lessons which he gave, he conquered from an adverse faculty at Saragossa, desirous of his failure, first his degree of Bachelor of Arts and Sciences, and very soon after that of Bache- lor of Laws.

He went to Madrid; in the very Capital he drew that touching invitation to prayer for the souls of the eight students shot in Havana in 1871, and on the morning of that anniversary there was no church or public building in the Spanish metropolis, on which the tremen- dous accusation was not affixed; this was the courageous act of the few surviving companions and of José Marti.

When the Republic was established, a Republic which proved better than anything else the incapacity of the Spaniards to govern themselves, Marti raised his voice against an impossible declaration of the Cubans in favor of the Spanish Republic, which was aimed to weaken the Cuban Revolution. For seven hours the young orator, with wonderful eloquence and convincing logic, thwarted the plans of the enemies of the war. The museums where he studied art, and the theatre of which he was so fond, were the only amusements which his hard and reduced life permitted.

He was more than a friend to the Cuban young men studying in the universities, an adviser who practiced what he preached, a quiz-master, a nurse and a faithful companion.   Many a one to-day recalls the abnegation with which he cared for them when ill, how he would scold them when they left their books, how he established a lodge for the Cubans, in which night classes were given to the children of Madrid.   Many a physician and lawyer to-day earns his living with the diploma that José Marti made them obtain !

Preparing for a New Uprising.

In 1873, he escaped and went to Mexico, where he called his family to his side and worked for their support.   He is remembered there by the brilliancy of his journalism, by the refined talent which he showed in the drama, by his feeling verses and by his magnificent orations.   Unwilling to accept any Government position which would prevent him from working for the interests of Cuba, he nevertheless accepted the representation of the workingmen in a labor congress.

He now visited Central America.   In Guatemala he became Professor of Philosophy in the University and vrote a historical drama on the independence of that section of America.

When peace was signed at " El Zanjon," he returned to Havana. He knew that this was only a temporary armistice ; that the Cubans had been duped; that the war would be kindled again ; that it was necessary to commence on the morrow of the defeat, to accumulate the elements for an uprising which was sooner or later to come. His voice rang with clarion tones in the literary societies; he refused to enter the Home Rule Party, knowing how futile would be its efforts, and on becoming known that if sent to the Spanish Cortes, he would demand for the good of Spain as much as for the Island, their complete separation, his name was withdrawn from the list of candidates; nevertheless there were then men in the Province of Santiago de Cuba who would only cast their votes for him.

Marti became the centre of the new conspiracy; General Blanco, seeing the danger of having such a man within the Island, sent him to Spain in connnement; from there he escaped by way of France and arrived in New York City, where with General Calixto Garcia he prepared a new invasion of the Island. After its failure he went to Venezuela, where he devoted himself to teaching and to newspaper work; but not submitting to the exigencies of Guzman, he returned to New York City, where he established himself definitely in 1880 until, in the month of January, 1895, he left on his last voyage.

In these fifteen years the amount of his labors was marvelous; his unequaled activity exerted itself in many walks; but whether as a teacher, a poet, an author, a diplomat or an orator, all converged to place the cause of Cuba before the world, and to acquire sympathies for her impending revolution.

Masterly Essays and Orations.

In the "Hour" he wrote, in his then quaint English, delicious articles on art, and that generous American, Mr. Charles A. Dana, patronized him, offering him the columns of his paper, where he wrote memorable articles on art and literature.

His labor as a correspondent for South and Central American newspapers is a complete review of all the contemporaneous events in the United States. These articles, when collected into a book, will form one of the most profound, entertaining and just studies of this country. But Marti, in the midst of this work with which he earned his bread, had time to write the tenderest thoughts in poetry to his child, to publish, in some lines which he entitled "Simple Verses," the decisive moments of his life, and in his oratory and prose of fire, brilliant with images and filigree composition, he put all that colossal mind of his, with its new and high ideas, and his soul as grand, as brave as his imagination was vivid and rich.

The Spanish-American Republics vied with each other to do him honor and to offer him a permanent home, but he lived not for position or wealth, but for his country; and this man, who had been poor all his life, when he was rewarded by Argentina and Uruguay with their consulates, which allowed him to live more comfortably, to give more time to the colored Cubans whom he used to teach in a small room in an out-of-the-way street of New York City, and to be still more charitable and kind to those who would never go away from his door unaided, when Marti was the official representative of those Republics, and it was necessary to either give up his welfare or his convictions as a Cuban, then this great man preferred to remain with his only means of livelihood, which was a class in a night-school, than to cease being a patriot.

Revolution in the Air.

His pure, his sincere, his noble life was indeed devoted to Cuba. For her he had suffered imprisonment and banishment; now he was to commence the final labor of bringing together the Cubans within the Island and abroad, organized in such a manner that when the hour arrived for the uprising the soldiers of freedom would not want the arms with which to make effective their enthusiasm. Marti had an exquisite nervous temperament, and had at the same time that rarer quality of being able to bridle his impulses, and the even more difficult gift of knowing how long to wait and when to strike. In three years he put in tangible shape what he had been preparing for so many. And it was time, because the people of Cuba had now reached the point which Marti had foretold, when the Home Rule Party could no longer restrain the natural indignation of a long-deceived country; when the veterans of the last revolution were preparing their arms; when the youth of this generation—vigorous and determined—were already exercising themselves for the battle of the future; when there floated over the Island the soul of that protest, which was now again to drench with blood the most unfortunate, the most martyrized of American lands.

Marti was ready. While others hoped and waited with their arms crossed, the visionary, the lunatic, as he was called by some of his skeptical countrymen, had done the work for all. He had established the Cuban Revolutionary Party upon whose bases and by-laws he had united all the Cuban Revolutionary elements; he had collected slowly but surely the money with which to make the first stand.

At his words, as of an apostle, the heroes of the last decade had answered that when the moment came their places would not be vacant; the loved leaders who more than once had led them to victory, did not shrink from this new proof of their loyalty to the cause; the gray-haired General-in-Chief felt that he could still mount with dash his war charger; his brave lieutenants, the bronzed giants of the East; the old companions of hardships, of victory and of hope,—all responded.

Marti may not have made the Revolution, but he was the one who, thoroughly disinterested, brought together in a sublime embrace those of yesterday and to-day, those who wield the sword without which no nation can attain its independence, and those who will make the laws, without which no independence can be maintained nor the Republic founded.

Still Enthusiastic for Freedom.

The temporary drawback that he received when the vessels in which he was to take the arms and the leaders to Cuba were captured, could not discourage his stout heart. The day he saw all his plans fall to the ground, through treachery or cowardice, on that day when he was so great in his suffering, he turned to the only friends in whom he confided, to the venerable Tomas Estrada Palma, to his faithful "brother," Benjamin J. Guerra, to whom this revolution owes so much, to Horatio S. Rubens, the distinguished American lawyer, who has been the truest ally of Cuba, and to myself, his "son," and only asked, full of emotion: "Do you have faith in me still ? Will you help me again ?"

When I asked in his name these very questions, six weeks afterwards, to the thousands of our countrymen who had already contributed so liberally to the party, the answer was unanimous and effective. Marti, who had left for Santo Domingo, with Generals Collazo and José M. Rodriguez, to see General Gomez and inform him of the condition of affairs, found on his arrival there that the Cubans loved him more than ever; that they had absolute confidence in his words; that they would continue to support him; that they gave him the funds with which to go with the Commander-in-Chief to the Island.

The Island, surprised as well as Spain, at the magnitude of the plans of Marti, ripe and impatient, was clamoring for the word. When the letters of Marti, which I took to Key West, and from there were sent by a trusted messenger across, were received in Cuba, Generals Gomez and Marti were getting ready for their departure. In those last days when Marti was with me, in January of 1895, I saw him in another light, so different from the others before, and the man grew in grandeur; indeed, it could be said of him, that to know him was to appreciate him, to know him well was to love him forever.

And it could not be his enthusiasm of a believer, nor his dreams as patriot, nor his eloquence, nor his constant and unobtrusive teaching which drew those who were around him more closely to his heart. No; those were times of doubt, of discouragement and of defeat, and yet who could fail to admire that man who would not leave his friends alone in trouble, in Florida, but would rush to share with them their sadness?

His Love for Cuba.

Who does not admire this man when you see him? Who would not feel his heart ache when at night, after the day's worry and work, he would try to rest? His fertile brain was no more under the control of his strong will, and he gave vent to those rending wails in which he exclaimed, " The traitor, how he struck the bosom of Cuba!" Only then, in that kind of somnolence, did I ever here him complain.

The last two weeks of his life in New York he passed at my house, unknown, only to his few trusted friends. In the midst of the blow no one caressed my little child with such softness; no cavalier could be more polite to the ladies; no one more mindful of the comforts of others. In the evening, he, whose thoughts were only in Cuba and was fretting under the delay, would read to them in his melodious and sonorous voice the superb lines in which he has translated Moore's " Lalla Rookh," and then he would prepare the chocolate; while he waited for the milk to boil he would read Franklin's autobiography.

The remembrance of his last farewell on board of the steamer, of his kiss of good-bye, open now the fountains of my heart. Marti was to enter in the last phase of his varied and splendid career. Only one thing could be said of him—he had not proved his valor in the field; he had never fought with rifle or sword.

In a small schooner, on the first of April, Marti, General Gomez, Generals Angel Guerra, Paquito Borrero, Cesar Salas and a dominican, Marcos Rosario, left from a desert shore on the frontier of Hayti. The passages were filled with men of war; the Spanish Consuls were advised of their movements; the captain was a scoundrel; he brought them to Inagua, where the crew at the instigation of the mate deserted; it was impossible to obtain any seamen; the Cubans were trapped in the arid Island; they could not possibly reach Cuba, and Cuba was desperate, expecting their promised coming.

Landed by Night.

When General Gomez was writing, "I have lost all hope!" Marti had made arrangements with a steamer that took them to Hayti; here they had to hide, for fear of arrest by the authorities; another vessel took them there. On the night of the 11th of April, the six men, in a row-boat, were placed on the coast of Cuba. They rowed with all their life; the lady hands of Marti directed one of the oars; in a short time they landed; Marti had kept his word; he had practiced what he preached; he was in his place!

His letters describing the landing; the welcome which the Cuban forces in that section gave him; his appointment as Major General of the army; his excursion through the East; his judgment of men and things; his faithful pictures of nature, are literary gems. Wherever he went he was received with admiration and love; in his excursions through the East he met with enthusiastic receptions, and with demonstrations of warm affection. Marti spoke to the assembled patriots; his orations were now short harangues, full of that irresistible magnetism that swayed the masses; they were like the sparks of the clashing of the machete and the sabre; they were delivered from the saddle of battle to the defenders of liberty; they are engraved in the minds of those legions never to be forgotten.

The statesman now revealed himself. On leaving Santo Domingo he gave to Cuba his famous declaration of principles of the revolution, dated at Monte Christi, on the 25th of March · in paragraphs in which every phrase is packed with ideas, in a massive language, he proclaimed the ability of the Cubans to carry on the war, their capacity for creating a stable government the day after the victory, the antagonism between the mother country and the colony, due to their peculiar relations, the belief and proof that in Cuba there could neither be a military despotism nor a war of races, the assurance that the Spaniard would find in the Cuban not an enemy, but a friend, and the determination of the patriots to renew the war, with its consequent sufferings and miseries, not for a mere dream or poetic aspiration of independence, but because the dignity and salvation of the country demanded it, and because the Cubans were convinced, after years of patient and useless waiting, that only by fire and sword could the happiness and freedom of the Island be obtained.

Concealed in a Hut.

In the month and a half that he breathed the invigorating air of our republic, Marti spent most of his time, while not on the march, in the humble hut of the peasant, writing on a board of palm those decrees calling the resident Spaniards to help make the nationality of their children, promising that the property of friends and neutrals would be protected; and above all the one prescribing that any one presenting himself to any Cuban chief with any proposition of peace, other than that based on absolute independence, should be summarily tried as a traitor. His last public utterances, embodied in a lengthy and lucid document, appealing to the justice of republicans and of America, was published in the United States on the 19th of May, the very day when the prime founder of Cuba was sealing his words with his blood, when José Marti was dying like a soldier!

"Under the palms, on a white steed, with my face to the sun," as he wished it, he fell. There, where our only majestic river, the

Cauto, opens its arms, where from the rising ground, the valleys, like a motherly bosom, invite the eternal rest, canopied by a gray firmament, there, where the world seems to dilate, José Marti battled for the last time against Spanish tyranny.

The Cuban troops had just heard his words of faith; the mountains still echoed with the applause; now he was to march West to fan the embers into a conflagration in the Central provinces, to establish the Civil Government.   But the enemy has been advised by a spy of the presence of the Cubans; the camp appears surrounded; the Commander-in-Chief mounts hurriedly and goes to the front; he is followed by his gallant lieutenants.   Gomez tells Marti to wait for his return.   José Marti is not the man to remain quiet while others fight and are in danger.   " A Major-General in the Cuban Army can not stay behind."

A Martyr to Freedom.

While Gomez is attacking one of the flanks of the Spaniards which is completely broken, General José Marti advances with a few followers by another road; he charges; his spirited horse carries him ahead of his men; it is his first engagement, it is his last victory; he rolls from his horse, fallen, wounded; his breast is riddled with bullets; the murderous lead entering under his chin has disfigured the firm mouth; the heavy mustache is burnt; his golden tongue is forever silent!

Let us hope that it is false that he was picked up by his enemies, unconscious, but still with life, and that they cruelly ended his existence.   Let us hope that it is false, for the honor of those officers who barefacedly appropriated his ring and his time-piece and who did not respect even the papers which he had next to his bleeding heart!

To expose the deformed mass of human flesh, in order to terrorize his countrymen and to hypocritically speak before his corpse is not chivalry.   Real chivalry cannot exist in men who desecrate and plunder the body of the generous opponent!

The cemetery of the City of Santiago, in the Eastern end of Cuba, is the depository of the mortal remains of José Marti, born in Havana, in the Western end of Cuba ; but over all the Island there palpitates with the same patriotism and fervor to-day as a year ago, as it will while a single Cuban lives, the spiritual José Marti, who guides, from above, our armies to victory ; who consoles the suffer ing, the exiled, the orphan, the widow ; who watches with unceasing vigilance for the welfare of his children ; who welcomes his brothers-in-arms who have joined him in the heaven of immortality ! José Marti, oh father ! you live in us, you can only die when, consumed by the flames or submerged in the waves, Cuba shall be no more !

General Maximo Gomez.

Who is this wiry man, tall, sun-burnt by twenty years of fighting, with gray hair, mustache and imperial ; who, alone in his tent, leans his well-formed head on his hands, resting on the handle of his erect sword ?   Who is this warrior who has given orders that no one shall enter his pavilion while he laments the loss of his friend ?   It is the dominican, it is the Cuban General-in-Chief, Maximo Gomez.   More distressed by the loss of Marti than by his wounds, he prefers to grieve alone for his noble companion.   Suddenly he rises ; he gives orders to his aids, he is on the march again to the West ; the way to do honor to the memory of the illustrious Cuban is to continue and finish the work.

Gomez rides silently for many days ; his officers do not speak to him ; they know that he is thinking of the blow which will prevent Spain from taking moral advantage of the death of Marti.   With his eyes of an eagle he chooses the direction ; with the cunningness of the fox he covers his tracks ; when the Spaniards are announcing his death and the end of the revolution, the veteran General sends his horse across the river Jobabo ; he is in Puerto Principe ; he has caught Martinez Campos napping ; two days afterwards he embraces again the grand old man of Cuba, Salvador Cismeros Betancourt, the ex-Marquis of Santa Lucia ; the veterans flock to his standard ; it is here that his renowned exploits of Las Guasimas, Naranjo, La Sacra and Palo Seco took place ; it is here that he will mature his plans.

When his old companions of sixteen years ago surround him in the starred evenings to hear him speak in his charming manner, he becomes reminiscent; he tells them how, when he sheathed the sword, he went away without a dollar to Panama with his Cuban wife and his Cuban children; "one of them will soon be fighting by my side," he exclaimed with pride; how he struggled with the fevers, how he wandered striving hard to make ends meet in Central America, Jamaica and Santo Domingo.

But he does not say that he has abandoned his plantation, that he has left his family to the care of his sons; he does not tell how his wife prefers to live poorly from their work rather than accept from the grateful Cubans any money which "can be employed in buying war material;" he never relates the abnegation of that model home and when he is through his peregrinations he brusquely says : "and I am here again." "When I gave up in 1868 my uniform and rank as Major of the Spanish Army, it was because I knew that if I kept them I would have some day to meet my own children in the field and combat against their just desire for liberty. Now, with my many years, I have come to lead and counsel the new generation to ultimate victory."

Iron Hand and Velvet Glove.

It is that confidence in the cause he defends which has made the rigid disciplinarian the idol of his soldiers; it is that generosity with which he has served Cuba which had conquered for him their eternal gratitude. He who has refused to preside over the destinies of his native land because that of his adoption is not free, is well worthy of being considered, as every native of the Island considers him, as the very best of Cubans.

General Gomez's reputation does not merely rest as a fortunate guerrilla chief; he is a tactician capable of planning an intricate campaign and of organizing large bodies of troops which he can manage with consummate ability. But General Gomez believes in attaining the end with the means at his disposal, and he is to be praised for that patience with which he has waited, and waits, until his raw

troops are organized, and until he has equipped them with arms captured from the enemy.

He is fond of sudden surprises which yield him excellent results.
In a circular operation which he made in Puerto Principe he collected
enough weapons for his Camagueyan cavalry; yet these brilliant
coups which make him dangerous are apparently followed by periods
of inaction; for almost three months during the summer of 1895, he
seems to have retired from active work, but when he had finished his
calculations, he mounted his horse, and, together with General
Antonio Maceo, paraded through Puerto Principe, Santa Clara and
Matanzas and encamped within sight of the Morro Castle lighthouse !

Right, and Then Goes Ahead.

So well measured and disposed were his steps, that one hundred
thousand Spanish soldiers were impotent to detain him.   He seldom
promises to do anything or prophesy, but when he does one or the
other he keeps his word;   he does not brag nor exaggerate like his
opponents, but once he makes up his mind that a certain course is
right he pursues it to the end.

Spain must be deprived of resources to carry on the war; the only
way to do it is by preventing the sugar crops from being harvested;
the Government relies on his military arm for the enforcement of the
order, and General Gomez, who is the first to obey and swear allegiance to the civil authorities, refuses every and all advances, sternly
follows the instructions, whether it be foe or friend who complains,
and proves with his army that the Cuban Republic is the supreme
law of the land because it has power to see that its decrees are complied with !   And yet not one prisoner has been killed by the army
under him ! not even when his men are butchered !

The affectionate interest that he takes in his soldiers is proverbial;
he eats what they eat ; and he sleeps where they sleep.   Of his marvelous energy and tireless physique, these thousand of miles which
he has traversed on horseback, fighting wherever the enemy would
dare to stand, are abundant proof that all the stories of his failing
health are as false as the calumny that he is a condotierri, like the

paid Generals of Spain, who come to the Island to make hay while
the sun shines, and who return to Spain, as more than fifty have
already done, as soon as by a mere scratch, or a run, or a massacre
of defenseless country people, they are promoted or obtain a pen-
sioned cross.

The horses that are killed under the firm stirrup of the veteran
warrior, and the wounds which he receives, charging always at the
head of his dashing staff, only have as rewards the blessings of a
people, which when emancipated will call him the Liberator of Cuba!

General Antonio Maceo.

He is a lion; and he is unconquerable. And he is the favorite child
of fortune.   He is a mulatto and commenced life as a donkey-driver.
By his courage, coolness, military subordination and talents he rose
from the ranks to a Major-General in the last war.   His worth must
indeed be indisputable, when against all possible drawbacks he rose
to such high command; the favorite disciple of Gomez, he is the
Lieutenant-General of the Cuban Army.   The Spanish use his name
to prove that this is a war headed by negroes and of race tendencies.

It is well that they should thus revenge themselves from their
feared foe; it is easier than to face him like the brave Spanish General Santoscildes, and to be killed; it is far better to remain like
Weyler in the comfortable palace, protected by thousands of soldiers
and Krupp guns, than to be carried away on a litter, disguised, as
"our glorious" Martinez Campos was at Bayamo, to save himself
from being captured, or to retreat in a panic at the second trial in
Caliseo; it is safer than to be wounded as General Cornell was in the
breast, or have the leg bored as General Luque, or be in peril of
drowning as Col. Devos was by being whipped into the sea! That
is the "mulatto," as they contemptuously refer to him, their terror
and constant nightmare.

Antonio Maceo is not only a lucky fighter—he is a tenacious ad-
versary who can never be bought.   I said he was a lion, and I recall
him now in the arena of Cuba, in his Eastern mountains as the Coliseum, for eleven months after the treaty of peace holding out with a

34

thousand faithful against thirty thousand soldiers, against all Spain. And I said he was unconquerable, for the lion did not surrender ; he made no terms with the master ; the master was satisfied to let him go in peace.

With Gomez he attempted to initiate another movement in 1884 ; the time was not ripe when Marti went to see him at Costa Rica, where he was trying to develop a great colony ; he found him willing and anxious. With his fearless brother José and the lamented Flor Crombet, he landed in April, 1895, in Baracoa. Hosts went to receive him ; he was again in the arena ; but now the spectators were his allies, and the old master, Martinez Campos, was the one who went, not with honors as did Maceo, but disgraced, discouraged, defeated !

In these years of exile, General Antonio Maceo has traveled extensively, has mastered several languages, has studied the military theories, which he has already applied ; has attained an enviable degree of culture and writes in a most concise and elegant style. He is a self-made man ; a self-made great man. His herculean figure has been the centre of attraction of this revolution ; around him the best families of Cuba fight ; he has been the scourge of the Spaniard, the support of the revolution, and the patriot army honors him.

Generals Calixto Garcia, Serafin Sanchez, Francisco Carrillo and José Maria Rodriguez.

Cuba has many other distinguished leaders, who, if the misfortunes of war should deprive her of the great commanders, would take their places and go on with the campaign where it was left by them. Garcia, Sanchez, Carrillo and Rodriguez are veterans of the last revotion and are identified with the present plans. Their names are a guarantee of their devotion and a convincing proof that the families of position and respect are as much interested in the success of the war as the masses of the people.

GENERAL CALIXTO GARCIA, for seven years, to 1875, was the Chief of the Eastern Department ; under him, the Maceos and the expert General Rabi, learned the art of war.

He was fond of large engagements and of attacking the important towns.   At a critical period of the revolution, by a series of rapid and succsssful operations around Holguin, Jiguani and Manzanillo, where he is the idol, he did a great deal to restore the *morale* to the forces. Surprised and surrounded by a Spanish column, with only his escort, the victor of Los Melones fought desperately until he saw that he could not escape; then he placed the muzzle of his revolver under his chin and discharged the last chamber—the bullet came out between the eyebrows.

For many months he hung between life and death, but finally recovered.   He was sent to Spain as a prisoner of war; in 1879, after the peace, he came to New York City, from where he took a small expedition to Cuba in the hope of renewing the struggle.   He arrived too late; without any response he gave up, so as to save his few surviving companions. Banished again to Spain, he supported his family by giving lessons—his refined education alone saving him from hunger. A believer in Marti, he placed himself under his orders. Near the close of 1895, evading the Spanish authorities, he escaped to France, and from there came to this country.

He Outlives Shipwreck.

Various attempts were made to send him to the Cuban army; that of the " Hawkins," sunk by paid hands of Spain, which declared that General Garcia would never reach the Island.   In the terrible shipwreck, in which ten lives were sacrificed by Spanish criminality, the figure of the chief stood out magnificently, washed by the furious waves; he stood on the bridge, tall, massive, with his fair face in its frame of silvery hair and beard, and in tones which were heard above the rumbling of the sea and the whistling wind, he said: " My boys, it is the same to perish here as there, it is for Cuba!"

But he was not to perish; after another attempt, in which he was arrested, he arrived in Cuba on the 25th of March, with his eldest son by his side.

GENERAL SERAFIN SANCHEZ is from Sancti Spiritus; of portly appearance, of serene valor, an organizer, and a man of intelligence and education; he is at the same time a man on whom the new republic can count for its definite order and progress. His life in its activities is an example of what all these soldiers will do when Cuba is free. Like some of the others, he became a planter first, and afterwards was employed in the cigar factories of Key West; he did not dishonor himself by that; he preferred to earn his living rather than to receive it from his compatriots. In the prime of his life, from him, as well as from Carrillo and Rodriguez, much is to be expected in this war.

Skillful Commanders.

CARRILLO AND RODRIGUEZ.—By an association of ideas easily explained, it is difficult to speak of one without thinking of the other; yet the first was born in Remedios, and the other in Santiago. Besides being contemporaneous, their only resemblance, physically, is that they are both short of stature and wear a beard like Stonewall Jackson, in common with whom they have many traits. Carrillo is stout, with a round head, prematurely bald, a high forehead, soft blue eyes, a perfect nose, a small mouth, a pronounced blonde beard and a magnificent manly face.

Mayia, as his friends call Rodriguez, has a long head, thick black hair and beard, tinged with white here and there; the narrow forehead broadens; the gray eyes sparkle; the nose is of a decided temper; his body is thin, almost emaciated; he walks painfully, his knee-cap was shattered by a bullet at the charge in which he covered himself with laurels at Naranjo; he has never since recovered the full use of his leg; and he fought four years in that condition, and when Gomez remonstrated that he could not bring with him an invalid, the subordinate hardly controlled himself, but said, sadly: "General, if you do not take me, I will die; if you do not give me the means, I will go across in a boat." The General sent him as his personal representative when the preparations were being made; after the failure he returned to Santo Domingo, and landed finally in Cuba!

Carrillo and Rodriguez are the best cavalry leaders of Cuba; they are aggressive, honest, of the best military schools of Cuba; they are adored by the rank and file. It is such men on whom the new generation counts for the final triumph; while they live, others will try to imitate them, and as General Gomez, speaking of the death of Marti and Borrero, said truthfully : " Do not despair, many will have to fall; I and perhaps some of my lieutenants will not reach the end of the journey, but there will be plenty who will take our places and reach the goal of our ambition ! "

Salvador Cisneros Betancourt.

The " grand old man" of Cuba !   There is no bluer blood in Spain than his; his estates, ruined now by confiscation and destruction, were once of the most extensive of the Island; a Cisneros and a Quesada ceded to the Government the land on which is situated the port of Santa Cruz in Puerto Principe.   But the ex-Marquis of Santa Lucia is nobler by his deeds than by his title and escutcheons.   Of the seventy years he has lived, fifty have been devoted to the cause of liberty in his country.   He came to Philadelphia when a boy and graduated as a Civil Engineer, the first in his class; few equal him in mathematics.

In the United States he learned to love—as all of us—the institutions which give every one his due and foster the advancement of the people's interest.   His mind, not brilliant, but a persistent, quiet and deep one, has been as steadfast in its convictions as his heart, generous to the point of prodigality.   El Lugareno, his relative, Gaspar Betancourt Cisneros, who sowed the seeds in Puerto Principe, found in the young man an ardent devotee.

Returning to his native city, he was the promoter of all that could advance the material, intellectual or political prosperity of his countrymen; he founded radical newspapers, contributing sharp articles against the abuses of the authorities; of the Lyceums he was a powerful factor; of the fairs, where the improvement of the cattle industries and agricultural products was encouraged, he was one of the founders; he was a benefactor.

In every separatist movement he can be found until the present; his motto seems to be, If you fail, try again.   On account of the attempts in 1848, he was banished; when he came back he conspired year after year, until, in 1867, the work commenced to be shaped;

again he wielded the pen.   He created the Revolutionary Committee of Camaguey, of which he was the moving spirit.   He traveled from place to place bringing together the conspirators, and when on the 4th of November, 1868, Camaguey answered the call, the Marquis led the seventy-two young men who first defied the Government.

He is not a soldier, and yet as a member of the Assembly, as President of the Republic, he has gone into the thickest of the fight; collecting the arms left by the enemy, or picking up and caring for the wounded; it is unknown that he has ever shot a cartridge; he has the highest valor; without firing he receives with imperturbable coolness the enemy's fusillade; he was wounded in the arm in the attack of Pinto.

A Wise Statesman.

But if he is not a military chief, he is one of the corner-stones of the Republic; for he jealously provides that the civil power shall have its place in the embryo constitution of Cuba.   In the last revolution, as in this, he insisted on having the law paramount to the sword; he is conducting the Ship of State so that in the future there can never be dictators in the Island or military oligarchies, but a real democracy and a republic in fact, and not in name only.

He is inflexible.   After the peace he came to this country; his life was a hard fight against misery; stooped already by hardships and age, he could be seen in summer with his winter coat from which he had removed the lining; he would exist on one meal a day, and not very nutritious at that, but he was too proud to accept charity, not because of himself, but because of his Cuba!

In those days of despair, when only a few would meet in a lowly hall to honor the memories of the heroes, he used to take me, a child then,—he who had lost all his children—and would place me by his side on the wooden benches, and his bony hands would pat me kindly on the shoulders, and he would say in his peculiar voice: "Hear, do not allow the happiness of the American people and their liberty which you enjoy, make you forget that you do not deserve them until you have acquired them by your own effort; hear well and be a Cuban."

When he went back to Puerto Principe, after the last hopes of a new uprising had failed in 1885, the Marquis (that is the way we affectionately called him in the army) gave up his magnificent house, now the Spanish Casino; divided into colonies his estates in Las Minas for the use of the veterans, would not enter any political party, and when a negro captain died, a Cuban soldier noted for his devotion and gallantry, and it was fitting that he should have a tomb worthy of his merits, it was the carriage of Cisneros that was at the head of the funeral; he helped to place the casket of the humble negro by the side of those of his titled ancestors, in the niche of the Marquises of Santa Lucia!

When, in 1893, he was written to, he answered that they could always count upon Camaguey, but that there were no arms. This was the reason why this province did not respond until June, and then it was with *machetes* only, and very few cartridges. The venerable Marquis was the first to unfurl again the flag in Puerto Principe.

The Government Well Organized.

Devoting all his energies to the formation of the Civil Government, postponed on account of the death of José Marti, delegates from all the provinces met at Jimaguayu under his chairmanship, and drew the provisional constitution; while at the same time, leaving the military all liberty of action, it subordinates it to the civil delegates of the people, who elect all the officers of the Republic for two years.

An indefatigable organizer, he has extended the civil machinery all over the portions of the Island in control of the Cubans; by a system of prefectures regulated by wise rules, the army always finds horses and food on its marches; those who do not bear arms are employed in farming and manufacturing; a complete system of post-offices is in operation throughout the Island; taxes are collected; civil marriage determines the relations of the sexes; the citizen is taught to respect the civil functionaries, and to see them respected by the military chiefs, and while the sword and the torch destroy and purify the existing germs of corruption and colonial despotism, the country is being prepared for a natural evolution into the life of a modern and orderly nation, without the necessity of passing through periods of struggle and doubt, of disquiet, or temporary anarchy.

It is well to do away with the rotten elements, but it is the work of the statesman to put in their place the solid and healthy foundations for the future. Such is the ambition and endeavor of the President of the Provisional Government of Cuba, Salvador Cisneros Betancourt.

Tomas Estrada Palma.

The Cuban Revolution is not only fought in Cuba; it is fought all over the world, and especially in the United States. The Spanish domination in America would cease the day when Madrid would be cut off from Havana; on the supply of arms and ammunition which reaches the patriots, depends the rapid termination of the unequal war. The representative of the Cuban Republic abroad is the collaborator of most importance perhaps.

Spain must be met wherever she has her agents; her lies and detractions, propagated in press and book to dishonor the Cuban cause, must be answered; her detectives must be fooled, and war material, a legitimate merchandise, must be sent to Cuba, to the thousands of men who are clamoring for it; to those patriots who shed tears when they see that one ship has not brought enough for all. The duel between Spain and Cuba is also an economic war; wherever and whenever Spain has to spend her last millions, there the battle is being waged. Every day that passes is a victory won by the Cubans, for it represents so many hundred thousands of dollars to the Royal Treasury, which Spain must borrow.

Her children, she does not mind if they are killed; she can replace them from the poor peasantry of her deserted and impoverished fields; but a dollar—a dollar is one more piled to her enormous debt; with every one spent it is harder to get the loan of another. So every spy, every cable, every *secret service* abroad, is an unconscious contributor to the bankruptcy of Spain, and Cuba's independence. This is a duel in which the Spaniards, to win, must spend money, and the Cubans use their brains.

No better man could have been chosen by the Cubans abroad to succeed José Marti, than the tried patriot, Tomas Estrada Palma. This selection was so ratified by the unanimous appointment he received from the Constituent Assembly, as Delegate Plenipotentiary of the Cuban Republic in foreign countries; that is to say, the Government gave him the amplest powers.   Only on a man of the history of Palma could such a confidence be conferred; but the Cubans who knew well his past history, and the Americans who have learned to love him in Central Valley, New York, are proud and satisfied that the selection should have fallen on him.

Palma unites with the fervor of the first apostles of Cuban liberty —of whom he was one—the mature deliberation of the man who by experience knows why the last revolution did not succeed; and his labor has been directed to see that no division may arise between the Cubans who are fighting in the field and the Cubans abroad, who should be an auxiliary wing of the army of liberation; and he has with consummate skill softened the natural antagonisms among men, overcome difficulties and brought together all the Cubans to a common labor.   While there existst his union, equal to the one in the ranks, the Cuban cause is invincible.   While Tomas Estrada Palma remains in his present position, his name is the guarantee of such union.

A Self-sacrificing Patriot.

The disinterestedness with which he serves his country in this epoch is more to be admired than when he abandoned, young then, his vast estate; when he made his house the meeting-place for the conspirators; when he, the only son and heir, gave up all for his Cuba.   And he did not only suffer in those years when the fortitude of constitutions, not as frail as his, was vanquished by the miseries of war, but he received the cruelest of wounds.

Since then there is a tinge of sadness in his eyes.   His mother was, for his sake, a victim of Spanish brutality; she could not part from the only consolation of her life; she followed him to the rebel woods; sick and an invalid she was made a prisoner; her captors dragged the unfortunate woman through the road inhumanly; she died of their ill-treatment!

Tomas Estrada for many a month bowed his head in silent despair; but when Spanish soldiers were captured, he was the first to intercede in their behalf; he would not insult his mother's saintly memory, her virtue, her martyrdom, by revenge.   They say that to-day the venerable patrician keeps next to his heart a little wallet, with relics of his mother's love, his treasures; when he needs encouragement, he thinks of her; he reverently kisses the time-worn trinkets; he sheds tears and is comforted and strengthened.

Independence First, then Peace.

With the same constancy Palma loves his Cuba; had he not been captured, perhaps the Spaniards never would have had a chance to present propositions of peace; it was this little man, who, previous to his Presidency, when Secretary of State, drew the " Sportuno decree," re-enacted by Marti and Gomez, incorporated in another form in Article X. of the present Constitution : " No peace but on the basis of independence."   Inflexible in its compliance, a relative of his was the first to suffer its consequences, for bringing other propositions; he was tried and executed; with Palma there are no relatives or influences that can make him waver; his conscience is his only counsellor.

Sent to Spain, he was confined in a castle until the end of the war. Palma refused all aid that the Government offered him; when the census was being taken he was asked his occupation.   " President of the Republic of Cuba," he answered proudly; thrice, and each time to a higher officer, the prisoner answered, " President of the Republic of Cuba."   They could not persuade him to change his reply, either by coaxing or threats !   While the Prime Minister at Madrid was expecting him to confer as to the best way of dealing with separatism in the Island, and to offer him a fine position in the Cuban administration, Tomas Estrada Palma was crossing the frontier to France in a third-class coach, with hardly enough money to reach Paris.

In Honduras, where he found the affectionate companion of his home, he was made Postmaster-General of the Republic, and commenced his pedagogic career, to which he was, by his kindness and patience, more inclined than to the tricks and aggressiveness of the profession of the law.

By dint of economy and perseverance he realized finally his dream: the establishment of a school for Spanish Americans and Cuban children in the United States, where they would be educated in the midst of liberty, and see how the people govern themselves; would be taught letters, as well as the love for agricultural work, and where they would not lose their home customs or their veneration for the fatherland.

To contemplate him there in the picturesque valley, with the mountains surrounding it, in his spacious and neat home, with his pupils, to whom he is an elder brother, rising with the sun, overseeing the tasks of his employees, alert, benevolent, advising with paternal solicitude, teaching with amiability and clearness, nursing his wards and caring for them with as much interest as for his own dear ones, is to believe in the existence in this world of virtue and perfection.

No Glory but that of Sacrifice.

And from this model home, from his school, from his family that he adores, from his orchards, from his cows, from his lake, from tranquillity and happiness, his countrymen called him to enter the turmoil of revolutionary agitation, to become the bull's eye of the enemy, to worry, to incessant work night and day, to the grave responsibilities of a position fraught with unavoidable difficulties and with no glory but that of sacrifice. Estrada Palma accepted it, and he did it conscious of the obstacles in the way, of the hard road which he had to travel. But could it be worse than the one which led his friend Marti to martyrdom and the one of his sweet, magnanimous mother?

For the first days he groped his way as if studying the situation; the office full of envious people was not the quiet school-room with the smiles of his scholars; the buzz of the city, the nervous life, the unrest, the agitation took him by surprise; but his wonderful adaptability vanquished everything; soon he had mastered the details of the vast and complicated labor; he was again not the schoolmaster, but the same executive officer of twenty years ago!

An able judge of men, his initial steps were to carefully choose his coadjutors. In Benjamin Guerra, he found a treasurer of that integrity which is Palma's essential requisite; struggling people are always poor, but they have sufficient if their savings are defended ; and not one cent of Cuba's money is spent but in forwarding its cause. Guerra's face has much of the determination of the mastiff, and he watches the money of the patriots with such tact and fidelity that he has been repeatedly elected unanimously to his high position of trust. Benjamin J. Guerra is besides a man of cool and wise counsel, whose opinions carry weight, not only by his patriotic history, but by the moderation and conservatism of his tendencies.

All in the Service of Liberty.

Mr. Palma has also had the happy faculty of not removing those who have done good service or shown themselves fitted for their positions. Horatio S. Rubens had been the legal adviser of Marti, who implicitly confided in the young lawyer ; Palma kept him by his side. In this revolution the Americans have not as yet occupied in the Cuban Army the commands which Jordan, Reeves, Johnston and Humphries did in the last; but this American, Rubens, has done so much for the success of the independence of the Island, that his name, cherished by Generals, cheered by the soldiers, dear to the Cubans abroad, will occupy one of the most brilliant pages in the history of Cuba. He has given up his future for liberty ; he has placed his legal talent at the service of the patriots.

Emileo Nunez, who has well earned his title of General, by his successful landing of arms in Cuba ; Joaquin Castillo, who has helped him ; Dr. Juan Guiteras, a scientific glory of America and a proved patriot, have all contributed to Palma's success. Palma has accomplished more than his predecessors in 1868–78; he has landed more cargoes of war material ; he has floated a loan, aided by Ponce de Leon, Zaldo, Zayas, active and distinguished Cubans ; and he has obtained from the American people, through both Houses of Congress, the declaration of sympathy, its opinion that the Cubans are entitled to belligerency, and that the United States desire the independence of the Island.

What more could be expected in a year? And Tomas Estrada alma has done this in his quiet, unassuming way, without flattering anybody, without the dignity of his country suffering. The following address will give an idea of the stand Palma has taken in this revolution:

"To the People of the United States:

"The persistency with which the American press has, during the last few days, been treating of supposed administrative reforms to be introduced in Cuba by the Government of Spain compels me to request the publication of the following declarations which I make in behalf of my Government, of the army of liberation of Cuba, and of the Cuban Revolutionary Party.

Not Reforms but Independence.

"The question of the proposed reforms is not a matter which at all concerns those who have already established an independent government in Cuba and have resolved to shrink from no sacrifice of property or life in order to emancipate the whole Island from the Spanish yoke. If the Spanish residents of the Island, who are favored by the Spanish Government with all sorts of privileges and monopolies, and if the handful of Cubans, too pusillanimous or too proud to acknowledge their error, or a few foreigners guided only by selfish interests, are satisfied that Cuba should remain under Spanish domination, we, who fight under the flag of the solitary star, we, who already constitute the Republic of Cuba, and belong to a free people with its own Government and its own laws, are firmly resolved to listen to no compromise and to treat with Spain on the basis of absolute independence for Cuba.

"If Spain has power to exterminate us, then let her convert the Island into a vast cemetery; if she has not, and wishes to terminate the war before the whole country is reduced to ashes, then let her adopt the only measure that will put an end to it and recognize our independence. Spain must know by this time that while there is a single living Cuban with dignity—and there are many thousands of them—there will not be peace in Cuba, nor even the hope of it.

"All good causes must finally triumph, and ours is a good cause. It is the cause of justice treated with contempt, of right suppressed by force, and of the dignity of a people offended to the last degree.

"We Cubans have a thousandfold more reason in our endeavors to free ourselves from the Spanish yoke than the people of the thirteen colonies had when, in 1776, they rose in arms against the British Government.

The American Revolution and the Cuban.

"The people of these colonies were in full enjoyment of all the rights of man; they had liberty of conscience, freedom of speech, liberty of the press, the right of public meeting, and the right of free locomotion; they elected those who governed them, they made their own laws, and, in fact, enjoyed the blessings of self-government. They were not under the sway of a Captain-General with arbitrary powers, who, at his will, could imprison them, deport them to penal colonies, or order their execution, even without the semblance of a court-martial. They did not have to pay a permanent army and navy that they might be kept in subjection, nor to feed a swarm of hungry employees yearly sent over from the metropolis, to prey upon the country.

"They were never subjected to a stupid and crushing customs tariff which compelled them to go to the home markets for millions of merchandise annually which they could buy much cheaper elsewhere; they were never compelled to cover a budget of $26,000,000 or $30,000,000 a year without the consent of the taxpayers, and for the purpose of defraying the expenses of the army and navy of the oppressor, to pay the salaries of thousands of worthless European employees, the whole interest on a debt not incurred by the colony, and other expenditures from which the Island received no benefit whatever; for out of all those millions only the paltry sum of $700,000 was apparently applied for works of internal improvement, and one-half of which invariably went into the pockets of the Spanish employees.

"We have thrown ourselves into the struggle advisedly and deliberately; we knew what we would have to face, and we decided unflinchingly to persevere until we should emancipate ourselves from the Spanish Government. And we know that we are able to do it, as we know that we are competent to govern ourselves.

Capable of Managing Organizations.

"Among other proofs which could be adduced of the capacity of the Cuban white and colored to rule themselves is the strong organization of the Cuban revolutionary party in America. It is composed of more than 20,000 Cubans living in different countries of the New World, and formed into clubs, the members of which yearly elect their leader. This organization has an existence of over five years, during which every member has strictly discharged his duties, has respected, without any interruption, the regulations, and obeyed the elected delegate loyally and faithfully. Among the members of the clubs there are several Spaniards, who enjoy the same rights as the Cubans, and who live with them in fraternal harmony.

"This fact, and those of the many Spaniards incorporated into our army, fully demonstrate that our revolution is not the result of personal hatred, but an uprising inspired only by the natural love of liberty and free institutions. The war in Cuba has for its only object the overthrow of Spanish power, and to establish an independent republic, under whose beneficent laws the Spaniards may continue to live side by side with the Cubans as members of the same community and citizens of the same nation. This is our programme, and we strictly adhere to it.

"The revolution is powerful and deeply rooted in the hearts of the Cuban people, and there is no Spanish power—no power in the world —that can stop its march. The war, since General Weyler took command of the Spanish army, has assumed a cruel character; his troops shoot the Cuban prisoners, pursue and kill the sick and wounded, assassinate the unarmed, and burn their houses. The

Cuban troops, on their part, destroy, as a war measure, the machinery and buildings of the sugar plantations, and are firmly resolved not to leave one stone upon another during their campaign.

"Let those who can put an end to this war reflect that our liberty is being gained with the blood of thousands of Cuban victims, among whom is numbered José Marti, the apostle and martyr of our revolution. Let them consider that, before the sacred memory of this new redeemer, there is not a single Cuban who will withdraw from the work of emancipation without feeling ashamed of abandoning the flag which, on the 24th of February, was raised by the beloved master.

"It is time for the Cuban people to satisfy their just desire for a place among the free nations of the world, and let them not be accused if, to accomplish their noble purpose, they are obliged to reduce to ashes the Cuban land.   T. ESTRADA PALMA."

Like Franklin, Palma puts his faith in the justice of his cause rather than in the pomp of language, or on the show of dress. He always dresses in black; he uses neither the silk hat nor the evening dress; he wears no jewels; his fourteen-year old boy is by his side, that he may accompany him; he always finds time, as did Lord Nelson in the midst of the perils of the sea and vicissitudes of combat, to write to his lady; every night he kisses the sacred wallet!

Noble and pure soul! Of such are the founders of Cuba's liberty.
                              GONZALO DE QUESADA.

Appendix.

Latest Events in the Cuban Revolution, including Military Operations, Battles, Secret Expeditions and Arrests of American Citizens.

THE next event of importance following the history of the Cuban conflict narrated in the first part of this volume, was the arrest at Havana of Rev. Alberto J. Diaz, a Baptist missionary and a citizen of the United States. Subsequently, at a public meeting in Philadelphia, Mr. Diaz told a dramatic story of escape from military death in Cuba, of the cunning and brutality of the Spanish General Weyler and his fear of the United States.

Dr. Diaz and his brother were imprisoned in Cuba for preaching civil and religious liberty, and were only saved from death by the services of a member of his church disguised as a Spanish sentry. In Havana the members of the church, founded under the auspices of the Southern Baptist Missionary Society, were divided in sympathy between the Spanish and insurgents. Dr. Diaz preached true liberty to both factions alike, and although often warned against it he persisted in expounding the doctrines of liberty and claimed the right of uttering his honest sentiments.

Said he, "About three o'clock one morning I was aroused by a knock at the door of my house, and when I opened it I saw some fifty or sixty Spanish soldiers, with their guns leveled at me. I quickly shut the door and talked through it. The captain said he must search the house, and I consented to let three men come in. They spent seven hours looking through two trunks full of sermons and other papers, and when the search was completed they had found no incriminating documents."

Not notified, the soldiers led Dr. Diaz and his brother away to the prison cell in the now famous Morro Castle. They were placed face to a wall with sentinels all about them. For twenty-four hours they sat there without eating, for they were afraid to eat lest their food had been poisoned, as it had often been before. Finding that they did not eat, the soldiers allowed the doctor's wife to send in their meals.

One day Dr. Diaz saw two black coffins and saw all arrangements for his execution and supposed that day was his last on earth. Feeling that death was so near he laid aside prison rules and talked with his brother, and the two men sang hymns until they lay down for what they believed would be their last sleep.

A Secret Telegram.

" But," says Dr. Diaz, " I was not quite asleep when I was startled by some one kissing my hand. I started up, but a finger was laid on my lips as a signal for quiet. A soldier was by my side sobbing bitterly. At last he whispered, ' Don't you know me ? I belong to your church.' " Bending low the Doctor recognized the soldier, who then said : " You are to die to-morrow, is there anything I can do ? " Dr. Diaz asked for pencil and paper and wrote a telegram, " Diaz in jail ; about to be executed," and directed it to the President of the Southern Baptist Missionary Society, in Atlanta. The sentry promised to smuggle the telegram through, and he succeeded. Just what reply was received Dr. Diaz did not say, but following the receipt of the message the prisoners were allowed everything but their liberty.

Dr. Diaz wrote another telegram to Secretary of State Olney, stating the conditions of his imprisonment, and that he was an American citizen, but it was returned and reported that Weyler had said: " If that telegram is sent it will involve us in war with the United States."

Dr. Diaz told the messenger the message must be smuggled over to Key West. Soldiers were everywhere, and the messenger retreated, but later gave the telegram to two men who were not known, and they were allowed to go on board the steamer. The messenger wanted to send a message of his own and went on board the boat and was searched, but nothing found on him. When the boat was out of sight he told the Spaniards that the message was on the steamer bound for Key West.

The news was carried to General Weyler, who immediately anticipated the demand and telegraphed to Washington: " Diaz released." Forthwith Dr. Diaz was released and went directly to his church, where a monster prayer-meeting was held. The next day General Weyler ordered Diaz, his brother and family to leave Cuba on the next steamer. Dr. Diaz could not leave and went fishing until the boat left and then had to wait for three days. By this time all arrangements were completed and the whole family left for the United States. The story created great interest and the congregation congratulated him on his marvelous escape from death.

General Lee Sent to Cuba.

In April, 1896, a change of consuls at Havana excited comment. The appointment of General Fitzhugh Lee to succeed Consul General Williams, was regarded by Americans as well as by the authorities at the Palace, as an adroit way of sending a military commissioner from the States to Cuba. When there was an intimation that Mr. Cleveland contemplated sending a commissioner to learn officially what was going on, the officials at Madrid said very plainly that no military or other commission would be accepted by them, or permitted to pry into affairs in Cuba. There was, therefore, some curiosity as to how General Lee would be received, and as to what facilities would be accorded him for learning what was transpiring outside of the city of Havana. The American residents of Havana welcomed General Lee with open arms. The following is a summing up of the situation on May 1st, by a press correspondent:

"Three conclusions force themselves upon me as the result of observation of the progress of the revolution in Cuba. The insurgents are making a remarkably good fight. Spain has demonstrated her inability to put them down, and Cuba is surely slipping away from Spain. When I left Havana a week ago, the insurrection was more formidable, and apparently more promising of success, than at any time in the fourteen months since the Cubans rose against Spain.

"Before the arrival of General Weyler, correspondents were per‑ mitted to accompany Spanish columns. Since the enemy has grown from scattered bands to organized and fairly-well armed and drilled columns it is a matter of life and death for a correspondent to penetrate the rebel lines. I have had experience with four Captains-General— Calleja, Campos, Marin and Weyler. The last is the only one of them who made the life of a war correspondent burdensome. Polite in his reception of all Americans, yet he had a way of impressing upon a correspondent, without putting it into words, that it would conduce to his personal safety to make a practice of reporting nothing but Spanish official news.

"As these fail to mention a single insurgent success from the be‑ ginning, and are a record of many Spanish victories, which exist on paper only, the correspondent who accepts them at face value beguiles his readers. If the affair at Guatao was a battle and not a butchery, why were two correspondents thrown into Morro Castle, charged with having visited the place, which is only twelve miles from Havana? Every effort is made to keep the world in darkness as to what is being done in Cuba. Every cable despatch is carefully edited before it can be transmitted. Everything unfavorable to Spain or favorable to the Cuban cause is eliminated. The mails are searched to prevent news‑ paper correspondence being sent off. But with all these precautions the truth cannot be suppressed.

Spain's Immense Army.

"Spain has sent 140,000 regulars and 60,000 volunteers have been raised in the cities of the Island. The latter are used almost entirely for home defence. Of the regulars approximately 25,000 have suc‑ cumbed to bullets and disease during the year, 15,000 are in the hos‑ pitals or have been relieved from duty, and about 100,000 are available for active operations.

"The establishment of the latest trocha, that between Mariel and Majana, absorbs 30,000 regulars for the defence of the line. There are about 10,000 regulars divided into flying columns of 1,500 to 2,000 men each, operating aggressively against Maceo just west of the trocha in Pinar del Rio, and in all of the other provinces there are not more than 15,000 troops in the field against the enemy.

" Gomez, Lacret, José Maceo, Calixto Garcia and other insurgent leaders with large forces are unopposed. The number of insurgents under arms is now fully 45,000. Spaniards say that Cubans will not fight, but I have seen many trainloads of wounded Spanish soldiers brought into Havana and other cities, and American planters declare that the Cubans are reckless under fire.

" The entire interior of the Island is either in actual possession of insurgents or is in sympathy with them. In the large cities are many men who are thoroughly in sympathy with the insurgent cause. In the early days of the war the better class of Cubans declared the rising to be premature. Within three months there has been a decided change of opinion. Sons of leading families, and in some cases, heads of families themselves, have joined the insurgents. A gentleman, who owns a sugar plantation worth $2,000,000, said to me recently that he had become convinced that Cuba must be free or annexed to the United States, or every planter on the Island would be ruined.

Cruelty of the Spanish Commanders.

" The rabid Spaniards are the ones who forced the recall of General Martinez Campos. They have recently attacked General Weyler, accusing him of being as lenient as Campos. The General has been between two fires ever since he took command. He has endeavored to satisfy Spaniards and at the same time avoid bringing down the wrath of the United States on his head. He has succeeded in both fairly well."

The correspondent then gives details of acts of cruelty charged against Spanish commanders which have been reported from time to time. He continues:

" The ultra-Spaniards urge General Weyler to do more of this kind of work. They declare without hesitancy that all Cubans should be exterminated. They urge Spanish merchants to discharge their Cuban clerks and employ Spaniards. They look upon Cuba as a place to be plucked, and would drive every native from the Island and confiscate his property for themselves. These Spaniards are the dominant faction at present, but they are only a small minority in Cuba. The more liberal Spaniards and those with property interests at stake have different views."

The reader will be interested in a detailed account of the capture of the filibustering schooner "Competitor" by a Spanish gunboat. Several aboard the captured vessel claimed American citizenship, and among them were those who declared they were on lawful business and were not in any sense aiding the insurgents.

General Weyler was much pleased at the capture. He embraced Commander Butron, of the gunboat "Mensagera," and presented him with the cross Maria Cristina. Commander Butron said the papers seized were very valuable. Among them were letters to Maceo, circulars, many flags and other things besides the arms. The expedition started three times from Key West. Dr. Vedia, the Key West newspaper correspondent, was on board in all the attempts, and once was kept at sea twenty days.

Story of the Capture.

Commander Butron's story of the capture is as follows: "The Mensagera' was directed to watch the coast between Cayo Julia and Morrillo, about one hundred miles. It was heard on the afternoon of April 25, that a suspicious schooner had been seen near Quebrados de Uvas. The gunboat followed and found the 'Competitor.' The usual signals were made, but the schooner tried to get closer in shore so as to land a rapid fire-gun.

"The 'Mensagera' was then moved forward and fired a shot, which struck the schooner and exploded a box of cartridges which the men were trying to take ashore. Several occupants of the schooner became alarmed, and threw themselves into the water, fearing an explosion of dynamite. The gunboat's crew seized rifles and began shooting, killing three men. Several others reached shore.

"Three men were aboard the schooner when it was overhauled, and they surrendered without resistance. Among them was Owen Milton, editor of the Key West *Mosquito*. Sailors were sent ashore to capture the arms landed. In a skirmish two men, supposed to be filibusters, and a horse were killed. They secured several abandoned cases of cartridges. A body of insurgents had come to watch the landing of the boat's crew. The 'Mensagera' came to Havana with the arms and prisoners, who were very seasick. The schooner was towed to Havana by the gunboat 'Vicente Yanez.' It is regarded as an object of great curiosity by the crowds. It had the Spanish flag floating when captured. It is a neat, strong boat, and looks fast. One of the prisoners captured steadily refuses to give his name."

Trial of the Prisoners.

A despatch from Havana under date of May 8th, was as follows:

"The court opened at the Arsenal. The prisoners were Alfredo Laborde, born in New Orleans; Owen Milton, of Kansas; William Kinlea, an Englishman, and Elias Vedia and Teodoro Dela Maza, both Cubans. Captain Ruiz acted as president of the court, which consisted of nine other military and naval officers. The trial of the five filibusters captured aboard the 'Competitor' was proceeded with against the formal protest presented by Consul General Williams, who declared that the trial was illegal and in violation of the treaty between Spain and the United States.

"The prisoners were not served with a copy of the charges against them and were not allowed to select their own counsel, but were represented by a naval officer appointed by the government. They were not permitted to call witnesses for their defence, the prosecution calling all the witnesses. Owen Milton, of Kansas, testified through an interpreter that he came on the expedition only in order to correspond for a newspaper. William Kinlea, when called, was in his shirt sleeves. He arose and said in English, 'I do not recognize your authority and appeal for protection to the American and English consuls.'"

A few days later it was announced from Madrid that the Spanish and American Governments had arrived at an amicable understanding regarding the trial of the prisoners, who would be tried again, this time by a civil court under the provisions of the existing treaties between the two countries. The prompt action of our Government undoubtedly saved the lives of several, if not all, of the prisoners.

Early in May the Spaniards succeeded in capturing Cacarajicara, Maceo's fort in the western mountains, being led by General Inclan. The insurgents made an attack upon the Spanish artillerymen with their machetes, but were driven back from the cannon forty feet by a wall of troops. A tall, bearded man, stick in hand, urged the insurgents to fall on the Spaniards, but they refused and retreated.

Hand to Hand Fighting.

A bayonet charge was then ordered and the soldiers patriotically rushed into the ditch, driving out the insurgents. One of those who defended the fort and who fled with the others was a woman. The defence is said to have been conducted by Maceo, Socarras and Quintin Bandera. The return march was very difficult, the enemy being scattered all through the hills and firing from every point. The progress was slow on account of the wounded soldiers. The official report says 2,000 Spanish and 6,000 to 8,000 insurgents were engaged in all. Socarras is said to have been gravely wounded in the face. A ball struck Pilar Rojas in the stomach, seriously wounding him. General Inclan made an address, thanking his soldiers for their valor, which, he said, "deserves a place in the best pages of Spanish history."

The situation in Cuba in the middle of July is fully stated by a press correspondent, who furnished, among other accounts of important events, the details of the death of General José Maceo, brother of the famous General Antonio Maceo, and himself a dashing leader scarcely less renowned than his illustrious brother.

"I went out," says the correspondent, "with General Agustin Cebreco on June 20, and arrived the next day at the Aguacate estate by the Cauto River, where we pitched our camp. We started out the next day and marched to San Luis, where we met General José Maceo's forces, who were returning from conveying the war material landed from the steamer 'Three Friends.'

"I met Colonel Rafael Portuondo, who was the leader of the expedition. It was the largest ever brought to Cuba, and according to Portuondo himself there were seventy men. The expedition left Jacksonville on the 23d of May, and consisted of the following:— 1,052 rifles, 24 cases of hardware, 200 suits of clothes, 200 hammocks, 525,000 cartridges, 2 rapid-fire guns, 800 shells, 1,000 dynamite shells, 1,000,000 dynamite caps and one ton of medical stores, presented to the Cubans by an American wholesale drug firm. There was enough morphine and quinine for an army. There were also 200 Mauser rifles of French make, which have a longer range than the German gun.

"The 'Three Friends' effected a landing at a place called Bacunao, between Santiago de Cuba and Guanbanamo on May 30, at dawn. It took two and a half hours to send everything ashore; it took three hours more to hide it in a place of safety. Members of the expedition then started out in search of the Cuban forces, but none were found in the neighborhood until six days later.

"José Maceo and 2,000 men passed near the place and were notified of the landing Colonel Portuondo is a lawyer of Santiago de Cuba, who rose in arms last February. He was elected later Secretary of Foreign Relations and was afterward sent by the government on a mission to Washington. He has been successful in all his undertakings.

Some Incidents of the March.

"The day before we met José Maceo, 250 of his men met 102 Spaniards and fought them, killing twenty-five of their number and capturing twenty-six horses. On June 23, I went with 1,800 men of Maceo and Cebreco's commands to forage in the Spanish cultivated zone near the Santa Anna estate. The soldiers in the fort at this place fled from the Cubans when they approached. Not one shot was fired at us. We also visited a coffee plantation owned by a Frenchman named Benjamin Cagnet, who tried to be friendly toward us and render us some assistance.

"We encamped that night in the town of Cauto Abajo, which is now in ashes. On June 24th, St. John's Day, José Maceo's army had marched through the camp, where the following generals had

pitched their tents :—Agustin Cebreco, Periquito Perez, Serafin Sanchez, Matias Vegas and Higinio Vasquez. We started for Canasta
the next day, where a meeting was to take place between the Cuban
forces from the Western and Eastern departments. The place is on
the Cauto River, where there is plenty to eat and drink for men and
horses.

Successful Assault on a Gunboat.

"The condition of the roads was so bad on going to the meeting
place that many horses were left stuck in the mud and others died
from exhaustion. The mules are more suitable for the Cuban roads
in the rainy season. Maceo employed three hundred mules in transporting Portuondo's expedition. June 26 we reached Canasta, after
five hours' march from San Felipe, where we encamped last night.
Here we met Major General Jesus Rabi, with 1,700 men, cavalry and
infantry. He had been waiting for us one day. The following day
all the troops were formed on parade and the arms and ammunition
were distributed among them.

"General Rabi told me some interesting details about the capture
of the gunboat 'Belico' by General Rios. The Spanish gunboat was
steaming up the Cauto River, carrying provisions and ammunition for
the garrison in Bayamo. The Cubans in large numbers assaulted
the gunboat in the narrowest part of the river and wounded the commander in the breast. He surrendered, and the crew were made
prisoners. The captain was afterward released, and is now nursing
his wound in Bayamo.

"Rabi is a tall, well-built man, in complexion like an Arab. His
beard, like his hair, jet black. He is reputed as a brave and dashing
officer. He is liked by all who come in contact with him. He is a
veteran of the Ten Years' War, and is so kind in nature that all the
Spaniards who desert the Spanish ranks seek him. He has more
than five hundred Spaniards in his ranks. He rose in arms in February last with 300 men in his native place, Santa Rita, Santiago
province.

"On the same day he entered Jiguani and captured Baire, where his
ranks swelled to three thousand men. At Cacao he defeated the

Spaniards and captured 200 rifles and 115 prisoners.   The Spaniards say he was born in Spain.

"On June 28, 800 men from the eastern army were sent out to join the army which is to go as reinforcements to the western end of the Island.   The next day General Serafin Sanchez left for Las Villas with the reinforcements.   General Rabi went toward Tunas, where he will meet Calixto Garcia and Maximo Gomez, José Maceo, Periquito Perez, Matias Vegas and Higinio Vasquez.

"It is surprising to see so many lawyers, doctors, merchants, students and others, who a year ago were working at their offices, now turned into soldiers for the cause of freedom.   Early in the morning, June 30, we were informed that the enemy was coming toward us. Our men were aching for a fight, but no enemy made its appearance.

"Reveille was sounded at 3 A. M. on July 1, and camp was struck at once.   We marched all day until the afternoon, when we halted at a place called Curia, where we had our mess of plantains and yuca root. Our men captured at this place a Spanish courier bearing important dispatches.

Hurrying for Life to the Woods.

"We started after mess and halted for the night at a place known as El Hondon.   When I awoke on July 2 I found my leg was considerably swollen from a wound I inflicted on myself in jumping a barbed wire fence.   It had become inflamed in walking six miles in the scorching sun.   As I found it utterly impossible for me to move on I was ordered by General Maceo to remain at a prefect's house, on the road, where the inmates said they would look after me.   An officer of the general staff, however, was detailed to see that I was duly cared for.   The army surgeon, Porfirio Valiente, of General Maceo's staff, dressed my wound and I was left at the house of the prefect.   The Cuban forces continued on their march.

"Soon after they had gone a courier from the main body rushed into the house and directed me to run for safety into the woods near by, as a body of guerrillas would probably pass the place where I was and might do harm to me and the other inmates of the prefect's house, who were men unable to fight, and women.

"The prefect, an old man, at once sounded the alarm, and everybody in the neighborhood rushed for the nearest woods. While I was hiding my personal effects near the house, a volley from the approaching guerrilla band warned me to run for my life. At the same time that the Spaniards rushed toward the house a body of Cuban cavalry, which had been ordered to protect it, charged them from an opposite direction, and, as I had no time to lose on account of my disabled condition, I started for the woods, guided by a young girl, a daughter of the prefect, who took me by a narrow path in the woods to the rebel camp, where there were about thirty families.

"From the hiding-place we could hear the firing and even the voices of the combatants. Shortly afterward it began to rain copiously and the firing ceased. I spent the night in the woods.

The Spanish Troops Retreat.

"Early on July 3 I went to the prefect's house. Couriers had been sent in all directions searching for me. At the house I was told that the affair of the previous day had been only a skirmish; that the Spaniards had withdrawn as soon as they noticed there was resistance shown them. When they found that General Maceo was waiting to give them battle they changed their course and went to the town of Songo, which is fortified.

"Going over the ground where the fighting had taken place, the previous day, it was found that there were five dead horses, one belonging to an officer, who left his pearl-handled revolver by the horse's side. Pools of blood were seen all around, and the body of a dead Spanish soldier was found in the tall grass. The Spaniards' loss cannot be estimated, but, judging by the pools of blood, they had many dead and wounded. The Cubans lost Major José Ines Echevarria, and a sergeant killed and three privates wounded.

"General Maceo was in ambush three miles away from the place and had placed two rapid-fire guns in commanding positions, but the enemy changed front and evaded the encounter. He sent several detachments of his men after the Spaniards, who harassed their column as they retreated to Songo. On July 4, which marks American Independence, all was joy in camp at dawn and sadness at night. Maceo's forces, which kept hunting for the Spaniards, were informed while halting at the Triunfo estate, owned by an American—Mr. Whiting—that two Spanish columns were encamped at Loma del Gato, near the town of Cristo. Maceo at once ordered his men to move in that direction.

"When General Maceo reached the place the Spaniards were engaged in burning all the houses by the roadside. Maceo charged them with his own body guard and part of General Cebreco's cavalry. The Spanish cavalry fled before the Cuban horsemen's charge. The Spaniards then began to work two rapid-fire guns.

"Maceo's intentions were to carry the enemy's position by assault, and he charged several times, hewing down many of his opponents at each cavalry onslaught. During one of the charges Maceo, who was riding a superb white horse, was struck in the head by a bullet, which lodged in his brain. He was taken down from his horse by one of his aides, while the fight continued under the direction of General Cebreco.

Death of General José Maceo.

"Maceo was taken into the town of Ti Arriba, which was held by the Cubans. He died shortly afterward, without uttering a word. The General died as he often said he would like to die, fighting for Cuban freedom. General Periquito Perez was by the side of Maceo until the end. The Spaniards retired into the town of Cristo, carrying many wounded. The Spanish loss was undoubtedly heavy. The Cubans lost, beside General Maceo, three privates killed and twenty-four wounded.

"Maceo's death has exasperated his men so much that they are fretting to meet the Spaniards again to avenge their commander's fate. I learned that a fierce fight had taken place near Mayari some days ago. Generals Maximo Gomez and Calixto Garcia are coming toward us, and General Rabi would meet them. It was expected that, combining their forces, they will strike a heavy blow at some important place. The Spaniards tried to move this morning toward the point where we were encamped, but a section of cavalry from Las

Villas on their way to meet us met them, and, after a skirmish, drove them back to their fortified town."

Similar operations, involving skirmishes without decisive results, were carried on notwithstanding the rainy season and the outbreak of yellow fever. The insurgents continued to receive arms and ammunition from secret expeditions sent out from various parts of the United States. The Spanish Government more than intimated that our Government at Washington was not exercising all possible vigilance to prevent filibustering expeditions, which, it was maintained by our officials at Washington, was a groundless charge.

A great stir was caused at Madrid on October 17th, by the statement in a dispatch from Washington that President Cleveland intended to intervene in Cuba in a manner tantamount to the recognition of the independence of the insurgents. The *Imparcial*, a semi-official journal at Madrid, commenting on the report, declared that Spain ought to demand a full explanation of the Washington Government.

Anger in Madrid.

"She cannot brook such a threat over her head," continued the *Imparcial*, "even for a single day. By what right do the United States define the time for Spain to settle a question of her internal administration? It must be affirmed before the whole world that the American Government cannot impose any sort of terms upon us."

After denouncing the United States' "fictional neutrality," the *Imparcial* concluded as follows:

"The conduct of the United States will arouse general indignation. If Spain should remain alone in a conflict with the United States, Spaniards by their own efforts will know how to mark the difference between the noble defenders of their own property and the vile traffickers at Washington."

Such expressions were not calculated to cement more closely the bonds of peace between the two nations. The resolutions in the platforms of the Republican and Democratic parties expressing strong sympathy with the Cubans in their conflict, still further irritated the Spanish Government and pointed to a possible rupture between the two nations. Mr. Cleveland was plainly resolved to take no notice of the angry mutterings of thoughtless partizans. His policy was non-interference, equal justice to all and a peaceful attitude on the part of our Foreign Office. Such an attitude would be approved after the clamor of the hour had subsided.

With the election of Mr. McKinley fresh alarm was felt in Spain and new hope among the friends of Cuba. Would belligerent rights be granted to the insurgents? Would there be a formal and authoritative expression of the sympathy of the American people for the gallant patriots struggling for life and liberty against the tyranny and oppression of Spain? It was conceded to be more likely that active measures in behalf of Cuba would be adopted and vigorously enforced under the new administration. It was possible that Mr. McKinley would adopt a policy intended to secure to Cuba freedom and independence. Spain was stirred to a half desperation and the patriot army of Cuba nerved itself afresh for the sword and victory.

News from the Battle-field.

Under the most recent advices, a close observer of Cuban affairs makes the following statement of the situation:

" The Cubans can continue to use the ' fight-when-you-please ' tactics that have enabled them to carry the revolution through the 750 miles of narrow Cuba against Spanish masses, which, if not so large, were even better equipped with railroads, telephone and telegraph lines than are the Weyler hosts to-day.

" Spain has 200,000 troops in Cuba. Two-thirds of them are needed to guard the fortified towns and the trocha. The other third form General Weyler's army of operations, of 50,000 men, picked troops, guerrillas, regular cavalry, infantry and mountain artillery. This force cannot well be increased in numbers without large reinforcements from Spain, for to withdraw or to weaken a single garrison means the destroying of a town by the Cubans and the loss to Spain of a stronghold, a storehouse and a base of possible operations.

" The trocha garrisons might be brought into active service without weakening Spain's chances, but the ' trocha idea ' seems to fill such a large part of the Spanish military brain that it is not likely to be done. The Cuban leaders, too, may be relied upon to keep up a vast amount of demonstration near these alleged military 'strong' lines to foster the Spanish notion that 50,000 useless trocha soldiers are useful. Of Spain's 50,000 soldiers now available for active duty 30,000 are now being sent against Maceo's mountains in Eastern Pinar del Rio, just west of the Mariel (Weyler's) trocha. The other 20,000 are scattered.

Odds in Favor of the Insurgents.

"Weyler has taken the field. His forces are near the Rubi Mountains. He cannot hope to win, even should Maceo be killed, for then the Cuban army would merely split up, would be all the harder to catch and would occupy the province. The war would only last the longer. It is likely that Maceo will have an easy time of it shortly. Unless Weyler deserts his Eastern trocha or abandons many towns, he must move most of his force out of Pinar del Rio province, across the Mariel trocha and into East Central Cuba to use them against the westward movement in three columns of General Gomez, whose advance guard is already in Matanzas province.

"Even should Weyler abandon the eastern trocha, collect all his available scattered columns and immediately mass 80,000 men against Maceo, it is not at all likely that he would crush, or even corner and starve out the Cuban General, such are the wonderful strategic advantages of Cuba's Western wooded mountains. Weyler may even mass this number of men against Gomez. This move would seem equally unavailing, for last year he tried it without success with over 125,000 men and with railroads, telephones and telegraphs at his disposal.

"The Cuban farmers have stuck to their fields despite positive orders to leave them for Spain's fortified towns, and they have not even been intimidated by wholesale butcheries in stopping their all-important service to their brethren in arms."

GENERAL ANTONIO MACEO.

C LOSELY following the events narrated in the foregoing pages, came reports of the death of the renowned Cuban leader, General Antonio Maceo. The death of the brother of this famous chieftain has already been recorded. Each was a tower of strength to the cause of independence in Cuba, and with their death it was believed in Spanish circles that a fatal blow had been struck to the cause of the insurgents.

It is not surprising that there was great joy both in Havana and in Madrid when it was reported that Antonio Maceo had fallen on the field of battle. The report was, however, received with reserve, as this was the sixth time in which he had been reported killed. His ability to rise from death appeared to be like that of the fabled Phœnix, which sprang from its own ashes, and spread its wings with renewed youth and vigor. Soon the question agitated two continents, "Is Maceo really dead?" The public mind was in a state of uncertainty, and eagerly awaited confirmation or denial of the news.

In forty-eight hours it was stated by the representatives of the republic of Cuba, that Maceo had been foully assassinated, and circumstantial details were reported. It was affirmed that he had been lured into ambush under pretense of discussing with him terms of peace, and in open violation of the laws of civilized warfare, his flag of truce had been disregarded, and he had been slain by the foulest treachery. It was declared that the physician on his staff, Dr. Zertucha, was a prime mover in the intrigue that cost Maceo his life.

Conflicting Reports.

It was not long before reports came that the great leader was still alive, and although he had disappeared from the scene of his recent operations, he was still at the head of his troops, and was dealing sturdy blows at the forces of General Weyler. That he had lost his life seemed to be confirmed by a letter purporting to have been written by young Gomez, son of General Maximo Gomez, chief in command of the insurgents. The body of young Gomez was found with that of Maceo, and the letter stated that he had taken his own life rather than be separated from the slain body of his leader. Various documents were also said to have been found which proved that one of the bodies found was that of General Maceo. Still, many Cuban sympathizers throughout the country refused to believe he had met his death.

The following despatch, in detail confirmatory of his previous advices, was received by the Spanish Minister DeLome, at Washington, from the Spanish Minister of Foreign Affairs at Madrid:

"The insurgent leader, Antonio Maceo, realizing the impossibility of remaining in Pinar Del Rio Province, and being constantly pursued by Spanish columns, crossed the trocha on the 4th instant. He was at the head of over two thousand men, whom he had recruited from the local bands of the western part of the Province of Havana, when he was overtaken by Major Cirujeda's column, 350 men strong. Maceo's forces were routed, the leader being killed in the engagement, and Maximo Gomez's son committing suicide after being wounded.

"The corpses have been identified, and their clothing, arms, and the documents found in their possession were taken by the Spaniards. The remainder of the brave band dispersed in consequence of this brilliant victory of our troops."

Details of Maceo's Death.

This intelligence was supplemented by a trustworthy despatch from Havana, as follows:

"The confident claim of the Spanish officials that they have abundant proof of the death of Antonio Maceo and his young aide, Francisco Gomez, son of Maximo Gomez, continues. The details which are announced, however, of the facts relied upon for the identification of the two Cubans have caused an undercurrent of doubt in this city.

"Major Cirujeda, who commanded the Spanish forces in the engagement at Punta Brava, and whose troops discovered the two bodies and gave the evidence of identification, has consented to be interviewed on the circumstances of the case. He said to a news-paper correspondent that when the insurgents were routed it was evident that the body of the chief was abandoned on the field. The Spanish column, without stopping to explore the field, went in hot pursuit of the insurgents, and followed them for a mile or more. Meantime young Gomez is supposed to have committed suicide by Maceo's side. While the troops were returning to Guatao, after the pursuit had ceased, various guerrillas belonging to Major Cirujeda's command, went over the field where the rout of the insurgents had occurred, and searched the bodies remaining there for anything of importance.

" 'The body of Maceo,' Major Cirujeda continued, 'was relieved of a ring, clothing, etc. The guerrillas who performed the act were at the time quite unaware that the body was that of Maceo. In fact, little attention was paid to the identity of the bodies. It was already dark on the field, and it was raining also. Various other bodies were also searched.'

Indignities Offered to the Slain.

" It was an adjutant, according to Major Cirujeda's further statement, who insisted that the above-mentioned body and the other, which was lying by its side, were evidently of importance, and that they must not be left thus without identification. 'The two bodies were, therefore, tied by the feet to the tails of some horses,' Major Cirujeda went on to relate, 'and thus dragged over the ground, the intention being to carry them to town for identification. But, after proceeding for a while, the horses became tired with their burden, and the bodies were therefore cut loose and left in the road.'

" When the troops reached Guatao Major Cirujeda proceeded to read the documents which had been found upon the bodies. They included a letter addressed to ' Dear Panchot,' and signed M. Gomez, a diary of Maceo's operations from November 28 to December 7 and a note in pencil, found on the body of the younger man, saying he died rather than abandon the body of his general.

" The undershirt and socks on the body of the elder man were marked with the initials ' A. M.,' and a ring on the finger contained the engraved inscription, ' Antonio y Maria.' After reading these documents Major Cirujeda says he became convinced that the bodies which the troops had abandoned were those of Antonio Maceo and the young Gomez. But it was then too late to return and recover them. Major Cirujeda, however, expresses the firm conviction that they were those of Maceo and Gomez's son.

"With the insurgents in the battle, Major Cirujeda says, was a beautiful Amazon about 22 years of age, who urged the rebels 'a la machete,' but at the same time interposed to prevent the killing of the prisoners. Major Cirujeda has taken charge of the objects found on the body said to be that of Maceo for further examination. There were a gold watch, a splendid pair of cuff buttons made by Moreau Torin, Paris, with five-pointed stars on them and enclosed in a big strapped leather case, a hunting knife with an ebony handle and gold mounted, and a good waterproof coat. All of these were taken from the body by the scout Santa Ana. It is thus seen that there has been no actual identification of the bodies themselves, the conviction as to identity resting upon the evidence of documents and articles found upon them.

A Most Striking Character.

"There is no doubt, however, of the assurance of the general public here that Maceo is dead. It is pointed out that he met his death in a manner similar to that of José Marti and Zyas. His loss is considered as the heaviest blow the revolution has received, and it is felt that his continued life was all that could save the insurgent movement. He was the most striking personal character of the outbreak.

"Major Cirujeda telegraphed to headquarters that after the battle at Punta Brava he had been obliged to abandon the bodies which in the course of a reconnoissance his troops had discovered to be the bodies of Maceo and Francisco Gomez. The guide of the column said that the body looked like Maceo. Some one standing by observed that Maceo was in Pinar del Rio, but it is nevertheless believed that the bodies were those of the Cuban leaders. The bugler of the battalion of San Quentin was taking away from the fallen Cuban a ring, when he found that he was still alive. He thereupon killed him with the machete. The insurgents, upon noting the small force of the reconnoitering party, rushed in with a large number on the troops and succeeded in carrying away the body said to be Maceo's, but without securing any of the jewels and papers which had been found upon it.

"Major Cirujeda, in order not to abandon his dead and wounded, was compelled to retreat to Punta Brava. At Punta Brava the soldiers delivered the jewels and documents which they had found with the two bodies and then the chief of the column became convinced of the death of Maceo."

Following is a copy of the letter written in pencil which was found on the body of the youth supposed to be Francisco Gomez:

"Dear Mamma, Papa, Dear Brothers: I die at my post. I did not want to abandon the body of General Maceo, and I stayed with him. I was wounded in two places, and as I did not fall into the hands of the enemy I have killed myself. I am dying. I die pleased at being in the defense of the Cuban cause. I wait for you in the other world.   Your son,   "FRANCISCO GOMEZ.

"Torro in San Domingo."

("Friends or foes, please transmit to its destination, as requested by one dead.")

Ovation to General Weyler.

General Weyler, who was absent from Havana when Maceo's death was reported, immediately returned, arriving at half-past five in the afternoon. He rode into the city on horseback, accompanied by two squadrons of cavalry. His coming had been made known to the public, and large crowds gathered to welcome him. He was given a popular ovation from the time he reached the city limits until he arrived at the Palace. At some places along his route girls strewed flowers in his pathway, and he was in other ways treated as a popular hero.

Calle Obispo, Calle O'Reilly, the other streets in the vicinity of the Palace, and the Plaza de Armas were jammed with people, who enthusiastically cheered the Captain-General as he rode along. When he arrived near the Palace the enthusiastic crowd surrounded him, despite the military, and he was compelled to stop his horse in order not to ride down his admirers, who greeted him with all manner of loyal cries. A passage-way was finally opened, and General Weyler proceeded to the Palace. Shortly after he had entered the building he appeared upon a balcony, and was greeted with the most tumultuous cheering.

Rejoicings at Havana.

The city at night presented a most animated aspect, reflecting the joy felt by the Spaniards because of Maceo's death and General Weyler's triumph over the insurgents in the western province. Casa Blanca, the little village under the walls of the Cabala fortress, and Regla, on the southern side of the bay, held little demonstrations of their own in honor of the victorious return of General Weyler.

Further details of General Maceo's untimely death were soon after received, and were as follows:

Dr. Maximo Zertucha, formerly the physician of Antonio Maceo, the second in command of the insurgent forces, who, after the death of Maceo, surrendered to General Tort, at San Felipe, was interviewed by a reporter of *La Lucha*, one of the leading newspapers of Havana. Dr. Zertucha said that Maceo intended to attempt to cross the trocha on December 3, but was prevented by sickness from doing so. On the next day, however, it was announced that he would not march across the trocha with his men, but would go by water around the end of the trocha and meet an insurgent force on the Havana side of the line. Two boats were accordingly prepared, they being painted black in order to prevent their being seen, and the oars were muffled so they could not be heard while playing in the row-locks. At night Maceo and twenty-six men embarked in the boats, and passed in front of the town of Mariel, at the northern extremity of the western trocha, without being seen by any of the Spanish sentries thereabouts. The insurgent leader, Miro, and several other commanders, accompanied Maceo. The short voyage was accomplished without the slightest mishap, and the insurgent party landed at the point selected without being discovered.

When, on December 4, the engagement took place between the insurgents and Major Cirujeda's command, Maceo was encamped with 2,000 men. When the Spanish force appeared, Maceo divided his men into two wings, his intention being to surround the Spanish column. He remained alone with his staff for a moment, watching the fighting, and exclaimed, " This goes well."

Shortly afterwards he was hit by two bullets, one striking him on the chin, breaking his jaw and passing out at the junction of the neck and shoulder, and the other striking him in the abdomen. Either wound would have caused death, and the insurgent leader expired in a short time.

Maceo's Body Recovered.

The insurgents who were fighting desperately against the Spanish attack, were panic-stricken when they heard of the death of their chief. They fled in disorder, not making any attempt then to take Maceo's body with them. The Spaniards then returned to Punta Brava with their dead and wounded. When the field was clear some of the insurgents returned and carried Maceo's body off with them. Dr. Zertucha said that he did not know where the remains were buried, and thus far the search made by the Spaniards has proved fruitless.

From other accounts it appears that Maceo and his staff were encamped in the hills and expecting the arrival of Cuban reinforcements, under Brigadier-General Sanchez and others, ordered by General Aguirre to receive and escort the noted Pinar del Rio chief to the east. Major Cirujeda was totally ignorant of Maceo's presence in the district, believing him to be still west of the trocha. But learning that a Spanish fort on the San Pedro had been fired upon that morning by insurgents, he started out on a reconnoitering tour at the head of a remnant of the San Quentin battalion, accompanied by a force of local guerrillas under Captain Peral. The latter's men were dressed in a manner very similar to that of the insurgent troops, and they marched in the vanguard of the Spanish column.

Mistaking these for Sanchez's vanguard, challenges having been made and countersigns given satisfactorily, Maceo, surrounded by members of his staff and a handful of followers, advanced with all confidence to meet his friends, when the guerrillas received them with a rifle volley. Maceo fell at the first fire, his men, temporarily disconcerted with surprise, retiring by the flanks. Young Gomez, though he had been previously wounded at the trocha and still had his arm in a sling, assisted, as the engagement became general, in dragging his chief to a place of temporary safety on the grass, and remained by his side until, realizing that they had been abandoned, Gomez wrote the note to his parents, which has been previously referred to, and then committed suicide by shooting himself with a revolver.

"I Die for Cuba and Independence."

After the fight the Spanish scout, Santa Ana, accompanied by the bugler of the San Quentin battalion, while reconnoitering the field in quest of documents and other objects of importance or value, ran upon the body of Maceo, who was still alive. As the bugler pulled the ring from his finger, Maceo asked in an agonized tone if they were Spaniards or Cubans.

"Spaniards," said the bugler, and he raised his machete as the dying chief said: "I die for Cuba and independence."

As the knife came down, almost severing the victim's head from his body, the scout, interposing, remarked: "That man resembles Maceo." "Impossible," responded the bugler. "Maceo is in Pinar del Rio."

The scout insisted that at least it was a chief of some importance, and, tying the body by the feet to his horse's tail, he proceeded. Meanwhile, the insurgents, learning that their chief's body was in Spanish hands, and being evidently reinforced, rallied and made a new attack and succeeded in recovering the body. The Spanish officers, unaware of its importance, cut it loose as an unnecessary impediment

It thus seems that Major Cirujeda did not know that his forces had encountered and killed Maceo till after reaching Guatao at nightfall and reading the documents, etc. The full statements of Dr. Zertucha were not allowed to be telegraphed even to Madrid.

General Antonio Maceo.

BY GONZALO DE QUESADA,

Charge D'Affaires of the Republic of Cuba.

THERE is one dark day that will be forever remembered by the Cubans. On that day fell General Antonio Maceo. The life of this hero was cut short by treachery in the moments in which he was to astonish the world by a most brilliant blow to Spanish domination—an attack on the suburbs of Havana.

Antonio Maceo was the son of Mariana Grajales, who will go to posterity for having given fourteen children to the cause of liberty. His father was Marcos Maceo, a cattle-driver. He was born in Santiago de Cuba on the 14th of Juiy, 1848, the anniversary of the fall of the Bastile. When the revolution of Yara broke out Antonio was a stalwart youth, who had followed his father's occupation, and revealed already the qualities which afterwards made him famous— sagacity and fearlessness. Some days after the outbreak, Marcos assembled his children. His house had been burned; his family had been ill-treated by the Spaniards; his native land was in arms against the tyrant. His own children and his step-sons took the oath of fighting to the last for Cuba's independence, and not one failed to keep the word!

In the first engagement Antonio, a private, so distinguished himself in the front rank of the patriots that General Donato Marniol congratulated him. Without ever enjoying a furlough, without having been reprimanded, without any favoritism, he rose by sheer merit to the highest rank in the Army of the Republic. His twenty-four scars and three bullets in his body were the best testimonies of his invaluable services to his country. He fought those ten years like a lion. His deeds read like a novel or the feats of some superhuman being. The bullets seemed to caress him, but never to wish him much harm.

When the treaty of El Zanjon was signed, while the Cubans were being duped by Spanish promises of reforms, General Antonio Maceo remained firm, with some hundreds of his loyal followers. The battalion of San Quintin—curiously enough the one which twenty years after killed him—was decimated in two days of constant firing. The Spaniards reported that when Maceo charged he would cry out to the Spanish officers: "This is the way the brave of San Ulpiano surrender!"

Defied the Forces of Spain.

All efforts to induce him to capitulate were useless. He protested at the famous Baragua against the compact entered into; he fought four months alone against all the forces of Spain, in the midst of his indifferent compatriots. The Spanish commander attempted to propose money to him. Maceo answered to the Spanish Brigadier-General Fuenks: "You take advantage of the distance and the slight acquaintance there exists between us to offend my honor in a way I shall never forget. Do the Spanish believe that men who fight for a principle and military glory, who respect their reputation and honor, can sell themselves when they have the hope yet of saving their principles, or to die in the attempt without degrading themselves? No; men who, like me, fight for the sacred cause of liberty will break their weapons when they are impotent to win before degrading themselves."

And when, finally, he left for Jamaica to see if he could obtain new means for the war, with his faithful companion, General Ruis Rivera, a man of the same temper, he wrote: "I did not submit to the treaty nor to the terrible situation. I left because my friends deceived me with a commission, when, in reality, they wished to save my life."

Maceo, during the peace, traveled in several South American countries; in Honduras he held an important government position; in Costa Rica he devoted himself to the establishment of a tobacco colony, aided by the government. During these years he studied languages, tactics, strategy, and was a devourer of the best literature; but never for one moment did he give up his ideal, not even when he enjoyed the blessings of the happiest of companionship with his wife, the virtuous and patriotic Maria Cabral.

In 1884, with General Gomez, he tried to renew the war, but the country was not ready yet; in 1890 he went to Havana and Santiago de Cuba, and was preparing to rebel, when he was banished. He then returned to Central America, where, in July, 1893, Marti conferred with him. Maceo commenced immediately to prepare for the coming revolution. The following year the Spaniards tried to assassinate him in San Jose, Costa Rica. On leaving the theatre the Cubans and Spaniards clashed; General Maceo was assisting a lady who had fainted; a treacherous Spaniard fired his revolver at the general's back, and the bullet he then received he carried with him to the day of his death.

On the 31st day of March, 1895, he landed at Duaba, on the northern coast of Baracoa, with a few followers. As soon as he met people he sent a despatch to the Spanish commander: "Maceo is here." The Spanish troops were defeated in the first engagement, but they sent thousands after him; they thought they had him caught; he was reported killed and buried. Finally, after a series of hardships, and suffering enough to discourage any other mortal, he joined the nucleus of the Cuban army; two weeks afterwards his presence alone in the Island had increased the army in the Eastern Department to seven thousand men; when Marti and Gomez met him they were organized and ready for ten years of war, if necessary.

His Brilliant Victories.

The story of his exploits during this Revolution are current history: ne fought Marshal Martinez Campos at Peralejos, inflicting a tremendous defeat on the Spaniards, in which General Santosceldes was killed; he was General Gomez's coadjutor in the great invasion of the Western provinces, defeating Martinez Campos again at Coliseo, Generals Cornell, Lugue, Echague, and whipping Colonel Deods to the sea.

After reaching the westernmost part of the Island, Mantua, he returned to the provinces of Havana and Matanzas. General Weyler, having proclaimed the pacification of Havana and Pinar del Rio in order to influence the action of both houses at Washington, General Maceo retraced his steps and again entered Pinar del Rio. Then he became the central figure of the revolution; the eyes of the world were all fixed on this giant, who defied the whole power of Spain and her best generals with a few thousands of patriots; the military trocha constructed to keep him from returning to Havana, killed as many thousands of Spanish soldiers as the total of Maceo's army; every time a Spanish column dared attack him it was destroyed, leaving hundreds of arms in Maceo's possession.

A Victim of Treason.

Finally, Weyler decided to take the field against him, but Weyler returned to Havana without finding the astute Cuban, who would not give battle except when he was sure of victory. The clamor of Spain and the requests of her ministers forced Weyler to again go in his quest. Maceo, who had thoroughly organized his forces in the provinces, and had under him General Ruis Rivera, in whom he absolutely confided, resolved to discredit General Weyler completely; he would cross the so-called impenetrable trocha, would appear in Havana, burn the outskirts, and then join General Gomez for the winter campaign. General Weyler would be looking for him among the hills, and the authorities at Madrid would say that Maceo had burned Mariana.

He crossed the line on the 4th of December; on the 5th he celebrated the event, on the 6th and 7th he was joined by Cuban forces of Havana province, about four hundred in number. As yet the Spaniards were not aware of his crossing; here the work of treason commenced; to all appearances the man in whom he had entire confidence, his physician, Dr. Zertucha, communicated to the Spaniards the news and details of where General Maceo would be; in those days desertions had occurred from the Spanish ranks; it was easy to simulate a Cuban force with Spanish regulars.

General Maceo was marching with his men on the 7th, when they met Major Cirujeda with six hundred of the San Quintin regiment, famous for its killing of *pacificos;* at first General Maceo took them to be Cubans; soon was the error discovered. A fierce battle followed, General Maceo commanding the centre; the outlook was so bright that General Maceo exclaimed, " This goes well." To decide the engagement, he charged, his machete on high, at the head of his staff, as he had done a hundred times before. Fifty paces from the enemy a terrific volley laid him low, with the valiant Francisco Gomez, the son of the general-in-chief. Only General Miró escaped, wounded.

The Spaniards, defeated, were forced to retreat to Punta Brava; the Cubans recovered the body, which they secretly buried. This is the story from the best sources in the absence of official reports. Thus died the wonderful mulatto, the most illustrious, perhaps, of his race, superior to Toussaint L'Ouverture. His public life was consecrated to liberty; he knew no vice or mean action; he would not permit any around him. When he landed, he was told there were no arms. " I will get them with my machete," he answered, and he left 5,000 to his country, conquered by the power of his arm.

He was modest: when some young flatterer told him: " You are by right the general-in-chief, because you were the last to surrender in the last war," he replied, " My sword can never compare with that of General Máximo Gomez." He was a man of lofty ideal: when the Spanish press propagated the calumny that he was aiming at a colored republic, he sent me word to then and always assert over my signature that: " General Maceo is neither black nor white; he is a Cuban." That is the man, a Cuban, and for that reason it is fitting that General Miró should have saturated his handkerchief with the blood of the patriot, so that he could show it to his countrymen as the symbol of sacrifice, and that it may serve to keep them alive to their duty of dying like the hero, Antonio Maceo, who never surrendered to the Spanish tyrant !

GENERAL WEYLER'S TROCHA ACROSS THE ISLAND OF CUBA.

574

Description of the Famous Trocha—Inhuman Treat ment of American Citizens—Consul-General Lee's Prompt and Resolute Action.

THE peculiar methods of warfare adopted by the Cuban insurgents led General Weyler to construct his famous barricade, known as the trocha. It has not been the plan of the Cuban army ever to risk a great battle against the immense army of Spain, for the reason that they were much fewer in number, and for a long time were but poorly equipped with arms and ammunition. Still, with their cavalry and scattered bands, they were able to occupy a large part of the Island, and even to threaten the city of Havana. General Weyler's plan was to construct a trocha, extending from a point on the North coast to the Southern coast, thus dividing a small part of the Island from the remainder. The Western section, known as the Province of Pinar del Rio, could then, it was thought, be pacified, and the insurgents driven out. It would be impossible for them to pass the trocha, and they could be pursued and captured. The reader will be interested in a description of this formidable barricade.

The trocha is a cleared space, 150 to 200 yards wide, which stretches through what is apparently an impassable jungle for 50 miles. The trees, which have been cut down in clearing this passageway, have been piled up at each side of the cleared space and laid in parallel rows, forming a barrier of tree trunks and roots and branches higher than a man's head. It would take a man some time to pick his way over these barriers, and a horse could no more do it than it could cross a jam of floating logs in a river. The object was to make the obstacles insurmountable to the insurgent cavalry, and to armed bodies of infantry, presenting an effectual check upon the transportation of artillery, and in fact upon all their offensive movements.

Between the fallen trees lies the single track of the military railroad, and on one side of that are the line of forts, and a few feet beyond them a maze of barbed wire. Beyond the barbed wire again is the other barrier of fallen trees, and the jungle. In its unfinished state, this is not an insurmountable barricade. Gomez crossed it by daylight with 600 men, and with but the loss of 27 killed, and as many wounded. Where it has been completed, it is almost impossible to cross it, except at the sacrifice of a great loss of life.

Three Styles of Forts.

The forts are of three kinds. They are best described as the forts, the block-houses and the little forts. A big fort consists of two stories, with a cellar below, and a watch-tower above. It is made of stone and adobe, and it is painted a glaring white. One of these is placed at intervals of every half mile along the trocha, and on a clear day the sentry in the watch-tower of each can see the three forts on his either side.

Midway between the big forts, at a distance of a quarter of a mile from each, is a block-house of two stories, with the upper story of wood, overhanging the lower foundation of mud. These are placed at right angles to the railroad, instead of facing it, as do the forts.

Between each block-house and each fort are three little forts of mud and planks, surrounded by a ditch. They look something like a farmer's ice-house, as we see them at home, and they are about as hot inside as the other is cold. They hold five men, and are within hailing distance of one another. Back of them are three rows of stout wooden stakes, with barbed wire stretching from one row to the other, interlacing and crossing and running in and out above and below, like an intricate cats' cradle of wire.

A Barbed-Wire Barricade.

One can judge how closely knit it is by the fact that to every twelve yards of posts there are 450 yards of barbed fencing. The forts are most completely equipped in their way, and twelve men in the jungle would find it quite easy to keep twelve men securely imprisoned in one of them for an indefinite length of time.

The walls are about twelve feet high with a cellar below and a vault above the cellar. The roof of the vault forms a platform, around which the four walls rise to the height of a man's shoulder. There are loopholes for rifles in the sides of the vault and where the platform joins the walls. These latter allow the men in the fort to fire down almost directly upon the head of any one who might rush up close to the wall of the fort, and where, without these holes in the floor, it would be impossible to fire on him except by leaning far over the rampart.

Above the platform is an iron or zinc roof, supported by iron pillars, and in the centre of this is the watch-tower. The only approach to the fort is by a movable ladder, which hangs over the side like the gangway of a ship of war and which can be raised by those on the inside by means of a rope suspended over a wheel in the roof. The opening in the wall at the head of the ladder is closed at the time of an attack by an iron platform, to which the ladder leads, and which also can be raised by a pulley. The Spanish hope to have calcium lights in the watch-towers of the forts with sufficient power to throw a search-light over a quarter of a mile, or to the next block-house, and so light the trocha by night as well as day. With their immense army it would not be difficult to do this.

Bomb Death Traps.

As a further protection against the insurgents the Spaniards have distributed a number of bombs along the trocha. These are placed at those points in the trocha where the jungle is less thickly grown, and where the insurgents might be expected to pass. Each bomb is fitted with an explosive cap, and five or six wires are attached to this and staked down on the ground. Any one stumbling over one of these wires explodes the bomb and throws a charge of broken iron to a distance of fifty feet. This, in brief, was General Weyler's scheme for preventing the insurgents roaming at will from one end of the Island to the other, but to make the plan effective he would have to construct several trochas, which would be an almost impossible task. The length of time required for constructing the trocha, and

37

the necessity of watching it at every point, has led military officers to doubt whether the barricade does not cost more than it is worth.

Outrages Upon American Citizens.

Much excitement was caused throughout the United States by Weyler's imprisonment of American citizens, alleging that they were giving aid and encouragement to the Cuban forces. One of the prisoners, whose case excited universal interest, was Dr. Ricardo Ruiz, who, it was reported, had been murdered in a dungeon at Guanabacoa. He was for five years a resident of Philadelphia, having come from Cuba in 1875, at the time when the former war was rendering the Island a place almost uninhabitable, bringing with him letters of introduction from well-known parties in Cuba. He studied dentistry, and in 1878 obtained a diploma from the Pennsylvania College of Dental Surgery. After having practiced his profession for two years he returned to Cuba, but previous to this, after five years' residence in the United States, he secured naturalization papers and became an American citizen. He settled in Guanabacoa as a dentist, and married a lady to whom he had been engaged before leaving the Island. All accounts go to show that he was a man of peaceable disposition.

He was arrested and confined in prison on suspicion of sympathizing with the insurgents, where he remained two years, when his death was reported. It was claimed by his friends that he had died from violence, and that his imprisonment was illegal, as he had never had an impartial trial. These reports created indignation in the United States, which the Spanish authorities endeavored to allay by affirming that an examination after death showed that Dr. Ruiz died from natural causes.

The Case of Julio Sanguilly.

Almost immediately came a report that another American citizen had been sentenced to imprisonment for life, and that, too, in direct violation of our treaty with Spain, which has been in operation for a hundred years, and therefore has all the sanction of time-honored precedent. This treaty specifies the tribunal before which a person charged with treason shall be tried, and it was maintained that the provisions of the compact had been unjustly set aside through the operation of martial law, by which General Weyler was attempting to govern Cuba.

The Committee on Foreign Relations in the United States Senate passed a resolution demanding the immediate release of Julio Sanguilly, who had been sentenced to life imprisonment. Hot words were uttered on the floor of the Senate, and much bitter feeling was engendered in the debate which followed the introduction of the resolution. Notwithstanding the request from the State Department to suspend action in the case for a few days, the Senators took the question in their own hands and proceeded to act. A multitude of eager listeners were present.

The United States Humiliated.

Senator Daniel, of Virginia, took the floor in behalf of the adoption of the resolution. He said: "Two years ago yesterday Julio Sanguilly, an American citizen, was thrown into prison. Two years have gone by, and this government has done practically nothing for this citizen. Great Britain would have released him as soon as one of her battleships could reach Havana. He has been brutally treated and condemned on unsworn testimony before military tribunals. This country and all civilization have been disgraced by the treatment meted out to this unfortunate man. Every citizen of this country would have patriotically applauded the President if he had sent a fleet of American battleships and compelled the release of this American citizen, whose country has been insulted by the treatment accorded to him and to our representative in Cuba."

Senator Gray, of Delaware, said he was informed that Sanguilly's counsel had withdrawn his appeal to Madrid in order to facilitate his release. Thereupon, with increased force and manifestly increased anger, Senator Daniel said: " If that is true, it is a humiliation to the United States that one of her citizens has been compelled by sickness and poverty, and delay on the part of this government, to withdraw his appeal for justice, in order to secure his release from prison. It means that he has concluded that the United States has abandoned her citizen, her legal child, and that he despairs of justice. His appeal should not be withdrawn. The people of this country should compel his unconditional release."

It was at this point that Senator Frye, of Maine, electrified the Senate by saying: " If Sanguilly's counsel has withdrawn the appeal of his client, he has done an unjust act which is inexcusable. For, by that withdrawal, he leaves Sanguilly a convicted criminal, liable to imprisonment for life, and surrenders for Sanguilly and for his family all claims for damages against Spain. He surrenders all that Spain has contended for. Here, we are contending that Sanguilly has been unjustly treated, and that all international law has been violated in his case, when his discouraged counsel withdraws his appeal for justice. If I had my way, a ship of war would start immediately to Havana and deliver him."

The outbreak in the galleries was such as has not been paralleled in years. They were filled with Daughters of the American Revolution, and they would not be quieted. Messengers and doorkeepers warned them, and finally had to force some of them into their seats that order might be restored. Their strong sympathy for Cuba was much in evidence.

News of Sanguilly's Release.

Later in the day it was announced that the government at Madrid, concluding that discretion was sometimes better than valor, had ordered General Weyler to release Sanguilly. This had a tendency to somewhat allay the excitement, yet a very uneasy feeling and excited state of the public mind was apparent, which a breath might inflame into a wild burst of indignation.

General Sanguilly soon arrived at Key West. He was made a cripple by the former war, and he now appeared to be in an enfeebled condition. Before he descended the gang-plank he was lifted up on the shoulders of friends and conveyed to a carriage. In reply to a request for a speech, he said he was too fatigued after a rough sea voyage, but thanked his countrymen for the hearty welcome accorded, which he did not take for himself, but, he said, as an evidence of the loyalty to the cause dear to the heart of every Cuban.

On March 1st the President transmitted to Congress important dispatches from Consul-General Lee, including telegrams relating to the case of Charles Scott. These awakened unusual interest in the Senate.

On February 20th Mr. Lee telegraphed as follows to the State Department: "Charles Scott, a citizen of the United States, arrested at Regla. No charge given. He has been without communication in jail at Havana 264 hours. I cannot stand another Ruiz murder, and have demanded his release. How many war vessels at Key West or within reach, and will they be ordered here at once if necessary to sustain demand?"

General Lee Threatens to Leave Havana.

On the 23d General Lee said in a cable message: "Situation simple. Experience at Guanabacoa made it my duty to demand, before too late, that another American who has been incommunicado (without communication with friends) 264 hours, be released from said incommunicado, and did so in courteous terms. If you support it and Scott is so released, the trouble will terminate. If you do not I must depart. All others arrested with Scott have been put in communication. Why should the only American in the lot not be? He has been incommunicado now 338 hours."

Later on the same day, the 23d Feb., Mr. Lee wired: "Demand complied with. Scott released from incommunicado to-day, on demand, after fourteen days' solitary confinement in cell five feet by eleven, damp, water on bottom of cell. Not allowed anything to sleep on or chair. Was charged with having Cuban postage stamps in the house. Scott says he went always twelve hours without water; once two days. He was employee of the American Gas Company."

General Lee's determination to see that every American citizen in Cuba should have his rights fully protected, met with a hearty response from all classes of the American people.

General Weyler's Career.

General Valeriano Weyler was appointed Captain-General of Cuba to succeed General Martinez Campos in January, 1896. He arrived in Havana February 10th, and took the oath of office the following day. In November he took the field against Maceo. He learned that General Maceo was in the western part of Pinar del Rio. Spanish journals were quite certain that the Cuban leader was in a trap from which escape was impossible. General Weyler marched his troops into the province to entrap Maceo. Other forces were concentrated in the vicinity of the military line of Mariel and the Batabano Railroad. The Spanish general, however, paid no attention to Gomez, the rebel commander-in-chief, who was in the province of Havana.

Ten desperate engagements were fought in the space of fifteen days after the actual beginning of the campaign, and in none did the Spanish gain an advantage. After the battle of Neuva Empressa the Cuban leader had little difficulty in moving his men wherever he desired. The Spaniards were left in the rear, and Maceo again entered Havana province, crossing in his route the western trocha near Quivicar. This crossing was made in full view of a large Spanish column stationed there to intercept Maceo.

After a succession of operations in which General Weyler was not successful in pacifying the western provinces, the rainy season stopped further progress in the work of conquering the rebellion. Then began on the part of the Spanish Government a wonderful movement of reinforcements to the Spanish coast, and as soon as a propitious season arrived these were despatched across the ocean to Cuba.

With the troops already in the field in the Island the force at General Weyler's command at the opening of the fall campaign of 1896-7 was not short of two hundred thousand men. Then General Weyler decided to take the field in person. It was said at the time that he had been ordered to do so by the Spanish Government. This, however, was denied. General Weyler proceded toward the mountainous region of Pinar del Rio. He made his headquarters near the line of the main railway from Havana to Pinar del Rio city.

Thence he sent out columns to search for the rebels, but he was not successful in finding them in force, nor did he fight any decisive engagement.

While he was in the west Maceo met his death at the hands of Spanish troops under Major Cirujada. When General Weyler finally gave up active operations and seated himself in the palace at Havana he announced that Pinar del Rio was practically free from rebel bands It was officially announced by General Weyler on January 11, that three provinces were practically pacified, and then, by a seeming paradox, he took the field again on January 19. The bulletins issued from the Palace announced sweeping victories for the Spanish in Matanzas and the other provinces which he had declared pacified, showing that the insurgents there were still active.

The last personal campaign, like the first, was one of destruction, and the torch played an important part. When the Captain-General left Havana, he did so with the avowed intention of meeting General Gomez in Matanzas, but there was no engagement of consequence. Gomez eluded the Spanish forces, which outnumbered his own by several thousand, and there were only a few skirmishes. In all of these the officials in the Palace in Havana claimed victories for Spain, with heavy losses to the insurgents.

General Ruis Rivera.

This veteran, who succeeded General Antonio Maceo in the command of the Cuban forces in the province of Pinar del Rio, was born in Puerto Rico in 1847. General Rivera is the son of a wealthy Spanish family; his father was a Spanish colonel. Young Rivera was sent to Spain to be educated as a lawyer. When the revolution of 1868 broke out, he was studying law in Barcelona; he gave up his college career and sailed for Cuba.

Rivera fought valiantly; he displayed at the head of his troops remarkable ability. When the ten years were ended, in 1878, he stood out with Maceo in his refusal to accept the terms of the treaty. He left the Island without surrendering, and before going he handed his machete to Col. Figueredo, his faithful friend, with this injunction:

" This is my true weapon. If I ever return to Cuba to fight for her freedom, you shall return it to me. If you ever fight with it, and are forced to surrender or leave the fields of Cuba, break it in twain and bury it. Let it never fall into the hands of the enemy."

Rivera saw the war renewed sixteen years after; as soon as he was called to his post he left Honduras, where he was prosperous in business; he took an expedition to Maceo, which materially strengthened the patriots in the west. His long experience and his splendid qualifications have made him conspicuous. He is a man of great personal magnetism, and a natural successor to his life-long companion, General Antonio Maceo.

The Brave General Captured.

It was the fate of General Rivera soon to be captured, the story of which is dramatic. General Hernandez Velasco left San Cristobal under secret orders at noon March 18th, with the Castillo Reina battalion and two field pieces and pitched his camp amid the Brujito Hills. The insurgents attacked the regulars from the very outset of the advance. The Spanish column marched upon Perico Pozo, where General Ruiz Rivera awaited them in a strongly entrenched position. The result of the engagement that ensued was the defeat of the insurgents and the capture of General Rivera.

Rivera opened fire immediately on seeing the head of the column. Colonel Jose Roco advanced with the extreme vanguard, Major Sanchez Bernal leading another division under the protection of artillery, which shelled the trenches held by Rivera, who was already wounded in the thigh.

One company of the cavalry galloped forward, capturing the trenches and seizing as prisoners five men who lay severely mutilated by the shells. Colonel Bacallao, on learning that Rivera had been wounded, hurried to the trenches and begged the soldiers not to kill him. Rivera and Colonel Bacallao were taken into the presence of General Velasco, who shook hands with Rivera and introduced him to the officers of his staff, giving instructions that the first thing to be done was to give him surgical relief. Lieutenant Terry and

Colonel Bacallao were also wounded in a fight at the same place on March 15th.

The Castillo battalion secured important documents as well as the arms and money of General Ruiz Rivera. The money consisted mostly of American gold coin. A number of splendid watches were left with General Velasco. The villagers of San Cristobal, who went out to receive the small column of Spanish troops, enthusiastically cheered the victors.

He was Accorded the Honors of War.

General Rivera, who remained quietly in prison, eulogized the escort of Spanish soldiers. He said the troops treated him with the greatest consideration. He also said the families of the insurgents in the camp of the Cubans were in a critical situation. They suffered greatly from hunger, and were compelled to go out in search of vegetables whenever it was possible to avoid the Spanish troops. The insurgents were well supplied with meat, but had no spices.

General Rivera would say nothing concerning the war or Cuban political matters. When asked his name by General Velasco, Rivera replied, and made the following request:

"Give me the honors of war and stretch out to me your hand."

Rivera afterward conversed with some of the chief officers, and offered them tips for services rendered. Velasco, noticing this, said: "Soldiers need not money, but honor, which they have."

One of the shells exploded in the insurgent camp, wounding many members of Rivera's staff. Rivera himself received a Mauser ball, which caused three serious wounds in the thigh. The moment the Spanish infantry entered the trenches Colonel Bacallao raised General Rivera on his shoulders as if to carry him off. After his capture General Rivera, speaking of the Spanish soldiery, said: "They have treated me very carefully." He complained much of the pain of his wounds.

Captain-General Weyler received the news of Rivera's capture at Cienfuegos, where the intelligence was loudly cheered. The Captain-General was described as "satisfied" with the result, and received cablegrams of congratulations from the Spanish Minister of War and the Spanish Premier, who congratulated him in the name of the Queen of Spain. Lieutenant Henry Terry died from his wounds. He was a naturalized American.

President McKinley on the Cuban Situation.

The long-standing case of Cuba again came to the front in the United States Senate on May 17. President McKinley gave the first indication of his policy by a special message asking Congress to appropriate $50,000 for the relief of suffering Americans in Cuba. The President's message read thus :

" Official information from our Consuls in Cuba establishes the fact that a large number of American citizens in the island are in a state of destitution, suffering for want of food and medicines. This applies particularly to the rural districts of the central and eastern parts.

" The agricultural classes have been forced from their farms into the nearest towns where they are without work or money. The local authorities of the several towns, however kindly disposed, are unable to relieve the needs of their own people, and are altogether powerless to help our citizens. The latest report of Consul-General Lee estimates that 600 to 800 are without means of support. I have assured him that provision would be made at once to relieve them. To that end I recommend that Congress make an appropriation of not less than $50,000, to be immediately available for use under the direction of the Secretary of State.

" It is desirable that a part of the sum which may be appropriated by Congress should, in the discretion of the Secretary of State, also be used for the transportation of American citizens who, desiring to return to the United States, are without means to do so."

The public interest in the subject was shown by the great crowds which besieged the galleries throughout the day. Among the occupants of the diplomatic gallery were Sir Julian Pauncefote, the British Ambassador, and Minister Hatch, of Hawaii, and in the reserved gallery were General Dan Sickles, ex-United States Minister to Spain. Neither the Spanish Legation nor the Cuban Bureau in Washington was represented in the galleries, so far as could be observed.

A STARVING AMERICAN FAMILY IN CUBA.

587

Two phases of the subject were presented.   First came the question of relief to destitute and starving Americans in Cuba.   This was presented in the President's message as soon as the session opened.   Immediately following the reading of the message, Mr. Davis, chairman oi the Committee of Foreign Relations, presented a favorable report on the joint resolution originally introduced by Mr. Gallinger, appropriating $50,000 for the relief of American citizens in Cuba.   There was only one brief speech—from Mr. Gallinger— and then the resolution went through by unanimous vote, there being no response to the call for nays.   It took exactly eighteen minutes for the reading of the message, the presentation of the committee report, the brief speech and the final passage of the resolution.

A New Departure.

In the House of Representatives the resolution was passed without dissent.

Speaking of the President's message, one of our leading journals commented as follows : " It is an essentially new departure in international affairs, and it is in order for the sticklers for precedent to enter fussy protestation, as they did in connection with the Venezuelan question, against the Monroe doctrine, declaring that it was not to be found in the code of international law.   It is certainly very unusual, if not unprecedented, for the Government to make a relief appropriation for its own people in some foreign land.   The truth is, this Cuban situation is wholly exceptional.   Here is a little island in a state of civil war.   It is largely a sectional war, one part of the island being in possession of one of the belligerents and the other section in the possession of the other belligerent.

" Several hundreds of our American citizens are in that section of the island occupied by Spanish armies, and are suffering, in common with the Cubans themselves, from a deliberate policy of starvation. Weyler is trying to conquer by famine.   That is his fixed purpose, and, from the nature of the case, no discrimination is made between Spanish subjects in rebellion and American citizens sojourning in the island.   If the policy of starvation can not be maintained without this indiscrimination, then so much the worse for Weyler and his policy. Congress has only to make the appropriation asked for, and the relief will go forward, without regard to any collateral consequences."

The second phase of the Cuban subject came up in the Senate when the Morgan resolution, declaring that a state of war exists in Cuba, was taken up. Mr. Wellington, the new senator from Maryland, came forward for his initial speech in the Senate, making a vigorous protest against the resolution, on the ground that it threatened war with Spain. He said the first duty of Congress was to pass the tariff bill. The senator condemned "jingoism," and gave his indorsement to President Cleveland's conservatism on the Cuban question.

Warm Words in Behalf of Cuba.

Senator Daniel, of Virginia, said the senator from Maryland (Wellington) had "taken a shot at creation" while presumably discussing the pending resolution. He had gone into the tariff, currency, the late and the present administrations in their various ramifications. Mr. Daniel asserted that the Maryland senator entirely misapprehended the resolution in declaring that it involved hostility to Spain. In sarcastic tones Mr. Daniel referred to Mr. Wellington's statement that some debt of gratitude existed because Spain had produced a Christopher Columbus. "It were better had there been no Columbus," said Mr. Daniel, "if America was to continue a savagery that prevailed here before the country was discovered." The senator then took up the legal questions involved in the recognition of belligerency.

After concluding his legal argument on the powers of Congress and the President, Mr. Daniel branched to the general subject of Cuba, and again aroused the keenest attention by his vigorous words. The diplomacy of Spain had succeeded for two and one-half years, he said, in blinding American diplomacy in the belief that war did not exist in Cuba. But the world knew that war existed there, highhanded, red-handed, bloody, cruel war. It is a war in which Spain employs more troops than England employed in seeking to put down the American revolution.

And yet senators were met with the statement that a recognition of a state of war in Cuba would be inimical to Spain. He denied that the recognition of an existing fact could be construed as a hostile act, but in any event the fact should be recognized and the great influence of the United States thrown toward the cause of civilized and Christian usage. It might subject some American vessels to search, but this would be a small matter compared with the results achieved. It might give Spain a right to blockade Cuba, but in that Spain would suffer more than the United States.

A Calamity Greater than War.

"It is said this means war," continued Mr. Daniel. "I deny it. If Spain should declare war against us because we recognized the belligerency of her former subjects, who had carried on a war for two and one-half years, she would have an unjust cause of complaint and war against us, and we will have a just cause of complaint and war against her. I do not wish to see the American people involved in war. I look upon war as one of the greatest calamities that can befall a people. But it is a greater calamity for the high public spirit of a great nation to be so deadened that it can look upon murder and arson and pillage with indifference and for the public spirit of that nation to be so dead as to delay one instant in doing an act of justice because of fear of war."

During the debate Senator Mason, of Illinois, made a bold, patriotic and eloquent speech, denouncing Spanish atrocities in Cuba. The inhuman barbarities inflicted upon innocent people, the savage attacks made upon them and their expulsion from their own homes, condemned to suffering and starvation, were depicted in burning language. Among other things he said: "Here is the proof in the communication of the President, stating that 800 citizens of the United States have been driven from their homes, and are destitute. Who forced them there? Was it the Insurgents? Then, there is war in Cuba. Was it the Spaniards? Then, if there is no war, there ought to be, and with us. Eight hundred Americans driven from home starving, and still some senators say it is not much of a war."

Again and again the galleries broke into loud applause as the sturdy Senator expressed in eloquent terms the feeling of the American people. The excitement was at white heat; handkerchiefs waved; cheers burst forth that could not be repressed.

Senator Foraker, of Ohio, produced an unpublished letter of Secretary Olney, addressed to the Spanish government in April, 1896, in which the President offered to Spain the mediation of the United States to bring the war to a close, which was firmly refused by the Spanish government, who stated, through their minister at Washington, that there was no effectual way to pacify the Cubans except upon the condition that they should first submit to the mother country.

The Morgan Resolution.

Mr. Foraker's speech was delivered with much warmth and earnestness. Several of his well-rounded periods, in which sympathy was expressed with the struggling Cubans, and in which the cruelties and barbarities of the Spanish military forces were denounced, called forth demonstrations from the galleries.

The Morgan resolution declared: "That a condition of public war exists between the Government of Spain and the Government proclaimed and for some time maintained by force of arms by the people of Cuba, and that the United States of America shall maintain a strict neutrality between the contending parties, according to each all the rights of belligerents in the ports and territory of the United States."

The resolution received in its favor the votes of 18 Republicans, 19 Democrats, and 4 Populists; 12 Republicans and 2 Democrats voted against it—a total vote of 41 to 14.

Early in May President McKinley sent Hon. W. J. Calhoun, of Illinois, as a special commissioner to Cuba, who was charged primarily with helping Consul-General Lee to investigate the circumstances surrounding the death of Dr. Albert Ruiz in a Spanish prison. The Spanish government was represented by Dr. Congosto, Spanish Consul at Philadelphia. Under date of May 28th a reliable correspondent in Cuba made public the following communication:

"There will be trouble over the Ruiz investigation. In fact, there has been trouble already. It will be set down in the future as an irritant in the relations between Spain and the United States, whereas President McKinley built hope of another kind upon it.

"In ten days the joint commission, of which General Lee and Dr. Congosto are the heads, has had exactly one session, which had little result beyond showing General Lee and Mr. Calhoun how little they might expect.

"The delay has been caused by Dr. Congosto on the flimsiest pretext, and the Spanish representative, too, by talking recklessly about General Lee, and other Consuls came within an ace of being told that the American representatives would have nothing more to do with him personally and officially.

Dr. Ruiz in His Cell.

"Ruiz died, according to the surgeons, from congestion of the brain, caused by a blow or blows. When General Lee and Mr. Calhoun visited the jail in Guanabacoa, they were shown the cell in which the Spanish say that Ruiz died.

"The guard explained to General Lee and Mr. Calhoun that he heard thumping on the inside of the door, and when he opened it and went in, Ruiz was running at the heavy door and butting it with his head.

"Ruiz had only one wound on the top of his head. Had he butted this door, as the jailor says he did, his scalp must necessarily have been lacerated in several places.

"The American representatives have decided that they will not ask a single question of the guards if they are called, feeling it absurd to waste time on them under the circumstances. Dr. Congosto has been told plainly that from all that is known the testimony of these men would not be received in any court in the United States, unless they were prisoners and chose to speak in their own defence.

"The Americans asked for the official record of the arrest of Ruiz and the charges made against him. Dr. Congosto said that the record was in Madrid. It has not been furnished."

General Weyler succeeded for ten days in concealing from every one in Havana the startling news that the city of Santiago de Cuba, a Spanish stronghold considered to be as impregnable as Havana itself, was raided and practically captured early in September by the insurgents. They remained there nearly all day, and retired only after securing a very large amount of valuable plunder.

Capture of Arms and Ammunition.

The insurgents entered Santiago de Cuba, most unexpectedly to the Spaniards, on September 8, by way of El Sueno ward, and, dispersing the detachments from the garrison that attempted to check them, they advanced to the Marte Square, which is in the heart of the city. There a strong body of the Spanish garrison was defeated, and the Spanish took refuge in the forts. Two Spanish gunboats which were in the port approached the city to bombard it upon the first order from the Spanish military commander. Meanwhile the insurgents were plundering the principal stores and capturing arms and ammunition from the volunteers, who were scattered through the city. When they had completed their work they retired, because the bombardment from the Spanish forts and gunboats would surely damage the many Cuban families living in their own houses in the city.

Murders were committed by the Spanish in Cuban hospitals every day, and the terrible retaliation of the insurgents on the Spanish guerrillas continued. The guerrillas were slain whenever they were caught by the Spanish soldiers.

Among the hills of Lastra, between La Salud and Quivican, Havana province, a Spanish spy discovered a Cuban hospital, and immediately piloted the dreadful guerrillas of Bejugal to the place. Thirty-two Cubans, sick and wounded, with their wives and children, were assassinated. Near Guane, in Pinar del Rio province, after a hard fight in which the Cubans, commanded by Major Luis Laza, surrounded the Spanish forts, a Spanish detachment of twenty-five guerrillas was captured, and all the prisoners were killed with the machete.

General Montaner, with 2,000 Spanish soldiers tried to capture a filibustering expedition near Harmonia, Santa Clara province. He

38

arrived too late, and found only twenty-six empty boxes and one small open boat left on shore by the filibustering steamer. On returning from the coast the insurgents, under Alvarez, attacked him, and a fierce fight ensued, in which eleven Spanish guerrillas of the " Guerrilla of Death," well known throughout the province for their massacres of peaceful citizens and their raids on Cuban hospitals, fell into the hands of the revolutionists. Two hours later they were all hanged in the neighboring forest.

A train was blown up with dynamite by the insurgents between Mangas and Punta Brava, Pinar del Rio province. The locomotive was shattered and many Spanish soldiers were killed and wounded. The Spanish forces of Candelaria advanced to attack the Cubans, who were under command of General Perico Diaz. A hard fight was the result. It lasted several hours, with heavy losses on both sides.

President McKinley's Decisive Action.

When President McKinley appointed General Woodford Minister to Spain, it was commonly believed that vigorous measures would be adopted by our Government to bring the war in Cuba to a close. General Weyler, with his army of 200,000 Spanish troops, appeared to be no nearer subduing the revolutionists than when he landed on the Island. Bombastic reports had been sent by him to Spain affirming that several provinces had been brought into subjection, and the long and bloody struggle was nearly ended. Facts, however, disproved these statements, as facts in so many instances before had shown that statements sent out from the Governor's palace at Havana were false.

There was a universal feeling in the United States that our country was losing much by the continuance of the war. Very little trade was carried on with Cuba and the Island was desolated from one end to the other. The torch had consumed beautiful residences; the finest plantations had been destroyed; thousands had lost their lives, and multitudes were impoverished; peaceful citizens had been driven into the towns where, unable to obtain food, they were in danger of starvation. A reign of terror existed in nearly every part of the island.

Under these circumstances it is not strange that the people of the United States hoped that President McKinley's administration would adopt most rigorous measures to end the long and terrible struggle. It was understood that instructions to this effect had been given to General Woodford before he left New York for Madrid. Unusual measures were taken to protect him on his journey from San Sebastian to the Spanish capital, but the trip was quite uneventful. A party of gendarmes, commanded by a sub-lieutenant, guarded the Southern Express, on which he was a passenger. Secret police were posted at the station, and the prefect of police was in waiting to escort him to his hotel. The drive through the streets was marked by no special incident, though several people saluted him, receiving a bow in return.

Fear of Anarchists.

The Spanish Government protected our Minister, as it does all prominent officials; not because of fear that public sentiment might crystallize into mob violence, but because Spain and other European countries are infested with Socialists and Anarchists, any one of whom might be unexpectedly guilty of some overt act.

The Government of Spain fully understands that any act of violence upon the Minister from this country might arouse our populace beyond the bounds of reason, and possibly beyond the control and direction of our conservative administration. Therefore, our Minister was carefully guarded, so that there might be neither excuse nor palliation for complaint on the part of this Government in the event that some irresponsible person should make himself infamous by seeking to become famous. So it was stated at Madrid, yet there is no denying that the public feeling was profoundly excited.

General Woodford immediately called upon the Spanish authorities and presented his credentials. He stated afterward that his conference with the Duke of Tetuan, the Foreign Minister, was of the most satisfactory character. The unexpected bitterness of the press and of public opinion painfully impressed him, but he hoped this would soon be allayed, as he considered his mission favorable to

Spanish interests, and could not believe that Spain would reject mediation designed to end an impoverishing war. He did not name any time at which the war must be terminated, but he trusted, as the result of his friendly offices, that it would be ended quickly.

He gave the Spanish Government to understand that the war was inflicting great losses upon the United States, and that it was impossible to prevent filibustering expeditions. While our Government wished to abide by international law and maintain peace with a friendly nation, so many were the friends of Cuba in our country and so great were the opportunities for sending expeditions to aid the insurgents, that it was impossible to prevent all filibustering.

Downfall of the Government at Madrid.

On September 29 it was announced at Madrid that the Spanish Cabinet had resigned. The news was startling, for it was instantly felt that there was a crisis in the Cuban revolution and that Minister Woodford was making his power felt in Spain. It was well understood that the administration thus suddenly brought to a close had been friendly to General Weyler, and had supported him in all his severe measures for conquering the Cuban people. If the Liberals in Spain came into power, it was believed that General Weyler would be recalled and there would be an earnest effort to find some means of bringing the war to a close.

The Queen Regent of Spain accepted the resignations of her Ministry and called Senor Sagasta to be the head of the new Government. The prospect of his returning to power was well received in political and financial circles, and the decision shown by the Queen Regent in hastening the solution of the Cabinet crisis was much praised.

People jumped to the conclusion that a change of Government at Madrid would immediately affect Cuban affairs and the relations of the Spanish Government with this Republic. There was no apparent ground for such inferences or conclusions. Sagasta did not pledge himself to make any great changes in the Spanish policy toward Cuba, yet it will soon be seen that he was dissatisfied with the situation.

There is much evidence to show that from the first it was the policy of President McKinley to endeavor to secure self-government for Cuba, while causing the Island to remain a colonial possession of Spain, with a Governor-General to be appointed by the Crown. This would render Cuba practically free, and Spain would enjoy the fiction of sovereignty over her last American possession.

On September 30 it was announced that General Nunez, head of the department of Cuban supplies, had returned from Cuba where he had a lengthy interview with Generals Gomez and Garcia and officers of the Republican Government. " The present crisis in Spain," he said, " is due entirely to the presence of Mr. Woodford at Madrid and his conference with the Minister of Foreign Affairs, the Duke of Tetuan. Undoubtedly Mr. Woodford has demanded several concessions from the Spanish Government which have embarrassed the Cabinet to such an extent that they resigned rather than try to grant them.

Possible Settlement of the Conflict.

" I think Mr Woodford has taken a decisive step and it is high time, as the United States has been in a most embarrassing position for many months. The people of the country favor Cuban freedom, the Executive and Congress fail to interfere."

General Nunez was asked if he had heard of a rumor to the effect that an important communication had been received by the Spanish Government from the leaders of the Cuban insurgents suggesting the basis of a possible settlement of the difficulties ?

" That is entirely possible," he said, " and I would not be surprised if General Gomez has made an offer. He communicated with the United States Government to the same effect during Cleveland's administration, and the Cubans are willing to buy their freedom. Remember they will have freedom and any negotiations must be to that effect. Cuba will never, never accept anything less than positive freedom from Spain. If the present war should not bring it a later one will. We fought twelve years in one struggle and are prepared to keep up the conflict until we gain the desired end."

It was known that the new Spanish Premier, Sagasta, before he assumed the reins of government, was dissatisfied with the conduct of the war. As late as September 14th, referring to the Cuban insurrection, he said the uprising, instead of dying out, was spreading considerably. He added that the situation in the Philippine Islands was serious. He asserted that the Carlist propaganda in Spain could not be viewed with indifference, and he expressed the belief that a reconciliation between the political parties in Spain was impossible so long as the Conservatives were in power.

Captain Wiborg Liberated.

While the public were awaiting the action of the new Spanish Cabinet an incident occurred which will be of interest to all readers. Captain Wiborg, an alleged filibuster, was arrested in Philadelphia, in November, 1895, by Deputy United States Marshall Lloyd, on the charge of violating the neutrality laws in carrying arms and ammunition to Cuba while serving as commander of the steamship Horsa. He was tried in the United States Court, before Judge Butler, in March, 1896, and, after being found guilty, he was sentenced to sixteen months' imprisonment. On March 19th, after serving two days of his sentence, he was released from the Eastern Penitentiary, his case having been taken to the Supreme Court by his counsel, W. W. Ker, when a stay was granted.

The Supreme Court, at its next session, sustained the action of the lower court, and on July 6, 1896, Captain Wiborg began serving his term of sixteen months' imprisonment. In the meanwhile he had been honored by being one of the distinguished guests at a public meeting of one of the city's most fashionable clubs.

He served out his sentence, but was unable to pay the fine that had been imposed. Commenting on this, one of the public journals said: "Last Saturday, in the Eastern Penitentiary of the great Keystone Commonwealth, there expired the regular term of imprisonment of a bronze-bearded Dane, who risked his liberty in behalf of the freedom of the oppressed people of the Star of the Caribbean Sea. On that day Captain J. H. J Wiborg, of Holstein, Denmark, commander of the steamship Horsa, alleged to have been engaged in aiding Americans to help Cubans to throw off the yoke of the Spanish Kingdom, finished the term of imprisonment of sixteen months placed upon him by a United States court. Yet he still languishes in jail, because there was added, as a penalty for his alleged misdemeanor, a fine of $300 and costs, making a total of $500, which, unless paid, will subject him to an additional imprisonment of thirty days. No one has come forward to say that this man's confinement shall no longer continue; probably because no one has been informed of the fact."

Friends Come to the Rescue.

A public subscription was immediately started and tne next day the same journal said: "Friends of Cuba and lovers of liberty and fair play have been quick to respond to the call for subscriptions to pay the fine, his inability to pay which would keep him behind prison bars for another month. His term has expired. He has paid the penalty, so far as time is concerned, of aiding the struggling patriots of Cuba to wage war against the tyrannies of Spanish rule. But there is money to be paid. A fine and the costs of the case.

"The former captain of the steamer Horsa spent his last penny in defending his case, but the law says that he must pay now or locks and bars will keep him from freedom for thirty days. The captain's wife is living on the charity of friends and must continue to so live until he regains his liberty and can again earn the wages or a thorough seaman."

On the day following the same journal made the pleasant announcement: "Wiborg is free. He, the daring captain of the celebrated Horsa; he, the Cuban aider and patriot; he, the lover of liberty, was last night released from the Eastern Penitentiary, where for fifteen months and two days he had been imprisoned, deprived of the very freedom for which he had so valiantly and untiringly contended.

"It was a happy moment for the representatives of this journal when, as the big gong rang out the hour of 10 through the whitewashed corridors of the prison, they presented the release to the authorities and were led to Wiborg's cell; it was a still happier moment for Wiborg himself, and all the more so on account of the surprising nature of the glad tidings, for, although he had been informed of the efforts in his behalf, he had not hoped to become free again for at least another twenty-four hours. Indeed, while our representatives were making their way to his cell he was wrapped in sleep, all unconscious of the freedom awaiting him just outside the bolted door of his whitewashed cell.

"Cuba Will be Free."

"When first awakened he did not grasp the full meaning of the words addressed to him. Five minutes later he did though, for then it was that he stepped forth, in company with friends, from the last prison door between durance vile and the outer world and liberty. And then it was that the hale upholder of freedom said in answer to a question, while a smile, full of meaning spread over his honest features : '" Yes, I'm free, and Cuba will be free, too." '

In a few seconds the big doors of the gruesome-looking structure swung behind Captain Wiborg and his friends, and once again the Danish skipper, who had risked his life and served a term of imprisonment because he had assisted the Cubans in their heroic struggle for liberty, was a free man.

At midnight, October 8th, it was announced at Madrid that the Cabinet had decided upon the immediate recall of General Weyler from Cuba, and a decree would be issued, appointing Captain-General Blanco Governor General of the island. The Queen Regent would sign the decree at once. It was also stated that 20,000 reinforcements would accompany General Blanco to Cuba.

Already there had been a demonstration in Havana in favor of retaining General Weyler, which, it was shrewdly suspected, had not only been authorized, but even inspired by himself. It was openly asserted that he found his position too profitable to be willing to part with it. The demonstration was spectacular and was a good deal overdone, much after the manner of a party demonstration in which the followers of some political " boss " have received orders to hurrah.

Nevertheless Captain-General Weyler found it necessary to resign. In the course of the cable message sent by him to Premier Sagasta, placing his post in Cuba at the disposal of the Government he said:

" If the functions with which the government had entrusted me had been merely those of Governor General of Cuba, I should have hastened to resign. But the twofold character of my mission and my duty as commander-in-chief in the face of the enemy prevent my tendering a resignation.

General Weyler Resigns his Office.

" Nevertheless, although I can rely upon the absolute, unconditional support of the autonomist and constitutional parties, as well as upon public opinion, this would be insufficient without the confidence of the Government, now more than ever necessary to me after the censure of which I have been made the object by the members and journals of the Liberal party and by public opinion in the United States, which latter is largely influenced by the former. This confidence would be necessary to enable me to put an end to the war, which has already been virtually concluded from our lines at Jucaro to Cape Antonio."

Senor Sagasta replied : " I thank you for your explanation and value your frankness, I wish to assure you that the Government recognizes your services and values them as they deserve, but it thinks a change of policy, in order to succeed, requires that the authorities should be at one with the ministry."

Captain General Ramon Blanco, successor to General Weyler, has had his chief experience in the Philippines, where he was for a time Governor General, ending his career there in 1894, and for his services, receiving the rank of Marshal in May, 1895. In August, 1896, he reported to the Spanish Minister of the Colonies the existence of an extensive plot aiming at the independence of the islands. This rapidly took on the proportions of a formidable insurrection, which the efforts of General Blanco were powerless to check. In September of that year he narrowly escaped assassination.

A plot was formed to surprise the garrison at Manila, to seize the headquarters, and to murder the Captain-General. It was discovered just in the nick of time, and more than one hundred persons were arrested for complicity in it. Prior to this, General Blanco had not resorted to extreme measures; but, spurred on by the personal danger to which he had been exposed, he issued a decree ordering that all property belonging to residents of the Philippine Islands who had been implicated in the rebellion should be forfeited for the benefit of the Government, a week's grace being offered to those who were willing to surrender.

Story of Evangelina Cisneros.

But neither this decree nor General Blanco's military tactics nor other exceptional measures which he took to repress the rebellion prevented it from spreading, and in December, after a broad hint from the Government that his methods were not sufficiently severe, he tendered his resignation. Shortly after this Marshal Blanco was appointed Chief of the Military Household of the Queen Regent. He has been described as the " softest-hearted soldier in Spain," and his whole career indicates his disposition to employ mild rather than violent measures.

An incident occurred in October which plainly showed the interest taken by the American people in Cuban affairs, and their sympathy for the cause of the insurgents. Evangelina Cisneros, niece of President Cisneros of the Cuban Republic, accompanied her father to the Isle of Pines whither he had been banished by the Spanish authorities at Havana.

His offence, of course, was his love of liberty and his efforts in behalf of Cuban Independence. His daughter, well educated, cultivated, popular socially, and remarkable for her striking personal appearance, clung to her father and determined to share his sufferings in his exile. It was reported, and subsequent events confirmed the report, that a Spanish officer became charmed with her, showed her many attentions, and, to gain her favor, granted her father many liberties. Her love for Cuba, however, was as ardent as ever and was not to be bought.

She rejected the attentions of the officer, and particularly his proposal that she should compromise her honor. Failing to gain his ends, he became the avowed enemy of Miss Cisneros, accused her of plotting against the cause of Spain, and she was arrested and sent to a prison in Havana.

Public Indignation.

It is not surprising that such a high-handed outrage became known and awakened indignation. The family of the young lady is one of best known and influential in Cuba. When the story of her wrongs was published in this country it created universal comment. The friends of Cuba were aroused and adopted active measures to secure the fair prisoner's release. In fact, so much was said, and so profound was public interest in the case, that it was likely to have a bearing on the relations of Spain with our own country. Quite likely some of the statements and some of the demands of the public press ware extravagant, yet the main facts were well authenticated, and there was a wide public demand that Miss Cisneros should receive her liberty and should not suffer for the heroic part she had been acting in favor of the country she and her people loved so much.

The story of her escape from the prison in Havana is thrilling and romantic. One day two gentlemen, respectable in appearance, rented a house adjoining the prison. No questions appear to have been asked concerning the use they intended to make of it, and no suspicions were awakened. The sequel proved that this house would not have been rented if it had not adjoined the prison in which the niece of the President of Cuba was confined. She was allowed some privileges not ordinarily granted to insurgents who are incarcerated, and seems to have known that outside friends were making efforts to liberate her. A New York journal had a correspondent in Havana, whom we will allow at this point to tell his story:

"I have broken the bars of prison and have set free the beautiful captive of Monster Weyler, restoring her to her friends and relatives, and doing by strength, skill and strategy what could not be accomplished by petition and urgent request of the Pope. Weyler could blind the Queen to the real character of Evangelina, but he could not build a jail that would hold against enterprise when properly set to work.

"To-night all Havana rings with the story. It is the one topic of conversation. Everything else pales into insignificance. No one remembers that there has been a change in the Ministry. What matter if Weyler is to go? Evangelina Cisneros has escaped from the jail, thought by everyone to be impregnable. A plot has been hatched right in the heart of Havana—a desperate plot—as shown by the revolver found on the roof of the house through which the escape was effected, and as the result of this plot, put into effect under the very nose of Spanish guards, Evangelina is free. How was it done? How could it have been done?

Kept in Concealment.

"These are questions asked to-night by the frequenters of the cafes throughout the city, where the people of Havana congregate. It is conceded by all, by the officials of the palace included, to be the most daring coup in the history of the war, and the audacity of the deed is paralyzing. No one knows where Evangelina is now, nor can know.

"To tell the story of the escape briefly, I came here three weeks ago, having been told to go to Cuba and rescue from her prison Miss Cisneros, a tenderly-reared girl, descended from one of the best families in the Island, and herself a martyr to the unsatisfied desires of a beast in a Spanish uniform. I arrived at Cienfugos late in September, telegraphed to a known and tried man in Santiago de Cuba to meet me in Havana, and then went to Santa Clara, where I picked up a second man, known to be as gritty as Sahara, and then proceeded to Havana.

"Here I remained in almost absolute concealment, so as to avoid the spies that dog one's steps wherever one may go, and make impossible any clever work of this kind. Both the men who accompanied me, Joseph Hernandon and Harrison Mallory, pursued the same course, and remained quiet until all plans had been completed.

"The fact that Miss Cisneros was incommunicado made the attempt seem at first beyond the possibility of success, but we finally, through Hernandon, who was born on the Island and speaks Spanish like a native, succeeded in sending a note to her through an old negress, who called upon one of her friends in the prison. A keeper got this note through two hands to Miss Cisneros, and three keepers later got to her a package of drugged sweets. Having established communication with her, we began work without losing a day."

Over Two Roofs to Freedom.

The drugged candies were passed around to the other inmates of the room in which Miss Cisneros was confined—eleven women charged with political offences—and they slept soundly on the night appointed for the escape. By sawing the prison bars and making use of a rope ladder and wooden bridge, the young lady passed over the roofs of the two buildings and placed herself in the custody of her daring captors.

She soon after arrived in New York, her coming being chronicled as follows in one of the city journals: "Evangelina Cisneros, one week ago a prisoner among the outcast wretches in a Havana prison, is a guest at the Waldorf Hotel. Surrounded by the luxury and elegance, she is alternately laughing and crying over the events of one short week. One week ago last night a correspondent broke the bars of her cell and led her to liberty over the flat roofs of the Cuban capital. It is the memory of those thrilling few minutes that meant for her a lifetime of captivity or a future of peace and liberty that most often occurs to her now.

"She arrived to-day on the Ward liner, *Seneca*, and was taken from the steamer by a boat at quarantine, thanks to the courtesy of the Government and quarantine authorities. When the *Seneca* sailed from Havana there figured on the passenger list one Juan Sola. A girl who signed the name Juana Sola to the declaration, exacted by the Custom House officers, was the nearest passenger to making good the lost one. Her declaration was that she brought nothing dutiable into the country.

" If ever that declaration was truthfully made, it was made in the case of this brown-eyed, chestnut-haired girl, who was so anxious to please the man who made her sign. All she had was the simple red gown she had on her back and a bundle that contained a suit of clothes such as a planter's son might have worn.

" Those were the clothes that Juan Sola wore when he run up the gang-plank in Havana, with a big hat slouched over the chestnut hair that even danger of discovery could not tempt her to cut, and a fat cigar between a red, laughing pair of lips that accidentally, maybe, blew a cloud of smoke into the face of the chief of police, who was watching that plank and made the features of the young man very indistinct indeed.

" There was no reason the chief of police should scan too closely the young man with the big cigar. Juan Sola's passport had been duly issued by the Spanish Government, and as far as the papers showed there was no reason to suspect him.

Disguised in a Boy's Suit of Clothes.

" Of course, Juan Sola was the girl the correspondent had rescued from prison, and the fame of whose escape was on every tongue in Havana, the girl for whose capture the police had for three days been breaking into houses and guarding the roads, and yet she passed under their noses with no disguise but a boy's suit of clothes.

" Miss Cisneros did not court danger any more than was necessary, and at once went to her cabin. The next day, however, when Morro Castle was left far behind, she appeared on deck, transformed into Senorita Juana Sola, alias Evangelina Cisneros.

" When the ship sighted Cape Hatteras light the young woman asked what light it was, and when told that it was an American beacon she knelt down in the saloon and prayed. After that she wept for joy. She must have been all strung up with excitement over her experiences, and when she saw the light she could contain herself no longer, but simply overflowed.

" Nothing could be seen of the Cuban girl as the *Seneca* slowed opposite quarantine to permit the boarding of the health officer.

The other passengers after the habit of ocean travelers, grouped amidships to scan the vessel of the tyrant, who had it in his power to lock them all up in quarantine. The girl was hidden away in her stateroom, wondering what reception awaited her in the big city whose sky-line broke the horizon ahead.

"The people on board were kind to her from the moment she revealed her identity, but at this moment when she had reached the haven of refuge, to gain which she and her gallant rescuers had risked death itself, she fled from the new-found friends and would not even look out the door of her stateroom."

Details of her Imprisonment and Escape.

On the way to the hotel she told the story of her imprisonment and release.

"It is a dream, a happy dream," she said, as she settled down into the cushions of her carriage. "It has all gone so quickly. It seems as if I must wake up and find myself looking out through those bars again and wondering if I should ever see the sky uncrossed by iron

"It was only yesterday or it seems so, that I was hiding in the house of those good friends of mine in Havana, while the whole city was hunting me as if I was a vicious animal that must be taken or the whole city would be in danger.

"To-day I'm here riding up the most beautiful street I ever dreamed of, where every building seems a palace reaching to the skies, in the midst of people all happy, all comfortable, all content."

She spoke of the mother she had never known and of the kind family in Saqua that brought her up as their own daughter. She traveled all over the Island. Then she went back to her father. He was not as wealthy as her foster parents, but he had had enough to provide for her and her sisters comfortably, and this father whom she had scarcely known became dear to her.

Then the dark time came and he was seized, and on suspicion that the heart of the patriot burned in his bosom, he was exiled to the Isle of Pines, a sort of purgatory between liberty in Cuba and the hell of the African penal settlements. She could not bear to be apart from her father, and soon she went to share his exile.

The next day after her arrival in New York she was accorded a great public reception in which many thousands participated.

It was commonly believed that there would not be any international complications, or trouble of any sort about the escape of Miss Cisneros from the Cuban prison in Havana, for the very good reason that those who helped her out, as well as those who held her as a prisoner, practically agreed that her escape was a necessity.

Quite Willing to have her Escape.

It would have been utterly impossible for Miss Cisneros to escape from the Cuban prison, to walk on a vessel in the port of Havana in open day, and pass the inspection of the Cuban police and detectives, even to the extent of examining her passport two days after she had escaped from prison, if the Spanish officials had not been made to understand that it was necessary for them not to recognize her at any time until she had successfully fled from the Island.

Neither General Weyler nor any of the Spanish authorities in Cuba dared publicly confess that they actively or passively aided the escape of Miss Cisneros, and the official proclamation from the Military Judge of Havana calling upon her to return to prison was simply playing for the galleries. High Spanish officials in Cuba would have been seriously compromised if the true story of the indignities offered to Miss Cisneros, when a voluntary prisoner with her father, was crystallized in history, and the whole civilized world took up her cause with such earnestness that the only hope of escape from very serious complications was in practically opening the doors for her freedom.

Of course she was taken out of prison through a top window and down over the roof of the prison, and plausible appearances of a miraculous escape were presented. Generous means were at hand to meet the emergency, and to help some of the Spanish officials to escape a worse fate than that suffered by the young lady who became the hero of the hour in this country, not only among the ardent friends of Cuban independence, but among all American men and women with whom love for chivalric justice and fair play to women is paramount.

As already stated, it was understood that General Blanco would adopt peaceful measures for the suppression of the great insurrection in Cuba, General Weyler's harsh measures having failed even in those provinces which he boasted he had subdued. It was also understood that the new Spanish Cabinet would offer through General Blanco to the people of Cuba a system of autonomy, or self-government, by which the one great desire for independence on the part of Cuba would be satisfied.

Certain reforms were promised and certain rights and privileges were to be guaranteed, and, with these, the Spanish Government, with charming innocence, supposed the insurgents would be delighted and would at once lay down their arms. But the insurgents knew something of Spanish promises and how much, or rather how little, they meant. When General Blanco attempted to introduce this wonderful system of self-government, the insurgents not only treated it with scorn, but warned the messengers who were sent with it to various parts of the Island that they would be treated as Spanish spies. Absolute independence, and not a false and hypocritical system of self-government, offered by Spain to cheat them into submission, was what the Cuban people wanted and were determined to have if it cost the last drop of blood.

It Means Extermination.

Very little fighting was done, but multitudes have perished by an enemy as brutal as the sword, that of starvation. General Weyler had ordered that in all the provinces still under Spanish authority the people should be driven into the towns and fortified strongholds where they could be guarded and could be prevented by Spanish troops from making further trouble. This infamous order proved to be one of extermination, for the innocent people were left to die of disease and starvation.

Meanwhile, much was said both in Spain and in our own country concerning the friendly relations existing between the two Governments. Our Government at Washington had endeavored to the utmost to fulfill every obligation, yet it was openly asserted by the

39

Spanish newspaper press that the insurrection would have been stamped out long ago except for the aid secretly furnished from this country to the Cuban patriots. It has been evident from the first that almost the entire American people have been in hearty sympathy with the cause of freedom in Cuba. As an evidence of this President McKinley issued an urgent appeal to the American people to send relief to the starving multitudes in Cuba whose sufferings were described as being most pitiable.

Honorable Charles W. Russell, Assistant United States Attorney in the Department of Justice, went to Cuba on a tour of personal investigation to ascertain the true condition of the Island. Under date of January 11th, 1898, Mr. Russell put forth the following statement:

" I feel it a solemn duty to humanity to make the American people realize the terrible distress which exists there. Much has been written on the subject, but, judging others by myself, I feel quite sure that because we do not commit, and have not in our history committed, such atrocities as Spain is committing on that Island the American reading public regards the reports as biased by the preconceived opinions of newspapers or grossly exaggerated.

Sickening Spectacles.

" I spent just two weeks in Cuba, visited Havana, went south to Jaruco, southwest to Guines, northeast to Matanzas, eastwardly about two hundred miles through the middle of the country to San Domingo, Santa Clara and Sagua la Grande. I visited Marianao, a short distance west of Havana, and saw along the railroads thirty or forty towns or stations. In Havana I visited the Fossos, the hospital prison at Aldecoa, where I talked with the father of Evangelina Cisneros, and a place called the Jacoba. I found reconcentrados (people who had been driven into the towns) at all three places, and begging everywhere about the streets of Havana.

" The spectacle at the Fossos and Jacoba houses, of women and children emaciated to skeletons and suffering from diseases produced by starvation, was sickening. In Sagua I saw some sick and emaciated little girls in a children's hospital, started three days before by

charitable Cubans, and saw a crowd of miserable looking reconcentrados with tin buckets and other receptacles getting small allowances
of food doled out to them in a yard.   In the same city, in an old
sugar warehouse, I saw stationed around the inside walls the remnants
of twenty or thirty Cuban families.

" In one case the remnant consisted of two little children, seven or
eight years old.   In another case, where I talked to the people in
broken Spanish, there were four individuals, a mother, a girl of fourteen, and two quite small girls.   The smallest was then suffering from
malarial fever.   The next had the signs on her hands, with which I
had become familiar, of having had that dreadful disease, the beriberi.   These four were all that the order of cencentration had left
alive of eleven.   At San Domingo, where two railroads join, the
depot was crowded with women and children, one of the latter, as I
remember, being swollen up with the beri-beri, begging in the most
earnest way of the few passengers.

No Means of Subsistence.

"San Domingo is little more than a railroad station in times of
peace, but at present it has a considerable population living in cabins
thatched with the tops of royal palm trees, composed of the survivors
of the reconcentrados.   The huts are arranged close together in a
little clump, and the concentration order required and apparently still
requires these people to live within a circle of small block houses
commonly dignified in the dispatches by the name of forts.   They
had no work to do, no soil to till, no seed to plant, and only begging
to live on.   I do not know the exact measure of the dead-line circle
drawn around them, but there was certainly nothing within it upon
which a human being could subsist.

" Practically they are prisoners.   At every one of the numerous
stopping places along the road a similar collection of huts could be
seen, and at most of them beggars, often nice-looking women and
beautiful children, invaded the cars.   Between the stations, although
I traveled always by daylight, as the trains do not run at night, and
was observing as carefully as possible, I saw no signs of the recon-

centrados g ing away from the forts.   If they had gone, it takes seeu,
instruments, land and three or four months to raise the vegetable
which could be soonest produced, and nowhere away from the block-
houses was there any sign of vegetables growing.   Near the larger
towns the circle of concentration seemed to be somewhat larger, and
some planting of vegetables, tobacco, etc., seemed to be going on.
At this a very few persons, possibly some of them reconcentrados,
found employment.

The Whole Land Lying Idle.

" All along the railroad as far as could be seen, were stretches of
the most fertile and beautiful country, with very few trees, even on
the low mountains, and most of these the royal palms.   I saw many
dozens of burned cane fields, and one evening, going from Guines to
Havana, saw the sky all lighted up along the road with fires principally of the tall grass of the country, but partly of cane.   The whole
land was lying perfectly idle except that I saw two or three or four
sugar mills where cane was growing, but in all such instances the
mill and cane were surrounded by forts, manned by soldiers who are
paid, as I was told, by the owners.   Except in the cities I saw no
indication that any relief whatever was being afforded to the starving
people.   Neither in Havana nor elsewhere did any priest, religious
woman or other person seem to be paying any attention to the wants
of the starving except that at the Fossos and some other places
charitable Cubans were nursing the sick.

" The Church, being a State institution, was, so far as I could see,
leaving the victims without either bodily or spiritual relief.   In fact
the general air of indifference to suffering which seemed to prevail
everywhere was astonishing.

An Appalling Loss of Life.

" As the country was stripped of its population by the order of
concentration, it is easy to believe that 400,000 persons were gathered
behind the forts without being given food, medicine, or means of any
kind to earn a living, except where in the larger cities some few could

find employment in menial offices.   Judging by the orphans I was
shown at Jacoba, Aidecoa and elsewhere, and from all I saw and
heard, I believe that half of the 400,000 have died as the result of starvation.   I know from the official register of the city of Santa Clara,
which ordinarily has a population of about 14,000, that the deaths for
November were over 1000, and the number of deaths for December
was over 900, and showed an increase, considering the loss of the
former 1000 from its total population.

"The exact figures for December are 971.   At that city the Government was distributing 500 single rations per day out of a total
appropriation for the purpose of $15,000.   This was not relief, but a
mere prolongation of the sufferings of a small part of the reconcentrados of that city.

Neither Food nor Medicine Provided.

"So far as any evidence of relief was visible to my eyes or was
even heard of by me in all my talks on the Island the surviving
200,000 people are in the same condition and have the same prospect
of starvation before them as had their kindred who have died.
There is as much need of medicine now as of food, and they are
getting neither.

"The reason given by the Spanish sympathizers in Cuba is that
the troops must first be fed, and it is certain that many of the soldiers
are sick and suffering for want of proper food.   I saw many myself
that looked so.   I was informed on all sides that they had not been
paid for about eight months, and that most of the civil officials had
not been paid for a similar period.   It is, therefore, most probable
that Spain is practically unable to supply the millions which are immediately necessary to prevent the death of most of the surviving
reconcentrados, but this leads to political questions, which I desire
to avoid.

Something Must be Done.

"I wish merely to state in such a way as to be convincing that in
consequence of the concentration of the people some 200,000 Cubans
are daily suffering and dying from diseases produced by a lack of

nourishment in the midst of what I think must be the most fertile country in the world, and that something must be done for them on a large scale, and at once, or a few months will see their extermination.

"So far as I could see they are a patient, amiable, intelligent set of people, some of them whom I saw begging having faces like Madonnas. They are Americans, probably the oldest Americans of European descent. Constant intercourse with the United States has made them sympathize with and appreciate us, who are but six hours by boat from them, if we do not sympathize with or care for them. No order or permission from General Blanco can save the lives of many of them. Indeed, many are too far gone to be saved by the best care and treatment.

The Outlook Hopeless for Many of the Sufferers.

"There was no indication of a cessation of hostilities by the insurgents. If they do not voluntarily cease, their tactics are such that Spain cannot conquer them, if at all, before the reconcentrados will have had the finishing stroke. But even the speedy termination of the war would not save many of them. What they need is instant pecuniary assistance to the extent of $20,000 a day, distributed by our consuls. Private charity will hardly, it seems, produce that amount. Twenty thousand dollars would be but ten cents a piece for medicine, clothes and food. When I left Havana I was informed that Consul General Lee had received $5000 and some hundreds of cans of condensed milk. As there are about 30,000 sufferers in Havana alone, the inadequacy of such contributions is manifest. Whether Congress should make an appropriation, as in the case of the San Domingo refugees and other cases, it is not for me to say, but I beg the charitable to believe the statements of facts which I have made and try to realize what they mean."

The foregoing statement made by one of the Government officials at Washington reveals a state of things in Cuba that may well arouse not only the sympathy but the indignation of our whole country. It is the statement of an impartial observer and can be relied upon as truthful.

A story of the bravery of Americans serving under General Gomez and General Calixto Garcia in the eastern provinces of Cuba, and an account of the death of W. Dana Osgood, the famous University of Pennsylvania football player, was told by Lieutenant-Colonel Frederick Funston, who arrived in New York early in January, 1898.

The Colonel had landed in Camaguey in August, 1896, with the expedition of Raphael Cabrera, and went at once to Gomez, who was then in force near the coast. After Cascorro, Gomez and Garcia formed a junction in the early part of October, they moved toward Guimaro. Garcia had with him a twelve-pound Hotchkiss rifle and four American artillerymen—W. Dana Osgood, the famous University of Pennsylvania athlete and football player; Latrobe and Janney, of Baltimore, and Devine, of Texas.

The Cubans attacked Guimaro on the morning of October 17th, using two of their three guns only because ammunition was scarce. They had about 2000 infantry. They opened fire in the morning at ranges of from 400 yards to 700 yards, the infantry being protected by a breastwork of earth, in which openings were left for the guns.

Hot Firing all Day.

The Spanish garrison consisted of 200 men in 11 forts, and they maintained a hot rifle fire all day. Gradually, however, the Hotchkiss rifle, the fire of which was directed by Osgood, made the largest and nearest fort untenable, and it was abandoned by the garrison and immediately occupied by Colonel Menocal and forty men.

One of the Cuban guns was moved forward and stationed in this fort in the night, and from that point of vantage the other forts were shelled on the following day.

Naturally the rifles of the garrison were trained most of the time upon the man sighting the Hotchkiss in the captured fort, and there, leaning over the gun in the early morning, the intrepid Osgood was shot through the head. He was carried off by his comrades under fire, and died four hours later. The death of this gallant young American was universally lamented, yet many others of similar spirit have held themselves ready to enlist in the cause of Cuban independence.

On the 12th of January, 1898, a riot broke out in Havana, and for a time it was feared that Americans residing there were in danger from the mob. The Spanish Minister called on the Secretary of State in Washington, and conveyed to him the latest information from Havana. The Minister told Mr. Sherman that the Havana military government would see to it that the danger would be confined to the Spaniards themselves, and that measures had been taken to suppress the ardor of the officers who were chafing under newspaper criticism, and especially the gathering of mobs on the streets.

He also assured the Secretary that there would be ample protection to the American Consulate and American interests in the event of any demonstrations against them, but he added that the riot was in no sense an anti-American one, and was merely an outbreak on the part of the extreme pro-Spanish element against several of the autonomist newspapers.

Reassuring Despatches from General Lee.

General Lee sent two cipher dispatches to the State Department concerning the troubles. One simply gave the facts of the riot briefly and added that everything had quieted down. In addition to this, General Lee telegraphed the State Department that if he needed a war vessel he would cable.

One of the State Department officials said that the news, although the rioting was confined to the Spaniards themselves, was the most interesting that had been sent to Washington since the beginning of the war. It showed that the way was open for internal dissensions in the only city of importance in Cuba, and that the spirit of the rioting, meaning the suppression of free speech, demonstrated that the Spaniards would need another army to repress the malcontents made by the audacious attitude of the military officers toward the independent press. Every effort was made by the Spanish authorities at Havana to belittle the riotous demonstration, but it is plain that it was an ominous uprising.

In February an incident occurred which created universal comment and threw all other public questions into the background. First, there came a rumor that the Spanish Minister in Washington, Senor Dupuy De Lome, had written a letter reflecting severely upon President McKinley and our Government at Washington, on account of the policy they were pursuing toward the war in Cuba.

It was thought by many that the rumor was unfounded, as the action of President McKinley and his Cabinet was so conservative that no possible occasion of offence could have been given to Spain, and, therefore, it was not believed that the Spanish Minister could be guilty of a gross insult to the United States. The rumors, however, multiplied and in a short time were confirmed. It was openly asserted that such a letter had been written, and had fallen into the hands of the Cuban Junta in New York and that its text would soon be transmitted to Washington.

The Notorious Letter of the Spanish Minister.

Very soon the public were permitted to read the following most extraordinary communication addressed by the Spanish Minister to Jose Canelejas, editor of a newspaper at Madrid, who, after having traveled in the United States, had gone to Havana, where the letter in question was sent. Its translation was as follows:

" My distinguished and dear friend: You need not apologize for not having written to me. I ought to have written to you, but have not done so on account of being weighed down with work.

" The situation here continues unchanged. Everything depends on the political and military success in Cuba. The prologue of this second method of warfare will end the day that the Colonial Cabinet will be appointed, and it relieves us in the eyes of this country of a part of the responsibility of what may happen there, and they must cast the responsibility upon the Cubans, whom they believe to be so immaculate.

" Until then we will not be able to see clearly, and I consider it to be a loss of time and an advance by the wrong road, the sending of emissaries to the rebel field, the negotiating with the autonomists, not yet declared to be legally constituted, and the discovery of the intentions and purposes of this government. The exiles will return one by one, and when they return will come walking into the sheep-fold, and the chiefs will gradually return.

"Neither of these had the courage to leave *en masse*, and they will not have the courage to thus return. The President's message has undeceived the insurgents, who expected something else, and has paralyzed the action of Congress, but I consider it bad.

"Besides the natural and inevitable coarseness with which he repeats all that the press and public opinion of Spain has said of Weyler, it shows once more what McKinley is—weak and catering to the rabble, and, besides, a low politician, who desires to leave a door open to me and to stand well with the jingoes of his party. Nevertheless, as a matter of fact it will only depend on ourselves whether he will prove bad and adverse to us.

Talking only for Effect.

"I agree entirely with you that without a military success nothing will be accomplished there, and without military and political success there is here always danger that the insurgents will be encouraged, if not by the Government, at least by part of the public opinion. I do not believe you pay enough attention to the role of England. Nearly all that newspaper canaille, which swarm in your hotel, are English, and while they are correspondents of American journals, they are also correspondents of the best newspapers and reviews of London.

"Thus it has been since the beginning. To my mind the only object of England is that the Americans should occupy themselves with us and leave her in peace, and if there is a war, so much the better. That would further remove what is threatening her, although that will never happen. It would be most important that you should agitate the question of commercial relations, even though it would be only for effect, and that you should send here a man of importance, in order that I might use him to make a propaganda among the Senators and others, in opposition to the Junta and to win over exiles.

"There goes Amblarad. I believe he comes too deeply taken up with political matters, and there must be something great or we shall lose. Adela returns your salutation and we wish you in the new year to be a messenger of peace and take this new year's present to poor Spain.

" Always your attentive friend and servant, who kisses your hands.

" ENRIQUE DUPUY DE LOME."

Profound Sensation Created by the Letter.

The authenticity of the letter was not doubted by the Junta. The letter at the Junta's office was said to be on the official stationery of the Spanish Legation. Its discovery created a profound sensation among New York Cubans. No news that had come from Cuba for a long time interested them so much.

The man to whom De Lome wrote was Jose Canelejas, editor of the *Heraldo* in Madrid, the acknowledged organ of the Sagasta Ministry. He has for years been an intimate friend and confidant of Sagasta, and was sent out as a sort of unofficial agent for Sagasta to sound the Cubans on the autonomy proposition. Armed with full credentials from the Madrid Ministry, he reached Havana early in December. It was there that he received this letter from his friend, Senor de Lome.

At first it was reported that the Spanish Minister denied having written any such letter, but soon afterwards finding that a letter in his own handwriting, containing all the allegations charged against him was in the hands of the Cuban Junta, and seeing that it was impossible to deny its authenticity, he at once admitted his guilt and instantly cabled his resignation to the Spanish Government. He also went to the State Department in Washington and withdrew his passports, thus preventing his abrupt dismissal, which would have added to his disgrace.

The insolent conduct of De Lome thoroughly aroused the indignation of the American people, and not a little surprise was expressed that a man who had represented his Government for twenty years at Washington, and was supposed to be a trained diplomat, should have so far forgotten himself as to fling an insult in the face of the President. The question was freely discussed whether his disgrace and re-tirement from his post would have any actual bearing upon the official relationship of the United States and Spain with reference to Cuba.

It was generally agreed that the message had opened the eyes of the American people to the duplicity of Spain's agents and their representations toward this country, and had already redounded to the benefit of the Cuban cause, inasmuch as it intensified the strong feeling of sympathy which has characterized the American people since the conflict in Cuba began.

How the Letter was Obtained.

As soon as the letter of De Lome was given out for publication by the Cuban Junta it was branded as a forgery by some of those who thought they knew Spain's Minister to this country. But De Lome acknowledged the authorship by the resignation of his post. When this startling news was flashed over the country it brought to the minds of all the next most interesting point in the affair: how was the letter obtained?

Half a dozen stories regarding this latter feature were published, but we are able to publish the true version of the matter. Its authority is a Cuban of the highest standing in the councils of his party and a leading and popular citizen. His information came directly from headquarters in New York. Here is the story of the getting of the famous letter, which aroused two continents and gave renewed strength to the cause of the struggling Cubans:

The letter was not stolen from the United States mails, but was secured by an agent of the Cuban Junta in the post office of Havana. Don Jose Canelejas, to whom the letter was addressed, never saw the original. He did not know until eight days after the letter reached Havana that such a letter from Spain's representative in Washington had been written him. De Lome wrote the letter in his private residence in Washington instead of at the Spanish Legation. The paper, however, was marked with the official type and read in the corner "Legation de Espana." The same inscription was upon the left-hand upper corner of the envelope.

Senor De Lome did not mail the letter from his house. In fact he had not quite completed it upon the morning it was written and carried it to the legation, where it was first seen and noticed by a person who was in the employ of the embassy, acting in a sub-official capacity. The letter lay upon the desk of the Minister in his inner office, the outer office being his place of reception to visitors. During an absence of half an hour from the inner office of De Lome the clerk in question saw the open letter and read some of it.

On its Way to Havana.

The next day this same person sent word to his Cuban associates in Washington to the effect that he had seen a letter from De Lome to Canelejas, in which President McKinley was villified and autonomy called a scheme. Several of the Cuban leaders got together and asked the employee of the Embassy to secure the letter. They did not believe implicitly in his story, although he urged them to come into the public print and make charges against De Lome. Because they did not have the letter in their possession the leaders refused to say anything about it. The employee of the Legation was urged to use all means in his power to secure the letter, although it was considered probable that the letter was already in the mails when the Cubans at the Hotel Raleigh were informed of its existence.

The clerk in the employ of Minister De Lome saw no more of the letter. His memorized abstracts were forwarded to New York, and it was quickly agreed that could possession of the letter be obtained and his statements proven to be true the letter would be of incalculable value to the Cuban cause as substantiating what Cuban leaders had maintained regarding autonomy and the general Spanish feeling, in official circles, toward this country and its officers. Immediately words of warning and urgings to be on the alert were sent to every Cuban who might be in a position to obtain track of or intercept the much-sought-for missive.

The letter reached Havana five days after its postmark in Washington. An agent of the Cuban party who is an employee of the Spanish post-office, knew that the letter was on the way, and when it came into his hands it was carried from the post-office and a copy was made of it. Word to this effect was sent to the Cuban leader in Jacksonville, Fla., who at once asked the secret Cuban Junta in Havana to secure the original letter—that a copy was not what was desired. The Havana post-office clerk was not willing to do this at first, but afterward consented, as he was obliged to account for a certain number of letters to other employees of the department.

Arrested and Discharged.

The original was then taken, several blank sheets were substituted in place of the paper upon which De Lome had written, and the letter finally postmarked in the Havana office and sent in its routine way. Eight days from its arrival in the Havana office the sealed envelope, properly addressed to Senor Canelejas, was delivered at the Hotel Inglaterra. Senor Canelejas did not regard the matter seriously at the time, although the hotel boy who brought him the letter, and the post-office employee who had last charge of it were arrested. So, also, was the hotel employee who went several times daily to the post-office for the mails. All three were discharged after an examination.

Senor Canelejas communicated almost immediately with Minister de Lome, and for several weeks letters and cablegrams passed between the two, but no trace of the letter could be obtained. Canelejas shortly thereafter left Havana, going to Madrid. It is not explained why the letter was kept by the Cubans for several weeks before it was given out for publication. An informant other than the person who gave the foregoing, but who is on the inside in Cuban official circles, declares that the delay was occasioned by a desire on the part of the Junta to be assured absolutely that the writing was that of the Spanish Minister, so that he might not have any chance to deny its authorship, and thus cause a reaction which undoubtedly would have been the result of the propagation of a fake.

Dr. John Guiteras, the Cuban leader in Philadelphia, commenting on the securing of the letter, said that it was clever work, and that the letter itself told the American people, in a better way than could any number of Cuban speeches or pamphlets, the inmost feelings of Spanish officials toward this country, its people and Government.

Commenting further on the letter, Dr. Guiteras said : " There are portions of the De Lome letter concerning which it cannot be said that the incident is closed. Nor can I understand how honest citizens in Spain can consider it closed whilst the present Ministry remains in office. That a Government should propose two important measures directed to an understanding with the United States, and that a representative of that Government should declare both these measures to be merely for effect, is a very serious matter.

" The said representative was in charge of both these measures—autonomy and a commercial treaty—as far as these measures concerned the United States, and he writes to a man prominent in politics, and who apparently was charged with some secret mission to that Government. Will the American people now believe what the Cubans have repeatedly said, namely, that autonomy is a farce?

Disparaging our Public Men.

" I would like to forget that part of De Lome's letter which refers in a disrespectful way to President McKinley. Although it is very offensive I do not believe it will have any influence upon the action of the Government. But there is a great lesson to be learned from this disagreeable incident. I do not hesitate to say that we are, ourselves to blame, for the boorish conduct of this foreign representative. We have a confirmed and pernicious habit of speaking in disparaging terms of our public men and our institutions. I have no doubt that Mr. de Lome has found in this country willing ears for such statements as he makes in his letter, if he has not himself frequently heard similar expressions from American lips.

" Freedom of speech is a great thing. The faults of our public men should be pointed out openly and without fear. Specific charges should be made, where there is a foundation for them. But there is a vast difference between this and the loose generalizations we hear so frequently. Men in office seem to be honored for a moment by the popular vote, only to be villified as public criminals. We lack patriotism. If we do not love and honor our institutions we cannot expect foreigners to respect them."

Justice Brewer, of the United States Supreme Court, in speaking ¬n the subject, said:

" No one knew better than Senor De Lome that President McKinley, instead of attempting to cater to the popular prejudice in connection with the Cuban agitation, was distinctly the one bold restraining figure which sought to check the growth of sentiment in this direction. He knew that it was President McKinley who opposed the jingo element in both branches of the National Legislature, and by whose firm, yet politic course, several dangerous crises in the relations between the two nations had been passed over with comparatively little friction. Why he should have written the letter was and is a mystery, and not to be explained on any reasonable hypothesis.

Hypocrisy Unmasked.

" Of course, its effect will be to add to the strain which already exists in the relations of the two countries. Apart from the natural resentment which will be felt in this country because of De Lome's references to President McKinley, are the unpleasant revelations the letter contains as to the motive for urging the reciprocity treaty with this country. It smacks so strongly of duplicity it will add greatly to the charges which have been made all along against Spain."

Meanwhile the terrible struggle in Cuba went on. The failure of Pando's campaign in the eastern part of Cuba was regarded as proof that in a military way Spain's condition was utterly hopeless. The mortality from starvation according to the latest official reports did not decrease. In the city of Santa Clara, which has only 12,000 inhabitants, the deaths numbered 1000 in January, as compared with 78 in the same month the year before.

There were ten thousand reconcentrados forced into Santa Clara city, and out of that number over 8000 died. That was the story from all parts of Cuba, and the starvation still went on. Before the war there were 200,000 resident Spaniards on the island, and according to the census just taken there were only about 137,000 left.

The sequel of the letter by the Spanish Minister already referred to deserves to be noted. Spain was compelled to officially disclaim in a positive manner the reflections contained in the letter and offer a suitable apology. The following is an abstract of the note sent by the Spanish Government to Minister Woodford, at Madrid:

"The Spanish Government on learning of the incident in which Minister Depuy De Lome was concerned, and being advised of his objectionable communication, with entire sincerity laments the incident, states that Minister De Lome had presented his resignation, and it had been accepted before the presentation of the matter by Minister Woodford. That the Spanish Ministry, in accepting the resignation of a functionary whose services they have been utilizing and valuing up to that time, leaves it perfectly well established that they do not share, and rather, on the contrary, disauthorize the criticisms tending to offend or censure the Chief of a friendly State, although such criticisms had been written within the field of friendship and had reached publicity by artful and criminal means.

"That this meaning had taken shape in a resolution by the Council of Ministers before General Woodford presented the matter, and at a time when the Spanish Government had only vague telegraphic reports concerning the sentiments alluded to. That the Spanish nation, with equal and greater reason, affirms its view and decision after reading the words contained in the letter reflecting upon the President of the United States.

New Commercial Treaty.

"As to the paragraph concerning the desirability of negotiations of commercial relations, if even for effect and importance of using a representative for the purpose stated in Senor Dupuy De Lome's letter, the Government expresses concern that in the light of its conduct, long after the writing of the letter, and in view of the unanswerable testimony of simultaneous and subsequent facts, any doubt should exist that the Spanish Government has given proof of its real desire and of its innermost convictions with respect to the new commercial system and the projected treaty of commerce.

40

"That the Spanish Government does now consider it necessary to lay stress upon, or to demonstrate anew the truth and sincerity of its purpose and the unstained good faith of its intentions.   That publicly and solemnly, the Government of Spain contracted before the mother country and its colonies a responsibility for the political and tariff changes which it has inaugurated in both Antilles, the natural ends of which, in domestic and international spheres, it pursues with firmness, which will ever inspire its conduct."

Closely following the resignation of the Spanish Minister came news of an appalling disaster in the harbor of Havana.   The American battleship "Maine" was lying in the harbor, having been sent on a friendly visit to Cuba.   On the evening of February 15th a terrific explosion took place on board the ship, by which upwards of two hundred and forty sailors and officers lost their lives and the vessel was wrecked.

Appalling Results of the Explosion.

The cause of the explosion was not apparent.   The wounded sailors of the "Maine" were unable to explain it.   It was believed that the battleship was totally destroyed.   The explosion shook the whole city.   The windows were broken in many of the houses.   The wounded sailors stated that the explosion took place while they were asleep, so that they could give no particulars as to the cause.

The Government at Washington and the whole country were horrified at the destruction of one of our largest cruisers and the loss of so many of our brave sailors.   The excitement throughout the country was intense.

The chief interest in the "Maine" disaster now centered upon the cause of the explosion that so quickly sent her to the bottom of Havana harbor.   With every day the reticence of the naval officials seemed to increase.   Secretary Long declined to express any opinion on the terrible affair, and all others in authority were similarly silent.

A naval board of inquiry was appointed to proceed at once to Havana to make a thorough investigation.   The navy officers who would talk were skeptical as a rule of the accident theory.   The story of a percussion hole in the " Maine's " side was not generally believed, but the sentiment was strong that the affair needed a strong light to dispel the ugly shadows. Every suggestion of a possible reason for an explosion seemed to be met by certain facts that controverted it.

A bill was introduced in the National House of Representatives to appropriate money for the heirs of the " Maine's " dead. The funeral of victims whose bodies were recovered was held at Havana. Messages of condolence were received at Washington from the rulers of most of the great nations of the world. King, Emperor, Sultan, President, united in a tribute to the devoted dead. Many Legislatures adopted resolutions of sympathy and regret for the disaster.

The message of Queen Victoria was as follows:

" Secretary State :—

"1 have the honor to inform you that I am commanded by the Queen to convey to the President the expression of her Majesty's sympathy with the American people on the occasion of the sad disaster which has befallen their navy by the loss of the battleship ' Maine' and of so many members of her crew. I request that you will be good enough to transmit the above message to its high destination.

" I have the honor to be, with the highest consideration, sir, your most obedient, humble servant,　　　　　　　　　　　　　　　　JULIAN PAUNCEFOTE."

The Emperor William, of German~, telegraphed as follows:

" BERLIN, February 17.

" President United States, Washington :—
" Let me express my sincere sympathy to you and your country at the terrible loss of the ' Maine' and the death of so many brave officers and men of your navy.
" WILLIAM, I. R."

The following dispatch came from Paris:

" PARIS, February 17.

" Sherman, Secretary, Washington :—
" President Faure asked personal interview in which he requested me to express his warmest sympathy and profound sense of condolence to President McKinley regarding the appalling catastrophe to the ' Maine,' and to convey assurance that the French people, especially the French navy, are deeply touched by the death of the gallant officers and men who lost their lives at their post of duty.
" PORTER."

Similar expressions of sympathy and condolence came from other rulers, all expressing horror at the catastrophe which resulted in the loss of so many lives.

The reader will be interested in a description of the United States battleship "Maine." She was launched at the Brooklyn Navy Yard in November, 1890, and was first commissioned September 17, 1895. She was a steel armored battleship, with two ten-inch barbette turrets. Her dimensions were: Length, 318 feet; beam, 57 feet; draft, 21 feet 6 inches; and displacement, 6,682 tons. She had eight steel horizontal boilers, vertical inverted cylinder direct-acting triple expansion twin-screw engines of 9,000 indicated horse-power. She carried 822 tons of coal, with which she could steam 2,770 knots at 14.8 knots an hour, or 7,000 knots at 10 knots an hour. She had a double bottom and numerous water-tight compartments.

A Formidable Naval Battery.

Her armor consisted of a side armor belt, twelve inches thick. Four ten-inch rifles, en barbette in turrets, constituted her main battery, and six six-inch rifles on the battery deck for the auxiliary battery. Four six-pounders, eight three-pounders and two one-pounder rapid fire guns, four revolving cannon and four Gatlings made up the second battery. There were armored tops on each of the two masts.

As a fighting machine the "Maine" was as formidable as any of her class. The hull was encased in an armor belt twelve inches in thickness, tapering to seven inches below the water-line. Like most vessels of her class, her ends were unprotected by side armor, but at both ends there were transverse armored bulkheads of sufficient thickness to deflect projectiles. A steel deck covered the vital parts of the ship and afforded protection to the machinery and boilers.

The barbette armor was twelve inches in thickness and the plates of the turret armor were eight inches thick. The armor of the forward barbette cost $125,000, that for the after barbette $122,000. The cost per gross ton was $575, plus 2¼ cents per pound for harveyizing the plates and ½ cent per pound for introducing nickel.

The "Maine" was propelled by twin screws of manganese bronze. A bulkhead divided the engine room, so that each set of the machinery was in a water-tight compartment by itself. The fire rooms were fitted for forced draught. The vessel was fitted for a flag ship, which means that she had a separate cabin for an admiral and additional state rooms for state officers. The cost of the "Maine" was $2,500,000.

Only a comparatively small number of bodies were recovered from the wreck of the "Maine," and many of these were mutilated beyond recognition. The scene was ghastly and sickening. The interment of the dead took place at 5 o'clock on the afternoon of February 17th. Shortly before that hour all Havana was moving. The flags on the public buildings were at half mast and many of the houses were draped in mourning. All classes were represented in the throngs that filled the streets along which the funeral procession passed to the cemetery. The order of the procession was as follows:

Funeral of the Victims at Havana.

The Municipal Guards on horseback, in full uniform, the city fire brigade, the municipal employees, the Aldermen in seven splendidly decorated firemen's cars, special cars bearing the bodies, the clergy, deputations consisting of the chief officers of the army, navy, and the volunteers, representatives of various official bureaus and of the custom house, a committee representing the Chamber of Commerce, a delegation representing the grocers.

Elaborate preparations had been made for the interment of the dead, the twenty-two bodies having been brought to the City Hall, where they rested in coffins covered with beautiful crowns of silk ribbons, with appropriate inscriptions. The crown from the City Council bore the inscription: "The people of Havana to the victims of the Maine." There was a handsome crown of silk ribbons in the Spanish national colors, with the inscription, "The Navy Department at Havana to the victims of the Maine."

The Marquis de Esteban, Mayor of Havana, headed the ceremonies, the burial expenses being paid by the municipality. General Solana assisted at the funeral, representing Captain General Blanco. Manuel Santander, the Bishop of Havana, had donated the ground for the burials.   The population that lined the route of the funeral procession, gave every indication of the profoundest respect.

The funeral cortege started from the principal entrance of the City Hall on Weyler Street, then turned to the right on Mercadores Street, then up O'Reilly Street along the right side of Central Park and finally to the right along San Rafael Street to the cemetery.

Consul General Lee, General Parrado, the Marquis Larinaga, Admiral Monterola, the chief officers of the " Maine," the representatives of foreign Government: and numerous other officials were present.   Two Spanish battalions furnished the bands.

The Investigation Begins.

A Naval Board of Inquiry, composed of Captain Sampson, of the "Iowa;" Captain Chadwick, of the "New York;" Captain Marix, of the "Vermont," and Lieutenant-Commander Potter, of the " New York," went to Havana, and proceeded promptly to investigate the causes of the explosion that destroyed the battleship.

The further the inquiry into the causes that led to the " Maine " disaster proceeded, the more remote appeared the chances that any evidence would be discovered to show that the disaster was due to accident.   Those divers who penetrated into the forward part of the wreck found that the whole forward end of the ship from a point just abaft the forward turret had been twisted fifteen or twenty degrees to starboard.   That part of the vessel was a wilderness of debris and curled and twisted plates.

The sharp, jagged edges of some of the plates added danger to the difficulties of the divers' getting life lines into a tangle and fraying the cords.   In one instance they almost cut through a rubber tube which supplied a diver with air.   One important discovery made was the position of the bodies found in the wreck, one hundred of which were floating about the torn compartments.   A full score of these were examined.

All of these bodies were in hammocks, and all had the arms curved upward.   They looked as if the men had been startled by some sudden shock of danger and were in the act of reaching up for their hammock hooks to swing themselves on deck when death came. This seemed to confirm what had already been said about there having been two explosions—the first startling the men into the act of arising from their hammocks, the other dashing the life out of them while they were in that position.

Before the explosion the ten-inch magazine was located on the starboard side forward and beneath the forward turret. What was left of the magazine seemed to have been driven toward the port bow, in a diagonal and upward direction. The six-inch magazine, which had its location in the port side of the ship forward, was hurled in a direction directly opposite to that of the ten-inch magazine. One of the copper cylindrical tanks for the six-inch magazine was found by the divers in the wreck of that structure. It contained no powder charge.

Strange Tales of the Shocking Disaster.

The ten-inch magazine was not closely examined, but such inspection of it as was made led to the belief that a big pile of twisted wreckage that lay about the top of it was composed of unexploded ten-inch charges.

It was believed that the six-inch magazine was exploded by the first shock that was felt and that there was another explosion in the ten-inch magazine.

Many strange tales of the disaster were brought out as the days wore on. One of these was made known publicly, when the captain of an English bark anchored in the harbor, nearly a mile distant from the " Maine," told how a man's jaw had fallen on the deck of his vessel. The captain was asked to appear as a witness before the Court of Inquiry.

Every one in Havana believed that a crisis would follow close upon the heels of the investigation. The Spanish authorities realized that Spain was perilously near a rupture with the United States, and the suppressed excitement was felt in the air.

Captain Sigsbee and other officers of the " Maine " were called by the Board of Inquiry, and it was evident no effort would be spared to get the most complete information concerning the causes of the explosion.

Photographs of the wreck having been taken, these were submitted to Mr. Charles H. Cramp, the well known shipbuilder, of Philadelphia, who made the following comments :

" Examination of the original photographs of the ship as she lies indicates much greater destruction than at first thought. From them it appears that the ship is completely wrecked as to her upper works for at least half her length forward, and much damaged for a considerable distance abaft the region of total wreck.

" The mainmast, though left standing, shows considerable injury, doubtless by flying pieces of wreckage from forward. The prostration of both smokestacks indicates very great damage, if not entire wreckage, in the boiler spaces. This could not happen without serious effect in the engine rooms, though the engines may not be totally disabled.

Damaged Beyond Repair.

" To sum up, the photographs indicate an area of effect that could not have been caused by a single explosion in the forepart of the ship. Such wrecking could be caused only by several stupendous forces acting in quick succession.

" The photographs also indicate that the ship is too badly wrecked, and through too great a part of her length, for successful raising and restoration. The submerged portion is doubtless filled to a depth of several feet with the silt and ooze which covers the bottom of the Havana harbor, and this alone would seriously impede raising operations, even if there was enough left of the ship forward to get hold of, which, from the surface conditions as shown by the photographs, does not appear probable.

" From the meagre information before me I think the only practicable mode of raising the ship will be that of building a coffer dam around the wreck, pumping out and then patching her up, so she will float. And even this may be found impracticable."

As the investigation proceeded, a strong public opinion was aroused in support of the Government at Washington,

REPORT OF THE NAVAL BOARD.

For upwards of twenty days the country awaited in profound suspense the result of the inquiry of the Naval Board. During this time all sorts of conflicting rumors were afloat, but it was well understood that the government at Washington was pursuing a conservative course, and would not plunge the country into war without the greatest provocation.

At length the investigation by the Naval Board was completed and was transmitted to Congress, accompanied by a message from President McKinley, as follows :

To the Congress of the United States :

For some time prior to the visit of the "Maine" to Havana harbor our consular representatives pointed out the advantages to flow from the visit of national ships to the Cuban waters, in accustoming the people to the presence of our flag as the symbol of good will and of our ships in the fulfillment of the mission of protection to American interests, even though no immediate need therefor might exist.

Accordingly on the 24th of January last, after conference with the Spanish Minister, in which the renewal of visits of our war vessels to Spanish waters was discussed and accepted, the peninsular authorities at Madrid and Havana were advised of the purpose of this government to resume friendly naval visits at Cuban ports, and that in that view the "Maine " would forthwith call at the port of Havana. This announcement was received by the Spanish Government with appreciation of the friendly character of the visit of the " Maine," and with notification of intention to return the courtesy by sending Spanish ships to the principal ports of the United States. Meanwhile the " Maine" entered the port of Havana on the 25th of January, her arrival being marked with no special incident besides the exchange of customary salutes and ceremonial visits.

The " Maine" continued in the harbor of H᷃ ana during the three weeks following her arrival. No appreciable excitement attended her stay; on the contrary, a feeling of relief and confidence followed the resumption of the long interrupted friendly intercourse. So noticeable was this immediate effect of her visit that the Consul General strongly urged that the presence of our ships in Cuban waters should be kept up by retaining the " Maine" at Havana, or, in the event of her recall, by sending another vessel there to take her place.

At forty minutes past nine in the evening of the 15th of February the " Maine" was destroyed by an explosion, by which the entire forward part of the ship was utterly wrecked. In this catastrophe two officers and two hundred and sixty-four of her crew perished, those who were not killed outright by her explosion being penned between decks by the tangle of wreckage and drowned by the immediate sinking of the hull.

Recovering the Bodies of the Dead.

Prompt assistance was rendered by the neighboring vessels anchored in the harbor, aid being especially given by the boats of the Spanish cruiser "Alphonse XII." and the Ward Line steamer "City of Washington," which lay not far distant. The wounded were generously cared for by the authorities of Havana, the hospitals being freely opened to them, while the earliest recovered bodies of the dead were interred by the municipality in the public cemetery in the city. Tributes of grief and sympathy were offered from all official quarters of the island.

The appalling calamity fell upon the people of our country with crushing force and for a brief time an intense excitement prevailed, which in a community less just and self-controlled than ours might have led to hasty acts of blind resentment. This spirit, however, soon gave way to the calmer processes of reason and to the resolve to investigate the facts and await material proof before forming a judgment as to the cause, the responsibility, and, if the facts warranted, the remedy. This course necessarily recommended itself from the outset to the Executive, for only in the light of a dispassionately ascertained certainty could it determine the nature and measure of its full duty in the matter.

The usual procedure was followed, as in all cases of casualty or disaster to national vessels of any maritime state. A Naval Court of

Inquiry was at once organized, composed of officers well qualified by rank and practical experience to discharge the duty imposed upon them. Aided by a strong force of wreckers and divers, the court proceeded to make a thorough investigation on the spot, employing every available means for the impartial and exact determination of the causes of the explosion. Its operations have been conducted with the utmost deliberation and judgment, and while independently pursued, no source of information was neglected and the fullest opportunity was allowed for a simultaneous investigation by the Spanish authorities.

Sudden Destruction of the Ship.

The finding of the Court of Inquiry was reached after twenty-three days of continuous labor, on the 21st of March, and having been approved on the 22d by the commander-in-chief of the United States naval force of the North Atlantic station, was transmitted to the Executive.

It is herewith laid before the Congress, together with the voluminous testimony taken before the court. Its purport is in brief as follows:

When the " Maine " arrived at Havana she was conducted by the regular government pilot to buoy No. 5, to which she was moored in from five and one-half to six fathoms of water. The state of discipline on board and the condition of her magazines, boilers, coal bunkers and storage compartments are passed in review, with the conclusion that excellent order prevailed and that no indication of any cause for an internal explosion existed in any quarter.

At eight o'clock in the evening of February 15th everything had been reported secure and all was quiet. At forty minutes past nine o'clock the vessel was suddenly destroyed. There were two distinct explosions with a brief interval between them. The first lifted the forward part of the ship very perceptibly; the second, which was more open, prolonged and of greater volume, is attributed by the court to the partial explosion of two or more of the forward magazines.

The evidence of the divers establishes that the after part of the ship was practically intact and sank in that condition a very few minutes after the explosion. The forward part was completely demolished. Upon the evidence of a concurrent external cause the finding of the court is as follows:

At frame seventeen the outer shell of the ship, from a point eleven and one-half feet from the middle line of the ship and six feet above the keel, when in its normal position, has been forced up so as to be now about four feet above the surface of the water; therefore about thirty-four feet above where it would be had the ship sunk uninjured.

The outside bottom plating is bent into a reversed V shape, the after wing of which, about fifteen feet broad and thirty-two feet in length (frame 17 to frame 25) is doubled back upon itself against the continuation of the same place extending forward. At frame 18 the vertical keel is broken in two and the flat keel bent into an angle similar to the angle formed by the outside bottom plates. This break is now about six feet below the surface of the water and about thirty feet above its normal position.

Caused by the Explosion of a Mine.

In the opinion of the Court this effect could have been produced only by the explosion of a mine situated under the bottom of the ship, at about frame 18 and somewhat on the port side of the ship.

The conclusion of the court are: That the loss of the "Maine" was not in any respect due to fault or negligence on the part of any of the officers or members of her crew:

That the ship was destroyed by the explosion of a submarine mine, which caused the partial explosion of two or more of her forward magazines; and

That no evidence has been obtainable fixing the responsibility for the destruction of the "Maine" upon any person or persons.

I have directed that the finding of the Court of Inquiry and the views of this government thereon be communicated to the government of her Majesty, the Queen Regent, and I do not permit myself to doubt that the sense of justice of the Spanish nation will dictate a course of action suggested by honor and the friendly relations of the two governments.

It will be the duty of the Executive to advise the Congress of the result, and in the meantime deliberate consideration is invoked.

Signed   WILLIAM McKINLEY.

EXECUTIVE MANSION, March 28, 1898.

Finding of the Court.

The following is the full text of the report of the Court of Inquiry appointed to investigate the disaster to the "Maine" at Havana:

U. S. S. "Iowa," first rate, Key West, Fla., Monday, March 21, 1898. —After full and mature consideration of all the testimony before it, the Court finds as follows:

1. That the United States battleship "Maine" arrived in the harbor of Havana, Cuba, on the twenty-fifth day of January, Eighteen Hundred and Ninety-eight, and was taken to Buoy No. 4, in from five and a half to six fathoms of water, by the regular government pilot. The United States Consul-General at Havana had notified the authorities at that place the previous evening of the intended arrival of the "Maine."

2. The state of discipline on board the "Maine" was excellent, and all orders and regulations in regard to the care and safety of the ship were strictly carried out. All ammunition was stowed in accordance with prescribed instructions, and proper care was taken whenever ammunition was handled. Nothing was stowed in any one of the magazines or shell rooms which was not permitted to be stowed there.

The magazine and shell rooms were always locked after having been opened, and after the destruction of the "Maine" the keys were found in their proper place in the captain's cabin, everything having been reported secure that evening at 8. P. M. The temperatures of the magazine and shell room were taken daily and reported. The only magazine which had an undue amount of heat was the after 10-inch magazine, and that did not explode at the time the "Maine" was destroyed.

The torpedo warheads were all stowed in the after part of the ship under the ward room, and neither caused nor participated in the destruction of the " Maine." The dry gun cotton primers and detonators were stowed in the cabin aft, and remote from the scene of the explosion.

Waste was carefully looked after on board the " Maine" to obviate danger. Special orders in regard to this had been given by the commanding officer. Varnishes, dryers, alcohol and other combustibles of this nature were stowed on or above the main deck and could not have had anything to do with the destruction of the " Maine." The medical stores were stored aft under the ward room and remote from the scene of the explosion. No dangerous stores of any kind were stowed below in any of the other store rooms.

Careful Inspection of the Bunkers.

The coal bunkers were inspected daily. Of those bunkers adjacent to the forward magazines and shell rooms four were empty, namely, " B3, B4, B5 and B6." " A5 " had been in use that day and " A16 " was full of new river coal. This coal had been carefully inspected before receiving it on board. The bunker in which it was stowed was accessible on three sides at all times, and the fourth side at this time, on account of bunkers " B4 " and " B6 " being empty This bunker, " A16," had been inspected Monday by the engineer officer on duty.

The fire alarms in the bunkers were in working order, and there had never been a case of spontaneous combustion of coal on board the " Maine." The two after boilers of the ship were in use at the time of the disaster, but for auxiliary purposes only, with a comparatively low pressure of steam and being tended by a reliable watch. These boilers could not have caused the explosion of the ship. The four forward boilers have since been found by the divers and are in a fair condition.

On the night of the destruction of the Maine everything had been reported secure for the night at 8 P. M. by reliable persons, through the proper authorities, to the commanding officer. At the time the " Maine " was destroyed the ship was quiet, and, therefore, least liable to accident caused by movements from those on board.

3. The destruction of the " Maine " occurred at 9.40 P. M. on the 15th day of February, 1898, in the harbor of Havana, Cuba, she being at the time moored to the same buoy to which she had been taken upon her arrival.

There were two explosions of a distinctly different character, with a very short but distinct interval between them, and the forward part of the ship was lifted to a marked degree at the time of the first explosion.

The first explosion was more in the nature of a report, like that of a gun, while the second explosion was more open, prolonged and of greater volume. This second explosion was, in the opinion of the court, caused by the partial explosion of two or more of the forward magazines of the " Maine."

Wreck of the Forward Part.

The evidence bearing upon this, being principally obtained from divers, did not enable the court to form a definite conclusion as to the condition of the wreck, although it was established that the after part of the ship was practically intact and sank in that condition a very few minutes after the destruction of the forward part.

4. The following facts in regard to the forward part of the ship are, however, established by the testimony : That portion of the port side of the protective deck which extends from about frame 30 to about frame 41 was blown up aft, and over to port, the main deck from about frame 30 to about frame 41 was blown up aft, and slightly over to starboard, folding the forward part of the middle superstructure over and on top of the after part.

This was, in the opinion of the court, caused by the partial explosion of two or more of the forward magazines of the " Maine."

5. At frame 17 the outer shell of the ship, from a point eleven and one-half feet from the middle line of the ship and six feet above the keel when in its normal position, has been forced up so as to be now about four feet above the surface of the water, therefore, about thirty-

four feet above where it would be had the ship sunk uninjured. The outside bottom plating is bent into a reversed V shape, the after wing of which, about fifteen feet broad and thirty-two feet in length (from frame 17 to frame 25) is doubled back upon itself against the continuation of the same plating extending forward.

Not Due to Negligence on Board.

At frame 18 the vertical keel is broken in two and the flat keel bent into an angle similar to the angle formed by the outside bottom plating. This break is now about six feet below the surface of the water and about thirty feet above its normal position.

In the opinion of the court this effect could have been produced only by the explosion of a mine situated under the bottom of the ship at about frame 18, and somewhat on the port side of the ship.

6. The court finds that the loss of the "Maine" on the occasion named was not in any respect due to fault or negligence on the part of the officers or men of the crew of said vessel.

7. In the opinion of the court the "Maine" was destroyed by the explosion of a submarine mine, which caused the partial explosion of two of her forward magazines.

8. The court has been unable to obtain evidence fixing the responsibility for the destruction of the "Maine" upon any person or persons.

W. T. SAMPSON,

Captain U. S. N., President.

A. MARIX,

Lieutenant Commander U. S. N., Judge Advocate.

Important Message from President McKinley.

Following the destruction of the battleship " Maine," which, as already noted, stirred the resentment of the entire country to a marked degree, negotiations were continued by our government with Spain for the purpose of putting an end to the war in Cuba, which, it was admitted by all, had been attended with intolerable cruelties. Perhaps the exact number of those who perished by starvation, as the result of the Spanish policy in that Island, will never be known; suffice it to say, that the land was in desolation; starvation and death on every side aroused the indignation of the civilized world.

Meanwhile there was a very restless feeling in Congress, and definite action toward intervention between Spain and Cuba was delayed only by the expectation of a message from President McKinley that would deal vigorously with the whole question. The message was held back in order that the views of our government might, if possible, be accepted by Spain and the issues between the two governments settled by diplomacy.

On the 11th of April, 1898, the President transmitted to Congress his message, which contained the following statements and recommendations :

To the Congress of the United States :

Obedient to that precept of the Constitution which commands the President to give from time to time to the Congress information of the state of the Union and to recommend to their consideration such measures as he shall judge necessary and expedient, it becomes my duty now to address your body with regard to the grave crisis that has arisen in the relations of the United States to Spain by reason of the warfare that for more than three years has raged in the neighboring island of Cuba. I do so because of the intimate connection of the Cuban question with the state of our own Union, and the grave relation the course which it is now incumbent upon the nation to adopt must needs bear to the traditional policy of our Government if it is to accord with the precepts laid down by the founders of the Republic and religiously observed by succeeding administrations to the present day.

41

The present revolution is but the successor of other similar insurrections which have occurred in Cuba against the dominion of Spain, extending over a period of nearly half a century, each of which during its progress has subjected the United States to great effort and expense in enforcing its neutrality laws, caused enormous losses to American trade and commerce, caused irritation, annoyance, and disturbance among our citizens, and by the exercise of cruel, barbarous, and uncivilized practices of warfare, shocked the sensibilities and offended the humane sympathies of our people.

Ravages of Fire and Sword.

Since the present revolution began, in February, 1895, this country has seen the fertile domain at our threshold ravaged by fire and sword in the course of a struggle unequalled in the history of the island, and rarely paralleled as to the number of the combatants and the bitterness of the contest by any revolution of modern times, where a dependent people striving to be free have been oppressed by the power of the sovereign State. Our people have beheld a once prosperous community reduced to comparative want, its lucrative commerce virtually paralyzed, its exceptional productiveness diminished, its fields laid waste, its mills in ruins, and its people perishing by tens of thousands from hunger and destitution. We have found ourselves constrained in the observance of that strict neutrality which our laws enjoin, and which the law of nations commands, to police our waters and watch our own seaports in prevention of any unlawful act in aid of the Cubans.

Our trade has suffered, the capital invested by our citizens in Cuba has been largely lost, and the temper and forbearance of our people have been so seriously tried as to beget a perilous unrest among our own citizens, which has inevitably found its expression from time to time in the National Legislature, so that issues wholly external to our own body politic stand in the way of that close devotion to domestic advancement that becomes a self-contained Commonwealth, whose primal maxim has been the avoidance of all foreign entanglements. All this must needs awaken, and has indeed aroused, the utmost concern on the part of this Government as well during my predecessor's term as in my own.

In April, 1896, the evils from which our country suffered through the Cuban war became so onerous that my predecessor made an effort to bring about a peace through the mediation of this Government in any way that might tend to an honorable adjustment of the contest between Spain and her revolted colony, on the basis of some effective scheme of self-government for Cuba under the flag and sovereignty of Spain. It failed, through the refusal of the Spanish Government then in power to consider any form of mediation or, indeed, any plan of settlement which did not begin with the actual submission of the insurgents to the mother country, and then only on such terms as Spain herself might see fit to grant. The war continued unabated. The resistance of the insurgents was in no wise diminished.

The efforts of Spain were increased both by the despatch of fresh levies to Cuba and by the addition to the horrors of the strife of a new and inhuman phase, happily unprecedented in the modern history of civilized Christian peoples. The policy of devastation and concentration by the Captain-General's bando of October, 1896, in the province of Pinar del Rio was thence extended to embrace all of the island to which the power of the Spanish arms was able to reach by occupation or by military operations. The peasantry, including all dwelling in the open agricultural interior, were driven into the garrison towns or isolated places held by the troops. The raising and moving of provisions of all kinds were interdicted. The fields were laid waste, dwellings unroofed and fired, mills destroyed, and, in short, everything that could desolate the land and render it unfit for human habitation or support was commanded by one or the other of the contending parties and executed by all the powers at their disposal.

Misery and Starvation.

By the time the present Administration took office a year ago, reconcentration—so-called—had been made effective over the better part of the four central and western provinces, Santa Clara, Mantanzas, Havana and Pinar del Rio. The agricultural population, to the estimated number of 300,000 or more, was herded within the towns and their immediate vicinage, deprived of the means of support, rendered destitute of shelter, left poorly clad, and exposed to the most unsanitary conditions. As the scarcity of food increased with the devastation of the depopulated areas of production, destitution and want became misery and starvation.

Month by month the death rate increased in an alarming ratio. By March, 1897, according to conservative estimate from official Spanish sources, the mortality among the reconcentrados, from starvation and the diseases thereto incident, exceeded 50 per centum of their total number. No practiced relief was accorded to the destitute. The overburdened towns, already suffering from the general dearth, could give no aid.

In this state of affairs my administration found itself confronted with the grave problem of its duty. My message of last December reviewed the situation, and narrated the steps taken with a view to relieving its acuteness and opening the way to some form of honorable settlement. The assassination of the Prime Minister. Canovas, led to a change of Government in Spain. The former Administration pledged to subjugation without concession gave place to that of a more liberal party committed long in advance to a policy of reform involving the wider principle of home rule for Cuba and Porto Rico.

Relief for the Suffering Cubans.

The overtures of this Government made through its new Envoy, General Woodford, and looking to an immediate and effective amelioration of the condition of the island, although not accepted to the extent of admitted meditation in any shape, were met by assurances that home rule, in an advanced phase, would be forthwith offered to Cuba, without waiting for the war to end, and that more humane methods should thenceforth prevail in the conduct of hostilities.

While these negotiations were in progress, the increasing destitution of the unfortunate reconcentrados and the alarming mortality among them claimed earnest attention. The success which had attended the limited measure of relief extended to the suffering American citizens among them by the judicious expenditure through the Consular agencies of the money appropriated expressly for their succor by the joint resolution approved May 24, 1897, prompted the humane extension of a similar scheme of aid to the great body of sufferers. A suggestion to this end was acquiesced in by the Spanish authorities. On the 24th of December last I caused to be issued an appeal to the American people inviting contributions in money or in kind for the succor of the starving sufferers in Cuba, following this on the 8th of January by a similar public announcement of the formation of a Central Cuban Relief Committee, with headquarters in New York City, composed of three members representing the National Red Cross and the religious and business elements of the community.

Coincidently with these declarations, the new Government of Spain continued to complete the policy already begun by its predecessor of testifying friendly regard for this nation by releasing American citizens held under one charge or another connected with the insurrection, so that, by the end of November, not a single person entitled in any way to our national protection remained in a Spanish prison.

The war in Cuba is of such a nature that short of subjugation or extermination a final military victory for either side seems impracticable. The alternative lies in the physical exhaustion of the one or the other party, or perhaps of both—a condition which in effect ended the ten years' war by the truce of Zanjon. The prospect of such a protraction and conclusion of the present strife is a contingency hardly to be contemplated with equanimity by the civilized world, and least of all by the United States, affected and injured as we are, deeply and intimately by its very existence.

Realizing this, it appeared to be my duty in a spirit of true friendliness, no less to Spain than to the Cubans who have so much to lose by the prolongation of the struggle, to seek to bring about an immediate termination of the war. To this end I submitted on the 27th ultimo, as a result of much representation and correspondence through the United States Minister at Madrid, propositions to the Spanish Government looking to an armistice until October 1, for the negotiation of peace with the good offices of the President.

Measures Proposed by Spain.

In addition I asked the immediate revocation of the order of reconcentration so as to permit the people to return to their farms and the needy to be relieved with provisions and supplies from the United States, co-operating with the Spanish authorities so as to afford full relief.

The reply of the Spanish Cabinet was received on the night of the 31st ultimo. It offers as the means to bring about peace in Cuba, to confide the preparation thereof to the Insular Parliament, inasmuch as the concurrence of that body would be necessary to reach a final result, it being, however, understood that the powers reserved by the Constitution to the central Government are not lessened or diminished. As the Cuban Parliament does not meet until the 4th of May next, the Spanish Government would not object for its part to accept at once a suspension of hostilities if asked for by the insurgents from the General-in-Chief, to whom it would pertain in such case to determine the duration and conditions of the armistice.

The propositions submitted by General Woodford and the reply of the Spanish Government were both in the form of brief memoranda, the texts of which are before me, and are substantially in the language above given.

There remain the alternative forms of intervention to end the war, either as an impartial neutral by imposing a rational compromise between the contestants, or as the active ally of the one party or the other.

As to the first, it is not to be forgotten that during the last few months the relation of the United States has virtually been one of friendly intervention in many ways, each not of itself conclusive, but all tending to the exertion of a potential influence toward an ultimate pacific result just and honorable to all interests concerned. The spirit of all our acts hitherto has been an earnest, unselfish desire for peace and prosperity in Cuba, untarnished by differences between us and Spain and unstained by the blood of American citizens.

The forcible intervention of the United States as a neutral, to stop the war, according to the large dictates of humanity and following many historical precedents where neighboring States have interfered to check the hopeless sacrifices of life by internecine conflicts beyond their borders, is justifiable on rational grounds. It involves, however, hostile constraint upon both the parties to the contest as well to enforce a truce as to guide the eventual settlement.

Intervention to End the War.

The grounds for such intervention may be briefly summarized as follows: First. In the cause of humanity and to put an end to the barbarities, bloodshed, starvation, and horrible miseries now existing there, and which the parties to the conflict are either unable to or unwilling to stop or mitigate. It is no answer to say this is all in another country, belonging to another nation, and is therefore none of our business. It is specially our duty, for it is right at our door.

Second. We owe it to our citizens in Cuba to afford them that protection and indemnity for life and property which no government there can or will afford, and to that end to terminate the conditions that deprive them of legal protection.

Third. The right to intervene may be justified by the very serious injury to the commerce, trade, and business of our people, and by the wanton destruction of property and devastation of the island.

Fourth. Aid which is of the utmost importance. The present condition of affairs in Cuba is a constant menace to our peace and entails upon this Government an enormous expense. With such a conflict waged for years in an island so near us and with which our people have such trade and business relations: when the lives and liberty of our citizens are in constant danger and their property destroyed and themselves ruined; where our trading vessels are liable to seizure and are seized at our very door by warships of a foreign nation, the expeditions of filibustering that we are powerless altogether to prevent, and the irritating questions and entanglements thus arising—all these and others that I need not mention, with the resulting strained relations, are a constant menace to our peace and compel us to keep on a semi-war footing with a nation with which we are at peace.

The Maine Tragedy.

These elements of danger and disorder already pointed out have been strikingly illustrated by a tragic event which has deeply and justly moved the American people. I have already transmitted to Congress the report of the Naval Court of Inquiry on the destruction of the battleship " Maine " in the harbor of Havana during the night of the 15th of February. The destruction of that noble vessel has filled the national heart with inexpressible horror. Two hundred and fifty-eight brave sailors and marines and two officers of our navy, reposing in the fancied security of a friendly harbor, have been hurled to death, grief and want brought to their homes and sorrow to the nation.

The Naval Court of Inquiry, which, it is needless to say, commands the unqualified confidence of the Government, was unanimous in its conclusions that the destruction of the " Maine " was caused by an exterior explosion—that of a submarine mine. It did not assume to place the responsibility. That remains to be fixed.

In any event the destruction of the " Maine," by whatever exterior cause, is a patent and impressive proof of a state of things in Cuba that is intolerable. That condition is thus shown to be such that the Spanish Government cannot assure safety and security to a vessel of the American Navy in the harbor of Havana on a mission of peace and rightfully there.

Further referring in this connection to recent diplomatic correspondence, a despatch from our Minister to Spain, of the 26th ultimo, contained the statement that the Spanish Minister for Foreign Affairs assured him positively that Spain will do all that the highest honor and justice required in the matter of the Maine. The reply above referred to of the 31st ultimo also contained an expression of the readiness of Spain to submit to an arbitration all the differences which can arise in this matter, which is subsequently explained by the note of the Spanish Minister at Washington of the 10th instant as follows :—

As to the question of fact which springs from the diversity of views between the report of the American and Spanish boards, Spain proposes that the fact be ascertained by an impartial investigation by experts, whose decision Spain accepts in advance. To this I have made no reply.

In view of these facts and of these considerations, I ask the Congress to authorize and empower the President to take measures to secure a full and final termination of hostilities between the government of Spain and the people of Cuba, and to secure in the island the establishment of a stable government capable of maintaining order and observing its international obligations, insuring peace and tranquillity and the security of its citizens as well as our own, and to use the military and naval forces of the United States as may be necessary for these purposes.

And in the interest of humanity and to aid in preserving the lives of the starving people of the Island I recommend that the distribution of food and supplies be continued, and that an appropriation be made out of the public treasury to supplement the charity of our citizens. The issue is now with Congress. It is a solemn responsibility. I have exhausted every effort to relieve the intolerable condition of affairs which is at our doors.

Prepared to execute every obligation imposed upon me by the Constitution and the law, I await your action.

The Addenda.

Yesterday, and since the preparation of the foregoing message official information was received by me that the latest decree of the Queen Regent of Spain directs General Blanco in order to prepare and facilitate peace, to proclaim a suspension of hostilities, the duration and details of which have not yet been communicated to me. This fact, with every other pertinent consideration, will, I am sure, have your just and careful attention in the solemn deliberations upon which you are about to enter. If this measure attains a successful result, then our aspirations as a Christian, peace-loving people will be realized. If it fails, it will be only another justificat'on for our contemplated action.

(Signed)   WILLIAM M'KINLEY,

Executive Mansion, April 11, 1898.

Prompt Action of Congress on the Message.

Congress acted at once upon the President's message. The House of Representatives passed unanimously a resolution embodying the recommendations contained in the message, authorizing the President to use the land and naval forces of the United States to put an end to the war in Cuba and establish an independent government on the Island. The Senate, however, desired that stronger action should be taken, and a resolution was passed recognizing the Republic of Cuba and granting the President authority to employ the military forces of the United States for the purpose of giving effect to the resolution.

Then followed an earnest effort on the part of the two branches of Congress to come to an agreement. After one of the hardest fought battles between the two Houses known in many years, Congress at an early hour on the morning of April 19th, came to an agreement upon the most momentous question it has dealt with in a third of a century. The Cuban resolution was passed and sent to the President. Its provisions meant the expulsion of Spain from the island of Cuba by the armed forces of the United States. There were many roll calls in both Houses and each body held tenaciously for its own resolution.

The conference had great difficulty in agreeing. The first conference showed a determination on the part of the House not to yield a single point, and it was only after long consultations with the House leaders that they agreed to allow the little words " are and " in the first section of the Senate resolution, which declares that the people of Cuba are, and of right ought to be, free and independent.

The resolution as finally adopted was that reported from the Senate Committee on Foreign Relations, with the addition of the fourth section, known as the Teller amendment, disclaiming any intention on the part of the United States to acquire Cuba. The conference report was adopted in the Senate by a vote of 42 ayes to 35 noes. In the House the report was adopted by a vote of 310 to 6,

The Resolutions.

The resolutions as finally passed are as follows : Joint resolutio.. for the recognition of the independence of the people of Cuba, demanding that the Government of Spain relinquish its authority and government in the island of Cuba, and withdraw its land and naval forces from Cuba and Cuban waters, and directing the President of the United States to use the land and naval forces of the United States to carry these resolutions into effect.

WHEREAS, The abhorrent conditions which have existed for more than three years in the Island of Cuba, so near our own borders, have shocked the moral sense of the people of the United States, have been a disgrace to Christian civilization, culminating, as they have, in the destruction of a United States battle ship with 263 of its officers and crew while on a friendly visit in the harbor of Havana, and cannot longer be endured, as has been set forth by the President of the United States in message to Congress of April 11, 1898, upon which the action of Congress was invited ; therefore,

Resolved, By the Senate and House of Representatives of the United States of America in Congress assembled,

First, That the people of the Island of Cuba are, and of right ought to be, free and independent.

Second, That it is the duty of the United States to demand, and the Government of the United States does hereby demand that the Government of Spain at once relinquish its authority and government in the Island of Cuba, and withdraw its land and naval forces from Cuba and Cuban waters.

Third, That the President of the United States be, and he hereby is, directed and empowered to use the entire land and naval forces of the United States, and to call into the actual service of the United States the militia of the several States to such extent as may be necessary to carry these resolutions into effect.

Fourth, That the United States hereby disclaims any disposition or intention to exercise sovereignty, jurisdiction or control over said Island, except for the pacification thereof, and asserts its determination, when that is accomplished, to leave the government and control of the Island to its people.

At 1.15 o'clock in the morning the Senate received the report of the Conference Committee of the two branches of the Congress, and twelve minutes afterwards had adopted it. There was a fight to the last minute, however, the advocates of recognition of the independence of the Island Republic standing their ground until they were fairly knocked down by a vote of 43 to 35.

The minority vote was cast by those who wanted radical action and insisted that the resolution should carry with it recognition of the independence of the Cuban Republic. Upon this a split developed which very nearly proved fatal to any action at all. The adoption of the conference report brought to a close one of the most interesting and tumultuous sessions of the Senate held in years. Such scenes of confusion and excitement have rarely been witnessed in the ordinarily staid and dignified body as characterized its proceedings from noon until nearly 2 o'clock in the morning.

Settlement of the Great Question.

Interest in all other questions was dwarfed into insignificance by the one overwhelming question of war—war which all now regarded to be absolutely inevitable. A feeling of bitterness grew up between the Senate and the House during the late afternoon and evening that at one time seemed likely to delay action. Cooler councils prevailed, however, and determination of the momentous question was finally reached.

Those who were fighting for recognition of the Island Republic early decided that the Senate should not take the initiative in requesting a conference between the two Houses. They further resolved that, when the Senate conferees were finally appointed, at least two of them should represent the majority sentiment of the body.

The radical advocates of independence slowly, but none the less surely, lost ground, however, being swept back by the powerful and compact minority opposed to them. They yielded only after one of the bitterest contests in the history of the Senate. They capitulated, but did not surrender.

The House was held true to the Administration mainly through the efforts of Speaker Reed. By a vote of 178 to 156 the Senate resolutions, amended so as to strike out the clause recognizing the Republic of Cuba, were adopted. The acceptance of the Senate resolution by the House was an invitation to harmony of action that should have been accepted, but the Republican Senators who voted originally for recognition met in Senator Quay's room and ten of them voted to continue to act with the Democrats, Populists and Silverites in upholding the Cuban Junta, without regard to the effect of such action upon their own country. The Senate refused to concur in the amended resolutions as returned from the House by a vote of 32 yeas to 46 nays.

The Senate also refused to ask for a conference, and the resolutions were sent back to the House. An effort was made to secure concurrence in the Senate resolutions, including that recognizing the Cuban Republic, but the administration forces stood firm, the vote resulting —yeas, 148; nays, 172. The House asked for a conference, and a Conference Committee was appointed, consisting of Messrs. Adams, Heatwole and Dinsmore, the latter having voted for the Senate resolutions unamended.

A Final Vote.

The Senate acceded to the request for a conference, and the Vice-President appointed, on the part of the Senate, Messrs. Davis, Foraker and Morgan. After a full and free discussion the conferees reported to the respective Houses that it was impossible to agree. The Senate conferees yielded the clause explicitly recognizing the Republic of Cuba, but insisted that the words "are, and," should remain, making the first section of the House resolution read : " That the people of the island of Cuba ' are, and ' of right ought to be, free and independent."

The House stood firm on a test vote after the report of disagreement by its conferees, and gave no signs of weakening. A second conference resulted in an agreement declaring that the people of the island of Cuba are, and of right ought to be, free and independent, but omitting the recognition of Cuban independence. The Senate accepted this report, thus receding from its original position. There was objection, however, to this reading as embarrassing the President, who could not consistently refuse recognition.

The President's message to Congress on Cuba had long been awaited, the delay for several days having occurred in order that General Lee and other consuls might escape from Cuba before hostilities broke out. On April 11th the message was finally sent, and a week later resolutions passed both houses of Congress calling upon our Government to intervene and demand independence for Cuba.

Our ultimatum to Spain embodying the demands of the resolutions of Congress was delivered to the Spanish minister at Washington on the 20th. He immediately called for and received his passports, and left for Canada. The same ultimatum was sent to the Spanish Government at Madrid, and on April 21st Minister Woodford was curtly handed his passports, thereby severing all diplomatic relations between the two governments.

The President's Call for Volunteers.

Aggressive measures were at once adopted by the authorities at Washington, and on April 22nd Admiral Sampson blockaded the port of Havana with the North Atlantic squadron. On the same date the United States gunboat "Nashville" captured the Spanish merchantman "Buena Ventura" in the Gulf of Mexico. In this capture the first gun of the war was fired.

On the next day President McKinley promulgated a resolution of Congress calling for 125,000 volunteers. The same day two more Spanish vessels were captured off Havana and towed into Key West. Also on that date Morro Castle, commanding the entrance to Havana harbor, fired on the United States flagship New York, but without inflicting any damage. Several other captures of Spanish vessels followed, chief of which was the steamship "Panama," which was taken by the "Mangrove," and proved to be a very rich prize.

These captures of Spanish vessels proved the activity of the smaller United States vessels attached to Admiral Sampson's squadron, and served to create enthusiasm on all the ships of the fleet, at the same time affording the country assurance that the war was to be prosecuted with vigor.

The next event of importance was the bombardment of Matanzas by the cruiser "New York," the flagship of Rear Admiral Sampson the monitor "Puritan," and the cruiser "Cincinnati," on April 27th From the fact that the Spaniards opened fire on our ships while the latter were making a reconnoissance in force, and when the vessels were nearly five miles out from the batteries, led to the belief that the enemy thought that all that was necessary to induce the United States fleet to move further away was for the batteries to open fire on them.

Opened Fire with a Vengeance.

But if, from former experience, they reached this conclusion, they found that forbearance had reached the limit, and they must have been intensely astonished when the "New York," being the farthest west, but the nearest in shore, opened fire with her batteries with a vengeance, and, steaming nearer shore, accompanied by her consorts, made such excellent practice with her guns that in eighteen minutes every Spanish gun was silenced.

While there are no casualties reported on board any of the attacking boats, the loss of life on the Spanish side must have been large. The guns of the monitor "Puritan" are believed to have caused the most havoc on the shore, but the markmanship of all the boats was superb.

The attack began shortly before 1 o'clock, and was concluded in less than twenty minutes. The Spaniards had been actively at work on the fortifications at Punta Gorda, and it was the knowledge of this fact that led Admiral Sampson to shell the place, the purpose being to prevent their completion. A small battery on the eastern side of the bay opened fire on the "New York," and the flagship quickly responded with her heavy guns. Probably twenty-five 8-inch shells were sent from the battery at our ships, but all of them fell short. A few blank shells were also fired from the incomplete battery. One or two of these whizzed over Admiral Sampson's flagship.

While the "New York" and the "Cincinnati" were locating the defences of Matanzas, the monitor "Puritan" attacked the Point Maya fortifications. The flagship then went in close and shelled Rubalcaya Point, while the "Cincinnati" was soon at work shelling the fortification on the west side of the bay. The range at the beginning of the engagement was about 7,000 yards, but it was reduced to about 3,000 when it was seen that the shots from the batteries fell wide of their mark.

The last shot fired from the shore was from Point Rubalcaya. The monitor "Puritan" let go with a shot from one of her 12-inch guns. Its effect was seen when a part of the fortification went into the air. The target practice of the flagship was an inspiring sight. At every shot from her batteries clouds of dust and big pieces of stone showed where the Spanish forts were suffering. The "New York" fired shells at the rate of three a minute. Cadet Boone, on the flagship, fired the first gun in answer to the Spanish batteries.

The Great Battle of Manila.

On May 1st, the American squadron, commanded by Dewey, won a complete and glorious victory over the Spanish fleet in the Philippines. The fighting was of the fiercest character, beginning in the early morning and lasting several hours. The bravery of the American seamen was of the highest character, and, led by the intrepid Dewey, inflicted upon the enemy a blow that may be termed almost a veritable rout.

The news of the battle, which came through Government sources and by way of the Spanish cable, showed that the attack was terrible in its energy. Signalling for the American transports to keep well out, and that the "Olympia" and "Baltimore" would engage the Spanish admiral's flagship, the "Reina Christina," and the "Castilla," the largest of the enemy's fleet, the American warships moved in line of battle on the Spaniards. On both sides of Manila are erected forts well manned, though the reports as to the strength of the armament were conflicting.

As soon as his ships had been worked around so that their starboard batteries presented a broadside to the enemy, Commodore Dewey began a terrific cannonading of the enemy's ships and the Spanish forts. Every shot told. The "Olympia's" battery consisted of four 8-inch rifles, ten 5-inch rapid-fire guns, fourteen six-pounders, six one-pounders, four machine guns and six torpedo tubes. The heaviest battery of the enemy was on the " Reina Christina," which had twenty-one guns and five torpedo tubes.

Commodore Dewey directed the movements of the squadron from the conning tower of the "Olympia." He moved his ship close up to the " Reina Christina" and sent shell after shell ploughing into the Spanish admiral's hull. Captain Charles V. Gridley, of the " Olympia," was with him. The superior aim and heavier projectiles of the " Olympia " soon began to tell, and the fire from the Spanish grew more wild and somewhat slower.

Captain Dyer, of the " Baltimore," put his ship in close fighting distance to the " Castilla." The " Baltimore" had four 8-inch and six 6-inch guns in her main battery to the "Castilla's " four 5.9-inch Krupp guns and two 4.7-inch and three 2.2-inch guns. Both ships had good secondary batteries for cruisers.

Loud Thunders of Battle.

The din of battle was terrific. All the while the Spanish forts were keeping up an incessant fire on the American fleet. The ships were enveloped in a cloud of smoke, weighted by the early morning air, and the incessant crack of the rapid-fire guns and booming of the big guns mingled into voluminous thunder.

The hot work on the " Olympia " brought the end of the " Reina Christina." A shot from the American exploded a magazine on the latter boat, and she took fire. Despite the efforts of the Spaniards the flames made rapid headway. Captain Gridley worked his ship around to rake the Spaniard. He fought the Spanish ship with one battery, and kept up a fire on the forts with the other. The masts on the American boats were shot away, but few shells got through the armor.

Several of the Spanish ships were deliberately blown up to prevent their capture by the American fleet. Pouring a murderous fire into the forts, the American flagship and several more of the boats forced the entrance to the harbor. They steamed to the west side of the bay and there landed their wounded. The victory of the American squadron was complete, and the Spanish fleet was annihilated.

Further details of the great battle at Manila fully confirmed the first reports. In the first assault Admiral Dewey's flagship, the Olympia, took the lead, the other vessels following in her wake at four ships' length. The Spanish fleet was approached by laps, each turn bringing the contestants nearer. By this plan the American vessels frequently poured broadsides into the enemy, but were themselves more exposed to fire.

At one time the smoke became so dense that it was necessary to draw aside, allowing the cloud to lift. The vessels were examined, and it was found that they had sustained no damage. Breakfast was served to the men, and in a few minutes they re-entered the fight with the greatest enthusiasm. The second fight was even more fierce than the first. It was in that that the Baltimore was struck.

A Shell that Did Terrible Execution.

During the first fight the Spanish Admiral's ship put bravely out of the line to meet the Olympia. The entire American fleet concentrated fire on her, and she was so badly injured that she turned around to put back. At this juncture the Olympia let fly an 8-inch shell, which struck her stern and pierced through almost her entire length, exploding finally in the engine room, wrecking her machinery. This shell killed the captain and sixty men, and set the vessel on fire.

In the heat of the fight the two torpedo boats moved out to attack the fleet. They were allowed to come within 800 yards, when a fusilade from the Olympia sent one to the bottom with all on board, and riddled the other. The second boat was later found turned upon the beach covered with blood.

In the second fight the Baltimore was sent to silence the fort at Cavite. She plunged into a cloud of smoke, and opened all her batteries on the fortifications. In a very few minutes a shell struck the ammunition, and the fort blew up with a deafening roar.

The work on the Baltimore was glorious. After the principal ships had been destroyed the Concord, Raleigh and Petrel, being of light draft, were sent in to handle the remaining vessels of the fleet. They made quick work of them. In taking possession of the land

42

forts several hundred wounded Spaniards fell into the hands of the Americans, and nearly 200 dead were accounted for on the spot.

Several shots struck the Olympia, and she was pierced a number of times.   One shell struck the side of the ship against the hospital ward.   The chaplain and nurses who were watching the fight through a port hole a few inches away were stunned by the concussion. Experts figured out the fighting volume of the guns of the respective sides as three for the Americans against seven for the Spanish.

In honor of his distinguished services Commodore Dewey was raised to the rank of Admiral, and Congress passed a series of resolutions thanking him and his men for services rendered their country.

Death of Ensign Bagley.

On May 11th Ensign Bagley, of the torpedo boat Winslow, and five men were killed, and five others were wounded, in Cardenas harbor, on the northern coast of Cuba, in an engagement with Spanish gunboats.   The Americans displayed great bravery in the face of danger, the action of the United States gunboat Hudson being especially notable in going to the rescue of the Winslow, and towing her out of range of the enemy's fire.   Ensign Bagley was the first to lose his life in the war.   On the same date there was an engagement between United States vessels and Spanish troops at Cienfuegos, on the southern coast of Cuba.   One American was killed, and six badly wounded.   The object of the expedition, however, was successful in cutting the cable from that point.

On May 12th General Wesley Merritt was appointed Military Governor of the Philippines, and orders were given for troops to be sent to Manila for the purpose of capturing the town and occupying the Island.   Agreeably to this order the cruiser Charleston sailed on May 18th for Manila, loaded with supplies and ammunition.

On May 12th Admiral Sampson's squadron arrived off Porto Rico, and for three hours bombarded the forts of San Juan, inflicting serious damage upon them and the town.   The Admiral then withdrew, stating that his object was not to capture San Juan, but to find, if possible, the Spanish fleet which had sailed some days previously from the Cape Verde Islands. Great mystery attended the movements of the Spanish squadron.

On May 19th the long suspense occasioned by the difficulty of ascertaining what Admiral Cervera intended to do with his fleet was over, and it was definitely known that his vessels were entrapped in the harbor of Santiago. The government resolved to send troops at once to that point to aid the fleet in capturing the town. While it was known that the Spanish vessels were inside the harbor of San-

LIEUT. R. P. HOBSON.

tiago it was considered impossible for our battleships to enter the harbor on account of mines which had been planted, and the formidable attack sure to be made by batteries on shore.

The entrance to the harbor of Santiago is very narrow, and vessels are compelled at one point to go through a channel not much over three hundred feet wide. Here occurred on the morning of June 3d one of the most gallant acts recorded in the annals of naval warfare. Lieutenant Hobson, naval constructor on the flagship of Admiral Sampson, conceived the plan of blocking this narrow entrance by sinking the collier Merrimac, thus "bottling up" Cervera and his fleet. The reader will be interested in a detailed account of this remarkable exploit.

When the Admiral's consent for making the daring venture was obtained, Mr. Hobson became impatient of all delay, and that very night, after the moon went down, he set the time for the attempt. Volunteers were called for on all the ships of the fleet. Whole cheering crews stepped forward at the summons for the extra-hazardous duty. About three hundred on board the New York, one hundred and eighty on board the Iowa, and a like proportion from the other ships volunteered, but Mr. Hobson decided to risk as few lives as possible.

He picked three men from the New York and three from the Merrimac. The latter were green in the service, but they knew the ship and had pleaded hard to go, and one man stowed away on board the collier.

Six other men selected from various ships, with Ensign Powell in command, manned the launch, which was to lie at the harbor mouth and take off those who escaped. The Merrimac was made ready. Six torpedoes were strung along her port side, with wire connections to the bridge. Her anchors were lashed at the bow and stern. Her cargo of coal was shifted, and her cargo ports were opened so that she would more readily fill when the time came to cut her anchor lashings, open the seacocks and torpedo her bulkheads.

A Critical Moment.

The work was not completed until after four o'clock Thursday morning; but, with the sky paling in the east, Mr. Hobson headed in on his desperate mission.

On board the ships of the fleet picketed about the entrance every officer and man, with many warm heart beats for their brave comrades, awaited the issue, with eyes anxiously fixed on the jutting headlands that marked the entrance of the harbor. But as the Merrimac steamed forward Rear Admiral Sampson, pacing the deck of the flag-ship, looked at his watch and at the streaks in the east, and decided that the Merrimac could not reach the entrance before broad daylight. Consequently the torpedo boat Porter, which was alongside, was despatched to recall the daring officer. Mr. Hobson sent back a protest, with a request for permission to proceed. But the Admiral declined to allow him to take the risk, and slowly the Merrimac swung about.

During the day Lieutenant Hobson went aboard the flagship. So absorbed was he in the task ahead of him that, unmindful of his appearance and of all ceremony and naval etiquette, he told the Admiral in a tone of command that he must not again be interfered with.

UNIFORMS OF UNITED STATES MARINES AND NAVAL OFFICERS.

661

"I can carry this thing through," said he, "but there must be no more recalls. My men have been keyed up for twenty-four hours and under a tremendous strain. Iron will break at last." When Mr. Hobson left the ship and the extended hands of his shipmates, more than one of the latter turned hastily to hide the unbidden tear. But the Lieutenant waved them adieu with a smile on his handsome face.

The Merrimac started in shortly after three o'clock Friday morning. The full moon had disappeared behind a black cloud-bank in the west. Three thousand strained eyes strove to pierce the deep veil of night.

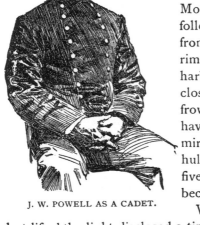

Suddenly there were several shots from the rocky eminence on which Morro Castle is situated. They were followed by jets and streams of fire from the batteries opposite. The Merrimac had reached the entrance of the harbor. She must have passed so close that a stone loosened from the frowning parapet of the Castle would have fallen on her deck. It seems a miracle that her apparently riddled hull could have reached the goal. After five minutes the firing ceased and all became dark again.

J. W. POWELL AS A CADET.

When the curtain of the night was at last lifted the light disclosed a tiny steam launch riding the waves at the very throat of the entrance of the harbor. In an instant the guns of the shore batteries were turned upon her, and, with a last lingering, vain look for the crew of the Merrimac, Ensign Powell headed his launch close along shore to the westward. In this lay his salvation. The guns of the batteries to the westward could not be depressed enough to hit the little launch, and the guns on Morro Castle would not bear upon her.

But the Spaniards, nevertheless, fired wildly, overshooting the

launch, until the latter was fully two miles up the coast.   Then some
of the shells began to drop fairly close, and one of them threw a cloud
of spray on board the small craft.   In the meantime the ships of the
fleet had drawn on until the New York, Massachusetts, Texas and
Marblehead were barely three miles from Morro Castle.

HARBOR AND FORTIFICATIONS OF SANTIAGO.
The star shows where the Merrimac was sunk.

The fire of the great guns continued, but the gunnery seemed to
grow worse, until the Spaniards became tired.   They were not rash
enough, except in two instances, to fire at the fleet, fearing probably
to provoke an antagonist with the strength of Admiral Sampson.
Knowing Hobson's desperate plan, the despatch boat had taken up
a position opposite the narrow harbor entrance and just outside the
line of the blockading war ships.

From here the Merrimac was seen entering the harbor.   A few
minutes later the fire of the Spanish batteries was seen to be concentrated westward close to the shore.   There a tiny thread of smoke
disclosed their target.   It was the New York's launch which Ensign
Powell had gallantly held close under Morro's walls until after daylight, when, driven out by the fire of the big guns, he had run far up
the shore, under the partial cover of the bluffs and had turned and

eventually boarded the Texas out of range. Then he passed the New York. The brave fellow was broken-hearted at not finding Hobson and his men.

Lying closer in than the war ships, Powell had seen the firing when the Merrimac and her dare-devil crew, then well inside Morro Castle, were probably first discovered by the Spaniards. He also heard an explosion, which may have been caused by Hobson's torpedoes. The Ensign was not sure. He waited vainly, hoping to rescue the heroes of the Merrimac, until he was shelled out by the forts.

The work, however, was done. The big vessel had been swung across the narrow entrance to the harbor, the torpedoes had been fired, the explosion had come, the great collier was sinking at just the right point; and her gallant crew, having jumped into the water to save their lives, were taken on board the flagship of the Spanish Admiral, who praised their bravery, and sent an officer under flag of truce to assure Admiral Sampson that the heroic band was safe and would be well cared for. Spanish chivalry was forced to admiration.

Bombardment of Forts at Santiago.

On June 6th Admiral Sampson's vessels made a combined attack on the forts at Santiago. The bombardment lasted for about three hours and nearly all the fortifications at the entrance of the harbor were silenced, more than half of the guns being dismounted and rendered useless. During the last hour of the bombardment the forts failed to reply, as the gunners were driven from their places by shot and shell from the American ships. In stately style the vessels moved to the attack; the marksmanship of Sampson's fleet was remarkably effective considering that heavy mist and rain obscured the batteries and the battle may be said to have been fought in the clouds.

As our ships steamed away some of the Spaniards returned to their guns and fired a parting shot; none of the American vessels were seriously injured and not a life was lost. Admiral Sampson's official report stated that he had silenced the enemy's works.

On June 13th, about 15,000 men under General Shafter left Key West for Santiago, and on June 22d the troops were landed at Baiquiri, on the southern coast of Cuba. The landing was very successful, having been accomplished in two days, with the loss of only two men, and that by accident. Preparations were immediately made to move the army forward towards Santiago, with a view to capturing the town.

It was not long after General Shafter's army landed before the United States troops were engaged in active service and had a sharp conflict with the enemy. The initial fight of Colonel Wood's Rough Riders and the troopers of the First and Tenth regular cavalry will be known in history as the Battle of La Quasina. That it did not end in the complete slaughter of the Americans was not due to any miscalculation in the plan of the Spaniards, for as perfect an ambuscade as was ever formed in the brain of an Apache Indian was prepared and Lieutenant-Colonel Roosevelt and his men walked squarely into it.

For an hour and a half they held their ground under a perfect storm of bullets from the front and sides, and then Colonel Wood, at the right, and Lieutenant-Colonel Roosevelt at the left, led a charge which turned the tide of battle and sent the enemy flying over the hills toward Santiago.

Number of Killed and Wounded.

It is definitely known that sixteen men on the American side were killed, while sixty were wounded or reported to be missing. It is impossible to calculate the Spanish losses, but it is known that they were far heavier than those of the Americans, at least as regards actual loss of life. Thirty-seven dead Spanish soldiers were found and buried, while many others were undoubtedly lying in the thick under-brush on the side of the gully and on the slope of the hill.

That the Spaniards were thoroughly posted as to the route to be taken by the Americans in their movements towards Sevilla was evident, as shown by the careful preparation they had made. The main body of the Spaniards was posted on a hill, on the heavily wooded slopes of which had been erect d two block houses, flanked by irregular intrenchments of stone and fallen trees. At the bottom of these hills run two roads, along which Lieutenant-Colonel Roosevelt's men and eight troops of the Eighth and Tenth Cavalry, with a battery of four howitzers, advanced.

These roads are but little more than gullies, rough and narrow, and at places almost impassable. In these trails the fight occurred. Nearly half a mile separated Roosevelt's men from the regulars, and between them and on both sides of the road in the thick underbrush was concealed a force of Spaniards that must have been large, judging from the terrific and constant fire they poured in on the Americans.

Beginning of the Battle.

The fight was opened by the First and Tenth Cavalry, under General Young. A force of Spaniards was known to be in the vicinity of La Quasina, and early in the morning Lieutenant-Colonel Roosevelt's men started off up the precipitous bluff back of Siboney to attack the Spaniards on their right flank, General Young at the same time taking the road at the foot of the hill

About two and one-half miles out from Siboney, some Cubans, breathless and excited, rushed into camp with the announcement that the Spaniards were but a little way in front and were strongly entrenched. Quickly the Hotchkiss guns out in the front were brought to the rear, while a strong scouting line was thrown out.

Then cautiously and in silence the troops moved forward until a bend in the road disclosed a hill where the Spaniards were located. The guns were again brought to the front and placed in position, while the men crouched down in the road, waiting impatiently to give Roosevelt's men, who were toiling over the little trail along the crest of the ridge, time to get up.

At 7.30 A. M., General Young gave the command to the men at the Hotchkiss guns to open fire. That command was the signal for a fight that for stubbornness has seldom been equaled. The instant the Hotchkiss guns were fired, from the hillsides commanding the road came volley after volley from the Mausers of the Spaniards.

"Don't shoot until you see something to shoot at," yelled General Young, and the men, with set jaws and gleaming eyes, obeyed the order. Crawling along the edge of the road, and protecting themselves as much as possible from the fearful fire of the Spaniards, the troopers some of them stripped to the waist, watched the base of the hill, and when any part of a Spaniard became visible, they fired. Never for an instant did they falter.

One dusky warrior of the Tenth Cavalry, with a rugged wound in his thigh, coolly knelt behind a rock, loading and firing, and when told by one of his comrades that he was wounded, laughed and said: "Oh, that's all right. That's been there for some time."

In the meantime, away off to the left could be heard the crack of the rifles of Colonel Wood's men and the regu-

NEW GATLING GUN READY FOR ACTION.

lar, deeper-toned volley-firing by the Spaniards. Over there the American losses were the greatest. Colonel Wood's men, with an advance guard well out in front and two Cuban guards before them, but apparently with no flankers, went squarely into the trap set for them by the Spanish, and only the unfaltering courage of the men in the face of a fire that would even make a veteran quail, prevented what might easily have been a disaster. As it was, Troop L, the advance guard under the unfortunate Captain Capron, was almost surrounded, and but for the reinforcements hurriedly sent forward every man would have probably been killed or wounded.

"There must have been nearly 1,500 Spanish in front and to the sides of us," said Lieutenant-Colonel Roosevelt when discussing the fight. "They held the ridges with rifle pits and machine guns, and hid a body of men in ambush in the thick jungle at the sides of the road over which we were advancing.

"Our advance guard struck the men in ambush and drove them out. But they lost Captain Capron, Lieutenant Thomas and about fifteen men killed or wounded. The Spanish firing was accurate, so accurate indeed that it surprised me, and their firing was fearfully heavy.

"I want to say a word for our own men," continued Lieutenant-Colonel Roosevelt. "Every officer and man did his duty up to the handle. Not a man flinched."

Gallant Charge on the Enemy.

From another officer who took a prominent part in the fighting more details were obtained. "When the firing began," said he, "Lieutenant-Colonel Roosevelt took the right wings with Troops G and K, under Captains Llewelyn and Jenkins, and moved to the support of Captain Capron, who was getting it hard. At the same time Colonel Wood and Major Brodie took the left wing and advanced in open order on the Spanish right wing. Major Brodie was wounded before the troops had advanced one hundred yards. Colonel Wood then took the right wing and shifted Colonel Roosevelt to the left.

"In the meantime the fire of the Spaniards had increased in volume, but, notwithstanding this, an order for a general charge was given, and with a yell the men sprang forward. Colonel Roosevelt, in front of his men, snatched a rifle and ammunition belt from a wounded soldier and, cheering and yelling with his men, led the advance.

"For a moment the bullets were singing like a swarm of bees all around them and every instant some poor fellow went down. On the right wing Captain McClintock had his leg broken by a bullet from a machine gun, while four of his men went down. At the same time Captain Luna lost nine of his men.

"Then the reserves, Troops K and E, were ordered up. There was no more hesitation. Colonel Wood, with the right wing, charged straight at a block-house about eight hundred yards away, and Colonel Roosevelt, on the left, charged at the same time. Up the men went, yelling like fiends and never stopping to return the fire of the Spaniards, but keeping on with a grim determination to capture that block-house.

"That charge was the end. When within five hundred yards of the coveted point the Spaniards broke and ran, and for the first time we had the pleasure which the Spaniards had been experiencing all through the engagement of shooting with the enemy in sight."

Deeds of Heroism.

In the two hours' fighting, during which the volunteers battled against their concealed enemy, enough deeds of heroism were done to fill a volume. One of the men of Troop E, desperately wounded, was lying squarely between the lines of fire. Surgeon Church hurried to his side, and, with bullets pelting all around him, dressed the man's wound, bandaged it, and walked unconcernedly back, soon returning with two men and a litter. The wounded man was placed on the litter and brought into our lines. Another soldier of Troop L, concealing himself as best he could behind a tree, gave up his place to a wounded companion, and a moment or two later was himself wounded.

Sergeant Bell stood by the side of Captain Capron when the latter was mortally hit. He had seen that he was fighting against terrible odds, but he never flinched. "Give me your gun a minute," he said to the sergeant, and, kneeling down, he deliberately aimed and fired two shots in quick succession. At each a Spaniard was seen to fall. Bell in the meantime had seized a dead comrade's gun and knelt beside his captain and fired steadily.

When Captain Capron fell he gave the sergeant a parting message to his wife and father, and bade the sergeant good-bye in a cheerful voice, and was then borne away dying.

Sergeant Hamilton Fish, Jr., was the first man killed by the

Spanish fire.   He was near the head of the column as it turned from the woodside into the range of the Spanish ambuscade.   He shot one Spaniard who was firing from the cover of a dense patch of underbrush.   When a bullet struck his breast he sank at the foot of a tree with his back against it.   Captain Capron stood over him shooting and others rallied around him, covering the wounded man. The ground was thick with empty shells where Fish lay.   He lived twenty minutes.   He gave a small lady's hunting case watch from his belt to a messmate as a last souvenir.

Impressive Burial Service.

With the exception of Captain Capron all the Rough Riders killed in the fight were buried the following morning on the field of action. Their bodies were laid in one long trench, each wrapped in a blanket. Palm leaves lined the trenches and were heaped in profusion over the dead heroes.   Chaplain Brown read the beautiful burial service for the dead, and as he knelt in prayer every trooper, with bared head, knelt around the trench.   When the chaplain announced the hymn, " Nearer My God to Thee," the deep bass voices of the men gave a most impressive rendering of the music.

The dead Rough Riders rest right on the summit of the hill where they fell.   The site is most beautiful.   A growth of rich, luxuriant grass and flowers covers the slopes, and from the top a far-reaching view is had over the tropical forest   Captain Brown marked each grave and preserved complete records for the benefit of friends of the dead soldiers.

Captain Capron's body was brought into Juragua, but it was deemed inadvisable to send the remains north at this season and the interment took place on a hillside near the seashore, back of the provisional hospital.   After a brief service a parting volley was fired over the grave of the dead captain and a bugle sounded " Taps " as the sun sank over the mountain tops beyond Santiago.

The valor of the American troops had been tested, and so far from being found wanting, it was found that the volunteers acted with as great bravery as is commonly shown by veterans.

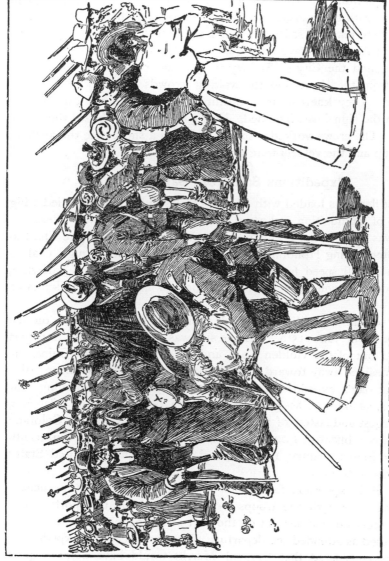

UNITED STATES TROOPS LEAVING SAN FRANCISCO FOR MANILA.

Troops from the Pacific slope were ordered to San Francisco, and on May 25th the transports which were to carry them to the Philippines were ready to sail. At four o'clock in the afternoon Brigadier-General Anderson gave the signal from the Australia for the City of Peking and the City of Sydney to get under way. The signal was seen from the shore and the waiting crowds commenced to cheer wildly. They knew what it meant as well as the sea captains for whom the signal was intended. No time was lost on board the transports. The crews worked with a will, and in a short time the anchors were up and the vessels were under way.

Expeditions Sail from San Francisco.

The fleet was loaded with supplies to last a year, and carried a big cargo of ammunition and naval stores for Admiral Dewey's fleet.

It was thought the fleet would not keep company with the Charleston after leaving Honolulu. All the vessels carried enough coal to steam at full speed from Honolulu to Manila, while the Charleston, in order to economize coal, would not go faster than ten knots an hour.

A second expedition weighed anchor at San Francisco on the afternoon of June 15th. As the sun was setting the last transport passed out of the Golden Gate, and, led by the flagship China, the fleet steamed away toward Honolulu, where the vessels will recoal.

That day's expedition carried 3,500 men, distributed among four vessels, as follows: assigned to the China, General Greene's flagship, the largest and fastest of the fleet, were the First Regiment Colorado Volunteer Infantry, 1,022 men; half a battalion of the Eighteenth United States Infantry, 150 men, and a detachment of United States Engineers, 20 men.

A third expedition for Manila was made ready at San Francisco, and on June 25th the troops went on board the transports. The same scenes of enthusiasm on the part of the people of the city were witnessed as attended the departure of the two preceding expeditions. It was considered that General Merritt would have a force quite sufficient to enable him to capture and hold Manila.

Admiral Sampson ascertained that Admiral Cervera's fleet had moved into the upper harbor of Santiago. General Shafter in his despatches to the Secretary of War complimented the fleet for its assistance in landing troops. With the soldiers landed from the Yale, and General Garcia's army transported from the westward, twenty-one thousand men in all had been disembarked in the vicinity of Santiago on June 29.

The American officers showed the utmost energy in preparing for the attack on Santiago; by July 1st everything was in readiness, and General Shafter ordered a forward movement with a view of investing and capturing the town. The advance was made in two divisions, the left storming the works at San Juan. Our forces in this assault were composed of the Rough Riders, commanded by Lieutenant-Colonel Roosevelt, and the First, Third, Sixth, Ninth and Tenth dismounted cavalry. Catching the enthusiasm and boldness of the Rough Riders, these men rushed against the San Juan defences with a fury that was irresistible.

Desperate Resistance by the Spaniards.

Their fierce assault was met by the Spaniards with a stubbornness born of desperation. Hour after hour the troops on both sides fought fiercely. In the early morning the Rough Riders met with a similar, though less costly, experience to the one they had at La Quasina just a week before. They found themselves the target for a terrific Spanish fire, to resist which for a time was the work of madmen. But the Rough Riders did not flinch. Fighting like demons, they held their ground tenaciously, now pressing forward a few feet, then falling back, under the enemy's fire, to the position they held a few moments before.

The Spaniards were no match for the Roosevelt fighters, however, and, as had been the case at La Quasina, the Western cowboys and Eastern " dandies " hammered the enemy from their path. Straight ahead they advanced, until by noon they were well along toward San Juan, the capture of which was their immediate object.

There was terrible fighting about the heights during the next two

43

hours. While the Rough Riders were playing such havoc in the enemy's lines, the First, Third, Sixth, Ninth and Tenth cavalry gallantly pressed forward to right and left.

Before the afternoon was far gone these organizations made one grand rush all along the line, carrying the Spaniards off their feet, capturing the San Juan fortifications, and sending the enemy in mad haste off toward Santiago. It was but three o'clock when these troops were able to send word to General Shafter that they had taken possession of the position he had given them a day to capture.

In this attack the cavalrymen were supported by the Sixth and Sixteenth infantry, who made a brilliant charge at the crucial moment. The advance was up a long steep slope, through a heavy underbrush. Our men were subjected to a terrific fire from the enemy's trenches, and the Rough Riders and the Sixth cavalry suffered severely.

Enemy Driven Back into the Village.

There was no artillery to support the attack. The dynamite gun, which a detachment of Rough Riders, under charge of Sergeant Hallett Alsop Borrowe, had hauled up from the coast with such tremendous effort, was jammed during the opening hours of the engagement and rendered useless for the time.

On the right General Lawton's division, supported by Van Horne's brigade, under command temporarily of Colonel Ludlow, of the Engineers, drove the enemy from in front of Caney, forcing them back into the village. There the Spaniards for a time were able to hold their own, but early in the afternoon the American troops stormed the village defences, driving the enemy out and taking possession of the place. Gaining the direct road into Santiago, they established their lines within three-quarters of a mile of the city at sunset.

While the battle was raging about Caney, Cuban scouts brought in the report that General Pando was hastening to the relief of the Spanish commander, General Linares, with four thousand trained Spanish troops. These reinforcements, the scouts reported, were within ten miles of the city.

General Shafter's advance against the City of Santiago was resumed soon after daybreak on the morning of July 2d. The American troops renewed the attack on the Spanish defences with impetuous enthusiasm. They were not daunted by the heavy losses sustained in the first day's fighting. Inspired by the great advantages they had gained on the preceding day, the American troops were eager to make the final assault on the city itself.

When the attack began the command of General Lawton occupied a position between Caney and Santiago, within three-quarters of a mile of the city. The Rough Riders, with Lieutenant-Colonel Roosevelt in command, were but a short distance further from the city, to the northwest of Aguadores. Between these troops, presenting a solid front along the entire eastern side of the city, was the main body of General Shafter's army.

Successes of Shafter's Troops.

Our forces began the day's fighting, hoping that the city would fall into their hands before dark. Their advance had been an uninterrupted series of successes, they having forced the Spaniards to retreat from each new position as fast as it had been taken. Admiral Sampson, with his entire fleet, joined in the attack.

General Shafter, by sending forces to the south of Caney during the first day's fighting, made it impossible for the Spaniards in that village to fall back into Santiago when they were driven from their position. They had to retreat toward the west, where an attempt was made to form a junction with four thousand of General Pando's troops, who were hurrying forward to reinforce General Linares.

It was estimated that the American losses in the first day's fighting, including killed and wounded, were over one thousand. The battles before the intrenchments around Santiago resulted in advantage to General Shafter's army. Gradually he approached the c ty, holding every foot of ground gained. In the fighting of July 2d, the Spanish were forced back into the town, their commanding general was wounded, and the day closed with the certainty that soon our flag would float over Santiago.

The fleet of Admiral Cervera had long been shut up in the harbor, and during the two days' fighting gave effective aid to the Spanish infantry by throwing shells into the ranks of the Americans.   On the morning of July 3d, another great naval victory was added to the successes of the American arms, a victory no less complete and memorable than that achieved by Dewey at Manila.

Admiral Cervera's fleet, consisting of the armored cruisers Cristobal Colon, Almirante Oquendo, Infanta Maria Teresa and Viscaya, and two torpedo-boat destroyers, the Furor and the Pluton, which had been held in the harbor of Santiago de Cuba for six weeks by the combined squadrons of Rear-Admiral Sampson and Commodore Schley, was sent to the bottom of the Caribbean Sea off the southern coast of Cuba.

Hurricane of Shells from Sampson's Fleet.

The Spanish admiral was made a prisoner of war on the auxiliary gunboat Gloucester, and 1,000 to 1,500 other Spanish officers and sailors, all who escaped the frightful carnage caused by the shells from the American warships, were also made prisoners of war by the United States navy.

The American victory was complete, and the American vessels were practically untouched, and only one man was killed, though the ships were subjected to the heavy fire of the Spaniards all the time the battle lasted.

Admiral Cervera made as gallant a dash for liberty and for the preservation of the ships as has ever occurred in the history of naval warfare.   In the face of overwhelming odds, with nothing before him but inevitable destruction or surrender if he remained any longer in the trap in which the American fleet held him, he made a bold dash from the harbor at the time the Americans least expected him to do so, and, fighting every inch of his way, even when his ship was ablaze and sinking, he tried to escape the doom which was written on the muzzle of every American gun trained upon his vessels.

The Americans saw him the moment he left the harbor and commenced their work of destruction immediately.   For an hour or two they followed the flying Spaniards to the westward along the shore line, sending shot after shot into their blazing hulls, tearing great holes in their steel sides and covering their decks with the blood of the killed and wounded.

At no time did the Spaniards show any indication that they intended to do otherwise than fight to the last. They displayed no signals to surrender even when their ships commenced to sink and the great clouds of smoke pouring from their sides showed they were on fire. But they turned their heads toward the shore, less than a mile away, and ran them on the beach and rocks, where their destruction was soon completed.

Spaniards Escape to the Shore.

The officers and men on board then escaped to the shore as well as they could with the assistance of boats sent from the American men-of-war, and then threw themselves upon the mercy of their captors, who not only extended to them the gracious hand of American chivalry, but sent them a guard to protect them from the murderous bands of Cuban soldiers hiding in the bush on the hillside eager to rush down and attack the unarmed, defeated, but valorous foe.

One after another of the Spanish ships became the victims of the awful rain of shells which the American battleships, cruisers and gunboats poured upon them, and two hours after the first of the fleet had started out of Santiago harbor three cruisers and two torpedo-boat destroyers were lying on the shore ten to fifteen miles west of Morro Castle, pounding to pieces, smoke and flame pouring from every part of them and covering the entire coast line with a mist which could be seen for miles.

Heavy explosions of ammunition occurred every few minutes, sending curls of dense white smoke a hundred feet in the air and causing a shower of broken iron and steel to fall in the water on every side. The bluffs on the coast line echoed with the roar of every explosion, and the Spanish vessels sank deeper and deeper into the sand or else the rocks ground their hulls to pieces as they rolled or pitched forward or sideways with every wave that washed upon them from the open sea.

Admiral Cervera escaped to the shore in a boat sent by the Gloucester to the assistance of the Infanta Maria Teresa, and as soon as he touched the beach he surrendered himself and his command to Lieutenant Morton and asked to be taken on board the Gloucester, which was the only American vessel near him at the time, with several of his officers, including the captain of the flagship. The Spanish admiral, who was wounded in the arm, was taken to the Gloucester, and was received at her gangway by her commander, Lieutenant Commander Richard Wainwright, who grasped the hand of the graybearded admiral and said to him:

"I congratulate you, sir, upon having made as gallant a fight as was ever witnessed on the sea."

Wainwright's Wonderful Fight.

Lieutenant Commander Wainwright then placed his cabin at the disposal of the Spanish officers. At that time the Spanish flagship and four other Spanish vessels had been aground and burning for two hours, and the only one of the escaping fleet which could not be seen at this point was the Cristobal Colon. But half a dozen curls of smoke far down on the western horizon showed the fate that was awaiting her.

The Cristobal Colon was the fastest of the Spanish ships, and she soon obtained a lead over the others after leaving the harbor, and escaped the effect of the shots which destroyed the other vessels. She steamed away at great speed with the Oregon, New York, Brooklyn and several other ships in pursuit, all of them firing at her constantly and receiving fire themselves from her after guns.

There seemed no possibility whatever for her escape, and while her fate was not definitely known for some time, it was predicted from the words of Captain Robley D. Evans, of the Iowa, who returned from the westward with 340 prisoners from the Vizcaya.

In answer to an inquiry, he shouted through the megaphone: "I left the Cristobal Colon far to the westward an hour ago, and the

Oregon was giving her hell. She has undoubtedly gone with the others, and we will have a Fourth of July celebration in Santiago to-morrow."

Captain Evans, who had been in the thick of the engagement up to the time he took the Vizcaya's officers and crew from the shore, said that to the best of his knowledge not one American ship had been struck. The torpedo-boat Ericsson, which also returned from the westward at about the same time, made a similar report, saying it was believed no man was injured on board the American ships, though another report had it that one man was killed aboard the Brooklyn. This report was afterward confirmed.

Decks Strewn with Dead and Wounded.

There was no means of telling what the Spanish loss was, but it was believed to have been very heavy, as the prisoners in custody reported their decks strewn with dead and wounded in great numbers, and besides, there was a statement that many bodies could be seen fastened to pieces of wreckage floating in the sea after the fight was over. A large number of the Spanish wounded were removed to the American ships.

Another account by an eye-witness gives additional particulars of the great battle :

"Three of the Spanish cruisers that were bottled up in Santiago harbor and two torpedo-boat destroyers were pounded into helpless hulks by the guns of Admiral Sampson's fleet on Sunday in a vain attempt to escape from the harbor. The vessels were beached in a last effort to save as many of the lives of the crews as possible.

"Admiral Cervera, on board the Maria Teresa, headed his fleet in the attempt to get away at about half-past 9 o'clock. So little were the Americans expecting the dash that the flagship New York was cruising up the coast to the east and returned only in time to see the finish of the fight and to fire a shot or two at the torpedo-boat destroyers.

"The Iowa, Indiana, Oregon, Massachusetts, Texas, Brooklyn and the converted yacht Gloucester, formerly the Corsair, formed in position to give battle as soon as the Colon was sighted rounding the wreck of the Merrimac.

"The American vessels did not open fire at once; they waited until Cervera's ships were out of the range of Morro's guns before giving battle. Cervera headed to the west, the Colon in the lead, followed by the Vizcaya and Oquendo and the destroyers, all firing rapidly.

"All of the American battleships opened fire at once, and the Spanish were soon in a hurricane of shot and shell, but the Teresa kept on bravely till when ten miles from the westward of Morro Castle, Admiral Cervera turned his vessel to the shore and beached her. She was blazing in a score of places, but her guns kept at work and the white flag never showed until she was completely disabled.

Desperate Bravery on Both Sides.

"The Oquendo and Vizcaya were opposed to the Iowa, Texas and Indiana and went down to defeat with fearful swiftness, covering only about half the distance made by the Colon before their captains ran them ashore. Their crews fought with desperate bravery, but their courage was no match for the courage of our men, added to their superb gunnery. The Spanish shells went wild for the most part, but the American gun-fire was marked by merciless precision. The two cruisers, both on fire, were beached not more than one-quarter of a mile apart.

"A most dramatic feature of the battle was the contest between the torpedo-boat destroyers and the Gloucester. The latter was struck several times and is the only American vessel reported damaged. At first the Gloucester fired upon them with her six pounders, but they ran past her and engaged the battleships.

"Finding the fire too hot, they turned and attacked the Gloucester again until both destroyers were afire and had to be beached. Their crews threw themselves into the surf to save their lives. Just before this the New York came up and assisted in giving the finish blow to the destroyers. There was explosion after explosion from the beached vessels."

General Shafter at noon, July 5th, repeated his demand for the surrender of the city, and notified General Linares that unless Santiago surrendered, hostilities would be resumed at noon on that day. Conferences with the Consuls of the foreign powers were conducted near General Wheeler's headquarters. The Consuls said there were 31,000 men, women and children foreign subjects in the city, and they required a cessation of hostilities in order to enable them to be removed outside Santiago, and to be placed under the protection of the United States. This was definitely refused by the American commander, who declined to accept any such responsibility.

Consuls Insist on Surrender.

The Consuls were told that it rested with them to insist upon General Linares' surrender. The conference was resumed at 9 o'clock next morning, when the Consuls expressed grave doubts as to General Linares' surrender, on account of the false telegrams in regard to Spanish victories and yellow fever among the American troops sent daily to Madrid, which caused the Spaniards to think they dare not surrender and return to Spain.

However, the foreign Consuls demanded the surrender of the city, but it was doubtful whether they would prevail. All the negotiations were submitted direct to Washington, thus causing some delay. General Shafter denied the existence of a regular armistice under the white flag, and it was believed hostilities would recommence on Tuesday, July 5th, at 10 o'clock in the morning, before which time the exodus of the 31,000 foreigners would be accomplished.

General Garcia's appearance at Dos Palmas was in accordance with plans agreed upon by General Shafter and the Cuban commander. It was feared by both generals that the Cubans under Garcia would be unable to prevent General Pando from forcing his way into the city, owing to superior numbers. But General Shafter believed that Garcia would be able to hold Pando in check long enough to enable the American forces to the east of the city to gain material advantages.

From the news brought by the refugees it was impossible to give particulars of the fight at Dos Palmas between the Cubans and

Pando's men.   All that was known was that Garcia's band, though outnumbered two to one, made a bold stand against the advancing Spaniards, and contested the way for a considerable distance.   The Spaniards finally broke through the Cuban lines, however, and pressed
on toward Santiago, effecting an entrance to the city from the west.

GENERAL WILLIAM R. SHAFTER.

General Pando was at the head of his troops in the fight with the
Cubans.   He passed along the line often, seeking to encourage his
men at those points where the fighting was fiercest.   His men were
discouraged when he fell to the ground, suffering from a wound in
his arm, but they quickly rallied and forced their way through the
Cuban columns.   General Pando was the third conspicuous Spanish
leader to fall in battle in the attack upon Santiago.

Considerable comment was caused among the officials of the War

Department, at Washington, by the great loss of American officers in the two days of fighting at Santiago. Official reports received indicated that fifty-eight American officers were either killed or wounded, and the list was only partial.

Speaking of the matter, Adjutant-General Corbin said that a finer lot of officers than was with General Shafter's corps in Cuba never wore shoulder straps. They were, he said, brave, aggressive, and brilliant, and were well worthy to carry the honor of the stars and stripes. General Corbin did not forget the enlisted men in his command, saying that the great majority of Shafter's force was the pick of the regular army—strong, resolute, admirably disciplined, and thoroughly enthusiastic and patriotic.

Heavy Losses of Our Army.

Shafter's army was laboring at great disadvantage, not only on account of the intense heat and the shock of a great battle, but also on account of the loss and disability of so many officers. While none of the general officers had been wounded, no less than five of them were ill, and were they at home would be in bed.

The heavy loss of officers was due to the dash and bravery of the officers themselves. Instance after instance was disclosed of officers springing in front of their commands and leading them in brilliant sorties against the enemy. Quite naturally the Spanish sharp-shooters singled out the officers as targets, and the result was that the American forces suffered particularly heavy in this respect.

Intelligence was received on July 6th that between 12,000 and 15,000 innocent victims of the war had fled to El Caney, just outside the city, in wild panic to escape the terrors of the threatened bombardment of Santiago, and they were confronted by the horrors of starvation. In their hopeless confusion they were appealing to General Shafter for succor. Most of them were foreigners, principally French, or with an admixture of foreign blood, and their interests were being looked after by their Consuls.

When they were informed that General Toral refused to consider the question of surrendering they swarmed out of the north gate of the city all day, and trudged under the blazing sun over the road, which in many places was ankle-deep in mud. Tottering old men and women were supported by children, and mothers with babes at their breasts struggled on toward El Caney, San Luis and other towns. Most of them reached El Caney on July 5th, and over five thousand of them slept in the village, which, under ordinary circumstances, hardly accommodates three hundred people.

They were crowded together in the houses, upon the verandas and in the streets. At daylight those who had been overtaken by darkness on the wayside began to pour into the village, numbering more than 15,000. They were not allowed to bring food with them, and those who had money were as destitute as those who were without. Rich and poor, cultured and ignorant, white and black, were huddled together, choking the passage-ways between the houses, all with gaunt despair written on their countenances.

Pathetic Sights on Every Side.

The ignorant desired only to be fed and the cultured wanted to get away, anywhere, anyhow, away from the war which had driven them from their homes. Pathetic sights were witnessed on all sides. There were ladies of good birth and education, supported by frail girls who hid their faces from the vulgar gaze of others who surged about them. In the eyes of both mothers and daughters was the haunted look which wild animals have when driven to bay.

Admiral Cervera sent to General Blanco at Havana the following report of the naval battle at Santiago:

"In compliance with your orders I went out yesterday from Santiago de Cuba with all the squadron, and after an unequaled combat against forces more than triple mine had all my squadron destroyed by fire. Teresa, Oquendo and Vizcaya beached and the Colon fleeing. I accordingly informed the Americans and went ashore and gave myself up. The torpedo-chasers foundered.

"I do not know how many people were lost, but it will surely reach 600 dead and many wounded. Although not in such great numbers, the living are prisoners of the Americans. The conduct of the crews rose to a height that won the most enthusiastic plaudits of the enemy. The commander of the Vizcaya surrendered his vessel. His crew are very grateful for the noble generosity with which they are treated. Among the dead is Villimil and I believe Lasaga (spelling uncertain), and among the wounded Concas and Eulate. We have lost all; are necessarily depressed. "CERVERA."

Exchange of Hobson and his Brave Men.

Assistant Naval Constructor Richmond P. Hobson, of the flagship New York, and the seven seamen, who, with him, sailed the collier Merrimac into the channel of the harbor of Santiago de Cuba on June 3d last, and sank her there, were surrendered by the Spanish military authorities, July 7th, in exchange for prisoners captured by the American forces.

Hobson and his men were escorted through the American lines by Captain Chadwick, of the New York, who was awaiting them. Every step of their journey was marked by the wildest demonstrations on the part of the American soldiers, who threw aside all semblance of order, scrambled out of the entrenchments, knocked over tent guys, and other camp paraphernalia in their eagerness to see the returning heroes, and sent up cheer after cheer for the men who had passed safely through the jaws of death in their desire to serve their country.

As Hobson and the men of the Merrimac approached the first line of entrenchments, occupied by the Rough Riders, low murmurs ran from one end of the line of cowboys and Eastern athletes to the other, and by the time the returning party reached them every man was on his feet, refusing to be restrained by the admonishing of the officers, cheering wildly and rushing over every obstacle that chanced to be in their way, in their efforts to reach Hobson and his party and grasp them by the hand. The released prisoners were soon surrounded and compelled to stop to receive the greetings, congratulations and vigorous, heartfelt handshaking of men they had never seen before.

Hobson, so far as possible, grasped each hand extended towards him, and neither he nor his men made any protest against the most uncomfortable crowding and jostling which they had to undergo.

If the young officer, whose home is in Alabama, had any race prejudice, he certainly forgot all about it as he passed through the lines of soldiers on his way to General Wheeler's headquarters. He saw it was the uniform of the United States army, and he cared not for the color of its wearers, grasping the hands of the ebony-hued troopers of the Ninth and Tenth Cavalry, and expressing his thanks for their patriotic welcome with as much heartiness as he displayed towards men of his own race. He and all of his men were completely overcome by the reception accorded them, and tears rolled down their cheeks as the soldiers crowded around them.

Hearty Cheers from Sailors and Marines.

The same scenes of enthusiasm were repeated upon the arrival of the men at the hospital station and at our base at Juragua. Hobson, who reached there in advance of his companions, was taken on board the New York immediately. The flagship's decks were lined with officers and men, and as Hobson clambered up her side and stepped on board his vessel the harbor rang with the shouts and cheers of his comrades, which were echoed by the crews of a dozen transports lying near-by. Hobson had little to say in regard to his experiences except that he and his companions had been well treated by the Spaniards and that they were all in excellent health.

In conducting the exchange Colonel John Jacob Astor and Lieutenant Miloy, accompanied by Interpreter Maestro, were in charge of the Spanish prisoners. These consisted of Lieutenants Amelio Volez and Aurelius, a German, belonging to the Twenty-ninth Regular Infantry, who were captured at El Caney on Friday last, and Lieutenant Adolfo Aries, of the First Provisional Regiment of Barcelona, one of the most aristocratic military organizations of the Spanish army, and fourteen non-commissioned officers and privates. Lieutenant Aries and a number of the men were wounded in the fight at El Caney. The Spanish prisoners were taken through the American lines mounted and blindfolded.

The meeting between Colonel Astor and Major Irles was extremely courteous, but very formal, and no attempt was made by either of them to discuss anything but the matter in hand. Major Irles was given his choice of three Spanish lieutenants in exchange for Hobson and was also informed that he could have all of the fourteen men in exchange for the American sailors. The Spanish officers selected Lieutenant Aries, and the other two Spanish officers were conducted back to Juragua.

It was then not later than 4 o'clock, and just as everything was finished and the two parties were separating, Major Irles turned and said courteously enough, but in a tone which indicated considerable defiance, and gave his hearers the impression that he desired hostilities to be renewed at once: "Our understanding is, gentlemen, that this truce comes to an end at 5 o'clock."

Siege Guns Ready for the Fight.

Colonel Astor looked at his watch, bowed to the Spanish officer, without making a reply, and then started back slowly to the American lines with Hobson and his companions following. The meeting of the two parties and the exchange of prisoners had taken place in full view of both the American and Spanish soldiers, who were entrenched near the meeting place, and the keenest interest was taken in the episode.

During the truce which General Shafter effected with General Linares, the Spanish commander at Santiago, the American land and sea forces perfected plans to deal a smashing blow upon the city of Santiago. It is impossible to tell yet just when this blow will be delivered, but it was expected to fall at noon on Saturday, July 9th.

General Shafter succeeded in getting his siege guns in commanding positions at the front, and Sergeant Hallet Alsop Borrowe had his dynamite guns repaired and in position on San Juan Hill. Our troops also fortified themselves with protected rifle pits, from which they would be able to do the enemy much harm without themselves being especially exposed to the enemy's fire.

In addition to these advantages gained on land by General Shafter he arranged with Admiral Sampson for the fleet to participate in the attack on the city. It was found impracticable for the fleet to shell Santiago from the bay, owing to the presence of mines and the stationing of Spanish riflemen to protect the mine fields. To get around this difficulty Admiral Sampson decided to bombard Santiago from off Aquadores, from which point the guns of the fleet would be able to do great damage in the beleaguered city.

The results of the operations against Santiago were foreseen by General Toral, who at once put himself in communication with the Spanish Government for the purpose of deciding whether to surrender or continue a hopeless conflict. After attempting to save the Spanish troops from being included in the terms of capitulation, General Toral, on July 14th, made an unconditional surrender to General Shafter.

Surrender of Santiago.

Cervera took his ships to Santiago on May 19, and on May 30 Commodore Schley reported that he had the Spanish Admiral bottled up. That was just six weeks before the surrender. On June 3, the Merrimac was sunk in the mouth of the harbor in an attempt to cork the bottle, which was not entirely successful. Shafter's troops began landing at Baiquiri, fifteen miles from Santiago, on June 22, and Cervera's fleet was taken out of the harbor and destroyed on July 3, after a sanguinary battle by the land forces, lasting two days, July 1 and 2.

After that time there was no fighting of consequence, ten days having been consumed in negotiations for the surrender of the city. The campaign really lasted no more than twelve days—from June 20 to July 3—but the losses were very heavy, aggregating at least 1,800 out of the army of 16,500 originally landed. The appearance of yellow fever was an admonition that these losses would be greatly increased if the army should be kept at Santiago.

By the terms of surrender our Government agreed to transport the ten or twelve thousand soldiers captured back to Spain. The downfall of Santiago was hailed with delight throughout the country.

We are able to furnish a reliable account of the preliminaries that preceded the surrender. It appears that on Monday, July 11th, General Shafter did not again demand the unconditional surrender of Santiago, which General Toral had refused on Sunday; but he offered, as an alternative proposition, to accept the capitulation of the enemy and to transport the Spanish officers and troops to Spain, they to leave all their arms behind. He offered also to accept their parole. This proposition General Toral declined.

Notable Council of War.

It was decided next morning to hold a personal interview with General Toral. General Miles and his staff, accompanied by General Shafter and his staff, rode out to the front shortly before eight o'clock under a flag of truce.

A request for a personal interview with the Spanish commander-in-chief was made and acceded to, and about nine o'clock General Miles, General Shafter, General Wheeler, General Gilmour, Colonel Morse, Captain Wiley and Colonel Mestre rode up, passed over our entrenchments and went down into the valley beyond. They were met by General Toral and his chief of staff under a spreading mango tree, at the bottom of the valley, about half way between the lines. The interview that followed lasted almost an hour.

The situation was placed frankly before General Toral, and he was offered the alternative of being sent home with his garrison or being attacked by the combined American forces. The only condition imposed was that he should not destroy the existing fortifications and should leave his arms behind. This latter condition the Spanish general, who does not speak English, explained through his interpreter, was impossible. He said the laws of Spain gave a general no discretion. He might abandon a place when he found it untenable, but he could not leave his arms behind without subjecting himself to the penalty of being court-martialled and shot. His government, he said, had granted him permission to evacuate Santiago. That was all. Further than that he was powerless to go.

Without saying so in words, General Miles stated that the tenor of

44

General Toral's remarks all betrayed his realization that he could not hold out long. When General Shafter explained that our reinforcements were coming up, that he was completely surrounded, and that new batteries were being posted, General Toral simply shrugged his shoulders. "I am but a subordinate," said he, "and I obey my government. If it is necessary we can die at our posts."

The Spanish General.

General Toral is sixty years old, with a strong, rugged face, and fine soldierly bearing. His brave words inspired a feeling of respect and admiration in the hearts of his adversaries. Nevertheless, the Spanish General's anxiety to avoid further sacrifice of life in his command was manifest, and he did not hesitate to ask for time to communicate the situation to Madrid, although he dubiously shook his head when he spoke of the probable response.

During the course of an interview General Toral said the bombardment of Sunday and Monday had done little damage. He admitted the shells from the guns of the fleet had destroyed four houses, but he asserted that only half a dozen soldiers of the garrison had been injured. He also volunteered the information when General Miles gallantly inquired after General Linares' condition that the latter would probably have his left arm amputated at the shoulder.

General Miles at the interview did not attempt to assume the direction of the negotiations, but, as General of the United States Army, he vouched for the conditions General Shafter offered. Upon the return of our commanders to the American lines an important consultation was held at General Wheeler's headquarters. Generals Garcia and Castillo, with their staff, had ridden around from the extreme right to see General Miles. It was a notable group gathered under the protecting awning of General Wheeler's tent.

General Toral was made to see that it would be madness for him to attempt to continue the struggle, that the American army was master of the situation, and the downfall of Santiago was only a question of time. There was but one thing for General Toral to do, and that was to surrender.

After the first announcement that General Toral would surrender, and commissioners had been appointed to arrange the details, the negotiations were halted by the urgent request of the Spanish commander that his troops be allowed to retain their arms. This request was peremptorily refused by our Government, and after further parleying, the Spanish government, seeing that continued resistance was useless, consented to the terms proposed by General Shafter.

The formal sanction by the Madrid government of the terms of capitulation unraveled the tangled skeins of demands and counter-demands between the opposing commanders which threatened to end the negotiations and compel a return to arms.

Terms of Santiago's Surrender.

The agreement consisted of nine articles:

The first declared that all hostilities should cease pending the agreement of final capitulation.

Second. That the capitulation includes all the Spanish forces and the surrender of all war material within the prescribed limits.

Third. The transportation of the troops to Spain at the earliest possible moment, each force to be embarked at the nearest port.

Fourth. That the Spanish officers shall retain their side arms and the enlisted men their personal property.

Fifth. That after the final capitulation the Spanish forces shall assist in the removal of all obstructions to navigation in Santiago harbor.

Sixth. That after the final capitulation, the commanding officers shall furnish a complete inventory of all arms and munitions of war, and a roster of all the soldiers in the district.

Seventh. That the Spanish general shall be permitted to take the military archives and records with him.

Eighth. That all guerrillas and Spanish irregulars shall be permitted to remain in Cuba if they so elect, giving a parole that they will not again take up arms against the United States unless properly released from parole.

Ninth. That the Spanish forces shall be permitted to march out with all the honors of war, depositing their arms to be disposed of by the United States in the future, the American commissioners to recommend to their government that the arms of the soldiers be returned to those "who so bravely defended them."

On the evening of July 17th the War Department at Washington posted the following despatches from General Shafter:

"I have the honor to announce that the American flag has been this instant, 12 o'clock noon, raised over the House of the Civil Government in the city of Santiago. An immense concourse of people was present, a squadron of cavalry and a regiment of infantry presenting arms and a band playing national airs. The light battery fired a salute of twenty-one guns.

The Situation.

"Perfect order is being maintained by the municipal government. The distress is very great, but there is little sickness in the town. Scarcely any yellow fever. A small gunboat and about two hundred seamen, left by Cervera, have surrendered to me. Obstructions are being removed from the mouth of the harbor.

"Upon coming into the city I discovered a perfect entanglement of defences. Fighting as the Spaniards did the first day it would have cost five thousand lives to have taken it. Battalions of Spanish troops have been depositing arms since daylight in the armory over which I have guard. General Toral formally surrendered the plaza and all stores at 9 A.M."

Amid impressive ceremonies the Spanish troops laid down their arms between the lines of the Spanish and American forces at nine o'clock in the morning of July 17th. General Shafter and the American division and brigade commanders and their staffs were escorted by a troop of cavalry, and General Toral and his staff by one hundred picked men. Trumpeters on both sides saluted with flourishes.

General Shafter returned to General Toral the latter's sword after it had been handed to the American commander. Our troops, lined up at the trenches, were eye-witnesses to the ceremony. General

Shafter and his escort, accompanied by General Toral, rode through the city, taking formal possession. The city had been sacked, before they arrived, by the Spaniards. General McKibben was appointed temporary military governor.

The ceremony of hoisting the Stars and Stripes was worth all the blood and treasure it cost. A vast concourse of 10,000 people witnessed the stirring and thrilling scene, that will live forever in the minds of all the Americans present. A finer stage-setting for a dramatic episode it would be difficult to imagine. The palace, a picturesque old dwelling, in the Moorish style of architecture, faces the Plaza de la Reina, the principal public square. Opposite rises the imposing Catholic Cathedral.

Raising the Stars and Stripes.

On one side is a quaint, brilliantly painted building, with broad verandas—the club of San Carlos; on the other a building of much the same description—the Cafe De La Venus. Across the plaza was drawn up the Ninth Infantry, headed by the Sixth Cavalry Band. In the street facing the palace stood a picked troop of the Second Cavalry, with drawn sabres, under command of Captain Brett. Massed on the stone flagging, between the band and the line of horsemen, were the brigade commanders of General Shafter's division, with their staffs.

On the red tiled roof of the palace stood Captain McKittrick, Lieutenant Miley and Lieutenant Wheeler; immediately above them, upon the flagstaff, the illuminated Spanish arms and the legend "Vive Alfonso XIII." All about, pressing against the veranda rails, crowding the windows and doors and lining the roofs, were the people of the town, principally women and non-combatants. The chimes of the old cathedral rang out the hour of twelve; the infantry and cavalry presented arms. Every American uncovered, and Captain McKittrick hoisted the Stars and Stripes.

As the brilliant folds unfurled in a gentle breeze against a fleckless sky, the cavalry band broke into the strains of "The Star Spangled Banner," making the American pulse leap and the American heart thrill with joy. At the same instant the sound of the distant booming of Captain Capron's battery, firing a salute of twenty-one guns, drifted in.

When the music ceased from all directions around our line came floating across the plaza the strains of the regimental bands and the muffled, hoarse cheers of our troops. The infantry came to "order arms" a moment later, after the flag was up, and the band played "Rally Round the Flag, Boys." Instantly General McKibben called for three cheers for General Shafter, which were given with great enthusiasm, the band playing "Stars and Stripes Forever."

Hungry Army of Refugees.

Since 4 o'clock in the morning a stream of refugees had been pouring into the city, some naked, and all hungry. Many had fallen by the wayside. The town of Santiago presented a dismal sight. Most of the houses had been sacked and the stores had all been looted and nothing to eat could be had. In the streets of the city, at the entrenchments, at the breastworks and at every hundred feet or so of the barbed wire fences were the living skeletons of Spanish soldiers.

Among the arrivals were the German, Japanese and Portuguese Consuls and their families, the British and French Consuls having arrived two days before.

Three thousand five hundred men from Manzanillo arrived on July 3d, making the total garrison 7,000. The contact mines in the harbor were removed the day Admiral Cervera left, but two chains of electric mines, one from Estrella Point and the other from Socapa, were still down.

Twenty-two thousand refugees were quartered at El Caney, 5,000 at Firmeza and 5,000 at Cuabitas El Bonito and San Vincente, where they had been living for a fortnight. In one case 500 were crowded into one building. The Spanish troops were encamped two miles outside the city limits, under guard, awaiting their embarkation.

The docks were crowded by incoming refugees in a starving condition, awaiting the arrival in the harbor of the Red Cross Society's steamer State of Texas with eatables.

OFFICIAL REPORTS OF THE DESTRUCTION OF CERVERA'S FLEET.

Official reports made by Rear Admiral Sampson and Commodore Schley on the destruction of the Spanish fleet at Santiago on July 3d were not made public until July 27th. They tell in detail of the work of each American ship in that great sea fight.

U. S. FLAGSHIP NEW YORK, First Rate. }
Off Santiago de Cuba, Cuba, July 15, 1898. }

SIR—I have the honor to make the following report upon the battle with and the destruction of the Spanish squadron commanded by Admiral Cervera off Santiago de Cuba on Sunday, July 3, 1898:—

2. The enemy's vessels came out of the harbor between twenty-five minutes to ten and ten A. M., the head of the column appearing around Cay Smith at twenty-nine minutes to ten, and emerging from the channel five or six minutes later.

3. The positions of the vessels of my command off Santiago at that moment were as follows:—The flagship New York was four miles east of her blockading station, and about seven miles from the harbor entrance. She had started for Siboney, where I intended to land, accompanied by several of my staff, and to go to the front to consult with General Shafter. A discussion of the situation and a more definite understanding between us of the operations proposed had been rendered necessary by the unexpectedly strong resistance of the Spanish garrison of Santiago.

I had the day before arranged to go to General Shafter's headquarters, and my flagship was in the position mentioned above when the Spanish squadron appeared in the channel.

Position of the Fleet.

The remaining vessels were in or near their usual blockading positions; distributed in a semi-circle about the harbor entrance, counting from the eastward to the westward in the following order:—The Indiana about a mile and a half from the shore, the Oregon—the New York's place between these two—the Iowa, Texas and Brooklyn, the latter two miles from the shore west of Santiago. The distance of the vessels from the harbor entrance was from two and one-half to four miles—the latter being the limit of day blockading distance.

The length of the arc formed by the ships was about eight miles. The Massachusetts had left at four A.M. for Guantanamo for coal. Her station was between the Iowa and Texas. The auxiliaries Gloucester and Vixen lay close to the land and nearer the harbor entrance than the large vessels, the Gloucester to the eastward and the Vixen to the westward.

The torpedo boat Ericsson was in company with the flagship, and remained with her during the chase until ordered to discontinue, when she rendered very efficient service in rescuing prisoners from the burning Vizcaya. I enclose a diagram showing approximately the positions of the vessels as described above.

4. The Spanish vessels came rapidly out of the harbor, at a speed estimated at from eight to ten knots and in the following order: —Infanta Maria Teresa (flagship), Vizcaya, Cristobal Colon and the Almirante Oquendo. The distance between these ships was about eight hundred yards, which means that from the time the first one became visible in the upper reach of the channel until the last one was out of the harbor an interval of only about twelve minutes elapsed. Following the Oquendo, at a distance of about twelve hundred yards, came the torpedo-boat destroyer Pluton, and after her the Furor.

Shrouded in Smoke.

The armored cruisers, as rapidly as they could bring their guns to bear, opened a vigorous fire upon the blockading vessels, and emerged from the channel shrouded in the smoke from their guns.

5. The men of our ships in front of the port were at Sunday "quarters for inspection." The signal was made simultaneously from several vessels, "Enemy's ships escaping," and a general quarters was sounded. The men cheered as they sprang to their guns, and fire was opened probably within eight minutes by the vessels whose guns commanded the entrance.

The New York turned about and steamed for the escaping fleet, flying the signal, "Close in toward harbor entrance and attack vessels," and gradually increasing speed, until, toward the end of the chase, she was making sixteen and one-half knots, and was rapidly closing on the Cristobal Colon. She was not, at any time, within the range of the heavy Spanish ships, and her only part in the firing was to receive the undivided fire from the forts in passing the harbor entrance, and to fire a few shots at one of the destroyers, thought at the moment to be attempting to escape from the Gloucester.

Turned into a Chase.

6. The Spanish vessels, upon clearing the harbor, turned to the westward in column, increasing their speed to the full power of their engines. The heavy blockading vessels, which had closed in toward the Morro at the instant of the enemy's appearance, and at their best speed, delivered a rapid fire, well sustained and destructive, which speedily overwhelmed and silenced the Spanish fire.

The initial speed of the Spaniards carried them rapidly past the blockading vessels, and the battle developed into a chase, in which the Brooklyn and Texas had at the start the advantage of position. The Brooklyn maintained this lead. The Oregon, steaming with amazing speed from the commencement of the action, took first place.

The Iowa and the Indiana, having done good work, and not having the speed of the other ships, were directed by me, in succession, at about the time the Vizcaya was beached, to drop out of the chase and resume blockading stations. These vessels rescued many prisoners. The Vixen, finding that the rush of the Spanish ships would put her between two fires, ran outside of our own column, and remained there during the battle and chase.

7. The skillful handling and gallant fighting of the Gloucester excited the admiration of every one who witnessed it and merits the commendation of the Navy Department. She is a fast and entirely unprotected auxiliary vessel—the yacht Corsair—and has a good battery of light rapid-fire guns. She was lying about two miles from the harbor entrance, to the southward and eastward, and immediately steamed in, opening fire upon the large ships.

Anticipating the appearance of the Pluton and Furor, the Gloucester was slowed, thereby gaining more rapidly a high pressure of steam, and when the destroyers came out she steamed for them at full speed and was able to close to short range, where her fire was accurate, deadly and of great volume. During this fight the Gloucester was under the fire of the Socapa battery.

Destroying the Destroyers.

Within twenty minutes from the time they emerged from Santiago harbor, the careers of the Furor and Pluton were ended, and two-thirds of their people killed. The Furor was beached and sunk in the surf; the Pluton sank in deep water a few minutes later.

The destroyers probably suffered much injury from the fire of the secondary batteries of the battleships Iowa, Indiana and the Texas, yet I think a very considerable factor in their speedy destruction was the fire, at close range, of the Gloucester's battery. After rescuing the survivors of the destroyers, the Gloucester did excellent service in landing and securing the crew of the Infanta Maria Teresa.

8. The method of escape attempted by the Spaniards—all steering in the same direction and in formation—removed all tactical doubts or difficulties, and made plain the duty of every United States vessel to close in, immediately engage and pursue. This was promptly and effectively done.

As already stated, the first rush of the Spanish squadron carried it past a number of the blockading ships, which could not immediately work up to their best speed; but they suffered heavily in passing, and the Infanta Maria Teresa and the Oquendo were probably set on fire by shells fired during the first fifteen minutes of the engagement. It was afterward learned that the Infanta Maria Teresa's fire-main had been cut by one of our first shots, and that she was unable to extinguish fire.

With large volumes of smoke rising from their lower decks aft, these vessels gave up both fight and flight and ran in on the beach— the Infanta Maria Teresa at about fifteen minutes past ten A. M., at Nima Nima, six and one-half miles from Santiago Harbor entrance, and the Almirante Oquendo at about half past ten A. M., at Juan Gonzales, seven miles from the port.

9. The Vizcaya was still under the fire of the leading vessels. The Cristobal Colon had drawn ahead, leading the chase, and soon passed beyond the range of the guns of the leading American ships. The Vizcaya was soon set on fire, and at fifteen minutes after eleven she turned in shore and was beached at Aserraderos, fifteen miles from Santiago, burning fiercely, and with her reserves of ammunition on deck already beginning to explode.

When about ten miles west of Santiago the Indiana had been signalled to go back to the harbor entrance, and at Aserraderos the Iowa was signalled to resume blockading station. The Iowa, assisted by the Ericsson and the Hist, took off the crew of the Vizcaya, while the Harvard and the Gloucester rescued those of the Infanta Maria Teresa and the Almirante Oquendo.

Brave Rescue of Prisoners.

This rescue of prisoners, including the wounded, from the burning Spanish vessels was the occasion of some of the most daring and gallant conduct of the day. The ships were burning fore and aft, their guns and reserve ammunition were exploding, and it was not known at what moment the fire would reach the main magazines. In addition to this a heavy surf was running just inside of the Spanish ships. But no risk deterred our officers and men until their work of humanity was complete.

10. There remained now of the Spanish ships only the Cristobal Colan—but she was their best and fastest vessel. Forced by the situation to hug the Cuban coast, her only chance of escape was by superior and sustained speed. When the Vizcaya went ashore the Colon was about six miles ahead of the Brooklyn and the Oregon; but her spurt was finished, and the American ships were now gaining upon her.

Behind the Brooklyn and the Oregon came the Texas, Vixen and New York. It was evident from the bridge of the New York that all the American ships were gradually overhauling the chase, and that she had no chance of escape. At ten minutes to one the Brooklyn and the Oregon opened fire and got her range—the Oregon's heavy shell striking beyond her—and at twenty minutes after one she gave up without firing another shot, hauled down her colors, and ran ashore at Rio Torquino, forty-eight miles from Santiago.

Enemy's Last Ship Lost.

Captain Cook, of the Brooklyn, went on board to receive the surrender. While his boat was along side I came up in the New York, received his report, and placed the Oregon in charge of the wreck, to save her, if possible ; and directed the prisoners to be transferred to the Resolute, which had followed the chase.

Commodore Schley, whose chief of staff had gone on board to receive the surrender, had directed that all their personal effects should be retained by the officers. This order I did not modify.

The Cristobal Colon was not injured by our firing, and probably is not much injured by beaching, though she ran ashore at high speed. The beach was so steep that she came off by the working of the sea. But her sea valves were opened and broken, treacherously, I am sure, after her surrender, and, despite all efforts, she sank.

When it became evident that she could not be kept afloat, she was pushed by the New York bodily up on the beach—the New York's stem being placed against her for this purpose, the ship being handled by Captain Chadwick with admirable judgment—and sank in shoal water and may be saved. Had this not been done she would have gone down in deep water, and would have been, to a certainty, a total loss.

11. I regard this complete and important victory over the Spanish forces as the successful finish of several weeks of arduous and close blockade, so stringent and effective during the night that the enemy was deterred from making the attempt to escape at night, and deliberately elected to make the attempt in daylight. That this was the case I was informed by the commanding officer of the Cristobal Colon.

12. It seems proper to briefly describe here the manner in which

this was accomplished. The harbor of Santiago is naturally easy to blockade—there being but one entrance, and that a narrow one, and the deep water extending close up to the shore line, presenting no difficulties of navigation outside of the entrance.

Method of the Blockade.

At the time of my arrival before the port—June 1—the moon was at its full, and there was sufficient light during the night to enable any movement outside of the entrance to be detected; but with the waning of the moon and the coming of dark nights there was opportunity for the enemy to escape, or for his torpedo boats to make an attack upon the blockading vessels.

It was ascertained with fair conclusiveness that the Merrimac, so gallantly taken into the channel on June 3d, did not obstruct it. I therefore maintained the blockade as follows: To the battleships was assigned the duty, in turn, of lighting the channel. Moving up to the port, at a distance of from one to two miles from the Morro, dependent upon the condition of the atmosphere, they threw a search-light beam directly up the channel, and held it steadily there. This lightened up the entire breadth of the channel for half a mile inside of the entrance so brilliantly that the movement of small boats could be detected. Why the batteries never opened fire upon the search-light ship was always a matter of surprise to me, but they never did.

Stationed close to the entrance of the port were three picket launches, and at a little distance farther out three small picket vessels, usually converted yachts, and when they were available one or two of our torpedo boats. With this arrangement there was at least a certainty that nothing could get out of the harbor undetected.

After the arrival of the army, when the situation forced upon the Spanish admiral a decision, our vigilance increased. The night blockading distance was reduced to two miles for all vessels, and a battleship was placed alongside the searchlight ship, with her broadside trained upon the channel in readiness to fire the instant a Spanish ship should appear.

The commanding officers merit the greatest praise for the perfect manner in which they entered into this plan and put it into execution. The Massachusetts, which, according to routine, was sent that morning to coal at Guantanamo, like the others had spent weary nights upon this work, and deserved a better fate than to be absent that morning.

I enclose, for the information of the department, copies of orders and memoranda issued from time to time relating to the manner of maintaining the blockade.

All Did Good Work.

13. When all the work was done so well it is difficult to discriminate in praise. The object of the blockade of Cervera's squadron was fully accomplished, and each individual bore well his part in it—the commodore in command of the second division, the captains of ships, their officers and men. The fire of the battleships was powerful and destructive, and the resistance of the Spanish squadron was in great part broken almost before they had got beyond the range of their own forts.

The fine speed of the Oregon enabled her to take a front position in the chase, and the Cristobal Colon did not give up until the Oregon had thrown a 13-inch shell beyond her. This performance adds to the already brilliant record of this fine battleship, and speaks highly of the skill and care with which her admirable efficiency has been maintained during a service unprecedented in the history of vessels of her class.

The Brooklyn's westerly blockading position gave her an advantage in the chase, which she maintained to the end, and she employed her fine battery with telling effect. The Texas and the New York were gaining on the chase during the last hour, and had any accident befallen the Brooklyn or the Oregon would have speedily overhauled the Cristobal Colon.

From the moment the Spanish vessel exhausted her first burst of speed the result was never in doubt. She fell, in fact, far below what might reasonably have been expected of her. Careful measurements of time and distance give her an average speed from the time she cleared the harbor mouth until the time she was run on shore at Rio Tarquino of 13.7 knots.

Lost No Time in Starting.

Neither the New York nor the Brooklyn stopped to couple up her forward engines, but ran out the chase with one pair, getting steam, of course, as rapidly as possible on all boilers. To stop to couple up the forward engines would have meant a delay of fifteen minutes, or four miles, in the chase.

14. Several of the ships were struck, the Brooklyn more often than the others, but very slight material injury was done, the greatest being aboard the Iowa. Our loss was one man killed and one wounded, both on the Brooklyn.

It is difficult to explain this immunity from loss of life or injury to ships in a combat with modern vessels of the best type; but Spanish gunnery is poor at the best, and the superior weight and accuracy of our fire speedily drove the men from their guns and silenced their fire. This is borne out by the statements of prisoners.

The Spanish vessels, as they dashed out of the harbor, were covered with the smoke from their own guns, but this speedily diminished in volume and soon almost disappeared. The fire from the rapid-fire batteries of the battleships appears to have been remarkably destructive. An examination of the stranded vessels shows that the Almirante Oquendo especially had suffered terribly from this fire. Her sides are everywhere pierced and her decks were strewn with the charred remains of those who had fallen.

15. The reports of Commodore W. S. Schley and of the commanding officers are enclosed.

16. A board appointed by me several days ago has made a critical examination of the stranded vessels, both with a view of reporting upon the result of our fire and the military features involved, and of reporting upon the chance of saving any of them and of wrecking the remainder. The report of the Board will be speedily forwarded.

Very respectfully,   W. T. SAMPSON,

Rear Admiral, U. S. N.; Commander in Chief U. S. Naval Force, North Atlantic Station.
THE SECRETARY OF THE NAVY, Navy Department, Washington, D. C.

Commodore Schley's Report to Admiral Sampson.

NORTH ATLANTIC FLEET, SECOND SQUADRON,
U. S. Flagship Brooklyn,
Guantanamo Bay, Cuba, July 6, 1898.

SIR :—I have the honor to make the following report of that part of the squadron under your command which came under my observation during the engagement with the Spanish fleet on July 3, 1898 :

2. At 9 35 A.M. Admiral Cervera, with the Infanta Maria Teresa, Vizcaya, Oquendo, Cristobal Colon and two torpedo-boat destroyers came out of the harbor of Santiago de Cuba in column at distance and attempted to escape to the westward. Signal was made from the Iowa that the enemy was coming out, but his movement had been discovered from this ship at the same moment.

This vessel was the furthest west, except the Vixen, in the blockading line : signal was made to the western division as prescribed in your General Orders, and there was immediate and rapid movement inward by your squadron and a general engagement, at ranges beginning at eleven hundred yards and varying to three thousand, until the Vizcaya was destroyed, about 10.50 A.M. The concentration of the fire of the squadron upon the ships coming out was most furious and terrific, and great damage was done them.

Beginning the Destruction.

3. About twenty or twenty-five minutes after the engagement began, two vessels, thought to be the Teresa and Oquendo, and since verified as such, took fire from the effective shell fire of the squadron, and were forced to run on the beach, some six or seven miles west of the harbor entrance, where they burned and blew up later. The torpedo-boat destroyers were destroyed early in the action, but the smoke was so dense in their direction that I cannot say to which vessel or vessels the credit belongs. This, doubtless, was better seen from your flagship.

4. The Vizcaya and Colon, perceiving the disaster to their con-

sorts, continued at full speed to the westward to escape, and were followed and engaged in a running fight with the Brooklyn, Texas Iowa and Oregon until ten minutes of eleven, when the Vizcaya took fire from our shells.   She put her helm to port, and with a heavy list to port, stood in shore and ran aground at Aserraderos, about twenty one miles west of Santiago, on fire fore and aft, and where she blew up during the night.   Observing that she had struck her colors, and that several vessels were nearing her to capture and save her crew, signal was made to cease firing.

The Oregon, having proved vastly faster than the other battle-ships, she and the Brooklyn, together with the Texas and another vessel, which proved to be your flagship, continued westward in pursuit of the Colon, which had run close in shore, evidently seeking some good spot to beach, if she should fail to elude her pursuers.

End of the Chase.

5. This pursuit continued with increasing speed in the Brooklyn, Oregon and other ships, and soon the Brooklyn and the Oregon were within long range of the Colon, when the Oregon opened fire with her thirteen-inch guns, landing a shell close to the Colon.   A moment afterwards the Brooklyn opened fire with her eight-inch guns, landing a shell just ahead of her.   Several other shells were fired at the Colon, now in range of the Brooklyn's and Oregon's guns.

Her commander, seeing all chances of escape cut off, and destruction awaiting his ship, fired a lee gun and struck her flag at a quarter past one P.M., and ran ashore at a point some fifty miles west of Santiago Harbor.   Your flagship was coming up rapidly at the time, as were also the Texas and Vixen.   A little later, after your arrival, the Cristobal Colon, which had stuck to the Brooklyn and the Oregon, was turned over to you as one of the trophies of this great victory of the squadron under your command.

6.   During my official visit, a little later, Commander Eaton, of the Resolute, appeared, and reported to you the presence of a Spanish battleship near Altares.   Your orders to me were to take the Oregon

45

and go eastward to meet her, and this was done by the Brooklyn, with the result that the vessel reported as an enemy was discovered to be the Austrian cruiser Infanta Maria Teresa, seeking the commander-in-chief.

7. I would mention for your consideration that the Brooklyn occupied the most westward blockading position with the Vixen, and, being more directly in the route taken by the Spanish squadron, was exposed for some minutes, possibly ten, to the gun fire of three of the Spanish ships and the west battery at a range of fifteen hundred yards from the ships, and about three thousand yards from the batteries, but the vessels of the entire squadron, closing in rapidly, soon diverted this fire and did magnificent work at close range.

Deadly Shots from Our Fleet.

I have never before witnessed such deadly and fatally accurate shooting as was done by the ships of your command as they closed in on the Spanish squadron, and I deem it a high privilege to commend to you for such action as you may deem proper, the gallantry and dashing courage, the prompt decision and the skillful handling of their respective vessels, of Captain Philip, Captain Evans, Captain Clark, and especially of my chief of staff, Captain Cook, who was directly under my personal observation, and whose coolness, promptness and courage were of the highest order.

The dense smoke of the combat shut out from my view the Indiana and the Gloucester, but as these vessels were closer to your flagship, no doubt their part in the conflict was under your immediate observation.

8. Lieutenant Sharp, commanding the Vixen, acted with conspicuous courage; although unable to engage the heavier ships of the enemy with his light guns, nevertheless was close in to the battle line under heavy fire, and many of the enemy's shot passed beyond his vessel.

9. I beg to invite special attention to the conduct of my flag lieutenant, James H. Sears, and Ensign Edward McCauley, Jr., aid, who were constantly at my side during the engagement, and who exposed

themselves fearlessly in discharging their duties; and also to the splendid behaviour of my secretary, Lieutenant B. W. Wells, Jr., who commanded and directed the fighting of the Fourth division with splendid effect.

10. I would commend the highly meritorious conduct and courage in the engagement of Lieutenant Commander N. E. Mason, the executive officer, whose presence everywhere over the ship during its continuance did much to secure the good result of this ship's part in the victory.

11. The navigator, Lieutenant A. C. Hodgson, and the division officers, Lieutenant T. D. Griffin, Lieutenant W. R. Rush, Lieutenant Edward Simpson, Lieutenant J. G. Doyle, Ensign Charles Webster, and the junior divisional officers were most steady and conspicuous in every detail of duty contributing to the accurate firing of this ship in her part of the great victory of your forces.

Brave and Competent Officers.

12. The officers of the Medical, Pay and Engineer and Marine Corps responded to every demand of the occasion, and were fearless in exposing themselves. The warrant officers, Boatswain William L. Hill, Carpenter G. H. Warford and Gunner F. T. Applegate, were everywhere exposed in watching for damage, reports of which were promptly conveyed to me.

13. I have never in my life served with a braver, better or worthier crew than that of the Brooklyn. During the combat, lasting from thirty-five minutes past nine until fifteen minutes past one, much of the time under fire, they never flagged for a moment, and were apparently undisturbed by the storm of projectiles passing ahead, astern and over the ship.

14. The result of the engagement was the destruction of the Spanish squadron and the capture of the Admiral and some thirteen hunhundred to fifteen hundred prisoners, with the loss of several hundred killed, estimated by Admiral Cervera at six hundred men.

15. The casualties on board this ship were G. H. Ellis, chief yeoman, killed; J. Burns, fireman first class, severely wounded. The

marks and scars show that the ship was struck about twenty-five times, and she bears in all forty-one scars as the result of her participation in the great victory of your force on July 3, 1898. The speed cone halliards were shot away, and nearly all the signal halliards. The ensign at the main was so shattered that in hauling it down at the close of the action it fell in pieces.

16. I congratulate you most sincerely upon this great victory to the squadron under your command, and I am glad that I had an opportunity to contribute in the least to a victory that seems big enough for all of us.

17. I have the honor to transmit herewith the report of the commanding officer, and a drawing in profile of the ship, showing the location of hits and scars; also a memorandum of the ammunition expended and the amount to fill her allowance.

Planned to Ram the Brooklyn.

18. Since reaching this place and holding conversation with several of the captains—viz.: Captain Eulate, of the Vizcaya, and the second in command of the Colon, Commander Contreras, I have learned that the Spanish admiral's scheme was to concentrate all fire for a while on the Brooklyn, and the Vizcaya to ram her, in hope that if they could destroy her the chance of escape would be increased, as it was supposed she was the swiftest ship of your squadron.

This explains the heavy fire mentioned and the Vizcaya's action in the earlier moments of the engagement. The execution of this purpose was promptly defeated by the fact that all the ships of the squadron advanced into close range and opened a terrific fire upon the enemy's squadron as it was coming out of the harbor.

21. I cannot close this report without mentioning in high terms of praise the splendid conduct and support of Captain C. E. Clark, of the Oregon. Her speed was wonderful and her accurate fire splendidly destructive. Very respectfully,

Commodore United States Navy, Commanding Second Squadron, North Atlantic Fleet.
To the Commander-in-Chief, United States Naval Force, North Atlantic Station.

CAPTAINS TELL OF OUR NAVAL VICTORY.

The following are the reports of Captain Chadwick, of the New York; Captain Taylor, of the Indiana; Captain Philip, of the Texas; Lieutenant-Commander Wainwright, of the Gloucester; Captain Clark, of the Oregon; and Captain Evans, of the Iowa, on the destruction of Cervera's fleet, which were included in Admiral Sampson's report.

Captain Chadwick's report was as follows : The ship had started at 9.30 A. M. for the army landing at Siboney, the commander-in-chief having an appointment with the general commanding the army. A few minutes after the crew had been called to quarters for Sunday inspection, firing was heard, and a ship was seen leaving the harbor entrance. The helm was at once put over, the crew called to general quarters, signal " Close in towards the harbor entrance and attack vessels " made, orders given to spread all fires, and the ship headed back for the enemy, whose ships were seen successively coming out at a high speed.

The Flagship on Fire.

The nearer ships had immediately engaged, and by the time we were off the entrance one, the flagship, was already afire and was soon ashore; the Indiana and Gloucester were actively engaged with the torpedo boats. This ship fired some 4-inch shells at the one nearer the port, towards which she was already headed, and seemed attempting to return; but she was already practically out of the fight, the boiler of the more advanced one having blown up, showing a vast column of condensed steam. During this time the batteries, whose line of fire we had crossed close to, repeatedly fired upon us, but without effect. This ship stood on, leaving the Gloucester, which had shown herself so capable, to look after the survivors in the torpedo-boats.

By this time a second cruiser was ashore and burning (the Almirante Oquendo), while the third, the Vizcaya, and the Cristobal Colon were still steaming rapidly westward. The Indiana was now signaled (11.26 A.M.) to return to her blockading position, to look after anything which might be there. Very shortly the Vizcaya turned shoreward, smoke began to issue from her after part, and, by the time that she was ashore on the reef at Acerraderos (fifteen miles west of Santiago), she was ablaze. The Iowa had signaled a little before that she had surrendered, and stopped off this place, where she gave much assistance in the rescue of the Vizcaya's people.

This ship stood on in chase of the Cristobal Colon, with ahead of us the Brooklyn, Oregon, Texas and Vixen, the Oregon being much nearer inshore of the two headmost ships, but not in gunshot. We were rapidly increasing our speed.

Spanish Ship Struck Her Colors.

About 12.50 the Oregon opened fire, and some of her shells were observed to strike beyond the Colon; this made her capture a foregone conclusion, and shortly after 1 o'clock she turned in towards shore and soon struck her colors. She had been beached at a small inlet known as Rio Torquino. By the time we arrived a boat was alongside of her from the Brooklyn, and Captain Cook, the boarding officer, came alongside this and reported. This ship then sent a boat to take possession, the commanding officer going in the boat. I was received by the commodore of the squadron, the captain, Captain De Navio Don Emilo Moreu, and Captain De Navio, of the first-class Don Jose de Paredes y Chacon (which latter had been civil governor of Santiago and had only just been attached to the squadron).

I arranged for the transfer of the crew and officers, a division to each ship present, and the engineer force to be left aboard. While aboard, however, the Resolute arrived, and it was arranged to transfer the whole number to her.

Though the ship was not able to come to action with any of the larger ships on account of her distance to the eastward, every nerve was strained to do so, and all was done that could be done; our speed had rapidly increased, so that we were going sixteen knots at the end. We were immediately astern while all others were considerably to seaward. We were thus in a position to prevent a possible doubling to the rear and escape to the southeast. The officers and crew, as they always have done, acted in the most enthusiastic and commendable manner.

The Indiana's Part.

Captain H. C. Taylor, commanding the United States steamship Indiana, first rate, reported as follows:

The Spanish squadron was seen emerging from the harbor at 9.37, and in a few moments a general action ensued. The leading ship, which proved to be the Infanta Teresa, flying the flag of Vice Admiral Cervera, was followed by the other vessels of the squadron as follows: Vizcaya, Cristobal Colon, Oquendo and the torpedo-boat destroyers Furor and Pluton. The enemy's vessels headed to the westward. This ship fired on all of them as they came out one by one, and continued the action later by firing principally on the Maria Teresa, Oquendo, Furor and Pluton. Several of our shells were seen to take effect on these vessels.

Our secondary battery guns were directed principally on the destroyers, as also were the "6" guns. The destroyers were sunk through the agency of our guns and those of the Gloucester, which vessel had come up and engaged them close aboard. The initial fire of the last two ships was directed at this vessel, and although falling very close, only striking the ship twice without any injury to ship or crew. One of our "13" shells was seen to enter the Maria Teresa under the quarter deck and explode, and that ship was observed on fire very shortly afterwards.

About 10.15 A.M. observed the Maria Teresa and Oquendo on fire and heading for the beach, the fire from their guns having ceased. We then devoted our special attention to prevent the escape of the destroyers, which appeared more than a match for the Gloucester, she being the only small vessel near to engage them. They were soon seen to blow up, apparently struck by our "6" and 6-pounders. We now fired our large guns at the Vizcaya, which was at long range; she made for the shore soon after, on fire and battery silenced. These ships hauled down their colors as they made for the beach. The Spanish flagship hoisted the white flag as she grounded.

We now ceased firing. The Colon was observed well over the western horizon, closely pursued by the Brooklyn, Oregon and Texas, off shore of her. The flagship New York, steaming full speed to the westward as soon as the Vizcaya surrendered, signaled us, " Go back and guard entrance of harbor." Several explosions were observed on board the burning ships. At noon turned and stood to the eastward for our station in obedience to the above signal. Observed the Harvard and several transports standing to the westward. During this action we used no armor-piercing shells, except the smokeless powder 6-pounders, and the good effect of the common shell is shown by the fires on the enemy's ships and the short time taken to disable them without piercing their armor and with almost no injury to our ships.

Captain Taylor commended all his officers and crew, and especially Lieutenant-Commander John A. Rodgers, the executive officer.

What the Texas Did.

Captain J. W. Philip, commanding the United States battleship Texas, the sister ship to the Maine, destroyed in Havana harbor, reported to Admiral Sampson as follows:

Just at 9.35 as general signal No. 250 was made the Texas, which was lying 5,100 yards distant from Morro, the enemy's ships were sighted standing out of the harbor. As the leader bearing the admiral's flag appeared in the entrance she opened fire, which was at 9.40 returned by the Texas at range of 4,200 yards, while closing in. The ship leading was of the Vizcaya class and the flagship. Four ships came out, evidently the Vizcaya, the Oquendo, Maria Teresa and Colon, followed by two torpedo-boat destroyers.

Upon seeing these two we immediately opened fire upon them with our secondary battery, the main battery at the time being engaged with the second and third ships in line; owing to our secondary battery, together with the Iowa and Gloucester, these two destroyers were forced to beach, and sunk.

While warmly engaged with the third in line, which was abreast and engaging the Texas, our fire was blanketed for a short time by the Oregon forging ahead and engaging the second ship. This third ship, after a spirited fire, sheered in shore, and at 10.35 ran up a white flag. We then ceased fire on the third, and opened fire with our forward guns at long range (6,000 yards) on the ship (which was then engaged with the Oregon) until 11.05, when she (enemy's second ship) sheered into the beach on fire.

At 11.10 she struck her colors, we ceased fire, and gave chase with Brooklyn and Oregon for the leading ship until 1.20, when the Colon sheered into the beach and hauled down her colors, leaving them on deck at the foot of her flagstaff. We shut off forced draught and proceeded at moderate speed to close up. I would state that during this chase the Texas was holding her own with the Colon, she leading us about four miles at the start.

Captain Philip concluded with expressing the approval of the bearing and performance of duty of all his officers.

The Gloucester's Plucky Fight.

Lieutenant Commander Richard Wainwright, formerly of the Maine when that ship was destroyed in Havana harbor, and who commanded the Gloucester, the converted yacht, in the plucky fight with Cervera's two torpedo-boat destroyers, reported as follows :

It was the plain duty of the Gloucester to look after the destroyers, and she was held back, gaining steam, until they appeared at the entrance. The Indiana poured in a hot fire from all her secondary battery upon the destroyers, but Captain Taylor's signal, " Gunboats close in," gave security that we would not be fired upon by our own ships. The escape of the Gloucester was due mainly to the accuracy and rapidity of the fire. The efficiency of this fire, as well as that of the ship generally, was largely due to the intelligent and unremitting efforts of the executive officer, Lieutenant Harry P. Huse.

The result is more to his credit when it is remembered that a large proportion of the officers and men were untrained when the Gloucester was commissioned. Throughout the action he was on the bridge and carried out my orders with great coolness. That we were able to close in with the destroyers—and until we did so they were not seriously injured—was largely due to the skill and constant attention of Passed Assistant Engineer, George W. McElroy. The blowers were put on and the speed increased to seventeen knots without causing a tube to leak or a brass to heat. Lieutenant Thomas C. Wood, Lieutenant George H. Norman, Jr., and Ensign John T. Edson, not only controlled the fire of the guns in their divisions and prevented the waste of ammunition, but they also did some excellent shooting themselves.

Acting Assistant Surgeon J. F. Bransford took charge of one of the guns and fired it himself occasionally. Acting Assistant Paymaster Alexander Brown had charge of the two Colt guns, firing one himself, and they did excellent work. Assistant Engineer A. M. Proctor carried my orders from the bridge and occasionally fired a gun, when I found it was not being served quite satisfactorily. All were cool and active at a time when they could have had but little hope of escaping uninjured.

Lieutenants Wood and Norman, Ensign Edson and Assistant Engineer Proctor were in charge of the boats engaged in saving life. They all risked their lives repeatedly in boarding and remaining near the two destroyers and the two armored cruisers when their guns were being discharged by the heat and their magazines and boilers were exploding. They also showed great skill in landing and taking off the prisoners through the surf.

The wounded and exhausted prisoners were well and skillfully tended by Assistant Surgeon Bransford, assisted by Ensign Edson, who is also a surgeon. The admiral, his officers and men were treated with all consideration and care possible. They were fed and clothed as far as our limited means would permit.

Part the Oregon Took.

Captain Clark, of the famous Oregon, reported as follows:

I have the honor to report that at 9.30 A. M. yesterday the Spanish fleet was discovered standing out of the harbor of Santiago de Cuba. They turned to the westward and opened fire, to which our ships replied vigorously. For a short time there was an almost continuous flight of projectiles over this ship, but when our line was fairly engaged, and the Iowa had made a swift advance as if to ram or close, the enemy's fire became defective in train as well as range. The ship was only struck three times, and at least two of them were by fragments of shells. We had no casualties.

As soon as it was evident that the enemy's ships were trying to break through and escape to the westward we went ahead at full speed with the determination of carrying out to the utmost your order: " If the enemy tries to escape the ships must close and engage as soon as possible and endeavor to sink his vessels or force them to run ashore." We soon passed all our ships, except the Brooklyn, bearing the broad pennant of Commodore Schley. At first we only used our main battery, but when it was discovered that the enemy's torpedo boats were following their ships we used our rapid-fire guns as well as the six upon them with telling effect.

Driven Headlong on the Beach.

As we ranged up near the sternmost of their ships she headed for the beach, evidently on fire. We raked her as we passed, pushing on for the next ahead, using our starboard guns as they were brought to bear, and before we had her fairly abeam she, too, was making for the beach. The two remaining vessels were now some distance ahead, but our speed had increased to sixteen knots, and our fire, added to that of the Brooklyn, soon sent another, the Vizcaya, to the shore in flames.

Only the Cristobal Colon was left, and for a time it seemed as if she might escape, but when we opened with our forward turret guns and the Brooklyn followed she began to edge in towards the coast and her capture or destruction was assured. As she struck the beach her flag came down and the Brooklyn signaled " cease firing," following it with " congratulations for the grand victory; thanks for your splendid assistance."

The Brooklyn sent a boat to her, and when the admiral came up with the New York and Texas and Vixen she was taken possession of.   A prize crew was put on board from this ship under Lieutenant Commander Cogswell, the executive officer, but before 11 P. M. the ship, which had been filling in spite of all efforts to stop leaks, was abandoned, and just as the crew left her she went over on her side.

I cannot speak in too high terms of the bearing and conduct of all on board this ship.   When they found the Oregon had pushed to the front and was hurrying to a succession of conflicts with the enemy's vessels if they could be overtaken and would engage, their enthusiasm was intense.

As these vessels were so much more heavily armored than the Brooklyn, they might have concentrated upon and overpowered her, and consequently I am persuaded that but for the way the officers and men of the Oregon steamed and steered the ship and fought and supplied her batteries, the Colon and perhaps the Vizcaya would have escaped.   Therefore I feel that they rendered meritorious service to the country, and while I cannot mention the name of each officer and man individually, I am going to append a list of the officers, with their stations that they occupied, hoping that they may be of service to them should the claims of others for advancement above them ever be considered.

The Iowa Fired the First Shot.

Captain Evans' official statement of his ship's work in the destruction of Cervera's fleet, was as follows:

I have the honor to make the following report of the engagement with the Spanish squadron off Santiago de Cuba on the 3d of July.

On the morning of the 3d, while the crew was at quarters for Sunday inspection, the leading vessel of the Spanish squadron was sighted at 9.30 coming out of the harbor of Santiago de Cuba.   Signal "Enemy's ships coming out" was immediately hoisted and a gun fired to attract attention.   The call to general quarters was sounded immediately, the battery made ready for firing, and the engines rung full speed ahead.

The position of this vessel at the time of sighting the squadron was the usual blockading station off the entrance of the harbor, Morro

Castle bearing about north and distant about three to four miles. The steam at this time in the boilers was sufficient for a speed of five knots.

After sighting the leading vessel, the Infanta Maria Teresa, Admiral Cervera's flagship, it was observed that she was followed in succession by the remaining three vessels of the Spanish squadron, the Vizcaya, Cristobal Colon and Almirante Oquendo. The Spanish ships moved at a speed of about eight to ten knots, which was steadily increased as they cleared the harbor entrance and stood to the westward. They maintained a distance of about 800 yards between vessels. The squadron moved with precision, and stations were well kept.

Immediately upon sighting the leading vessel fires were spread and the Iowa headed toward the leading Spanish ship. About 9.40 the first shot was fired from this ship at a distance of about 6,000 yards. The course of this vessel was so laid that the range speedily diminished. A number of shots were fired at ranges varying between 6,000 and 4,000 yards. The range was rapidly reduced to 2,500 yards and subsequently to 2,000 and to 1,200 yards.

Heavy Broadsides From the Iowa.

When it was certain that the Maria Teresa would pass ahead of us, the helm was put to starboard, and the starboard broadside delivered at a range of 2 500 yards. The helm was then put to port, and the ship headed across the bow of the second ship, and as she drew ahead the helm was again put to starboard, and she received in turn the full weight of our starboard broadside at a range of about 1,800 yards. The Iowa was again headed off with port helm for the third ship, and as she approached the helm was put to starboard until our course was approximately that of the Spanish ship. In this position, at a range of 1,400 yards, the fire of the entire battery, including rapid-fire guns, was poured into the enemy's ship.

About 10 o'clock the enemy's torpedo-boat destroyers Furor and Pluton were observed to have left the harbor, and to be following the Spanish squadron. At the time they were observed, and in fact most of the time that they were under fire, they were at a distance varying from 4,500 and 4,000 yards. As soon as they were discovered the secondary battery of the ship was turned upon them, while the main battery continued to engage the Vizcaya, Oquendo and Maria Teresa.

The fire of the main battery of the ship, when the range was below 2,500 yards, was most effective and destructive, and, after a continuance of this fire for perhaps twenty minutes, it was noticed that the Maria Teresa and Oquendo were in flames, and were being headed for the beach. Their colors were struck about 10.20, and they were beached about eight miles west of Santiago. About the same time (about 10.25) the fire of this vessel, together with that of the Gloucester and another smaller vessel, proved so destructive that one of the torpedo-boat destroyers (Pluton) was sunk, and the Furor was so much damaged that she was run upon the rocks.

Rescuing Defeated Spaniards.

After having passed, at 10.35, the Oquendo and Maria Teresa, on fire and ashore, this vessel continued to chase and fire upon the Vizcaya until 10.36, when signal to cease firing was sounded on board, it having been discovered that the Vizcaya had at length struck her colors.

At 11 o'clock the Iowa arrived in the vicinity of the Vizcaya, which had been run ashore, and it was evident that she could not catch the Cristobal Colon and that the Oregon, Brooklyn and New York would, two steam cutters and three cutters were immediately hoisted out and sent to the Vizcaya to rescue her crew. Our boats succeeded in bringing off a large number of officers and men of that ship's company, and in placing many of them on board the torpedo boat Ericsson and the auxiliary dispatch vessel Hist.

About 11.30 the New York passed in chase of the Cristobal Colon, which was endeavoring to escape from the Oregon, Brooklyn and Texas. We received on board this vessel from the Vizcaya Captain Eulate, the commanding officer, and twenty-three officers, together with about 248 petty officers and men.

The United States military expedition under the command of Major General Nelson A. Miles, commanding the Army of the United States, which left Guantanamo Bay during the evening of Thursday last, July 21, was landed successfully at Guanica, July 25, after a skirmish with a detachment of the Spanish troops and a crew of thirty belonging to the launch of the United States auxiliary gunboat Gloucester. Four of the Spaniards were killed and no Americans were hurt.

General Miles' Army Lands in Porto Rico.

At noon on the 24th, General Miles called for a consultation, announcing that he was determined not to go by San Juan Cape, but by the Mona Passage instead, land there, surprise the Spaniards and deceive their military authorities. The course was then changed and the Dixie was sent to warn General Brooke and the transports conveying our troops, which had been ordered to Cape San Juan.

Early in the morning the Gloucester, in charge of Lieutenant Commander Wainwright, steamed into Guanica harbor in order to reconnoitre the place. With the fleet waiting outside, the gallant little fighting yacht Gloucester braved the mines which were supposed to be in this harbor and found that there were five fathoms of water close in shore. Guanica Bay is a quiet place, surrounded by cultivated lands. In the rear are high mountains, and close to the beach nestles a village of about twenty-one houses.

The Spaniards were taken completely by surprise. Almost the first they knew of the approach of the army of invasion was in the announcement contained in the firing of a gun from the Gloucester, demanding that the Spaniards haul down their flag, which was floating from the flagstaff in front of a block-house standing to the east of the village.

The first couple of three-pounders were fired into the hills right and left of the bay, purposely avoiding the town, lest the projectiles hurt women or children. The Gloucester then hove to within about six hundred yards of the shore and lowered a launch, having on board a Colt rapid-fire gun and thirty men, under the command of Lieutenant Huse, which was sent ashore without encountering opposition.

Quartermaster Beck thereupon told Yeoman Lacy to haul down the Spanish flag, which was done, and they then raised on the flag-staff the first United States flag to float over Porto Rican soil. Suddenly about thirty Spaniards opened fire with Mauser rifles on the American party. Lieutenant Huse and his men responded with great gallantry, the Colt gun doing effective work. Almost immediately after the Spaniards fired on the Americans the Gloucester opened fire on the enemy with all her 3 and 6-pounders which could be brought to bear, shelling the town and also dropping shells into the hills to the west of Guanica, where a number of Spanish cavalry were to be seen hastening toward the spot where the Americans had landed.

Built a Fort for Defense.

Lieutenant Huse then threw up a little fort, which he named Fort Wainwright, and laid barbed wire in the street in front of it in order to repel the expected cavalry attack. The lieutenant also mounted the Colt gun and signaled for reinforcements, which were sent from the Gloucester.

While the Mausers were peppering all round, Lieutenant-Commander Wainwright called to the Associated Press correspondent, and said : "They fired on us after their flag was down and ours was up and after I had spared the town for the sake of the women and children. The next town I strike I will blow up."

Presently a few of the Spanish cavalry joined those who were fighting in the street of Guanica, but the Colt fired to a purpose killing our of them. By that time the Gloucester had the range of the town, and of the blockhouse, and all her guns were spitting fire, the doctor and the paymaster helping to serve the guns.

Soon afterwards white-coated galloping cavalrymen were seen climbing the hills to the westward, and the foot soldiers were scurrying along the fences from the town. By 9.45, with the exception of a few guerrilla shots, the town was won, and the enemy was driven out of its neighborhood. The Red Cross nurses on the Lampasas and a detachment of regulars were the first to land from the transports.

After Lieutenant Huse had captured the place he deployed his small force into the suburbs. But he was soon reinforced by the regulars, who were followed by Company G of the Sixth Illinois, and then by other troops in quick succession. All the boats of the men-of-war and the transports were used in the work of landing the troops, each steam launch towing four or five boats loaded to the rails with soldiers. But everything progressed in an orderly manner, and according to the plans of General Miles. The latter went ashore about noon, after stopping to board the Gloucester and thank Lieutenant-Commander Wainwright for his gallant action.

Report from General Miles.

The War Department at Washington at 11.30 posted the following:

St. Thomas, July 26, 1898, 9.35 P.M.

Secretary of War, Washington:

Circumstances were such that I deemed it advisable to take the harbor of Guanica first, fifteen miles west of Ponce, which was successfully accomplished between daylight and 11 o'clock. Spaniards surprised. The Gloucester, Commander Wainwright, first entered the harbor; met with slight resistance; fired a few shots. All the transports are now in the harbor, and infantry and artillery rapidly going ashore. This is a well-protected harbor. Water sufficiently deep for all transports and heavy vessels to anchor within two hundred yards of the shore. The Spanish flag was lowered and the American flag raised at 11 o'clock to-day. Captain Higginson, with his fleet, has rendered able and earnest assistance. Troops in good health and best of spirits. No casualties.

MILES, Major-General Commanding.

Coincident with the landing of our troops at Guanica the Spanish Government made a move to end the war and secure peace. The proposition was formally submitted to the President at 3 o'clock July 25th, by the French Ambassador, M. Jules Cambon, who had received instructions from the foreign office at Paris to deliver to the United States Government the tender of peace formulated by the Spanish Cabinet. President McKinley and his advisors immediately took the proposition into consideration.

46

Major General Miles made his invasion of Porto Rico a triumphal procession. Having landed a force at Guanica, that pushed on against some ineffective opposition and took possession of the railroad at Yauco, he sailed to Ponce with the other troops that had arrived in the meantime. The Dixie first entered the port and secured its surrender and General Miles then landed and occupied the town, the Spanish garrison withdrawing hastily and the inhabitants welcoming the Americans as deliverers.

On July 29th, the Navy Department at Washington posted the following bulletin:

"St. Thomas, July 29, U. S. S. Massachusetts, Ponce, Porto Rico, July 28.

"Commander Davis with Dixie, Annapolis, Wasp and Gloucester, left Guanica, July 27, to blockade Ponce and capture lighters for United States army. City of Ponce and Playa surrendered to Commander Davis upon demand. American flag hoisted 6 A. M., 28th. Spanish garrison evacuated. Provisional articles of surrender until occupation by army:

"First—Garrison to be allowed to retire. Second—Civil government to remain in force. Third—Police and fire brigade to be maintained without arms. Fourth—Captain of Port not to be made prisoner.

"Arrived at Ponce from Guanica with Massachusetts and Cincinnati, General Miles, and General Wilson, and transports at 6.40 A. M., 28th. Commenced landing army in captured sugar lighters. No resistance. Troops welcomed by inhabitants, great enthusiasm. Captured sixty lighters, twenty sailing vessels and 120 tons of coal.

HIGGINSON."

General Miles Reports His Victory.

The War Department received the following dispatch from General Miles :

"Port Ponce, Porto Rico, *via* St. Thomas, July 29.

"On the 26th Garretson had a spirited engagement on the skirmish line. Our casualties were four wounded, all doing well. The Spanish loss was three killed, thirteen wounded. Yauco was occupied yesterday Henry's division is there to-day. Last evening Commander Davis, of the Dixie, moved into this port, followed by Captain Higginson with his fleet early this morning. General Wilson with Ernst brigade now rapidly disembarking.

"Spanish troops are retreating from the southern part of Porto Rico. The populace received the troops and saluted the flag with wild enthusiasm. Navy has several prizes, also seventy lighters. Railway stock partly destroyed now restored. Telegraph communication also being restored. Cable instruments destroyed. Have sent to Jamaica for others. This is a prosperous and beautiful country. The army will soon be in the mountain region; weather delightful; troops in best of health and spirits; anticipate no insurmountable obstacles in future. Results thus far have been accomplished without the loss of a single life.

"NELSON A. MILES, Major General."

Another dispatch which was received at the War Department Washington, read as follows:

"In the affair of the 26th, Captain Edward J. Gibson, Company A, was wounded in left hip. Captain J. H. Prior, Company L, slightly wounded in hand. Private James Drummond, Company K, two wounds in neck, and Private Benjamin F. Bosbick, Company L, slight wound in right arm. All of Sixth Massachusetts. All doing well. The Spanish retreat from this place was precipitous, they leaving rifles and ammunition in barracks and forty or fifty sick in hospital. The people are enjoying a holiday in honor of our arrival.

"MILES."

The Sixth Massachusetts and Sixth Illinois went to Porto Rico on the Dixie.

American Flag Welcomed.

The following general dispatch was also received at Washington:

PORT OF PONCE, ISLAND OF PORTO RICO, July 28,
via the Island of St. Thomas, Danish West Indies.

"The Port of Ponce surrendered to Commander C. H. Davis, of the auxiliary gunboat Dixie, yesterday. There was no resistance, and the Americans were welcomed with enthusiasm.

" Major General Miles arrived here this morning at daylight with General Ernst's brigade and General Wilson's division on board transports. General Ernst's brigade immediately started for the town of Ponce, three miles inland, which capitulated this afternoon.

" The American troops are pushing towards the mountains and will join General Henry with his brigade at Yauco, which has been captured by our troops.

" A fight before the latter place on Thursday last was won by the American volunteers. The Spaniards ambushed eight companies of the Massachusetts and Illinois regiments, but the enemy was repulsed and driven back a mile to a ridge, where the Spanish cavalry charged and were routed by our infantry.

" General Garretson led the fight with the men from Illinois and Massachusetts, and the enemy retreated to Yauco, leaving four dead on the field and several wounded. None of our men were killed and only three were slightly wounded. The wounded are: Captain Gihon Barrett, Private James Drummond, Private H. C. Gary.

" The Porto Ricans are glad the American troops have landed, and say they are all Americans and will join our army. The roads are good for military purposes. Our troops are healthy and General Miles says the campaign will be short and vigorous."

Proclamation by General Miles.

General Miles issued the following proclamation :

" In the prosecution of the war against the Kingdom of Spain by the people of the United States, in the cause of liberty, justice and humanity, its military forces have come to occupy the island of Porto Rico. They come bearing the banners of freedom, inspired by a noble purpose, to seek the enemies of our government and of yours, and to destroy or capture all in armed resistance. They bring you the fostering arms of a free people, whose greatest power is justice and humanity to all living within their fold. Hence they release you from your former political relations, and it is hoped this will be followed by your cheerful acceptance of the government of the United States.

"The chief object of the American military forces will be to overthrow the armed authority of Spain and give the people of your beautiful island the largest measure of liberty consistent with this military occupation. They have not come to make war on the people of the country, who for centuries have been oppressed, but, on the contrary, they bring protection not only to yourselves, but to your property, promote your prosperity and bestow the immunities and blessings of our enlightenment and liberal institutions and government.

"It is not their purpose to interfere with the existing laws and customs, which are wholesome and beneficial to the people, so long as they conform to the rules of the military administration, order and justice. This is not a war of devastation and desolation, but one to give all within the control of the military and naval forces the advantages and blessings of enlightened civilization."

Towns Captured by American Troops.

Without seeing or hearing anything of the enemy the advance guard of General Henry's division, which landed at Guanica on July 26th, arrived at Ponce on the 29th, taking en route the cities of Yauco, Tallaboa, Sabana Grande and Ponuelas. Attempts by the Spaniards to blow up bridges aud otherwise destroy the railroad between Yauco and Ponce failed, only a few flat cars being burned. Our troops fired up the locomotives, and began operating the road from end to end, carrying supplies, messages and men.

At Yauco the Americans were welcomed in an address made by the Alcalde, and a public proclamation was issued, dated, "Yauco, Porto Rico, United States of America, July 27." Major Webb Hayes, of the Sixth Ohio, son of former President Hayes, hauled up the flag on the palace amid cheers from the populace. The people seemed really glad that the Americans had arrived; but they feared an uprising of the natives in the interior, who, it was asserted, would rob, kill, and destroy property in revenge for many years of Spanish misrule.

General Miles was in constant command of all his forces, and kept the artillery steadily in advance. He acted throughout with a promptness that promised success.

After Admiral Dewey's great victory at Manila on May 1st, there was no more fighting between the Americans and Spaniards until July 31st. Meanwhile, as already stated, several expeditions had sailed for the Philippines from the Pacific coast. These were under command of Major-General Wesley Merritt, who arrived at Manila on July 25th, and upon the arrival of the third expedition

GENERAL WESLEY MERRITT.

had 11,500 troops with which to conduct operations for the capture of the city.

General Merritt and Admiral Dewey consulted as to the best method of procedure, and it was agreed that all the interests of foreigners and non-combatants in the city should be protected as far as possible.

The fight on the night of July 31st indicated a degree of vigor on the part of the Spanish garrison for which they have not been given credit. It was a night attack on the flank of the American line. The insurgents were not fighting that day, it being one of their holidays, and they withdrew to enjoy it at leisure. The Spanish improved the opportunity to attack, but they found the American soldiers, as usual, equal to the occasion, and General Merritt reported the result with quiet gratification. The first intelligence of this important engagement came in a despatch dated Hong Kong, August 9th, as follows:

"Word has been received here to the effect that there was a heavy land engagement between the American and Spanish forces on the night of July 31st at Manila. The Spanish led in the attack, attempting to turn our right. After three hours of fighting, the Spanish were repulsed, with the loss of over 200 killed and 300 wounded. Our loss was only nine killed and forty-four wounded.

A Glorious Defence.

"The American troops engaged were the Tenth Pennsylvania, First California Battalion, Third Artillery, United States Regulars, and Battery A of Utah. Our volunteers made a glorious defence against upwards of 3,000 men, who composed the attacking force.

"The Spaniards made several desperate charges upon the American lines, but each time the fire of the American troops drove the Spaniards back, and finally broke the Spanish centre and the enemy retreated. Later, however, the Spaniards made a second attack, but were again repulsed and retreated into the bush, keeping up an incessant fire on the road leading to Manila, over which they apparently expected the American troops to advance. Some estimates placed the Spanish losses at over five hundred killed and wounded."

General Green's force, numbering 4,000 men, had been advancing and entrenching. The arrival of the third expedition filled the Spaniards with rage, and they determined to give battle before Camp Dewey could be reinforced. The trenches extended from the beach, three hundred yards to the left flank of the insurgents. Sunday was the insurgents' feast day, and their left flank withdrew, leaving the American right flank exposed.

Companies A and E, of the Tenth Pennsylvania and Utah Battery, were ordered to reinforce the right flank. In the midst of a raging typhoon, with a tremendous downpour of rain, the enemy's force, estimated at 3,000 men, attempted to surprise the camp. Our pickets were driven in and the trenches assaulted.

The brave Pennsylvania men never flinched, but stood their ground under a withering fire. The alarm spread, and the First California Regiment, with two companies of artillery, who fought with rifles, were sent up to reinforce the Pennsylvanians. The enemy were on top of the trenches when these reinforcements arrived, and never was the discipline of the regulars better demonstrated than by the work of the Third Artillery under Captain O'Hara. Nothing could be seen but flashes of Mauser rifles.

The Enemy Repulsed.

Men ran right up to the attacking Spaniards and mowed them down with regular volleys. The Utah Battery, under Captain Young, covered itself with glory. The men pulled their guns through mud axle deep. Two guns were sent around in flank and poured in a destructive enfilading fire. The enemy was repulsed, and retreated in disorder. Our infantry had exhausted its ammunition, and did not follow the enemy.

Not an inch of ground was lost, but the scene in the trenches was one never to be forgotten. During flashes of lightning the dead and wounded could be seen lying in blood-red water, but neither the elements of Heaven, nor the destructive power of man, could ring a cry of protest from the wounded. They encouraged their comrades to fight, and handed over their cartridge belts.

During the night the Spanish scouts were seen carrying off dead and wounded of the enemy. The American dead were buried next day in the convent of Maracaban. On the night of August 1st, the fighting was renewed, but the enemy had been taught a lesson, and made the attack at long range with heavy artillery   The Utat Battery replied, and the artillery duel lasted an hour.

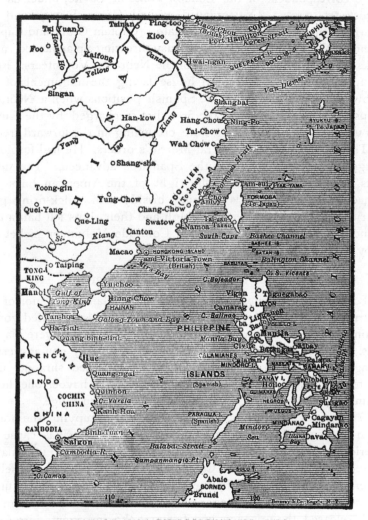

MAP OF THE PHILIPPINE ISLANDS.

729

The correspondent of the London *Times* at Cavite, under date of August 1st, wrote: "Yesterday I visited Camp Dewey and the American entrenchments before Malate. Captain Grant and Captain Young, of the Utah Artillery, were busy throwing up advanced earthworks for guns, under protection of the Nebraska Volunteers. From the upper floor of a European house facing the alignment of the earthworks I was observing the Spanish positions when a Nebraska sharpshooter beside me fired the first shot discharged by the Americans upon the Spaniards, who were crouching in the forward trench.

"This was contrary to General Merritt's orders. He had forbidden an aggressive attitude unless the Spaniards advanced. The insurgents now in force inland on the right of the American lines also opened fire, the Spaniards replying briskly with quick-firing guns and rifles, but their shooting was high and their shots fell half a mile behind the entrenchments, where a Colorado Volunteer picket was hit by a Mauser bullet.

Cool in the Face of Danger.

"Personally I was impressed by the nonchalant demeanor of the Americans in the fighting line. They were like high-spirited youths out on a picnic, while groups lying in the second line were playing cards. Had the Spaniards, who were unaccountably non-aggressive during the American landing and advance, dropped shrapnel from Malate fort, they would have wrought terrible havoc, one house forming a conspicuous mark, being within easy gun range.

"The natives follow the American advance, occupying the houses within the fighting line. General Aguinaldo's guerrillas cause the Americans considerable trouble. While I was in camp information was received that a party of California volunteers, engaged in felling timber, had been arrested by the insurgents. Colonel Smith, under General Green's instructions, ordered out an armed detachment, which released the prisoners and brought the insurgents into Camp Dewey. General Green sent a message to General Aguinaldo saying that if the Americans were further molested he would disarm the whole Filipinos."

The same correspondent, under date of August 3d, wrote: "A heavy monsoon has been blowing since Sunday, and deluges of rain have greatly increased the difficulty of landing and moving the

ADMIRAL MONTOJO, COMMANDER OF THE SPANISH FLEET.

United States troops and multiplied the discomforts in camp, which were already almost unendurable.

"Saturday was comparatively quiet, and so was Sunday until nightfall, when the Tenth Pennsylvania, Colonel Hawkins commanding, occupied the trenches after some desultory picket firing. At 11.30 P. M , the enemy opened fire vigorously, under cover of the dense undergrowth. Their movements were further hidden by the floods of rain. The Pennsylvanians met the attack with a succession of volleys, covering their right with two companies stationed in the swamp beyond the entrenchments.

"After about three-quarters of an hour two companies of the Third regular artillery, under Major O'Hara, arrived at double quick to relieve the Pennsylvanians, whose ammunition was almost exhausted. They soon silenced the enemy's fire, the First California, under Colonel Smith, and the First Colorado, under Colonel Hale, acting as supports. The affair lasted two hours. But notwithstanding the tremendous fusillade and the heavy shell fire, only nine Americans were killed and forty-seven wounded, though there were some casualties among the supports during the advance of the relieving battalions.

"Although the engagement scarcely attained the importance of a battle, it thoroughly tested the quality of the United States troops and had an excellent effect, stimulating their zeal and enthusiasm and inspiring them with confidence.

Sharp Fire from Spanish Guns.

"The Spaniards, whose losses in the engagement are not known, are adopting tactics intended to irritate the Americans. Every night they maintain an annoying fire. They have now got the true range of the earthworks, and their shell and shrapnel fire is very accurate.

"General MacArthur's brigade, which arrived Sunday, is landing to-day through the heavy surf. Nothing more serious than a thorough wetting has occurred as yet, although the operation is not without considerable danger. Hardly any cases of sickness are reported."

Malate, where the engagement took place, is a small suburb of Manila on the road between that city and Cavite. It was there that the family of Captain-General Augusti was captured by the rebels two months before. The place had been strongly fortified and held by the insurgents, and was occupied by our troops on their arrival from the transports.

General Green issued the following address to our troops:

STREET SCENE IN MANILA—PHILIPPINE ISLANDS.

733

" The brigadier-general commanding desires to thank the troops engaged last night for gallantry and skill displayed by them in repelling
such a vigorous attack by largely superior forces of Spaniards.   Not
an inch of ground was yielded by the Tenth Pennsylvania Infantry
and Utah Artillery stationed in the trenches.

" A battalion of the Third Artillery and First Regiment California
Infantry moved forward to their support through a galling fire with
the utmost intrepidity.   The courage and steadiness shown by all in
their first engagement is worthy of the highest commendation."

" Mr. Williams, formerly United States Consul at Manila, has
called the leaders in fifteen provinces of the Philippines to a conference, from which good results are hoped."

The scarcity of food was affecting even the richest class in Manila.
There was no meat, bread or flour, except a very small reserve,
chiefly laid under requisition for the Spanish troops.

Famine and Epidemic.

The newspapers, though rigidly censored, admitted that the famine
and the unprecedented rains were causing an epidemic.   They pretended that the disorders were trivial intestinal ailments, but it is
believed most of them were dysentery, due to the wretched food and
the dangerous character of the water.   A number of important persons were ill.

An abattoir was established for slaughtering horses and dogs.
The newspapers admitted that the military bakers were reduced to the
necessity of using rice, the stock of which would shortly be exhausted. The stock of fuel, too, was exhausted, and bakers were burning doors and window frames.   It is impossible to eat uncooked rice.

A decree was issued authorizing the entry of private premises
and the seizure of cattle and horses there, for nominal payments,
made in worthless drafts. Several animals belonging to British
owners were taken, though there were plenty belonging to Spanish
owners that had not been seized. An attempt was made to seize the
indispensable pony of the consular physician, and considerable indignation was expressed.

In an engagement five miles beyond Guayama on August 8th, five of the Fourth Ohio Volunteers were wounded. The Americans were caught in an ambuscade, and the only wonder is that half of Companies A and C, of the Fourth Ohio, were not wiped out. Ever since Guayama had been occupied three days before, the natives were most demonstrative in praising the Americans, and in showing how delighted they were at the retreat of the Spaniards. Soon there came a change, which was not at all surprising to those who know the character of the Porto Ricans.

It was just 1 o'clock in the afternoon when a horseman came galloping into the town, shouting: "Send the dynamite guns at once! The Fourth Ohio is being annihilated!"

Soldiers Hurry to Their Quarters.

In less than five minutes the alarm had spread throughout the town, and the streets were filled with soldiers hurrying to their quarters. The natives disappeared as if by magic, not a single one of them remaining in sight. Shutters were hurriedly put up on all the shops that were open, the hackmen rushed their horses to their stables, and everywhere the natives showed by their actions that they anticipated the recapture of the town by the Spaniards. The fears of some of the women led them to seek protection in the cathedral, where they spent the time in prayer.

The Spanish attack grew out of the fact that Colonel Coit, Major Dean and Lieutenant Wardman of General Brooke's staff, had, with Companies A and C of the Fourth Ohio, started early in the morning to reconnoitre to the northward with the object of ascertaining the truth of the reports that the Spaniards had mined the bridges on the road to Cayey, whither General Brooke's command was bound. On account of the smallness of the reconnoitring party, the report that they had been attacked by the Spaniards caused consternation at the Guayama headquarters.

A srtong force was, however, at once hurried to the front. There were no horses to haul the dynamite guns, but the men buckled to and dragged them over the hills for five miles to the scene of action.

On the way several privates of Company C were met. They reported that that company and Company A had been practically annihilated by Spanish artillery. They declared that they were too tired to fight any more. At 2 o'clock the reinforcements reached a turn of the road, and the whole scene of the engagement lay before them. They stood directly on the spot where the first ambuscade had been made. The road here takes a sudden turn to the right, while 300 yards further on it makes a quick turn to the left. Thus the marching troops were exposed at both turns to fire from the hills on either side.

The Spaniards were about 600 yards away. They were intrenched on one side behind a blockhouse and on the other behind earthworks on top of a hill. Nothing but a shallow ditch on the left side of the road saved the American troops. That the fire had been blistering hot there was shown by the trees, whose leaves and boughs had been torn away by the Spanish shot. For the greater part of two hours the Americans lay in the ditch, the Spaniards meanwhile directing a hot fire against them, but not attempting to charge them.

Hot Fire from the Blockhouse.

A stampede was started in Company C by the collapse of Captain Biddle, who was prostrated by the heat. When he fell it was generally believed that he had been shot, and the effect on the men might have been serious had it not been for Lieutenant Wardman, who assumed command of the company and fought gallantly through the engagement. As soon as the reinforcements arrived he pressed forward with his men to the top of the hill. Some time before this the enemy had stopped their cross-fire, but as soon as the Americans climbed the hill the Spaniards opened a hot fire from the blockhouse. The Americans rushed through the hail of bullets toward the block-house, and the Spaniards started to retreat.

Just at this time the dynamite guns got into action. The first shell landed at one side of the blockhouse and exploded with a terrific roar. The Spaniards were simply thrown into a state of panic by the explosion of the shell and were seen fleeing from the hill at top speed in all directions except toward the Americans. They could hardly be derided for evincing such a presiding desire to get out of range. The shell tore a hole in the ground for a distance of fifty feet and the shock of the explosion could be felt where the Americans stood.

From the place in the road where the guns were fired the sight was a beautiful one. All up the hill the American soldiers, their brown hats silhouetted against the sky, kept volleying away at the enemy and chatting at the same time in a manner to shock regular troops.

Welcome to our Troops.

After the third shot from the dynamite guns the Spaniards were in full retreat. The Americans then retired to Guayama for the night. They found the houses still closed as tight as traps. Not until the dynamite guns appeared would the natives even open their windows. Then one by one they straggled out, shouting: "Long live the Americans!" and displaying the American colors. Captain Biddle had just left the hospital, and was scarcely in condition to command his company.

That the Spaniards intended to put up a fight to prevent the advance of the Americans was evident. Natives reported this morning that 400 infantry and 150 cavalry camped within four miles of Guayama the night before. They also reported that there were heavy artillery intrenchments within five miles of the town. No artillery or cavalry was engaged in the fighting. The Americans crossed three bridges, and upon examination found that none of them had been mined or otherwise tampered with.

There was a two hours' fight before day-break at Cape San Juan August 9th, in which the Spaniards were worsted. Eight hundred Spaniards attempted to retake the lighthouse, which was guarded by forty of our sailors, commanded by Lieutenant Atwater. The Spaniards were driven back by shells from the Amphitrite, Cincinnati and Leyden. Refugees reported that one hundred Spaniards were killed. The Spanish advance began from Rio Grande, whither the Spaniards had retreated after the first landing of troops at Cape San Juan the week before. They marched through Luquillo and pulled down the American flag at Fajardo and replaced the Spanish flag.

47

The terrified refugees warned the light-house force that the Spanish were coming. Sixty women and children were in an outbuilding of the lighthouse during the fight. The Spaniards opened with a machine gun at a distance of three hundred yards. The Leyden, Ensign Crosley commanding, rushed within one hundred yards of the shore and poured one-pounders into the Spaniards. Captain Barclay, of the Amphitrite, used six-pounders and the Cincinnati five-inch guns.

The ships landed two hundred and fifty men during the fight and reinforced the lighthouse. A machine gun, rifles and ammunition were left by the retreating Spaniards. Ensign Crosley took the refugees off at daybreak and went to Ponce. Our flag was still on the lighthouse, but the forces were withdrawn. The Amphitrite guns covered the lighthouse, ready to annihilate it if our flag was hauled down. It is one of the most important lights on the island.

An Engagement Suddenly Stopped.

Hostilities were brought to an end at Guayama, Porto Rico, August 14th, amid the groans and murmurings of the soldiers under General Brooke, who were about to begin a movement whose end seemed certain victory.

Spaniards, massed in strong defences, lay right before our lines, in easy range. Light Battery B, of Pennsylvania, had been ordered into position to begin the engagement. The guns of the first section had been brought up and a gun had been unlimbered. A shell had been placed in the chamber.

A Pennsylvanian stood ready to fire. Suddenly there was a shout from the rear. Two men on horseback dashed into view, frantically waving their arms. The men at the guns waited. The horsemen were Signal Lieutenant McLaughlin and an orderly. They had ridden hard from the end of the military wire that was built in the field to General Brooke's headquarters.

The order to commence firing had been given when the lieutenant and orderly reached the gun. "Cease action!" shouted the lieutenant. Then to the wondering artillerymen he explained that the war was over. A message had been received from General Miles by General Brooke, he said, directing that all hostile military operations should be stopped. The peace protocol had been signed by representatives of both governments.

The Pennsylvanians, officers and men, howled with disgust, and when the lieutenant delivered General Brooke's order that they should return to the camp at Guayama they sullenly wheeled the guns about and went, sullenly, to the rear. The position of these men was superb. Brooke had thrown out three strong columns to the left of Guayama. His plan was to shell and rush his way to Cayey, where he was to form a junction with General Wilson.

His main column, himself in command, consisting of three light batteries, three regiments of infantry and two troops of cavalry, advanced over a mountain road, with its flanks effectually protected. It met with no opposition. Three miles out beyond the scene of Monday's fight the enemy was discovered, intrenched in a splendid defensive position on the top of a mountain, but the range was easy.

It was then that the notice of peace arrived and sent the soldiers sadly back with the gun that was to have sent the first shell on the way to victory.

The Dawn of Peace.

The Department of State at Washington, on the afternoon of August 2d, issued a statement announcing officially the President's terms of peace which were handed to Ambassador Cambon. They were that Spanish sovereignty must be forever relinquished in the Western Indies; that the United States should have a coaling station in the Ladrones, and that this country would occupy Manila's bay and harbor, as well as the city, pending the determination of the control, disposition and government of the Philippines. The statement was as follows:

"In order to remove any misapprehension in regard to the negotiations as to peace between the United States and Spain, it is deemed proper to say that the terms offered by the United States to Spain in the note tendered the French Ambassador on Saturday last are in substance as follows:

"The President does not now put forward any claim for pecuniary indemnity, but requires the relinquishment of all claim of sovereignty over or title to the Island of Cuba, as well as the immediate evacuation by Spain of the Island; the cession to the United States and immediate evacuation of Porto Rico and other islands under Spanish sovereignty in the West Indies, and the like cession of an island in the Ladrones.

"The United States will occupy and hold the city, bay and harbor of Manila, pending the conclusion of a treaty of peace which shall determine the control, disposition and government of the Philippines.

"If these are accepted by Spain in their entirety, commissioners will be named by the United States to meet commissioners on the part of Spain for the purpose of concluding a treaty of peace on the basis above indicated."

Spain Expected to Agree to Terms.

The announcement on August 7th, from Madrid, that the Spanish Ministry had formally decided to accept the proposition of the United States for a peace convention relieved the anxiety that was felt for a definite decision. No doubt was entertained that Spain would agree to the terms offered by President McKinley, nor was the faith of the President shaken in the ultimate outcome by reason of what the impatient public regarded as delay on the part of Spain in making answer. The public were not admitted to all the councils of the government and therefore were not prepared to form an intelligent opinion.

There were reasons why an immediate reply could not be made to the American proposition, and these reasons were understood and appreciated by the President and Secretary Day. Convinced that Spain would accept the terms there was no disposition on the part of the President to insist upon hasty action. It was felt that the reply would be made within a reasonable time, and the good judgment and sagacity of the President were vindicated by the action of the Spanish Cabinet.

On the evening of August 12th, 1898, President McKinley issued the following proclamation:

" By the President of the United States of America.

" A Proclamation.

" Whereas, By a protocol concluded and signed August 12th, 1898, by William R. Day, Secretary of State of the United States, and His Excellency, Jules Cambon, Ambassador Extraordinary and Minister Plenipotentiary of the Republic of France at Washington, respectively representing for this purpose the Government of the United States and the Government of Spain, the United States and Spain have formally agreed upon the terms on which negotiations for the establishment of peace between the two countries shall be undertaken; and

" Whereas, It is in said protocol agreed that upon its conclusion and signature hostilities between the two countries shall be suspended, and that notice to that effect shall be given as soon as possible by each government to the commanders of its military and naval forces;

" Now, therefore, I, William McKinley, President of the United States, do, in accordance with the stipulations of the protocol, declare and proclaim on the part of the United States a suspension of hostilities, and do hereby command that orders be immediately given through the proper channels to the commanders of the military and naval forces of the United States to abstain from all acts inconsistent with this proclamation.

" In witness whereof, I have hereunto set my hand and caused the seal of the United States to be affixed.

" Done in the city of Washington, this 12th day of August, in the year of our Lord one thousand eight hundred and ninety-eight, and of the Independence of the United States the one hundred and twenty-third.   William McKinley."

" By the President, William R. Day, Secretary of State."

Provisions Stated in the Protocol.

The protocol, signed by Secretary Day on behalf of the United States and by Ambassador Cambon on behalf of Spain, contains the following provisions:

That Spain will relinquish all claim of sovereignty over and title to Cuba.

That Porto Rico and other Spanish islands in the West Indies, and an island in the Ladrones to be selected by the United States, shall be ceded to the latter.

That the United States will occupy and hold the city, bay and harbor of Manila pending the conclusion of the treaty of peace, which shall determine the control, disposition and government of the Philippines.

That Cuba, Porto Rico and other Spanish Islands in the West Indies shall be immediately evacuated, and that commissioners, to be appointed within ten days, shall, within thirty days from the signing of the protocol, meet at Havana and San Juan, respectively, to arrange and execute the details of the evacuation.

That the United States and Spain will each appoint not more than five commissioners to negotiate and conclude a treaty of peace. The commissioners are to meet at Paris not later than the 1st of October.

On the signing of the protocol, hostilities will be suspended and notice to that effect will be given as soon as possible by each government to the commanders of its military and naval forces.

The closing chapter of events that led up to the signature of the protocol and the cessation of hostilities were full of interest. There were rumors in the early morning that over night the French Embassy had received the long-expected final instructions from Madrid, but these, upon inquiry, proved groundless, and it was not until half-past 12 that the note began to come from Madrid in small lots.

The Formal Ceremony.

At 2.45 o'clock Secretary Thiebaut, of the French Embassy, appeared at the State Department to inform Secretary Day that the Ambassador was in full possession of the note, was fully empowered to sign the protocol for Spain, and only awaited the pleasure of the State Department. He intimated that the Ambassador would be pleased to have the final ceremony conducted in the presence of President McKinley, where the negotiations were begun.

Leaving the Secretary of Embassy in his own office, Secretary Day made a short visit to the White House to learn the President's wishes in the matter. The latter immediately consented to accept the suggestion, and M. Thiebaut hastened to inform his principal that the President would receive him at the White House at 4 o'clock.

At the appointed hour a driving rain storm prevailed, obliging all the parties to resort to carriages for transportation to the White House. Secretary Day came first, with a large portfolio under his arm, enclosing copies of the protocol, of the proclamation to be issued by the President stopping hostilities, and some other necessary papers. He was accompanied by Assistant Secretary Moore, Second Assistant Secretary Adee and Third Assistant Secretary Cridler. They were shown immediately into the Cabinet room, where the President sat in waiting.

When Ambassador Cambon reached the White House the rain was still violent, and the Ambassador abandoned his usual custom of alighting at the outer gates of the Executive grounds. He was driven under the porte cochere, passing through a cordon of newspaper men, before he and Secretary Thiebaut were ushered inside. They went direct to the library adjoining the Cabinet room on the upper floor. At 4.05 they were announced to the waiting party in the Cabinet room, and were ushered into their presence.

After an exchange of diplomatic courtesies no unnecessary loss of time occurred and Assistant Secretary of State Cridler, on the part of the United States, and First Secretary Thiebaut, on the part of Spain, retired to a window, where there was a critical formal examination of the protocol. This inspection had all the outward formalities due a document of this importance and was considered proper in a matter of such grave importance.

How the Protocol Was Arranged.

It was prepared in duplicate at the State Department, one copy to be retained by the United States Government, and the other to become the property of Spain. The text was handsomely engrossed in a running Old English script. Each copy of the protocol was arranged in double column, French and English standing alongside for easy comparison as to the exactness of the translation.

The protocol sent to Spain was accompanied by the credentials issued by President McKinley, specially empowering the Secretary of State to affix his signature to this document. The authorization was brief and in type-writing, save for the President's characteristic bold signature. Written credentials of the Spanish government were sent to M. Cambon bearing the signature of Cristina. The cable dispatch received by him conferred full authority to sign the protocol, and stated that the written authorization would follow, signed by the Queen Regent in the name of the King.

The examination of the protocol was satisfactory, and the document was handed to M. Cambon first, and then to SecretaryDay, who affixed signatures in that order to each side of the two copies. Then the last detail in making the protocol binding was administered by Assistant Secretary Cridler, in charge of the chancery work, who attached the seal of the United States.

Throughout the ceremony all but the two signers remained standing. M. Cambon, in signing for Spain, occupied the seat which Secretary of the Navy, Long, now away on a vacation, usually occupied. The President stood at the left hand corner at the head of the great Cabinet table. Secretary Day, M. Thiebaut and M. Cambon, in the order named, on the left side of the table. The rest of the party were standing in other portions of the room.

The Signatures Are Attached.

It was 4.23 o'clock when the final signatures were attached to the protocol, and within the knowledge of all the officials present this was the first time that a protocol or treaty had been signed at the White House.

As this ceremony concluded, Acting Secretary Allen, of the Navy Department; Secretary Alger and Adjutant General Corbin appeared having been summoned to the White House by the President, and they were admitted into the Cabinet room just in season to witness one of the most impressive features of the ceremony.

The President requested the hand of the Ambassador and through him returned thanks to the sister republic of France for the exercise of her good offices in bringing about peace. He also thanked the Ambassador personally for the important part he has played in this matter, and the latter replied in suitable terms. As a further mark of his disposition, President McKinley called for the proclamation which he had caused to be drawn up suspending hostilities, and signed it in the presence of M. Cambon, who expressed his appreciation of the action.

The following are fac-similes of the signatures of the French Ambassador and Secretary Day, which were attached to the Protocol:

Jules Cambon

12 août 1898

William R. Day

Aug. 12. 1898.

President McKinley Praises the Troops.

The following official correspondence between President McKinley and General Breckinridge, in which the President pays tribute to the troops who could not be sent to the front, was made public August 12th.

"THE PRESIDENT: "CHICKAMAUGA PARK, GA., August 10, 1898.

"May I not ask you, in the name and behalf of the forty thousand men of this command, to visit it while it is still intact ? There is much to be said showing how beneficial and needed such a visit is ; but you will appreciate better than I can tell you the disappointment and consequent depression many men must feel, especially the sick, when they joined together for a purpose, and have done so much to show their readiness and worthiness to serve their country in the field, but find themselves leaving the military service without a battle or campaign. All who see them must recognize their merit and personal interest, must encourage all if you can find time to review this command.

"BRECKINRIDGE, Major General Commanding."

The following is the President's reply :

"EXECUTIVE MANSION, Washington, August 11, 1898.

"MAJOR GENERAL BRECKINRIDGE, Chickamauga Park :

"Replying to your invitation I beg to say that it would give me great pleasure to show by a personal visit to Chickamauga Park, my high regard for the forty thousand troops of your command, who so patriotically responded to the call for volunteers and who have been for upwards of two months ready for any service and sacrifice the country might require. My duties, however, will not admit of absence from Washington at this time.

" The highest tribute that can be paid to a soldier is to say that he performed his full duty. The field of duty is determined by his government, and wherever that chances to be is the place of honor. All have helped in the great cause, whether in camp or battle, and when peace comes all will be alike entitled to the nation's gratitude.　　　　　　　　　　　　　" WILLIAM McKINLEY."

On Saturday, August 13th, another and very important victory was added to those already gained by our military and naval forces. Manila fell before the guns of Dewey's fleet and the assaults of General Merritt's troops. No news having reached the Philippines of the end of the war by the signing of the protocol on August 12th, the long deferred attack upon Manila was made, and after a spirited resistance by the Spanish troops, the city surrendered.

Early in the morning Dewey's fleet, which had blockaded the town since May 1st, advanced and signalled a demand for a surrender, which was refused. The forts were then bombarded with great effect, and the city was taken by our land forces. The Spanish General Augusti, was taken off by a German cruiser late at night and with his family went to Hong Kong.

The capture of Manila completed a series of military events of the most brilliant description and destined to change the map of the world, placing America in the front rank of naval and military powers, a position which she had not held up to the time of our War with Spain, owing to the fact that it has never been necessary for us to take on the character of a military nation.

Condensed Record of the Events of the War.

The following is a condensed record of the Events of the War, including the dates on which all the principal events took place:

February 15, 1898.—Destruction of the Battleship Maine in the harbor of Havana.

February 17th.—Court of Inquiry on Maine explosion appointed.

March 28th.—Court of Inquiry reports Maine blown up by external causes.

April 5th.—Consul-General Lee recalled from Havana.

April 10th.—Consul-General Lee sails from Cuba.

April 11th.—President McKinley sends a message to Congress on the Cuban question.

April 16th.—Senate passes the Belligerency resolutions.

April 18th.—House refuses to recognize the belligerency of the Cubans. Spain sends memorandum to the Powers.

April 19th.—Congress adopts conference report.

April 20th.—The President signs the Cuban bill, and sends an ultimatum to Spain in accordance therewith. He also makes public notification of blockade of Cuban ports.

April 21st.—Passports sent Minister Woodford.

April 23d.—Havana blockaded by North Atlantic Squadron, and cruiser Nashville fires first shot of the war, taking as prize steamer Buena Ventura. The President issues proclamation calling for 125,000 men.

April 24th.—Spain makes declaration of war.

April 25th.—Congress declares war against Spain dating from April 21st.

April 26th.—Congress passes Army Reorganization bill, and the President proclaims adherence to the Declaration of Paris. England proclaims neutrality.

April 27th.—Matanzas fortifications bombarded by New York, Puritan and Cincinnati. Admiral Dewey sails from Mirs Bay to Manila to engage Spanish fleet.

April 28th.—France declares neutrality. Congress passes Naval Appropriation bill.

April 29th.—Admiral Dewey arrives off Philippine Islands. Army moves from Chattanooga for Tampa. Portugal declares neutrality. Fleet under command of Admiral Cervera sails from Cape Verde Islands for West India waters.

April 30th.—Battleship Oregon and the Marietta reach Rio from San Francisco.

May 1st.—Admiral Dewey's fleet entirely destroys the Spanish fleet in Manila Bay.

May 2d.—Admiral Dewey demands surrender of fortifications in harbor of Manila, and cuts cable to Hong Kong

May 3d.—Government decides to send an army to the Philippines.

May 4th.—Oregon and Marietta leave Rio.

May 5th.—Gunboat Wilmington covers landing of arms from tug Leyden for the Cubans.   Spaniards routed.

May 7th.—Admiral Dewey announces the capture of Cavite.

May 9th.—At the request of President Congress unanimously gives vote of thanks to Admiral Dewey.   Torpedo boat Winslow has a fight with Spanish vessels in Cardenas harbor.

May 11th.—Ensign Bagley and four of the crew of the Winslow killed during an engagement in Cardenas harbor.   Cable at Cienfuegos cut.

May 12th.—Admiral Sampson bombards San Juan de Porto Rico. General Merritt accepts command of Philippine Islands army.

May 13th.—Commodore Schley sails from Hampton Roads with Flying Squadron.

May 14th.—Admiral Cervera's fleet reported at Curacoa.

May 17th.—Censorship of Cable messages established.

May 18th.—Alabama launched.   Cables cut by St. Louis and Wampatuck under heavy fire.

May 19th.—Commodore Schley's fleet at Key West.   Cervera's fleet reported at Santiago.

May 20th.—Six regiments of immunes ordered raised.

May 22d.—Cruiser Charleston sails from San Francisco to Manila.

May 24th.—Battleship Oregon arrives at Jupiter, Fla.

May 25th.—President calls for 75,000 additional volunteers.   First expedition of troops sailed for Manila.

May 26th.—Colonel Lacret lands in Cuba with 432 men.

May 29th.—Commodore Schley reports finding Admiral Cervera's fleet in Santiago Bay.

May 30th.—General Shafter ordered to embark with 15,000 or more men for Santiago campaign.

May 31st. — Commodore Schley bombards fortifications at Santiago.

June 1st.—Admiral Sampson takes command at Santiago.

June 2d.—House passes urgent deficiency bill of nearly $18,000.-
000. Spain makes another appeal to the Powers to intervene in
her behalf.

June 3d.—Hobson and crew of seven men sink Merrimac in entrance
of Santiago harbor to prevent egress of Cervera's fleet, and are
captured by Spanish.

June 6th.—Santiago fortifications again bombarded and Spanish
cruiser Reina Mercedes sunk. Admiral Dewey reports insurgent
successes around Manila.

June 7th.—Fortifications at Caimanera in Guantanamo Bay destroyed.
Monitor Monterey sails for Manila.

June 10th.—Congress passes war revenue bill. Six hundred marines
land at Caimanera.

June 11th.—Spanish troops attack marines, but repulsed with heavy
loss. Four Americans killed.

June 12th.—Attack renewed, but Spanish troops again repulsed.
Philippine insurgents declare independence and choose Aguinaldo President.

June 13th.—Attack on marines at Caimanera at night. Two Americans killed and 15 Spaniards. Latter repulsed.

June 14th.—General Shafter sails from Tampa for Santiago with
15,000 men. American marines and Cubans storm blockhouse
at Caimanera, capture it and rout the enemy.

June 15th.—Second expedition for the Philippines sails. House
passes Hawaiian resolutions by vote of 209 to 91. The exchange of Lieutenant Hobson is authorized by the Spanish
Government.

June 16th.—The Cadiz squadron, under Admiral Camara, sails for
the Philippines.

June 19th.—Admiral Sampson and General Garcia confer.

June 20th.—General Shafter's army lands at Baiquiri.

June 21st.—Forts at Nipe Bay silenced and Spanish vessel Jorge
Juan sunk. Sampson and Shafter visit Garcia. Cruiser Charleston captures Guam, Ladrone Islands.

June 22d.—Part of General Shafter's army disembarks. The St. Paul disables the Terror in harbor of San Juan, Porto Rico.

June 23d.—General Shafter's troops all landed without accident. Monitor Monadnock sails for Manila.

June 24th.—Battle of La Quisima, 16 Rough Riders and Regulars killed and 40 wounded.

June 27th.—Commodore Watson ordered to command squadron to proceed to Spain. Third expedition for Manila sails.

June 28th.—President orders Cuban Blockade extended.

June 29th.—General Merritt sails for Manila.

June 30th.—First expedition to Manila arrives. General Shafter's army advances near Santiago. The Egyptian Government orders Camara's squadron to stop coaling in its waters.

July 1st.—Battle of Santiago begun. General Lawton's division storms and captures El Caney, and another division, including Regulars and Rough Riders, storm and capture San Juan. American troops lose about 1,800 men.

July 2d.—Spanish forces try unsuccessfully to recapture San Juan.

July 3d —Commodore Schley destroys Admiral Cervera's fleet.

July 4th.—Spanish cruiser Alphonso XII. sunk off Havana by the Hornet.

July 6th.—Senate votes affirmatively on Hawaiian resolutions Hobson exchanged. President McKinley issues a Thanksgiving proclamation.

July 7th.—Admiral Dewey captures Isla Grande, Subig Bay, and forces German cruiser Irene to retire. President McKinley signs Hawaiian resolutions of annexation.

July 8th.—Congress adjourns. Camara's squadron sails back to Spain.

July 11th.—General Miles arrives at Santiago.

July 13th.—General Shafter reports yellow fever among the troops.

July 14th.—General Toral surrenders the Spanish army in the greater part of Santiago province, including the city to General Shafter.

July 15th.—The fourth expedition for Manila sails.

July 17th.—The American flag raised in Santiago.

July 18th.—The President issues a proclamation regarding the government of Santiago.

July 20th.—Troops sail from Tampa for Porto Rico.

July 21st.—General Miles sails with troops for Porto Rico from Guantanamo Bay.

July 25th.—General Miles lands at Guanica, Porto Rico, and General Merritt reaches Manila.

July 26th.—Spain sues for peace through French Ambassador Cambon.

July 27th.—Nearly 3,000 fever cases among American troops at Santiago.

July 29th.—Ponce, Porto Rico, surrenders, and inhabitants give warm welcome to General Miles

July 30th.—President McKinley makes reply to Spain's plea for peace.

July 31st.—Battle of Malate, an outskirt of Manila. Spanish troops attack at night and repulsed with heavy loss, estimated at 500 killed and wounded. American loss, 14 killed and 44 wounded.

August 2d.—General Merritt asks for 30,000 more troops. Spain intimates she will accept the terms of peace demanded by the United States.

August 3d.—Colonel Roosevelt and Generals under General Shafter unite in a Round Robin, asking that troops be sent home on account of yellow fever.

August 5th.—Embarkation of Shafter's troops for home begins. General Hains captures Guanama after a sharp skirmish.

August 9th —Spain sends long reply to United States terms of peace.

August 12th.—Peace protocol signed in Washington. War and Navy Departments cable Generals and Admirals to suspend hostilities. Blockade of Havana raised.

August 13th.—Hot battle between Spanish and American forces at Asmonte Ridge, Porto Rico. Americans victorious. Mayagues captured. Havana batteries open fire on American warships, and one shot strikes the San Francisco, but injures no one. Flag of truce announcing peace then sent in. Bombardments of the forts at Manila by Admiral Dewey's fleet and a capture of the city after an assault by General Merritt's troops.

Before the attack on Manila August 13th, detailed in the foregoing pages, General Merritt issued the following order to his army :

"In view of the extraordinary conditions under which this army is operating, its commanding General desires to acquaint the officers and men with the expectations he entertains as to their conduct.

"You are assembled on foreign soil, situated within the western confines of a vast ocean separating you from your native land. You have come not as despoilers or oppressors, but simply as the instruments of a strong, free government, whose purposes are beneficent and which declared itself in this war champion of those oppressed by Spanish misrule.

"It is therefore the intention of this order to appeal directly to your pride in your position as representatives of a high civilization, in the hope and with the firm conviction that you will so conduct yourselves in your relations with the inhabitants of these islands as to convince them of the lofty nature of the mission you have come to execute.

"It is not believed any acts of pillage, rapine or violence will be committed by soldiers or others in the employ of the United States, but should there be persons with this command who prove themselves unworthy of this confidence, their acts will be considered not only as crimes against the sufferers, but as direct insults to the United States flag and be punished on the spot with the maximum penalties known to military law."

Dewey's Terrific Bombardment.

Further details of the battle before Manila show that with a loss of eight killed, fifty wounded and not even a shroud carried away on one of the warships, the American land and naval forces captured the city. Seven thousand prisoners, twelve thousand rifles, a number of field guns and an immense quantity of ammunition fell into the hands of the victors.

The fortifications and shore defenses and part of the city itself were destroyed by American shot and shell during a terrific bombardment of two hours by eight ships of Admiral Dewey's fleet. The Americans killed lost their lives in storming the Spanish trenches, when they swept everything before them like a whirlwind, and gave the Spaniards and Filipinos a splendid exhibition of Yankee valor.

Three demands for the surrender of the city were made by Admiral Dewey before Manila was attacked. The first was made on August 7th. In it the Spaniards were given forty-eight hours to lay down their arms. The German Consul immediately embarked all German subjects on the German warships for protection. On the afternoon of August 9th the demand for surrender was again made. The Spaniards asked a delay to enable them to get instructions from Madrid. This was refused.

On the 13th the final demand was made. A message was sent to the Spanish commander at 8 o'clock. The Spaniards were given one hour in which to surrender. They immediately refused to do so. The American squadron promptly cleared for action. They moved into a line between Malate and Old Manila. There were eight vessels in the squadron— the Olympia, the flagship; the Monterey, the Boston, Baltimore, Charleston, Petrel, Raleigh and Hugh McCulloch. The German and French vessels lay north of the Passig river. The greatest excitement prevailed among the vessels of the foreign fleet, which lay across the bay. The British and Japanese warships were nearest the American fleet.

Signal to Open Fire

At 9.30 o'clock the signal to open fire fluttered from the signal lines of the Olympia. The flags were scarcely set when there was a roar from the big guns of the flagship herself. Instantly all the other vessels opened, and a shower of steel missiles sped toward the doomed city. At the same time along the line of the American entrenchments the field guns opened on the Spanish position, and the American infantry were massed in the intrenchments ready for the final assault.

The din was terrific. The heavier guns of the warships roared at intervals, while the rapid-fires barked viciously and the guns of the secondary batteries spat and sputtered fast and furiously. Through the awful noise the great 13-inch guns of the big monitor Monterey

48

could be heard distinctly like great thunderclaps, and the awe-inspiring shrieks of her immense shells could be readily distinguished from the tenor and alto songs of the smaller missles.

Great gaps were torn in the Spanish fortifications as the shells struck and exploded, and buildings in the outskirts of the city could be seen to tumble or rise in the air as the shells passed through or exploded within them. In the midst of the bombardment the order to storm the Spanish trenches was given to the American soldiers. The Spanish lines extended a distance of ten miles around the city, and from two to four miles outside the walls.

Grand Assault by Americans.

With a cheer the Americans sprang from their trenches and dashed for the Spanish earthworks. The First Colorado Volunteers were in the van. A deadly fire was poured in from the heights occupied by the Spaniards, and it was this that caused the American losses.

But the men never hesitated. They swept the enemy from the outer line of intrenchments to the second line of defense. This was at once attacked, and from there the Spaniards were driven into the walled city. Then the Spanish commander saw that further resistance was useless, and he sent up a white flag. The bombardment was at once stopped, and soon afterward the American forces entered the city. General Merritt assumed command and temporarily restored the civil laws.

The Spanish forces numbered about 7,000 men, but they were well intrenched. Nearly 10,000 Americans were engaged in the assault, and their losses under the circumstances are considered small. The Colorado troops were the first to storm the trenches, and every man was a hero.

On August 18th the War Department at Washington received the following official report from General Merritt:

" MANILA, August 13.

" ADJUTANT-GENERAL, Washington :

" On 7th instant Admiral Dewey joined me in forty-eight hour notification to Spanish commander to remove non-combatents from city. Same date reply received expressing thanks for humane sentiments and stating Spanish without places of refuge for non-combatants now within walled town.

"On 9th instant sent joint note inviting attention to suffering in store for sick and non-combatants in case it became our duty to reduce the defences, also setting forth hopeless condition of Spanish forces, surrounded on all sides, fleet in front, no prospect of reinforcements, and demanded surrender as due to every consideration of humanity; same date received reply admitting their situation, but stating council of defence declares request for surrender cannot be granted, but offered to consult Government if time was granted necessary to communicate *via* Hong Kong. Joint note in reply declining.

"On the 13th joined with navy in attack, with following result: After about half-hour's accurate shelling of Spanish lines, McArthur's brigade on right and Greene's on left, under Anderson, made vigorous attack and carried Spanish works. Loss not accurately known—about fifty in all.

"Behavior of troops excellent; co-operation of the navy most valuable. Troops advanced rapidly on walled city, upon which white flag was shown and town capitulated. Troops occupy Malate, Binondo, walled city San Miguel. All important centres protected. Insurgents kept out. No disorder or pillage.   MERRITT."

What Is Thought of Our Soldiers.

A correspondent of the Hong Kong *Telegraph*, writing from Manila, furnishes the following estimate of the United States soldiers who were sent to the Philippines:

"In the early part of the day the raw recruits from Roaring Camp or Dead Man's Gulch are being 'licked into shape' by Sergeant Whatshisname, with a California twang. In the afternoon they have a rest, and may prowl about the native town, or bathe in the bay, or exercise their ingenuity in finding something else to do. They are a fine, big, strong-looking lot, of about the toughest type of the Wild West, I should imagine; splendid fellows, no doubt, thorough

'rough diamonds,' extremely rougb.   Great, hulking backwoodsmen, bull-punchers, diggers, cargo-lumpers from 'Frisco, farm hands from San Diego, and all apparently selected for their size.   Among the lithe little Philipinos they are an army of Goliaths.

"A strapping six-footer in non-commissioned officer's uniform came and asked us some questions in very broken English, with a Norwegian accent, and, after giving him the information he desired, we asked him, jokingly, 'Have any of your soldiers ever been in America?'   He stared for a minute or two, pondering over the true inwardness of the query, and then replied: 'Ve vas all Amurricans. Vat you dinks?'   In some trepidation, as I gauged the man's height and fighting weight, I replied, 'I begs bardon, I dinks you vas some Norske shib's garbenders.'   He took it quite goodnaturedly, and laughed as we parted.

Mixture of Nationalities.

"It is impossible to guess how many of these troops are of American birth.   Possibly we miscalculated.   (I say 'we' because I had a companion in all my peregrinations, an excellent and invaluable friend.)   We guessed that there might be a fairly thick sprinkling of aliens, say 10 or 15 per cent., British and a similar proportion of Continental Europeans; the rest, 70 or 80 per cent. American born. They look as if they should make the finest troops in the world, after being drilled and disciplined; strong, brave, intelligent, and with plenty of 'go,' not merely clay to be moulded like Chinese or Egyptian raw material, but full of fire and life.

"At present, however, roughness is the chief characteristic noticeable about them.   Their uniform intensifies the impression; it is a coarse brown canvas, beside which our Indian campaigning dress of khaki is as silk beside floor matting.   The color is darker than khaki, and I think better for invisibility; but the material is altogether too much like coal sacks.

"The Americans seem to carry their republicanism to such extreme lengths as to studiously avoid any suggestion of spruce or smart appearance; they could be dressed quite as plainly and still be neat and trim. I am not finding fault with the California Volunteer , nor do I overlook the fact that they had only just landed from a very long voyage. But, after making all allowances, it must be recognized that they are dressed in coarse canvas which after being worn some time looks slouchy. It is nothing against their fighting qualities; as I have said, they seemed to me to be magnificent fighters."

Our Regular Army.

The regular army did not receive the credit it deserved for the part it played in the war with Spain. Nearly all the reports received gave glowing and deserved accounts of the bravery, dash and efficiency of the volunteers, but almost wholly neglected the performances of the regulars. Yet a careful study of the campaign will show indisputably that it was mainly through the discipline and steadiness of the regulars that the volunteers were able to give such an heroic account of themselves, and that a threatened disaster was turned into a glorious victory. Few realized the splendid and invaluable character of the work performed by the regulars in the Santiago campaign, but when all is known these brave men should and will receive the full credit due them, and their true worth will be appreciated. While there was a large number of regiments of the regular army engaged in the battles near Santiago there were only three volunteer regiments.

It was natural perhaps under the circumstances that at the outset the volunteers should receive the greatest attention from the public, and there was not the slightest reason to suppose there was any intention to glorify them at the expense of the regulars. The latter are the pride of the nation—always excepting the practical politician, who can see no personal profit in their existence; but it was almost purely sentimental considerations that gave the most enthusiastic praise to the volunteers. In a sense the volunteers are closer to the mass of the citizens. Every regiment almost is composed of fathers, brothers, husbands, neighbors and friends of the people of a certain locality, while the members of a regiment of regulars are recruited from all parts of the country.

As much was not expected from the volunteers as from the regulars, for they had not the same training in the art of war.

Without detracting in the least from the courage and valor of the volunteer forces, it is evident that both were strengthened and sustained by the coolness, the magnificent discipline and long military training of the regulars. It is generally admitted that it was the clearheaded, cool conduct of the regulars that gave strength and confidence to the Rough Riders and the other volunteers, even if they had been disposed for a moment to waver during the terrible and bloody charge up San Juan Hill to that glorious victory.

Commissioners Appointed by Our Government.

The commissioners appointed in behalf of the United States to arrange for the Spanish evacuation of Cuba are Rear-Admiral Sampson and Major-Generals Wade and Butler. The commissioners for Porto Rico are Rear-Admiral Schley and Major-Generals Brooke and Gordon. The Commissioners appointed by Spain were as follows: For Cuba: Major General Gonzales Parrado, Rear Admiral Pastor y Landero, Marquis Montoro. For Porto Rico: Major General Ortega y Diaz, Commodore of First Rank Vallarino y Carrasco, Judge Advocate Sanchez del Aguila y Leon.

On August 24th it was announced that the following American Peace Commissioners to settle the future of the Philippine Islands had been selected by President McKinley: William R. Day, of Canton, Ohio, Secretary of State; Cushman K. Davis, United States Senator from Minnesota, Chairman of the Foreign Relations Committee; William P. Frye, United States Senator from Maine, member of the Foreign Relations Committee. He has served ten years in the House of Representatives and fifteen in the Senate; succeeded James G. Blaine in the Senate; Whitelaw Reid, of New York, for several years American Ambassador to the French Republic; and George Gray, United States Senator from Delaware, who succeeded Thomas F. Bayard in the Senate in 1885. The sessions of the Peace Commission are to be held in Paris, commencing not later than October first and continuing until an agreement is reached.